# Managing Beyond Compliance:

The Ethical and Legal Dimensions
of Corporate Responsibility

# Managing Beyond Compliance:

## The Ethical and Legal Dimensions of Corporate Responsibility

**Alfred Marcus**
University of Minnesota

**Sheryl Kaiser**
Loyola College

**NCP**
NorthCoast
Publishers, Inc.
GARFIELD HEIGHTS, OH

Published by:     NorthCoast Publishers, Inc.
                  5063 Turney Road, Garfield Heights, OH 44125
                  (216) 332.0323 (V) • (216) 332.0324 (Fax)
                  cservice1@northcoastpub.com

Address inquiries to:
College Permissions: NorthCoast Publishers, Inc.
 5063 Turney Road,
Garfield Heights, OH 44125.

Printed in the United States of America          B C D E F G E
ISBN 1933583290

This publication is designed to provide accurate and authoritative information with regard to the subject matter involved. It is sold with the understanding that the publisher is not engaged in rendering legal, accounting or other professional advice. If legal advice or other expert assistance is required, the services of a qualified professional person should be sought.

—From: **A Declaration of Principles**, jointly adopted by a Committee of the American Bar Association and a Committee of Publishers and Associations.

Visit our home page at: http://www.northcoastpub.com

# Contents – Brief

# Contents – Expanded

## Part Three: Case Studies and Exercises in Corporate Social Responsibility

# Preface and Perspective

The phrase *Beyond Compliance* in the title of this text was chosen with care, with the intention of conveying a particular perspective about the role of business in the twenty-first century. The phrase, having gained popularity in the post-Enron era of U.S. capitalism, risks becoming another catchy, empty buzzword like so many others of the past. It deserves better. It merits consideration as a core guideline for business behavior.

At the turn of the twenty-first century, U.S. business is undergoing a profound transformation. Its original conception as a profit-seeking institution and its commitment to the free market economy remain as strong as ever. Nonetheless, notions about the obligations of business to those it affects are evolving in response to increased recognition of the pivotal and far-reaching role business plays in society and the individual lives of citizens—as investors, employees, consumers, and community members.

The obligations people have to one another are the essential questions of ethics. In his magnum opus *A Theory of Justice*, John Rawls defined ethics as "...a conception of the person, the relations among persons, and the general goals and ends of social cooperation." The dominant ethics of the society inform the social and polit-ical consciousness of citizens, who shape laws in response to their ideals. As ethics shift and evolve, social consciousness changes as well, as does the form and substance of the law. "Rare is the legal victory that is not the careful byproduct of an emerging social consensus."[1]

Law reflects ethics, but it does so imperfectly. Law is imperfect first because it is reactionary and not preemptory in nature. Therefore, lags and gaps often exist between what is legally restricted or required and what would constitute ethical comportment. As former U.S. Supreme Court Justice Potter Stewart once said, "There is a big difference between what we have the right to do and what is right." Many corporate abuses that led to the avalanche of financial disasters in 2002 and 2003 were not technically prohibited at the time they were undertaken. They may have been unethical; and there is no question that they caused the demise of some of the largest corporations in the world, costing stakeholders hundreds of billions of dollars. Nonetheless, tax and securities regulations, accounting standards, and other regulatory controls did not specifically prohibit many schemes intending to defraud investors and creditors. In response to clear ethical transgressions, laws have been changed and new laws

---

1. O'Connor, Hon. Justice Sandra Day. (2003). *The majesty of the law: Reflections of a supreme court justice.* New York: Random House.

have been enacted to prevent future abuses.

In business, laws reflect ethics imperfectly because businesspeople tend to be wary of government intervention and regulation. They prefer *laissez-faire*—let the market alone—because ethical and legal obligations can translate into costs that chip away at profits. Social responsibility may not be compatible with short-term profitability. Many businesspeople seek to use their political influence to thwart regulation aimed at their companies, which is another reason for the imperfect reflection of ethics in the law. Even so, few businesspeople will deny that some rules are required to keep the market free. They have to reconcile themselves to the limitations that law and public policy impose on their conduct. Businesspeople are rarely advocates for self-regulation. They would prefer that the laws be introduced and enforced by government authorities.

In the continuum of ethics, political consciousness, and law, the gap of where the law ends or does not yet speak is an area that is "beyond compliance." For corporations to function in an ethically responsible manner, business managers must recognize that the technical limits of law do not set a moral floor for their behavior. Operating beyond compliance requires recognition that although some moral obligations may not be codified, that fact does not make their observance any less imperative.

Managing beyond compliance requires that business organizations progress beyond a culture of gamesmanship where they hypertechnically parse the law to see what they can get away with. Unethical behavior poses a risk to the vitality and perpetuity of businesses. An organization that encourages its members to take advantage of what the law allows, without regard for ethics, will find itself outside the law. Many financial disasters that beset U.S. firms are the result of a no-holds-barred management style that rewards the discovery and exploitation of legal tricks and loopholes.

Mere compliance is dangerous. When a company causes personal harm, it can get stung. Tobacco companies did not violate any legal regulation when they failed to warn the public of the known health risks posed by cigarettes. Nonetheless, they now face billions of dollars in

punitive damage judgments for their negligence. Companies that dispose of toxic waste in water or soil in a manner that causes personal injury or property damage can be held legally liable for such harm regardless of the legality of the original dumping. Examples abound of situations where a company's activities resulted in financial liability that far exceeded the original cost-benefit calculation factored into corporate decision making.

There is also a trend toward conferring legal reward for operating beyond compliance. Increasingly, companies are held accountable for their actions whether their agents knew of the misdeeds or not. To alleviate the harshness of this liability, statutes and court decisions have recognized that the financial damages may be mitigated to the extent that the organizations affirmatively attempted to prevent the illicit behavior—that is, to the extent that they operated beyond the bare floor of legal compliance. For example, the guidelines enacted by the United States Sentencing Commission in 1991 take this approach to punishing white-collar crime. The guidelines impose strict liability on corporations and other organizations (for example, labor unions, pension funds, partnerships, and nonprofits) for violations of federal law, regardless of the knowledge and complicity of management; yet they also provide for leniency in sentencing if, at the time of the offense, the convicted organization had implemented an "effective program to prevent and detect violations of the law." For white-collar crime, such programs may consist of a heightened and more independent compliance office, training in fraud detection and prevention for employees and managers, an independent ombudsman to handle reports of wrongdoing confidentially without retaliation against whistle-blowers, and similar measures. All of those measures are above anything required of the organization by law.

In *Burlington Industries v. Ellerth*, 524 U.S. 742 (1998), the Supreme Court took a similar approach to punishing a corporation for sexual harassment. The Court imposed strict liability on the employer for an actionable hostile environment. However, corporate culpability can be lessened to the extent that the employer shows that it took steps to prevent and promptly correct any sexually harassing behavior in the workplace. The types of affirmative, proactive preventative policies and practices that serve as a mitigating defense—employee sensitivity training, meaningful and confidential grievance procedures, and published and consistently followed codes of conduct on sexual harassment—are not required by law. Nonetheless, there seems little doubt that reasonable and responsible managers must now implement such measures if they are to serve the best interests of the corporation.

The goal of this text is not to educate you in the technical requirements of law—that is better left to business law and legal environment courses. Instead, the purpose is to persuade you to identify and consider the ethical foundations of regulation. A secondary purpose is to enable you to understand the obligations of the corporation to those it affects, to better anticipate the likely evolution of law and policy, and to lead companies with a vision of good corporate citizenship.

The format of this text consists of three parts.

Part One explores basic theories of ethics and corporate social responsibility, the role of the government as an external control, and the role of corporate culture as an internal check on behavior. Part Two addresses ongoing issues as they relate to stakeholders. The obligations managers have to owners, employees, customers, the community, and society at large are considered as are the special ethical considerations of multinationals operating in less developed countries. Part Three contains cases that relate to managerial obligations to stakeholders.

In no way does this book include all issues involving corporations and their constituencies—only a few representative topics are highlighted and examined. The goal is to guide you by (1) providing moral dilemmas raised by corporate action; (2) encouraging your consideration of the perspectives of affected constituencies; and (3) guiding you to an informed and educated decision based not on what the law permits or does not yet prohibit, but on reasoned principles.

# PART 1

## Foundations

### Introduction

Jokes abound about business ethics. Like *military intelligence,* business ethics is supposed to be an oxymoron. Enron had a 64-page "Code of Corporate Ethics," dozens of copies of which, in mint condition and obviously never read, were auctioned by former employees on eBay when the company went under. Although ethics are universally regarded as important, in a business context, they often are slighted. A businessperson may maintain that so long as a company does not violate the law or engage in shameful acts, it has the right to do whatever it can to make a profit—that there is no obligation to stop and consider who might get hurt. A businessperson may believe that the only reason to develop amicable relations with employees, customers, suppliers, and competitors is to enhance profits. That person may contend that if an opportunity exists for profit, the opportunity should be pursued regardless of the consequences. Some businesspeople even rationalize that if they don't pursue the opportunity, someone else will; therefore, they exclude ethics in favor of economic efficacy because it is "just plain good business sense."

This compartmentalization of ethics requires a view of business as something outside of and unrelated to the well-being of society. Yet business plays a pervasive role in modern society. Business is a vital and indispensable institution whose position in society belies the partitioning and marginalizing of ethics. If anything, the important role of business establishes a strong rationale for ethics' central place.

Part One of this text consists of five chapters that examine the role of the corporation in society. Chapter One deals specifically with ethics and explains why ethics matter in business. Chapter Two provides methods of reasoning about ethics and discusses their relevance. Chapter Three is an exploration of theories about corporate social responsibility; these ideas are further developed in Part Two of the text. Chapter Four examines the role of the government in influencing corporate conduct *and* the role of business in influencing government policy. Chapter Five examines corporate culture as it affects corporate behavior, attempting to explain why otherwise ethical people would take part in unethical business dealings.

# Chapter 1

## Why Do Ethics Matter?

*"To be or not to be, that is the question.*
*Whether 'tis nobler in the mind to suffer*
*The slings and arrows of outrageous fortune,*
*Or to take arms against a sea of troubles,*
*And, by opposing, end them?"*

— William Shakespeare, *Hamlet*

Ethical inquiry dates back to the earliest eras of recorded history. Humans have long pondered their place in the universe and their obligations to others. Plato's *The Republic* devoted itself to the question, What is justice? One of the first questions posed in the Old Testament is "Am I my brother's keeper?"—that is, what are my obligations to my fellow human beings?

Every tradition seeks to discover universal principles to define proper human behavior. Many propound a version of the Golden Rule—that your first duty is to love your neighbor as yourself.

The Hindu scripture professes, "Men... should always treat others as they themselves wish to be treated."

Confucius warned, "What you do not want done to yourself, do not do to others."

The Jewish sage Hillel said that the essence of religion was "What you yourself hate, do not do to your neighbor."

The New Testament maintains, "Do unto others as you would have them do unto you."

Immanuel Kant, the eighteenth-century philosopher, put forth a secular principle of human conduct—the categorical imperative that you should never act except in such a way that your actions can be a "maxim" for "universal law." That principle admits to no exceptions. You should act only in a way that you would want everyone to act under the same circumstances. Kant was formulating an erudite version of the Golden Rule.

## What Is Ethics?

Ethics is reflection on what you should do. The Greek philosopher Socrates called it the "examined life."[1] This ancient Greek (circa 400 BCE) proposed that you should not act just out of habit or just on the basis of what society expects

---

1. Twentieth-century analytical philosophy—as exemplified by such thinkers as Moore (1873–1958), Russell (1872–1970), Wittgenstein (1889–1951), and Ayer (1910–1989)—has been concerned with clarifying the meaning of everyday ethical concepts and commonplace language. Russell used logic and mathematics to criticize and clarify notions that were apt to be regarded as fundamental and accepted uncritically. Wittgenstein searched for the meaning of words such as *duty, obligation, right,* and *good* and the way they were used. Ayer pointed to the "emotive" and "commanding" elements in moral language and maintained that people could not show others that they had the wrong ethical feelings. All they could do was argue about the "facts."

or just because some authority figure commands certain behavior. You cannot be ruled simply by emotions or desires or induced to follow popular tastes and opinion. Rather, you have a duty to examine *why* you act as you do, to examine the implications of your actions, and to ensure that your behavior is consistent with your beliefs about society and your role in it. You also must seek to understand why others behave as they do and what their beliefs are. Indeed, all of your values and beliefs should be examined in light of those of the people around you; and on that basis, you should arrive at principles to govern your actions.[2]

As discussed in the Preface, ethics is "...a conception of the person, the relations among persons, and the general goals and ends of social cooperation."[3] The quest for ethics is a quest for universal principles to justify your actions. Your ethical ideas must be supported by consistent and well-grounded principles. Reaching conclusions about those matters requires that you engage in a *continuous* search. You cannot just rigidly hold on to beliefs—critical thinking requires room for change based on the evidence. Ethics refers to this search for the principles that ought to govern your behavior.[4] But it also means that you must reflect on your actions to make sure that you can abide by the principles to which you adhere. You have a duty to act on the basis of the principles you espouse.

## Ethical Dilemmas in Business

Today the state of business ethics is under intense scrutiny. Some of this stems from scandals involving a seemingly endless list of companies—Enron, WorldCom, Arthur Andersen, Adelphia, Global Crossing, ImClone, Hallibur-

ton, and Tyco—whose advisors, creditors, and partners also were implicated in the crimes to which their companies were accused. Those companies have been charged with manipulating financial data and intentionally engaging in fraud and other deceptive actions with the intent of the individuals involved to achieve personal gain at the expense of shareholders, clients, and employees.

Some of the heightened attention to ethics is also due to the increased public coverage of business in an age of mass media. The public is regularly and continuously kept abreast of Wall Street scandals, setbacks, and sweet deals, as well as protests and dire economic conditions of people around the world. The late 1980s saw similar soul-searching on the part of some executives, prompted by insider trading scandals on Wall Street and environmental catastrophes such as the *Exxon Valdez* in Prince William Sound and the Union Carbide plant in Bhopal, India. At that time, executives promised to be better corporate citizens and improved stewards of the environment. Today they are promising greater financial integrity and more accountability.

But has the message really sunk in? The pressure to cut corners to enhance short-term profitability has not abated. As long as a company does not get caught, why shouldn't it violate laws and encroach on generally accepted ethical values? The challenge of business ethics has not gone away. Recent polls have found widespread disenchantment with corporate managers. A high percentage of those surveyed believe that managers lack moral principles and that they are incapable of dealing with ethical dilemmas.[5]

The ethical situations that managers face are not as dramatic as the well-publicized cases portrayed in the media. Ethical dilemmas are situa-

---

2. Thus, ethics involves both a search for meaning and value in one's life and the passing of judgment – the evaluation of other people's lives and behaviors. In this latter sense, ethics can be a weapon that does much harm. Can people justly evaluate others' lives and behaviors unless they understand everything about the others' circumstances? If people do judge others, do they not have an obligation to intervene? Along with judging must there not also be caring?

3. John Rawls, the American philosopher, has defined *ethics* in this manner.

4. The Danish theologian and philosopher Søren Kierkegaard (1813–1855) argued that the authentic person chooses himself or herself. That person clarifies and creates values, grasps freedom, orders priorities, and creates an identity. He or she keeps from meaningless social roles and the petty pursuit of wealth. The twentieth-century existentialist Jean Paul Sartre (1905–1980) held that people have to struggle to make themselves. The self is not a stable, solid, or lasting creation, but is made and remade from moment to moment. According to Sartre, people make the world and themselves by bestowing values upon it. He maintained that by giving meaning, people are heroes. However, because he believed that no values were better than any other, people also experience anguish.

tions that consist of actual or potential harm to others. They entail actions that may affect the freedom and well-being of others. They arise when you want to do what is right but you do not know for certain what that action is or whether you have the power to carry it out. Ethical dilemmas exist when there are conflicts between values, between means and ends, and between groups and individuals to whom you are obligated.

The commonplace ethical dilemmas found in organizations are troubling. Nonetheless, employees may be reluctant to discuss the dilemmas in ethical terms. The workers relegate those matters to the practical and are concerned with the organization's interests and economic good sense. The situations with which employees deal are labeled as judgment calls, professional matters, or strategic issues rather than ethical concerns.

Many managers are "mute" with regard to ethical discussion. They may prefer to avoid the use of ethical language, defining the conflicts they face in nonethical terms. Aside from the harm they may be doing to others, managers may experience negative consequences—stress and personal conflict—from their failure to confront ethical issues directly.

When you confront an ethical dilemma, diverse and sometimes conflicting factors affect what you should do: obligations to yourself, to the organization, to professional or occupational norms, to laws, to society, and to religious beliefs. At an abstract level, the principles that govern your behavior may be clear; but their application to the concrete case may be difficult. When moving from abstract principles to the concrete case, complications may arise: qualifications, limitations, reasons for making exceptions, inadequacies in the factual basis for deciding, and lack of good grounds for a judgment.

The following vignettes are examples of how hard it is to resolve even simple ethical dilemmas. Think through these dilemmas before you give your answer. What would you do and why?

### #1 Revealing Everything You Know about a Product

You sell medical products to surgeons who carry out very specialized procedures. Often they ask your advice on the best devices to use. A prominent surgeon with whom you work tells you about a particularly difficult operation that she must perform. She asks if your product is the best one available for the procedure. You know that your product is adequate for the task, but you have just seen a demonstration of a new product developed by a competitor. You believe that the competitor's product is better because it entails less risk to the patient and provides a quicker recovery time.

### #2 Choosing between Jobs and the Environment

You are the manager of an unprofitable paper mill owned by a large diversified multinational. The paper mill is an old facility that needs updating if it is to be competitive globally with new facilities in nations with far lower pay structures than in the United States. Corporate headquarters says that you must make severe cost cuts; otherwise, your mill will be shut down within the next three months and nearly all employees will be laid off. You are caught in the middle. If you make the radical cost reductions that corporate expects, you likely won't meet the stringent pollution control requirements recently imposed by the government. On the other hand, not complying with the pollution control requirements could damage the health of local residents. You live in the community, as do most of your employees. Your plant uses chemicals with proven negative health effects.

### #3 Taking a Competitor's Plan

You are a salesperson for a large computer company that is in financial trouble. At a trade association meeting, the marketing director of a major competitor inadvertently leaves a copy of his company's internal marketing plan on the table. The plan is clearly marked "Confiden-

---

5. "Possession of an MBA or business background has become as much a detriment today as it once stood for qualification. It now certifies membership in a corporate elite that is rapidly losing the trust of American voters."—Alan Heslop, professor of government at Claremont McKenna College.

tial—For Internal Eyes Only." However, you could easily pick it up without being observed. You suspect that the document will provide invaluable information. It may allow your company to thwart a major new marketing campaign begun by your competitor, who has recently made many gains in the industry.

### #4 Giving a Gift to a Customer

You are a sales agent for a large sporting goods concern that has outlets throughout the United States, Latin America, and Europe. One outlet in particular is your best account; 80 percent of the goods you sell move through this company. Although your compensation is partially based on commission, you obtain bonuses and other rewards for exceeding sales quotas. The newest and hottest product your company is selling is a set of premium high-tech golf clubs. Sales have begun to increase, and the product has great potential. The main purchasing agent for the sporting goods company asks you for a set of these $1,100 golf clubs. He wants to try them out "on a more or less permanent basis." This person's goodwill is critical. If he should turn against you, you could lose the account to a competitor that is offering its own line of premium golf clubs. You could sneak the golf clubs out of your company's warehouse without telling anyone, but you suspect it would violate the company's policy of not giving gifts worth more than $15 to customers.

### #5 Giving a Small Gift to Family and Friends

In a tight job market, you find employment as an assistant buyer for a large retail chain. The job could launch your career with the company, which is known to treat its employees well. The only problem is that the salary is not quite what you expected. A compensation for the low level of pay is that you can buy anything the company offers at a substantial discount. Upon revealing the perk to your family and friends, they tell you that they are eager to take advantage of it; some of them ask you to buy items for them, using your discount. You know that many of your fellow employees use the discount in this way. They make purchases not only for themselves, but also for family and friends. Though

this practice is against company policy, you don't see the policy being enforced; the company doesn't seem to care.

Determining how to resolve these kinds of dilemmas in a fair and ethical manner can be difficult. Conflicting loyalties to self, the family, the organization, and the community make it hard to prioritize one's obligations. Common rationalizations are used as safe harbors against taking responsibility. You may say to yourself such things as "Everybody else does it," "If we don't do it, someone else will," or "I was just following orders." As you will see in the ensuing chapters, such common rationalizations do not have an ethical foundation.

The following frameworks for dealing with ethical dilemmas provide a starting point for your deliberations. The criteria used in the frameworks—identifying the stakeholders affected, considering the obligations owed, and recognizing the actual and perceived effects of action or inaction—are used throughout this text.

## Frameworks for Dealing with Ethical Dilemmas in Business

Useful frameworks for confronting ethical dilemmas are presented below. Each differs somewhat in focus and factors to be considered. These approaches resonate with different people. They may be more relevant to one situation than another. Read each model carefully and reflect on it. After you have studied the frameworks, review the previous vignettes, trying to apply the frameworks to those real-life issues. They are not abstractions. They require real-life application.

Model 1 works for basic ethical questions. However, because it focuses on the individual, it is not always appropriate in a business context, where you may have an obligation to act for others and not just in your own best interest.

### MODEL 1
**SEVEN ETHICAL QUESTIONS**
1. What is going on here? (What are the relevant facts?)
   Who are the players?
   What are their intentions?
   What are they saying?

To what extent is it to be believed?
What are they likely to do?
What are the likely consequences?
2. How do I feel?
3. What are my goals?
4. What should I do regardless of how I feel or what my goals are?
5. What principles should I abide by?
6. What are the likely effects of what I am going to do (on the situation and/or on my character)?
   Will I be a "better" person?
7. Will I be able to accept responsibility for what I have done?
   Can I live with my decision?
   How does my decision make me feel about myself?
   How does my decision make me feel about others?

Model 2 is shorter and more generic. It focuses on the future implications of your actions and your ability to explain and justify them. This framework rests heavily on the "disclosure rule"; that is, if you are going to be uncomfortable with an action after associates, friends, and family become aware of it, you shouldn't do it. This framework and the variation that immediately follows it (What Is at Stake?) both work well in a business context because they compel you to consider your firm's constituencies and your ethical obligations to them.

## *MODEL 2*
### JUSTIFYING ONE'S ACTIONS
- Who has a stake in the outcome (groups/and or individuals)?
- As a manager, whom am I serving?
- As a manager, whom might I injure (and how badly)?
- What principles should I use in making a decision?
- Are those principles clear?
- Could I describe them to the company's board of directors and to my family?
- Could I explain them in court?
- Could I explain them to the media?
- Could I explain them to fellow workers?
- Will the decision I make seem right a year from now?

- Will the decision seem right 20 years from now if someone writes a history of the company?

### WHAT IS AT STAKE?
- What is to be gained by the action or the decision not to act?
- Who is affected by the action or the decision not to act?
- What is the extent of any adverse effects?
- What is the obligation to those harmed?
- What is the balance between the effects of taking the action versus the effects of not taking the action?

Model 3 comes from a pocket guide 3M distributed to its employees after they attended a training session on ethics. Employees were expected to put this card in their wallets and carry it with them at all times.

## *MODEL 3*
### THE POCKET GUIDE TO CORPORATE ETHICS
- 3M's values are based on a commitment to:
- Satisfying our customers with superior value.
- Providing investors with an attractive return through sustained, high-quality growth.
- Respecting the social and physical environment.
- Being a company that employees are proud to be a part of.

We want you to:
1. Identify all the critical facts.
2. Identify the key values of all the players.
3. Identify the driving forces in the situation.
4. Work through a worst-case scenario and its effects on the players.
5. Identify key values and ethical principles you would uphold.
6. Write down an outline of your action plan.
7. Identify organizational changes that could prevent this situation in the future.

Our ethics checklist consists of the following:
1. Is it legal?
2. Is my action the right thing to do?
3. Can my action stand public scrutiny?

4. Will my action protect 3M's reputation as an ethical company?

*Source: Modified from internal 3M document.*

Model 4 comes from Texas Instruments (TI). This framework is unusual in that it encourages employees to openly discuss a situation. It tells employees that if they do not know what to do, they should ask—and they should keep asking until the situation becomes clear and they can resolve it satisfactorily. This framework suggests that ethical dilemmas often need clarification and that the best way to approach them is through open and ongoing discussion.

### MODEL 4
### TEXAS INSTRUMENTS' QUICK TEST
- Is the action legal?
- Does it comply with our values?
- If you do it, will you feel bad?
- How will it look in the newspaper?
- If you know it is wrong, don't do it.
- If you're not sure, ask.
- Keep asking till you get an answer.
    > Ask your co-workers.
    > Ask legal.
    > Ask human resources.
    > Call the ethics office.
    > Ask your friends.
    > Ask your family.
    > Don't feel like you have to carry all that pressure yourself.

*Source: Modified from internal Texas Instrument document.*

### Beyond Compliance

Note that the last two models begin their analysis with the question, Is it (the action) legal? That is the "compliance" question: Is the action or any of the options contemplated prohibited by law? Generally, if the answer is no, the analy- sis stops there; but this misses an important point. There are unethical laws—for example, racial and gender apartheid—that may morally require noncompliance. Companies operating in a compliance mode often end their decision making when the answer to the question is that the action is legal. The wisest among them may add the follow-up question, How close of a call is it? But social responsibility mandates that for any decision with adverse effects, critical con- sideration be given to ethics. That is what it means to operate beyond compliance. So in addition to asking whether contemplated options are legal and how close of a call they are, you should think through who is affected and whether the effects are worth the aims you are trying to achieve. Consider how you would want the situation to turn out if you were on the receiving end of the actions, regardless of whether they were legal.

## Conclusion: Why Be Ethical in Business?

In the mid-twentieth century, the image of business as a game of sport or chance was pop- ularized.[6] While a competitive spirit thrives in everyone, the analogy between sports and busi- ness has to be carefully analyzed. Often time in sports, there are few implications outside the playing field. Once the game is over, it is over. But business activities involve risks to external parties, many of whom have not willingly agreed to be involved. The risks are long-term. They do not end after a transaction has been completed. The pure self-interest model that fuels winning in games does not work in the marketplace; business should not succeed by causing harm to others. A corporation has recip- rocal relations with employees, customers, gov- ernment officials, bankers, investors, the community and other important constituen-

---

6. Albert Carr compared business to the game of poker: "While both have a large element of chance, in the long run, the winner is the man who plays with steady skill. In both games, ultimate victory requires intimate knowledge of the rules, insight into the psy- chology of the other players, a bold front, a considerable amount of self-discipline, and the ability to respond swiftly and effectively to opportunities provided by chance. . . . Poker's own brand of ethics is different from the ethical ideals of civilized human relationships. Cunning deception and concealment of one's strength and intentions, not kindness and openheartedness, are vital in poker. No one thinks any worse of poker on that account. And no one should think any worse of the game of business because its standards of right and wrong differ from the prevailing traditions of morality and society"... See Carr, A. (1968, January/February). Is business bluffing eth- ical? *Harvard Business Review.*

cies. A company cannot expect sustained profitability unless it develops sound long-term ties built on trust and respect with these stakeholders. Deception, manipulation, and fraud will harm the company in the long run.

Why be ethical in business? There are many good, practical, and philosophical reasons, which you will explore in this text.

# Chapter 2

## Ethical Theory and Principles of Social and Economic Justice

*"Every rational being exists as an end in himself and not merely as a means to be arbitrarily used by this or that will. In all his actions, whether they are directed to himself or to other rational beings, a human being must always be regarded at the same time as an end... i.e... . an object of respect."*

— Immanuel Kant, eighteenth-century German philosopher

*"If the hypothesis were offered us of a world in which... millions kept permanently happy on the one simple condition that a certain lost soul on the far-off edge of things should lead a life of lonely torture... even though an impulse arose within us to clutch at the happiness so offered, how hideous a thing would be its enjoyment when deliberately accepted as the fruit of such a bargain."*

— William James, nineteenth-century American philosopher and psychologist[1]

### Means versus Ends

The two traditions of ethical theory most evident in American law and public policy are the teleological and the deontological theories. Both are examined in some detail in this chapter. There are other ethical traditions—the Greek concept of cultivating ethical "virtues" as the way to achieving moral excellence and the feminist "ethic of care" that places care, compassion, and human relationships at the core of all ethical considerations. But the teleological model, sometimes called "consequentialism" or "utilitarianism," and the deontological model, sometimes referred to as the "rights-based approach," remain the cornerstone in Western thought.

The most fundamental difference between the two theories is in the way that they measure justice. For utilitarians/consequentialists, the focus is on *the ends*. If the end result maximizes good for most people and minimizes harm, then that end result justifies the means. For deontologists, *the means* are what matter. People are entitled to be treated as ends in themselves, not merely as means. Thus, the means used to pursue a goal cannot transgress a person's basic rights without his or her consent. For deontologists, the end result is less important than respecting those rights. Kant's statement above reflects that tradition.

The primary criticism of utilitarianism is that it could accept violation of basic human rights in the service of the greater good. The example commonly used is slavery. If it could be shown

---

1. James, W. (1956, June). The moral philosopher and the moral life. In *The will to believe and other essays in popular philosophy: human understanding.* Mineola, NY: Dover Publications.

that some level of slave labor would maximize good for most of th2e people, would it be ethical to pursue that policy? There is no question that such a position would be unjust.

Nonetheless, examples of utilitarian ethical analysis abound in public and private policy making. During World War II, the U.S. government imprisoned thousands of Japanese Americans in concentration camps in California based solely upon their Japanese ancestry.[2] The U.S. Supreme Court acknowledged that the equal protection rights of those individuals, many of whom were citizens of the United States, had been violated, but found that violation was legally justified because of a "compelling governmental interest" in national security. The "greater good" of national security outweighed the harm caused to those individuals. Private business decisions made on utilitarian principles may also yield results patently unjust to some. Unocal Corporation justified its decision to construct a pipeline in Burma as achieving the greater goods of development and job creation. Unocal took that position at a time when Burma was under martial law, had been sanctioned by the international community, and had experienced divestment from most companies in the developed world. In fact, Unocal's "job creation" consisted of forced, uncompensated labor by displaced villagers conscripted into the workforce by the Burmese military junta. As a result of its actions, Unocal faced serious repercussions for its complicity in human rights violations.[3]

Deontologists reject such justifications, viewing freedom and equal treatment as fundamental rights and humans as an end in themselves. For deontologists, whatever the greater good, it must be achieved only with means that respect fundamental rights.

The opening quote by William James points to the tragic character of the teleological dilemma. The sacrifice of one life to lonely torture for the good of the many is theoretically justifiable in utilitarian terms. Yet even if a group decides that its happiness justifies an individual's suffering, can the group easily live with that decision? Its happiness is muted by the consciousness of the unhappy bargain it has had to strike. There is grave injustice in the nonconsensual sacrifice of even one. What if you are that one lost soul? Would you be willing to sacrifice your life for the good of the many? Would it be fair for your parent, sibling, or child to make that sacrifice?

## The Limitations of Moral Common Sense

The starting point for reasoning about ethics is common sense. Most people do not want to cause harm to others. They respect others' rights. They do not want to lie or cheat. They intend to keep their promises and contracts, obey the law, help others in need, and be fair. But how do they reconcile conflicts between those desires? What if avoiding harm to others requires lying and cheating? To save the lives of hostages, it may be necessary for negotiators to lie, cheat, and even strike back violently—all seemingly morally justified. What if the risk of harm to others is small compared to the good to be achieved? How should values be weighed against values in a particular instance? Those are the questions that make ethical inquiry and discourse necessary. Ethical theories seek to provide a framework for deciding the proper course of action.

Two different but related questions are central to this pursuit: What is right or wrong, and what is good or bad? The history of ethical study has examples of thinkers who have been primarily concerned with the question of action and its rightness and thinkers who have been primarily concerned with the ends or goals of action and their goodness. The deontological model concerns itself with the rightness of action; the teleological or consequentialist model, with the goodness of end result. Yet much of political and

---

2. *Korematsu v. United States*, 323 US 214 (1944). Decades later Congress authorized payments in reparation to the Japanese Americans who suffered internment.

3. This case is discussed in depth in the case study "Lying Down with Dogs...Getting Up with Lawsuits: Unocal and the Alien Tort Claims Act" in Part Three of this text.

religious thought cannot be categorized simply on one side or the other. While the deontological model is often associated with the Western religious traditions of Judaism and Christianity, those religions are also concerned with good results. And while the teleological model is often associated with classical Greek thought, Greek writers such as Plato often concerned themselves with duty. Ethical inquiry requires reflection on both of these elements—what is right and wrong *and* what is good and bad.

## Teleological Ethics: Utilitarianism

John Dewey, twentieth-century American philosopher and educator, argued that it is not so much motives—the intention to treat people with respect—that are important, but deliberation on consequences: "We are reasonable when we estimate the import or significance of any present desire or impulse by forecasting what it would come or amount to if carried out."[4] Dewey advised deliberation on a proposed action by means of an "imaginative rehearsal"— something that might be referred to today as visualization. People should consider the result of their actions in terms of their "likes and dislikes... desires and aversions," developing within them "a running commentary" based on their values of "good or evil." Dewey explained:

> We give way, in our mind, to some impulse; we try in our mind some plan. Following its career through various steps, we find ourselves in imagination in the presence of the consequences that would follow; and as we then like and approve, or dislike and disapprove, these consequences, we find the original impulse or plan good or bad... .

Dewey's views are *teleological* in that they focus on the outcome of actions. Moral worth, or "goodness," is determined by a consideration of the action's consequences, not the actor's intentions.

### Identifying Good and Bad

But what constitutes a "good" or "bad" result? The word *good* is used in many different contexts—a good meal, a good job, a good feeling. The teleological concept of good distinguishes between things valued for what they are "good for" and final goods, things with value in and of themselves. The ancient Greeks called them *intrinsic* goods, which have in inherent value as opposed to *extrinsic* goods, which derive their value from what they can lead to. Aristotle distinguished between intrinsic and extrinsic goods as follows:

> If then there is some end of the things which we desire for its own sake (everything else being desired for the sake of this), and if we do not choose everything for the sake of something else (for at that rate the process would go on to infinity, so that our desire would be empty and vain), clearly this must be the good and the chief good. Will not the knowledge of it, then, have a great influence on life?[5]

Extrinsic goods are means to an end, rather than ends unto themselves. Thus, people go to the dentist not because doing so is a final good, but because it allows them to achieve another more important aim—good health. People may take a "good" job solely to provide for themselves and their children and to improve the quality of their lives, not because they value the work or the money in and of themselves. Plato, Aristotle, and other classic philosophers believed that the highest good was wisdom and that virtuous behavior ultimately produced wisdom.

The "virtues" are attitudes, dispositions, or character traits that enable people to develop their potential. They provide people with the ability to pursue the ideals they have adopted. Honesty, courage, compassion, generosity, fidelity, integrity, fairness, self-control, and prudence are all examples of virtues.

---

4. Dewey, J., & Tufts, J. (1993). *Ethics*. Originally published in 1908 by H. Holt, New York. In L. Hickman & T. Alexander (Eds.). (1998). *The essential Dewey: ethics, logic, psychology, Volume 2*. Bloomington, IN: Indiana University Press.

5. Aristotle. (1962). *The Nicomachean ethics*. (M. Ostwald, Trans.). Indianapolis: Bobbs-Merrill. (All quotes in this section are from Books I and II.)

To engage in virtuous behavior, according to Aristotle, one needs to comport oneself with moderation in all things—to find the mean between extremes. Virtue is "concerned with passions and actions and in these there is excess, defect, and the intermediate," according to Aristotle. He believed that "excess and defect are characteristics of vice, and the mean of virtue." Virtuous behavior is not mediocrity; it calls for harmony and balance. A *suppressed* person controls his or her desires too vigorously. A *weak-willed* person cannot control his or her desires. A *temperate* individual directs his or her desires toward that which is good naturally through habit and toward that which becomes second nature.

Finding the mean between an overabundance of a quality and a deficiency can be tricky. The virtue of generosity is a mean between extravagance and stinginess; the virtue of high-mindedness is a mean between pettiness and vanity; the virtue of gentleness is a mean between short temper and apathy; the virtue of friendliness is a mean between obsequiousness and grouchiness; the virtue of truthfulness is a mean between boastfulness and self-deprecation; the virtue of wittiness is a mean between buffoonery and boorishness; etc. Aristotle believed that those virtues are developed through practice; they are habituated. That is, once they are acquired, they become characteristic of a person. Just as the ability to run a marathon is developed through training and practice, so, too, does one's capacity to be fair, courageous, or compassionate. Therefore, it is by the consistent habit of *acting* virtuously that one becomes virtuous. A person who has developed virtues will be naturally disposed to act in ways that are consistent with those moral principles, and that virtuous person is the ethical person.

Unlike the ancient Greeks, who understood the good to consist of those qualities that led to moral excellence and intellectual wisdom, later teleologists focused on pleasure and pain, happiness and harm as the defining characteristics of good and bad.

### Bentham and Mill

Jeremy Bentham, the eighteenth-century English philosopher and jurist, maintained:

> An action is right from an ethical point of view if and only if the sum total of utilities produced by that act is greater than the sum total of utilities produced by any other act the agent could have performed in its place.

This formulation determines that the action with the greatest aggregate or net utility is the right one, regardless of who gets the benefits. Utility, according to Bentham, derives from the capacity to cause pleasure and pain:

> Nature has placed mankind under the governance of two sovereign masters, pain and pleasure. It is for them alone to point out what we ought to do as well as to determine what we shall do.[6]

John Stuart Mill, a nineteenth-century economist and philosopher, developed the Greatest Happiness Principle: "Actions are right in proportion as they tend to promote happiness, wrong as they tend to produce the reverse of happiness."[7]

Happiness equates with pleasure, but there are degrees of pleasure. Distinguishing among and ranking their relative merit requires inquiry. Public policy equates the interest of the community as the "greatest good for the greatest number."[8] As a society, people should add together quantitative units of happiness and subtract quantitative units of unhappiness to arrive at a measure of total happiness or total pain and pleasure. Such a calculation will enable them to make more rational decisions.

6. Bentham, J. (1974). An *introduction to the principles of morals and legislation*. In O.A. Johnson. (2003). *Ethics: selections from classical and contemporary writers* (3rd ed.). New York: Holt, Rinehart and Winston, pp. iv8–iv39.

7. Mill, J. (1986). *Utilitarianism*. Oxford, England: Basil Blackwell.

8. Ibid.

*Is there the assumption that basic needs are met in all of this — if people lose their homes to build a mall?*

Is public happiness equivalent with the gross domestic product (GDP)?[9] Money and property may well be pleasures that bring happiness, but they are not ranked as the "greatest good" by ethical theorists. Most ethical thought, beginning with the ancient Greeks, holds intellectual pleasure to be superior to physical pleasure. Mill's quip was that it was better to be an unsatisfied Socrates than a satisfied pig. So how should *happiness* be defined? The twentieth-century English philosopher G. E. Moore, a friend and mentor of the acclaimed economist John Maynard Keynes, maintained that happiness came from maximizing values such as freedom, knowledge, justice, and beauty. The value of such goods is, however, priceless and immeasurable.

### Criticisms of Utilitarianism

The major criticisms of utilitarianism include its acceptance of certain injustice and its nebulous measure of values, as follows:

- Where the "greatest good for the greatest number" necessitates harm or hardship for some, can it be morally justified? Can a person be used ethically as a means to another's pleasure or happiness without giving informed consent to the arrangement?
- What is "the good"? How is it defined, ranked, and measured? Who makes those decisions?

Bentham and Mill envisioned a quasi-democratic approach to those matters, but the utilitarian model is extremely vulnerable to the "tyranny of majority." In the Constitution, the Founders of the U.S. government took that into account in creating a republic and not a democracy. The distinguishing features of a republic are pluralism, divided power, checks and balances, tolerance, and protection of minority rights.

The difficulty of ranking and quantifying values also represents a shortcoming of teleological ethics in the context of fundamental rights and social justice. In its most inartful form, utilitarianism breaks down into cost-benefit analysis. Cost-benefit analysis requires comparing, weighing, and balancing, using a common denominator. In some cases, there can be no common denominator—how does one value a life, for example? In such a case, the problem of measuring relative values is exacerbated by attempting simplistic quantification.

*How do you quantify "the greater good"?*

One of the most infamous examples of this kind of application of utilitarian analysis occurred in the Ford Pinto case, presented below. Although the case is dated, it is a classic example of utilitarianism gone awry.[10]

## Deontological Ethics— Rights and Duties

The Golden Rule, or "Do unto others as you would have them do unto you," is a universal idea with origins in many religious traditions. In Buddhism, it is expressed as "Hurt not others with that which pains yourself." The "excellent" companies in Peters and Waterman's best-selling book *In Search of Excellence: Lessons from America's Best-Run Companies* often displayed the Golden Rule as a core value—with managers treating employees, customers, suppliers, shareholders, and other stakeholders with the same respect they would have liked to receive.[11] All but the most extreme cynics believe that

---

9. The nation measures its collective well-being by the gross domestic product (GDP), an indicator of the national economic results of commerce and expenditures. A 1995 article in *The Atlantic Monthly* proposed a change to GDP in keeping with the values of the citizenry. In "If the Economy Is Up, Why Is America Down?" authors Clifford Cobb, Tad Halstead, and Jonathan Rowe proposed a different measure for the country: a Genuine Progress Indicator (GPI). The GPI would add up the nation's expenses (GDP), factor in sectors that are usually excluded from the market economy (such as housework and volunteering), then subtract social ills (crime, natural resource depletion, and loss of leisure time). When calculations were made under both indicators, the disparity in results suggested that GDP was no longer an accurate gauge of economic progress.

10. Ford was not applying utilitarian ethics to its reasoning, but rather a simple cost-benefit analysis—maximizing the good of the bottom line for shareholders is not an application of utilitarian ethics. There are many examples of use of cost-benefit analysis that have nothing to do with utilitarian ethical decision making. In addition to the idea of maximizing the good of the shareholders, one occasionally hears a quasi-nationalistic argument for "maximizing the good of Americans," often in the context of the relatively cheap price of goods that can be obtained from overseas sweatshop labor. From whatever perspective such a maxim might be argued, it is not an ethical one. The ethical theory of utilitarianism seeks to maximize the overall good of all, not a select group.

11. Peters, T. J., & Waterman, R. H. (1982 ). *In search of excellence: lessons from America's best-run companies.* New York: Harper & Row.

---

**The Ford Pinto Case—A Teleological Terror**

In the late 1960s, foreign competition in smaller and cheaper cars was beginning to make serious inroads on the U.S. domestic automobile market. Ford Motor Company, then headed by Lee Iacocca, came up with a plan to meet the competition head on: to develop, build, and sell an automobile "weighing no more than 2000 pounds and costing no more than $2000." That automobile was the Ford Pinto. To meet an artificially imposed deadline of the 1971 model year (to get a jump on the competition), the normal drawing-to-production time for the Pinto was drastically compressed into two years, from the usual schedule requiring almost twice that long. The compressed schedule meant that tooling for production was occurring simultaneously with design, curtailing the ability to accommodate design problems along the way. When completed, crash-testing of the models proved problematic: ruptured gas tanks and dangerous leaks occurred at almost any speed of impact. The problem was obviously the location of the tank. Yet modifying the design to change the tank location and to rectify the problem would require retooling, more money, and a later public introduction of the Pinto—none of which were acceptable to management.

After considering the costs and benefits, Ford did nothing to change the defective design. As a result, in the first seven years after the introduction of the Pinto, upwards of 500 fire-related deaths were attributable to its defective design. Ford engineers later testified that 95 percent of the victims would have survived if the fuel tank had been relocated on the vehicles. Further, the regulatory oversight agency for automotive safety, the National Highway Traffic Safety Administration (NHTSA), later amended its standards to require rupture-proof tanks on the Pinto and cars like it, prompting a massive recall by Ford. As a result of tragic deaths in Pintos, dozens and dozens of civil lawsuits were filed against Ford and millions of dollars in punitive damages were awarded to victims. It is estimated that the case ultimately cost the company more than $1 billion. In addition, in at least one case, Ford was charged with criminal homicide when, in 1978, seven years after the introduction of the dangerous and defective vehicle, three teenage girls burned to death when their 1973 Pinto was struck from behind by a van.

Ford's defenses ranged from a claim that the Pinto was "no more unsafe" than any other vehicle of its class (foreshadowing Ford's defense of its SUV)[a] to the fact that it met federally established standards for crash safety (standards that the company and its competitors had lobbied hard to keep well below the state of the art).

The actors in this real-life tragedy did not employ ethical reasoning.

---

a. A separate and in-depth case study on the Ford/Firestone product liability case is included in the case study "Auto Safety at Ford" in Part Three of this text.

---

humans should do what is right by treating others with dignity. People have a duty, a moral obligation, to do so. In everyday discussion, that duty is signified by the word *ought*. In the Judeo-Christian tradition this "ought" is positively expressed: people are obligated to love their neighbors as themselves; people ought to treat others as they would want to be treated.

### The Inadequacies of the Golden Rule
However, in the New Testament, Jesus had a more demanding standard—not simply to love your *neighbors*, but also your *enemies:*

I say unto you love your enemies, bless them that curse you, do good to them that hate you, and pray for them that despitefully use you and persecute you.... For if you love those who love you, what reward have you? Do not even the common people do the same? Be you therefore perfect....

Loving one's own or those that reciprocate love is expected. According to Jesus, the ethical dimension of the rule is as applied to "others," or those outside one's conventional circle of caring.[12]

Modern critics also point to the narrowness and potential chauvinism of concepts of the Golden Rule. There is an implicit premise in the rule that people want and expect *the same* treatment as others. Modern and post-modern concepts of humanity and history are more inclusive of the diverse and multicultural wants and expectations of people. At the time most of these ethical theories were conceived, they were, in fact, fairly narrowly directed. The ancient Greek concept of ethical virtue and moral and intellectual excellence was reserved for white, male, propertied Greeks only—no women, no slaves, no foreigners. For the most part, it was only in the twentieth century that a more inclusive concept of human rights emerged to include all people.

A corollary of the Golden Rule is ethical testing of an action by "stepping into another's shoes." With a broader and more inclusive vision of the goals of society, "stepping into the shoes" requires not just considering what would be preferable to a person, but what would be preferable to that person if he or she had the wants and expectations of the individual affected.

Immanuel Kant also was concerned that the Golden Rule would be perversely applied. A sadomasochist, for instance, desires to hurt and to be hurt; thus, that person could rationalize that it is right to harm others and to be harmed because hurting and being hurt is how he or she wants to be treated. A businessperson, too, might believe that inflicting economic harm and being the recipient of that harm is acceptable since it is part of the dog-eat-dog order of the business world.

Kant's categorical imperative, first discussed in Chapter 1, was at least, in part, an attempt to combat the possibility of this kind of corruption of the Golden Rule. Kant addressed this inherent problem by building his universal rule on basic premises regarding the fundamental rights and duties of people—something that the common understanding of the Golden Rule lacked.

### The Categorical Imperative

The Kantian formulation of the Golden Rule, *the categorical imperative*, states:

> One ought to act such that the principle of one's act could become a universal law of human action in a world in which one would hope to live.[13]

Kant's categorical imperative admits of no exceptions. It requires that a person ask whether a proposed action is consistent with universal standards of conduct. Would a person be willing to live in a world where *everyone* behaved in the manner contemplated? Would a person be willing to live in a world where everyone used violent means to get his or her way or in a world where everyone lied, cheated, or engaged in bribery? If one person may break a promise, then the rule would permit everyone to do so—there can be no exceptions. And if breaking promises was justified for everyone, there could be no trust, social order would disintegrate, and society would not function. If a person is not willing to permit others the right to a particular type of behavior, he or she may not make an exception for himself or herself.

Application of the categorical imperative is premised on Kant's second formulation:

One ought to treat others as having intrinsic value in themselves, and not merely as a means to achieve an end.

Kant believed people to be equal in their freedom and basic rights as rational human beings.

---

12. In *Plato's Republic*, Socrates imagined that one of the ways to achieve this universal "love," or care for the other, would be to abolish the traditional notion of parents—mothers and fathers would not know the identity of their own biological children, presumably encouraging a love of *all* children.

13. See Kant's Critique of Practical Reason (1788); *The Metaphysics of Morals* (1785); and, more recently, *Foundations of the Metaphysics of Morals* (2d ed.). (1989). (L. W. Black, Trans.). Upper Saddle River, NJ: Pearson Education.

As Kant expressed it, the duty to regard other human beings with respect, as ends and not merely as means, is unconditional. With the term *not merely* as means, Kant admitted the pragmatic inevitability that, to some extent, people would be treated by others as means and people might agree or consent to be used as means to another end in different situations and capacities. Nonetheless, given basic equal freedom, dignity, and rationality under the deontological model, each person has the right to decide to what extent they are willing to be so treated and in exchange for what.

Kant was interested less in the results produced by ethical behavior—what the right action would produce—than in the means used to achieve it. Kant believed that the *means* of moral reasoning and not its *ends* was what mattered. The capacity to reason morally made people human. It distinguished them from animals. For Kant, the unique qualities that gave people their potential for morality were rationality, their ability to give reasons for what they did, the freedom to act against instinct, and the ability to engage in actions based on reasons they gave. Doing what they were *inclined* to do was not a sign of a moral act. If you do "good" out of natural impulse or inclination, you may deserve praise, but you do not deserve esteem. It is only when you act against natural inclination and impulse to do the right thing that moral reasoning has been exercised.[14]

Kant lived and wrote at the time of the American and the French Revolutions; and his ideas are, in large measure, in accord with the ideas of those uprisings. The Declaration of Independence holds "these truths to be self-evident... that all men are created equal... they are endowed by their Creator with certain alienable rights... among these are life, liberty, and the pursuit of happiness." The leaders of the French Revolution similarly proclaimed human beings to have natural rights to "liberty, property, security, and resistance to oppression."[15] *Liberty* is defined as "the power to do anything that does not injure others."[16] The rights-based theory of ethics, represented by Kant and the leaders of the American and French Revolutions, holds that individuals have rights to free consent, privacy, freedom of conscience, freedom of speech, and due process.

"Contractarian" deontology seeks to apply the basic deontological principles to determine the best or most just arrangement of society by defining the terms of the human "social contract." Where Kant envisioned each person to determine ethical behavior by moral reasoning, contractarians imagine a time before organized society—a "state of nature"—where people are born equal in their basic freedom and rationality but without the means to individually secure those rights for themselves. Accordingly, they knowingly and voluntarily agree to bind together under agreed rules to preserve their security and property.[17] Under the basic precepts of deontological thought, each person—a rational entity deserving of rights—enters into the social contract entitled to the greatest freedom and equality coextensive with that of another. Rights exist to the extent that they do not unreasonably infringe on another's basic rights. The social contract that creates government and civil society exists to preserve this: "Governments derive their just power from the consent of the governed."[18]

The Lockean view of the social contract is a limited one: the role of the rules (those imposed by the State and by commonly understood moral principles of society) is to go only as far

---

14. "But assume that the mind of that friend to mankind was clouded by a sorrow of his own which extinguished all sympathy with the lot of others, and though he still had the power to benefit others in distress, their need left him untouched because he was preoccupied with his own. Now suppose him to tear himself, unsolicited by inclination, out of his dead insensibility and to do this action only from duty and without any inclination—then for the first time his action has genuine moral worth." *Kant: foundations of the metaphysics of morals* (2d ed.). (1989). (L. W. Beck, Trans.). Upper Saddle River, NJ: Pearson Education.

15. *Declaration of the Rights of Man and Citizen* (1789).

16. Id.

17. Thomas Hobbes, a seventeenth-century English philosopher, described life in the state of nature as "nasty, brutish, and short." *Leviathan* (1650). Little wonder then the impetus for man to enter into the social contract.

18. *Declaration of Independence.* (1776).

## The Lockheed Bribery Case

The conflict between deontological ethics and teleological ethics may arise in business situations that have little to do with human rights abuse or fundamental harms. In the case of foreign bribery, business managers face cultural differences in ethical norms as well as legal obstacles. A classic business case involving the ethics of foreign bribery is the Lockheed bribery case. Most people would agree that there are circumstances where immoral means are necessary to achieve a moral end, such as the personal security of another. For example, few would argue that it is morally impermissible to lie to protect the safety of a child against a kidnapper. Where the end goal is a business purpose, such as obtaining contracts and developing new business, where should one draw the line? Whether to engage in the payment of illegal bribes to obtain contracts is one such dilemma.[a] From a fairness perspective, bribery seems axiomatically unethical whether it is legal or not. Yet in the service of a greater good, might it be justified? The Lockheed bribery scandal provides a clear example of a company wrestling with this dilemma.

In the early 1970s, Lockheed Aircraft Corporation was in desperate straits as a company; it had just been bailed out by a federal government loan guarantee, and the company's very existence was at stake.[b] Many jobs would be lost if the company did not obtain a sufficient number of orders for its L-1011 Tristar commercial aircraft. Lockheed had attempted but failed to obtain contracts for the L-1011 from Italy, Germany, and Sweden; and a large order was essential to bring unit sales close to the break-even point and to at least partially repay the expense of designing and building the aircraft. A contract with Japan's Air Nippon was viewed as essential by Carl Kotchian, Lockheed's president. If the Nippon order, which meant more than $430 million in revenues, was not forthcoming, it would mean a slowdown in new design projects and layoffs for many Lockheed engineers and production workers.

Kotchian did not go to Japan, intending to bribe Japanese officials. Although directly responsible for the negotiations for the sale of the planes, he did not speak Japanese and had to rely on advice and representation from executives of a Japanese trading company that had been retained as an agent for Lockheed. The trading company represented Lockheed in all deliberations with the prime minister and the prime minister's office, and Kotchian did not have direct contact with the government officials who would make the actual decision. His contact was limited to the technical and functional representatives of Japan's airlines. The negotiations extended over a period of 70 days, during which time Kotchian stayed in a hotel room in downtown Tokyo. He was subjected to hurried meetings and continued comments that the decision would soon be made, except that "something," an unnamed "something," was not in place.

Kotchian had no firm knowledge of whether his competitors had supplied that unnamed "something," but he suspected they had or would be willing to do so. Lockheed maintained a large workforce in Burbank, California, which Kotchian felt obligated to protect. If Lock-

---

a. Until 1997, such payments were legal by corporations in most of the developed countries. The Foreign Corrupt Practices Act of 1977 (FCPA), an amendment to the Securities Exchange Act of 1934, made bribery illegal. Indeed, many industrialized nations permitted a deduction on the corporate tax return for foreign bribes paid until very recently. The Organisation for Economic Co-operation and Development's (OECD's) Accord on Foreign Bribery (June 1997) was not legally binding on any country; but by 2000, all of the OECD signatory countries (most of the industrialized nations) had passed national legislation similar to the FCPA.

b. Pendergast, B. (1976, November). *Lockheed aircraft corporation* (rev. ed.). Boston: Harvard Business School Case 9-37iv-013.

## The Lockheed Bribery Case (continued)

heed lost its fourth foreign order in a row, the jobs of the workers in Burbank would be in danger; Kotchian's own job would be in jeopardy as well. Kotchian believed that less than 1 percent of the face value of the order as a bribe was a small price to pay when so much else was at stake. Ultimately, Kotchian would authorize Lockheed's payment of $3.8 million in bribes to Japanese officials.

Mark Pastin, a business ethicist at the University of Arizona, believes Kotchian's decision was justified.[c] He argues that most ethical rules are not categorical. Even rules stating that people should keep their promises (or not lie, cheat, bribe, and violate the law) have clear exceptions: "A sound ethics requires that rules sometimes be broken." Pastin distinguishes between categorical rules and prima facie rules: categorical rules cannot be violated under any circumstances, whereas prima facie rules can be "violated in favor of more pressing obligations." Prima facie rules should not be violated if other things are equal; however, in the "complex circumstances of international business," situations "do not conform to simple maxims." Under those circumstances, "violating an ethical rule may be ethical or ethically required."

According to Pastin, the Lockheed situation should be assessed from a utilitarian perspective. Using that perspective, one can argue that the positive ends of getting the Japanese business and preserving Lockheed jobs (and perhaps the company's very existence) outweigh the unethical means of bribery. The costs are moral ones—a corporation engaged in lying, covering up, and cheating to get what it wants takes unfair advantage of its competitors. In addition, the company would be doing harm by helping corrupt officials stay in power. As well, the costs of the bribe are passed along to consumers. Balanced against those costs are positive outcomes: the health of American businesses that engage in international trade; the overall health of the U.S. economy; and the benefits of the sale to management, stockholders, and employees. The $400 million that Lockheed would receive for the planes would go a long way toward restoring Lockheed's fiscal health and provide savings to taxpayers by generating revenues and avoiding payment of unemployment benefits. From the stance of "endpoint" ethics, Pastin argues that "such payments are ethical if the product is good and someone else would have made the bribe anyhow." Others argue that the only defense to Lockheed's conduct is "necessity"; that is, the company had no other choice because of the economic factors.[d] The company cannot be defended on a moral basis; nor can it be defended on the rightness or wrongness of its decision. Mitroff and Kilmann maintain that resolving ethical dilemmas such as whether to engage in bribery requires a "dialectical" inquiry within a company.

The company should consider the following questions:

- What is the worst thing that can happen if the company engages in bribery?
- What will be the effect on future business?
- What will be the effect on the company's image?
- How will it affect the corporation's philosophy of management?
- How will it affect the control that managers have over the corporation?
- How will it affect the kinds of employees the company attracts?
- How will it affect the company's customers?

---

c. Pastin, M. (1986). *The hard problems of management: gaining the ethics edge.* San Francisco: Jossey-Bass Publishers.

d. Mitroff, I.I., & Kilmann, R.H. (1977). Teaching managers to do policy analysis: the case of corporate bribery. *California Management Review, 20*(1), 47–54.

**The Lockheed Bribery Case (continued)**

- How will it affect the company's relationships with competitors?
- What will it do to the managers as human beings? Will it erode moral fiber?
- How will it affect the status and quality of products, R&D, and innovation in the company?
- Is this the kind of practice with which the company wants to be identified?

Mitroff and Kilmann are convinced that if managers probe those questions deeply and thoughtfully, they will find that bribery is not a justifiable form of doing business.

**That Was Then... This Is Now**
**Overseas Bribery since the FCPA**

The passage of the FCPA prohibiting foreign bribery brought certainty, but also complaints of unfairness from much of the business community. The United States was among the few countries in the world to have such a law in the 1970s, and business generally lamented that the ban placed U.S. corporations at a competitive disadvantage in relation to non-U.S. multinationals vying for foreign contracts. Into the 1990s, most industrialized nations permitted bribery of foreign officials in exchange for business contracts and several still permitted a deduction on the corporate income tax return for foreign bribes paid! In 1997, each nation of the OECD voluntarily agreed to enact national legislation in its respective country similar to that of the FCPA—banning bribery of foreign officials for discretionary contracts and barring a deduction against taxes for any such payments.[e] By 2000, all member nations had enacted a home country law reflecting that agreement, and once again the global playing field seemed level for multinationals from the wealthiest nations.

But the field is level only for those playing by the rules. And there is much evidence that the FCPA is a rule often flouted by American business. Given the fact that the illicit activities are, by their very nature, clandestine and that most often take place overseas, the law is difficult to enforce. The same can be said of its international legislative counterparts.

Violations of the FCPA abound. In 2003, the oil industry was scandalized with allegations of overseas bribery. Two American executives were indicted in connection with the bribery of Kazakstan officials in the 1990s. The indictment in the country alleged that nearly $80 million was paid to the Kazakstan president, the prime minister, and senior members of the administration on behalf of the U.S. oil companies ExxonMobil, ConocoPhillips, Amoco (now part of British Petroleum (BP)), and Texaco (now ChevronTexaco) in connection with rights to oil and gas fields.

All of the companies have denied any knowledge of the payments. Charges in the indictments include violations of the FCPA and money laundering statutes. The wide-ranging investigation has implicated several European oil firms and banks as well.[f]

Before its demise, Enron faced charges of bribery in connection with energy projects in India, Bolivia, Ghana, and the Dominican Republic. (CEO Jeffrey Skilling once boasted that Enron's "ethics" should be apparent to all, given the company's successful defense against bribery charges in 11 different countries.) Xerox reported improper foreign payments of

---

e. This is a voluntary consortium of more than 30 of the most industrialized nations that agree to abide by mutual rules of commercial engagement for the sake of expediting global business. The topic is discussed in greater detail in Chapter Ten.

f. Telvick, M. (2003, April 7). Indictments allege bribes were paid for Kazakstan oil. *San Francisco Chronicle*.

---

### The Lockheed Bribery Case (continued)

$700,000 in India. Tyco is alleged to have bribed Venezuelan officials for its contract to build a $200 million water-treatment facility in that country.[g] Ironically, in 2004, Lockheed was forced to scrap a proposed merger with defense contractor Titan because of a pending FCPA bribery investigation of Titan by the government. Also in 2004, Lucent fired its two top executives in China and two other executives in the wake of an FCPA bribery scandal.[h]

Pastin and others argue that the question of compliance with the FCPA comes down to a cost-benefit analysis by the companies involved. Millions, often billions, of revenues are at stake. In the case of Kazakstan, U.S. oil companies have billions of dollars invested in the former Soviet republic. Oil reserves in Kazakstan are estimated at between 9 billion and 25 billion barrels. The financial stakes are enormous for contracts in many of those countries. The payment of a few (or even several) million dollars for a payoff of billions heavily tips the cost-benefit balance sheet. Factor in the likelihood of detection (pretty low) and the cost of fines and penalties if you are caught and successfully prosecuted (comparatively light), and the calculus favors noncompliance.[i]

Moreover, many rationalize bribery as a victimless crime—perhaps statutorily prohibited but not inherently evil. And, indeed, bribing foreign executives may not rise to the level of abusing human rights or poisoning the environment as examples of invidious corporate behavior; but prohibiting them is, nonetheless, an essential ethical rule needed to keep the free market free. Whether intrinsically bad or not, bribery is unfair; it rigs the system artificially; it countermands transparency; it abets corruption; it is a form of cheating.[j]

---

g. Drutman, L., & Cray, C. (2002, December). Top ten financial scams of the 2002 crime wave. *Multinational Monitor.*

h. Brown K., & Lee, G. L. (2004, April 7). Lucent fired top China executives. *Wall Street Journal.*

i. Incongruously, the "war on terror" may also hinder enforcement of the FCPA. In the case against the Americans for bribing the Kazakstan government, the American attorney representing the President of Kazakstan has requested that the Bush Administration intercede to dismiss the case so as not to scandalize a Kazakstani government that is providing U.S. flyover space to Afghanistan.

j. "If activities that are permitted in other countries violate the morality of the marketplace—for example, undermine contracts or involve freeloading on the rules of the market—they, nonetheless, are morally prohibited to multinationals that operate there. Such multinationals are obligated to follow the moral norms of the market. Contrary behavior is inconsistent and ultimately self-defeating." Bowie, N. (1988). *The moral obligations of multinational corporations.* In *Ethical theory and business* (5th ed.). (1997). Beauchamp. T. and Bowie, N. (Eds.). Upper Saddle River, NJ: Prentice Hall.

---

as necessary to preserve the basic rights of each person. This restrained approach is reflected in the language of the U.S. Bill of Rights, which imposes no affirmative duties on the State toward it members, but, instead, consists entirely of a series of negative injunctions—"No person shall deprive another...; "No state shall deprive an individual..."—all setting limits on what the State or members of society may do to impinge on the basic rights of others. Ultimate-

ly, however, those restrictions on *means* have a teleological end of securing the rights of all.

### *Criticisms of the Deontological Theory of Ethics (or "You Kant always get what you want.")*

Many twentieth-century thinkers rejected Kantian morality and returned to the early notion that people are driven by impulses beyond their control and, thus, are incapable of freedom and

---

19. Others such as Karl Marx rejected the whole concept of the state of nature as a false and self-serving fiction and explained the emergence of the social structure, instead, in terms of historical materialism and class struggle.

free will. Sigmund Freud, the twentieth-century Austrian neurologist and psychotherapist, wrote "... the innermost essence of human nature consists of elemental instincts, which are common to all men and aim at the satisfaction of certain primal needs."[20] Humans, according to Freud's view, are driven by impulses, not reflection.

This tendency to denigrate rationality and to view humans as bundles of elementary drives and instincts has been criticized by post-World War II European intellectuals. Dutch thinker Julien Benda complained of "the teaching of modern metaphysics which exhorts man to feel comparatively little esteem for the truly thinking portion of himself and to honor the active and willing part of himself."[21] In *The Road to Serfdom*, Nobel Prize-winning economist Friedrich Hayek wrote that the instinctual element in human behavior was harnessed by totalitarian dictatorships to impose their will. In a totalitarian society, a person has no choice to do good or evil, but merely to follow the will of the State if they are to preserve themselves. Such a regime deprives a person of the ability to exercise moral judgment. Before human beings can be ethical, they must be free.[22]

The main criticism of Kantian ethics is its exclusive focus on motives and neglect of consequences. In much the same fashion that utilitarianism can be criticized for countenancing some injustice, so might the Kantian formulation, which could theoretically have unjust outcomes despite the ethics of the means used to achieve them. In not taking into account the "greater good," social and economic injustice could flourish. Security of the basic rights of freedom and autonomy and respect do little to address inherent arbitrary political, social, and economic inequalities in the structure of society. This lack of a guiding paradigm of intrinsic fairness in deontology is addressed by principles of social and economic justice.

### John Rawls: Modern Social Justice

Modern contractarian deontologists have also used the "thought experiment" of a state of nature and its basic premises of equal freedom and rationality to determine universal principles of social justice for ethical decision making.[19] John Rawls, whose theories of social justice as fairness inform much of modern thought, imagined a "model" state of nature in order to produce the principles and rules to which reasonable, rational beings would universally agree in order to ensure the most fairness to themselves and others.

## Principles of Social and Economic Justice

The universal principles put forth by utilitarianism and the rights-based theory of ethics may both be criticized for accepting the possibility of injustice for some in their application—whether in *the means* used to achieve overall good or in *the ends* actually achieved. Principles of social justice embrace justice as fairness and seek to ensure that the societal structure is at least minimally *fair* to all, regardless of one's lot in life, in the basic distribution of social benefits and burdens. Principles of social justice address the question of the fairest distribution of political power, social resources, and economic resources among individuals and groups in society. *Fairness* does not necessarily mean *equality* in all respects, and theories of justice recognize and

---

20. "We assume that human instincts are of two kinds: those that conserve and unify, which we call erotic or else 'sexual,' and secondly the instincts to destroy and kill, which we associate as the aggressive or destructive instincts. These impulses represent the desire to love and hate. They are too complex to be called either good or bad." Freud, S. (1915). *Thoughts for the times on war and death.*

21. Modern thinkers tend to assign "a secondary rank to the mind." Benda condemned "... a whole literature (that) has assiduously proclaimed the superiority of instinct, the unconscious, intuition, the will as opposed to intelligence." Benda, J. (1990). *The treason of the intellectuals.* (R. Aldington, Trans.). New York: Norton & Co.

22. Nazi and Communist totalitarianism deprived people of their autonomy and took away their ability to exercise moral judgment. In those societies, Hayek believed, people "have no title to praise.... Outside the sphere of individual responsibility there is neither goodness nor badness nor opportunity for moral merit.... Only where we ourselves are responsible for our own interests and are free to sacrifice them has our decision moral value.... . [Morals] can exist only in the sphere in which the individual is free to decide for himself and is called upon voluntarily to sacrifice personal advantage to the observance of a moral rule." It is instructive to note, too, that the Nazis knew their enemies well—all of Kant's books were burned when the regime took power. Instead, the Nazis employed a manipulated and mutant understanding of the teachings of Friedrich Nietzsche, Kant's greatest critic, to support their ideology.

do not universally seek to redress inequalities in wealth and economic power. Principles of *economic justice*—ideas about the fairest way to distribute economic benefits and burdens in society—are subsumed within the overall considerations of social justice, as an essential aspect of liberty and the ability to participate in political life.

## The Amorality of the Market Model

*"But while they prate of economic laws, men and women are starving. We must lay hold of the fact that economic laws are not made by nature. They are made by human beings."*
— Franklin D. Roosevelt, Presidential nomination acceptance speech (1932)

In 1776, Adam Smith, Professor of Moral Philosophy at the University of Glasgow, wrote *An Inquiry into the Nature and Origins of the Wealth of Nations*. This book provided a defense of profit making at a time when the dominant religious ethics condemned even money lending and believed it easier for a camel to pass through the eye of a needle than for a rich man to get to heaven. Smith based much of his economic analysis on the natural inclination of man to self-interested actions in commerce. In one of the most famous passages, he asserted how this principle operates in commerce:

> It is not from the benevolence of the butcher, the brewer, or the baker, that we expect our dinner, but from their regard to their own interest. We address ourselves, not to their humanity, but to their self-love, and never talk to them of our own necessities but of their advantages.[23]

Smith explained the division of labor in society, "from which so many advantages are derived," as an inevitable result of the human "propensity to truck, barter and exchange one thing for another." Smith explained that, unlike other creatures, which once matured have no natural need of others, "man has almost constant occasion for the help of his brethren, and it is vain for him to expect it from their benevolence only. He will be more likely to prevail if he can interest their self-love in his favor and show them that it is for their advantage to do for him what he requires of them. Whoever offers another a bargain of any kind, proposes to do this. Give me that which I want, and you shall have that which you want, is the meaning of every such offer."[24]

In pursuing one's own self-interest in industry and in appealing to the self-interest of others, Smith believed that the public interest may well be served.

> Every individual is continually exerting himself to find the most advantageous employment for whatever capital he can command. It is his own advantage, indeed, and not that of the society, which he has in view. But the study of his own advantage, naturally, or rather necessarily, leads him to prefer the employment which is most advantageous to the society.[25]

Smith asserted that the individual's desire to protect and secure his or her property and for the highest and most efficient use of the resources to produce the greatest value for himself or herself, nonetheless benefit society: "… he intends only his own gain, and he is in this, as in many other cases, led by an invisible hand to promote an end which was no part of his intention."

Smith was a professor of moral philosophy. Before, during, and after publication of the *Wealth of Nations*, he published editions of his *Theory of Moral Sentiments*, a massive inquiry into ethics and morality that recognized the need to go beyond profit maximization toward greater goods that are more useful to others,

---

23. Smith, A. (2000). *The wealth of nations*, Book I, Chapter II. New York: Random House. (Original work published 1776).
24. Ibid.
25. Ibid., Book IV, Chapter II.

---

**Economic Justice and Fairness**
**Wealth and Income Inequality in the United States—2003 Statistics\***

*The share of national wealth owned by the richest 1% of Americans has doubled in the past three decades. The top 5% of Americans own more than half of all wealth in the United States—the remaining 95% hold the other 41%. The top 20% own 80% of the wealth—the remaining 80% own 20%.*

*With regard to income, the average black family in the United States earns 60% of what the average white family earns. In wealth distribution, however, the average black family owns only 18% of the wealth owned by the average white family.*

*The richest 10% of Americans own 85% of all corporate stock.*

*The United States has substantially more disparity than any other developed country—a recent development since the late 1970s when the U.S. ratio was better than Great Britain's and even Sweden's. The United States also has lower taxes than most developed countries.*

Many argue that such a gaping disparity in wealth is unfair. Moreover, many believe that such a high level of inequality is harmful to the well-being of society as a whole. There is empirical support for this assertion in the fact that more unequal societies have lower rates of economic growth. One likely reason for this is that in less disparate countries, educational opportunities are more equally distributed, thus fostering greater development of human capital.

Many reasons are given for the astonishing increase in wealth and income disparity in the United States, including falling levels of unionization, corporate globalization and global free trade, and declining minimum wages—issues that are examined in greater detail in Part Two of the text.

\*From "Wealth and Income Inequalities in the USA" and "The Wealth Divide: The Growing Gap in the United States between the Rich and the Rest," *Multinational Monitor*, May 2003.

---

such as justice and benevolence. Smith placed the highest value on justice; benevolence in relationships; and prudence, by which he meant self-interest based on self-respect and self-love, not selfishness. Smith was aware that self-interest does not address (nor lay claim to cover) the *rules* or *necessary moral conditions* for operation of the free market. Moral prerequisites for effective operation of the invisible hand include honesty, disclosure, fairness, and voluntariness—ethical behavior that creates the implicit mutual trust and confidence necessary for exchange to occur. The need for these rules and ethical principles to govern commercial behavior is most clearly evidenced in emerging free market economies, where background institutions are lacking and economic development is hampered on account of it.

### Justice as Fairness

Rawls sought to construct a theory of justice on the basic deontological principles of human dignity and respect as well as the premise that *the means* matter much more than the ends.[26] Upon that foundation, he posited that as long as the procedure is fair for establishing the social structure and the rules that govern it, the system is fair and justice is served. The fairness of the process engenders fairness in the outcome. To determine what a fair process would

---

26. The discussion of Rawls and his quotes in this section are taken from his most famous work, *A Theory of Justice,* (Harvard University Press, 1971). See also Rawls, J. (1999). *A theory of justice* (rev. ed.). Cambridge, MA: Harvard University Press [revised by the author].

look like, Rawls returned to the imaginary "state of nature"—that prepolitical state conjured by the Enlightenment thinkers. Rawls considered what rules for distribution of political, social, and economic benefits and burdens people in this original condition would voluntarily consent to abide by. In the state of nature, all people are equal in their freedom and rationality. All people being equally free, establishment of the rules for protecting these rights must be unanimous—no one can be coerced to agree to them. Further, each person deliberates on the matter from behind a "veil of ignorance"; that is, without knowledge of who they are; nor knowledge of any of their distinguishing characteristics, talents, and shortcomings; nor knowledge of how they would fare by the choice made.[27]

> Among the essential features of this situation is that no one knows his place in society, his class position or social status, nor does anyone know his fortune in the distribution of natural assets and abilities, his intelligence, strength, and the like. I shall even assume that the parties do not know their conceptions of the good or their special psychological propensities.

When the principles of justice that govern society are established from this original position of complete equality, "the fundamental agreements reached in it are fair."

Rawls argued that in such a situation, an egalitarian balance would be struck: people would not agree to rules that gave more to another than to themselves, nor to rules that gave less to themselves than to others. Acting from self-interest (albeit veiled and speculative) in this original position and seeking the best rules for themselves (but not knowing how the rule might apply to them), people will seek to ensure at least the minimal dignity and benefits and burdens for the least off in society, being unsure where their own position may lie.[28]

The two universal principles that Rawls described are as follows:

1. Each person is to have an equal right to the most extensive basic liberty compatible with a similar liberty for others.
2. Social and economic inequalities are to be arranged so they are (a) reasonably expected to be to everyone's advantage and (b) attached to positions open to all...

The first principle for Rawls addresses basic liberty and political rights—the right to vote and to hold political office, the right to express free speech and assembly, and the right to due process; those rights are equal among all members of society. The second principle recognizes that some social and economic inequality is inevitable, but that rational people would agree to permit it only to the extent that such inequality benefits everyone.

### The Difference Principle, Unearned Privilege, and Social Justice

Historically, in most societies, legal and political civil rights have been denied on the basis of immutable characteristics that one has no control over—mere accidents of birth (race, color, national origin, sex, able-bodiedness, age, sexual orientation, etc.). Institutional inequalities that benefit people on account of family wealth and position (again, accidents of birth) proliferate in access to education, property and capital, and political power. While people may be inherently unequal in their natural intelligence, physical ability, physical attractiveness, and similar attributes, institutional discrimination based on the caprice of nature is unjust. It also gives rise to a corollary "unearned privilege" for those arbitrarily benefited by the discriminatory treatment. The deprivation of one necessari-

---

27. For a simplified modern example of applying the "veil of ignorance," assume a debate over whether to prohibit employment discrimination against the disabled and to require an employer to make reasonable accommodations for disabled employees. In determining the most ethical course of action under Rawls' theory, one would have to weigh the possibilities veiled from the knowledge of whether the person were disabled and would benefit from the policy or whether he or she were the owner of a small business that would have to finance such accommodations.

28. Note that this benefit of everyone does not involve a utilitarian analysis—it is not the greater good of the most, but rather each member's welfare being enhanced.

| TYPES OF UNEARNED PRIVILEGE | DOMINANT GROUP | SUBORDINATE GROUP |
|---|---|---|
| Sex | Males | Females |
| Race | Whites (People of European Descent) | People of Color; Biracial, Multiracial People |
| Heterosexuality | Heterosexuals | Gays, Lesbians, Bisexuals, Transgendered People |
| Class | Middle and Upper Classes | Poor and Working Classes |
| Age | People in Early and Middle Adulthood | Children and Elders |
| Able-bodied | Able-bodied/ Nondisabled People | People with Disabilities |
| Religion | Christians | Non-Christians |

From D. Goodman, *Promoting Diversity and Social Justice: Educating People from Privileged Groups.*

ly enriches the other, whether intentionally or not. If a bias deprives women, the benefit runs to men; if a bias exists against blacks, the benefit of that bias runs to whites. Where the discrimination that gives rise to the benefit is arbitrary—not based on any concept of merit or on anything attributable to characteristics over which a person has control—the associated privilege is "unearned" or simply fortuitous and of no moral import.[29]

Peggy McIntosh has studied the concept of unearned privilege and the failure of those who enjoy it to recognize it.[30] She cataloged some of the daily effects of white privilege that she herself has experienced and came up with dozens of seemingly commonplace activities and expectations on which she could count—and on which people of color could not. McIntosh identified

similar comforts and benefits in the social structure for men, due to biases against women, and for heterosexuals, due to biases against homosexuality. There was no discriminatory animus in these experiences. They simply reflected social institutionalization of the values, concerns, and biases of the dominant group. Nonetheless, the result was a form of injustice, however inadvertent and unconscious.

## Beyond Compliance

This chapter ends as it began. Ethical dilemmas are difficult. They involve conflicts between deeply held and often opposing principles. There is no easy resolution, and yet one must still give an account for what one has done. One must provide a justification. Two different but

---

29. "Systems of oppression are characterized by dominant-subordinate relations. There are unequal power relationships that allow one group to benefit at the expense of another... The group that receives the privilege—earned or not—is the dominant group. It has greater social power and it sets the social norms... Its values, images, and experiences are most pervasive in and representative of the culture—in other words, dominant." Goodman, D. J. (2001). *Promoting diversity and social justice: educating people from privileged groups.* Thousand Oaks, CA: Sage Publications.

30. McIntosh, P. (1988). White privilege and male privilege: a personal account of coming to see correspondences through work in women's studies. Reprinted in Donaldson, T., & Werhane, P. *Managing Beyond Compliance.*

related questions are central to the pursuit of the rules that ought to govern human action and the goods that are worth seeking in human life: what is right or wrong, and what is good or bad? You have seen that the history of ethical study contains examples of thinkers who have been primarily concerned with the question of action and its rightness and of thinkers who have been primarily concerned with the ends or goals of action and their goodness. Yet ethical reasoning often requires critical analysis of the implications of both means and ends. Consideration of what one does does not necessarily preclude consideration of the other. One can accept the basic premises of humans as ends in themselves, entitled to the greatest liberty coextensive with that of others, and still apply utilitarian analysis to the situation, with those basic premises of human rights as an inherent limit on means that might justify the ends.

A general framework for ethical decision making, which you may want to keep in mind, involves inquiry into the following:
- What is to be gained by the action or the decision not to act?
  - Make sure you have all of the facts available.
    *What are the short-term implications?*
    *What are the long-term implications?*
- Who is affected by the action or the decision not to act?
  - Identify all of the parties benefited and harmed.
- What is the extent of any adverse effects?
  - How are the adverse effects balanced against what is to be gained?
    *Is the action or inaction in the best inter-*

*est of the most people affected?*
*Are any fundamental rights violated in acting or in not acting?*
- What is the obligation to those harmed (legally and ethically)?
  - Who are you, as a professional, serving? What are your fiduciary obligations?
  - What is the obligation of the company to those harmed by the action or inaction?

When in doubt and faced with little time for moral contemplation, at the very least, consider the following common ethical guidelines, which were described earlier, in evaluating your proposed course of action:

### The Golden Rule
Treat others as you would want to be treated.

Test actions by "stepping into the shoes" of those affected—put yourself on the receiving end of your actions.

### The Public Disclosure Test
How would you feel if your actions or the actions of your company appeared on the front page of major newspapers?

### The Universalization Test
Is the action one that *everyone* should follow?

If everyone took the same action that you are contemplating, is it a world in which you'd want to live? Is it a world you'd want for your loved ones?

Apply the concepts you learned in this chapter to the five scenarios below.

---

### Exercise in Ethics: Ends-Means Dilemmas

For each scenario, identify the ethical dilemmas and apply the various ethical theories, maxims, and methods to determine the most appropriate action.

1. *A Fundamental Breakthrough.* You are the research director for a pharmaceutical company. You believe that the company's claims about a product you helped develop, if not outright mendacious, are exaggerated. The product could endanger the lives of people it is

## Exercise in Ethics: Ends-Means Dilemmas (continued)

supposed to help. You are also aware that the pharmaceutical company is no longer growing as rapidly as it once was; that it has had few major new products reach the market in recent years; and that as an insider in the industry, its exaggerations are typical. You also recognize that millions of dollars in profit are needed from successful products to recoup the losses from unsuccessful ones. Product development is a very expensive proposition, and "misses" outnumber "hits" by a wide margin. Only by making substantial profits from its few successful products can the company afford the research needed to keep your team adequately funded. But that is not the only issue. You believe that only through an adequately funded research team can your company benefit society, and your team may be close to a fundamental breakthrough in the fight against AIDS.

2. *Managing New Ventures.* You work for Brighten Enterprises, a Fortune 500 company with annual sales of more than $23 billion. Your company has been on the cutting edge in new product innovation. It has grown rapidly and has produced many good jobs that help stimulate the local economy. Recently, you persuaded a small company with about $1 million in sales to purchase, finance, install, and maintain new equipment that will be used almost exclusively for deals with Brighten. You told Sunshine Electronic Devices and Precision Equipment that it could earn as much as $70 million in sales over ten years. The total cost of the equipment was about $15 million. Although this was a big step for Sunshine, the company was eager to take it. You got along well with Sunshine's managers and looked forward to working with them. The negotiations lasted more than 18 months, and you were pleased with the capability of Sunshine's people. The equipment was more than 65 percent installed when Brighten Enterprises was hit with some bad news. Marketing forecasts were not met, and revenues were 10.5 percent lower than anticipated. Your unit was hardest hit; sales were down 31 percent. Although your business is cyclical, those numbers surprised you.

Top management at Brighten decided that your unit could not afford any new investments. All new projects were terminated until a fuller evaluation could be carried out and decisions made about restructuring. Though your job was secure because of your strong track record in product development, Sunshine was sure to suffer. Without the Brighten contracts, Sunshine could not service its debt. It faced bankruptcy. More than 300 Sunshine workers could lose their jobs. You thought this scenario had probably been played out before. Sunshine had taken a chance; while Brighten, cautious as usual, had cut its losses. It was a brilliant way to manage the risk of new ventures. Brighten is the local powerhouse, the engine that gives dynamism to the economy and provides many people with jobs. Its impact is also large at the national and international level.

3. *A Tight Schedule.* An American war on foreign soil is raging, and your job is to meet specifications for a large-scale military contract on a very tight schedule. A second manufacturer waits for components produced by your company to assemble the final product. The government had been dissatisfied with late delivery by previous component suppliers. Your company was chosen chiefly because of its ability to deliver goods on time. The specifications for the component require work from a certified welder. Unfortunately, the two welders with whom you usually work are unavailable. One is on vacation; and the other, who has a long history of unexplained absences, called in sick. You are in luck, however, because the apprentice welder is available. He has worked with you for more than two years and does excellent

**Exercise in Ethics: Ends-Means Dilemmas (continued)**

work. In fact, you believe that his work is better than that of the certified welders. You trust him completely. You allow the apprentice to weld the component, but you check that the job is done correctly. X-ray inspection shows that the job appears perfect. As closing time approaches, more than 99 hours of the 100 inspection hours specified in the contract have been completed. The component has to be shipped by the end of the day, or there will be production bottlenecks. The 100-hour inspection requirement, you believe, is arbitrary: 99-plus hours is just as good. The driver in your carpool is ready to leave. You start to sign the certification papers, to apply the inspection sticker, and to call shipping to pick up the welded component. You will be awarded a bonus for meeting the deadline.

4. *Where Highways Dare Not Go.* You are a marketing professional who is offered a promotion as the leader of a team developing a new recreational vehicle. This vehicle has a rough ride and few amenities, but it can travel at high speeds and take people to places "where highways dare not go." The vehicle will be marketed to young consumers who are interested in thrills and adventure. The product must sell at a low price, so there will be severe limits on engineering and material costs. The vehicle may have safety problems. Foreign competition has created financial difficulties, but your company is betting that this product will become very profitable. Accepting the promotion would put you in line for a top management spot.

5. *Risk Perception.* You work for a small but prestigious and respected marketing research firm. An attorney from a legal firm representing the cigarette manufacturers' association asks your supervisor whether your firm would conduct a study of the scientific literature on risk perception. The request seems odd because it is not the kind of work your company usually does. Moreover, your supervisor is reluctant to do work for a firm that represents the cigarette manufacturers. He tells the attorney to look elsewhere. The attorney persists, saying that she wants your firm to do the study. Your supervisor then demands a huge fee, expecting that the attorney will back off. Surprisingly, the attorney accepts the demand. Your firm certainly could use the business because of the current down cycle in the economy. Your supervisor confides to you that if his wife knew he was accepting this job, she would be extremely upset. Her father smoked two packs of cigarettes a day and died of lung cancer at the age of 50. However, your supervisor rationalizes that it is "only an academic survey" and that he won't get further involved even if it means testifying in court. You know from your sister, who is an attorney, that risk perception is a hot topic in the courts and that your supervisor could easily become embroiled in a trial. The cigarette manufacturers have escaped paying damages to people who contracted diseases from smoking because of the warning label on the package. That label shifts the burden of proof to the smoker, who is assumed to know the risks and to have assumed them voluntarily. If an attorney for a person harmed by smoking could prove that the warning label was not adequate in communicating the risk of smoking, cigarette manufacturers could face huge liabilities.

Your supervisor asks you to do the literature review and suggests that you take the lead in client contact. This may be an opportunity for you to develop some business on your own and to create an independent reputation. However, you also understand that the evidence you unearth could be very helpful to the law firm, which will use it only to advance the interests of the cigarette manufacturers.

# Chapter 3

## Principles of Corporate Social Responsibility

*"In its broadest sense, corporate social responsibility (CSR) represents a concern with the needs and goals of society which goes beyond the merely economic. Insofar as the business system as it exists today can only survive in an effectively functioning free society, the CSR movement represents a broad concern with business's role in supporting and improving that social order."*

— Eells (1974)[1]

*"The contemporary challenge to giant business is quite modest compared to historical movements in our past. There is no strong demand for basic ownership changes.... The principal call is almost primitive in its simplicity. It is a call for corporations to stop stealing, stop deceiving, stop corrupting politicians with money, stop monopolizing, stop poisoning the earth, air, and water, stop selling dangerous products, stop exposing workers to cruel hazards, stop tyrannizing people of conscience within the company, and start respecting long-range survival needs and rights of present and future generations."*

— Ralph Nader (1980)[2]

## Evolving Conceptions of Corporate Social Responsibility

One of the primary purposes of the corporation must be to make a profit. But that goal need not be pursued wearing social blinders. Corporate social responsibility (CSR) principles limit the means that may be used to pursue corporate ends where those means pose a risk to the interests of society.

### Early Notions of Corporate Purpose

The quid pro quo for legal recognition of the corporation is the obligation to serve the public as well as the private interest. In the early nineteenth century, the state gave charters of limited liability to business enterprises for special purposes. The charter advantage, such as a government subsidy (and sometimes, in addition to one), generally was given for endeavors that furthered the public good. Legislatures used corporate charters to encourage the development of roads, bridges, and banks, for example, as these were profitable enterprises that benefited the public.[3]

---

1. Eells, R. (1974). *Conceptual foundations in business.* Homewood, IL: Irwin.

2. Nader, R. (1980, March 29). Corporate power in America. *The Nation.*

3. For more detailed discussion of this development, see Hovenkamp, H. (1991). *Enterprise and American law 1836–1937.* Cambridge, MA: Harvard University Press.

As the nineteenth century progressed, oil, steel, railroads, and other industries used corporate charters to assemble large amounts of capital. But charges of political cronyism and unfairness took place. Those charges led to broad liberalization of the conditions under which corporate status was granted. States then started to compete for charter revenue with lenient and scant requirements. Delaware won "the 'race to the bottom' in the early 1900s and it remains the domicile of many of the world's largest corporations."[4] Today all 51 state incorporation statutes (the District of Columbia included) require no other purpose for achieving corporate status than that of a corporation being organized and empowered to do what is permitted by law.

### Shareholder Primacy

In the case of *Dodge v. Ford Motor Co.*, 204 Mich. 459, 170 N.W. 668, 3 A.L.R. 413 (1919), the Michigan Supreme Court started a movement toward establishing shareholder primacy. The purpose of the corporation was to maximize returns to investors. In 1916, the board of directors of the Ford Motor Company approved a plan to reduce the selling price of its automobiles. Henry Ford, owner of 58 percent of the company's stock and in control of the board, explained the move as one that would sell more cars and, in doing so, would "employ still more men, spread the benefits of the industrial system to the greatest number, and help them to build up their lives and their homes."

Though regular dividends would continue with the price reduction, the move would result in no further payments of special dividends on the stock—something to which shareholders had grown accustomed. The Dodge brothers, 10 percent owners of the company, filed suit claiming that the price reduction was against shareholder interests.[5] In deciding in favor of the Dodge brothers, the court said:

> A business corporation is organized and carried on primarily for the profit of the shareholders. The powers of the directors are to be employed to that end.

The concept of profit maximization as the corporation's purpose grew with the expansion of business. The term was elevated from a legal precept to a business principle in Milton Friedman's classic 1970 article "The Social Responsibility of Business Is to Increase Its Profits."[6] Friedman argued that corporate executives were employees of the owners of the business and had direct responsibility to them. "That responsibility is to conduct the business in accordance with their desires, which generally means to make as much money as possible while conforming to the basic rules of society, both those embodied in law and those embodied in ethical custom."

Friedman maintained that it was irresponsible for a corporation to act on social issues such as controlling pollution or training the unemployed because those were political functions that should have been left to the government. Corporations were not designed or equipped for such considerations. Under Friedman's model, areas of social concern and social responsibility should be left to governmental regulation. The sole corporate focus should be on making profits within the confines of rules and the "ethical custom" of society.

---

4. Nader, R. (1980, March 29). Corporate power in America. *The Nation*. Hovenkamp (previous note) observes that with the proliferation of these permissive statutes, "acquiring corporate status became easier than entering into business itself."

5. It should be noted that the Dodge brothers planned to use this money to set up their own competing automobile company. Henry Ford knew this, which may cast some suspicion on his altruism.

6. *New York Times Magazine*. (1970, September 13).

## The Private Assumption of Public Functions: The Social Responsibility of Halliburton

Where the paying customer is the tax-paying public, does a corporation have an obligation to serve the public interest as well as the private interest? The question is not hypothetical. Increasingly, governmental functions have been privatized in the global economy. This widespread diffusion of private ownership and stewardship of public functions triggers questions about business responsibilities.

> Countries that once thought only governments could operate... airports, seaports, railroads, and public utilities are rushing to turn these functions over to the private sector.... In the United States, privatization of... core government functions like criminal justice and education has become a subject of experiment.... The trend toward privatization has led... to... blurring of the line between business and government. The implications... are... not... clearly understood. If voters are no longer the ultimate source of accountability for privatized functions, who is? Should shareholders of the companies exercising formerly public functions have different expectations in terms of return than do shareholders of other types of companies?[a]

The United States Armed Services has experienced a move toward privatization. Halliburton is a large defense contractor serving the needs of the armed forces. Under the first President Bush, Secretary of Defense Dick Cheney awarded a $3.9 million contract to the company to study the feasibility of private contracting for military food and laundry. Halliburton declared the privatization "feasible" and was awarded defense contracts worth more than $2 billion. After leaving office, Cheney served as the CEO of the company from 1995 until 2000, when he took the office of vice president under George W. Bush.

Since the war on Iraq began in 2003, Halliburton and its subsidiaries have received the majority of troop maintenance and rebuilding contracts that provide logistical support ranging from food to oil. The contracts to Halliburton have been awarded on a no-bid or short-bid basis, meaning they have been subject to little or no competition. The awarding of these contracts in this way has raised accusations of political patronage because of the Cheney connection and the history of Halliburton.

The Halliburton subsidiary awarded the fuel contract for American military forces in Iraq has been accused of overcharging the U.S. government by more than $61 million. It has repaid $6.2 million in overcharges. The company reimbursed the government for admitted overcharges of $27.4 million for meals that were never actually served at five locations. In 2004, Pentagon auditors concluded that the company had not adequately accounted for more than $1.8 billion of work in Iraq and Kuwait. That same year, relying on high-level whistle-blowers, the FBI opened a wide-ranging investigation into the improper awarding of the no-bid contracts in Iraq. Despite ongoing Congressional and governmental investigations into the company's activities, Halliburton continues to receive additional U.S. government contracts.

Halliburton remains active in Burma despite U.S. sanctions against investment activities there since 1997. Despite sanctions forbidding U.S. corporations from doing business with other governments such as Iran, Libya, and Iraq, Halliburton has continued to do business with those countries. In 1998 and 1999, a Halliburton subsidiary sold $23.8 million of

[a]Schwartz P., & Gibb, B. (1999). *When good companies do bad things: responsibility and risk in an age of globalization.* New York: Wiley & Sons.

## The Private Assumption of Public Functions:
## The Social Responsibility of Halliburton (continued)

equipment to Saddam Hussein's government.

Throughout the 1990s, Halliburton faced charges of foreign bribery and corruption stemming from $180 million in improper payments to Nigerian officials in connection with building a natural gas plant in Nigeria. In 2002, the SEC began a multiyear investigation of accounting fraud by the company. Halliburton was alleged to have engaged in deceptive accounting. (Like Enron, it also used the accounting firm of Arthur Andersen.) The SEC estimated that Halliburton overstated revenues by as much as $450 million from 1999 to the end of 2001. In 2004, the company agreed to pay $7.5 million to settle accounting fraud charges relating to 1998. In 2004, the company and several top executives were sued in a shareholder class action suit for intentionally engaging in "serial accounting fraud" from 1998 to 2001.

Privatizing public functions may be a necessity in the global economy of the twenty-first century, but should not such private activity be accomplished with the public interest in mind? When acting on behalf of the government, as the government's *agent*, the contracting company takes on the responsibility of fulfilling the obligations of its *principal*—the client: here, the government. Should not that obligation be to serve the interests of the public?

*Authored collaboratively by Professor Sheryl Kaiser and Mary Katherine Nugent (Loyola College 2004).

Sources: "Occupation, Inc." by Pratap Chatterjee and Herbert Docena; "The New War Profiteers" by Chris Kromm, both in *Southern Exposure*, Winter 2003/3004; "The Profitable Connections of Halliburton" by Peter Carlson, "Pentagon to Probe Halliburton for Alleged Fraud in Iraq Deals," "Contracts to Rebuild Iraq Go To Chosen Few" by Jackie Spinner, "Halliburton to Return $27.4 Million to Government," and "Halliburton Reports $85 Million Profit"—all in *The Washington Post* (February–April 2004); "Contract Sport: What Did the Vice-President Do For Halliburton?" by Jane Mayer, *New Yorker*, February 16 and 23, 2004; "Halliburton Settles SEC Charges" by Kevin Drawbaugh and John Poirier, *Reuters*, August 11, 2004; "Halliburton Accused of Fraud in Lawsuit" by Jonathan Stempel, *Reuters*, August 3, 2004; "Pentagon Questions $1.8B of Halliburton's Iraq Work" by Neil King Jr., *Wall Street Journal*, August 11, 2004; "FBI Investigating Halliburton Contracts" by Larry Margasak, *Associated Press*, October 29, 2004; "Halliburton Says Nigeria Payments Were Possible" by Russell Gold, *Wall Street Journal*, November 8, 2004.

## Criticisms of Shareholder Primacy

The shareholder-centric model relies on the limits of laws to define permissible business practices.[7] This reliance on laws presupposes a meaningful and active government concerned with social needs and obligations. But what if the law is lacking or has not yet evolved to cover a social issue or is simply not enforced? Is the appropriate means to conduct business simply to obey legal minimums?

Particularly for enterprises doing business in nations that have not meaningfully developed laws and institutions, the gap "between what one has a right to do and what is right to do" is huge. The gap between law and ethics is amplified whenever a country does not have a well-developed legal system to protect its citizens. Environmental degradation, human rights abuse of the workforce, and dangerous and exploitative marketing to vulnerable populations all might be within the limits of the law.[8]

## Moral Minimums

Theories of morally minimum corporate behavior apply under all circumstances, but especially when the law is underdeveloped. These theories do not renounce shareholder primacy; instead, they seek to lay down a moral floor on the means of profit making in situations where the law ends or is lacking. When the law does not cover moral minimums, the corporation still must do so.

Most theories of moral minimums begin with the premise that a corporation should avoid causing harm; and for harm that the corporation does cause, it should pay compensation. These theories also include ethical ground rules for respecting human rights (whether the applicable law does or does not) and principles for ethical operations in a foreign country. The rules and principles include contributing constructively to the country's development and encouraging (or at least cooperating with) governmental initiatives aimed at social welfare, including taxation.[9]

---

7. Marjorie Kelly is the co-founder and publisher of the magazine *Business Ethics,* a columnist for the *Minneapolis Star-Tribune,* and the author of *The Divine Right of Capital: Dethroning the Corporate Aristocracy.* She has criticized the shareholder-centric model for what she terms is its "aristocratic bias." In an interview with her (see *Multinational Monitor,* July/August 2002 (Vol. 23, Nos. 7 and 8)), she explains: "An aristocratic world is a property-based world. Like a feudal estate, a corporation is considered a piece of property—not a human community—so it can be owned and sold by the property class. This picture of the corporation as property was accurate at the turn of the last century. In 1900, three quarters of the companies listed on the New York stock exchange were railroads, which are pretty tangible. But today, three quarters of the market capitalization of the S&P 500 is in intangibles. A lot of the value is employee knowledge, and the notion that stockholders can own that is dubious at best."

In the corporate structure, only the members of the (property) ownership class may vote. As well, they are the only class with the right to sue the corporate managers for not serving their interests. According to Kelly, this is a vestige of aristocratic privilege. "Stockholders claim wealth which they do little to create—that's privilege, the privilege of receiving gains detached from productive contribution. Even though they're considered the sole members of corporate society, stockholders contribute very little." Employees, customers, and others harmed by the corporation may sue under the laws of negligence or worker or consumer protection laws to the extent that they exist. Those people have no right to sue the company for failing to take their interests into account or failing to operate the company in accordance with their best interests, as do the shareholders. In *The Divine Right of Capital,* Kelly recorded that of all the dollars trading on public stock exchanges, more than 99 percent is purely speculative—and that it simply goes from one speculator to another, never actually reaching companies to fund growth or operations.

Other commentators have challenged this property-rights approach to corporate obligation, arguing that the passive nature of corporate ownership—its separation from control and responsibility—dilutes accountability. See Boatright, J. R. (1994). Fiduciary duties and the shareholder management relation: or, what's so special about shareholders?" *Business Ethics Quarterly,* 4. The justification for a special, exclusive obligation to shareholders under principles of equity, contract, or agency has been examined and found wanting. Boatright contends that there is a public policy argument for a fiduciary obligation of management to owners. That argument goes on to say that management should not act in its own self-interest, but that such a fiduciary obligation would not be compromised by imposing obligations on corporate management to act with prudence and due diligence toward the interests of other affected constituencies. Others maintain that the model is not efficient. The ability of a business concern to externalize costs of production (for example, in the form of pollution) is a poor use of resources. Unequal knowledge as between sellers and buyers, particularly with regard to safety, is another problem. See Arrow, K. J. (Summer 1973). Social responsibility and economic efficiency. *Public Policy,* 21.

8. The amplified role of ethics and social responsibility for multinational enterprises and particular theories of moral minimums are examined in detail in Chapter Ten of this book, "Ethical Considerations in Multinational Operations."

9. In the 1980s, this became known as the "neoclassical view"—that corporations should pursue profits while avoiding inflicting harm. See, for example, Bowie, N. (1991, July/August). New directions in corporate social responsibility. *Business Horizons,* 34.

Theories of moral minimums are grounded in the principle that everyone is equally obligated to avoid or correct a social injury that he or she causes. That principle has its source in the ethics of compensatory justice, which is prominently reflected in the Western legal tradition. It is a negative injunction, which prohibits injurious activities, as opposed to an affirmative duty, which compels certain behaviors or actions. The U.S. Bill of Rights and the Ten Commandments are two examples of laws framed as negative injunctions. Tort law (see Chapter Seven and Chapter Eight) also provides means of legal redress for those who fail to abide by the negative injunction against causing harm.[10]

Business ethicists list obligations in ascending order of difficulty: avoiding harm, preventing harm, and doing good. They claim that avoiding harm is a moral minimum. "No one has a right to render harm on another unless there is a compelling overriding moral reason to do so."[11]

"The negative injunction to avoid and correct social injury threads its way through all morality.... Although reasons may exist why certain persons or institutions cannot or should not be required to pursue moral or social good in all situations, there are many fewer reasons why one should be excused from the negative injunction against injuring others. Any citizen, individual or institutional, may have competing obligations which could, under some circumstances, override this negative injunction. But these special circumstances do not wipe away the prima facie obligation to avoid harming others."[12]

Much of the argument against corporate social responsibility by Friedman and others is focused on the danger of putting concern for the public good in the hands of corporate management.[13] Executives, Friedman and others argued, were ill-equipped to make decisions that would "restrain inflation, improve the environment, fight poverty, and so on and on."[14] But those activities involve affirmative duties. By couching corporate social responsibility as a choice between proactively serving the public interest versus making a profit, the critics of corporate social responsibility miss "that business activity may at times injure others and that it may be necessary to regulate the social consequences of one's business activities accordingly."[15]

Theories of moral minimums are firmly rooted in the deontological ethical tradition, which are premised on the value of human beings as ends in themselves worthy of basic dignity, equality, and freedom. Those principles are universal regardless of the state of applicable law.[16]

---

10. The obligations of the tort law are reflected as negative injunctions (there is an obligation not to cause foreseeable harm, at least not without the informed consent of the person placed at risk), but there is no affirmative duty to assist one in harm's way (no legal requirement to be a Good Samaritan). Only when one's own actions caused the peril or harm is there a legal obligation to assist or compensate the victim.

11. Bowie, N. (1990). Money, morality, and motorcars. *Business, ethics and the environment: the public policy debate.* Hoffman M., & Petry, E., Jr. (Eds.). New York: Quorum Books.

12. Simon, J. G., Powers, C. W., & Gunnemann, J. P. (1972). The responsibilities of corporations and their owners. In *The ethical investor: universities and corporate responsibility.* New Haven, CT: Yale University Press.

13. See also Levitt, T. (1958, September–October). The dangers of social responsibility. *Harvard Business Review.*

14. Friedman, infra.

15. Simon, et al.

16. For example, the principles for avoiding and correcting social injury are acutely relevant for some of the worker safety and worker compensation issues raised in Chapter Seven of this book, "Obligations to the Employees of the Corporation," in the several states where there is little or no legal protection for workers injured on the job.

## The Stakeholder Model

In countries with developed social welfare laws, stakeholder constituencies have to receive consideration if the corporation is to operate.[17] Laws protect stakeholder interests. There are worker health and safety laws and antidiscrimination laws that protect the interests of employees, product liability laws that protect the interests of consumers, and environmental laws that protect the interests of the community in which the corporation operates. Internalizing those considerations into the structure of the corporation is an acknowledgment of the firm's moral obligations to the groups. From an economic standpoint, the laws are needed for the market to remain free and competitive. The ability of businesses to externalize costs, coupled with the tendency of business toward monopoly and oligopoly, serve as obstacles to efficiency and competition. Both are mitigated by laws that protect stakeholder interests.

The stakeholder theory posits that stakeholders and the firm have reciprocal obligations to each other. They can benefit and harm each other, as shown above. The stakeholder theory aims to have managers consider the interests of constituencies other than shareholders. Those that affect and are affected by corporate decisions—employees, customers, suppliers, and the community in which the corporation operates—must be taken into account.[18] The stakeholder theory finds its ethical basis in the deontological tradition that each stakeholder group "has a right not to be treated as a means to some end." Accordingly, each has a right to participate in corporate decision making that has an impact on it.

| RECIPROCAL STAKES | AT STAKE FOR THE CONSTITUENCY | AT STAKE FOR THE CORPORATION |
|---|---|---|
| Financial investment with expectation of monetary gain | Shareholders | Source of capital resources |
| Wages, benefits, and job security | Employees | Skills, labor, and loyalty |
| Reliable, affordable, quality products and services | Customers | Revenues to keep the firm profitable |
| Dependence on company for business operations | Business Partners | Dependent on partners for business operations |
| Tax base and economic and social benefit of the community and its members | Community | Right to build facilities and to operate in an environment (schools, roads, housing) conducive to a productive and competent workforce |

---

17. Skeptics of the profit-centric model emerged fairly early in the twentieth century. The proliferation of the corporate form and the dramatic growth in size, complexity, and resources of industry spurred a critical rethinking of the approach that had made such sense a few decades earlier. In 1932, Berle and Means observed: "Corporations have ceased to be merely legal devices through which the private business transactions of individuals may be carried on.... the corporation has, in fact, become both a method of property tenure and a means of organizing economic life. Grown to tremendous proportion, there may be said to have evolved a "corporate system"—which has attracted to itself a combination of attributes and powers, and has attained a degree of prominence entitling it to be dealt with as a major social institution." See Berle, A. A., Jr., & Means, G. C. (1932). *The modern corporation and private property.* Somerset, NJ: Transaction Publishers. William Gossett, the vice president of Ford Motor Company in the 1950s, described the corporation as the dominant institution of American society. By the second half of the twentieth century, the notion that the corporate purpose could extend beyond merely making a profit within the limits of the law gained wide attention.

18. R. Edward Freeman, foremost proponent of the theory, set it forth as a need to "reconceptualize the firm around the question, For whose benefit and at whose expense should the firm be managed? Evan, W. E., & Freeman, R. E. A stakeholder theory of the modern corporation: Kantian capitalism. Excerpted in Beauchamp T., & Bowie, N. (2003). *Ethical theory in business* (7th ed.). Upper Saddle River, NJ: Pearson, pp. 56–65.

## Conflicts among Stakeholders

In the stakeholder model, management (a stakeholder group itself) must balance the interests of diverse constituencies. The interest of no single group is given automatic priority over another. Thus, the model necessitates management's consideration of the various interests affected by corporate decision making.

The main criticism of the stakeholder theory is the difficulty of applying it in real-life situations, where the interests of stakeholders often are in conflict. The upcoming "Exercise in CSR," which deals with relocation of a plant, illustrates some of these tensions.

Ed Freeman, a leading stakeholder theorist, proposes resolution of conflicts among stakeholders with a "doctrine of fair contracts"—a set of basic contractual principles within which to frame consideration of the respective rights and responsibilities of stakeholders. This "doctrine" would include principles for engagement of and exit from relationships, for governance of those arrangements, and for bargaining by groups for costs and benefits. What makes the "doctrine" "fair" is that the principles are established under a Rawlsian "veil of ignorance." An arrangement is deemed fair "if parties to the contract would agree to it in ignorance of their actual stakes."[19]

Kenneth Goodpaster has identified the practical problem associated with resolving stakeholder conflict as the "stakeholder paradox."[20] On the one hand, it is incumbent on management to employ a profit-maximizing approach for the health of the enterprise. On the other hand, ethics require that management consider the interests of all affected constituencies as equals and not simply from the perspective of their influence on the ability of the firm to make a profit. The impartiality required by the stakeholder approach may be unethical because of the breach of the fiduciary duty owed to shareholders. As Goodpaster writes, "It seems essential, yet in some ways illegitimate, to orient corporate decisions by ethical values that go beyond strategic shareholder considerations...."

According to Goodpaster, management is damned if it takes a shareholder approach and damned if it takes a stakeholder approach. He has suggested that resolution of the paradox may take the form of preserving the fiduciary duty to shareholders while recognizing non-fiduciary, but nonetheless morally significant, obligations to stakeholders.[21]

The current U.S. corporate legal model retains the primacy of shareholders and recognizes fiduciary duties only to them, with a few exceptions. A handful of states, including Minnesota, have adopted constituency statutes that require corporate management to consider stakeholders other than shareholders in certain situations such as plant closings and takeover attempts. Some courts have been willing to take a broader and more long-term view of what advances the best interests of the corporation. These decisions have widened the parameters of management discretion in how it fulfills the corporate purpose from the narrow view dictated by *Dodge v. Ford Motor Co.*[22] Protections for other stakeholders consist of externally imposed regulation of the workplace, employee rights, the environment, and the marketplace.

---

19. The aggregated constituencies would agree to the terms that control the relations among them without knowledge of their particular role or position in the organization. As Rawls intended, such an approach would "ensure the basic equality among stakeholders in terms of their moral rights... and recognize that inequalities among stakeholders are justified if they raise the level of the least well-off stakeholder." Rawls, *Theories of Justice*, infra. Refer also to the discussion of Rawls and the veil of ignorance in Chapter Two, "Ethical Theory and Principles of Social and Economic Justice."

20. Goodpaster, K. E. (1991, January). Business ethics and stakeholder analysis. *Business Ethics Quarterly*, 1.

21. Boatright refined this approach by suggesting that the fiduciary obligation to shareholders be limited only to matters concerning management's duty of loyalty—to avoid and disclose conflicts of interest and to prohibit management's self-dealing—and that all other fiduciary obligations of management—to exercise due care, diligence, and prudence in corporate decision making—could be extended to other stakeholders without usurping or infringing on the duty of loyalty.

22. See, for example, *A.P. Smith Mfgr. Co. v. Barlow*, 98 A.2d 581 (N.J. Supreme Ct. 1953). In upholding a board-approved donation by the corporation to the local Princeton University maintenance fund., the Court said: "It seems to us that just as the conditions prevailing when corporations were originally created required that they serve public as well as private interests, modern conditions acknowledge and discharge social as well as private responsibilities as members of the communities within which they operate."

## Exercise in CSR
## Plant Relocation

The contrast between the shareholder and the stakeholder theory of the firm is starkly illustrated in management's decisions about whether to close a facility. These situations are not hypothetical, but occur regularly in the United States and around the world.

The relationship between a company and its employees and the community in which it operates has positive and negative symbiotic, interdependent aspects. The company contributes to the tax base for municipal services, provides jobs, creates business-to-business opportunities, and represents a source of support for civic and charitable causes. In return, the community adjusts infrastructure, roads, and zoning around the operation; provides public services such as water and police and fire protection; and generally accommodates the corporation as necessary. Employees then give their professional loyalty and skill to the firm; and they build neighborhoods, schools, and community services around and in reliance on the companies for which they work.

How corporate management views those relationships—whether it assumes any obligations in consideration of them—is often determinative of a decision to relocate. A profit maximizing approach may lead to a different decision than a theory of moral minimums or a stakeholder theory.

*Put yourself in the position of a director of a corporation considering whether to close an aging plant that is badly in need of repair and modernization in favor of moving operations overseas for cheaper production and distribution costs. Assume that the plant has been operating in the town for many years and is one of the chief employers in a town with few other employment opportunities. Analyze the issue from the perspective of the shareholder-centric model, the moral minimum model, and the stakeholder model. Determine the company's options. Consider and compare the advantages and disadvantages of each option. What facts might you need to know to make an informed and prudent decision?*

The idea for this exercise has been derived from "Ethical Issues in Plant Relocation" by John P. Kavanagh, excerpted in *Moral Issues in Business*, 7th ed., William Shaw and Vincent Barry (Eds.) (Belmont, CA: Wadsworth). In it, Kavanagh has argued that at a minimum, the corporation has an obligation not to harm the employees or the community. Accordingly, the corporation has an obligation to "replace its divot" when it decides to relocate. The ethical corporation will (1) take into account the impact of the move on employees and the community, (2) avoid the move if possible, (3) notify the affected parties as early as possible, and (4) make efforts to ameliorate the effects of the move. The company should take into account all possible options: whether it can rebuild or modernize the existing plant or build a new plant in the same community, renegotiate labor contracts, obtain financial assistance for the government, be granted special incentives, or even report less of a profit. Ameliorating the negative effects of the move may involve plans for income maintenance, job placement, job training, or even the search for a business willing to take its place in the community.

Corporate management takes these interests into account because they are bound to by law, but there is no internal obligation at the core of the corporate mission and purpose to do so.[23]

The law thus seems to lag behind the political and social consciousness of the citizenry. In August 2002, *Business Week* conducted a Harris Poll positing the following two statements, asking a wide range of Americans which statement they most agreed with.

---

23. Of course, in the corporate charter, the corporation can *voluntarily* adopt, amend, or ratify any purposes and any limits on the means of achieving them that it wants, subject to shareholder approval.

> *Corporations should have only one pur-*
> *pose—to make the most profit for the*
> *shareholders—and the pursuit of that goal*
> *will be the best for America in the long run.*
> OR
> *Corporations should have more than one*
> *purpose. They also owe something to their*
> *workers and the communities in which they*
> *operate and should sometimes sacrifice*
> *some profit for the sake of making things*
> *better for their workers and communities.*

Only 5 percent of those polled agreed with the first statement (the current law); 95 percent agreed with the second. This sentiment is even more evident in other nations where U.S. corporations operate.

## Current Conceptions of Corporate Social Responsibility

Current conceptions of CSR are broken into two camps: those that would limit the means of corporate profit making to ensure that it does not come at the expense of the public interest (the negative injunction) and those that would reconceptualize the corporate purpose to include operating in the best interest of the public welfare (the affirmative duty).

For those advocating greater restraint only— simply better-defined limits on corporate undertakings that may cause harm—the essential corporate mission remains maximizing returns to shareholders. Ken Hinkley has proposed that this could be accomplished with the mere addition of "28 words" to the legal obligations of corporate directors set forth in state incorporation statutes. The duty of directors is to make profits for the shareholders, ". . . but not at the expense of the environment, human rights, the public health or safety, the communities in which the corporation operates or the dignity of its employees."[24]

Corporations enjoy the same constitutional rights and legal protections as individual citizens. Why should they not be held accountable in the same manner as other citizens to those adversely affected by their actions? They operate with limited liability for harm caused or debt owed, though their capacity to cause harm and incur debt exceeds the potential of a single individual.[25]

On the other side of CSR, advocates of more affirmative corporate obligations maintain that corporations must serve and improve and enhance the public interest, not just avoid causing harm to it.[26] Although the particulars of this conception of CSR vary, the basic premises are that:

- Corporations have meaningful responsibilities to a broad range of stakeholders.
- Those responsibilities attach to all aspects of business operations, including doing business in the global economy.[27]

Major issues covered in CSR are many and include bribery and corruption, labor rights, environmental justice, genetic engineering, child labor, water, health, and education.

---

24. Hinkley, R. (2002, July–August). 28 words to redefine corporate duties: the proposal for a code for corporate citizenship. *Multinational Monitor* (Nos. 7 and 8). Several states have begun to see similarly structured initiatives for corporate reform on their ballots. Such a change in law would provide direct legal recourse for stakeholders adversely affected by corporate action—in the same manner as a derivative suit may be brought on behalf of shareholders against the corporation now.

25. Friedman originally posited that the limit of corporate obligation was "conforming to the basic rules of society, both those embodied in law and those embodied in ethical custom." Since that time, the rules have changed, the ethical conceptions have shifted, and societal expectations of industry have evolved. Times have, indeed, changed. Friedman began the 1970 piece, "When I hear *businessmen* speak eloquently..."

26. Norman Bowie even proposed a justification for socially responsible corporate activism, using a sort of "enlightened Friedmanite" perspective (although clothing any Friedmanite, enlightened or otherwise, with the vestments of social activism is a bit reminiscent of the film *Weekend at Bernie's*). Bowie observed that the social problems faced in this country (drug use, lack of education, poverty, crime, and racial and ethnic tensions) have a severe effect on the quality of the workforce, which is industry's most valued asset in the future global marketplace. As well as the effect on a productive workforce in the future, many of these problems adversely affect productivity now. Bowie further observed that there is little political incentive for elected officials to address the problems. There is little political will to make sacrifices now for results that will not be realized before the end of one's term of office. So Bowie concluded, by default, that business must address itself to these social issues for the protection of its profitability. Corporate America is one of the few institutions big enough, powerful enough, and with enough resources to do so. Bowie, N. (1991, July/August). New directions in corporate social responsibility. *Business Horizons*, 34.

27. There are significant rewards and penalties for companies that do this well or poorly. David Monsma, Loyola College in Maryland. (2003).

## Sustainable Development

*Sustainable development* means "meeting the needs of the present without compromising the ability of future generations to meet their needs."[28] This concept falls squarely into the more progressive or affirmative CSR camp. The cornerstone of sustainable development is a concept of three interlocking spheres: the environmental, the social, and the economic. Consciously mindful and interdependent development of each of those spheres in a harmonious fashion is the objective. The three spheres are sometimes referred to as the "triple bottom line."[29]

The Global Reporting Initiative Sustainability Reporting Guidelines (July 2002) describe these considerations as follows:

### Environment

Organizations create environmental impacts at various scales, including local, national, regional, and international. These occur in relation to air, water, land, and biodiversity resources. Some are well understood, while others present substantial measurement challenges owing to their complexity, uncertainty, and synergies.

### Social

The social dimension of sustainability captures the impact of an organization's activity on society, including on employees, customers, community, supply chain and business partners. Social performance is a key ingredient in assuring an organization's license to operate, and supports the organization's ability to deliver high-quality environmental and economic performance.

### Economic

Organizations affect the economies in which they operate in many ways, including through their use of resources and creation of wealth. These impacts, however, are not fully captured and disclosed by conventional financial accounting and reporting. Thus, additional measures are required to capture the full range of an organization's economic impacts.[30]

**ENVIRONMENTAL**

**SOCIAL**          **ECONOMIC**

While sustainable development seeks synergies in the three spheres, invariably there is a give and take from each sector and sacrifices are made where interests conflict. The goal is to attempt to resolve those conflicts in a way that causes the least harm, benefits the most people, and respects fundamental rights, both for the present generation and for future generations. In many ways, however, it is the *process* of resolving the conflicts as much as the end result that is paramount. A company's commitment to sustainable development is a commitment to engage in critical and enlightened examination of its actions and its viable options and impacts before determining its course of action. That commitment represents recognition of the interdependent nature of environmental, social, and economic spheres and a dedication to thoughtfully balancing that triple bottom line in making decisions. It signifies a willingness to challenge assumptions and rethink ways of accomplishing goals. Many of the largest companies in the world have signed on to voluntary pacts, guidelines, and organizations committed to sustainable development, though measurement standards for performance in this area are still weak.

Simon Zadek calls a corporation committed to those principles a *civil corporation*.[31] It seeks to

---

28. Brundtland Report of the UN World Commission on Environment and Development. (1987).

29. A phrase attributed to John Elkington, a leading international authority on sustainable development. (1994).

30. http://www.globalreporting.org

31. *The Civil Corporation: the New Economy of Corporate Citizenship*, Simon Zadek, (Earthscan Publications 2001).

use its resources, knowledge, and skill to find innovative ways to accomplish its objectives in ways that enhance society. Eco-entrepreneurism is a large part of sustainable development and a good example of such activism. (See the following feature.)

### The Hazards of Insularity

The notion that otherwise good companies can still do "bad things" is derived from the idea that competent management can be blindsided by a failure to recognize and respond to changes not yet in law that might, nonetheless, adversely affect the corporate bottom line. There are many examples of companies that faced public controversy and extensive, if not fatal, damage to their corporate reputation over activities that were not technically illegal. Royal Dutch Shell faced such a situation. It was implicated in the murder of nine native activists in Nigeria. The case of the Ogoni Nine in Nigeria involved the extrajudicial killing of nine activists protesting Shell's activities on native tribal lands, undertaken without just compensation and causing extreme and permanent environmental damage of the property. One of the tribesmen, Ken Saro Wiwa, was an internationally known businessman, statesman, and political activist. Shell's complicity in the murders had to do with the fact that the men were arrested at the behest of Shell; was on account of the men's activism against Shell; and that knowing of their arrest and the plan for execution without trial, Shell did nothing to stop the killings.[32]

Traditional risk management assesses the costs of risk that can be quantified: costs such as the risk of lawsuits, environmental cleanup, wage and benefit expenses, and public relations campaigns to counter bad publicity and the costs associated with such insurance. The process results in some quantifiable dollar amount associated with the risks presented by corporate activities. What traditional risk management fails to take into account are the unquantifiable costs of risk in the form of harm to reputation and brand value—intangible corporate assets of increasing importance in the global economy. Those items represent real, albeit unquantifiable risks—risks that do not translate easily into dollars and, therefore, do not fit easily into cost-benefit analysis. The point is that these unquantifiable risks can pose as big a threat to corporate success and perpetuity as the traditionally quantifiable ones. Thus, it is a grave management mistake to neglect their consideration in risk management strategy.

### Scenario Thinking

An alternative to traditional risk analysis is *scenario thinking*. In scenario thinking, a firm forces itself to consider, in a regular and continuous fashion, the question, What could happen in the future that would put us out of business? The analysis will take different forms for different types of businesses. But the concept compels a broader and longer-term view of the company's position and stability. The inquiry will involve the question, What could happen in the future that would implicate us—as a company or as individuals—in the suffering or death of human beings? (a sure bet "bad thing" to sully the shiniest of corporate brand images).

Businesses engaged in the production and sale of consumer products have to consider what practices are acceptable to their customers and whether their contractors and suppliers follow those practices. Businesses engaged in resource exploration and extraction must pay heed to issues of environmental protection and sustainable development, partnerships with the often-corrupt regimes of underdeveloped countries, and obligations to indigenous peoples.[33]

## Beyond Compliance

CSR is about beyond compliance management—there is no legal mandate for a corpora-

---

32. See the discussion of the case of *Saro-Wiwa v. Royal Dutch Shell*, filed under the U.S. Alien Tort Claims Act, in the case study "Lying Down with Dogs... Getting Up with Lawsuits: Unocal and the Alien Tort Claims Act" in Part Three of this text.

33. *When Good Companies Do Bad Things: Responsibility and Risk in an Age of Globalization*, Peter Schwartz and Blair Gibb (John Wiley & Sons 1999) ISBN 0-471-32332-2.

### Bill McDonough: Eco-Entrepreneur

"Fabrics you can eat. Buildings that generate more energy than they consume. Factories with wastewater clean enough to drink. Even toxic-free products that, instead of ending up as poison in a landfill, decompose as nutrients into the soil. No more waste. No more recycling. And no more regulation."[a]

Environmental designer Bill McDonough has a vision of green industrial growth. McDonough, a former dean of the architecture school at the University of Virginia, now works with some of the largest companies in the world to develop sustainable and environmentally responsible industrial materials and practices. His list of clients includes Ford, BP, DuPont, Nike, and BASF. His approach involves the use of double manufacturing loops— one that emits only biologically sound nutrients and the other that captures carcinogenic or toxic emissions, breaks them down, and recycles them for continuous use in the loop. McDonough calls this the "cradle-to-cradle" approach—which is also the name of the book published by McDonough and his business partner, renowned chemist Michael Braungart. McDonough contrasts this approach with the traditional cradle-to-grave linear manufacturing processes of the nineteenth and twentieth centuries.

One of the most notable accomplishments of McDonough was the redesign of Ford's Rouge River manufacturing plant, in operation for decades and traditionally one of the dirtiest operations in the country. (In the 1960s, Detroit's Rouge River actually caught fire due to the level of contamination from the Ford plant and many other manufacturing concerns along its banks.) In 1999, Ford Motor Company committed to rebuilding the obsolete and environmentally unsound plant into "a model of 21st century sustainable manufacturing" and an environmental showpiece.[b]

With the assistance of McDonough and his team, the Rouge plant was transformed.

- The plant has a "living roof" planted with 454,000 square feet (or 10.4 acres) of several varieties of sedum, covering the space of eight football fields. The sedum absorbs and filters rainwater. The roof holds more than 4 million gallons of runoff water. Solar panels heat the water, which is collected from the overflow off the plant's roof, for the building.
- The sedum also absorbs harmful carbon dioxide and airborne particles and returns oxygen to the air. The 16-acre plant parking lot performs in the same fashion. Made of porous material, storm water runs into the surface and is scoured and filtered before channeling into special vegetated ditches, which clean the water before it is deposited into the ground or the Rouge River.
- Ten huge and 36 smaller skylights provide the factory floor with natural light, proven to be beneficial to workers' eyes and moods; the natural light also greatly diminishes the plant's need for electricity.
- The plant's ductless air conditioning system utilizes fresh air over chilled water coils to keep the plant atmosphere from getting stale, keeping the workers healthier. The water in the system is chilled at low-demand hours for energy.
- Landscaping at the plant is designed around flora known to break down contaminants in the soil caused by the production of steel. Harmful microbes are absorbed by the plants instead of the soil and groundwater.

The renovations to the plant have resulted in substantial savings to Ford, prompting its CEO to comment, "This is not environmental philanthropy... it is sound business."[c] McDonough and others like him are environmental capitalists.

a. Conlin, M., & Raeburn, P. (2002, April 8). Industrial evolution. *BusinessWeek.*

b. Ford Rouge Center makes history again during launch of its unique redevelopment. http://www.ford.com

c. Conlin and Raeburn, op. cit.

tion to operate in a socially responsible way. Corporate charity, moreover, should not be confused with CSR. CSR involves a rethinking and an integration of a company's whole of operations in order to be in line with economic, environmental, and social values. (See "Waking Up the Coffee Industry," which follows.) An advantage to operating in a socially responsible way is that it may dramatically reduce the paperwork and bureaucracy associated with external governmental regulation. Only when industry operates in a socially responsible way will it be trusted to engage in self-regulation.

Different companies approach CSR in different ways and with varying degrees of commitment to different issues and constituencies. There may be economic benefits to operating in a socially responsible way, but the greatest motivation should come from within—from the owners, managers, and operators of a corporation who are also consumers, employees, residents of a community, citizens, and parents and great-great-grandparents of future generations.

It is imperative that consumers, as corporate stakeholders, accept certain responsibilities for their consumption and reward with their loyalty companies that manage beyond compliance. If you knew that the $3 difference in a $100 dress (or sport coat or watch or Barbie Dream House) meant the difference between a living wage and sweatshop wages for the person making it, would you be willing to pay the price? Would you be willing to pay the extra 3 cents for recyclable sandwich bags or a dollar or two extra for biodegradable diapers when the waste from cheaper alternatives would far outlive the users and generations of their descendents?

Increasingly, socially responsible firms are counting on increased public consciousness of the issue and are beginning to direct their marketing to the audience that says, "Yes, I am willing to pay that added increment to avoid harm or to do good." Particularly for higher-end goods aimed at more affluent consumers, socially conscious marketing is gaining a foothold. Companies such as Patagonia, a sports apparel and accessories company, are a good illustration of that approach.[34]

---

34. Bowie, N. (1991, July/August). New directions in corporate social responsibility. *Business Horizons, 34*. The consumer's obligation for social responsibility requires moving beyond mere price, and especially for pampered American consumers, the obligation will also require a willingness to sacrifice some convenience. Bowie puts forth examples of several well-intentioned but failed attempts at social responsibility—customers balking at Wendy's replacement of plasticware with more environmentally sound paper plates and cups; Kodak's ill-fated attempt to eliminate its trademark yellow-box packaging; and a general failure by the consuming public to reward businesses that contribute to the local community with their patronage, price considerations aside. Bowie includes among his examples Procter & Gamble's (P&G's) attempt to minimize packaging by offering a concentrated form of its best-selling fabric softener, Downy. The concentrated formulation required dilution with water for optimal use. Unlike their European counterparts who embraced the innovation, American consumers were slow to accept the extra step in the fabric-softening process in exchange for the environmental benefits; and U.S. sales lagged. Conlin, M., & Raeburn, P.

## Waking Up the Coffee Industry

Fair Trade Certification is one method by which a company can secure an imprimatur of socially responsible behavior. The fair trade movement has developed a process to provide assurances to trading partners and consumers that their products have been grown and processed in accord with the principles of sustainable development—that they are socially, environmentally, and economically sound.

Transfair, the sole independent Fair Trade certifier in the United States, explains the need for Fair Trade principles in the following statement:

> Throughout Latin America, Asia, and Africa, family farmers follow generations of tradition to cultivate the world's finest coffee, tea, bananas and other food products. Historically, however, the lack of market access and price volatility in global commodities markets, have prevented family farmers from receiving a fair price for their harvests. When local market prices fall below the cost of production, farming families struggle just to survive. Coffee is the second most heavily traded commodity in the world, after oil, and farmer prices have plummeted to their lowest level in recorded history, forcing millions of coffee farmers off the land and into poverty.

The principles governing fair trade are developed by the Fairtrade Labeling Organizations International (FLO), which is headquartered in Bonn, Germany. The FLO establishes standards for Fair Trade certification; then non-governmental organizations (NGOs) such as Transfair and its counterparts throughout the rest of the world implement the principles and monitor growers, producers, and importers for compliance. Transfair currently certifies coffee, tea, chocolate, bananas, and other fresh fruit in the United States.

Fair trade balances the three spheres of sustainable development by ensuring:

1. *A fair price—a living wage that permits farmers and workers to adequately support their families and permits children to attend school instead of working the fields.*
2. *Quality products—the fair price permits high-quality goods.*
3. *Care for the environment—most of the Fair Trade-certified products are organic; most are also shade-grown (coffee, tea, and chocolate), maintaining biodiversity and helping to reduce global warming.*
4. *Community impact—the redirection of agriculture from the drug trade takes place; there is community reinvestment in healthcare and education and in training others in their methods.*

From an economic perspective, a cost is associated with the fairness of fair trade. Fair Trade coffee sells for up to 25 percent more than regular supermarket brands. The FLO has set a minimum price of $1.26 a pound for coffee, which means that farmers make close to $1.00 per pound. Comparatively, farmers selling their coffee at market price can expect to make less than 25 cents per pound. Given the fact that the costs to produce coffee run between 50 cents and 80 cents per pound, many farmers facing losses on the open market simply abandon their crops, abandon their farms, and seek work in the often overcrowded and jobless cities.

The cost may be incremental (in the United States, Starbucks absorbs the additional expense and does not pass it along to the consumer—or at least not only to that consumer). But the amount represents the difference between productive and healthy lives for those

**Waking Up the Coffee Industry  (continued)**

who farm as a profession versus poverty and the eventual demise of all but multinational corporate agriculture.

The fair trade movement has gained tremendous ground in the two decades or so since its founding. In 2003, P&G introduced a Fair Trade certified coffee called "Mountain Moonlight." The first of the big supermarket coffee producers to do so, P&G had been under pressure from its shareholders to adopt the Fair Trade principles; but the shareholders withdrew their resolution when the company compromised by adding a Fair Trade brand line in addition to their existing coffees. Starbucks serves Fair Trade coffee, and Dunkin' Donuts introduced Fair Trade espresso beverages last year. Sales of Fair Trade coffee have risen dramatically over the past several years, with coffee roasters increasing their purchases of the certified beans. Fair Trade-certified products have been sold in retail outlets throughout the United States.

Wholesalers and retailers can and do charge a premium for Fair Trade certified products, and several have been the subject of criticism alleging that the increased profit collected is not properly passed along to the growers. Claims abound that companies are capitalizing on the public relations value of fair trade without practicing its principles. And some may be accurate. Nonetheless, the theory of fair trade and its growing acceptance in the community of consumers is a reason for some optimism in the field of sustainable agriculture—and a relatively small price to pay for a cup of good conscience....

Sources: http://www.transfairusa.org; "Fair Trade Coffee Buzz Gaining Momentum" by Missy Ryan, *World Environment News*; and special thanks for conceptual inspiration to Laurie Cherpock (Loyola College 2004) and her essay "Grounds for Change, or Should We Say Dollars?"

# Chapter 4

## External Control of the Corporation: Government Regulation

*"Nothing is false than the antagonism too often presented between legal authority and individual liberty. Quite on the contrary, liberty (we mean genuine liberty, which it is society's duty to have respected) is itself the product of regulation. I can only be free to the extent that others are forbidden to profit from their physical, economic, or other superiority to the detriment of my liberty. But only social rules can prevent abuses of power. It is now known what complicated regulation is needed to assure individuals the economic independence without which their liberty is only nominal."*

— Emile Durkheim, *Anomie and the Modern Division of Labor* (1902)

*"Wherever Law ends, Tyranny begins."*
— John Locke, *Second Treatise of Government* (1690)

### The Role of the State in Regulating Commerce

What does it mean to say that "Governments derive their just power from the consent of the governed."[1] Governments exist by virtue of a *social contract*. By the time of the American founding in the eighteenth century, the social contract theory was firmly rooted in America. This theory posits that human beings are born with certain inalienable rights—among them the right to life, liberty, and physical security. Unable to secure these rights individually, people agree to form governments and grant authority and power to the state to enact and enforce rules that people agree to accept. The state thus derives its legitimacy from the people. The obligation of the state is to serve the public interest by providing the maximum amount of liberty and equality compatible with the rights of others. Thus, the overarching role of government is protection of people's selves, people's liberty, and people's property.

Protection of property rights includes more than tangible and real property. People are possessed of property rights in jobs, benefits, ideas, even government subsidies; and those protections have been extended to corporations, too, as "artificial persons."

Corporations did not exist in the United States at the time of its founding, and no reference is made to corporate or commercial forms in the nation's founding documents. Nonetheless, judicial decisions have conferred upon corporate entities "personhood" and virtually all of

---

1. *Declaration of Independence.* (1776).

45

the constitutionally protected rights enjoyed by human beings.[2]

Adam Smith's *Inquiry into the Nature and Origins of the Wealth of Nations* appeared the same year as the Declaration of Independence. As the United States grew, so did its economy, influenced significantly by Smith's free market model. The founders recognized the value of commerce and its potentialities, but they reserved to the federal government regulation of interstate commerce. (See Article I, Section 8 of the Constitution, the "Commerce Clause.") At the end of the nineteenth century, the power of the federal government to regulate business started to be exercised in a meaningful way.

In a capitalist free market system, the means of production and distribution of goods are in private hands. A socialist economy features public ownership of the means of production and centralized planning rather than the market system to allocate resources and distribute income. Heilbroner asserts that the triumph of capitalism in the twentieth century is, in part, attributable to democratic institutions tempering the excesses of the market by means of regulation.[3] So, for example, the United States has minimum wage regulation, worker rights and worker safety laws, laws that protect the right of labor to collectively bargain, graduated income taxes, free public education, and a democratic government with significant economic control. As business expanded, so, too, did the scope and reach of governmental regulation. The historical development of major areas of business regulation in the United States over the decades included the antitrust laws of 1890 and 1914, the securities laws and labor laws of the 1930s, antidiscrimination and consumer protection laws in the 1960s,

and environmental laws in the 1970s.

Most of the world's economy today embraces capitalism. This chapter is about government regulation and how it has tempered capitalism's excesses.

## Advantages of a Regulated Market

Proponents of the free market system generally prefer decentralized decision making by consumers in the marketplace to the centralized control of the government. This preference is based on the efficiency advantages of markets, but is broader than that and includes economic and technological progress, a rising standard of living, social mobility, and political freedom.[4] There are a number of efficiency advantages of markets. First, they tend to achieve particular purposes at lower costs than government or to accomplish those purposes better for the same costs. In this way, they outperform government in "static" efficiency terms. However, they also outperform government in terms of "dynamic" efficiency; that is, they are better than government at promoting new technologies, improving product quality, and creating new products.[5] Finally, they outperform government by stimulating organizational improvements, increasing worker and management motivation, and enhancing business decision making. This capability has been referred to as "X-efficiency" to distinguish it from the static and dynamic efficiency advantages just mentioned.[6]

Economic efficiency requires competition, which requires that there be no obstacles to the free entry of new market participants, full market knowledge, and full market power by exist-

2. In *Santa Clara County v. Southern Pacific Railroad*, without hearing argument on the issue, the Court simply decreed that a corporation is a person for purposes of the Fourteenth Amendment: "The court does not wish to hear argument on the question whether the provision in the fourteenth amendment to the Constitution, which forbids a State to deny to any person within its jurisdiction the equal protection of the laws, applies to these corporations. We are all of the opinion that it does."

3. Heilbroner, R. (1989). Reflections on the triumph of capitalism. Originally published in *The New Yorker*.

4. Friedman, M., & Friedman, R. (1979). *Free to choose: a personal statement*. New York: Avon Books.

5. Dear landlord. (1991, February 9). *The Economist*, 75–76; Bhagwati, J. (1982). A review of directly unproductive profit-seeking activities. *Journal of Political Economy*, 90; Wolf, C. Jr. (1988). *Markets or governments: choosing between imperfect alternatives*. Cambridge, MA: The MIT Press.

6. Leibenstein, H. (1979). A branch of economics is missing: micro-micro theory. *Journal of Economic Literature*, 477–502.

ing producers and consumers. However, these conditions are rarely fully met by markets.[7] Another defect of markets is that they tend to be short-sighted and fail to adequately protect future rights and interests. Government intervention may be justified because private and public perspectives on the valuation of the present and future differ. Left to their own devices, markets also do not provide adequate amounts of public goods that anyone can use—clean air and water, schools, roads, and national defense.[8] Private goods are competitive goods; thus, the market does an efficient job of distributing them. Public goods, on the other hand, are noncompetitive; and the free market fails in their allocation because the highest bidder does not always represent the highest or best or even most efficient use.

Perhaps the most inefficient facet of private markets is the creation of so-called "spillovers," or "externalities." A positive spillover or externality exists when a producer cannot appropriate all benefits of the activities it has undertaken. An example is research and development that yields benefits to society (for example, employment in subsidiary industries) that the producer cannot capture. Thus, the producer's incentive is to underinvest in the activity unless government subsidizes it. With positive externalities, too little of the good in question is produced. With negative externalities, too much is made. Negative externalities, like air pollution, occur when the producer cannot be charged all of the costs. Since the external costs do not enter into the calculations the producer makes, the producer manufactures more of the good than is socially beneficial. In cases of both positive and negative externalities, market outcomes need to be corrected in order to be efficient.

Many, but not all, economists recognize two additional market defects. By themselves, markets may not guarantee a high level of employ-ment, price stability, and a socially desired rate of growth. Thus, to correct for apparent instabilities in the business cycle, the government can implement a variety of fiscal and monetary policies. An additional defect is that market outcomes may violate cherished values about equality and justice. In the market, a person's distribution of goods depends on factor endowments (skill and inherited wealth) and the relative prices the goods command. Society, however, may consider this distribution neither fair nor just. Thus, government may redistribute income via the tax code and other means, such as altering inheritance laws, providing social security benefits, providing welfare, and the like.[9]

In all of these instances where a rationale exists for government involvement, it does not necessarily follow that the government is capable of effectively correcting the defect. While markets are not perfect, governments, too, are not perfect. Governments suffer their own shortcomings, and the ability of governments to correct market imperfections is limited.[10]

## The Economic Role of the State— Three Perspectives

In each instance of a market defect, it is necessary to weigh whether the proposed government action would make things better. Improper government interference can be as dangerous to the stability of the market as the existence of the defects in the first place. There are three major schools of thought regarding the proper role of the government in regulating economic behavior: classic liberal, contemporary liberal, and neoconservative.

### The Classic Liberal View
The classic liberal view places individual freedom as the highest value worthy of governmental protection. The classic liberal view places great trust in the market system because the

7. Musgrave, R., & Musgrave, P. (1984). Fiscal functions: an overview from Musgrave & Musgrave. *Public finance in theory and practice* (4th ed.); Peretz, P. (Ed.). (1987). *The politics of American economic policy making.* Armonk, NY: M.E. Sharpe, Inc.

8. This principle is discussed in greater detail in Chapter Nine.

9. See the boxed feature in Chapter Two "Wealth and Income Inequality in the United States—2003."

10. Wolf, C. Jr. (1988). *Markets or governments: choosing between imperfect alternatives.* Cambridge, MA: The MIT Press.

market system values and promotes individual freedom. People enter the market to barter and exchange with others. They do this not because of social status, but because they are compelled by self-interest and because they offer each other a valuable good or service. It does not matter who is offering the good or service, so long as it is of high quality or low in price or has some other desirable feature.

Economist Milton Friedman is one of the foremost modern proponents of the classic liberal view. Despite his faith in the free market, however, even Friedman concedes the need for government regulation in some areas.

For example, Friedman accepts the cost of relying on government to preserve civil order, such as the need for police for internal security and for armies for external defense. As well, Friedman acknowledges that the government has a role to play as *rule-maker and umpire*. When individuals have disputes, someone has to resolve them. A judicial system is needed. Governments serve as arbiter where rights conflict. Friedman recognizes the government's constitutional responsibility "to coin money" and to maintain a monetary system as part of the responsibility to be a rule maker and umpire. Nonetheless, he does not favor using monetary policies for the purposes of stabilizing economic activity, believing instead that the government should maintain neutrality with regard to the money supply.[11]

Friedman acknowledges a proper regulatory role of government in correcting or compensating for free market shortcomings. He concedes the need for government antitrust regulation to counterbalance the tendency of capitalism toward monopoly. Another type of market defect that Friedman believes warrants governmental action is *neighborhood effects*. The classic example is pollution. The market is inefficient in dealing with the external costs.

The premise of a free market is that when two people voluntarily make a deal, they both benefit. If society gives everyone the right to make deals, society as a whole will benefit. Society becomes richer from the aggregation of the many mutually beneficial deals that have been made. In some cases, however, in consummating a mutually beneficial deal, there are negative or costly by-products to the transaction not accounted for in the equation. Where neither benefited party has an obligation to pay the costs of this by-product effect, the costs fall on society. The immediate parties to a transaction may be better off, but society as a whole foots the bill for some of the true expense associated with the deal. "The actions of individuals have effects on other individuals," Friedman writes, "for which it is not possible to charge or recompense them."

Friedman believes that to remedy the neighborhood effect, society must charge the individuals involved in the transaction the true costs of cleanup. Whatever damage is generated should be "internalized" in the price of the transaction. By doing so, the market defect or inefficiency (the price of pollution that is not counted in the transaction) is corrected. Only with those costs internally accounted for will the market reflect the true "social costs" of the activity. Actual U.S. policy relies on regulations and fines instead of the market to discourage adverse "neighborhood effects." But even a governmental approach that would tax polluters and others using common resources is inadequate, according to Friedman, since the extent of harm caused is often latent or long-term and the true diminution in value of the resource is often intangible and difficult to measure in monetary terms.

The market presupposes that people are rational and capable of caring for themselves. Given freedom, people are presumed to use it to further their self-interest. According to Friedman, for this reason, government involvement is also justified on *paternalistic* grounds for those who are incapable or incompetent to act for themselves. Children, the mentally incompetent, and other vulnerable populations may not be capable of the informed and voluntary decision making necessary for proper operation of the free market. For this reason, some govern-

---

11. Friedman, M. *Capitalism and freedom.* (1962). Chicago: University of Chicago Press (here and throughout the discussion of Friedman's classic liberal view).

mental regulation is warranted for protection of these groups.

Even with such qualifications, Friedman's vision of the role of the government in economic regulation is extensive. The government has a role to play in defending the nation, providing for law and order, defining property rights, adjudicating disputes, enforcing contracts, preserving competition, establishing a monetary framework, countering monopolies and neighborhood effects, and supplementing private charity by helping people who cannot otherwise help themselves. Friedman admits that his list of appropriate government functions is quite large, but not as large as the actual list of programs that the government of the United States carries out. For many functions of the U.S. government, Friedman can find no justification.

### The Contemporary Liberal View

Like classic liberals, the contemporary liberal school of economics also favors decentralized decision making and individual choice by consumers in the marketplace—with some significant exceptions. The justifications of contemporary liberals for governmental involvement stem from many of the same market imperfections identified by classic liberal thinkers, including:

#### Uncompetitive factor and product markets

There must be no obstacles to free entry and full market knowledge and no barriers to the free exertion of market power on the part of producers and consumers. Government is needed to assure competition and to expand the knowledge of producers and consumers. Thus, it is appropriate for government not only to endeavor to prevent monopoly, but also to require that warning labels be attached to cigarettes and other products when citizens are not otherwise aware of the full risks.

#### Public goods

It is appropriate for the government to provide such public goods as national defense, education, roads and canals, public space, and similar common goods. The market alone would not provide those goods in adequate quantity because, while use and enjoyment is shared by all, the costs of such goods would be borne by specific groups of providers.

Contemporary liberals differ most from classic liberals with their inclusion of the following justifications for governmental regulation of the economy:

#### Justice and equality

The invisible hand of the market guides exchange, not distribution; and the free market system does not distribute equally, oftentimes distributing quite unfairly as well. Thus, the state has a role in adjusting for some of the grosser inequalities by means of progressive tax structures, targeted tax policies, and similar devices.

#### Employment, price stability, and economic growth

The market system may not guarantee a high level of employment, price stability, and a socially desired rate of growth without government intervention to secure those objectives. To correct for instability in the business cycle, the government should decide to use a variety of fiscal and monetary policies to smooth the cycle.

Though committed to a larger scope for the government, even contemporary liberals admit that governments, no less than private markets, can err and be inefficient in attempting to remedy market defects.

Contemporary liberals such as Harvard economist Richard Musgrave and his wife and collaborator, Peggy Musgrave, divide the appropriate functions of government into three categories: allocation, distribution, and stabilization.[12] Resolving conflicts among those functions fairly and efficiently is a major challenge for government intervention.

---

12. Musgrave, R., & Musgrave, P. (1984). Fiscal functions: an overview from Musgrave & Musgrave. *Public finance in theory and practice* (4th ed.) (here and throughout the discussion of the Musgraves' views).

There is no disagreement between classic and contemporary liberals that the *allocation* of public goods should be approached collectively as opposed to individually. Government intervention in market action for those goods is required because they are "non-rival goods"—ownership of public goods is not limited to the individual who pays for them, but is shared broadly throughout society. With national defense, police protection, and other goods provided by the government, the resulting gain is available to everyone. If a single person or group of people paid for the benefits, they could not internalize the gain; they could not exclude others from enjoying the goods.

A distinction should be made, however, between public provision of goods and public production. Throughout the world, the *public provision* of goods such as education, roads, and national security is relatively high; yet not all of those goods and services are produced by the public sector. The United States, for instance, is roughly equivalent to other countries in the world with regard to the provision of public goods, but ranks low in public production (only 12 percent). Most public goods in the United States are purchased from the private sector.

The two schools of liberal economics diverge on the issue of the role of government in *distribution* of society's goods. Contemporary liberals argue that some alteration in the pattern of inequality is necessary for social justice. That distribution may take the form of progressive taxation and public welfare programs and benefits.

The two schools differ as well on the issue of *stabilization*. The business cycle is subject to substantial fluctuation. Contemporary liberals believe that the role of government is to try to control such fluctuations or to take counteractive measures to mitigate the detrimental effects of the instability (for example, unemployment and inflation). Classic liberals emphasize that government action in this area is imprecise at best and, accordingly, may lead to even greater economic instability.

Moreover, with the expansion of the global economy, it is difficult for any single national government to control its economy via macroeconomic stabilization (monetary and fiscal policies). International cooperation is now required for consistency and predictability in the markets—domestic and international. Increasingly, the countries of the world have recognized the need to act in concert for a stable global economy; but this recognition ebbs and flows, and the ability to act on it is unsteady.

### The Neoconservative View

Both classic and contemporary liberals recognize that government failure is possible. Neoconservatives assume it. They attempt to address government shortcomings as systematically as market shortcomings are treated. The views of neoconservatives are skillfully summarized by the Rand Institute economist Charles Wolf, Jr.[13] His criticisms of government intervention include:

- The fact that the government often is the exclusive provider of public goods and enjoys near monopoly status.
- The uncertainty that surrounds the means of providing these public goods (for example, education—what constitutes good teaching?—and defense—how much must be spent to guarantee national security?).
- The unanticipated side effects of government activities (for example, good intentions to provide for the poor may result in welfare dependency).

Neoconservatives assert that the government has grown too large, too complex, and too unwieldy to effectively address all market shortcomings. The systems government is attempting to influence are very complex. Efforts to correct market failures in one area may create unanticipated consequences in another. In addition, inequality of power and privilege among government officials can be as problematic as inequality of income. When one group has the right to command and coerce another, abuses are likely.

---

13. Wolf, C. Jr. (1988). *Markets or governments: choosing between imperfect alternatives.* Cambridge, MA: The MIT Press (here and throughout the discussion of Wolf's views).

Neoconservatives judge both markets and governments on the basis of equity and efficiency. The neoconservative conception of equity favors equality of opportunity over equality of outcome. With respect to efficiency, neoconservatives recognize that public goods require government intervention, and the market benefits from it. As Wolf points out, there are positive externalities from investments by the government in research and development—with benefits to be reaped by all. Nonetheless, conditions exist that lead to ineffective government management:

- Without competition, the government has difficulty achieving adequate levels of efficiency and quality in the provision of services.
- Defining and measuring the output of government programs is difficult.
- There is no bottom-line termination mechanism.

In a market, the costs of producing or sustaining an activity are linked to the prices charged for it. Consumers who decide what to buy provide the link. In the government, revenues come from non-price sources; that is, taxes, which are only indirectly related to the services that are provided. Taxpayers do not directly obtain goods and services for their tax dollars. All they can do to express their dissatisfaction is to vote out of office the politicians who supported the programs they opposed. The result is that government agencies are less accountable for their actions than are businesses in the marketplace.

Neoconservatives emphasize the limitations of what government can do to fix deficiencies in the market system. Simply because there is a market imperfection does not guarantee that the government can fix it. Nonetheless, neoconservatives accept a broad range of government involvement: environmental regulation (where there are externalities), food and drug safety controls (where consumers lack information), and radio and TV licensing (where there otherwise would be a monopoly). As well, neoconservatives accept government involvement in the production of pure public goods such as national defense, police protection, and the administration of justice. Neoconservatives also endorse government involvement in the provision of quasi-public goods such as education, postal services, and health research. Those goods may also be provided by the private sector (so there is some competition), but they would not be available in the quantities required by the whole of society. Finally, neoconservatives concede the need for some transfer programs such as social security and welfare. However, unlike classic liberal economists, neoconservatives justify government intervention on the grounds of equity, not paternalism.

## Economic Regulation: Not Whether, but How Much?

Almost all economists agree with the statement that the individual consumer should be sovereign. They use the term *consumer sovereignty* to distinguish this power from rule by government. They theorize that consumers should govern because individuals are best able to judge their needs and preferences through the transactions they choose to make in the marketplace. Through the invisible hand of the marketplace, where individual consumers are able to freely consummate deals that are in their best interests, society prospers. Reflective of those deals are the laws of the market, supply and demand, which move the goods of a society to their most productive uses. No central planning agency of government can accomplish this movement with the same wisdom and foresight that freely cooperating consumers achieve on their own.

Yet with respect to the role of government in the free market, economists are not anarchists. They see governmental regulation playing an important role. You can see that most accept that government should provide for the common defense (the armed forces), establish domestic order (police), make laws and settle disputes (legislatures and the courts), regulate unfair business practices, protect citizens from monopoly and the undesired side effects (externalities) of market activities, and provide citizens with some of the collective goods (for example, highways) that are necessary but that their voluntary behavior does not provide. Where people differ is in determining the proper mix of government and unrestrained market action in a well-functioning system.

---

**On Property and Poverty**

It is interesting to note that classic liberals and contemporary liberals both appeal to John Locke's views on property.[a] Locke believed that property was the result of people's hard work, applied skills, and unusual talent; therefore, people were entitled to the "fruits of their labor." On the other hand, he believed that no person should own more property than that person could properly use. According to this "spoilage principle," the government had the right to redistribute any excess. With regard to poverty, classic liberals would like to see problems such as poverty solved by the voluntary actions of private charities and social welfare agencies; but the classic liberal recognizes that government might have to play a role. Contemporary liberals stress that in an increasingly interdependent society, it is impossible for people to participate in the economy in isolation from one another. Whenever voluntary deals are made, they are likely to affect others who are not immediate parties to the deals. The right to freedom, moreover, is not sufficient if one does not also possess the means (that is, the resources and educational attainments) to express that freedom. Thus, government must give the disadvantaged a place to start in life so they can catch up with the more advantaged. Classic liberals, contemporary liberals, and neoconservatives all agree that unless the problems of the disadvantaged are addressed, society will face more crime, social conflict, and discord, which hurts everyone. Neoconservatives simply emphasize that there may be little that government can effectively do in that area.

a. Navarro P. (1984). *The policy game.* New York: John Wiley & Sons.

---

## Government in Theory versus Government in Practice

Government policies are not crafted by theoreticians, but by politicians. Fathoming what politicians do and why they do it is a complicated matter. The deliberations that determine political outcomes are influenced by the constitutional system of checks and balances instituted by the founders of the American Republic. The founders imagined a large country with diverse interests. Fearful of powerful majorities, they tried to create a system where no single faction could dominate. The participants in political controversies, therefore, are wide-ranging and diverse. They include citizens; corporations; labor organizations; trade associations; NGOs representing a broad array of social issues (the environment, civil rights, animal rights, disease control and prevention; etc.); federal bureaucrats; the media; and professional interests including scientists, physicians, engineers, and lawyers who not only speak on their own behalf, but also provide expert opinion. Sages, seers, and pundits of all kinds testify in front of congressional committees, appear on talk shows, and write columns for newspapers. Policy is affected by factual information, theory, beliefs, values, attitudes, conjectures, statistics, and anecdotes. The role of economists in this scheme is merely to play one part of the larger process.

Laws and regulations are enacted and implemented in myriad ways. The vast majority of legislation affecting business is not *enacted* by the elected legislature but, instead, *promulgated* by the various governmental agencies of the executive branch, which are charged with implementing the law. When Congress passes a bill, the bill usually is very broadly worded, without much detail about how it is to be executed. Laws passed by Congress contain a section authorizing the administrative agencies responsible for that area of law to develop regulations that will carry the law into effect. So, for example, when Congress passed the Clean Air Act, it directed the Environmental Protection Agency (EPA) to promulgate regulations to implement it; the EPA had to determine the actual air standards, their implementation by the states, the nature of enforcement actions, and all of the particulars. If Congress passes a tax bill rolling back capital gains, for example, it will be up to the Treasury Department to promulgate regulations that specify the types of property covered, calculation of holding periods, etc. Administrative agencies—sometimes called the "fourth branch of government" since they are neither executive, legislative, or judicial, yet they possess the powers of all three—provide the details; and the devil is in the details when it comes to law.

The regulations promulgated by government agencies have the force of law. If adopted in accordance with the principles of due process—with adequate public notice of the proposed action and adequate opportunity to be heard by all interested parties—the regulations are conferred the same authority as if enacted by the Congress. For most regulations of federal government agencies, the notice and opportunity-to-be-heard requirements are met with publication of the proposed regulation in the *Federal Register*, together with an invitation to interested parties to submit comments. In some cases, the agency conducts a more formal inquiry and hears public testimony from interested witnesses and experts. Once the comment period is over, the agency finalizes the regulation and republishes it in the *Federal Register*; thereafter it becomes law, codified in the *Code of Federal Regulations (CFR)*.

## The Role of Money

While all of those factors are important, it also is true that the role of money is large in the U.S. political system. Politicians must engage in almost constant campaigning and fund-raising is the sine qua non of this system.[14] Once elected, the quest for cash for reelection begins almost immediately. The political parties have become money machines, and a steady stream of campaign contributions is of paramount importance in ensuring a lawmaker's ability to serve and lead. Those who can provide that capital invariably have a favored position—and one might assume that some reciprocal obligation is due.

Over the past few decades, the political contributions of business and industry and organized unions have increased dramatically.[15] Those players enjoy a prominent position in the political arena because of their donations. Beginning in the 1970s and 1980s and ever-increasingly to this day, corporations have made use of political action committees, or PACs, to enhance their giving power.[16] The purpose of PACs is to make donations to political candidates. Companies are allowed to solicit funds for candidates from their employees, subject to limitations on the amount an individual employee can give to a particular candidate and various other reporting and disclosure requirements. Corporations and their management make political contributions through combinations of *hard money* and *soft money*—hard money being PAC dollars; soft money being donations to the political party itself, on which there are no dollar limitations.

By and large, the money needed to finance the increasingly expensive cost of acquiring political office "comes from big money sources, a combination of large individual wealthy contributors who write $1,000 checks, and from political action committees (PACs). Those wealthy individuals often come from the very same economic interests as are represented by the political action committees. The vast majority of Americans do not make a campaign con-

---

14. In 1996, campaign expenses for a House seat cost on average about $520,000; a Senate seat, $4.6 million. Following the money: an interview with Ellen Miller. (1996, October). *Multinational Monitor.* By 2002, the cost of a House seat increased to almost $1 million and the Senate to more than $5 million (http://www.crp.org).

15. Technically, corporations are somewhat limited in the ability to make direct political contributions. Accordingly, many of the top donors are corporate managers named as individual givers in the table Campaign Contributions: The Top 100 Donors.

16. Cohen, R. E. (1980, August 9). Congressional democrats beware—here come the corporate PACs. *National Journal,* 1305; Glen, M. (1979, December 24). The PACs are back richer and wiser to finance the 1980 elections. *National Journal,* 1982–1984; Matasar, A. Corporate responsibility gone away?: the corporate political action committee. Paper prepared for delivery at the 1981 Annual Meeting of the American Political Science Association, New York Hilton Hotel (September 3–6, 1981); Shockley, J. S. Corporate spending in the wake of the Bellotti decision: National implications. Paper prepared for the American Political Science Convention, New York (1978).

---

### Campaign Contributions: The Top 100 Donors

The Center for Responsive Politics, a nonprofit, nonpartisan watchdog group that tracks campaign contributions to federal candidates and PACs, released a report on the top 100 donors in October 2002. The report found that the top 100 had given more than $1 billion in contributions over the period 1989–2000.[a]

| *Top 10 Overall Donors* | in $millions |
|---|---|
| American Federation of State, County and Municipal Employees | $30.6 |
| National Education Association | 21.1 |
| National Association of Realtors | 20.4 |
| Association of Trial Lawyers of America | 19.9 |
| Phillip Morris | 18.9 |
| Teamsters Union | 18.8 |
| International Brotherhood of Electrical Workers | 18.3 |
| American Medical Association | 17.6 |
| Communications Workers of America | 17.5 |

| *Top 10 Individual Donors* | |
|---|---|
| Carl Lindner and Family (American Financial Group) | $4,110,240 |
| Richard DeVos and Family (Amway) | 2,388,120 |
| Jon and JoAnn Corzine (Goldman Sachs) | 935,050 |
| Philip and Tammy Murphy (Goldman Sachs) | 900,000 |
| Dwayne and Inez Andreas (Archer, Daniels, Midland Company | 896,950 |
| Kenneth and Linda Lay (Enron) | 887,390 |
| Paul Singer (Deloitte & Touche) | 743,790 |
| Alfred and Norma Lerner (MBNA) | 669,000 |
| William and Joan Schreyer (Merrill Lynch) | 584,180 |
| Alan and Cindy Horn (AOL Time Warner) | 538,780 |

a. "Under the hood: a look at the inner workings of government." (2002, October 23). *Washington Post.*

---

tribution at all, much less one at a level of $200 or more."[17]

### Other Forms of Corporate Involvement

Firms have also made grassroots efforts to motivate their employees, stockholders, customers, suppliers, and local citizens to become politically active.[18] Another notable development was the use of public policy advocacy advertising by corporations, unions, and other organized groups. Still another change was the involvement of chief executive officers (CEOs) in national political organizations such as the Business Roundtable and the Conference Board. CEOs became directly involved in establishing a political agenda for the American business com-

---

17. The big money in politics, along with self-financing, makes up about 80 percent of all money raised in Congressional races. Following the money: an interview with Ellen Miller. (1996, October). *Multinational Monitor.*

18. Keim, G., & Zeithaml, C. (1986). Corporate political strategy and legislative decision-making. *Academy of Management Review,* 11(4), 828–843; Marcus, A. A. (1984). *The adversary economy: business responses to changing government requirements.* Westport, CT: Quorum Books.

munity, taking positions on issues of vital concern, and personally lobbying Congress and government officials.

Aside from the money, the revolving door between public service and private industry also creates unparalleled access to former congressional bosses. The entry of former staffers and members of Congress into private sector lobbying (and sometimes back around again) creates an enormous opportunity for special access. Appointments to head administrative agencies often come from the world of business and then return back to the private sector, sometimes repeating the process many times.

### Lobbying, Campaign Financing, and the Corporate Right to Free Speech

The law is well settled that corporations have a First Amendment right to free speech. In 1978, the U.S. Supreme Court decided the case of *First National Bank of Boston v. Bellotti*,[19] holding that political contributions and expenditures were a form of political speech included within the First Amendment protections afforded by law to corporations. But not all corporate speech is so protected. Commercial speech, which is speech intended to promote the business of a corporation, may constitutionally be regulated as to truth (truth-in-advertising laws, for example) and time, manner, and place of delivery (for example, bans on certain tobacco advertising and limits on certain types of marketing to children).[20]

In *Bellotti*, the question before the court was whether a Massachusetts statute that prohibited businesses and banks from making contributions or expenditures for the purpose of influencing legislation represented an unconstitutional burden on the businesses' First Amendment rights of free speech. The plaintiff bank and other corporate interests were planning to make a significant investment to oppose an upcoming ballot initiative proposing that the state adopt a graduated income tax. The Massachusetts statute would have prevented them from legally doing so. In finding the Massachusetts statute unconstitutional, Justice Powell noted, "If the speakers here were not corporations, no one would suggest that the State could silence their proposed speech. It is the type of speech indispensable to decision making in a democracy, and this is no less true because the speech comes from a corporation rather than an individual."[21]

There are persuasive arguments against characterizing the expenditure of money as free speech, however:

> The notion that money equals speech is nonsensical. Since money is not evenly distributed, to have money be the determining factor of whose voice gets heard and how loud it gets heard is counter to our very basic democratic principles. We are not talking about free speech, we are talking about paid speech; and those who have more money get more paid speech. There are other constitutional principles at work here, and the very notion that money should equal speech in the political arena is absolutely contrary to the founding principles of this nation.[22]

Businesses have an obligation to act responsibly in politics, regardless of what has been codified in law. Be mindful of the political influence that permitted Enron's and Andersen's behavior to go unchecked.[23] Political contributions on Enron's behalf to federal candidates and parties totaled nearly $6 million in the decade from 1990 to 2000. A substantial percentage of those

---

19. 435 US 765 (1978).

20. The gray area between clearly political and clearly commercial speech was tested in the case of *Nike v. Kasky*, writ of certiorari *granted*, a case in which the U.S. Supreme Court granted *certiorari*, heard oral arguments, and then withdrew *certiorari*, claiming that the original writ to hear the case had been improvidently granted. 537 US 1099 (2002); *dismissed* 539 US 654 (2003). The case is discussed in detail in the Part Three case study "The Chilling Truth: Must Corporate Speech Be Honest?"

21. *First National Bank of Boston v. Bellotti*, 435 US 765 at 777 (1978).

22. Following the money: an interview with Ellen Miller. (1996, October). *Multinational Monitor*.

23. Data compiled by the Center for Responsive Politics from filings with the Federal Election Commission, except for lobby data, which is based on filings with the U.S. Senate. Wheat, A. (2002, January/February). System failure; deregulation, political corruption, corporate fraud and the Enron debacle. *Multinational Monitor*.

contributions went to members of Congress holding powerful positions in the committees charged with oversight of Enron's business activities. Throughout the 1990s, Enron lobbied hard for deregulation in the areas of its businesses, particularly that of the wholesale electricity market. The federal government began deregulation of those markets in 1992. California followed in 1996; Texas, in 1999.

Enron benefited from the revolving door, too. Beginning in 1992, Enron worked with the Commodities Futures Trading Commission (CFTC), then chaired by Wendy Gramm, wife of Texas Senator Phil Gramm, to exempt from regulation futures trading in energy derivatives.[24] The CFTC exempted such transactions and soon became one of Enron's most profitable activities. In 1993, Wendy Gramm stepped down from the CFTC and became a member of Enron's board of directors, where she remained through the 2001 collapse. Efforts in 2001 by the CFTC to reassert control over the trading in the energy derivatives were defeated by Congress, hindered largely by the Senate Banking Committee, then chaired by Senator Phil Gramm.

In the case of Enron and many of its other huge clients, Andersen served as both consultant and auditor—two roles often in conflict. Andersen's consulting revenues from Enron were many times greater than its audit fees, thus compromising its independent audit position. With respect to Enron's accountants—and the accounting industry in general—attempts to close the loopholes that permitted such financial chicanery were thwarted by the financial industry throughout the 1990s. A forceful effort by the Securities and Exchange Commission (SEC) in 2000 to separate audit and consulting practices by accounting firms was swiftly derailed.

## Beyond Compliance

The theme of this text is managing "beyond compliance"—that is, not relying on the government to protect society, but, instead, accepting that corporations and their management take some responsibility for social well-being as a member of society, irrespective of the limits set by law.

Even with the most comprehensive of regulations, there will still be a gap between law and ethics—due to the nature of law as a slow-moving phenomenon. The question for business ethicists is how to approach that gap. There are two ways:

Simply comply with the letter of the law; exploit the loopholes that exist legally; and take your chances that ethical transgressions, when discovered, will not be viewed as something that should be illegal and punished.

OR

Self-regulate—but if this is the course chosen, it must be undertaken responsibly. Responsible self-regulation requires strong ethical leadership throughout the organization. Without it, the temptations are too great.

### The Effectiveness of Self-Regulation

As discussed previously, there is a trend in the law toward rewarding companies that responsibly self-regulate. Increasingly, organizations are held accountable for the actions of their agents whether management knew of the misdeeds or not. To alleviate some of the harshness of such strict liability on the entity, statutes and court decisions have recognized that a company's financial damages may be mitigated to the extent that the organization affirmatively attempted to prevent the illicit behavior—that is, attempted self-regulation beyond mere compliance with the law.

These preventative, pro-active measures represent a bottom-line benefit to corporations faced with potential liability. Responsible managers have an obligation to implement such measures in the best interests of the corporation. Given the potential liability of the organization for the misdeeds of its agents, there has been a move toward adopting corporate ethics

---

24. A key source of income for Enron, *derivatives* are instruments that drive their value from the underlying commodity they represent and operate as a sort of hedge or insurance against unstable prices.

## Enron Total Contributions to Federal Candidates and Parties, 1989–2001

| Election Cycle | Total Contributions | Contributions from Individuals | Contributions from PACs | Soft Money Contributions | % to Democrats | % to Republicans |
|---|---|---|---|---|---|---|
| 1990 | $ 163,250 | $ 33,000 | $ 130,250 | n/a | 42% | 58% |
| 1992 | 281,009 | 75,350 | 130,550 | $ 75,109 | 42% | 58% |
| 1994 | 520,996 | 195,139 | 189,565 | 136,292 | 42% | 58% |
| 1996 | 1,141,016 | 281,900 | 171,671 | 687,445 | 18% | 81% |
| 1998 | 1,049,942 | 145,349 | 212,643 | 691,950 | 21% | 79% |
| 2000 | 2,441,398 | 489,800 | 280,043 | 1,671,555 | 28% | 72% |
| 2002 | 353,959 | 17,050 | 32,000 | 304,909 | 6% | 94% |
| Total | 5,951,570 | 1,237,588 | 1,146,722 | 3,567,260 | 26% | 74% |

## Enron Lobbying Expenditures, 1997–2001

| | |
|---|---|
| 1997 | $ 1,080,000 |
| 1998 | 1,600,000 |
| 1999 | 1,940,000 |
| 2000 | 2,130,000 |
| 2001 | 2,075,000* |

*Figures for first half of 2001 only

## Andersen Total Contributions to Federal Candidates and Parties, 1989–2001

| Election Cycle | Total Contributions | Contributions from Individuals | Contributions from PACs | Soft Money Contributions | % to Democrats | % to Republicans |
|---|---|---|---|---|---|---|
| 1990 | $ 252,780 | $ 123,975 | $ 128,805 | n/a | 43% | 57% |
| 1992 | 651,158 | 209,873 | 330,259 | $111,026 | 54% | 46% |
| 1994 | 584,361 | 344,010 | 240,351 | 0 | 50% | 50% |
| 1996 | 950,185 | 514,664 | 398,763 | 36,758 | 53% | 67% |
| 1998 | 825,056 | 442,086 | 275,720 | 107,250 | 31% | 69% |
| 2000 | 1,430,510 | 640,499 | 527,761 | 262,250 | 29% | 71% |
| 2002 | 525,442 | 347,775 | 45,405 | 132,262 | 31% | 68% |
| Total | 5,219,492 | 2,622,882 | 1,947,064 | 649,546 | 39% | 61% |

## Andersen Lobbying Expenditures, 1997–2001

| | |
|---|---|
| 1997 | $2,380,000 |
| 1998 | 1,985,000 |
| 1999 | 1,840,000 |
| 2000 | 2,480,000 |
| 2001 | 920,000* |

*Figures for first half of 2001 only

and legal compliance programs. However, even the most socially responsible managers face difficulties in implementing and assessing the effectiveness of these programs.

A study of companies that adopted such self-regulatory programs found that employees' attitudes and behavior toward the program were greatly affected by how they perceived the corporate culture. The authors of the study recorded positive employee response to ethics programs in organizations perceived to have ethical leadership, a commitment to fair treatment of employees, and a willingness to engage in open discussions of ethics in the organization. A negative perception of such programs prevailed where employees perceived that the corporate culture emphasized self-interest and unquestioning obedience to authority.[25] In such cases, corporate ethics programs were viewed by the rank-and-file members of the organization as existing only to protect top management from blame.[26]

The study characterized the two approaches to corporate ethics programs/self-regulation as either compliance-based or values-based. A *compliance-based* approach to corporate ethics programs focuses primarily on preventing, detecting, and punishing violations of the law. A *values-based* approach aims to define organizational values and encourage employee commitment to ethical aspirations. The values-based approach requires input from and participation of all employees in developing, encouraging, and rewarding ethical standards in the organization. The values-based approach, rooted in personal self-governance and integrity, aims to discern and validate the shared values of the company members and, thus, is more likely to motivate employees to behave in accordance with those values. The compliance-based approach, usually imposed from the top down (often from the company's legal department), is viewed by employees with suspicion and distrust; it is seen as yet another protection instituted for the benefit of top management.

A company that is able to achieve the shared values approach appears to be more effective in thwarting legal and ethical transgressions.

25. Trevino L., Weaver, G., Gibson, D., & Toffler, B. (2001). Managing ethics and legal compliance: what works and what hurts. *Ethical Theory and Business* (6th ed.). Beauchamp, T., & Bowie, N.E. (Eds.). Upper Saddle River, NJ: Prentice Hall (here and throughout the discussion of the study).

26. All of the characteristics of the bureaucratic ethic are discussed in Chapter Five.

# Chapter 5

## Internal Control of the Corporation—
## Management and Corporate Culture

*"On some positions, cowardice asks the question, is it expedient?*

*And then expedience comes along and asks the question, is it politic?*

*Vanity asks the question, is it popular?*

*Conscience asks the question, is it right?"*
—Dr. Martin Luther King, Jr.

*"All you need to start an asylum is an empty room and the right kind of people."*
—My Man Godfrey (1936)

Large-scale organizations have helped to make material progress possible and have provided many people with meaningful work and a sense of purpose and accomplishment. Yet there is also a dark side to large-scale organizations that novelists such as Franz Kafka and filmmakers such as Charlie Chaplin have masterfully portrayed. A large-scale organization, like a corporation, is inanimate and exists only on paper; it has no conscience of its own. Its conscience is a function of the attitudes and behaviors of the people who compose it. When the moral culture of those people is weak, employees place themselves in ethical jeopardy. They may be asked to engage in actions that conflict with their most deeply held values and convictions. Those types of dilemmas inevitably arise in organizations. How can a moral culture be created that mitigates them? What can be done to prevent the ethical lapses to

which large-scale organizations are prone? This chapter considers the laws that govern large-scale organizations, the issue of whistle-blowing, and the problem of moral responsibility in a bureaucratic organization structure.

### The Legal Relationship between the Corporation and Those Who Operate It

The legal relationship between the firm and those who operate it is based on agency principles. A firm can act only through human agents; thus, its directors, officers, managers, and other employees, as well as its attorneys, accountants, and bankers, are all *agents* of the corporation, which is the *principal* in the relationship.

Agents are responsible to the corporation, which is the principal. They must act in the best interests of the principal. That is the essence of the agency relationship. Agency law, a long-standing common-law tradition, recognizes the legal capacity of one person or entity to act on behalf of another person or entity. Anyone legally authorized to speak or act for another person or entity by an express or apparent grant of authority is considered an agent. The principal can authorize the agent to do anything that the principal legally could do.

There is great benefit to being able to have another work on one's behalf—modern business could not exist without the ability to have many agents acting on behalf of the corporation. The ability to make deals and to grow and prosper is contingent on the legal recognition of the principal as the beneficiary of the actions undertaken by its agents. There is, however, a price for this advantage. The quid pro quo is that the *principal* bears legal responsibility for *all* of the acts by one or more of its agents undertaken in its name and stead—both those that benefit and those that harm. This is the principle of *vicarious liability.* In exchange for legal recognition of the agent as one in the same as the principal, the principal bears responsibility for all actions of the agent in its name. Thus, job discrimination, sexual harassment, fraud, personal injury, or any such action undertaken by an agent may be charged against the principal as well.

Agents remain directly legally responsible for their actions. The liability of the principal is *vicarious,* or indirect, but also strict liability, meaning that there are generally no defenses available. The claim of "one rogue trader" or "one lecherous senior partner" is generally not a sufficient defense for a company whose agents are charged with such activity.[1]

The parties' obligations to each other in the agency relationship consist of the following:

*Obligations Owed by the Principal—*

### Compensation
Unless there is an agreement by the agent to render the services gratis, the principal has an obligation to pay fair compensation for services rendered. In the absence of a specific agreement as to amount, the amount owed is whatever would be considered "reasonable" for the nature of the services provided.

### Reimbursement and Indemnification
The principal is obligated to reimburse the agent for authorized expenditures made on behalf of the principal and indemnification against losses incurred while acting as directed by the principal unless—and this qualification is very important—said action is illegal or known by the agent to be wrong.

### Cooperation
To the extent that the principal's cooperation is required for the agent to render service properly, the principal has an obligation to accommodate.

### Preventing Avoidable Harm
Principals, like all others in society, have a general moral obligation not to cause preventable harm. In the case of the employment relationship, that duty is to provide safe working conditions for employees and to prevent harm on the job to the extent that harm is known by, avoidable by, and unacceptable to the affected worker or agent.[2]

*Obligations Owed by the Agent—*

### Duty of Diligence
Agents have a duty to exercise reasonable skill and care in conducting the business of the principal, including an obligation to be reasonably informed of all relevant facts and a duty to keep the principal informed of all relevant information and developments.

### Fiduciary Duty of Loyalty[3]
Agents are *fiduciaries* of the principal. A fiduciary position is one of trust and confidence—one person acting on behalf of and

1. As discussed earlier in the text, there is some trend in the law toward mitigating damages awarded against corporations under principles of vicarious liability where it is shown that the company went beyond the requirements of law in trying to prevent such activity by its agents. See, for example, the discussion of the Federal Sentencing Commission Guidelines of 1990 and the USSC case of *Burlington Industries v. Ellerth* in the Preface. In both the statutory and judicial approach, vicarious liability is strictly imposed whether or not the company knew of the wrongdoing. A company, however, may mitigate the extent of damages against itself by showing that it had implemented proactive affirmative measures to prevent and punish such behavior in the workplace. The defense is effective only when the implementation of those measures occurred *before* the wrongdoing.

2. These obligations owed by the principal to its agents are explored in detail in Chapter Eight, "Obligations to the Consumers of Corporate Goods and Services."

3. Ethical dilemmas in discharging the agent's fiduciary duties arise not only in determining the limits of the duty of loyalty, but also in determining to whom that duty is actually owed. Who is the principal: the owner-shareholders or the incumbent management running the company?

## The Agent's Duty of Obedience

"Just following orders" is a standard response to why people engage in otherwise dubious behavior. It took on a more sinister and chilling tone when it was used again and again as a defense in the Nazi war crimes trials—so much so that the "just following orders" claim became known as the "Nuremberg Defense." Post-Holocaust writers have tried to imagine how ordinary people could engage in such systematic atrocity. Modern writers contemplate the same questions with Rwanda, Bosnia, Tibet, Chechnya, and many other sites of mass genocide. Hannah Arendt identified the phenomenon as "the banality of evil" after covering Nazi Adolph Eichmann's war crimes trial in Jerusalem—observing that the most heinous evil may be accomplished without great moral suffering or dilemma on the part of the perpetrator, provided that person has the cover of legal sanction or some authority above.[a]

In a series of experiments conducted in the late 1950s, the social psychologist Stanley Milgram considered the tension between organizational requirements and individual conscience.[b] Over 1,000 subjects were involved in the experiments, which were repeated at numerous universities. The basic setting involved an individual being told that he or she was to inflict punishment on another person whenever that person made apparent learning errors. If the other person gave what seemed to be an incorrect answer, the subject in the experiment was instructed to increase the level of electric shock the person was to receive.

The purpose was to determine how far people would go to inflict increasing pain on a protesting victim. The electric shocks were simulated. The "victim" was a professional actor, and the inflictor/subject was a randomly chosen individual who had volunteered for the experiment. The actors were in on the experiment. The question that interested the researchers was whether people would stop inflicting pain after hearing grunts, verbal complaints, demands to be released, vehement and emotional protests, or agonizing screams from the victim?

As it turned out, a substantial number of the subjects, although they might display obvious distress and express outrage to the person in authority who was conducting the experiment, continued to inflict pain on the victims. The subjects continued to increase the level of the apparent electric shocks no matter how much pleading they heard from the "victim" to be released.

Milgram inferred from the experiments that people are unlikely to defy authority even in the face of an obvious moral imperative. Normal and otherwise reasonable people have a capacity for abhorrent, immoral acts committed simply because they are obeying authority.

What explains the apparent willingness of one person to inflict pain on another? First, people appear to be committed to doing their jobs and to doing them well (in this case, the job is to inflict pain when the victim makes an incorrect answer) even when the destructive consequences of what they are doing is clear to them. People want to be viewed as competent performers. They understand that society is broken up into individuals who are carrying out narrow and specialized jobs. The broader tasks of setting goals and assessing the morality of situations are entrusted to others. Someone else oversees what is taking place and assumes responsibility.

Second, while people may recognize that what they are doing is wrong, they have trouble carrying out the values they hold. "Binding factors," such as a desire to uphold the promise to conduct the experiment and the awkwardness of a withdrawal, lock people into the situation. They become consumed by the narrow technical details of their job and lose sight of the broader implications.

---

**The Agent's Duty of Obedience (continued)**

Third, as they become involved in the task, people lose a sense of responsibility. They believe themselves to be simply the agents of an external authority. They are just carrying out their duty. This point of view is the one often adopted by people operating in large organizations where they are locked into a subordinate status in the authority structure. Those people tend to believe that the activities of the organization are benevolent and useful to society and justify the inconvenience that any particular person suffers. "Quite" simply, the ends of the organization (as defined for them by others) justify the means the organization uses.

Finally, once having caused suffering to the victim, the perpetrators/subjects attempt to rationalize their guilt by imagining that the victim is unworthy—that the victim deserves punishment because he or she is unable to answer the question that has been given. The subjects come to see the victim as having some basic defect in intellect or character. The approach is not new: stereotyping victims as somehow deserving of their fate has long been a justification for the poor treatment of disadvantaged minorities in society.

a. Arendt, H. (1994). *Eichmann in Jerusalem: a report on the banality of evil.* New York: Penguin Classics. Originally published in 1963 by The Viking Press.

b. Milgram, S. (1975). *Obedience to authority.* New York: Harper & Row.

---

in the best interest of another. The agent's duty of loyalty requires that the agent avoid or fully disclose all conflicts of interest; not use confidential information for self-enrichment; disclose all financial benefits gained by the relationship; and observe a duty of obedience to act within the limits of the authority conferred, to follow reasonable instructions, and not to delegate responsibilities improperly. However—and this point is very important—the agent has no fiduciary obligation to obey illegal or unethical direction.

## The Legal Aspects of Whistle-Blowing

*"There comes a point when a man must refuse to answer his leader if he is also to answer his own conscience."*
—Sir Hartley Shawcross, British prosecutor
at the Nuremberg War Crimes trials
(opening statement)

The limits of employee loyalty are often tested in cases of whistle-blowing, where employees with knowledge of illegal or unethical behavior take the information to top management inside the company or to regulators or the media outside the company. Would-be whistle-blowers wrestle with their obligation of duty. They often are chastised, admonished, and exiled from the "team" because of it. Doing the right thing may come at great cost—both professionally and personally.

Where the terms of employment are clearly spelled out—in a written employment contract or in a union contract, for example—employees may be protected against being fired or demoted for illegitimate reasons such as discrimination or retaliation for whistle-blowing. For many workers, however, the terms of employment are at will; that is, there are no built-in protections. The at-will doctrine of employment law provides that lacking prior agreement by the parties, an employee can quit or be fired for any reason or for no reason at all without further legal recourse. For example, an at-will whistle-blower has little protection against being fired or demoted or from another detriment as a result of going public with his or her information.

The law recognizes several exceptions to the at-will doctrine. Most of the protection against retaliation afforded whistle-blowers is through the provision of particular statutes under which a violation is reported. The two main statutory exceptions are (1) the employment antidiscrimination laws—which prohibit discrimination in hiring, firing, or terms of employment on the basis of race, color, national origin, sex, religion, age, physical or mental disability, and (in some states but not at the federal level) sexual orientation and (2) the antiretaliation laws and provisions of laws that protect whistle-blowers. Firing an employee in violation of those laws gives rise to a cause of action by the employee for wrongful discharge or wrongful termination and a suit for damages or reinstatement against the employer. Antiretaliation laws make it unlawful to retaliate by firing, demoting, or changing the terms of employment detrimentally for one who reports illegal or unethical conduct.[4]

Many of the major pieces of federal legislation include provisions protecting those who report violations of the statute against retaliation. The National Labor Relations Act, the Occupational Safety and Health Act, the Clean Air Act, the Clean Water Act, the Railroad Retirement Act, the Employee Retirement Income Security Act of 1974 (ERISA), and many more include whistle-blower protection. The Corporate Fraud Accountability Act of 2002 also includes antiretaliation protection for employees who provide information to authorities or shareholders about corporate financial wrongdoing. But laws that protect whistle-blowers are something of a patchwork—providing protection only if the violation is of a statute with antiretaliation provisions or if the state provides some legal protection for the whistle-blower in its law.[5]

Retaliation can take many forms. Ostracizing the employee, assigning demeaning or meaningless work, transferring a person to Timbuktu—all are common organizational responses to whistle-blowing, which are not necessarily prohibited by law.[6]

### The Perils of Whistle-Blowing (or "Let no good deed go unpunished.")

The decision to blow the whistle on one's own organization often has been described as a choice between loyalty, dissent, or exit. When faced with ethically objectionable behavior, a person has the choice to go along with the behavior, dissent and risk the negative repercussions, or leave the organization so as to avoid moral compromise. None of those options is pleasant.

There are several types of whistle-blowing:[7]

- Internal versus external whistle-blowing—whether report of activity remains inside the company or goes outside to regulators or the public
- Personal versus impersonal whistle-blowing—whether the nature of the harm presents a danger to the public at large or

---

4. See, for example, the Civil Service Reform Act of 1978, the False Claims Act, and the Whistleblower Protection Act of 1989.

5. Where required by fairness and equity, the common law also recognizes some exceptions to the employment-at-will doctrine. For example, where application of the doctrine would subvert the public interest, the employment-at-will doctrine will not be recognized (the public policy exception); and where an employer has otherwise assured employees that they will be fired only for cause, the corporation can be legally held to that promise (the quasi-contract exception).

6. Some of the more famous examples include the following: Ernie Fitzgerald, the chief accountant for the Pentagon in the 1960s and 1970s, made public egregious overcharges by U.S. defense contractors; he was reassigned to auditing government-subsidized bowling alleys in Thailand in a windowless basement office. Roger Boisjoly, chief engineer for Morton Thiokol on the ill-fated *Challenger* space shuttle, testified truthfully under oath that Thiokol and NASA had known of the potential for explosion before the Challenger launch; Boisjoly, the former chief rocket scientist in the United States, was reassigned, blackballed from the space program, and eventually suffered a nervous breakdown. Dr. Jeffrey Wigand, chief of research for Brown & Williamson Tobacco, endured an unbelievable personal and professional smear campaign by the company when he went public about its use of chemicals to enhance the nicotine in its cigarettes; Wigand was black-listed from the industry, lost his home and family, and went from making $300,000 a year in the industry to making $30,000 a year teaching high school chemistry and Japanese. Jeffrey McMahon, the Enron accountant who first raised a red flag to superiors about the company's financial shell game, was promptly transferred to London. The automakers' decades-long and ultimately unsuccessful smear of consumer advocate Ralph Nader and the killing of Kerr-McGee worker-activist Karen Silkwood are two more extreme examples of the risks of whistle-blowing.

7. These characterizations are derived from the work of Richard DeGeorge, as put forth in his chapter "Whistleblowing" in *Business Ethics* (5th ed.), New York: Prentice Hall, 1999. Note that DeGeorge excludes from this discussion "governmental" whistle-blowers, acknowledging that the obligations one has to one's government and as a government employee are considerably different than those of a private employee to a private corporation.

personal harm to an individual or a group (for example, the risk of harm from the carcinogenic effects of tobacco to the public versus the harm from sexual harassment)

- Open versus anonymous whistle-blowing—whether the accuser openly reveals his or her identity and thus is subject to almost inevitable retaliation or, instead, makes the disclosure anonymously, leaving the source of the claims unknown and his or her credibility in question.

For many, the preferable method of whistle-blowing is to (1) address an impersonal harm of serious import in order to counter charges of self-interest;[8] (2) to undertake the action openly so that the accused may confront the accuser; or (3) to take the information outside the organization only after the exhaustion of internal channels, the idea being that organizations should have the opportunity for self-correction before the problem is made public.

When challenged with accusation, many corporations move to a defensive mode instead of critically examining the charges raised. Even if the whistle-blower is not fired, he or she generally is no longer trusted and, as a result, may have to give up hope of succeeding in the organization.

Open dissent identifies the whistle-blower for retaliation. Indeed, according to the Government Accountability Project, 90 percent of all whistle-blowers suffer reprisal—nearly half of those who blow the whistle are fired, half of those who are fired lose their homes, and half of that group suffers a separation or divorce.[9] Many get blackballed from the industry in which they have worked. There is rarely a happy ending. Nonetheless, ethical individuals make this personal sacrifice all the time.

Given the almost inevitable personal and professional sacrifice involved, reluctant whistle-blowers face great moral conflict—wanting to please the bosses and keep the job, yet wanting to do the "right" thing. Determining when one *may* and when one *must* blow the whistle on corporate action can be difficult to discern. When is there a moral *obligation* to blow the whistle on one's own organization?

Generally, whistle-blowing is agreed to be morally *permitted* provided that the allegations are true and provable and that disclosing them will not compromise some greater good. As well, many argue that:

- The nature of the risk of harm must be a *serious and considerable harm*; the likely harm to the organization should be substantially outweighed by the good of informing the public.
- An employee should first report the matter internally. The organization should be permitted the chance to correct the problem itself.

In comparison, a moral imperative that *requires* one to blow the whistle obtains if the above conditions are met, if there is no action is taken after the exhaustion of internal channels, and if:

- The would-be whistle-blower possesses or has access to documented evidence that would convince a reasonable impartial observer that the allegations are accurate.
- The would-be whistle-blower has good reason to believe that by going public, great harm will be prevented or the necessary changes will be brought about; the chance of success must outweigh the risks and dangers to which the whistle-blower is exposed. Without a good chance of preventing the harm or making those responsible for it pay, one is not *obligated* to suffer the potential consequences of going public.[10]

8. To the contrary, others argue not only that is there a moral obligation to speak out in cases of potential death or personal injury, but also that common torts and transgressions such as systemic discrimination, financial fraud, and violations of privacy also are whistle-worthy. See, for example, James, G. G. (1995). Defense of whistleblowing. Reprinted in *Contemporary issues in business ethics*. DesJardins, J., & McCall, J. (Eds.). Belmont, CA: Wadsworth.

9. Mayer, C. A., & Joyce A. (2002, February 10). Blowing the whistle. *The Washington Post*.

10. DeGeorge, *Business Ethics*. Other business ethicists would further require the whistle-blower to examine his or her own motives before blowing the whistle and would stress the need for a factual, well-documented, and nonmalicious disclosure by the whistle-blower. See, for example, Bok, S. (Summer 1980). Whistleblowing and professional responsibility. *New York University Education Quarterly*, 11.

---

**THINKING OF BLOWING THE WHISTLE?**

- Determine whether the situation involves an impersonal or a personal ethical issue. The greater the harm and the wider the potential pool of victims, the greater the obligation to speak up.
- Examine your motive in blowing the whistle. If some personal animosity is involved, make sure that is not coloring your view of the situation.
- Verify and document as much information as possible; and if it must be obtained or revealed illegally, make sure the potential harm posed by nondisclosure would justify the misappropriation.
- Determine the type of wrongdoing and to whom it should be reported—both inside and outside the organization, either regulatory agency or public interest group. Who is best in position to help or do something about the situation?
- State all allegations specifically and stick to the facts. Making untrue or unprovable claims will open you up to a suit for defamation. If you stick to the facts, the truth is always a defense against defamation.
- Decide whether internal or external whistle-blowing is more appropriate. This will depend on the nature of the organization, the nature of the harm, and the way the organization generally responds to such disclosures.
- To the extent that the company has in place an effective and confidential system for reporting, use it and make sure you follow the proper guidelines.
- Consult a lawyer and anticipate and document retaliation.

---

## The Double-Edged Sword of Loyalty, Dissent, or Exit

It is clear that the objecting employees' choices of dissent and exit leave them stranded and vulnerable. Increasingly, however, the choice of loyal obedience to management yields the same result. The price of loyalty for employees who object and then cave to management's misdeeds is sometimes criminal indictment right along with the corporate brass. Indeed, those employees are sometimes indicted *before* the corporate brass if the authorities are looking for a plea-dealing witness to testify against senior management.

In the massive fraud perpetrated by World-Com (now trading as MCI), which resulted in the largest bankruptcy in U.S. history, several of the relatively minor players in the financial scandal faced up to 15 years behind bars. Betty Vinson was a mid-level accountant at a small long-distance company that was taken over by WorldCom. Her new bosses at WorldCom told her to make false accounting entries. At first, she balked; then she caved in to keep her job. She and several others in similar positions with the company were indicted for accounting fraud.[11]

At Merrill Lynch, an employee who warned against the firm's financing of Enron deals because of apparent accounting manipulation, but was overruled and subsequently helped to complete the transactions, was indicted. At Adelphia Communications, where the Rigas family treated corporate assets as their personal piggy bank, an employee who objected to the executives' personal use of corporate funds ended up quitting his job rather than facilitate the embezzlement. His successor in the position, who stayed on despite this knowledge, was indicted along with the Rigas family.[12]

---

11. Pulliam, S. (2003, June 23). Over the line: a staffer ordered to commit fraud balked, then caved. *Wall Street Journal*.
12. Scanell, K., & Latour, A. (2004, April 21). Raising a red flag isn't enough. *Wall Street Journal*.

As prosecutors take a harder line on corporate fraud, it has become increasingly clear that raising red flags internally isn't enough to avoid criminal charges. Prosecutors have signaled again and again that they will go after anyone who is complicit or participates in fraud, even if they did so kicking and screaming under protest.[13]

For ethical employees facing corporate wrongdoing and deciding how to address an ethical dilemma not of their own making, the choice is Hellerian—damned if you are loyal, damned if you dissent, and damned if you exit—a true *Catch-22*.[14]

### Making the World Safe for Whistle-Blowing

Society depends on whistle-blowers to keep the system honest. Given the astonishing advances of technology and the correspondingly large risks they present, it is essential for public health and safety to ensure that ethical individuals within the organization are heard.

Changes have been proposed to the laws that protect whistle-blowers to make the laws stronger and more comprehensive. Most recently, the Corporate Fraud Accountability Act of 2002 contains a provision to protect employees against retaliation for providing information on illegal financial activities to regulators or shareholders.

One suggestion is legislation that would not only protect whistle-blowers from unjust punishment, but also reward them financially for coming forward. Professor Luigi Zingales of the University of Chicago has proposed that whistle-blowers be awarded a commission (say, 10 percent) of all fines and legal awards incurred

by the corporation on account of the fraud that the whistle-blower revealed.[15]

That system of "privatizing" the regulatory investigation function is already used in the False Claims Act, which covers employees of government contractors who report fraud. The Act confers on the whistle-blower 15 to 30 percent of the government's recovery against the company.[16] The arrangement is not that different from contingency fees charged by attorneys who take on big companies or the government for wrongdoing. Attorney fees in those cases generally run about 30 percent of the award to the plaintiff.[17] The legislation could be tailored to prevent false whistle-blowing/bounty-hunting by requiring that the whistle-blower's disclosure be made to the proper regulators only and the disclosure is not made to the general public. As well, in the case of false accusations, penalties could be imposed and the regular laws of defamation would apply.

## The Problem of Bureaucracy— the Bureaucratic Ethic

*"Bureaucracy, the rule of no one, has become the modern form of despotism."*
—Mary McCarthy

The fate of the would-be whistle-blower in the organization depends primarily on the organization itself. Whether the individual moved to act by conscience will end up as a contributor to the corporate conscience or be ridiculed as a traitor depends on how the organization prioritizes and cultivates ethics in its bureaucratic structure—not just on paper, but in actual practice.[18] In the best-

---

13. Id.

14. Joseph Heller wrote the novel *Catch-22* in 1955. By the 1970s, the term had entered the common vernacular; defined in the Oxford dictionary as "a dilemma or difficult circumstance from which there is no escape because of mutually conflicting or dependent conditions."

15. Zingales, L. (2004, January 18). Want to stop corporate fraud? Pay off those whistle blowers. *Washington Post*.

16. False Claim Act whistleblower stories have few happy endings—for example, a 67-year-old female janitor at a public hospital blew the whistle on its shoddy and dangerous disposal procedures for tainted blood. She was awarded $775,000 as her 15 percent of the fines and was finally able to retire.

17. Zingales, *Washington Post*.

18. Enron, aka "the Crooked E," had a 64-page Corporate Code of Ethics—and its executive team managed to violate most of its voluminous provisions.

### The Social Psychology of Irresponsible Behavior

Noted Harvard psychologist Lawrence Kohlberg explored the roots of behavior that discourage dissent in work that he did in the 1960s. Kohlberg theorized that ethical sensitivity develops in stages.[a] The problem is that very few people advance to the highest stage where they feel comfortable challenging illegitimate authority.

Kohlberg's theory is as follows: A child is influenced by praise and displeasure; he or she is mainly affected by *reward and punishment.* An adolescent focuses on *groups and group norms.* In trying to conform to the expectations of parents and peers, home, school, community, and church, an adolescent learns about right and wrong. The adolescent, like the child, gives in without understanding why. There is obedience to collective rules without an intrinsic understanding of them.

| | |
|---|---|
| Level One—<br>Pre-conventional | Stage One—avoidance of punishment<br>Stage Two—self-interest (what's in it for me?) |
| Level Two—<br>Conventional | Stage Three—desire for approval of others<br>Stage Four—obligation to act morally as a participant in the social world—understanding of the need for "law and order" and, for that reason, willingness to abide by social rules |
| Level Three—<br>Post-conventional | Stage Five—awareness of differences in value systems in the world—usual approach is that of utilitarian ethics—greatest good for the greatest number; recognition that the law is not always ethical and where it is not, one needn't follow it<br>Stage Six (highest level)—recognition and understanding of certain universal moral minimums and moral obligations; moral judgments are made in accordance with these principles regardless of current societal norms |

Kohlberg believed that only in an "adult stage" could a person truly comprehend the moral dimension of behavior and act on that basis. The people operating at that level accepted or rejected social conventions *not because society said so*, but because they understood the function and purpose of the conventions. Individuals functioning at that level engaged in moral inquiry and were able to give a rational defense of their actions and positions. They did not obey simply because of obedience.[b]

But how many people have truly advanced to the stage that Kohlberg considers that of an "adult?" Are not most people still children or adolescents in some important ways, and when they enter large-scale bureaucracies are not those tendencies amplified?

a. Kohlberg, L. (1968). Moral development. *International Encyclopedia of the Social Sciences*, 10. Sills, D. L. (Ed.). New York: Macmillan & Free Press; Kohlberg, L. (1983). *Moral stages: a current formulation and response to critics.* New York: Karger.

b. While some of the specifics of Kohlberg's stages may be open to discussion and controversial, Kohlberg's basic theory that cognitive development occurs in identifiable, sequential stages is widely accepted. In the 1980s, another Harvard scholar, Robert Kegan, theorized that process facilitating human moral development is one involving alternating periods of stability, instability, and temporary rebalance. "Individuals need a sense of confirmation, an environment of support, before moving on to situations of contradiction, conditions that challenge current meaning-making systems. They need a context for continuity that allows for transformation and re-equilibration."

managed companies, there is a much-diminished need for whistle-blowing; internal channels for communication of concerns are open and input is encouraged. These companies prefer to head off trouble before it presents itself. They rely on employees to keep the organization as a whole operating ethically and functioning properly.

Instead, the perils of whistle-blowing most often arise in organizations with a bureaucratic ethic—where a concerned or objecting employee is perceived as a traitor to the team. The bureaucratic ethic perceives any challenge to authority, merited or not, as a breach of loyalty worthy of punishment. When challenged with accusation, many corporations swing into a defensive mode, a siege mentality, instead of critically examining the charges raised.

In the mega-entities that dominate global commerce, layers stack upon layers in the organization, all with different lines of responsibility and accountability. The structure is vertical, hierarchical, with many levels between the highest and lowest rungs.[19]

Bureaucracy diminishes the need for excellence or virtue in the individual by creating a hierarchy for praise and blame—few are held responsible for their actions in a personal way. In the pyramidal structure, few are viewed in a personal way at all. Praise flows up, and blame flows down; and above all else, loyalty to superiors is paramount. No one makes gut decisions

unless necessary; and if forced to, the individual will attempt to set up a fall guy for blame.

The traditional virtues normally valued in social interaction and business commerce—honesty, reliability, trustworthiness, decency, modesty, prudence, and resourcefulness—have little place in the bureaucracy. Instead, according to Jackall, the virtues held in highest regard in the bureaucratic ethic consist of (1) appearance and dress—looking the part of management; (2) self-control—avoiding revealing one's true emotions and intentions; (3) perception as a team player—most often serving as a yes-man to the boss; (4) style—giving the appearance of quick and slick thinking ("giving the appearance of knowledge even in its absence"); and (5) patron power—picking a winning horse in the management race and riding with him to the top (right or wrong).[20]

Jackall maintains that the "bureaucratic ethic" separates substance from appearance, language from meaning, and action from responsibility.[21] Success in the bureaucratic ethic is the result of fealty or loyalty to the individual leaders, not to the organization as a whole and is dependent upon "how much one pleases and submits to one's employer and meets the exigencies of an impersonal market."[22]

Managers make use of a linguistic code in which honesty is replaced by a language that can be reinterpreted to keep one's options open.

---

19. Jackall, R. (1983, September/October). Moral mazes: bureaucracy and managerial work. *Harvard Business Review* (here and throughout this discussion of Jackall).

20. Jackall acknowledges that success in some of these aspects will also require a lot of (6) pure luck. Nonetheless, it is the appearance of style and success, rather than the actual achievement of substantive merit, that matters. Appearances are everything. In his political treatise on how to gain and hold power, Machiavelli counseled the young Medici, who would be *The Prince,* that an effective leader is one willing to accomplish his ends by whatever means necessary—however ruthless or deceptive the means, they are justified by the ends. Nonetheless, Machiavelli cautioned, to retain power, the leader must also cultivate a reputation for justice, whether earned or not. "Everyone sees what you appear to be, but few experience what you actually are." Appearances are everything. Machiavelli finished *The Prince* in 1514 and published it in 1532. A recent version is *Niccolo Machiavelli, The Prince.* (2003, January). (G. Bull, Trans.). New York: Penguin Classics.

21. Social critic Robert Jackall observed that the bureaucratization of the workplace has created its own "bureaucratic ethic." "This bureaucratization was heralded at first by a very small class of salaried managers, who were later joined by legions of clerks and still later technicians and professionals of every stripe. In this century, the process spilled over from the private to the public sector and government bureaucracies came to rival those of industry. This great transformation produced the decline of the old middle class of entrepreneurs, free professionals, independent farmers, and small independent businessmen . . . and the ascendance of a new middle class of salaried employees whose chief common characteristic was and is their dependence on the big organization.." Jackall, R. *Moral Mazes.*

22. In support of this assertion, Jackall cites several illustrations of the bureaucratic ethic and its divisive and harmful effects: Managers may play at "starving" a plant, whereby increased returns on assets are obtained by deferring capital expenditures while maintaining sales. Replacement of old or obsolete equipment is deferred to a successor's watch. "Milking" a plant involves selling a nonprofitable department to another with an agreement to buy product back—thus recharacterizing capital expenditure as operating expense and putting the problem on another's balance sheet (another within the same corporation).

| STOCK PHRASE | PROBABLE INTENDED MEANING |
|---|---|
| *Exceptionally well qualified* | Has committed no major blunders to date |
| *Tactful in dealing with superiors* | Knows when to keep mouth shut |
| *Quick thinking* | Offers plausible excuses for errors |
| *Meticulous attention to detail* | A nitpicker |
| *Slightly below average* | Stupid |
| *Unusually loyal* | Wanted by no one else |

Jackall argues that ability to speak this doubletalk is essential to success in the bureaucratic system. Managers operating in a bureaucratic ethic possess an uncanny ability to be inconsistent—to say one thing to one group and another to another group without moral unease.[23] Some of the "stock" phrases identified by Jackall can be found in the table above.

Jackall wrote his article in the early 1980s, yet the bureaucratic ethic lives on. In the great financial scandals of the turn of this century, the books of many of the world's largest companies were "starved" and "milked" into multi-billion-dollar bankruptcies. Many in modern corporate management have mastered the ability to say one thing and do another without apparent moral unease. Linguistic doublespeak and the parsing of legalese generally has made cracking the corporate language code a matter of gamesmanship.[24] Where the stakes are high, the consequences of a bureaucratic ethic can be grave. Organizational intransigence at NASA was identified as a key cause of its two space shuttle disasters.

---

23. Jackall's example is the industry response to the problem of brown lung disease from cotton dust. The industry fought clean-up mandates by OSHA in court, all the while denying that any problem existed, claiming that there were other less expensive ways to address it, blaming other causes for the problem, and threatening to move operations overseas if forced to address the issue. At the same time, the industry was investing in renovations for a few plants that it knew would make money—a side benefit of the renovation being an automated system that would reduce cotton-dust emissions to safe levels.

24. Meanings are stretched well beyond rational limits. The hypocrisy of saying one thing and doing another is barely blushed at. Tobacco company executives, with straight faces and under oath, denied knowledge of the addictive nature of nicotine, despite a documentary paper trail in their own archives that evidenced decades of science proving the fact. Those same executives wink at the suggestion that a cartoon character used to sell their cigarettes might be appealing to children. In the increasingly customer-service-conscious world of business, the examples of companies that adopt and claim publicly to adhere to a Code of Ethical Conduct in the organization but flout it in practice are too numerous to mention.

## NASA
### Lessons Learned?

On January 27, 1986 (the day before the launch was scheduled to occur), Roger Boisjoly and other senior engineers at Morton Thiokol, the firm spearheading development and maintenance of the space shuttle, strongly recommended that the launch of the shuttle Challenger be delayed. Temperatures at the launch site had dipped below freezing, and the engineers had solid evidence that the O-ring seals in the joints of the solid rocket boosters could crack in the cold. Examination of the equipment in previous launches had revealed a flaw in the O-ring that compromised its integrity at temperatures below freezing. As early as July 1985, in a confidential memorandum, Boisjoly had brought the O-ring problem to the attention of Thiokol's top management. Boisjoly had also addressed the issue at a conference of engineers in October 1985 and requested suggestions for resolution of the problem.

Top management at Thiokol and NASA overrode the engineers' January 27 recommendation against the launch. As everyone knows, early in the launch, the Challenger boosters exploded before the horrified eyes of the millions who watched the launch, killing the seven shuttle crew members. The subsequent government investigation of the incident by the Rogers Commission placed blame for the disaster squarely on Thiokol and the faulty O-rings. Testifying before the Commission, Thiokol's CEO, Charles Locke, took the position that Thiokol never agreed to the launch at that temperature and that the decision should have been referred to Thiokol's headquarters.

In his own testimony before the Commission, made against the wishes of his bosses, Boisjoly presented documentation that rebutted the interpretation given by Locke. He walked the Commission through the heated confrontation and debate of the launch eve and revealed that the risk was knowingly assumed by Thiokol and NASA. The Commission found that NASA had placed the shuttle astronauts at risk of life and limb for the sake of schedule and good appearances.

Roger Boisjoly, chief rocket scientist for Morton Thiokol on the ill-fated Challenger space shuttle, testified truthfully and under oath that Thiokol engineers had known of the potential for explosion and had tried to persuade NASA to delay the Challenger launch. Too high-profile to be fired, Boisjoly was relegated to assignments entirely unrelated to the space program, far from his former office and position. His boss was heard to complain that he had "aired the company's dirty laundry" and would not be trusted again. Boisjoly was blackballed from the profession and eventually suffered a nervous condition that forced his resignation.

After giving his testimony, Boisjoly endured increasing alienation from his coworkers and a demotion and reassignment to lesser responsibilities. He eventually ended up leaving the company with a traumatic nervous disorder. Formerly one of the chief space engineers in the country, he became virtually unemployable. The industry blackballed him, and he ended up lecturing on college campuses and serving as an engineering expert in product safety cases—a far cry from the rocket science he excelled at.

The Rogers Commission found an organizational culture at NASA that was hierarchical, secretive, and internally competitive. Information did not flow up or down the proper channels, and concern for meeting deadlines and securing appropriations far exceeded safety concerns. The combination of downplaying risk and suppressing dissent stifled any ethical concerns for the human component of the project: the astronauts.

With respect to Thiokol, in a May 1986 interview with *The Wall Street Journal*, Thiokol CEO Locke stated, "That shuttle thing will cost us 10 cents a share." NASA, for its part,

---

**NASA
Lessons Learned? (continued)**

promised a more responsible approach to safety and acceptable risks.

But on February 1, 2003, the world watched in horror as the space shuttle Columbia self-destructed—this time on entry, not launch. The speculation was that broken pieces of the shuttle's insulating foam, damaged on launch, caused the disaster. The final report of the Columbia Accident Investigation Board acknowledged the foam as the likely catalyst for the disaster, but cited the culture and bureaucratic ethic at NASA as the component that allowed the disaster to occur. It characterized the agency as having a "broken safety culture." The Commission concluded that the accident "was probably not an anomalous, random event . . . but rather likely rooted to some degree in NASA's history and the human space flight program's culture."[a]

Following are some of the more telling findings in the Commission's 250-page report:

"We are convinced that the management practices overseeing the space shuttle program were as much a cause of the accident as the foam that struck the left wing . . ."

"While it would be inaccurate to say that NASA managed the space shuttle program at the time of the Columbia accident in the same manner it did prior to Challenger, there are unfortunate similarities between the agency's performance and safety practices in both periods"

"In this board's opinion, unless the technical, organizational and cultural recommendations made in this report are implemented, little will have been accomplished to lessen the chance that another accident will follow."

a. Schwartz, J., & Wald, M. L. (2003, August 26). Panel sees dual failures that caused Columbia's break-up. *New York Times*. Quotes from the report.

---

## Beyond Compliance

The best organizational defense against whistle-blowing is to obviate the need for it. A corporate culture open to debate and dissent is likely to air and resolve concerns before somebody has to go public with them. A company that depends on internal "whistle-blowing" to protect itself from public accusations has an obligation to provide a regular forum for discussion of those issues—and one that poses no threat of retaliation or retribution. Such a company also has an obligation not to put unreasonable demands or goals on its employees that cannot be met within ethical limits. The organization should regularly assess and reassess any demands and make transparent disclosures to employees about company policies.[25]

Increasingly, there is recognition that highly complex, bureaucratic organizations have a

---

25. Nonetheless, in the pyramidal corporate structure, responsibility for "ethics" is often delegated to the human resources division. There is some logic to this inasmuch as human resources (HR) is the "people" department; but in reality, all of the divisions of the company are "people" departments, and ethics should be an issue for each of them. Added to the problem of centralization of the "ethics" function is the fact that HR is generally considered a "soft" department in the organization—concerned with support as opposed to real profit making. Accordingly, HR is often left out of the executive suite and out of the boardroom when strategic corporate decisions with potentially serious ethical consequences are considered. If the responsibility for corporate ethics is to lie primarily with HR, then the only way to ensure an ethical culture is to include that group in all senior management decision making. A 2003 survey of HR professionals by the Ethics Resource Center and the Society for Human Resource Management found that half of the HR managers charged with overseeing the company's "ethics" believe ethical conduct is still not valued in business today and is certainly not rewarded. A quarter of those polled said that they feel pressured to compromise ethical standards either all the time, fairly often, or periodically—double the number that gave the same response in 1997. Joyce, A. (2003, May 4). Life at work: rising pressure and falling standards. *Washington Post*.

need for high-level ethical leadership; but ethical leadership cannot simply come from the top down.[26] Especially in large organizations, there is a need for participatory two-way communication and an engaged relationship between those leading and those being led.

The thing about ethics is that *anyone and everyone are capable of ethical leadership.* The other thing about ethics is that those in leadership positions are often not the most *ethically* qualified to lead, though they may be well qualified in other respects. The ethical leaders of an organization may not be those in command. Ideally, ethical leadership is a characteristic possessed by the people who are chosen to lead because of their other skills, but that does not always occur in practice. In the best-organized companies, that fact is recognized and accounted for by giving voice to those ethical leaders in the organization not otherwise positioned to be heard.[27]

---

26. Gardner, J. (1995). Leadership in large-scale organizations. *The Leader's Companion: Insights on Leadership Through the Ages.* J. T. Wren (Ed.). New York and London: The Free Press.

27. The kinds of skills that make a person a good leader vary depending on the nature of the mission—managerial and financial acumen for a CEO; navigational expertise, resourcefulness, and survival skills for the leader of an expedition; vision, message, and political know-how for the leader of a country; discipline, respect, and loyalty for a military leader; and motorcycle, leather, and cigarettes for the leader of the pack. The traits possessed by leaders that qualify them in these capacities do not always qualify them for *ethical* leadership, however. Due to increased size and complexity of twenty-first-century organizations, competitive corporations will need to integrate thinking and acting at all levels of the organization. Peter Senge maintains that the problem with prevailing bureaucracies is that they are control-oriented from the top down, forcing those in the organization to "let the leaders do the thinking." Senge argues instead for "learning organizations" that are open to criticism, communication, and change.

The old days when a Henry Ford, Alfred Sloan, or Tom Watson *learned for the organization* are gone. In an increasingly dynamic, interdependent, and unpredictable world, it is simply no longer possible for anyone to "figure it all out at the top." The old model, "the top thinks and the local acts," must now give way to integrated thinking and acting at all levels. While the challenge is great, so is the potential payoff. "The person who figures out how to harness the collective genius of the people in his or her organization," according to Citibank CEO Walter Writson, "is going to blow the competition away."

Learning organizations make room for ethical leaders, even when they are not at the top of the organizational chart. Learning organizations strive to take advantage of full resources of all of the humans at all levels of the organization. The organizations think critically about policies and positions and display a willingness to be open and to learn and change. The learning organizations move beyond the blame of the bureaucratic ethic—rather than "who is responsible for this problem?" the question asked is "how do we make it better, for good?" Senge, P. (Fall 1990). The leader's new work: building learning organizations. *Sloan Management Review,* 32.

## WHAT SHOULD YOU DO?

### The Eccentric MBA

After looking for a job for six months, a new college graduate obtains the kind of work she has been seeking. It seems to her that this is a once-in-a-lifetime opportunity. She can get in on the ground floor in a new and expanding business that promises all of the challenges, excitement, and monetary remuneration she wants. The job pays extremely well for an entry-level position, so she will be able to get an apartment for herself and live without the restrictions imposed by parents and roommates. The catch is that the job is in a sensitive industry that requires high standards of personal conduct. The job demands conformity and integrity. The company recently was hurt and embarrassed by a scandal caused by an irresponsible employee. Image is critical to the industry. As a result of that experience, the company now requires new employees to take a personality test. The results are carefully scrutinized to determine whether the employee will fit in and be a good team player. The company cannot afford to hire people who will rock the boat; many controls are in place to ensure that employees play by the rules. For example, employees must adhere to a dress code and fill out a detailed form daily, accounting for their activities.

The new graduate admittedly is an eccentric who has carefully cultivated a lifestyle that makes her stand out from others. She is not used to being hemmed in by an organization. She does what she wants when she wants. Independent-minded, she resents being told how to behave. She is contemptuous of the personality test and does not see what relation it would have to her job performance. Nevertheless, she knows that if she guesses correctly at the expected responses on the test, she will be less likely to be questioned by the company's psychologist and more likely to be hired immediately. She also needs the job—even if it means curbing her independent ways and pretending to be like everyone else. Her failure to find work in the past six months has become stressful. At the same time, she wonders how well she will perform in a company that expects everyone to behave the same. What should she do?

### The Avid Environmentalist

You are the owner of a bank, and your best employee is president of a local environmental group. Recently, the group has protested vigorously against a hazardous waste dump owned by a company that is a subsidiary of your most important client. You believe that the environmental group's sensationalized campaign against your client is grossly unfair and is based on blatant lies and distortions, not on a true estimate of the risks involved in the situation. You are inclined to tell your employee that she will be fired if she does not cease her irresponsible actions as head of the environmental group. Just last year the media embarrassed you when they barged into your bank to interview an employee who was heavily involved in the pro-life movement. At that time, you explicitly told all employees to keep their private causes to themselves and away from the workplace. What should you do?

### A Tight-Knit Group of Brokers

You have worked with three other brokers at the same company for the past 12 years. The four of you are the best of friends, with strong personal ties going back 30 years; you grew up with these people, knew their families, and went to the same schools. Nevertheless, it is a surprise when one of your friends reveals that he has been successfully trading on "tips" from an unmentioned source. You know that your friend has been having personal financial difficulties, but his situation seemed to be improving. Now you think you know why. Your friend invites you and the other members of the group to join in the trades based on the tips. You, too, face financial challenges as your children approach college age and apply to private schools with high price tags. Your parents are aging and face a deteriorating financial situation. You have recently become concerned about dipping into your savings merely to meet monthly living expenses. One of your friends eagerly accepts the offer to trade based on tips, but another argues that doing so may be against the law. She says that the trades are not worth the risk of getting caught, that she is in no way interested in hurting her family or career, and that she might not participate in a cover-up if an investigation occurs. Your trader friend explains his scheme. It seems foolproof, though its legality may be doubtful. The risks of getting caught appear minimal. What should you do?

### Polishing an Image

You have just received your MBA. For the past year and a half, you have worked as a financial accountant for a company that is conducting talks about a proposed merger with another firm. A director of the company approaches you to enlist your support in "polishing the company's image" for the upcoming merger talks. She asks for "some terrific forecasts of industry growth and market share" to give her "some leverage" in the talks. She says, "Be a good team player and do what I say. It will all work out for the best." You are not naïve. You know that the figures you choose as the basis for the forecasts and the approach and techniques you employ can influence the results. On the one hand, you could massage the data to paint a fairly rosy picture of the company's future. On the other hand, you could analyze the data to show upcoming pitfalls and the prospects of rough going. While accounting standards exist for all accountants, the interpretation of how those standards apply varies. The rules applying to the numbers a person brings to the table in merger talks seem to give you substantial leeway. You like the job and the company. You have formed many close ties to the people involved, including the director, who is a role model for you. What should you do?

### Down the Drain

After a yearlong search, you finally find a job in the industry of your choice. The high-status industry is dynamic and has excellent growth potential. Landing a job in this industry makes you the envy of your fellow graduates in the MBA program. However, you discover that the company is using a recently banned chemical as a cleansing agent, which is then flushed down the drain. When you ask why the company is acting in this fashion, you are told that it has a large supply of the chemical in storage and that it is only using up the remaining amount—to toss what is left would be silly. To safely dispose of the cleansing agent is a bother, and the alternative compound proposed by the government is very expensive. Moreover, you are told that company officials believe the government has been overly cautious in banning the chemical because the company has had no reported health problems related to it. Your supervisor tells you, "Don't be naïve. Real companies operate differently than you expect. If you want to succeed in this company, you'll have to go along." What should you do?

# PART 2

## Ongoing Issues in Corporate Social Responsibility

Part One laid out a framework for analyzing the obligations of the organization in society. The topics covered included the philosophical and political grounds for recognizing social responsibility; various approaches to defining that level of responsibility; and the interactive and reciprocal relationships between government, business, and employees.

In Part Two, that framework is used to explore ongoing issues in relationships between the corporation and those most affected by it—the corporation's shareholder owners, employees, customers, and communities in which the corporation operates. Determining a company's ethical obligation to stakeholders requires the consideration of different perspectives and a willingness to challenge established norms.

Of the myriad aspects of social responsibility facing corporations today, only a select few are presented in Part Two. The goal of examining these issues is that the reader will gain a broader understanding of the nature of the relationships between stakeholders and the corporation and a more enlightened view of the societal role of business enterprises.

# Chapter 6

## Obligations to the Shareholders of the Corporation: Fiduciary Duties

*"Most men are individuals no longer so far as their business, its activities, or its moralities are concerned."*
—Woodrow Wilson (1910)

### The Great Financial Scandals of 2002 and Efforts at Reform

Enron's demise was just the first wave in a tsunami of financial scandals that deluged Wall Street. Among the more noteworthy scandals of the nearly 600 SEC investigations opened in 2002 (a record year) were the following:[1]

- Along with the demise of Enron came that of Arthur Andersen, one of the oldest and most revered public accounting firms in the country. Andersen's dual role of auditor and consultant compromised its ability to provide independent judgment and an objective evaluation of Enron for its public investors. Reports indicate that at the time of Enron's collapse, nearly three-quarters of the revenue generated by all of the largest public accounting firms consisted of fees for nonauditing services to their customers. Even with the passage of the Corporate Fraud Accountability Act of 2002 (discussed below), the largest firms continue to generate nearly half of their fees from nonauditing services.

- WorldCom revealed that it had improperly booked close to $4 billion of routine expenses as capital expenditures, giving rise to a restatement of earnings and an Enron-like implosion of the company. The number was later adjusted upward to at least $8 billion. The company sought bankruptcy protection in late 2002, the largest ever in U.S. history. In 2003, it renamed itself MCI.

- On the other side of the balance sheet, many companies used Enron's mark-to-market accounting approach to book uncertain revenues as current income. The practice was widespread throughout the energy sector.[2] AOL Time Warner was forced into a major restatement of earnings as a result of this practice.

- At ImClone, a pharmaceutical manufacturer, CEO Sam Waksal and family and friends were indicted for selling company shares before announcing an adverse Food and

---

1. Taken from Drutman, L., & Cray, C. (2002, December). The top 10 financial scams of the 2002 corporate crime wave. *Multinational Monitor.*

2. Halliburton, during the time the company was headed by Vice President Dick Cheney, used this approach to report more than $100 million of frontloaded income.

Drug Administration (FDA) ruling. Martha Stewart, homemaking guru and Waksal friend, was also implicated in insider transactions in ImClone stock. Insider trading investigations were legion in 2002 and reached the highest office in the land. President George W. Bush was investigated by the SEC for sales of more than 200,000 shares of Harken, where he served as a director. Company insiders had earlier been warned by Harken's outside attorneys not to sell, given their inside negative information about the company.

- Loans to corporate officers and directors also proliferated. More than three-quarters of the top 1,500 companies engaged in the practice of providing insiders with interest-free or otherwise preferential loans from corporate funds. Many of these loans were never repaid. At the time of WorldCom's implosion, CEO Bernie Ebbers had more than $400 million in outstanding company loans. Other companies that suffered financial disasters in 2002 had similar practices: at Adelphia, CEO John Rigas and family borrowed more than $263 million from the company, and Dennis Kozlowski at Tyco had $120 million outstanding.

- Other subtler forms of self-enrichment by corporate management were also employed. A practice known as IPO (initial public offering) "spinning" involved investment bankers giving preferential purchase options for lucrative initial public offerings to chief executives in exchange for their companies' business. While the legality of such transactions is questionable, the ethics are not. Rewards or opportunities that derive from the company belong to and should accrue to the benefit of all of the shareholders, not the inside managers.

- In 2003, New York Attorney General Eliot Spitzer and his small team of prosecutors charged an egregious abuse of trust by securities analysts in selling to unwitting clients stocks they believed unworthy (also known

as "putting lipstick on this pig"). The case resulted in a landmark settlement by the securities industry of $1.4 billion in fines (a mere fraction of the profits the securities analysts made on the transactions).

In the summer of 2002, Congress passed landmark legislation to regulate some of the areas of greatest corporate abuse in the Corporate Fraud Accountability Act (also known as the Sarbanes-Oxley Act, or Sarbox).

Responsibility for these scandals is partially attributable to managers not carrying out their fiduciary duties to shareholders. This chapter reviews those duties as they developed in law and practice.

## The Responsibility of Management to the Owners of the Corporation

Regardless of the corporate perspective on social responsibility to other stakeholders, the first obligation of those who operate the corporation is to those who own it. Directors and officers manage the company as *fiduciaries* for the owners. A fiduciary is a person in a position of trust and confidence, acting on behalf of and in the best interest of another or a group of others.

Shareholders are owners by their investment of capital in return for an interest in the business.[3] By law (usually a mechanism in the corporate bylaws), shareholders elect a board of directors to represent their interests. The board may then designate committees for oversight and appoint officers to carry out day-to-day management. While the board delegates these tasks and responsibilities to others, ultimate authority and responsibility for what the corporation does remains with the board.

## Legal Aspects of the Relationship

The legal aspects of the fiduciary duties of directors and officers are reflected as a duty of care and prudence and a duty of loyalty to the company." Each of those qualities is discussed next.

---

3. The owners of different business entities are known by different labels: limited liability companies have members; partnerships have partners. Every form of entity imposes fiduciary duties on those who manage it.

**Corporate Fraud Accountability Act of 2002**
*Sarbanes-Oxley Act of 2002*
**White-Collar Crime Penalty Enhancement Act of 2002**
*Corporate and Criminal Fraud Accountability Act of 2002*

*"To protect investors by improving the accuracy and reliability of corporate disclosures made pursuant to the securities laws, and for other purposes."*

### Establishes the Public Company Accounting Oversight Board

Creates a five-member board to oversee public accounting firms and audits of public companies, which operates under the authority and supervision of the SEC. Heretofore, the accounting profession was essentially only self-policed. The board is prohibited from having more than two certified public accountants (CPAs) as members, and all of its members serve full-time and exclusively on the board. Board imposition of sanctions and penalties are limited to cases of intentional misconduct or repeated instances of negligent conduct.

### Bars auditors from performing consulting and other services for an audit client to ensure independence

Prohibits contemporaneous audit and nonaudit representation, requires that all audit and nonaudit services be preapproved by independent audit committee (see below), and mandates rotation of audit partners every five years. Requires proactive disclosure to the audit committee of all critical or controversial positions or practices used in the audit and addresses the revolving-door problem by prohibiting audits if former employees of auditor serve as senior executives of the issuer.

### Requires that only independent members of the board of directors serve on the corporate audit committee

An independent director is defined as one who, other than in the capacity as a corporate director of the issuer, accepts no consulting, advisory, or other compensatory fee from the issuer, nor any affiliate or subsidiary of the issuer.

### Requires certification of financial statements and other financial filings by the corporate CEO and chief financial officer (CFO)

Certification includes statements regarding the veracity of the report and that it fairly represents the financial condition and obligations of the company; that the certifiers are responsible for ensuring that they have received all material information to which they are certifying; and that they have disclosed to the auditors and audit committee any internal control deficiencies or potential fraud. The act provides for criminal penalties including 10?20 years imprisonment for knowing violations of this provision. (An attempt by the Senate to include federal income tax returns among the reports requiring certification by the CEO failed.)

### Forfeits CEO and CFO compensation following violation of securities laws

Where the violation leads to an accounting restatement, CEO and CFO bonuses and compensation may be forfeited.

## Corporate Fraud Accountability Act of 2002 (continued)

### Bars further service as officer or director by corporate wrongdoers
The standard is whether the person's conduct demonstrates "unfitness" to serve. (The standard under prior law was "substantial unfitness.")

### Prohibits insider trades during pension fund blackout periods
Specifically in response to the Enron problem, if the pension plan cannot trade, then neither can corporate executives and board members. The act provides for disgorgement of profits realized from such trades.

### Uses attorneys as internal whistle-blowers
Requires the SEC to establish rules for attorneys who practice before the SEC to report securities or financial violations or breaches of fiduciary duty first to the CEO or chief legal counsel of the company, then, failing a response, to the audit committee of the board of directors of the company.

### Requires enhanced disclosure of off-balance sheet transactions
Standard for disclosure includes those items and relationships having a "material effect" on the financial status of an issue. Pro forma information must be reconcilable with the actual financial condition of the issuer under generally accepted accounting principles (GAAP).

### Prohibits personal loans by corporation to its officers and directors
Addresses a rampant problem of corporate management's self-dealing with corporate funds.

### Requires immediate disclosure of insider trades by senior management, directors, and principal stockholders
Electronic notification of the trades must be made within two days of the transaction. (Previously, public disclosure could take up to 13 months.)

### Directs the establishment of regulatory control over securities analysts' potential conflicts of interest
Requires the SEC to adopt rules to address the conflicts of interest inherent in firms that engage in both securities analysis and investment banking.

### Creates criminal penalties for the wrongful destruction of documents
Presumably, the act was specifically in response to Arthur Andersen's actions in the Enron case. The act imposes a five-year retention period for audit and work papers and directs the SEC to develop an industry-standard document retention policy.

### Provides antiretaliation protection for corporate whistle-blowers
Prohibits retaliation against an employee who assists or participates in a regulatory investigation of corporate wrongdoing or a shareholder suit for corporate wrongdoing.

## Fiduciary Duties of Directors and Officers

Directors and officers are bound by law to discharge their duties on behalf of the corporation in good faith, meaning with honesty and without deception. As representatives of the shareholders, they are bound to act with (1) the care an ordinarily prudent person would exercise under similar circumstances and (2) in a manner reasonably believed to be in the best interests of the corporation.[4] The duties of care and loyalty are the standards to which directors and officers are held and for which they are liable if the corporation fails to meet those standards.

### Duty of Care

The duty of care is also known as a duty of diligence. It requires that directors and officers use all available means to make informed and prudent decisions. Directors rely on information that officers provide. Directors also seek and obtain information from other employees, experts, accountants, attorneys, and board members. Directors are diligent to the extent that they inquire and have no reason to doubt the veracity of the information they obtain.[5] Officers may also rely on the information of others, but they are held to a higher standard of care given that they are insiders and have access to more information.

Directors and officers cannot guarantee or be certain of the outcomes of their decisions; they are simply obligated to be informed and diligent and to act in the corporation's best interest. They err all the time. To protect informed directors and officers whose business decisions turn sour, there is the business judgment rule (BJR). Where an officer or a director can show that he or she made an informed decision without any conflicts of interest and with a rational basis supporting the decision, the BJR creates a rebuttable presumption in law that the person is meeting the requisite duty of care and diligence required of a prudent manager. Even if it turns out that decisions made were wrong, the presumption in favor of the director or officer can be rebutted only by showing bad faith or negligence.

One of the most famous cases invoking the BJR involved a corporate decision about the installation of lights at Wrigley Field to enable the Cubs to play night games. Directors, after fully informing themselves about the neighborhood, traffic patterns, and other pros and cons, decided not to install lights, thus preventing night games and the potential television revenues. The decision was challenged by the shareholders in *Schlensky v. Wrigley Field,*[6] but the court ruled that the directors were protected by the BJR due to their diligence. The court noted that even a foolhardy decision is protected if made in an informed manner. Afterward the directors voluntarily reversed their decision and installed the lights.

In contrast, directors in *Smith v. VanGorkom*[7] were not given the shield of the BJR when they approved a cash-out merger of a company after only two hours of consideration. The court found that the directors acted without adequately determining the company's value, without benefit of expert opinions, without proper and adequate notice to the members of the board, and without the full attendance of the voting board members. The court ruled that the actions of the directors were neither sufficiently informed nor prudent for such a bet-your-company decision like a merger.

Will the presumption of the business judgment rule be available to former Enron directors? Evidence indicates that Enron's board of directors twice waived the corporate code of ethics to permit self-dealing transactions by the corporate officers (CFO Fastow made more than $30 million in otherwise prohibited deals) and that the board repeatedly failed to make inquiry into blatant and obvious accounting and financial irregularities in the corporate books.[8] If that was, in fact, the level of oversight authority

---

4. MBCA Secs. 8.30 and 8.42.

5. Id.

6. *Schlensky v. Wrigley Field,* 237 N.W.2d 776 (Ill. 1968).

7. *Smith v. VanGorkom,* 488 A.2d 858 (1985).

8. See more detailed discussion of this in the case study "The Collapse of Enron: A Business Ethics Perspective" in Part Three of this text.

exercised by the board over Enron's self-dealing officers and managers, it seems unlikely that the BJR will be an available defense.

## Duty of Loyalty

The fiduciary duty of loyalty requires that the directors and officers act in the best interests of the corporation and its owners and not in their own self-interest. Because managers both control and serve the corporation, the potential for conflicts of interest is great. Any undisclosed self-enrichment is a potential breach of loyalty. Conflicts of interest may take the form of contracts or other transactions with the corporation in which the director or officer (or someone related to him or her) benefits. The use of corporate assets for personal enrichment is a conflict. The board members cannot approve interest-free or later-forgiven loans to themselves and corporate executives. When World-Com CEO Bernie Ebbers stepped down in disgrace after presiding over the biggest bankruptcy in U.S. business history, he had outstanding loans to the corporation of $400 million.[9] The Corporate Fraud Act of 2002 now prohibits that type of loan.[10]

Executive compensation challenges the duty of loyalty. It is a prime area for self-interested back-scratching among managers—you vote for my pay package, and I'll vote for yours. Corporate governance reformers advocate independent directors on compensation committees to mitigate this conflict.

Directors and officers also have an obligation not to seize or usurp corporate opportunities for their own benefit. Opportunities for investments, diversification, discounts, commissions, premiums, or any other benefits that come to the attention of a director or an officer as a representative of the corporation belong to the corporation, for the benefit of all of its owners.

At one time, the common law viewed all conflicted director transactions as void or voidable. Modern law recognizes the possibility of a sort of informed consent to those transactions. Where all material facts of the transaction and director or officer involvement have been disclosed, subsequent approval of the transaction validates the transaction. Waiver of the conflict must be by (1) a majority of the directors who have no interest in or are not related to the transaction or director or (2) a majority vote of the shareholders.[11] Failure to waive the conflict of interest in one of those ways leaves the transaction and the parties vulnerable to challenge. The only defense, then, is proof of the inherent fairness of the transaction at the time it was undertaken. Fairness in price, terms, and benefit to the corporation must be shown, often with contemporaneous evidence of competitive or comparative bidding or similar documentation.

Subsequent approval of such deals is not easy. For some boards, no truly "disinterested" majority exists, particularly if a board is made up mainly of insiders. The prospect of voluntarily submitting to a vote of shareholders, when not otherwise required by law or corporate bylaw, is generally seen as unacceptable by corporate boards. Unless otherwise provided for in the corporate charter, shareholders have few rights with regard to voting on corporate actions (other than the right to elect the board);[12] and there is a general reticence on the part of management to permit shareholders a direct voice in the direction of the company's activities.[13]

---

9. Gross, D. (2001, January 14). Owing more than loyalty to a company you run. *New York Times*.

10. The Corporate Fraud Act of 2002 prohibits loans to corporate officers or directors on any terms other than those offered by the corporation to the general public.

11. MBCA Secs. 8.81-8.63.

12. Generally, these are limited to organic or fundamental changes to the corporate structure—amendment of the corporate charter, sale of substantially all corporate assets, dissolution, or a corporate merger if the corporation is the acquired entity (and, thus, will cease legal existence).

13. This issue is discussed in greater detail in later sections on corporate governance and securities laws. The restrictions on the submission of shareholder resolutions, for example, have eased from their once-draconian formality; nonetheless, even when approved by an overwhelming margin of the shareholders, such resolutions still have no binding authority on the board.

### Spinning Gold: Modern Rumplestiltskin

The misappropriation of corporate opportunities by senior management can take many forms. A prominent example in recent years involved the practice of "IPO spinning." Investment bankers, looking to acquire or shore up a business relationship with a company, would provide preferential opportunities for personal investment to the chief officers of those clients or prospective clients. The investment bankers offered corporate heads the chance to personally invest in "hot" new issues in order to curry their favor and gain the business of their companies. Although the practice may seem like bribery, it is not technically illegal (at least not for the enriched executive). It may, however, violate the internal codes of ethics of the recipient company. As well, if the personal windfall is neither disclosed to nor approved by the board, it could give rise to a breach of loyalty by a CEO.

The practice of spinning was widespread at the turn of this century. In a typical case in 1999, William Clay Ford, Jr., CEO of Ford Motor Company (FMC), was personally allocated coveted options for 400,000 shares in the IPO of Goldman Sachs. This award was the largest given to any individual and was equal in value to all of the stock Ford, Jr., owned in FMC. John Thornton, president and co-chief operating officer (COO) of Goldman Sachs, happened to sit on Ford's board and was an old prep-school friend of Ford, Jr. In the three years leading to this "spin," FMC constituted close to $100 million in revenues to Goldman Sachs, a business relationship that grew appreciably in 2000.

If the "spin" was granted in recognition of the valuable business FMC gave to Goldman Sachs, the benefit should have accrued to the company, not to an individual holding the post of CEO. The value of the company's business is an asset owned by all shareholders and does not belong to the CEO. At the time of the spin, FMC had the cash to invest in options and could have used the extra investment profits since its stock was at a ten-year low, the company's debt was veering close to junk status, and its reputation with Wall Street was flagging.[a]

Among the best-known spinners of the day was Frank Quattrone of Credit Suisse First Boston (CSFB). Quattrone, an investment banker, and his subordinates used the practice extensively to reward favored clients, despite knowing that "spinning was frowned on by the regulators."[b]

Quattrone ended up on trial, not for spinning, but for obstruction of justice. In 2000, the SEC undertook a probe of CSFB to determine whether, in exchange for spinning IPO stock to favored customers, it was receiving kickbacks via excessive compensation from hedge funds, a practice that was not only "frowned on," but also illegal. In response to the probe, Quattrone was alleged to have ordered his subordinates by e-mail to "clean up" their files—interpreted by them to mean "shred everything." Quattrone was charged with obstruction of justice for the order.[c] In May 2004, after his initial trial ended in a hung jury, he was convicted of the charge in a retrial.

Interestingly, also in May 2004, Google.com chose Quattrone's old company, CSFB, as the investment banking firm to underwrite its much ballyhooed IPO, but with a twist—options to participate in the IPO were publicly auctioned, and no private spinning was permitted.

In a perplexing policy flip-flop, at the same time that Quattrone's retrial was proceeding, the NASD, with the approval of the SEC, promulgated rules that would seem to condone the practice.[d]

a. Thomas, L., Jr. (2002, December 8). Ford and Goldman, so cozy at the top. *New York Times*, Section 3.
b. Masters, B. A. (2004, April 29). Prosecutors say IPOs were lures. *Washington Post*.
c Smith, R., & DeBaise C. (2004, April 28). Quattrone II: banker takes stand in retrial. *Wall Street Journal*.
d. Zuckerman, G. (2004, March 22). NASD opens door to profit for brokers on IPOs. *Wall Street Journal*.

### Using Corporate Assets to Preserve Management's Position

Perhaps nowhere is the duty of loyalty of corporate management tested more rigorously than in the sale of a corporation. When an offer is made to buy a company, directors and officers have the obligation to take action that is in the best interest of the corporation and not in their own self-interest, all the while knowing that if control of the corporation changes hands, they will likely lose their positions. Directors faced with takeover attempts in the 1980s responded to the threat by seeking injunctions and implementing poison pills and other antitakeover measures to thwart a buyout.

One such defensive tactic that has been employed by boards on the defensive is greenmail. *Greenmail* is the practice of buying out a shareholder who is making a bid for control or otherwise challenging the board, at a premium price, using corporate assets in payment. When EDS, the company founded and largely owned by Ross Perot, was acquired by General Motors (GM) in 1984, the exchange of stock netted Perot nearly 1 percent of the outstanding stock of GM as well as a seat on its board of directors. In due course, Perot's incessant criticism of the style and direction of GM's management became a matter of annoyance and embarrassment for GM's board. Perot advocated change and modernization and a new corporate management style steadfastly resisted by incumbent GM management. When Perot began to make his concerns public, potentially affecting GM's stock price, the directors took action. They would repurchase Perot's shares at a substantial premium over the market price if he (1) promised to stop criticizing the company publicly and (2) promised not to engage in any takeover activities against the incumbent board and management. Perot took the deal. The remaining 99.2 percent of the owners of the corporation were left out of the decision. Many filed suit, alleging breach of the duty of loyalty by the directors for using corporate funds to buy the silence of one difficult and disgruntled shareholder without the consent of the shareholders and without a similar offer extended to them.[14] The Delaware court ultimately protected GM's board under the business judgment rule.[15]

Breach of loyalty is an even more acute problem in management-led buyouts because those who are charged with representing the interests of the shareholders are the same individuals seeking to buy the company. The special problems with management-led buyouts are many:

- The practice presents a classic example of usurping a corporate opportunity. If a buyout is advantageous—that is, if the share price is below the value of the reorganized, releveraged, or liquidated company—then that value belongs to all shareholders. Management's obligation is to realize benefits to the owners of the corporation, not to appropriate the benefits for themselves.

- Management invariably has inside information—or at least a far superior knowledge of the workings and possibilities of the corporation than what is available to shareholders. That information belongs to and should be used for shareholder benefit.

- Management's obligation is to pay the shareholders the true value of the assets purchased—that is, a "fair price." Merely paying a premium, if it does not fully reflect the value, is not a "fair price."[16]

### *Director and Officer Indemnification and Insurance*

If the directors and officers abide by the duty of care and duty of loyalty, they should be legally protected against liability for their actions. Nonetheless, directors and officers are often named as defendants in suits against corporations by shareholders or by third-party complainants. The necessity and expense of

---

14. *Grobow v. Perot*, 539 A.2d 180 (Del. 1988).

15. A shareholder vote on antitakeover devices is a key issue for corporate reform. For the most part, shareholders are simply seeking to vote on whether to authorize use of such a device by the board. The timing for deploying such an antitakeover measure would still be left to the discretion of the board.

16. Bruner, R. F., & Paine, L. S. (1988). Management buyouts and managerial ethics. *California Management Review*, 30(2). The Regents of the University of California.

mounting a legal defense in those cases is a drawback to serving as director. To mitigate those effects, to some extent, corporations generally provide for indemnification of directors and officers.

All states require some indemnification of directors and officers, and all permit further indemnification to some extent. The variances in what is mandated, permitted, and forbidden indemnification usually depends on (1) whether the defense of the director or officer involves a third-party claim or a shareholder derivative suit, (2) whether the director or officer defense is successful on the merits or because of a procedural technicality (that is, statute of limitations), and (3) whether the defense involves civil claims as opposed to criminal charges. Under virtually all of the state corporate statutes, directors and officers are entitled to complete indemnification if their defense of either a derivative or a third-party suit is wholly successful on the merits. Where a defense is not successful, where a director has litigated and lost or has settled, states vary as to whether indemnification or only reimbursement of expenses or neither will be permitted. Some state statutes condition indemnification on a finding of no bad faith, no negligence, and no breach of duty of loyalty. Some treat a settlement of the case differently than an adjudication of liability.

The rules for indemnification are generally more liberal for third-party suits (by the government, by customers, and by employees) than they are for derivative suits; the reason for this is a practical one. In a shareholder derivative suit, the shareholders sue the directors and/or officers in the name of and on behalf of the corporation. If the defense is unsuccessful and the corporation wins the suit, the defendant directors or officers must pay the damage judgment to the plaintiff corporation. A payment to the corporation is viewed as a payment proportionately benefiting all of the shareholders by virtue of their ownership interest. If the corporation were then to indemnify and reimburse the defendants for the damages they were required to pay, it would effectively be giving back to those same defendants the money damages they just paid—all from the same pocket. The whole transaction becomes a wash; and the intended effect, holding a director or officer accountable for wrongful actions, is thwarted.

Where corporate indemnification is not available under a state statute, most states, nonetheless, permit a corporation to insure against director and officer liabilities.[17] The premiums for those liability insurance policies are extremely expensive and continue to climb yearly. The premiums are paid with corporate assets. An ethical issue is raised by the use of corporate assets to pay for indirect coverage of that which the corporation is, by law, prohibited from covering. This is particularly questionable given the lack of shareholder voice on issues of director and officer indemnification and insurance.

The avalanche of financial scandals of recent times—beginning before Enron and continuing today—is testing the limits of indemnification principles. Enron's insurance carriers are exploring ways to rescind their policies on Enron directors and avoid responsibility for paying legal judgments. Fraud on the part of the insured is the main grounds for rescinding, or voiding, these types of policies. In a recent case involving the carrier insuring the directors and officers of Adelphia Communications—the scandal-ridden publicly held company treated as a private bank account by the Rigas family—a judge ruled that a policy insuring directors and officers cannot be unilaterally rescinded by the insurance carrier. The ruling effectively makes litigation necessary before any claim of rescission may be made by an insurer. Thus, the ruling will require that the insurer cover all expenses, legal and otherwise, for the insured until final disposition of the case.[18]

---

17. "A corporation may purchase and maintain insurance on behalf of an individual who was or is a director, officer, employee, or agent of the corporation . . . against liability asserted against him or incurred by him in that capacity . . . whether or not the corporation would have the power to indemnify him against the same liability." MBCA Sec. 8.57.

18. Francis, T. (2004, March 24). Director's armor: Adelphia ruling shows legal bills must be covered. *Wall Street Journal.*

Shareholders of Xerox felt the double pang inflicted by indemnification provisions. Massive accounting improprieties and irregularities by corporate management had cost the shareholders billions of dollars of loss in share value. Then management informed the shareholders that they would be paying most of the $22 million in penalties assessed by the SEC against the six former Xerox executives most responsible for the accounting fraud. (Less than $3 million would be paid by the executives themselves.)[19]

## Ethical Obligations to Shareholders

The obligation of directors and officers to shareholders is an area where the law and ethics coincide quite closely, at least in theory. The ethical principles underlying the respective rights and responsibilities of corporate managers and corporate owners are agency relationships. The fiduciary obligation is a part of the bargained-for exchange in the relationship—for the agent, compensation and authority to act in the name and stead of another; for the principal, honest, loyal, and skilled service focused on pursuing the best interests of the principal.[20]

At the present time, most state incorporation statutes do not require a board of directors to consider in their deliberations any constituency other than the shareholders, though corporations may voluntarily adopt such provisions in their charter or bylaws.[21] The floor of compliance for corporate directors and officers, then, is their obligation only to the shareholders to serve in good faith and with loyalty, using due care and prudence. Nonetheless, corporate management often fails in performing even those very narrow and limited obligations. The gap between law and ethics in the context of corporate governance lies not in what the rules are, but in how they are carried out.

### Passive and Conflicted Boards
*"There is one thing all boards have in common, regardless of their legal position, they do not function."*
—Peter Drucker

The past six or seven decades have seen an increasing separation of ownership from control of the corporation, resulting in a steady erosion of shareholder power. As shareholder power erodes, so, too, does the means for holding directors and officers accountable for their actions in controlling and operating the corporation. Many scholars and commentators on law and business have observed and examined this phenomenon, and their observations and recommendations continue to form and inform the debate on corporate governance reform today.[22]

### Nature and History of the Problem
These commentators pointed out that the traditional theoretical structure of the corporation—shareholders electing the board, which then appoints officers—was inverted in actual practice—and, thus, the fiduciary obligations owed to the shareholders subverted. In practice, they argued that the shareholders do not control the board, nor does the board control the officers. Instead, it is officers who control the board; and the shareholders are mere passive owners who have little say in management or governance. The "loyalty" of the directors flows up to chief

---

19. Morgenson, G. (2004, March). Shareholders will pick up the bill this time, too. *Washington Post.*

20. There is much debate over the extent of management's duties to stakeholders other than shareholders. Business ethicist John R. Boatright makes a persuasive argument that while a fiduciary duty of loyalty may be owed only to the shareholders, the duty of care—the obligation for diligent and informed decision making—may be extended to all stakeholders without disturbing that primary relationship. Under that approach, directors and officers would be held to a standard requiring consideration of the interests of other affected constituencies and the business judgment rule would provide a defense for any well-considered but ill-fated decisions. Boatright, J. R. (1994). Fiduciary duties and the shareholder-management relation: or, what's so special about shareholders? *Business Ethics Quarterly, 4.*

21. There are a few states with constituency statutes for certain corporate actions—plant closings, relocations.

22. Notably among them, Supreme Court Justice William O. Douglas, Professor Myles Mace of the Harvard Business School, Professor Abram Chayes of the Harvard Law School, Yale political scientist Robert Dahl, Professor Christopher Stone of the University of Southern California Law School, and social advocate Ralph Nader. Two books, *Taming the Giant Corporation*, by Ralph Nader, Mark Green, and Joel Seligman, and *Where the Law Ends*, by Professor Christopher Stone, both published in the 1970s, exposed the problem of passive and conflicted boards to the consciousness of the investing public. Nader, R., Green, M., & Seligman, J. (1976). *Taming the giant corporation.* New York: W.W. Norton; Stone, C. (1975). *Where the law ends.* New York: Harper & Row.

officers instead of down to the shareholders. There are two reasons: (1) because the officers control who is on the board and (2) because the board members are more personally familiar with the officers of the company, many of whom may be fellow board members, than they are with faceless shareholders they are charged with representing.

The divergence between the board's legal obligation for loyalty to the shareholders and the board's actual loyalty to management creates the problem of conflicted and passive boards. The boards are unable to oversee management effectively because they are made up of or beholden to people in management. The boards may also be made up of outside directors who are ill-informed, inattentive, or stretched too thin to act as anything but a mere rubber stamp for the policies of management. Corporate governance requires a healthy friction between the board and the officers—the board should operate as a sort of "check and balance" in the interests of the company's health.

The proxy system for shareholder voting contributes greatly to the problem of passive and conflicted boards. One of the few rights legally afforded to shareholders is the right to elect directors to represent them. Nonetheless, only an infinitesimal percentage of shareholders actually attend annual meetings. Thus, the mode for election of directors and other matters subject to shareholder input is the written proxy cast by the absentee shareholder. In practice, however, management effectively nominates the slate of potential directors that will appear on the written proxy by which shareholders cast their votes. Shareholders have no meaningful ability to nominate directors whose

names will appear on the proxy.[23] Further, shareholders who attempt to put up their own slate of nominees or make an independent run for the board, for the most part, must use their own funds to wage the proxy contest. This can be prohibitively expensive in a widely held public company. Management, for its side of the proxy contest, is able to make use of whatever amount of corporate funds it deems necessary.[24]

With control over nominations for seats on the board, management effectively controls who will serve. Thus, directors owe their positions to management. As a result, director independence for oversight and "healthy friction" is compromised; and it is management who sets the corporate agenda, not the directors.

In addition to conflicts in loyalty, there is the matter of the informed decision maker. Many board members sit on many boards; many are chief officers in other corporations; many boards meet only one or twice a year, sometimes only for hours. The question is how informed or diligent can a director be in those circumstances? The answer, sometimes, is "not very."[25]

The board retains a right to veto choices, but rarely does. Choosing the chief officer of the company may be the board's most important responsibility. Nonetheless, often it is not the board that selects the president or chief officers, but the chief officer himself that selects his successor. An apt twenty-first century example is the replacement of Jack Welch at General Electric, one of the largest companies in the world. Welch, who reigned as CEO at the corporate giant for nearly 20 years, chose his own successor when he decided to retire. He presented the name to the board, which unanimously approved it. The choice may, in fact, have been

---

23. "Management so dominates the proxy machinery that corporate elections have come to resemble the Soviet Union's euphemistic 'Communist ballot'—that is, a ballot which lists only one slate of candidates." Nader, id. Nader further noted that "in 1973, 99.7 percent of the directorial elections in our largest corporations were uncontested." That number has not significantly changed over time.

24. Nader related a case where GM agreed to distribute a 100-word proxy solicitation by the Project on Corporate Responsibility, but included the paragraph within a 21-page booklet specifically rebutting each of the Project's charges. With 1.4 million shareholders in GM, any meaningful response by the Project to the 21-page booklet would have been prohibitively expensive. (GM management spent close to $500,000 in corporate funds to put out its side of the story.)

25. While R.J. Reynolds' management was hyping the prospects of its new "smokeless" cigarette (with full knowledge that the innovation was a bust), Reynolds' directors held their meetings at a variety of luxurious golf resorts—and spent much of their time on the greens—trusting the management hype and blissfully ignorant of the true state of corporate affairs. A dramatic enactment of this debacle, along with an entertaining exegesis of the whole takeover craze and conflicts in fiduciary duties, is the HBO film and the book *Barbarians at the Gate: The Fall of RJR Nabisco* by Brian Burroughs and John Helyer (New York: Harper-Collins, 1991).

a good one. Nonetheless, the process raises some doubt about how informed and diligent the directors were in making that decision and to whom they were loyal.[26]

Executive compensation is another area of board conflict and rubber stamping. Excessive and unchecked executive compensation remains the most common issue covered in shareholder resolutions to this day.[27] That fact lends credence to claims that often the board no more controls the corporate executives than the shareholders control the board.

## Early Recommendations for Change

In the quest to restore directors to their proper oversight function, many commentators recommended revamping the corporate board dramatically. Some suggested that the corporate board should consist of only full-time "professional directors" who are capable of maintaining an objective distance and putting in the time necessary to effectively monitor the performance of management.[28] Some argued the merits of having a federal agency appoint "public directors" to serve on the boards of the largest companies.[29] Others advocated the appointment of special public directors for oversight where a company is found to engage in repeated violations of the law.[30] Suggestions were also made to change the way the board is elected: either by permitting other stakeholder groups, such as employees or customers, to elect representative directors to the board (as is done in many European and South American companies) or at least by facilitating direct shareholder nomination of directors.

Less dramatic recommendations for governance reform urged limiting service on the board to only independent outside directors. An independent director would be one with no ties to the corporation other than as a director—no members of management or past management, no employees, no attorneys, no accountants, no representatives of the firm's underwriter or banker, and no other professional affiliation. Interlocking directorates would be prohibited, and the number of boards on which an individual might sit and the number of terms an individual could serve would be limited.

Also advocated was the designation of a specific area of responsibility and expertise for each director to "supplement, but not supplant the directors general duty" in acting in the best interest of the corporation. Under that approach, each director, in addition to his or her general director's responsibilities, would be assigned a particular corporate area for oversight: legal compliance, finance and audit, employee welfare, environmental protection and community relations, purchasing and marketing, planning and research, etc. The designated director would serve as the board's expert in this area of corporate activity, thus enhancing its abilities to make informed and prudent decisions.

For all but the most progressive of corporations, these observation and recommendations were confined to the arena of academic discourse for the next few decades.-

## The Market Response

Throughout the 1980s, the response to the problem of passive and conflicted boards was the hostile takeover. Investors with large amounts of capital and resources, sometimes

---

26. Welch himself was handpicked by his predecessor, the legendary Reginald Harold "Reg" Jones. Professor Mace suggested that these committees and the board that approves their recommendations do not act as "decision-making bodies."

27. *Survey of shareholder resolutions 2001, 2002.* Proxywatch, et al, www.thecorporatelibrary.com. Leonhardt, D. (2002, April 1). For the boss, happy days are still here. *New York Times* (Executive Pay: Special Report); Colvin. G. (2001, June 25). The great CEO pay heist. *FORTUNE.*

28. Nader notes that U.S. Supreme Court Justice William O. Douglas is often cited as the first to call for full-time "salaried, professional experts" as board members in 1940. Many others have subsequently endorsed that approach.

29. For every $1 billion in sales or assets, 10 percent of directors would be "public." Nader, R., Green, M., & Seligman, J. (1976). *Taming the giant corporation.*.New York: W.W. Norton.

30. Stone's call for special director oversight was met with ridicule and scorn at the time. Nonetheless, modern times have seen something that looks much like Stone's vision being implemented in cases of corporate wrongdoing. In the landmark settlements for race discrimination at Coca-Cola and Texaco and sex discrimination at Mitsubishi Motors, terms included the establishment of outside, independent "public-type" directors for board oversight of the areas of noncompliance. Stone has a well-earned reputation for this kind of prescience in many areas of the law.

called "corporate raiders," would identify underperforming companies and seek to take control of them, ousting the incumbent management and board and replacing them with individuals of their own choosing. Most often, these takeover attempts took the form of tender offers, whereby the offeror/raider made a sweetened offer to the public shareholders to purchase enough outstanding shares of the corporation to give it control of the machinery of management. Invariably, the tender offer bid was somewhere above the price at which the stock was currently trading on the market.

The motive for takeovers was generally the potential acquirer's belief that given the company's financial condition, it could be operated more profitably with more attentive management. Sometimes the plan of the acquirer called for a reorganization of the company: utilizing economies of scale, streamlining operations, laying off employees, closing obsolete plants, and/or selling off unproductive assets. Sometimes it called for releveraging the company's assets. And sometimes the plan meant to dismantle the company altogether. Regardless, the position of the acquirer was that management was not doing a proper job of maximizing profits for its shareholders and that a new team could do better.

While there may be other constituencies harmed in such takeovers—namely, employees and communities in the case of layoffs and plant closings—very rarely is a corporate board required to consider the effects of its decision on a buyout offer on any group but the shareholders. In a tender offer, the shareholders who sell out at a premium are generally happy with their profit and the shareholders who voluntarily stay with their investment in the corporation are simply subject to a new management team. In fact, the stakeholder group most detrimentally affected by takeovers is incumbent management, who will lose their positions with the company when a change in controlling ownership takes place. It is the incumbent directors and officers who have the most to lose in such a contest; yet it is those very individuals who determine whether a recommendation will be made to the shareholders to accept the tender offer or whether corporate funds will be used to fight the hostile acquisition.

The reaction of corporate boards and management (and their lawyers) to the hostile takeover phenomenon was quite often to use whatever corporate assets were available to thwart the takeover attempt. Little regard was given to the expedience or potential benefits of the proposed transaction for the shareholders or to the harm inflicted on the corporation in deploying the defense. A host of poison-pill type devices emerged—offering golden parachute agreements whereby the corporation would be obligated to pay millions of dollars to departing managers on a change in control, planning to restructure the corporation so as to effect deleterious tax consequences on a change in control, staggering board terms to ensure that incumbent directors could not be easily ousted, saddling the company with exorbitant debt that the new (and continuing) owners would have to repay, using corporate funds to pay greenmail to buy off the potential raider, and many other strategies.[31]

The upshot of much of this activity was that incumbent management was able to entrench itself and to ward off takeover attempts by legal device and not by business acumen or economic merit.[32] With this approach, the problem of passive and conflicted boards continued."

---

31. For example, *Moran v. Household International, Inc.*, 500 A.2d 1346 (Del. 1985) (the first case to uphold the use of a poison pill without shareholder approval) and *Hilton Hotels v. ITT Corp*, 978 F.Supp. 1342 (D. Nev. 1997) (the board's plan to split the company into three separate entities in order to create a multimillion dollar tax bill for anyone seeking to take over the company was held by the court to be an "organic" change in the corporate structure of such consequence as to require shareholder approval).

32. The names of antitakeover devices sound like something from an NFL playbook—the strategies themselves, like something from a war plan, suggesting corporate genocide or suicide is preferable to surrender. Some examples: the Crown Jewel defense, Golden Parachutes, the Pac-Man defense, Shark Repellent, and the Scorched Earth defense. The primary ethical objection to those devices is the fact that shareholders have virtually no say in whether and how their corporate managers utilize corporate assets for these often wasteful and self-destructive uses.

### Recent Trends in Reforming Corporate Governance

Deprived of a market mechanism to force management accountability, in the 1990s large institutional investors such as CALpers and TIAA-CREF—which have fiduciary duties to their own members to maximize returns—began to operate as a sort of governance watchdog. Investment funds and other shareholder activists evaluated the independence and oversight of corporate boards and made that information public.

The following provides an overview of the significant concerns of these groups and their recommendations.

- **Independence of the Board**
  - Majority independence—if a board composed entirely of independent outside directors is not possible, at least a majority of the directors should be independent (using the earlier definition of *independence*: no other ties to the company).
  - Committee independence—at a minimum, membership on certain key committees of the board should be limited to independent directors only—namely, the audit, compensation, nominating, and governance committees.
  - Chairman of the board independence—many, if not most, of the largest corporations permit the CEO to serve also as the chair of the board of directors. The conflicts for oversight are obvious.[33] For those cases where the CEO absolutely insists on the title and position of chair of the board, it is recommended that the board appoint an independent director to serve as a "lead" director in substitution of the chair for all decisions that might involve the CEO or oversight of management generally.
  - Term limits—these proposals take the form of both age limits and years-of-service limits on directors.[34]
  - Diversity in the board with regard to experience, race, gender, age, and background.[35]
  - Separate meetings and separate counsel for the independent directors on the board.
  - Ability of the independent directors to comment on proxy statements.[36]

- **Shareholder Rights**
  - Greenmail—shareholders should be given the right to approve corporate payments of greenmail to select investors.
  - Antitakeover measures—shareholders should be given the right to vote, at least initially, on whether and to what extent they want to empower the board to deploy poison pills and other measures designed to thwart takeover attempts.
  - Shareholder resolutions on the proxy statement—less restrictive rules should be implemented for getting a shareholder resolution on the proxy ballot.
  - Shareholder voting on executive compensation—Shareholders should be able to vote at least on the basic parameters of executives' packages in terms of stock options plans and bonuses and deferred compensation plans.[37]

---

33. In January 2003, a blue-ribbon panel issued the influential Report of the Conference Board Commission on Public Trust and Private Enterprise, which recommended in the strongest terms that the positions of chair and CEO be split and that the chair be an independent director. Elsewhere in the world, the practice is common. In the UK, 90 percent of the positions are split.

34. Perhaps more than any of the other proposals, this one is the most susceptible to challenge on the one-size-does-not-fit-all theory. Arbitrary age and term limits would sometimes exclude from service individuals with invaluable knowledge and experience to lend to the company. Nonetheless, a board predominated by aged and long-standing directors is often a stagnant one.

35. Closely related to the term limits proposal, this call for broad diversity on the board is intended to address the fact that boards have always been and continue largely to be "homogeneously white, male, and narrowly oriented." Nader referred to this as the problem of the "twelve grey-haired guys named George," a reference to news anchor Dan Rather's characterization of the Nixon cabinet.

36. Invariably, boards recommend a vote "against" virtually all shareholder resolutions that actually make it on to the proxy statement and a vote "for" the slate of director nominees and board-sponsored initiatives.

37. In 1980, the pay for the average CEO was 42 times that of his average worker; in 1990, it was 85 times as much; in 2000, 531 times as much. Tobias, A. (2003, March 2). How much is fair? *Parade.*

## Executive Compensation: Pay for Performance?

| Highest Paid U.S. CEOs | | | Largest Options Grants | | |
|---|---|---|---|---|---|
| Year | CEO and Company | Pay in Millions | Year | CEO and Company | Grants in Millions |
| 1990 | Steven Ross *TimeWarner* | $ 75 | 1990 | Steven Ross *TimeWarner* | $ 215 |
| 1991 | Roberto Goizueta *Coca-Cola* | 61 | 1991 | Leon Hirsch *US Surgical* | 170 |
| 1992 | Alan Greenberg *Bear Stearns* | 16 | 1992 | Roy Vagelos *Merck* | 35 |
| 1993 | George Fisher *Kodak* | 29 | 1993 | George Fisher *Kodak* | 67 |
| 1994 | Larry Bossidy *AlliedSignal* | 34 | 1994 | Larry Bossidy *AlliedSignal* | 63 |
| 1995 | Larry Coss *Green Tree* | 66 | 1995 | Mickey Drexler *GAP* | 79 |
| 1996 | Michael Eisner *Walt Disney* | 194 | 1996 | Michael Eisner *Walt Disney* | 506 |
| 1997 | Henry Silverman *Cendant* | 194 | 1997 | Henry Silverman *Cendant* | 570 |
| 1998 | Michael Dell *Dell Computer* | 94 | 1998 | Michael Dell *Dell Computer* | 272 |
| 1999 | Charles Wang *Computer Associates* | 507 | 1999 | Joseph Nacchio *Qwest* | 257 |

Issues of executive compensation remain at the top of the list of shareholder concerns. The Revenue Act of 1950 permitted companies to pay employees with stock options instead of or in addition to cash compensation. In 1993, the allowable deduction for cash executive compensation was capped at $1 million. A corporation could still pay its executives more than that, but it would not get the write-off on its tax return. That factor fueled a trend toward paying executives in stock. Equity compensation was viewed as having an added benefit as well—it would align the interests of management with shareholders. Managers would, at least theoretically, be acting in the interests of the other shareholders.

The ability of inside management to manipulate stock price and CEO pay packages that increase steadily despite company stock performance has rendered this compensation scheme problematic. Reasonable minds still disagree about the efficacy of director and officer equity ownership.[38] The magnitude and sheer

---

38. Increasingly, board members own stock in the companies on whose boards they sit. In a survey of more than 1,000 companies in 2000, the Corporate Library found that Enron tied for last place in director equity holdings. Nell Minow, head of the Corporate Library, reflected, "Institutional investors should have been looking at that, and calling them on it."

number of stock options awarded to executives and the fact that such options are neither disclosed to the shareholders nor reported as an expense of the company for tax purposes makes them ethically dubious.

*FORTUNE* magazine published the following list of the biggest pay packages for the previous decade. Since 2000, the numbers have only gotten bigger—often even when the company's performance was dismal and the organization suffered extensive layoffs and downsizing.[39]

### Maintaining a Healthy Friction

The crush of corporate scandals that rocked Wall Street in the beginning of the twenty-first century rallied forces for director independence, stricter scrutiny of management, and more accountability to shareholders and the public markets. The Corporate Fraud Accountability Act of 2002 (the Corporate Fraud Act)[40] was designed "to protect investors by improving the accuracy and reliability of corporate disclosures made pursuant to the securities laws... " The Act requires that the audit committee of the board of directors be comprised exclusively of independent directors and that at least one of them be a financial expert.[41] In addition, the New York Stock Exchange, the NASDAQ, and many voluntary organizations have also tightened rules on director independence, oversight responsibilities, and management accountability. One of the more practical developments has been a mandate for director education and training.[42]

Investors, too, have awakened to the importance of good corporate governance as an indication of financial soundness and stability. The Corporate Library has developed a system for rating board effectiveness based on an analysis of CEO employment contracts and compensation, outside director shareholdings, the board's structure and makeup, its accounting and audit oversight, and the soundness of its strategic decisions with regard to fundamental corporate actions.[43] The bond-rating agency Standard & Poor's started a corporate governance rating unit in 1998. The other major bond-rating agencies, Moody's Investors Service and Fitch Ratings, have also expanded to include corporate governance ratings.[44] Irrespective of accuracy in measuring corporate governance, one thing is clear: investors and their advisors now view corporate governance as a bottom-line factor in evaluating the worth of a company.

A continuing mass of evidence indicates that the scandals at the turn of this century were facilitated by the board's lax oversight of management—whether passive, conflicted, or passive-aggressive. Many of the corporate executives responsible for the financial frauds facing judges and juries are offering the defense that the board of directors said it was okay. In the case of Enron and other companies, the board did indeed waive the corporate Code of Ethics to permit management's self-dealing.

Board independence and a "healthy friction" between board and management are essential components for corporate integrity. Financial columnist James Surowiecki asserts that the characteristics of passive and conflicted

---

39. Source: Executive Compensation Advisory Services, *FORTUNE,* June 25, 2001.

40. Pub. Law 107-204 (7/30/2002), also known as the White-Collar Crime Penalty Enhancement Act of 2002 and the Criminal Fraud Accountability Act of 2002, is most commonly referred to as the Sarbanes-Oxley Act or Sarbox or Sox. Key provisions of the act are summarized in the opening section of this chapter.

41. Given the heightened scrutiny as well as the need for expertise, the difficulties boards have encountered in filling these posts has been substantial. See, for example, "More Work, More Pay" by Joann Lublin in *The Wall Street Journal Reports: Corporate Governance.* Special section R, February 24, 2003.

42. "NYSE Corporate Governance Rules Proposals, April 4, 2003," which became the Final NYSE Corporate Governance Rules (codified in section 303A of the *NYSE Listed Company Manual*) November 4, 2003. In the aftermath of one of the major corporate implosions of 2002, the presiding bankruptcy judge appointed a new CEO to lead WorldCom through its reorganization. One of the few remaining independent board members for the company, the dean of a prominent law school and a respected scholar, immediately resigned, saying she wanted to make room for the new CEO to "bring in his own board." The point here is that even the extremely erudite can be unclear on the proper relationship between the board and its officers—the new CEO works *for* the board, not the other way around.

43. *http://www.thecorporatelibrary.net.* Institutional Shareholder Services and several other independent firms also have rating services.

44. White, B. (2003, February 15). Bond rating firms get into corporate governance. *Washington Post.* None of these ratings services are independent; instead, the services are paid by the companies being rated.

boards—listening only to each other without outside input, falling prey to groupthink, and permitting undue influence or granting undeserved deference to the CEO—are a main cause of the rash of financial collapses. "Smart group decisions emerge out of disagreement, not consensus. But on too many corporate boards dissent is still seem as either superfluous or harmful."[45] Surowiecki recalls the words of the great Alfred Sloan, who ran GM from 1923 to 1956, when he said to his board,

> Gentlemen, I take it that we are all in complete agreement on the decision here. Then, I propose that we postpone further discussion... to give ourselves time to develop disagreement and perhaps gain some understanding of what the decision is all about.

## Obligations of Corporate Management under the Securities Laws

Securities laws protect investors' rights for honest and fair dealings from managers on their corporate payroll. Under securities laws, the fiduciary duties of loyalty and care form the basis for the legal obligations of management to investors. The duty of care and diligence is reflected in management's obligations to provide accurate and complete information in its offer of stock to the public. The duty of loyalty is reflected in management's obligations for truthful representations to its shareholders and prohibitions against insider trading.

The main securities laws in the United States were enacted in response to the stock market crash of 1929 and the ensuing Great Depression. The lack of regulation over the stock market made it fertile ground for scams and insider manipulation. The underlying theory for securities statutes is disclosure—complete and accurate information made available to owners and potential investors in the company. Disclosure is not intended to protect the foolhardy. It aims to provide the investor with the relevant information needed to make an informed decision about whether to buy or sell. The concept is analogous to that which underlies all notions of informed consent. In upholding the constitutionality of these laws, Supreme Court Justice Brandeis said, "Sunlight is said to be the best of disinfectants." Transparency and truthfulness are key values to ensuring market integrity and encouraging investor confidence.[46]

The scope and reach of the federal securities laws are significant. The term *security* is very broadly interpreted and includes almost all forms of equity and most forms of debt financing.[47]

### Statutory Framework of the Securities Laws

- **The Securities Act of 1933 (1933 Act)**
  Focuses on the mass distribution of securities offered to the public—covers the IPO of a security.[48]

- **The Securities Exchange Act of 1934 (1934 Act)**
  Focuses on the trading of securities after their IPO, including registration and periodic public reporting with the SEC, insider trading, and takeover rules; also establishes the framework for control of the largely self-regulating securities industry, including obligations of brokers, dealers, investment bankers, and accountants.

- **SEC Regulations and Rules**
  Focuses the rules and regulations promulgated by the SEC to flesh out these Acts.

---

45. Id.

46. The constitutional basis for federal securities regulation is the Commerce Clause. What constitutes *interstate* commerce in securities has been broadly interpreted, including use of the telephone, mail, and the Internet. Technically, a purely "intrastate" offering would be exempt from federal law; however, such offerings are rare and are subject to stringent requirements for exclusion.

47. Debt with a maturity of more than nine months is usually classified as a security. Most financial instruments tradable publicly will qualify as a security, with a few traditional exceptions such as home mortgages, consumer loans, and accounts receivable notes. *Reeves v. Ernst & Young*, 494 US 56 (1990).

48. An IPO of a security means that it is the first time *a particular security* is offered to the public, not the first time a company issues a security. Many public companies engage in several securities offerings throughout their existence. Each offering is subject to the 1933 Act unless otherwise exempt.

---

### Material Information under the 1933 Act
Required Disclosures in Registration

- A description of the nature of the security that is being offered and an explanation as to why it is offered—that is, the issuer's motivation for raising funds
- The position of the offered security in relation to the corporate capital structure
- An audited financial statement
- A list of corporate assets
- A description of the issuer's business
- Identification of management and inside ownership
- Information on pending lawsuits, governmental inquiries, and similar proceedings
- Any other information that a prospective investor would view as material to assessing the risk associated with purchase of the security

---

In addition to the federal securities laws, many states maintain their own securities laws, called "blue sky laws," requiring compliance with both federal and state law for issuers selling securities within the state.[49]

### The 1933 Act

Any initial offering of a security to the public must be registered with the SEC under the 1933 Act or claim as an exemption from it. If the offering is not exempt, the issuing company must comply with the requirements of the 1933 Act; namely, filing a registration statement and sample prospectus with the SEC. It is *illegal to offer to sell* a security unless the registration has been filed, *and* it is *illegal to sell* a security unless registration is effective. The interim between filing and effective date is called the "quiet period"; it is a transition time that, theoretically, gives time to investors to become acquainted with the prospectus. Management must be care-

ful to not run afoul of the stringent SEC restrictions on publicity, marketing, and solicitation during this period.[50]

*Securities fraud* under the 1933 Act may take a couple of different forms—either by putting forth a *misleading* registration statement or by selling a security through a *misleading* prospectus or a *misleading* oral communication. The 1933 Act provides for enforcement by the SEC as well as a private cause of action for damages by investors who were misled. For a person to sue, the misleading statement or omission must be the proximate *cause* of the investor's loss on the security and the investor must have actually suffered economic loss. *Misleading* is interpreted as a misrepresentation or an omission of a material fact. A material fact is a fact that a potential investor would view as significant to the mix of information he or she would consider when deciding whether to invest.[51]

To impose liability, the 1933 Act does not

---

49. The Capital Markets Efficiency Act, passed by Congress in 1996, requires considerable uniformity between the federal securities law requirements and the state law requirements. For the most part, state authority is somewhat preempted by the act and states are not permitted to require much more for approval of a public offering than is required under feral laws.

50. The much-anticipated IPO of salesforce.com was delayed by the SEC for several weeks and placed in jeopardy while securities regulators investigated whether public comments about the stock by the company's outspoken CEO, Marc Benioff, may have violated the quiet period. Bank, D. (2004, May 20). Disquiet period: salesforce.com IPO is delayed. *Wall Street Journal.*

51. Examples of "material facts" might include loans to insiders, business arrangements with insiders, an undisclosed use of the proceeds in the prospectus, failure to disclose debt or to identify uncollectible debt as such, competitive business interests owned by insiders, and misleading comparative market information.

require that the defendant intended to mislead.[52] Even inadvertent and unintended misrepresentations and omissions, if material, are sufficient for a violation. The range of potential defendants is expansive. It includes anyone who signed the registration statement; anyone who was required to sign the registration statement (whether he or she actually did); the issuer company; the underwriters of the offering; all directors and chief officers of the issuer; all of the experts used in preparation of the registration statement, including attorneys, accountants, and investment bankers; and anyone who controls any of them (that is, the companies they work for).

Defenses available to those charged with violating the 1933 Act are limited. The first line of defense lies in refuting some element of the claim—for example, that the proximate cause of the loss was something other than the misleading misstatement or that the omitted information was immaterial. In cases where the investor knew of the misrepresentation or omission at the time of investing and proceeded anyway, the investor is considered to have assumed the risk of loss and cannot later make a claim under the act. Failing that, the only defense remaining is that the defendant engaged in due diligence with respect to the offering—made reasonable investigation into the facts presented, believed in their veracity and completeness, and did not know and could not have known with due inquiry about the misrepresentation or omission.[53]

### The 1934 Act

The 1934 Act embodies just about all of the remaining securities regulation—basically anything occurring after the IPO of a security. The 1934 Act governs the reporting requirements for publicly traded companies, conditions for major stock acquisitions and/or takeover attempts, proxy solicitation rules and rules on shareholder resolutions, insider trading and other forms of fraud against shareholders by management, and the rules for self-regulation of those involved in the securities industry.

Reporting requirements of publicly traded companies under the 1934 Act and its regulations are fairly extensive, continuing the policy of disclosure of material information begun with the company's IPO under the 1933 Act. Noncompliance brings with it harsh penalties. Companies generally need professional assistance in keeping up with reporting obligations, which include regular unaudited quarterly financial statements; audited annual financial reports; filings upon trigger events such as a change in control, disposition of key assets, resignation of directors, amendments of Articles of Incorporation, and most organic corporate changes; and reporting for a myriad of other corporate activities.

A 1968 amendment to the 1934 Act, called the Williams Act, sets forth the rules for tender offers and takeovers by acquisition of stock. The Williams Act requires a filing evidencing the investor's intent in any stock acquisition involving more than 5 percent of a corporation's securities. The act sets forth rules for management's opposition to the tender offer and rules for tendering shares and generally seeks to ensure fair dealing in the transaction.[54]

The antifraud provisions cast a wide net for anyone attempting to defraud, deceive, or mislead in connection with the purchase or sale of a security. Anyone who manipulates the market may be found liable under the 1934 Act, including bankers, brokers, lawyers, and

---

52. The intent to mislead is technically referred to as "scienter" in securities law.

53. The due diligence defense permits nonexperts to rely on experts, within reason. The due diligence defense is not available to issuers—the issuing company itself will bear ultimate responsibility for whatever appears in its registration statement or prospectus. The requirements for successfully asserting the due diligence defense bear a striking resemblance to the business judgment rule that protects decision making that is fully informed, regardless of whether it ultimately proves poor.

54. Key provisions protecting stockholders and the integrity of the market itself are contained in the antifraud provisions of the 1934 Act; specifically, Section 10(b) and Rule 10b-5. Those provisions define, describe, and set penalties for fraudulent activities by individuals and corporations. The rule provides for a private cause of action as well as SEC enforcement; it also serves as the basis for the vast majority of securities fraud suits brought in the United States.

accountants.[55] Most claims under the antifraud provisions involve either (1) material misstatements by management or (2) insider trading. Both of those prohibited activities are rooted in the fiduciary obligation of corporate management and its agents to serve with loyalty to the corporate owners. For both material misstatements by management and insider trading, the victim of the offense is the shareholder—buying or selling without knowledge of the true facts of their investment.

## Material Misstatements by Management

The antifraud provisions are broad and cover any and all misleading representations and statements made about a company or its performance that may affect stock price. The provisions include statements made in press releases, public comments, media interviews, web postings, keynote addresses, etc. Besides management's liability for such misstatements or omissions, management's lawyers, accountants, and bankers can also be held liable if they meet the requirements of culpability—knowingly or recklessly putting forth misleading information to the investing public.[56]

The plaintiff must establish *all* of the following elements to prove a claim:

*The defendant made a misrepresentation or omission of a material fact.*

A material fact is generally considered to be any fact likely to affect market value of the stock. Misrepresentations can take the form of being misleadingly overcautious or misleadingly optimistic. In the case of *SEC v. Texas Gulf Sulphur*, 401 F.2d 833 (2d Cir. 1968), a drilling company, in its press release about the discovery, misleadingly played down the potential richness of a copper strike. Noting that the company had no obligation to discuss the strike publicly, the court said that once it did, it had an obligation to disclose all material facts about the strike accurately. This the company did not do. At the other end of deception is the misleadingly optimistic statement; for example, where a scientist working for a drug company indicates in an interview or elsewhere that FDA approval of a new drug is imminent, when in fact it is not.[57]

*The misleading statement was made with scienter.*

The misstatement or omission must be made knowing that it is likely to mislead. In most jurisdictions, reckless disregard for the truth or falsity of the statement is enough to find intent to mislead.

*The plaintiff acted in reliance on the misrepresentation.*

The plaintiff must prove that the misinformation was at least a part of the impetus for his or her purchase or sale of the security. That can take the form of evidence of plaintiff's direct reliance or may be shown with something called "fraud on the market"—that the market value of stock was not true or accurate because the market set the price based on the misleading statement or omission.

*The plaintiff engaged in a purchase or sale of the securities and suffered a causal loss.*

Causation is often the hardest element to prove—that the misstatement or omission was the proximate cause of the loss suffered by the plaintiff—because so many other factors in the market affect share value and price.

---

55. The standard of proof for fraud is significantly different from the 1933 Act, however, because it requires the element of *scienter*—the *intent* to mislead, deceive, or defraud. Unlike the 1933 Act, which may hold defendants liable for mere inadvertent misrepresentation or omission, the 1934 Act requires either a knowing misrepresentation or omission by the defendant or at least gross negligence in the form of reckless disregard for the truth or falsity of the information provided. Section 10-b(5) provides the following: It shall be unlawful for any person, directly or indirectly, by the use of any means or instrumentality of interstate commerce, or of the mails, or of any facility of any national securities exchange, (1) to employ any device, scheme, or artifice to defraud, (2) to make any untrue statement of a material fact or omit to state a material fact necessary in order to make the statements made, in light of the circumstances under which they were made, not misleading, or (3) to engage in any act, practice, or course of business which operates or would operate as a fraud or deceit upon any person, in connection with the purchase or sale of any security.

56. See, for example, *McGann v. Ernst & Young*, 102 F.3d 390 (9th Cir. 1996), *cert. denied*, 520 US 1181 (1997), wherein the court held that the company's auditors could be held liable for making a misleading statement in its audit opinion, where the misleading statement was included with knowledge that the opinion would be used by the company in public filings with the SEC.

57. Once you tell anything, you must tell everything; whether the statement is voluntary or obligatory. Partial disclosure is not an option.

Material misstatements by management played a key role in many of the financial scandals of recent years. The astonishing growth and wealth of software/media giant MicroStrategy in 2000 turned out to be the result of phantom income accounting tricks that overstated the company's profits by more than $60 million in 1998 and 1999. The SEC found that CEO Michael Saylor, CFO Mark Lynch, and cofounder Sanju Bansal were complicit in manipulating the company's accounts. "Each knew, or was reckless in not knowing, that MicroStrategy's financial statements were materially misleading...." The three executives settled the charges with the SEC—agreeing to pay $350,000 each in fines and to disgorge and return to the company a combined $10 million that they made on stock sales.

In the case of Enron, CEO and Chairman of the Board Kenneth Lay made public statements late in the fall of 2001 that the company was in great shape and that "the third quarter is looking great." Relying on that statement, investors—and especially Enron's employees—continued to hold and buy the company's stock. When the third quarter was actually reported, Enron revealed a loss of more than $600 million; the following day the company restated its balance sheet, reducing its reported assets by more than $1 billion. The company imploded from that point to its ultimate bankruptcy in December 2001.

As of this writing, it has not yet been revealed what Kenneth Lay knew about the grandly fraudulent accounting scheme at Enron or when he knew it, but it is clear that he was aware of the situation at least by August 2001. At that time, a day after the abrupt resignation of Jeffrey Skilling, Enron's CEO of six months, for "personal reasons," Vice President Sherron Watkins sent a confidential memo to Kenneth Lay, outlining the problems with the off-balance-sheet financial structures and their imminent breakdown. With great foresight, the memo warned that the company would "implode in a wave of accounting scandals."

## Rules against Insider Trading

The rules against insider trading are derived directly from the duty of loyalty owed to the owners of the company. The victim in insider trading is the person on the other side of the transaction from the insider—either a current or soon-to-be shareholder: a member of the very constituency that the insider has a duty to serve faithfully. Insider trading represents the ultimate breach of loyalty: self-enrichment at the expense of one's trusting beneficiary. The "inside information" involved in insider trading, whatever it may be—a pending approval of a company's miracle drug, a pending merger agreement, or a pending restatement of a company's financials in light of accounting improprieties—is considered to be information belonging to the corporation, not to its managers or employees. Any value associated with the information should inure, then, to the benefit of the company and its owners, not to the individual employed by the company who possesses it. The information is *proprietary* to the company, an asset belonging to all of the company's owners. The use of that information for personal self-enrichment by a fiduciary is a breach of fiduciary duty and a misappropriation of that intangible corporate asset. Both theories are used to prosecute cases of insider trading.

Insider trading laws are designed to prevent individuals with access to material, nonpublic information and who have some duty of disclosure to others from using the information in a such a way as to breach that duty. Insiders include officers, directors, controlling shareholders, employees, the corporation itself (if trading its own stock), as well as temporary insiders such as accountants, attorneys, investment bankers, contract labs, scientists, and consultants.

The prohibition on insider trading is to:
• Prohibit insiders (including temporary insiders) from trading in securities if they know or reasonably should know material facts either not yet made public or inaccurately publicized.
• Prohibit insiders from disclosing inside information to third parties who profit from trading.

Those trading in this second area are known as *tippees*. Their source of inside information is the *tipper*. The tipper need not make a profit on the transaction for both tipper and tippee to be liable under insider trading laws.

There are two theories upon which a person can be found liable for insider trading. The traditional theory is known as the *breach of fiduciary duty theory*. It involves proving that the person trading or the person tipping to another breached a fiduciary duty owed to the corporation. Thus, the "insider" had to be someone inside the company in whose stock he or she was trading or tipping. Management, employees, attorneys, consultants, and anyone else serving in an agency position with the company and possessing inside information are precluded from trading in the company's stock until that information is made public.

An alternative theory, recognized by the U.S. Supreme Court in the case of *United States v. O'Hagan*,[58] is the "misappropriation theory."

> The "misappropriation theory" holds that a person commits fraud "in connection with" a securities transaction, and thereby violates Section 10(b) and Rule 10b-5, when he misappropriates confidential information for securities trading purposes, in breach of a duty owed to the source of the information. Under this theory, a fiduciary's undisclosed, self-serving use of the principal's information to purchase or sell securities, in breach of a duty of loyalty and confidentiality, defrauds the principal of the exclusive use of that information. In lieu of premising liability on a fiduciary relationship between company insider and purchaser or seller of a company's stock, the misappropriation theory premises liability on a fiduciary-turned-trader's deception of

those who entrusted him with access to confidential information.[59]

*O'Hagan* involved trading and tipping by a lawyer in the law firm that represented a company seeking to take over another company. O'Hagan's fiduciary duty lay with the acquiring company. He purchased and tipped others to purchase options in the takeover target company, anticipating a rise in the value of the stock with the takeover announcement. In fact, O'Hagan and his tippees realized a profit of about $4 million on the investment.

The problem with prosecuting O'Hagan under the traditional breach of fiduciary duty theory is that he owed no fiduciary duty to the company in which he bought stock: the takeover target. Instead, under the misappropriation theory, the fact that O'Hagan breached a fiduciary duty to *his law firm* (he was an agent of the firm) by using its proprietary information for his own self-enrichment, without disclosure to the firm (the source of the information), was sufficient grounds to find him liable for insider trading. The high court's recognition of the misappropriation theory substantially widens the net of possible inside traders. Potentially any use of inside information that someone acquires in an agency capacity, without prior disclosure of the intent to trade, could be actionable.

The insider trading in which Enron executives engaged was a breach of fiduciary duty. In the two years before public disclosure of the company's long-running accounting fraud, Enron executives cashed out in a big way.[60] The SEC included charges of insider trading in its criminal complaints against Jeffrey Skilling, Andrew Fastow, and several other members of management that were indicted in the fraud. Several lower-level Enron executives have already settled insider trading charges with the SEC. A class action suit by Enron shareholders on the other side of the insider transactions was

---

58. 521 US 642, 117 S.Ct. 2199, 138 L.ed.2d 724 (1997).

59. *O'Hagan*, 521 US at 645.

60. An ex-Enron executive explained to *The Wall Street Journal* that former Enron executive Thomas E. White, who resigned to serve as Secretary of the Army, couldn't have been privy to the company's off-the-books deals. "If he really had inside information, he'd have sold out a lot sooner," the executive said. "The Fool's Defense," *Multinational Monitor*, June 2002.

## Gracious Entertaining in an Orange Jumpsuit

Poor Martha Stewart—she became to insider trading what Leona Helmsley was to tax evasion, what Lizzie Borden was to patricide, what Alexis Carrington was to *Dynasty*—everyone's favorite mean, greedy rhymes-with-witch.

Stewart was prosecuted, very publicly and at great expense, for engaging in Wall Street activity that goes on regularly, albeit usually on a much grander scale. The joke on the Street was that she did it for a couple thousand bucks—chump change to her—the cost of a nice dinner with friends in the Hamptons on a summer weekend.

Actually, Stewart was never convicted for insider trading; and the alternative theories of the case against her were shaky at best. What she was indicted on was lying to a federal agent about what she knew when she traded.

The case against Martha Stewart stemmed from a sale of fewer than 4,000 shares of ImClone stock that she made two days after Christmas in 2001. It was alleged that Stewart was informed through her broker, Peter Bacanovic of Merrill Lynch, that ImClone founder Sam Waksal, a Bacanovic client and a friend of Stewart's, was selling off a substantial portion of his ImClone shares. A ruling from the FDA on one of ImClone's most promising drug discoveries was imminent. It would later be shown in Waksal's trial for insider trading that he had advance notice of an unfavorable ruling, prompting his holiday sell-off.[a] On learning of Waksal's sales, Bacanovic asked his assistant, Douglas Faneuil, to notify Stewart about it, a practice also explicitly forbidden by Merrill Lynch's policies and codes. Faneuil would later plead guilty to taking a payoff to keep quiet about the circumstances of Stewart's trade. Bacanovic and Stewart defended the sale as prearranged. Bacanovic produced documents showing notations on worksheets that Stewart had made to put in a sell order any time the stock dipped below $60 per share. The government argued that the entry was made by Bacanovic after the investigation had begun in an attempted cover-up of the insider tip.

The government indicted Stewart and Bacanovic on nine counts, including the following: obstruction of justice; conspiracy to obstruct justice; making false statements; committing perjury; making and using false documents; and lastly, the oddest of the lot against Stewart, a charge of securities fraud in her capacity as the head of her publicly traded company Martha Stewart Living Omnimedia (MSLO). The theory of this charge was that (1) MSLO derives much of its intangible corporate value from the reputation of Martha Stewart and (2) Stewart made misleading public statements about her ImClone trades in order to maintain share value in MSLO. (She denied that the trades were insider trading.)

The government alleged that "STEWART made these false and misleading statements with the intent to defraud and deceive purchasers and sellers of MSLO common stock and to maintain the value of her own MSLO stock by preventing a decline in the market price of MSLO's stock." This allegation of material misstatement under Rule 10b-5 was the only allegation of securities fraud against Stewart or Bacanovic in the indictment. The count was ultimately dismissed by the trial judge as without merit.

Jurors convicted Stewart and Bacanovic on charges of obstructing justice and making false statements to federal officials.[b] The securities fraud charge against Stewart was thrown out, and the false documents charge against Bacanovic was not proved.

a. Waksal was eventually sentenced to seven years in prison for the violation.
b. A little-known felony used with increasing regularity in these kinds of cases, Section 1001 of the federal code prohibits lying to any federal agent, even by a person who is not under oath and even by a person who has committed no other crime. Berenson, A. (2004, March 7). There's a reason your mother told you not to lie. *New York Times*.

filed in 2002 against 30 of the company's directors and officers. The suits allege that at the same time the directors and officers were making false and misleading statements about the company's financial performance, the insiders sold more than 20 million shares of Enron stock, collecting trading proceeds just a bit shy of $2 billion.[61]

Some have argued against regulation of insider trading on the grounds that it helps to move share prices to their "correct" level. The price at which insiders trade represent the best indicator of its true market value:

> No other device can approach knowledgeable trading by insiders for efficiently and accurately pricing endogenous developments in a company. Insiders, driven by self-interest and competition among themselves will trade until the correct price is reached. This will be true even when the new information involves trading on bad news. You do not need whistleblowers if you have insider trading.[62]

The policy arguments that favor legalizing insider trading would be effective only when the trading was open and transparent and was immediately reflected in the market price of the stock. Insider trading remains illegal and is an enforcement priority with the SEC. Investors rely on the belief that proprietary corporate information is not being withheld from the market and used to the advantage of insiders.

## Beyond Compliance

Many of the corporate abuses that led to the avalanche of financial disasters at the turn of this century were not technically prohibited by law at the time they were undertaken. They may not have been prudent or diligent, and many of them were based purely on self-interest and were disloyal to the company; nonetheless, tax and securities regulations, accounting standards, and other regulatory schemes did not specifically prohibit many of the actions taken. The abuses were clearly unethical, but arguably legal. This is where business ethics and ethical dilemmas are most prevalent: *where the law ends, or does not yet speak to regulate conduct, is where ethics plays its most important role in corporate decision making.* If the players in these financial scams had considered their actions from an ethical perspective, many of the abuses may not have occurred.

The most ethical approach to discharging the corporate obligation to its owners is *transparency.* Of paramount importance is that the owners of the company be kept accurately apprised of what their investment is doing—and not only in terms of dollar value. Increasingly, the call for corporate reform includes a platform for a strategic change in the very nature of corporate reporting obligations—advocating a move away from mere dollars and cents toward reporting on qualitative factors that give value to the company like the skills and loyalty of the workforce, the environmental impacts (or the prevention of them) on the surrounding communities, the brand reputation, and so on.[63]

After all, "Sunlight is said to be the best of disinfectants..."[64]

---

61. See http://www.enronfraud.com/pdf/complaint.pdf. The named defendants and their securities activities in the two years preceding the company's implosion are set forth in detail in the class action complaint: CEO/COB Kenneth Lay sold 1,810,793 shares for $101 million; Skilling, 1,119,958 shares for $66.9 million; Fastow, 561,423 shares for $30.4 million; J. Clifford Baxter, the company's chief strategy officer, 577,436 shares for $35.2 million; Lou Pai, chair and CEO of a main Enron division, 5,031,105 shares for $353.7 million; and Kenneth Rice, chair and CEO of Enron Broadband, 1,138,370 shares for $72.7 million. Several more officers and ten of Enron's directors are also named as defendants in the suit, with sales ranging between $250,000 and $51 million (Robert Belfer, board of directors) to $79 million (Rebecca Mark, board of directors and former officer of the company).

62. "The Case for Insider Trading" by Henry G. Manne, *Wall Street Journal*, March 17, 2003.

63. Former Harvard professor and venture capitalist Robert Eccles has developed a model for change in reporting the value of corporate assets and activities in *The ValueReporting Revolution: Moving Beyond the Earnings Game*, 2001, New York: John Wiley & Sons.

64. One corporate governance group known as the Stakeholder Alliance has put forth what it calls "Sunshine Standards" for responsible corporate reporting. The standards seek to establish "a performance measurement system that reports benefits and costs to all those who are significantly affected by a corporation's actions—the stakeholders—instead of a system that reports only the effects on financial investors. . . . The Sunshine Standards call for corporate disclosure of information significant to stakeholders, such as environmental damage, statistics on workplace safety and health, consumer product safety andhe

# Chapter 7

## Obligations to the Employees of the Corporation

*"It is but equity... that those who feed, clothe and lodge the whole body of the people, should have such a share of the produce of their own labour as to be themselves tolerably well fed, clothed and lodged."*
—Adam Smith, *Wealth of Nations*, 1776

*"But it is the first function of the law to see that no one shall injure another unless provoked by some wrong."*
—Cicero, circa 45 BCE

## The Relationship between Corporate Management and Employees

The relationship between the managers of a corporation and the workforce has many facets. Both groups work toward the economic success of the firm; yet the two groups are also adversaries. While labor costs are deducted from revenues, management is interested in minimizing those costs at the same time employees want to maximize wages and employment conditions. In recognition of those opposing interests and the unequal bargaining position of workers, U.S. law imposes significant obligations on employers. Employment regulation in the United States prohibits discrimination on the basis of race, color, sex, national origin, religion, age, or disability.

Employers have obligations in the areas of child labor, minimum wages, overtime hours, family and medical leave, worker health and safety, worker disability and unemployment compensation, and collective bargaining.

Chapters Five and Six explored some of the obligations owed to the corporation by its agents—the fiduciary duty of loyalty and the duty of care—and some of the ethical conflicts that arise when individual values and obligations conflict with corporate means and goals. The corporation, as *principal* in the agency relationship, also has obligations. Among the most significant are the obligation to pay fair compensation to the workforce for services rendered and the obligation to provide a reasonably safe workplace. The duty to pay fair compensation is derived from moral precepts of human dignity and property rights in the fruits of one's labor. The obligation to provide a safe workplace comes from the moral obligation not to cause preventable harm. The duty to provide safe working conditions is to prevent harm on the job to the extent that harm is knowable, avoidable, and unaccepted. This chapter explores legal and ethical obligations to maintain a safe workplace and to pay fair compensation. It also examines aspects of labor unions and collective bargaining. In each of those areas, management beyond compliance may be required by a socially responsible company.

## The Obligation to Provide a Reasonably Safe Working Environment

The principle that everyone is equally obligated to avoid causing injury is a moral minimum. Ethical canons of compensatory justice further require correction and restoration by those causing harm. These are the ethics reflected in the common law of torts. The law sets forth an obligation not to cause foreseeable harm, at least not without the informed consent of the person placed at risk—but there is no affirmative duty to assist one in harm's way; no legal requirement to be a "good Samaritan." Only where one's own actions caused the peril or harm is there a legal obligation to assist or compensate the victim.[1]

### The Tort of Negligence

A tort is a wrong caused to a person or his or her property. The harmed party can sue the party that caused the harm (called a *tortfeasor*) for compensation. The punishment in civil actions is monetary damages. A jail sentence can result only through criminal actions brought by the government. The damages usually are compensatory. They are calculated to put the plaintiff in as good a position as he or she was before suffering the harm; that is, the compensatory awards are meant to make the victim whole. This might include awards for medical and health expenses, lost wages, and pain and suffering. Compensatory damages do not generally include attorneys' fees. The extent to which payment is made to an attorney is subtracted from the compensatory damages earned by the victim. Punitive damages also may be imposed depending on the defendant's culpability. Where the harm caused is intentional or made with extreme indifference to human health and safety, punitive damages may be awarded to punish the defendant and serve as a deterrent.[2]

The standard used to determine an individual's obligation to others is that of a "reasonable person"—what level of care would a reasonable person in the same circumstances have exercised to avoid harm? That standard is determined by the nature of the relationship, the circumstances under which the harm was inflicted and whether the resultant harm was foreseeable."

To prove negligence, a plaintiff generally must establish the following:
- A duty was owed by defendant to plaintiff, as determined by the proper standard of care
- A breach of that duty
- Actual harm in the form of injury or loss
- A direct causal connection between failing to meet the standard of care and harm

Failure to meet the standard of care has to be the proximate cause of the harm. Proximate care is an important principle that will receive more attention later in this chapter. The four elements above constitute the burden of proof (a prima facie case) that the plaintiff must satisfy to go forward with a case. If the plaintiff fails to satisfy any of these elements, the case may be dismissed.

### Duty: The Standard of Care

The plaintiff must first establish that the defendant had a duty not to cause harm. This is known as the *standard of care*. It is determined by considering what a reasonable person would do under the circumstances. The proper standard of care depends on circumstances and the relationship of the parties. Circumstances that present greater threats of harm warrant higher degrees of caution than those where risk is slight. Where relationships involve trust, reliance, or unequal awareness of risk and the ability to prevent harm, the standard of care is higher. Examples include doctor and patient, law enforcement officer and the community, and employers and employees.

Standards of care vary. The standard of care for manufacturers of potentially dangerous products such as automobiles is higher than for those manufacturing more innocuous goods.

---

1. "The law has consistently refused to recognize the moral obligation of common decency and common humanity to come to the aid of another human being who is in danger, even though the outcome is to cost him his life." Prosser on *Tort Law*.

2. A more detailed discussion of the difference between compensatory and punitive damages is included in Chapter Eight in the section "Tort Damages and Tort Damages Reform."

Likewise, the standard of care for products sold for use by children is higher than for products sold for use by adults.

### Breach of the Duty of Care

The plaintiff must establish that the defendant breached the duty of care. A breach of duty occurs if the defendant fails to exercise adequate caution in the undertaking, does not undertake adequate testing and precaution to make an activity or a product reasonably safe, or fails to provide adequate warning of known risks.

### Actual Harm or Loss

The plaintiff must suffer some actual, economically measurable loss in order to bring suit. Harm to the plaintiff may take the form of personal injury or property loss, medical expenses, disability, lost wages, pain and suffering, lost profits, or similar economically quantifiable harms.

### Proximate Cause

The plaintiff also must establish proximate cause—that the breach of duty actually caused the harm. Did the defendant's failure to exercise due care lead to injury? Without a clear connection between breach and harm, the defendant cannot be held liable for compensation. Proximate causation requires the "but for" test—*but for* the defendant's actions, the plaintiff would not have been harmed. This finding is further limited by a requirement of *foreseeability*. The defendant must be able to reasonably anticipate risk of harm to the plaintiff, but not the nature and extent of the harm.[3] Foreseeability focuses on recognizing the risk of harm, not on how much harm or how the harm might unfold. When the risk of harm is foreseeable but the plaintiff is injured in an unforeseen manner to a greater extent than anticipated, the defendant remains liable. However, when another event causing harm occurs after the defendant's negligence, it may supersede the defendant's responsibility as the proximate cause, thus relieving the defendant of liability.[4]

Proximate cause is a key issue when scientific proof of causality is less than absolute. In the Dow Corning breast implant case, the company argued that even if the implants were defective because they leaked silicone, a causal connection between silicone in the body and the alleged injuries did not exist.

### Defenses to Negligence

If a plaintiff can establish the four elements of a prima facie case for negligence, the burden of proof shifts to the defendant to establish a valid defense. The two main defenses focus on the plaintiff's actions. *Contributory negligence* or *comparative fault* assesses the conduct of the plaintiff to determine what role he or she played in contributing to the harm. In jurisdictions that follow contributory negligence, any fault on the part of the plaintiff will bar recovery and free the defendant of liability. In comparative fault jurisdictions, a plaintiff's recovery will be reduced by the amount of his or her own fault in the injury.[5]

The other main defense for negligence is *assumption of risk*. When a plaintiff is fully informed of the risks of harm involved and vol-

3. In *Palsgraf v. Long Island Railroad Co*, a man running for a departing train was boosted onto the moving car by two railroad attendants. Inadvertently, they knocked from his hands a plain-wrapped package. *Palsgraf v. Long Island Railroad Co.*, 248 N.Y. 339, 162 N.E. 99 (NY Ct of App 1928). The package contained fireworks, which exploded on the tracks. The vibration from the explosion caused a set of scales at the far end of the train platform to fall from their perch, striking and injuring Mrs. Palsgraf, who was waiting for a different train. The court found that the Long Island Railroad was not liable for Palsgraf's injuries. Nothing about the package gave any warning to the attendants that jostling or dislodging it might cause harm to a bystander at the far end of the train station. While the railroad may have owed other duties to Palsgraf as a passenger, this harm was too far removed to be within the realm of the railroad's duty. "In every instance, before negligence can be predicated of a given act, back of the act must be sought and found a duty to the individual complaining, the observance of which would have averted or avoided the injury." (Id.) Even if the railroad attendants' conduct was otherwise negligent as to the boarding man, harm on account of that to Mrs. Palsgraf was held not foreseeable enough to constitute proximate cause.

4. Superseding cause is fairly rare and is invoked only where the harm caused is different from the original kind of harm *and* the event and actors are independent and completely unrelated to the activities of the original defendant who caused harm to the plaintiff. For example, it is routinely held that negligent medical care provided to treat injuries caused by the negligence of others will not take the original negligent defendant off the hook.

5. Most jurisdictions in the United States have moved away from the strict and often harsh effect of contributory negligence, although several states still retain this common law rule. In applying comparative fault, a plaintiff must, of course, be less than 50 percent responsible for his or her own injuries in order to sue for negligence.

untarily acquiesces to them, the defendant is not held liable if the harm occurs. For assumption of risk to operate as a valid defense, the plaintiff's consent to the risk must be knowing (fully informed) and voluntary (without coercion or duress). This concept of *informed consent* is used regularly in medical treatment. A patient is fully apprised of all possible risks associated with a particular procedure and agrees to them by signing a waiver before undergoing treatment.

The assumption of risk defense works only when the actual harm suffered is assumed by the plaintiff. For example, extreme sports enthusiasts generally sign a waiver of liability acknowledging risks before bungee jumping. The risks warned of may include a variety of medical complications or problems arising from the jump. If, instead, the jumper is injured because the bungee operator used a 75-foot rope for a 50-foot fall, the operator cannot rely on the assumption of risk defense. The risk of crashing to the ground was not among those agreed to by the jumper—he or she was neither informed of the risk nor voluntarily assumed it.

The assumption of risk defense acknowledges potential plaintiffs as human ends in themselves, with free will and with the right not to be treated as a means to some other end without their consent. In the employer/employee relationship, the assumption of risk is explicitly bargained for in the negotiation of wages. Positions involving increased risk generally demand greater compensation. Workers tend to agree to wages that reflect the risk associated with their work.

If workers have given informed and voluntary consent to the risks posed by the workplace, employers will be protected against liability should those harms materialize. Yet it can be difficult to balance the employer's obligation for a safe work environment with the employees' free will to choose risks to which they subject themselves, as discussed in the following feature, "The Worker's Right to Choose." In the case of the *Automobile Workers v. Johnson Controls, Inc.*, the U.S. Supreme Court weighed the employer's obligation for a safe work environment against the employee's right to assume known risks. The

Court ruled in favor of informed and voluntary decisions of the worker.[6]

## Tort Principles in Employment Regulation

Federal and state laws are meant to provide employees with a safe work environment, adequate warning of job risks, and fair compensation should an employee be injured. These laws uphold basic ethical principles, but they often are weakly enforced. Inadequate enforcement provides firms with leeway to go beyond legal minimums and simple compliance. Some firms show a willingness to do more for their workers than the law dictates.

### Federal Occupational Safety & Health Administration (OSHA) Regulation

For most workers injured or killed on the job, occupational safety and health regulations and workers' compensation laws have preempted common law tort rights. The Occupational Safety and Health Act passed in 1970 incorporated a standard of care and workers' right to know. This act created a federal agency, the Occupational Safety & Health Administration (OSHA), to promulgate and enforce rules on what workers can be exposed to and what notice and warning must be given to them. The mission of OSHA is "to save lives, prevent injuries and protect the health of America's workers."

Under OSHA, employers are required to furnish employees with a workplace that is free from known hazards posing serious health risks. Employers must meet the various health and safety standards set under the act and keep records of injuries, deaths, accidents, illnesses, and specified hazards to which their workforce may be exposed. The tools available to OSHA for enforcement include the ability to inspect workplaces, cite violations, and impose penalties and fines for noncompliance with its standards. The agency cannot require immediate abatement of hazards or shut down a noncompliant workplace without a court order.

Prior to the passage of the Occupational Safety and Health Act, workplace health and safety was left to state regulation. Federal regulation

---

6. *UAW v. Johnson Controls, Inc.*, 499 U.S. 187 (1991). Read the case at 499 US 187—what do you think of the reasoning the Court employed in finding for the female workers?"

## The Worker's Right to Choose

Johnson Controls owned and operated a battery manufacturing plant. A primary ingredient in the manufacture of batteries is lead: an element known to pose serious health risks to humans. Occupational exposure to lead poses a threat not only to the health of workers, but also to the health of the fetus carried by a pregnant worker.

Prior to the 1964 Civil Rights Act, Johnson Controls refused to hire women to work in the plant. When sex discrimination was made illegal, the company employed women in the battery manufacturing process, but warned of the risks for those women planning to have children. The company required all women working in the plant to sign a consent and release form acknowledging that they were aware of the risk. In 1982, with more women working in the plant and several pregnancies, Johnson Controls changed the policy to exclude from employment in the battery plant all women "except those whose inability to bear children is medically documented."

Although workers compensation laws would limit the company's liability for harm to the workers, Johnson Controls feared liability for the consequences of lead exposure to children born to the exposed workers, to whom its liability would not be limited. Women workers at the plant filed suit, claiming the fetal protection policy was discriminatory. Several of the plaintiffs were women who had undergone sterilization to keep their jobs.

The U.S. Supreme Court found the fetal protection policy to have an obvious bias: Although lead exposure may also have a detrimental effect on male fertility, only women were banned from positions at the plant. Further, all women capable of having children were banned, regardless of their desire to have no children or no more children.

The Court found the company policy to be paternalistic, which was inappropriate in the employment context. Failure to treat all employees equally and fairly and failure to permit employees to make their own decisions on reproductive versus economic priorities constituted discrimination. With respect to potential liability for harm to children born to workers, the Court found assumption of risk to be an adequate defense.

brought greater coverage and consistency to the protection of the workforce. The rate of injuries in the workplace was 30 percent to 40 percent higher before the creation of OSHA. Nonetheless, the risk of injury and death on the job remain substantial.[7]

While OSHA has improved standards for workplace safety, there are limits to its reach. First, not all American workplaces are covered by the act. Small businesses with fewer than ten employees are exempt, as are federal, state, and municipal employers. As an agency of the federal government, OSHA is subject to congressional oversight and control of its budget. In addition, it has fewer employees today than it did in 1980, with the responsibility to cover more workplaces.[8]

Businesses often oppose OSHA regulation. For instance, in 1976, the National Institute for Occupational Safety and Health (NIOSH) recommended an emergency standard to limit work-

7. In 2000, "there were more than 5,000 workers who died from traumatic injuries, and an estimated 50,000 to 60,000 who died from occupational diseases. The number of reported workplace injuries was over 6 million, and that number is clearly understated. OSHA itself has estimated that reported injuries may understate the problem by one-half." An Interview with Margaret Seminario, Director of OSH for the AFL-CIO. (2003, June). Workers at risk: the dangers on the job when the regulators don't try very hard. *Multinational Monitor.*

8. "With their current budget and staffing—there are 2238 federal and state OSHA inspectors for 8 million workplaces—it would take OSHA 119 years to inspect every workplace." Cullen, L. (2002). *A job to die for: why so many Americans are killed, injured or made ill at work and what to do about it.* Monroe, ME: Common Courage Press.

place exposure to hexavalent chromium, a carcinogen causing liver, kidney, and lung cancer and other serious health problems. In 1993, when no action had been taken on the recommendation, several watchdog groups and unions petitioned OSHA to limit the chemical's exposure. After two lawsuits were filed in 2003, the agency began the process of lowering the exposure standard, but not to levels suggested as "safe" by medical science. OSHA, under court order, had until 2006 to promulgate a rule on exposure. In the meantime, more than 1 million workers each year were exposed to the toxin regularly.[9] The agency also took more than ten years to establish a workplace standard for tuberculosis testing for employees in hospitals, homeless shelters, prisons, and drug treatment centers, a regulatory process that began in 1993.[10]

A contested OSHA proceeding has not been able to establish standards to prevent repetitive stress injuries in the workplace. Muscular and skeletal disorders are a third of all serious workplace injuries. The Bush administration proposed ergonomic standards in 1990, and OSHA promulgated a regulation to identify workplace conditions that created repetitive stress injury risks and to reduce them. That regulation was made final in 2000, but it was overturned by the Bush II administration. This is a common practice among all incoming presidential administrations—to suspend, review, or overturn controversial regulations enacted as the previous administration is leaving office. Close to one-half of all workers' compensation costs are attributable to repetitive stress injuries. In the long run, employers are better off addressing the problem than fighting ergonomic standards: "Employers that have taken steps to address ergonomic hazards and musculoskeletal disorders generally see very good results, significantly reducing or even eliminating injuries. In six months to a year, they've got these investments paid for, because these injuries are so costly."[11] Thus, no such standard is in place.

## State Workers' Compensation Laws

The obligation to compensate employees injured or sickened on the job is left to state law." All 50 states have some form of workers' compensation. Eligibility for benefits and the amount available to the injured party vary from state to state. Employees have to prove that their injury or disease is work-related. The system, then, is no-fault—whether the injury was preventable or the risk was known to the employer is not relevant. Compensation is limited to medical expenses and lost income. Compensatory damages are not paid, and punitive damages are not available. Employers are shielded against further liability. Employer contributions fund the system based on an employer's workplace injury experience. The safer the workplace, the lower the employer's premium. That creates an incentive for a safe workplace, but it also leads employers to underreport injuries.

The system provides employees with a quick and simple means to resolve claims, without the expense and hardship of having to sue. However, it also provide employers with a shield against further liability. They are not held legally accountable for negligence or reckless disregard for worker safety. A shortcoming of the system is that work-related injuries and diseases do not always appear when an employee is working. When no longer on the job, the employee is no longer covered. Chronic injuries or progressive diseases that appear after the employee's tenure are undercompensated.

Some states permit employers to opt out of the system and self-insure. In states such as Texas, the workers' right to sue self-insured employers who fail to provide compensation has been effectively abolished.

## *Ethical Dimensions of Safe Work and Adequate Warning of Job Risks*

The obligation to provide a safe workplace is derived from the moral obligation not to cause preventable harm. That duty is to prevent harm

---

9. Skrzycki, C. (2004, November 9). OSHA slow to issue standards. *Washington Post.*

10. Golstein, A., & Cohen S. (2004, August 15). Bush forces a shift in regulatory thrust: OSHA made more business-friendly. *Washington Post.*

11. An Interview with Margaret Seminario, Director of OSH for the AFL-CIO. (2003, June). Workers at risk: the dangers on the job when the regulators don't try very hard. *Multinational Monitor.*

## Compensatory Justice: Texas-Style

The existence of federal workplace health and safety standards and state workers' compensation funds has improved the lot of many American workers over the past few decades. Nonetheless, for workers in some industries these protections remain elusive. Hardest hit are the most vulnerable populations—immigrant laborers, workers with past criminal records, and those living in areas without alternative employment opportunities. Some companies and industries have exploited these workers through intimidation, loopholes in the law, and the relative impotence of regulators. The effect of such exploitation is devastating, both on the workers themselves and on the society in which they live. Two recent exposes on the activities of such companies operating in Texas provide a chilling illustration of the tactics available to companies bent on avoiding legal and moral social responsibility for the impact of their commercial activities.[a]

### *Treated Like a Piece of Meat*
"According to the Bureau of Labor Statistics, meatpacking is the nation's most dangerous occupation. In 1999, more than one-quarter of America's nearly 150,000 meatpacking workers suffered a job-related injury or illness. The meatpacking industry not only has the highest injury rate, but also has by far the highest rate of serious injury—more than five times the national average, as measured in lost workdays. If you accept the official figures, about 40,000 meatpacking workers are injured on the job every year. But the actual number is most likely higher. The meatpacking industry has a well-documented history of discouraging injury reports, falsifying injury data, and putting injured workers back on the job quickly to minimize the reporting of lost workdays."[b]

In the span of little more than three decades, the job of meatpacking in the United States was transformed from one of the highest-paid industrial positions to one of the lowest. Where once workers in the industry enjoyed strong union representation, good benefits and fair working conditions, jobs in meatpacking are now mainly occupied by those with virtually no alternative means of support. Despite the economic desperation of its workforce, modern meatpacking also has one of the highest turnover rates in industrial production, with the typical plant replacing its workforce almost annually.

Beginning in the 1960s, the meatpacking industry dramatically changed its way of doing business. Industry operations traditionally located in urban centers moved to rural areas, where unemployment rates were higher and labor cheaper. The industry consolidated and is now concentrated in the hands of four major producers.[c] Union workers were largely replaced with an immigrant labor force and wages in the industry fell by as much as 50%.

The profitability of meatpacking depends upon the speed of slaughter. The tools of the trade for the work consist of knives, saws, grinders, conveyor belts, hide pullers, and boiling vats of chemicals. Increased production quotas coupled with an unskilled and untrained workforce makes the work especially dangerous. Injury and death by amputation, decapitation, burning, and crushing are not uncommon. As well, the nature of the work invariably involves repetitive and cumulative stress injuries from performing the same motion of cutting and lifting minute after minute, hour after hour, day after day.

"The rate of cumulative trauma injuries in meatpacking is the highest of any American industry. It is about 33 times higher than the national average. According to federal statistics, nearly 1 out of every 10 meatpacking workers suffers a cumulative trauma injury every year."[d]

Meatpacking is big business in the State of Texas. Texas slaughterhouses process close to

**Compensatory Justice: Texas-Style (continued)**

10 million animals annually, or about 25% of the cattle slaughtered in the US. Immigrant labor from Mexico is readily available in the state and the legal and regulatory climate of Texas is known to be business-friendly.

In 1989, the Texas legislature reformed the state workers' compensation system to permit companies to opt out of the state fund and self-insure. Iowa Beef Packers (IBP), one of the largest meatpacking concerns in the state, along with the other three major players in the industry, all have taken advantage of the ability to self-insure for worker injuries. As a result, the companies have a clear interest in minimizing workplace injuries—worker injuries have a direct and immediate impact on the bottom line. The problem is how the industry has gone about doing so. Instead of emphasizing the need for greater workplace safety, worker injury rates are held down by intimidation, discouraging injury reporting, and just plain failing to provide care for workers harmed on the job.

"When a worker is injured at an IBP plant in Texas, for example, he or she is immediately presented with a waiver. It reads: 'I have been injured at work and want to apply for the payments offered by IBP to me under its Workplace Injury Settlement Program. To qualify, I accept the rules of the Program....' Signing the waiver means forever surrendering your right—and the right of your family and heirs—to sue IBP on any grounds. Workers who sign the waiver may receive immediate medical care under IBP's program. Or they may not. Once they sign, IBP and its company-approved doctors have control over the worker's job-related medical treatment—for life."

For workers who refuse to sign the waiver, there is little recourse. They may be fired or retaliated against with harsh or demeaning job assignments. For illegal immigrants, the risk of retaliatory deportation looms large. Injured workers who quit in the face of retaliation risk losing eligibility for any medical benefits whatsoever.

### *Foundering in the Foundry*

In another part of Texas, the McWane Corporation operates its pipe foundry plants using similar tactics to those employed by the meatpacking industry. In the decade since McWane took control of Tyler Pipe in 1995, workers at McWane foundries have suffered more than 4600 injuries, hundreds of them serious, and at least nine on-the-job deaths. Federal health and safety inspectors have reported more than 400 workplace safety violations in McWane plants, considerably more than those recorded against all of its competitors combined.

McWane's turnaround strategy for its foundry business involved a slash-and-burn approach. It cut the workforce by more than one-half, moved three shifts of 8-hours into two 12-hour shifts, required employees to operate three machines instead of one, purged itself of personnel responsible for safety, quality, and pollution control, and cut back on cleaning and maintenance crews. Workplace "amenities" like water and ice for smelter workers, protective aprons, gloves, and boots, portable heaters in the winter and even toilet paper were eliminated. The results were a doubling of corporate profits and "a workplace that is part Dickens and part Darwin, a dim, dirty, hellishly hot place where men are regularly disfigured by amputations and burns, where turnover is so high that convicts are recruited from local prisons, where some workers urinate in their pants because their bosses refuse to let them step away from the manufacturing line for even a few minutes."[e]

The rash of dismemberment and deaths at McWane foundries brought the attention of OSHA. Since 1997, the agency has cited McWane for countless violations of workplace safety laws. The company's fatality rate is more than 6 times higher than others in its industry. OSHA

## Compensatory Justice: Texas-Style (continued)

records reveal that several of the deaths "resulted directly from McWane's deliberate violations of federal safety standards." In its plants outside of Texas, the problems were just as bad. McWane's Union Foundry plant in Alabama recorded more than 250 injuries among its 350 employees. Inspectors also found a deliberate corporate policy for underreporting serious injuries at the plants and a general indifference to worker safety. OSHA records show that the company policy "was not to correct anything until OSHA found it." As well, McWane's environmental record was abysmal. Company plants have been repeatedly deemed "EPA High-Priority Violators" and subject to fines for the environmental discharge of toxins including lead and arsenic. McWane has been cited for more than 450 environmental violations since 1995.

The company takes a pure cost-benefit approach to the health and safety of those affected by its activities.

> "McWane, current and former managers said, viewed the burden of regulatory fines as far less onerous than the cost of fully complying with safety and environmental rules.... company budget documents show, McWane calculated down to the penny per ton the cost of OSHA and environmental fines, along with raw materials.... the company has paid less than $10 million in fines and penalties for its safety and environmental violations and three criminal convictions — less than 1 percent of its annual revenues."[f]

McWane's exclusive concern for the bottom line was most glaringly apparent in its treatment of workers injured at its plants. Although shielding the company from legal liability to workers for the hazards it exposed them to in the workplace, Texas workers' comp laws nonetheless required the company to pay for the medical expenses and lost income of workers injured on the job. Given McWane's excessive workplace injury record compared to its competition, workers' comp premiums for the company amounted to millions of dollars. In an effort to reduce these costs, McWane "devised a system of workers' compensation cost control techniques that shifted responsibility for safety problems onto the workers themselves."

The overarching corporate strategy involved viewing all worker injuries with suspicion. Workers who reported on-the-job injuries were the subject of disciplinary actions, including firing, for violating workplace safety rules. "In 2000 and 2001, company records show, more than 350 workers were subjected to disciplinary actions — known as D.A.'s — after reporting injuries." The effect was not only to stifle employee injury reporting but also to create a turnover ratio in the plant of close to 75%.

In addition, McWane required injured employees to see only company doctors if medical attention was necessary. To this end, McWane hired a small start-up medical group called Occu-Safe to run its medical treatment for company workers. Occu-Safe was a new entity, run by an owner whose only prior business experience was a bankrupt air-conditioning company. McWane was by far its largest client. Records show that Occu-Safe's medical treatment of McWane employees was often dictated by McWane management. The types of pain-killers and medical treatment prescribed, the number of days an employee was permitted to recuperate away from work, and the medical information shared with the employee were all subject to approval by McWane management.

In one of the most egregious cases, a McWane foundry worker fell on the job and slammed his back into a piece of metal machinery. When he was seen by the Occu-Safe personnel he was weeping in pain, unable to walk, and obviously in shock. He was sent home for rest with some pain killers. More than three weeks after the injury, the employee was finally sent to a hospital for x-rays, which revealed that he had fractured his spine and was "within one hair"

---

**Compensatory Justice: Texas-Style (continued)**

of being paralyzed for the rest of his life. The fracture had worsened considerably since the accident. The employee is permanently disabled for life because of the medical malpractice.

### A Socially Responsible Alternative

One of McWane's main competitors in Texas is a foundry run by a company called Acipco. In contrast to the "McWane way," Acipco stresses worker safety on the job, provides a health club for employees, provides individual air-conditioners for employees working in the swelter of casting jobs, and generally runs on the principles of the Golden Rule. Turnover at Acipco is less than 1%, with a long wait-list of potential applicants when positions do open up. The company has 40 times fewer workplace safety violations than the McWane plants and was recently ranked sixth on Fortune Magazine's list of 100 best employers.

John Eagan founded Acipco in 1905. He "believed that if workers felt they had a genuine stake they would work harder and smarter and produce more. To carry out his plan, he decided to institute profit sharing for all employees. Upon his death, he declared, Acipco's workers would inherit the company."[g] Ironically, the President of Acipco at the founding was long-time employee J.R. McWane. Incensed by the plan for employee-ownership, J.R. McWane left Acipco to start up his own competing cast iron operation in Texas.

A century later, the companies remain competitors—different as night and day, different as life and death.

---

By Sheryl Kaiser, @2006, NorthCoast Publishers, Inc.

a. The two investigative reports that form the basis of this study are highly recommended as supplemental material for this chapter of the text. The meatpacking industry expose is based on the work of investigative journalist Eric Schlosser and can be found in his book Fast-Food Nation: the Dark Side of the All-American Meal (HarperCollins 2002). An article excerpted from the book, entitled "The Chain Never Stops" was published in Mother Jones Magazine (July/August 2001)—it is available online at www.motherjones.com ("Schlosser"). The McWane Pipe Foundry expose is based on a three-part series published by the New York Times during the week of January 8, 2003 by David Barstow and Lowell Bergman, with additional reporting by James Sandler and Robin Stein, see e.g. "At A Texas Foundry, an Indifference to Life" the New York Times, January 8, 2003 ("Barstow and Bergman"). The three-part series was made into a 60-minute documentary by Bill Moyers and Frontline entitled Dangerous Business. The documentary is also highly recommended as supplemental material for this chapter. A video of the documentary is available from www.pbs.org.

b. Schlosser.

c. "In 1970, the top four meatpackers controlled just 21% of the beef market. Today the top four—IBP, ConAgra, Excel (a subsidiary of Cargill) and National Beef—control about 85% of the market." Schlosser

d. Schlosser.

e. Barstow and Bergman.

f. Barstow and Bergman. OHSA fines, even for a worker's preventable death, are indeed minimal and likely encourage this kind of behavior in the worst of companies. The maximum sanction for a safety violation is $70,000, increased from $10,000 in 1990. "Under federal law, causing the death of a worker by willfully violating safety rules — a misdemeanor with a six-month maximum prison term — is a less serious crime than harassing a wild burro on federal lands, which is punishable by a year in prison."

g. Barstow and Bergman.

---

on the job to the extent that harm is knowable, avoidable, and unacceptable by the affected worker. The natural right to be treated as an end and not a means requires that workers be informed. Subjecting employees to harm, without their informed consent, contradicts the basic premise of deontological ethics. Workers' rights to be informed also are justified on utilitarian grounds. Workers aware of hazards will suffer fewer injuries.[12] They will heed warnings and make use of protective equipment to avoid exposure, the result being lower employer workers' compensation premiums. To the extent that workers are injured, the costs fall upon society in the form of public expenditures for health-care and other social services.

### The Obligation to Pay Fair Compensation

Without written terms of engagement, workers are at-will employees—they may quit or be fired at the discretion of their employers.[13] However, the framework of federal and state regulations governing employment practices place limits on employers' freedom to contract and sets a floor for working conditions beneath which employers may not reasonably bargain.[14]

### The Fair Labor Standards Act

The Fair Labor Standards Act (FLSA) enacted in 1938 imposes a minimum wage rate payable to workers covered by it. States have their own versions, which, if more protective of workers (for example, a higher rate), must be respected by employers within the state. The FLSA also sets limits on child labor, with age restrictions dependent on the type of work involved. For example, children under 14 may legally engage only in agricultural work. While the FLSA does not impose a maximum limit on the number of hours an employee may work in a day or week, it does mandate the payment of overtime for hours worked in excess of daily and weekly maximums. Under the FLSA, wages must be paid for *all* hours the employee worked.

Attempts to circumvent the mandates of the FLSA can result in large damage awards. For example, in 1997, Taco Bell was found liable for $13 million for shaving time off employees' time cards to avoid paying overtime. In 2001, Taco Bell settled a similar class action suit in California for $9 million in back wages and overtime.[15] In 1999, Nabisco paid a $5 million settlement for failure to pay overtime to 3,000 of its retail employees.

Currently, dozens of suits are pending against companies that attempted to circumvent application of the fair wage laws by classifying employees as "managers," a category deemed exempt from FLSA protections. Wal-Mart, Dollar General Stores, RadioShack, and several other large retailers have class action and individual suits pending against them for evading the payment of overtime through the use of the label "assistant manager."[16]

Attempts to semantically skirt the law on minimum compensation are not limited to large retailers. An article in *The Wall Street Journal* reports, "As businesses try to control labor costs, the practice of excluding low-level supervisors from overtime pay has accelerated across many industries, including restaurants, insurance, and

---

12. Boatright comments: "Employers can attract a sufficient supply of workers to perform hazardous work either by spending money to make the workplace safer, thereby reducing the risks, or by increasing wages to compensate workers for the greater risks. The choice is determined by the marginal utility of each kind of investment." Boatright, J. R. (2003). *Ethics and the conduct of business* (4th ed.). Saddle River, N: Pearson Education, Inc.

13. The doctrine of at-will employment is discussed in greater detail in chapter 5"..

14. Forced labor and slavery are universally condemned, and workers may expect fair pay for the labor tendered. If dissatisfied, they are free to seek employment elsewhere. The issue of modern forced labor is examined in the Part Three case study "Lying Down with Dogs ...Getting Up with Lawsuits." The issue of modern child slave labor is examined in the Part Three case study "St. Valentine's Day Massacre Redux: The Human Cost of Chocolates and Diamonds." Each case considers the obligations of multinational corporations to refrain from operations that exploit the practices of forced labor and child slave labor.

15. Similar cases are pending in several other states against the company. Schlosser, E. (2002). *Fast-food nation: the dark side of the all-American meal.* New York: HarperCollins.

16. The suits claim that there is very little difference between the job duties of hourly workers and assistant managers, especially the nighttime assistant managers, who, in most cases, are simply glorified stockers who unload trucks, move products into the store, and stock shelves. Under federal law, managers may be entitled to overtime pay if more than 40 percent of their time isn't spent supervising or if their jobs don't include decision making. Zimmerman, A. Big retailers face overtime suits as bosses do more "hourly" work. (2004, May 26). *Wall Street Journal.* In the Dollar General case, one store manager claimed that to keep his position, he was forced to work up to 90 hours per week without overtime, bonus, vacation, or sick time. In January 2003, the suit was certified as a class action. Wal-Mart has been named as a defendant in dozens of suits alleging work without pay. The company settled one case in Colorado for $50 million and faces a class action suit on similar grounds in Michigan. Wal-Mart is also defending against alleged illegal antiunion activities in several suits. In early 2005, Wal-Mart settled charges of child labor law abuses for a substantial fine. McDonough, S. (2005, February 12). Wal-Mart settles charges in child labor cases. Associated Press.

financial services."[17] The rules of legal construction, however, favor substance over form. If the "managers" are functioning as hourly employees, the law will generally afford them the protections of hourly employees, regardless of how the employer identifies them.[18]

## Minimum Wages

The minimum wage provisions of the FLSA are intended to assure workers "a fair day's pay for a fair day's work."[19] The goals of the law are to reduce poverty, bring the earnings of workers closer to the cost of living, and maintain their purchasing power. The principle of fair compensation for labor performed gained recognition internationally as a fundamental human right in the twentieth century.[20]

The idea that a minimum wage should be a "living wage"—one upon which, for a full day's work, a person makes enough to feed, clothe, and shelter himself or herself adequately—is not a new concept. The Norwegian Constitution of 1814 obligated the state to "create conditions that make it possible for every person who is able to work to earn his living by his work." The Mexican Constitution of 1917 mandated a minimum wage "sufficient to satisfy the normal necessities of life of the worker."[21] The 1948 Universal Declaration of Human Rights provides not only that everyone has the right to work and the right to work free of discrimination, but also that:

> Everyone who works has the right to just and favourable remuneration ensuring for himself and his family an existence worthy of human dignity and supplemented, if necessary, by other means of social protection.[22]

Many countries now have domestic minimum wage laws. When the FLSA was passed in 1938, the U.S. minimum wage was set at $0.25 per hour. The current rate (unchanged since 1997) is $5.15 per hour.

Until the early 1970s, the U.S. minimum wage kept pace with increases in worker productivity.

> Between 1947 and 1973, worker productivity rose 108 percent while the minimum wage rose 101 percent, adjusting for inflation.... Between 1973 and 2000, worker productivity rose 52 percent, but the minimum wage fell 17 percent and hourly average wages fell 10 percent, adjusting for inflation.... The current minimum wage of $5.15 an hour is lower than the real minimum wage of 1950 ($5.71).[23]

Approximately 30 million people in the United States work full-time and still earn poverty-level wages. A full-time position at the 2005 minimum wage rate pays $10,700 per

17. Zimmerman, A. (2004, May 26). Big retailers face overtime suits as bosses do more "hourly" work. *Wall Street Journal.*

18. Examples of the rule of construction favoring substance over form abound in tax law—status as a double-taxed corporation versus a single-taxed partnership depend on the functioning and characteristics of the entity, not what its originators label it. Similarly, characterizing a worker as an employee (with attendant tax-withholding responsibilities and benefit requirements) versus an independent contractor (for whom the company has no tax or benefit obligations) turns upon who controls the work and whether the worker is essentially functioning as other employees in the company.

19. From President Franklin Roosevelt's comments at the signing of the historic bill.

20. At that time, several factors converged to establish a fairly firm social consensus that there is some *minimum* wage beneath which lies exploitation of human rights. Among those factors are the abolition of slavery and forced labor; the rise of universal respect for the dignity of people as an end in themselves, not a means for others; and recognition of the economic rights of human beings, that the ability to feed and clothe and shelter oneself is an essential right for life and liberty. In the modern era, reasonable minds do not disagree on this point. Where they divide is over where to set the minimum level and which factors should have a hand in the determination.

21. Glendon, M. A. (2001). *A world made new: Eleanor Roosevelt and the Universal Declaration of Human Rights.* New York: Random House. Other early examples include French constitutions dating from the revolutionary period, the Bogota Declaration, and the founding principles of the International Labor Organization. Though absent from the U.S. Constitution, FDR's New Deal legislation sought to somewhat vindicate the lack of any constitutionally guaranteed economic rights for Americans. Dr. Martin Luther King, Jr., advocated for a living wage amendment to the Constitution in the 1960s.

22. Id. Article 23 of the Universal Declaration of Human Rights (UDHR). These principles have been incorporated into the International Covenant on Economic, Social, and Cultural Rights. It has the authority of binding international law on those countries that have ratified and adopted it—a group that includes most developed and many developing member nations of the United Nations (UN) (with the notable exception of the United States). The UDHR and international law are examined in general in Chapter Ten.

23. Sklar, H. (2003, June 26). Poverty wages are toxic. AlterNet. Independent Media Institute.

### Trading Places

"How does anyone live on the wages available to the unskilled?"

In her best-selling book, *Nickel and Dimed: On (Not) Getting By in America,* journalist Barbara Ehrenreich challenged herself to "do the old-fashioned kind of journalism" and go out there and try it for herself. For a year, Ehrenreich moved from city to city, working minimum wage jobs and attempting to live on what she earned.

"Highly educated and experienced, Ehrenreich applied and interviewed for the positions without benefit of her true resume. A writer with a Ph.D. in biology, she approached the task "in the spirit of science."

Rule one, obviously enough, was that I could not, in my search for jobs, fall back on any skills derived from my education or usual work—not that there were a lot of want ads for essayists anyway. Two, I had to take the highest paying job that was offered me and do my best to hold it .... Three, I had to take the cheapest accommodations I could find, at least the cheapest that offered an acceptable level of safety and privacy, though my standards in this regard were hazy and, as it turned out, prone to deterioration over time.

Ehrenreich worked as a waitress in Key West, Florida ($2.43 an hour—the minimum wage rate does not apply for positions that pay "tips"); a maid on a cleaning crew ($6.65 per hour); a sales associate at a Minneapolis Wal-Mart ($7 per hour); and several other low hourly wage positions. She lived in efficiency apartments, a half-sized trailer, a dormitory, and residential motels. Her diet consisted of chopped meat, beans, cheese, and noodles when she had a kitchen and fast-food when she didn't (at a cost of about $9 per day).

Ehrenreich found that she could not support herself, even in the most modest of terms, on one minimum wage job. That was the case despite the many advantages she enjoyed over much of the minimum wage workforce: she is white, she is a native English speaker, her children are grown and self-supporting, she is in good health, and she permitted herself a rent-a-wreck car for mobility.

"Just bear in mind when I stumble, that this is in fact the **best**-case scenario: a person with every advantage that ethnicity and education, health and motivation can confer attempting, in a time of exuberant national prosperity, to survive in the economy's lower depths."

Ehrenreich, B. *Nickel and Dimed: On (Not) Getting By in America.* Henry Holt & Co. 2001. All quoted material is from the book."

year. It would take $8.45 to match the minimum wage peak of 1968 in today's dollars.[24] The starting hourly wage at Wal-Mart is a bit above the minimum—at $6.25 an hour.[25] Using an "adequate but austere" budget for a family of three, "a single parent employed full-time at Salina's [Kansas] Wal-Mart and raising two children aged 4 and 12 does not earn enough money to supply the family's basic needs by shopping at that same Wal-Mart."[26] In the case of the Kansas Wal-Mart worker, the only way the family ekes out its austere living is with the

24. Adjusted for inflation, the minimum wage has dropped by more than 40 percent since 1968, while worker productivity has increased over the same period by more than 80 percent. Id.

25. Cox, S. (2003, June 10). Wal-Mart wages don't support Wal-Mart workers. AlterNet. Independent Media Institute.

26. The reporters found that the family of three would need a minimum of $1,136 per month to meet their basic needs, even shopping at discounters such as Wal-Mart. The $1,016 after-tax income of the full-time hourly Wal-Mart worker would not provide for those basic needs. Id.

supplement of the federal earned income tax credit (EITC) and childcare allowances provided by the state to impoverished parents.[27]

While the FLSA sets the federal minimum wage rate, states are free to impose their own minimums. The District of Columbia has always set its rate $1 above the federal rate.[28] Determining the number that provides a living wage for a U.S. worker can be a difficult calculation, however; and many variables have to be considered. The Atlanta Living Wage Coalition sets the number at $10.50 per hour.[29] Because minimum wages in the United States are so low, the fabric of family life has been worn thin where parents must work several jobs just to meet the subsistence needs of the family. The justification of low minimum wages offered by economists is that it stimulates more job creation. The United States has lower minimum wages and less unemployment than European nations that have higher minimum wages and more unemployment. When minimum wages are higher, employers are reluctant to create new jobs and to hire workers, according to most economists. Still, surviving on the low wages offered by many U.S. employers is becoming increasingly difficult.

## A Global Living Wage

The International Labor Organization (ILO) Treaty contains four basic principles that inform the rights of all workers:[30]

- The freedom of association and the right to collective bargaining
- The abolition of child labor
- The elimination of all forms of forced or compulsory labor
- Nondiscrimination in employment

The ILO and other labor groups, domestic and international, have called for an extra-territorial, transnational "minimum wage." The U.S. AFL-CIO endorses an international minimum wage (IMW), but cautions that such an international standard would need to reflect differences in the relative economic development of countries.[31]

The campus antisweatshop movement in the United States strives to ensure that items (apparel in particular) are not produced under sweatshop conditions. Principles governing the sweat-free campus movement are payment of a living wage, an end to discrimination against women in the workforce, transparency and accountability in transnational operations, and independent monitoring for compliance.[32]

Ian Maitland posits that there are three possible standards to apply to determine appropriate wage rates that companies from the US and other developed nations should pay to host country workers:

*Home Country Standard*—paying the

27. Id.

28. In recent years, as the federal rate remained unchanged, eight states raised their rate above the federal level; some more than once. As well, several cities have enacted their own rates for employers operating within the city borders. Uchitelle, L. (2003, September 8). Raising minimum wages, city by city. *New York Times*.

29. As one working mother in Atlanta put it: "I experienced working minimum wage jobs most of my working life. A job that pays $10 or more means I am not required, by necessity, to get a second job ...When I worked like that, I noticed that I wasn't able to spend any time with my children ...And when they were very little, one of my daughters, before I came home that evening, wrote a letter and left it on my nightstand, and when I got home she was already asleep because I was working graveyard shift, and it said 'I love you mommy, I miss you, and I want to see you again,' because she did not get to see me anymore, working the jobs I did.... A wage, around $10 an hour, it does make a difference ...It made a difference in my life.... I make in the neighborhood of $10 now, and I could use a little more help ...but I am not required to work a second job." "Waging a Fight" produced by James Hickey and Sharon Basco for http://www.tompaine.com (2002). "The St. Paul [MN]-based Jobs Now Coalition estimated that, in 1997, a 'living wage' for a single parent supporting a single child in the Twin cities metro area was $11.77 an hour." Ehrenreich, B. (2001). *Nickel and dimed: on (not) getting by in America.* New York: Henry Holt and Company, p. 127.

30. The International Labour Organization is the UN specialized agency that seeks the promotion of social justice and internationally recognized human and labor rights. It was founded in 1919 and is the only surviving major creation of the Treaty of Versailles and, later, the League of Nations. It became the first specialized agency of the UN in 1946.

31. The AFL-CIO also advocates an increase in the U.S. minimum wage to keep pace with inflation and to provide a decent standard of living for full-time workers and their families. "Call for Negotiations toward an International Minimum Wage," AFL-CIO Annual Meeting, March 11, 2004, Bal Harbour, Florida. "International negotiations should develop a fair and transparent process for determining the appropriate minimum wage for each country. The international minimum wage would be different for each country, based on its development level and standard of living?

32. Applebaum P., & Dreier, P. (1999, September–October). The campus anti-sweatshop movement. *American Prospect*, 46, 71–78. Excerpted in Beauchamp, T., & Bowie, N. (2001). *Ethical theory and business* (6th ed.). Upper Saddle River, NJ: Prentice Hall.

## U.S. Union Wage and Benefit Premium, 2001

|  | WAGES | INSURANCE | PENSION | TOTAL COMPENSATION |
|---|---|---|---|---|
| **All workers** | | | | |
| Union | $21.40 | $2.48 | $1.52 | $27.80 |
| Nonunion | 16.67 | 1.14 | 0.51 | 19.98 |
| Union premium | | | | |
| Dollars | 4.73 | 1.34 | 1.01 | 7.82 |
| Percent | 28.4% | 117.5% | 198.0% | 39.1% |
| **Blue Collar** | | | | |
| Union | $21.10 | $2.66 | $1.70 | $28.07 |
| Nonunion | 13.72 | 1.12 | 0.37 | 16.93 |
| Union premium | | | | |
| Dollars | 7.38 | 1.54 | 1.33 | 11.14 |
| Percent | 53.8% | 137.5% | 359.5% | 65.8% |
| Regression-adjusted | | | | |
| Union effect* | 21.0% | 51.3% | 20.3% | 27.8% |

Figures in 2001 dollars.

*Controlling for full-time employment, industry, occupation, public sector, region, and establishment size since 1994.

Source: Mishel, L., Bernstein, J., & Boushey, H. *State of working America 2002/2003*. (2003). Ithaca, NY: Cornell University Press, p. 191. Based on analysis of Bureau of Labor Statistics data and analysis from Brooks Pierce, "Compensation Inequality," Department of Labor, Bureau of Labor Statistics, 1998.a

a. Id.

same amount as is paid at home may operate as a disincentive to foreign investment. This approach also represents a sort of cultural imperialism by equating US standards with the minimum in the developing country. It also presents the possibility of irritating local competitors who are offering workers the local market rate.

*Living Wage Standard*—although a nebulous concept, there are clear moral parameters for at least subsistence-level compensation for basic human dignity.

*Classical Liberal Standard*—let the market set the wage, given an informed and voluntary decision by the workers to work for that amount.

The classic liberal view is that basically any work and wage will raise the standard of living for those otherwise deprived of the opportunity. As long as the work is "freely accepted by reasonably informed workers" then the market should set the wage rate under this standard. However, while it may be true that any job is better than no job, it is also true that in a country with no jobs and near total poverty, it is questionable whether one could ever "freely" accept anything?[33]

## The Relationship between Wages and the Workers' Right to Organize

Union workers command premium wage rates. A report by the Economics Policy Institute identified the premium for union wages at 28 percent.[34] A majority of unionized workers receive health-

33. Maitland, I. "The Great Non-Debate Over International Sweatshops." *British Academy of Management Annual Conference Proceedings*, September, pp. 240-265, 1997; excerpted in Beauchamp and Bowie, Ethical Theory and Business, 6th ed, PrenticeHall 2001.

34. An Interview with Kate Bronfenbrenner, Director of Labor Education Research at the New York State School of Industrial and

---

### The Universal Declaration of Human Rights – Worker Rights

**Article 23**

    (1) Everyone has the right to work, to free choice of employment, to just and favorable conditions of work and to protections against unemployment.

    (2) Everyone, without any discrimination, has the right to equal pay for equal work.

    (3) Everyone who works has the right to just and favorable remuneration ensuring for himself and his family an existence worthy of human dignity, and supplemented, if necessary, by other means of social protection.

    (4) Everyone has the right to form and join trade unions for protection of his interests.

**Article 24**

Everyone has the right to rest and leisure, including reasonable limitations of working hours and periodic holidays with pay.

**Article 25**

    (1) Everyone has the right to a standard of living adequate for the health and well-being of himself and his family, including food, clothing, housing and medical care and necessary social services, and the right to security in the event of unemployment, sickness, disability, widowhood, old age or other lack of livelihood in circumstances beyond his control....

---

care benefits and are paid substantially above the federal minimum wage. A 2001 comparison of union and nonunion worker compensation in 2001 is provided in the table above.

Despite the apparent economic benefits of union membership, the percentage of union workers in the American workplace has declined since the 1950s. Only 13 percent of the U.S. workforce is unionized—8.5 percent of private sector employees and 37 percent of public sector employees. The fastest-growing sectors of the market—retail and service industries—are not unionized. The sectors in greatest decline—American manufacturing—are traditional union shops. The decline of unions raises issues of social justice as well as economic issues.

## The Right to Organize as a Human Right

The right of workers to organize has been recognized as a fundamental human right.

While the political power of unions has declined in the United States, the labor movement on a world-wide scale has continued to strengthen. U.S. labor unions have suffered in recent years in comparison to those abroad.

### U.S. Labor Law

Four U.S, laws, enacted over a 25-year period, make up the National Labor Relations Act (NLRA):

*Norris LaGuardia (1932)* was enacted in response to judicial decisions that characterized unions as conspiracies in violation of the common law and antitrust laws (the predecessor of the Wagner Act).

*Wagner Act* (1935) gave employees the right to organize labor unions and to collectively bargain.

*Taft-Hartley Act* (1947) gave employees the right to refrain from union membership or activity and set forth a list of prohibited unfair labor practices *by* unions.

*Landrum-Griffin Act* (1959) proscribed certain kinds of illegal union activity, including racketeering, unfair election activities, financial fraud by union managers, and similar malfeasance.

| EMPLOYER UNFAIR LABOR PRACTICES | UNION UNFAIR LABOR PRACTICES |
|---|---|
| Interference with employees' rights to organize and collectively bargain | Restraint or coercion of employees' rights to organize and collectively bargain |
| Dominance of union | Compelling employer to discriminate on the basis on union or antiunion activity |
| Discrimination or retaliation for employees' union activities or complaints to the NLRB (whistle-blower protection) | Illegal strikes, pickets, and secondary boycotts<br>Excessive union dues |
| Failure to engage in good faith negotiation with union | Failure to engage in good faith negotiation with employer |

The NLRA and the regulations promulgated under it contain prohibitions on the activities of employers and unions that might thwart the workers' right to voluntarily engage in union membership and collective bargaining.

While the law recognizes the right to organize, many sectors of American business have been opposed to union representation. If it is in the interests of the workers to collectively bargain, they have the *right* to choose to do so; and companies must respect that right. If companies want to oppose a union, they must persuade their employees that the employees are better off without it. Many companies have made this argument to their employees. Indeed, some of the best-run and most socially responsible companies are those organized and operated in such a way as to need no union representation.

Unfortunately, some U.S. companies go beyond economic bargaining in their opposition of organized labor. A 1999 report issued by the Brussels-based International Confederation of Free Trade Unions (ICFTU), found U.S. enforcement of its labor law protections to be extremely wanting. The report criticized ineffective regulation and enforcement by the governing National Labor Relations Board (NLRB).

The NLRB consists of five members, appointed by the President for five-year terms. As such, the direction of the board reflects the political ideology of these appointees. In recent years, a Republican-dominated board has tilted in favor of employers. Democrat-dominated boards have tended to tilt in favor of employees.

Regardless, the NLRB's enforcement authority is weak and it has had little deterrent effect. For example, in the decade since 1995, the NLRB has dealt with 250 cases of alleged union-busting involving Wal-Mart. Despite evidence of wrongdoing, the company has suffered little punishment and remains union-free.

Several large multinational corporations have suits and investigations pending against them in connection with antiunion activities in the United States and abroad. In addition to Wal-Mart, McDonald's and others in the food service industry have faced suits for unlawfully thwarting union-organizing efforts. The Coca-Cola Company stands as a defendant in a wrongful death suit in the murder-for-hire of union organizers at its plant in Columbia, South America. Most of these companies do not deny being opposed to unions, but they say they do not use illegal tactics to prevent labor from organizing. The recent case of union busting in the United States by Smithfield Foods, the world's largest pork processor and hog producer, illustrates some of the illegal tactics companies have used.

## Beyond Compliance

Corporate management's obligation to the workforce is to treat employees as human beings—as an end in themselves and not merely as a means to another end. Employers must respect the rights of workers to life, freedom, and basic equality. Companies that grasp those ethical principles generally treat their workforce

## The Pinkertons of Pork

In 1997, workers in the world's largest hog processing plant in Tar Heel, North Carolina, sought to join the United Food and Commercial Workers International Union (UFCW). Smithfield Foods, owner of the plant, waged a campaign to thwart union organizing efforts. In December 2000, an NLRB judge issued a 400-page ruling, which found the company guilty of massive and flagrant violations of labor laws, as well as guilty of engaging in a conspiracy with local law enforcement to physically intimidate and assault union supporters. The ruling cited widespread perjury by Smithfield executives and managers and misconduct by its attorneys.

Several months later a separate NLRB tribunal overturned the union election results for the Smithfield plant in Wilson, North Carolina, citing an "illegal campaign carried out by high-level Smithfield officials to intimidate, coerce and harass workers from standing up for their legal right to have a union." The illegal activities undertaken by Smithfield included illegal threats of plant closure; illegal surveillance of workers' activities; illegal threats to workers of loss of jobs and retaliation for union support; illegal promises of reward in exchange for voting against the union; and illegal firing, disciplining, and denial of workers' compensation benefits in retaliation against union-supporting workers.

In March 2002, Smithfield Foods was found liable under a successor law to the Ku Klux Klan Act of 1871 for violating the civil rights of its workers. The federal district court jury found the company and its former security chief, Danny Priest, liable for the beating, false arrest, and imprisonment of two Smithfield employees involved in the 1997 UFCW organizing campaign. The jury awarded $755,000 in compensatory and punitive damages to the two Tar Heel employees.[a] Deputy sheriffs armed with shotguns were stationed around the plant property during the two days of balloting for the union. When the vote count on whether to institute union representation was in, company personnel stormed the counting area, creating a confrontation and engaging in the ensuing violent beating and arrest of the two union supporters. Smithfield was also found to have created a racially hostile environment in the plant to thwart organizing efforts.[b]

a. Zook, K. B. (Winter 2003). Hog-tied: battling it out at Smithfield Foods. *Amnesty Now.*
b. One Smithfield supervisor explained: "Smithfield keeps Black and Latino employees virtually separated in the plant with the Black workers on the kill floor and the Latinos in the cut and conversion departments. The word was that black workers were going to be replaced with Latino workers because blacks were more favorable toward unions. Sherri Buffkin, a Smithfield supervisor, blew the whistle on the company and testified before the NLRB and the U.S. Congress about the company's efforts to thwart the union. She testified that, as a supervisor, she was regularly ordered to fire union sympathizers Hill" Washington.

as a stakeholder group having a say in decisions that affect them. An organization that gives voice to this stakeholder group views the prosperity of the workforce as one of its many corporate goals and counts the loyalty of a trained workforce among its most valuable assets.

The moral obligation to warn the workforce of known or suspected risks and to reasonably protect against known hazards and preventable injuries requires management beyond mere compliance with OSHA regulations. As well, mere compliance with the minimum wage laws may not be a socially responsible position. Minimum wage in the United States does not provide a living wage for full-time workers. The additional costs of "living" are then borne by the larger society or simply not met by the unfortunate wage-earner. A company that is not willing to regulate itself in a responsible way, without exploiting the lack of law, will be left to cope with external regulation and inevitable litigation.

# Chapter 8

## Obligations to the Consumers of Corporate Goods and Services

*"The Reasonable Man invariably looks where he is going and is careful to examine the immediate foreground before he executes a leap or bound; who neither stargazes nor is lost in meditation when approaching trap doors or the margin of a dock; who never mounts a moving omnibus, and does not alight from any car while the train is in motion."*
— From "The Reasonable Man"
by Lord A.P. Herbert[1]

### The Relationship between the Corporation and the Stakeholders

The mutual dependence of the corporation and its customers is obvious—the corporation depends on this stakeholder group most directly for its bottom-line results in the form of sales revenues, and consumers rely on the corporation for goods and services essential to the conveniences and comforts of modern life. As discussed in preceding chapters, the negative injunction against causing avoidable harm is a universal moral norm that is equally applicable to individuals, institutions, organizations, and states. Determining the limits of responsibility for prevention and avoidance of harm depends on the circumstances of the situation. It also depends on the

nature of the relationship between the person undertaking the activities that pose the risk of harm and the person adversely affected by them. Where that relationship is one of seller and buyer and the circumstances of the transaction is the sale and purchase of goods or services, the questions become these: What is the extent of the seller's obligation to prevent avoidable harm to the buyer? What is the level of acceptable risk to the buyer in exchange for the goods or services? The law of products liability provides the legal floor for compliance with the negative injunction; however, the moral floor for business behavior in this area may, at times, extend beyond compliance.

### Legal Obligations Owed By the Corporation to Its Customers

The legal obligations to customers exist under contract law and tort law, with the most significant developments and impacts on the firm lying in the area of tort law. The law upholds important ethical principles of sharing information and warning consumers. It requires that corporations, at a minimum, not expose consumers to harms to which they have not offered their consent. If firms are aware of dangers and

---

1. Cooter, R., & Ulen, T. (1988). *Law and economics.* Glenview, IL: Scott, Foresman and Company.

they do not fully inform consumers, the firms can be subject to huge damage awards that threaten their financial viability.

### Obligations under Contract Law

The sale and consumption of goods has historically been viewed as a matter of legal contract—a voluntary agreement between parties with the capacity to contract. In a free market economy, decisions to sell or buy are matters of choice and free will, for the most part. Where the essential elements for a valid contract are met, regardless of the inherent fairness or foolhardiness of the bargain, a legally enforceable agreement is made. While the formalities of these essential elements have been liberalized over time, the intent behind them—to ensure a valid meeting of the minds between the parties as to the transaction—remains constant. The elements are (1) mutual assent—there is a shared understanding of the basis of the bargain being made and voluntary offer and acceptance of that bargain; (2) consideration—an exchange of value exists in the bargain, something beyond a mere gift, whether it be exchange of goods for cash, exchange of a promise to do something for compensation, or a promise to forebear from doing something one is legally permitted to do in exchange for value; (3) capacity to contract—the parties must be rational (that is, of legal age or status, mentally competent, and not intoxicated); and (4) legal objective—to be enforceable, the goal or accomplishing of the bargain must be legal (agreements to illegally collude or conspire, agreements for murder-for-hire, and the like are not legally valid).

With few exceptions, where those four elements exist, so does a valid contract, even when memorialized only with a handshake. Very few contracts are required to be in writing.[2] And only when the terms of the agreement are so patently lopsided and the bargaining power of the parties so dramatically unequal as to be deemed unconscionable will a contract be declared unenforceable.

The free-will aspect of contracting gave rise to the principle of *caveat emptor* for the ethics of the marketplace—let the buyer beware. Provided each of the rational parties enter into the agreement knowingly (informed about what they're giving and getting in return) and voluntarily (without duress, deceit, or manipulation), no moral questions are raised about the transaction.[3] The principle of caveat emptor puts the burden of risk on the buyer, assuming a moral floor of truth in dealings. In the case of a sale of goods, it is assumed that they are merchantable—of marketable quality and fit for the purpose intended—and will not cause unexpected harm. But nothing else is assumed of them unless the seller expressly warrants a quality or characteristic of the goods.

Under contract law principles, if the goods fail to be merchantable or fail to live up to an express warranty for performance (or even if they cause harm or loss or property damage), the buyer's recourse is to sue for breach of warranty. Note that only the buyer may sue. Contract principles include the requirement of *privity* between the parties—that they have a direct contractual relationship with each other. Accordingly, only the direct parties to the transaction may sue or be sued for harm or damage arising from it.[4] And if the party harmed by the goods, physically or economically, was not a party to the transaction, he or she has little recourse for redress and compensation under contract law.

The principle is illustrated in the famous case of *Winterbottom v. Wright*, decided in England in 1842.[5] The court held that a person thrown from

---

2. The various Statutes of Frauds determine the few types of agreements that must be in writing to be valid—usually included are contracts relating to the disposition of real estate, certain contracts that cannot be performed within one year, agreements to assume the debts of another, agreements for the sale of goods above a set value ($500 or $1,000, for example), and sometimes promises to marry.

3. Contract law is an inherently amoral discipline. Contract damages seek only to put the harmed party in as good a position as if the contract had been properly performed or in as good a position as before he or she entered into the ill-fated agreement. Contract damages do not, however, provide any compensation based on culpability of behavior or punitive damages. That remedy is left to tort law.

4. The principle of privity survives in modern law. Article 2 of the Uniform Commercial Code for Sales of Goods provides that one element a plaintiff must establish in order to bring a breach of warranty suit is that of privity with the defendant—that is, the plaintiff is within the group of foreseeable plaintiffs potentially harmed by the goods.

5. 10 Meesan & Welsby 109 (1842).

an imperfectly constructed wagon had no right to recovery against the wagon manufacturer because the wagon had been purchased from the retailer and not the manufacturer. Privity, and with it the ability to sue, existed in that case between the consumer and the retailer, not between the consumer and the manufacturer.

### Tort Law Obligations for Defective or Unreasonably Dangerous Products

With the vast expansion of commercial activity at the turn of the last century, particularly in the industrial and manufacturing sectors, principles of contract law were no longer adequate to regulate the proliferation of products on the market. The chain of mercantile distribution had widened and grown exponentially. In addition, the principle of privity was too constraining to provide effective legal remedy for dangerous or defective goods. Contract law and breach of warranty claims continued and continue to this day to have a meaningful place in the resolution of purely economic disputes between direct buyers and sellers. However, given the expanse of the market and its distribution systems, as well as the increasing risk posed by increasingly innovative products, contract law was forced to give way to tort law as a remedy for personal harm or loss on account of a defective or dangerous product.

The decision in *MacPherson v. Buick Motor Co.*[6] in 1916 marked the initial turning point from contract principles and requirements of privity toward tort principles for harm caused by an offending product. In *MacPherson*, Buick manufactured and sold an automobile with a defective wheel. Buick could have discovered the defect upon reasonable inspection when it received the wheels from its supplier, but the company failed to undertake one. Buick sold the automobile to a retailer who then sold it to MacPherson. The wheel collapsed while MacPherson was driving the car, causing serious injury to MacPherson. He sued Buick for negligence in failing to inspect and then selling the car with the defective wheel. Buick defended on the grounds that it

had no direct dealings with MacPherson and, thus, owed no duty to him. Justice Cardozo held for MacPherson stating:

> If the nature of a thing is such that it is reasonably certain to place life and limb in peril when negligently made, it is a thing of danger. If to the element of danger there is added knowledge that the thing will be used by persons other than the [direct] purchaser, then, irrespective of contract, the manufacturer is under a duty to make it carefully . . . The nature of an automobile gives warning of probable danger if its construction is defective. This automobile was designed to go 50 miles an hour. Unless its wheels were strong and sound, injury was almost certain. The defendant knew the danger. It knew the car would be used by persons other than the buyer, a dealer in cars. The dealer was indeed the one person of whom it might be said with some certainty by him that the car would not be used. Yet the defendant would have us say that he was the one person it was under a legal duty to protect.[7]

As well as whom to sue, who *can* sue changed with the turn toward tort law for products liability. Remote repurchasers and innocent bystanders harmed by defective or unreasonably products now had an avenue of legal redress as well.

### The Tort of Negligence and Unreasonably Dangerous or Defective Products

The basic principles of the law of negligence do not vary much in context. As discussed in the previous chapter, the essential elements for a claim of negligence require:

1. Establishment of the duty owed, the standard of care, which is based on the relationship of the parties and the circumstances in which they find themselves. What would a reasonable person in the plaintiff's position expect

---

6. 111 N.E. 1050 (N.Y. Ct. App. 1916).

7. Automobile manufacturers just can't seem to get the wheel thing right, even almost 100 years later. See the case study "Auto Safety at Ford" in Part Three for a modern version of *MacPherson v. Buick.*

in the form of information or protection or warning? What would a reasonable person in the defendant's position expect to be his or her obligation to inform, protect, or warn?
2. A breach of that duty by failure to meet the standard of care.
3. Actual harm in the form of injury or property loss.
4. The harm being the proximate cause of the breach—that there is a direct causal connection between them.

*Duty of Care.* The obligation here depends on the foreseeability of harm. Given that the manufacturer of the goods is putting them out into the chain of commerce for sale, what is the obligation for offering a product free of defects or unreasonable dangers? What are the expectations of a reasonable consumer for product safety? What are the obligations of a reasonable manufacturer to ensure that its product does not cause harm? In general, the obligation is viewed as one of selling goods that are neither in a defective nor unreasonably dangerous condition. A defective or unreasonably dangerous condition may exist on account of one of the following:
• A manufacturing defect that causes harm
• A design defect that causes harm
• A failure to warn of known or knowable risks of harm associated with use or consumption of the product

In the case of a manufacturing defect, the risk of harm is usually limited in some fashion by the limited number of lots made before the defect was discovered and corrected. In the case of a design defect, the potential pool of plaintiffs is much greater. Also, design defects may take longer to discover as a pattern before they are corrected. The case of the Ford Pinto, discussed in Chapter Two, is an extreme example of a design defect left uncorrected. The duty to warn of risks is the main reason why you cannot open a bottle of aspirin or a package of birth-control pills without unrolling a lengthy scroll of warnings and contraindications that put *War and Peace* to shame. It is the reason your hair dryer has a tag showing a picture of a bathtub with a large red *X* across it. It is also the reason for some of the more ludicrously self-evident warnings on everyday items.

---

**Caution:**

Cape does not enable user to fly.
*Instructions on a Batman costume*

This product can burn eyes.
*Warning on a curling iron*

Remove child before folding.
*Instruction tag on a baby stroller*

---

*Breach of the Duty of Care.* For breach of duty in a products liability case, the question is, Did the defendant know (or with reasonable care, *should* have known) of the defective or unreasonably dangerous condition? If the defendant exercised all reasonable due care, it will not be held responsible under negligence for harm caused. If the defendant failed to exercise such care—if it knew of the problem or should have known of the problem if the job was done correctly, then a breach of duty has occurred. For negligence, this element of culpability also determines damages. If the defendant's failure to produce a safe product or to warn of potential risks is merely careless or inadvertent but within the scope of its duty, it will be held responsible in negligence for compensatory damages—an economic award intended to make the plaintiff whole. If, instead, the defendant actually knew of the risk of harm but did nothing about it, ignored it, or failed to warn about it, then the defendant's culpability level rises measurably and punitive damages may be imposed, as discussed in more detail below.

*Proximate Cause.* One of the most difficult elements to prove in any negligence case is proximate cause, and this is no different for products liability claims. Proof that the defect or dangerous condition is the actual cause of the harm complained of can be challenging for a plaintiff. In one of the class action suits against the makers of silicone breast implants, a panel of independent experts in the scientific and medical field was unable to establish a direct nexus between the admittedly defective leaking silicone implants and the types of disease and injury claimed by the plaintiff patients. There was simply no scientific proof that silicone that leaked into the human body would necessarily produce the detrimental results complained of by the patients.

The issue of establishing proximate cause often devolves into a "battle of the experts"—with each side presenting expert testimony contradicting the other. The jury, having no expertise in the field and being ill-equipped for the task, is left to decide the scientific truth based on which side's experts are more convincing on the witness stand. For a price, an expert can usually be found who will take a particular side. Moreover, the rules on who qualifies as an expert are extremely liberal and vary from jurisdiction to jurisdiction. This issue is often debated in the context of tort reform.

In some circumstances, the plaintiff may be assisted in establishing a breach of the duty of care and proximate cause by a tort doctrine known as *res ipsa loquitur,* or "the thing speaks for itself."

The doctrine of *res ipsa loquitur* creates a rebuttable presumption or inference of negligence in favor of the plaintiff where:

1. The event that caused harm ordinarily would not occur in the absence of negligence.
2. The instrumentality that caused the harm was in the control or dominion of the defendant until the harm was caused and the plaintiff and other third-party causes of the harm have been ruled out.
3. The negligence that occurred is within scope of the defendant's duty to the plaintiff.

In the case of *Escola v. Coca-Cola,* a waitress in a restaurant was severely injured when a bottle of Coca-Cola exploded as she removed it from the case. It was established that the particular case of bottles had not been touched and sat undisturbed for the 36 hours since being delivered. The court held that in such a case, the jury could reasonably infer the defendant's negligence in filling the bottle.[8]

The doctrine of *res ipsa loquitur* creates a *rebuttable* presumption or inference; therefore, the doctrine may be overcome with a showing by the defendant of its use of due care.

*Harm.* Actionable harm in a products liability case is as for any other tort—personal injury, property damage, or other measurable economic loss. Unlike contract damages for harm, however, tort damages may include awards for pain and suffering and other consequential damages not recognized under contract law. In cases of gross negligence or reckless disregard on the part of the defendant, punitive damages, which are not available under contract law or strict liability in tort, may also be awarded in a negligence case.

### Defenses to Negligence for Unreasonably Dangerous or Defective Products

In the event the plaintiff is able to establish the prima facie case of negligent manufacture or design of a defective or unreasonably dangerous product or a knowing failure to warn of risks, the burden of proof then shifts to the defendant to establish a defense of its actions. The first line of defense is, of course, to challenge the plaintiff's prima facie case—to put into dispute one of the elements: that the standard of care owed did not include the risk presented; that with the exercise of reasonable care, the defendant could not have known of the defective or dangerous condition of the goods; that the defect was not the proximate cause of the harm to the plaintiff; or that no actual, measurable economic harm was suffered. Failing that, the defendant is left with two main defenses, both of which focus on the behavior of the plaintiff, not the defendant. The two defenses are (1) contributory negligence/comparative fault and (2) assumption of risk, also sometimes referred to as "informed consent."[9]

Contributory negligence is based on the premise that the plaintiff, too, has an obligation to act as a reasonable person under the circumstances. For products liability, misuse of the product is often the contributory negligence claimed. To be a valid defense, the misuse must not be reasonably foreseeable by the defendant; otherwise, the defendant would have an obligation to warn about it (reason again for those annoying, self-evident warnings on packaging).

The second defense available is assumption of

---

8. 150 P.2d 436 (1944). Judge Traynor's opinion in the *Escola* case is viewed by many as the precursor to the application of strict liability principles in tort to products liability cases. The opinion is discussed in detail in the next section.

9. These defenses are also discussed in Chapter Seven.

risk—that the plaintiff was aware of the risk of harm associated with use or consumption of the product and still decided to proceed. For assumption of risk to be a valid defense, the defendant must establish that the plaintiff's consent was both (1) knowing and (2) voluntary. Knowing implies adequate information to make a reasoned decision about use or consumption. It implies that all material facts are made known to the plaintiff and that armed with that knowledge, the plaintiff voluntarily proceeded. The question raised then is, How much information is enough? How much testing, how much research, how many warnings are adequate to meet the standard of care? How much did the plaintiff actually understand the information? Was the information calculated to reach the plaintiff in an effective way?

Informed consent or voluntary assumption of risk was a defense tactic used by the makers of silicone breast implants in the class action suits brought against them. The manufacturers claimed that certain warnings about the implants were provided to the doctors operating with them. The defense was unsuccessful for the implant makers on a couple of counts: first, because the warnings were not communicated in such a way as to reach the actual consumers of the product (the plaintiffs in the suit), but instead to their doctors; second, because the warnings did not address the specific types of problems that actually occurred with the devices; and third, because the companies failed to monitor and address ongoing problems with the devices (reported by doctors as well as by their own sales representatives) and failed to transmit that information to the proper regulatory authorities and to the women patients.

Assumption of risk has been a key defense for the tobacco industry in tort suits for the harm caused by cigarettes. At least since they began putting warning labels on the packaging (by regulatory order in the 1960s—long after the companies were aware of the dangers of smoking), tobacco manufacturers have been able to claim that smokers harmed by their unreasonably dan-

gerous product have knowingly and voluntarily done so.[10]

Additional defenses may be available depending on the circumstances. The statute of limitations may have tolled, particularly if the harm caused by the defect is latent and not discovered for many years or generations. A "government contract defense" is available to manufacturers who produce to meet government specifications. If there is a defect in the design specs, it will be considered the fault of the government and not the manufacturer. State-of-the-art may be another defense with a new or innovative product. Where technology has advanced only so far, society will accept a certain level of risk for the product. Finally, manufacturers of defective or unreasonably dangerous products may find a defense in asserting preemption by governmental regulation. Here the argument is that compliance with the existing safety regulations in force, regardless of knowledge of dangerousness beyond those precautions, will protect a company in bare compliance with them. For years, this was another valued defense tool for the tobacco companies. Hiding behind the weak and incomplete warning required on packaging by the Surgeon General in the 1960s was a defense to their failure to adequately inform the public of the known risks associated with smoking. The U.S. Supreme Court put the issue to rest in the case of *Cippolone v. Liggett Group*.

### Strict Liability in Tort and Defective or Unreasonably Dangerous Products

In addition to an action for negligence, tort law also recognizes an action in strict liability for harm caused by defective or unreasonably dangerous products. Strict liability in tort law holds the actor/defendant responsible for whatever harm may be caused by his or her activity. Use of due care is not a defense. Indeed, no fault or culpability need be proven to make the case in strict liability; and there are few defenses. The severity of strict liability obliges that it be used sparingly in law, and it is. U.S. law recognizes very few situations in which strict liability in

---

10. There is, of course, some controversy over the "voluntariness" of smoking, given the addictive qualities of nicotine; but that is a different issue.

## The Legacy of Rose Cippolone

*C*ippolone v. Liggett Group, 505 U.S. 504 (1992) proved to be a landmark for products liability cases against tobacco companies. A federal jury in Newark, New Jersey, awarded $400,000 in damages to Anthony Cippolone, whose wife died of lung cancer in 1964. The jury found the Liggett Group had wrongly implied that cigarettes were safe in the advertising it engaged in prior to 1966. The jury found that Liggett knew of and should have warned customers about the dangers of cigarette smoking prior to that year, when Congress first legally required that warning labels be put on cigarette packages.

Lawyers for the plaintiff spent about $3 million and five years gathering evidence to bring the *Cippolone* case. Their aim was to bring to light thousands of pages of internal documents showing that the cigarette manufacturers knew of the dangers of cigarette smoking prior to the congressional action and that they sold cigarettes to the public without a warning even though they had this knowledge. Once these documents were revealed, the lawyers for the plaintiffs hoped that it would be easier for other attorneys for the plaintiffs to win awards in future cases. And that has been the case. The *Cippolone* case began the archive of what is now the famous "Tobacco Papers," which form the basis for numerous individual suits against tobacco companies as well as the landmark multistate action by the states' attorneys general.

Cippolone's lawyers showed that the cigarette manufacturers' advertising made many implied promises about the safety of their products. For instance, in the 1940s, R.J. Reynolds claimed that "More Doctors Smoke Camels"; and in the 1950s, Lorillard Tobacco Company said that the micronite filter in Kent Cigarettes was "so safe, so effective it has been selected to help filter the air in hospital operating rooms." Those claims suggested that the cigarette manufacturers had established an explicit warranty with their customers about the safety of the product.

Liggett appealed the decision all the way to the U.S. Supreme Court with the argument that its compliance with governmental regulation in the area—the legally required warnings—preempted any further obligations to warn of harm. The Court held that some, but certainly not all, common law claims may be preempted by governmental regulation. Common law claims for fraudulent misrepresentation and breach of express warranties are not among those claims that can be preempted.

Cases such as the *Cippolone* case, and the plaintiffs and lawyers willing to bring them, can perform... the public." a valuable service in bringing the truth to light and protecting the public.

---

tort may be imposed, limited mainly to (1) harm that is caused by inherently dangerous or ultra-hazardous activities that, by their nature, cannot be made unfailingly safe[11] and (2) harm that is caused by the manufacture and sale of a defective or unreasonably dangerous product.

The earliest notions of strict liability in tort for dangerous or defective products began to emerge around the middle of the twentieth century. The 1944 opinion of Judge Traynor in *Escola v. Coca-Cola*, which permitted the use of *res ipsa loquitur* to find liability for an exploding bottle of soda, is viewed as among the earliest to recognize the concept that:

> ...a manufacturer incurs an absolute liability when an article that he has placed on the market, knowing that it is

---

11. Conducting blasting activities, test-firing rockets, generating and disposing of hazardous or toxic waste, and privately keeping wild animals are a few examples of activities subject to strict liability for any harm caused by them.

to be used without inspection, proves to have a defect that causes injury to human beings... Even if there is no negligence... public policy demands that responsibility be fixed wherever it will most effectively reduce the hazards...

It is evident that the manufacturer can anticipate some hazards and guard against the recurrence of others, as the public cannot. Those who suffer injury from defective products are unprepared to meet its consequences. The cost of an injury and the loss of time or health may be an overwhelming misfortune to the person injured and a needless one, for the risk of injury can be insured by the manufacturer and distributed among the public as a cost of doing business...

Consumers no longer approach products warily but accept them on faith, relying on the reputation of the manufacturer or the trademark... Manufacturers have sought to justify that faith by increasingly high standards of inspection and a readiness to make good on defective products by way of replacements and refunds... The manufacturer's obligation to the consumer must keep pace with the changing relationship between them...

Judge Traynor's opinion raised several of the justifications traditionally given for strict products liability. Efficiency, expediency, and fairness based on the expectations and resources of each side favor the imposition of strict liability for the manufacture and sale of defective or dangerous goods that cause harm. The actor undertaking the commercial activity (for profit) is in a better position not only to detect and correct product flaws, but also to insure against the risk of harm—and pass along the costs of such insurance to the consumer. The process is more efficient because the harmed consumer may sue the manufacturer directly or any and all in the commercial chain of the product and need only prove damage and causation, not fault. Legal proceedings should be less time-consuming and expensive; and while there may be more trials, the ease of their execution should reduce the total costs to society. Those considerations form the ethical and public policy foundations of strict products liability.

To carry the burden of proof, the plaintiff must establish all of the following elements of a prima facie case to sue in strict liability:

> The defendant was engaged in the business of selling or otherwise conducting commerce in the product—as manufacturer, distributor, or retailer—though some jurisdictions limit strict liability to the manufacturer only.
>
> The product was in a defective or unreasonably dangerous condition when it left the defendant's hands—the definition of defect here being the same as that for the negligence case: manufacturing defect, design defect, or failure to warn.
>
> The defect was the proximate cause of the harm suffered by the plaintiff. Actual economically measurable harm must be suffered.

In strict liability, there is no need to show the defendant's lack of care or breach of duty; if a defective or dangerous condition existed and the product proximately caused the harm complained of, the defendant will be liable for compensatory damages. The potential pool of defendants is considerably broader than that in a negligence action, as well. In most states, anyone in the chain of production, distribution, and sale of the product may be held jointly and severally liable for damages. In the case of a defectively manufactured product, all potential defendants in the chain of distribution would meet the plaintiff's prima facie case: engaged in the business of the product and defective when it left their hands (all through the chain, regardless of any particular defendant's role in the defect). As a practical matter, the intent is to make it as painless as possible for the injured party to seek recompense. As a business matter, it is left up to the group of defendants, all regular players in commerce, to fight it out among themselves as to who has ultimate liability after the plaintiff has been made whole. Most of them accomplish this through the terms of their contracts to do business together; others, with litigation. Most business contracts involving the manufacture or sale of goods have clauses providing for indemnification and reimbursement of a defendant lower down the distribution chain in the event of a manufacturing defect for which he or she is held liable to the consumer.

No punitive damages are awarded in a strict liability case because there is no "fault" at issue; no culpability is required. As such, strict liability provides for compensatory damages only.

In modern products liability lawsuits, there is no need for an election of remedies or an election of causes of action. If it can prove the relevant prima facie case, a plaintiff is free to sue under breach of warranty, negligence, *and* strict liability theories for harm caused by a defective or unreasonably dangerous product. Many do, though only one recovery is permitted per plaintiff for the same harm. The main differences between these causes of action involve the plaintiff's burden of proof and the measurement and imposition of damages.

### Strict Liability versus Absolute Liability

The legal doctrine of strict products liability is a matter of state law and varies by jurisdiction; however, its common law and statutory law foundations come from the 1965 Restatement (Second) of Torts put out by the American Law Institute (ALI).[12] Section 402A of the Restatement recognized a right of recovery against product manufacturers for harm caused by defective or unreasonably dangerous products, even where the manufacturer exercised "all possible care in the preparation and sale." This doctrine of strict products liability quickly gained wide acceptance throughout the country and has evolved into a legal principle embraced in some form in almost every U.S. jurisdiction.

Throughout its existence, the products liability provisions of the Second Restatement of Torts have been subject to debate and revision. Positions have alternated between the poles of pushing the legal doctrine in the direction of absolute liability—where the case is proven on a mere showing of use and harm and where no defense is available to the producer—versus expanding exculpatory defenses to liability. Unlike absolute liability, strict liability recognizes both contributory negligence (usually in the form of the plaintiff's unforeseeable misuse) and assumption of risk (usually in the form of a warning of the risk) as valid defenses for manufacturers. As well, strict liability, unlike absolute liability, recognizes that the determination of whether the product is, in fact, in a defective or unreasonably condition is subject to much the same analysis as that determination being made under principles of negligence—for example, whether the warning on the packaging is inadequate for risks presented. Manufacturers do not become insurers of *all* harmful outcomes under strict liability, and the state-of-the-art defense can still play an important role.[13]

In 1997, the ALI formally adopted the Restatement (Third) of Torts, which replaced the Second Restatement and Section 402A with a new Restatement of Products Liability consisting of 21 separate rules. The old Section 402A was viewed as consumer-friendly and representative of a trend toward ever-stricter liability for manufacturers.

The new Restatement (Third) on Torts is as follows: Products liability reflects something of a retreat from that position by narrowing the responsibility for design defects to those cases where "the foreseeable risks of harm posed by the product could have been reduced or avoided by the adoption of a reasonable alternative design by the seller or other distributor, or a predecessor

---

12. The ALI was created early in the twentieth century in an attempt to bring order and consistency to the common law of the nation. It consists of an elite group of law professors, practitioners, and judges working as a committee to survey, clarify, and simplify the general common law and to "restate" it—summarizing the principles in terms of the "majority" view, applied by most jurisdictions; the "minority" view, applied by some jurisdictions; and the "preferred" view, considered as the opinion of the ALI scholars. The ALI has since compiled Restatements on almost all areas of the common law and has gained significant stature as a source of law; often cited in Supreme Court opinions, in other court opinions, and in the legislative history of much statutory law.

13. In *Beshada v. Johns-Manville Products Corp*, 90 N.J. 191; 447 A. 2d 539 (N.J. Sup. Ct 1982), the defendant claimed that the dangers of asbestos were not known to science at the time. The court said that even if that claim were true (and it was of questionable veracity), the manufacturer would still be responsible for the harm caused by the product, implying that the manufacturer has an affirmative responsibility to discover unknown dangers and that a state-of-the-art defense may not protect it in that regard. The manufacturer may have the obligation to conduct testing on its products and processes and to warn workers and consumers if a problem exists, even if independent scientists have not yet discovered the problem.

in the commercial chain of distribution." This standard appears to recognize that no designs are entirely risk-free and that a certain amount of acceptable risk is built into production of goods. It is an approach favoring utility. Further, only where reasonable alternative designs are practical and available and ignored by the manufacturer will strict products liability be incurred. The new version likewise imposes a reasonableness test reflecting risk-utility analysis for defective conditions arising from a producer's failure to warn. The changes to the ALI position reflect a trend away from the imposition of absolute liability for unreasonably dangerous or defective products.

### Tort Damages and Tort Damages Reform

Available damages under tort law include compensatory damages, which are designed to put the plaintiff in as good a position as before the harm, and punitive damages, which are designed to punish the defendant's intentional or reckless failure to meet the standard of care. Compensatory damages are restitutional in nature and focus on the plaintiff's loss (although attorney's fees are not included). Punitive damages, instead, focus on the defendant's behavior and culpability for the harm caused. What did the defendant know, and when did he or she know it? The further the deviation from the standard of care, the more likely punitive damages will be awarded. For that reason, there are no punitive damages in strict liability, where the standard of care is all-encompassing and no proof of the defendant's knowledge of the defect is required for liability. In such a case, punitive damages would not have the desired deterrent effect.

Punitive damages exist because they are deemed the most effective way to punish businesses' bad behavior. There is no corporate death penalty (at least none that's ever been used by a state attorney general in response to corporate misbehavior). So the only way to punish and deter future bad behavior is to hit miscreant corporations where it hurts most: in the pocketbook.

Punitive damage awards are somewhat controversial. The criticisms of punitive damages are several. Punitive damages are known to be somewhat arbitrarily and capriciously awarded depending on the sentiments of a given jury. They are claimed to have a chilling effect on product innovation and development, particularly in the context of new pharmaceutical drug therapies and other innovations with high risk factors. It is argued that they create an unfair windfall to the plaintiff and its attorneys, who receive the entire amount of punitive damages awarded despite the fact that the award is made on the basis of the defendant's reprehensible behavior and may bear little relation to the extent of the plaintiff's harm. Further, as a practical matter, consumers end up paying for punitive damages in the form of increased costs that must be passed along somewhere in the commerce of the offending company.

Advocates in favor of punitive damages point out that they are the only meaningful way to punish reprehensible corporate behavior; regulatory fines are comparatively mere slaps on the corporate wrist. Moreover, between the ability to deduct parts of such payments for tax purposes and to pass along the costs in the price of goods, the punishment is not all that draconian after all.

Punitive damages also serve another very important societal function: They open the doors of the courthouse to those who might not otherwise have access to the law. Since U.S. law does not generally provide for a successful plaintiff's attorneys fees to be paid by the defendant and since few victims of defective products can afford to pay $400 or $500 an hour for an attorney to bring their case, punitive damages provide a motivation for attorneys to take cases on a contingency fee. In a contingency fee arrangement, the attorney agrees to represent the plaintiff and to cover all expenses associated with bringing that plaintiff's case in exchange for a percentage of the plaintiff's ultimate award—generally in the range of one-third to one-half of the plaintiff's damages.[14] If only compensatory damages are

---

14. The expenses of bringing suit against a large manufacturer can run into the millions and would be out of reach for most fee-per-hour, individual, noncorporate clients, who have neither access to corporate funds to pay the fees nor a corporate income tax deduction for the expenses incurred. An excellent narrative of such a case from the perspective of the plaintiff's law firm is *A Civil Action*, by journalist Jonathan Harr, which recounts the case against Beatrice and WR Grace by a community in Massachusetts stricken with an epidemic of childhood leukemia, allegedly caused by the companies' contamination of the community's water supply. A film version of the book, starring John Travolta, is also instructive on the issue, though it has the feel of "*Saturday Night Fever* Goes to Court."

## Products Liability Litigators—One Example
## The Law Firm of Robins, Kaplan, Miller, & Ciresi

A 200-member law firm in the Twin Cities—Robins, Kaplan, Miller, & Ciresi—achieved distinction when Solly Robins, one of its attorneys, won a case that established the principle of strict liability in Minnesota. The case, *Andrea McCormack v. Hankscraft,* involved a girl who had been scalded from hot water spilling out of a vaporizer. The court decided that it was unnecessary to prove negligence in the manufacture of the product. Product defect was enough to establish liability.

Michael Ciresi, another attorney for the firm, successfully challenged A.H. Robins Company, the manufacturer of the Dalkon Shield. His case was the first to win a major award against A.H. Robins. Eventually, Ciresi won over $37 million in settlements in 1988 Dalkon Shield cases; and A.H. Robins paid over $375 million before it filed for bankruptcy. Recently, Ciresi won an $8.75 million award from G.D. Searle & Company in the Esther Kociemba Copper-7 intrauterine device case.

A.H. Robins was a successful multinational enterprise that had more than $700 million in sales and 6,100 employees in 1985. Its strong product lines—ChapStick, Robitussin, and Sergeant's flea and tick collars—were well known to consumers. The intrauterine device (IUD), to which A. H. Robins had purchased the right, was called the Dalkon Shield. Invented by Dr. Hugh Davis, a professor at Johns Hopkins University, Davis did the first clinical trials of the Dalkon Shield, which he published in the *American Journal of Obstetrics and Gynecology.* He followed 640 users of the shield for five-and-a-half months, not long enough to discover if the low pregnancy rates he was observing, 1.1 percent, were accurate or to see if these women developed pelvic infections. A.H. Robins did not have to do any premarket testing because it was not required to do so at the time by the FDA. Ultimately, A. H. Robins sold 2.9 million Dalkon Shields in the United States and controlled 40 percent of the market for IUDs, selling the Dalkon Shield for $4.35 when it cost $0.25 to manufacture.

With more customers came more reports that the Dalkon Shield was not effective in preventing pregnancy. Worse still, it caused serious infections of the reproductive system and abdominal area. Many of those infections resulted in miscarriages, and many women were left sterile. The infections were often caused by a string on the Shield that was used as a safety device for doctors to determine whether the Shield had been properly placed. If not properly placed, the Shield could perforate a woman's uterus and enter the abdomen. The problem was that the string, unlike those on competitors' IUDs, was made of interwoven fibers that acted like a wick that drew bacteria into a woman's body.

Roughly 4 percent of the women who used the Shield suffered some type of injury. In the trials brought against the company, it was shown that top company officials ordered documents on the Shield's wicking tendencies be destroyed and that they knew of the dangers of the Shield. Before it filed for bankruptcy, A.H. Robins estimated that payouts to Shield victims would exceed $1 billion by the year 2002.

Ciresi then moved his attention to filing suit against G.D. Searle & Company for its Copper-7 IUD, representing 10 million female users of the Copper-7. Ciresi claimed the same kind of problems existed with the Copper-7 as were discovered with the Dalkon Shield. In preparing for the case, the Robins, Kaplan, Miller, & Ciresi attorneys reviewed more than 600,000 pages of Searle documents and found evidence that Searle officials knew of potential problems but decided not to warn the women who were users. Deleted from the label in the IUD package were phrases about the potential higher risks of infection and the increased

---

**Products Liability Litigators (continued)**

risks to women who had never had children. Also deleted were recommendations that young women, women who had never been pregnant, and women who had multiple sex partners should seek another birth control device.

Opponents of Ciresi accuse him of histrionics, combativeness in the courtroom, and over-aggressiveness. They also argue that his campaign against drug companies was making them too cautious. Important innovations that could help people are not coming to the market in a timely fashion because the manufacturers are afraid of litigation. Without advocates like Ciresi, however, the doors to the courtroom would remain closed to many victims.

*Sources:* Barrett, P. M. (1987, November 3). Hearings set in Robins chapter 11 case to fix amount of Dalkon Shield fund. *Wall Street Journal*, A4.

Warchol, G. (1988, August 24?30). Hit `em and hit `em hard. *Twin City Reader*, 10?12.

Schwadel, F. (1985, August 23). Robins and plaintiffs face uncertain future. *Wall Street Journal*.

Feder, B. J. (1987, December 13). What A.H. Robins has wrought. *Wall Street Journal*, F2.

Koenig, R., & Wermeil, S. (1989, November 7). Supreme Court refuses to hear challenges in A.H. Robins case. *Wall Street Journal*, A3.

Steiner, G. A., & Steiner, J. F. (1991). *Business, government, and society: a managerial perspective*. New York: McGraw-Hill, Inc.

---

available, the plaintiff will not, in fact, be made whole by the award, given that its attorneys will have to be paid for bringing the case. Thus, the possibility of punitive damages is viewed by advocates as ensuring that the worst of consumer product offenders will, indeed, see the inside of the courtroom. Though such contingency-fee attorneys are sometimes called ambulance chasers by their detractors, they serve an important role in society, as illustrated in the story of one firm of litigators.

The unfair-windfall-to-the-plaintiff and we-all-end-up-paying-for-it-anyway criticisms of punitive damages have engendered some rethinking about the way those damages are distributed. Some proposals would retain the underlying principle of imposing economic punishment so that it hurts the corporation, but would distribute the damages in a more communal or socially beneficial way. The plaintiff and his or her attorneys should clearly get a chunk for the time, effort, and resources expended in bringing the defendant to task for the reprehensible behavior. But the remainder of the damages could, instead, be paid into some form of constructive public trust

that would benefit more than just the plaintiff.

Many states have put a cap, or upper limit, on the amount that victims can recover, though some of those caps have been struck down as unconstitutional. From a policy standpoint, many argue that a cap on damages is no different from a ceiling on any price, such as rent control or other rate regulations, and that ceilings and caps are economically inefficient. Potential tort-feasors will not take sufficient precaution, but, instead, will merely factor in the limited damages in the same fashion as a regulatory fine.

Two recent U.S. Supreme Court cases in the area of punitive damages have injected further controversy into the remedy. The Supreme Court addressed the issue of constitutionality of punitive damages in two separate cases in the past seven years. In both cases, it held that excessive punitive damages constituted an unconstitutional denial of due process.

In 1996, the high Court decided the case of *BMW v. Gore*.[15] Dr. Gore purchased a "new" BMW from a dealer. Gore subsequently discovered that he had been intentionally deceived

---

15. 517 U.S. 559 (1996).

about a previous accident involving the vehicle; the dealer had had the car repaired before selling it to Gore. Indeed, it was shown at trial that it was the *policy and practice* of the company to hide this information from new car buyers. Actual harm to Gore amounted to $4,000—the difference between what he paid for the car and its actual fair market value given the accident and repairs. That amount was awarded by the jury in compensatory damages. The jury also awarded $4 million in punitive damages to punish the pattern and practice of intentional fraud by the company and to deter its recurrence. That award was later reduced on appeal to $2 million, and the case was appealed again to the U.S. Supreme Court. The Court held that the punitive damages in the case were unconstitutionally excessive on the following grounds:

1. Traditional notions of due process—that one has a right to notice of a potential taking of their property—are violated when punitive damages so dramatically exceed the amount of actual economic harm caused.
2. The jury mistakenly awarded punitive damages based on the defendant's conduct nationally (the practice was nationwide), instead of limiting its consideration to the company's reprehensible conduct only to that which occurred in the state where the plaintiff was harmed (in this case, Alabama).
3. The defendant's behavior was not as reprehensible as it could have been. The loss was economic and could only have been economic. No reckless disregard for human health or safety was involved. The Court specifically refused to draw a bright line for the proper ratio of compensatory damages to punitive damages, but said that the punitive damages here, 500 times the amount of the compensatory damages, was clearly excessive—at least where only economic harm is involved.

In 2003, the high Court again addressed the issue of excessive punitive damages in a case of economic harm in *State Farm v. Campbell*.[16] Curtis Campbell caused an automobile accident that left one of its victims permanently disabled. State Farm was Campbell's insurance company.

State Farm contested liability; declined to settle the ensuing claims for the $50,000 policy limit; ignored its own investigators' advice; and took the case to trial, assuring Campbell and his wife that they had no liability for the accident, that State Farm would represent their interests, and that the Campbells did not need separate counsel. In fact, a Utah jury returned a judgment for over three times the policy limit, and State Farm refused to appeal. The Campbells then sued State Farm for bad faith, fraud, and intentional infliction of emotional distress. The jury awarded the Campbells $2.6 million in compensatory damages and $145 million in punitive damages, subsequently reduced on appeal to $1 million compensatory and $145 million punitive. The Supreme Court held that a punitive damages award of $145 million, where full compensatory damages are $1 million, is excessive and violates the Due Process Clause of the Fourteenth Amendment.

The *State Farm* opinion reiterated the court's distinction between mere economic harm and physical harm.

> To determine a defendant's reprehensibility—the most important indicium of a punitive damages award's reasonableness—a court must consider whether: the harm was physical rather than economic; the tortious conduct evinced an indifference to or a reckless disregard of the health or safety of others; the conduct involved repeated actions or was an isolated incident; and the harm resulted from intentional malice, trickery, or deceit, or mere accident. *Gore*, 517 U. S., at 576-577. It should be presumed that a plaintiff has been made whole by compensatory damages, so punitive damages should be awarded only if the defendant's culpability is so reprehensible to warrant the imposition of further sanctions to achieve punishment or deterrence.

---

16. 538 U.S. 408 (2003).

Although the actions of State Farm in the case were indeed viewed as reprehensible—there was evidence of company-wide practices that breached its obligation of trustworthy representation to its client insureds—its punishment too far exceeded the actual harm caused. While the Court again expressed reluctance to establish a bright-line ratio between compensatory and punitive damages, it did acknowledge that in practice, few awards exceeding a single-digit ratio between punitive and compensatory damages will satisfy due process.

Justice Scalia and others dissented from and criticized both the *BMW* and *State Farm* opinions on the basis that requiring a relationship between compensatory and punitive damages proceeds from the faulty premise that they are related, when they are, in fact, not related at all. One focuses on the plaintiff and making him or her whole, while the other focuses on the defendant and punishing his or her behavior. As well, other dissenters noted a general hesitancy to infringe on an area that was traditionally the province of juries and fact finders. Whether there are any constitutional limits on punitive damages in cases where the reprehensible behavior poses harm to life and limb remains an open question for the Court.

What will this precedent mean? Different state courts will probably interpret it differently, and the "single-digit" guideline will not be followed in all cases. The precedent could have a huge impact on tobacco cases, however. Recently, an Oregon jury awarded a smoker $168,500 in compensatory damages and $100 million in punitive damages, a 500:1 ratio. Philip Morris will argue that the punitive damages should not exceed $1.5 million. In a class action suit in Florida, Philip Morris, based on its market share, was held responsible for $74 *billion* in a punitive damage award. The jury did not determine compensatory damages. Philip Morris will argue that without a compensatory damages award, it should have no liability for punitive damages.

Opponents of the tobacco industry hope that the high court rulings in *BMW* and *State Farm* will be limited to cases of economic harm. The tobacco cases, of course, are not limited to economic harm, but involve personal injury and death—the outcome of what the Department of Justice has called "more than 50 years of fraud."[178]

As a practical matter, some plaintiffs' attorneys believe that the impact of these Supreme Court cases will be slight because the punitive damages awarded in the cases it tries actually tend to be within a single-digit ratio. On appeal, judges often reduce the high punitive damage awards of juries; and in many cases, the punitive damages awarded simply do not greatly exceed the compensatory damages.

## Ethical Obligations Owed by the Corporation to Its Customers

At a moral minimum, the negative injunction against causing avoidable harm is a universal ethical norm—all of society, in all of its activities, has a duty to undertake those activities in such a way as not to cause undue harm to another person. For the most part, tort law sets the limits of responsibility of each actor for prevention and avoidance of harm. The level of obligation is dependant on the circumstances of the situation and the nature of the relationship between the one undertaking activities that pose the risk of harm and the one adversely affected by them. Only in very limited circumstances does the law impose an obligation to proactively prevent harm to another. Instead, tort law imposes responsibility only for a person's own role in the creation of peril or infliction of harm. Further, as explained in Chapter Seven, the moral norm of the negative injunction can be thwarted by law and regulation, as is the case with worker compensation laws and self-insured employers when harm is caused to workers.

In many ways, products liability laws have evolved more closely than most legal doctrines to their ethical foundations. The tripartite causes of action available—in contractual warranty, in negligence, and in strict liability—reflect quite transparently the requirements of the negative injunction against causing harm and the

---

17. There already is precedent in the tobacco cases for a greater-than-single-digit rule—$28 billion in punitive damages was awarded to the husband of a 64-year-old woman in a Los Angeles jury trial. The compensatory damage award in that case was $850 million, making the punitive-to-compensatory-damage ratio 33:1.

obligation to compensate for harm caused. The limits placed on those legal concepts likewise generally reflect the public consensus on what constitutes an "acceptable risk." Much in life presents some level of risk, and innovation inherently carries risk.

For practical purposes, all societies and communities must decide on what level of risk is acceptable in exchange for the product or activity, convenience or comfort. In negligence, determination of the acceptable level of risk is made under the "reasonable person" standard. That standard incorporates ethics—it forces some universalization; forces an individual to consider the "other"; and, to some extent, forces the individual into the other person's shoes. The human rationality that is the essential premise of the deontological tradition of ethics is what gives someone the capacity to determine the reasonable person standard. Ethical considerations, including teleological or utilitarian principles, are what give the group as a whole the ability to decide what is and what is not an acceptable risk.

### The Ethical Limits of Product Safety— Obligations of the Producer and the User

Just as each legal theory in products liability has its ethical and social policy underpinnings, each legal theory also has its ethical and political shortcomings. Philosopher and business ethicist Manuel Velasquez identifies the ultimate ethical issue in consumer product cases as where to draw the line between the consumer's duty to protect his or her own interests and the manufacturer's duty to protect the consumer's interests. Extremes in the debate range from caveat emptor to commercial paternalism.[18] Each of the three legal theories of liability for defective or unreasonably dangerous products (and the ethical foundations beneath them) strikes a different balance between the respective obligations of buyer and seller.

Contractual obligations are, by nature, voluntary and consensual. The moral constraints for contractual obligations require that:

1. Both of the parties to the contract have full knowledge of the nature of the agreement they are entering.
2. Neither party to a contract intentionally misrepresents the facts of the contractual situation to the other party.
3. Neither party to a contract is forced to enter the contract under duress or undue influence.[19]

Under the *contract* theory, the duty of a business to its customers includes only "the basic duties of complying with the terms of its sales contract, disclosing the nature of the product, avoiding misrepresentation, avoiding use of duress and undue influence. By acting in accordance with these duties, a business respects the right of consumers to be treated as free and equal persons, that is, in accordance with their right to be treated only as they have freely consented to be treated."[20]

The problem with using those principles to set the moral floor for products liability is that they are based on unrealistic assumptions about the way business is conducted. In the modern world of production and distribution, the direct relationship between manufacturer and end user is rare. When there is no contract between them, the notion of contractual obligation is artificial. In similar fashion, the practical ability of producers and sellers to disclaim any obligations for the goods sold—to sell goods as is or without any warranty of anything—undermines the moral minimum and allows those benefiting from commerce in the product to avoid any responsibility. The risk of harm lies entirely on the consumer. Finally, the assumption of equal knowledge between buyer and seller that permits a caveat emptor approach to sales is a sham.

> Sellers and buyers do not exhibit the equality these doctrines assume. A consumer who must purchase hundreds of different kinds of commodities cannot hope to be as knowledgeable as a manufacturer who specializes in producing a

---

18. Velasquez, M. (1998). The ethics of consumer production and marketing. In *Business ethics: concepts and cases* (4th ed.). Upper Saddle River, NJ: Prentice-Hall, pp. 318–341.

19. Id.

20. Id.

single product... Consumers, as a consequence, must usually rely on the judgment of the seller in making their purchase decisions, and are particularly vulnerable to being harmed by the seller. Equality, far from being the rule, as the contract theory assumes, is usually the exception.[21]

A cause of action in *negligence* for products liability is sourced in the "due care theory," reflecting more clearly the negative injunction against causing harm. It recognizes that buyers and sellers do not meet on equal ground in bargaining and knowledge and, thus, imposes a "duty" on the producer or seller to prevent avoidable injury.

The due care theory as the moral standard for selling obligations is also subject to criticism. First, determining the standard of care is difficult: Is there a higher standard for more dangerous risks, does it depend on the number of potential victims, can it vary geographically? And how much care is due care? Manufacturing knowledge and expertise about a product do not rise to the level of omniscience. Sometimes defects do not appear for years or generations. There is also some paternalism in this approach. It could evolve into an overprotectiveness that infringes on free will and freedom of choice. Cigarettes are, by their very nature, an inherently and perhaps unreasonably dangerous product. Should they just be banned altogether? What about guns? alcohol? Twinkies? The cultural ethos holds that the consumer should be able to voluntarily choose less safe products or activities and assume risk as long as his or her decision is rational and informed.[22]

*Strict liability* in products liability—without fault; you make it, you're responsible for whatever harm it causes—reflects a "social costs" theory of moral obligation, which Velasquez refers to as "a very strong version of the doctrine of *caveat vendor*: let the seller beware."[23] The social costs view derives from the utilitarian ethical tradition. Forcing manufacturers to internalize the costs of harm caused by a product they produce and sell, rather than permitting the costs of harm to be externalized and borne by the victim or the society, leads to the most efficient allocation of society's resources. This ability to externalize the costs of production and its consequences is a major criticism of laissez-faire economics, purely from the standpoint of economic efficiency.[24]

The social costs view posits that those engaged in the activity, those profiting from it, are in the best position to make it safe, to insure against loss from harm, and/or to recoup the costs of added safety precautions or compensatory payments made by passing along the costs in the product price. Strict liability for harm is also viewed as strong motivation for the production of safer products with more comprehensive warnings.

Criticisms of the social costs theory of manufacturers' liability for defective or unreasonably dangerous products include that it may actually encourage carelessness in consumers, who would be assured of compensation for injury (although whether just compensation for death is ever a possibility remains dubious). Thus,

---

21. Id.

22. Id. An examination of the balancing of obligations of producers versus consumers of fast food and junk food is contained in the Part Three case study "A Big Fat Problem."

23. Id.

24. The controversies surrounding strict products liability cut across political party affiliations and lines. Even the nature of the underlying cause of the modern movement toward greater manufacturer liability is a matter of controversy among otherwise like-minded conservative scholars. Professor Priest of Yale University maintains that manufacturer liability has gained acceptance not because it is the right doctrine, but because its proponents have been skillful in propagating it. Proponents of the doctrine can persuasively argue that manufacturers have unfair bargaining power over consumers, that they can absorb the losses better, and that they are in a better position to invest in precaution and in research in superior technology. Professor Priest believes those arguments are wrong because they take away the incentives consumers have for precaution and provide a sense of entitlement without a concomitant sense of responsibility. A contrary view is proposed by Professors Landes and Posner of the University of Chicago, who argue that the movement toward manufacturer liability promotes general economic efficiency. Their argument is that the expense for consumers of learning about product defects is greater than the expense for manufacturers when mechanization and the complexity of goods bought and sold are great. They hold that mass markets, which separate manufacturers from consumers, make the bargaining costs of allocating risks through contractual mechanisms prohibitively high. Thus, social welfare is served, in most cases, by a strict liability standard. *See* Landes, William M., & Posner, Richard A. (1987). *The economic structure of tort law.* Cambridge, MA: Harvard University Press.

there is no obligation of due care on a person's own behalf and little personal responsibility for a person's actions in general. However, that criticism neglects to consider that assumption of risk remains the primary defense for manufacturers in strict liability cases. The social costs view may also be criticized for its chilling effect on product innovation. The threat of a massive tort lawsuit for harm caused can theoretically bankrupt a company. Again, however, since there are no punitive damages in strict liability and the compensatory obligation is only to make the plaintiff whole, companies should be able to factor such damages into the costs of the product. From a public policy perspective, there is little question that the balance of equities of the commercial system favor placing the risk of loss from harm on the producer of the harm.[25]

All companies, regardless of the signals they send about their social responsibility, must keep the consumers' health and welfare at the top of their list of priorities. In a crisis, they must demonstrate their sincerity, as the following feature about Odwalla shows.

## Avoiding Both Legal and Moral Obligations to Consumers: The Threat of Bankruptcy

Bankruptcy among large American corporations has proliferated over the past few decades, culminating in the two largest corporate bankruptcies in U.S. history—Enron and WorldCom—at the turn of this century. The filing of a Chapter 11 bankruptcy petition is a frequent response to or a result of the loss of large products liability cases. Thus, understanding the laws of bankruptcy and the way they interact with the laws of products liability is important.

Standard economic theory assumes that if a firm goes bankrupt, its assets will be liquidated and the firm no longer will exist. The process of exiting from the market is an integral part of the discipline imposed on firms by the capitalist system. Investors have to accept risk; if the companies in which they invest do not succeed, they will lose large portions of their investment. New investors will then have the chance to purchase the liquidated assets at favorable terms; they can form new firms and enter the market. Because of some combination of lower costs, better management, and greater productivity, the new firm

---

### The Socially Responsible Response to Crisis
*One bad apple don't spoil the whole darn bunch...*

Stories about *good* corporate social responsibility rarely gain as much attention as those about corporate misbehavior. Products in the market are discovered in a defective or sis or potential crisis responsibly, with immediate concern for mitigating the harm they cause, get little press. Instead, the companies that grab most of the attention are those that have engaged in cover-ups, bribed the regulators, or oppressively gamed the legal system. Even *finding* the good companies can be difficult. But they are out there—outnumbering the bad, leading with integrity, and setting an example and benchmark for others.

---

25. As between the three potential parties to compensate for harm caused by a product—the manufacturer, the harmed party, or the government—a decision has been made as a society that the government is not to be held financially responsible. The lack of a national healthcare system in the United States plays a large role in the fact that the number of U.S. products liability cases dwarfs that of most other developed countries. Medical expenses are the largest component of compensatory damages in a products liability suit. If those healthcare costs were covered by the government, the impetus for litigation—to be made whole—would be largely removed. In the United States, however, medical expenses are the responsibility of the individual. So, as between the manufacturer and the victim, the equities favor placing the risk of harm on the person or entity that caused it. To do otherwise would disadvantage consumers in a way that would ultimately undermine the ability of that stakeholder group to participate meaningfully in the system of free exchange. Brenkert. G. Strict products liability and compensatory justice. Citing, in part, Boxhill, B. in The morality of reparation. Reprinted in Beauchamp, T., & Bowie, N. (2001). *Ethical theory and business* (6th ed.). Upper Saddle River, NJ: Prentice Hall, p. 189.

### The Socially Responsible Response to Crisis (continued)

The difference for those companies that choose to address a critical corporate problem in an ethical and socially responsible way is usually attributable to the management at the highest levels of the corporate ladder. The companies involved also generally have more than one corporate purpose—their goal is to make a profit, but it is also to provide a quality good or service and to maintain a loyal customer base. In achieving those ends, the managers understand that all affected corporate stakeholders need to be taken into account. The ordeal of Odwalla provides an instructive example of a responsible response to crisis.

Odwalla was an entrepreneurial venture started by three young Californians with a $200 juicer in the early 1980s. The company was founded on the ideas of committing to healthy products and nourishing the body. It built a strong base of customer trust and brand loyalty; and by the mid-1990s, its annual revenues neared $100 million.

In October 1996, Odwalla was informed of a possible link between its apple juice and an outbreak of *E. coli*, which had resulted in the death of one infant and the hospitalization of at least a dozen more. In the aftermath of the crisis, Odwalla would end up pleading guilty to criminal misdemeanor charges and paying a $1.5 million fine for shipping the tainted juice. Nonetheless, Odwalla's reputation remained intact, the company survived, and its brand emerged even stronger from the ordeal. That outcome is a direct consequence of how the company handled the crisis

As Odwalla's CEO, Stephen Williamson, explained when the company received the devastating news, "We had no crisis-management procedure in place, so I followed our vision statement and our core values of honesty, integrity, and sustainability. Our number-one concern was for the safety and well-being of people who drink our juices."[a]

Journalist Anni Layne examined the actions of Odwalla management in the immediate days following the crisis and attributed its success to the following steps:[b]

*Step One*

To deal with the onslaught of FDA investigations, product recalls, media criticism, and customer inquiries, the management team met several times an hour in the first days. Gradually, team members met less frequently, but they were always in regular communication. By the second day of the crisis, the CEO had instituted regular company-wide conference calls. Within 24 hours of the crisis, it had established a web site with information for the public about the contamination and assurances that the company would pay the medical expenses for anyone harmed by the tainted juice. The company *sought* publicity of the problem by speaking to the press, appearing on TV, setting up the web site, and using direct advertisements. One especially telling fact about the priorities of Odwalla's management was the fact that the company was at least two days into the crisis before they called their lawyers. The foremost concern of management was to ensure no further harm to its customers, regardless of the legal or economic consequences.

*Step Two*

Even during lean times, Odwalla had made the effort to keep its network of route delivery managers in-house. Although this was a more expensive alternative than contracting distribution, Layne identifies it as the saving grace for Odwalla's shelf space in the market after the crisis. "Immediately following the *E. coli* detection, Williamson asked route supervisors to yank apple and carrot products from coolers and to talk one-on-one with account managers.

## The Socially Responsible Response to Crisis (continued)

They revisited retail sites every day to deliver updates and to post public notes on Odwalla coolers. . . . Williamson says, 'For 15 years, we built a reservoir of goodwill in the Bay Area. When crisis struck, some of that goodwill drained away, but a lot of people still believed in Odwalla, partially because we never deceived or manipulated them. When things go bad, people want to look inside a company and to see whether its soul is good. Ours is.' "

### Step Three

At the first word of a possible link, well before scientific confirmation, Odwalla's management focused its response on transparency and its desire to avoid causing any further harm. The CEO of the company ordered a complete recall of the product, then divided company management into teams to oversee the most pressing needs: handling concerned customers and the media; dealing with health authorities; managing the existing business; and, most importantly, fixing the problem that facilitated the tainted juice. Just five weeks after the initial crisis in October, the company revamped its traditional method of juice production to ensure that the problem would not recur.

### Step Four

One of Odwalla's most valuable intangible assets was its reputation for ensuring absolute freshness in its products. The company believed that freshness was the quality that distinguished it from the competition and gave the product its edge. To stay true to that promise, the company's founders had refused to use the process of flash pasteurization, which would ensure the destruction of deadly bacteria such as *E. coli*. Instead, Odwalla relied on placing higher standards on the growers, pickers, sorters, and others involved in the manufacturing process of the juice. That approach obviously failed the company with the outbreak of *E. coli*.

"In the days following the *E. coli* outbreak, Odwalla did not try to defend its policy against pasteurization. The company admitted its fault, scrapped its operating system, and asked leading industry experts to help it start all over again—fast. Odwalla invested $1.5 million in new safety procedures within a year of the recall. Today, the company adheres to a Hazard Analysis and Critical Control Points program that exceeds FDA requirements, tests every batch of juice for purity, performs daily microbiological tests, and leads the charge for higher government standards across the juice industry."[c]

Odwalla has recovered from the crisis to grow and expand with more products in more geographic markets. In the year following the crisis, the company was named "Best Brand Name in the Bay Area" by *San Francisco Magazine*. The vision and mission of the company and the willingness of management to act in furtherance of them account for much of that resilience. That vision, according to the CEO, is for the company to be "the milkman of the 21st century... associated with health, home, and dependability. I want Odwalla to become synonymous with nourishment..."[d]

Whatever practices precipitated the problem (and admittedly the company was culpable), Odwalla's immediate and transparent response to the crisis is a worthy example of managing beyond compliance.

a. Layne, A. (2001, March). How to make your company more resilient. *Fast Company*.
b. Id. and throughout this passage with reference to Layne's findings and analysis.
c. Layne, id.
d. See also "Companies in Crisis—the Odwalla Case" at http://www.mallenbaker.com.

should be able to succeed where the old could not. In this way, capitalism is a dynamic system that perpetually revitalizes itself. It increases the growth and productivity of society at large by weeding out losing ownership teams and rewarding winning ones.

This form of discipline by the market, however, has been eroded by changes in the bankruptcy laws, which make it harder for firms to fail. Until 1893, the United States did not have a permanent bankruptcy law. Under common law, debtors were sent to prison. Efforts to create a permanent bankruptcy law (in 1800, 1841, and 1867) came to naught because of disputes between Jeffersonians, Jacksonians, and Southern and Western Democrats—who favored liberal bankruptcy laws—and Tories, High Federalists, Whigs, and Republicans—who opposed them. The first enduring national bankruptcy act called for strict liquidation of failing firms. It was not until 1938, in the midst of the Great Depression, that an alternative to strict liquidation was made part of law. The 1938 bankruptcy act is the predecessor to current laws. Passed in a period when many people were debtors and comparatively few were solvent, it allows for corporate reorganization rather than liquidation.

The 1938 bankruptcy act was amended in 1977 when a new bankruptcy code took effect. Under the new code, liquidation takes place under Chapter 7 proceedings; however, reorganization remains an alternative under Chapter 11. The 1977 amendments to the bankruptcy laws eliminate the need to be insolvent when filing for Chapter 11 status. As soon as a petition for bankruptcy is filed, a stay against collection of creditors' claims becomes automatic. Instead, financially troubled firms start a process of negotiations with committees of their creditors and those with claims against them—employees, suppliers, customers, shareholders, etc.—to arrive at some amount (always substantially less than what is legally owed) to resolve the debts and to start again with a clean slate. The last group to be paid back is the common shareholders. They are referred to as the "residual claimants," laying claim to remaining net profits when the firm is doing well and, in exchange, taking the risk of losing their entire investment when the firm

declares bankruptcy. In the case of bankruptcy brought on by a products liability judgment, the stakeholder group hit hardest by a Chapter 11 filing is often the harmed plaintiffs.

Two of the more significant bankruptcies in this area involved Johns Manville and its liability for asbestos in 1982 and A.H. Robins and its liability for the Dalkon Shield in 1986. Johns Manville faced an unpredictable number of claims relating to the damage caused by asbestos. At the time of the company's filing for bankruptcy, it had 16,500 existing asbestos claims against it, each of which was being settled at an average of $40,000 per suit. Five large punitive damage awards, however, had averaged over $600,000 since 1982. With 500 new claims being made every month, the total number of estimated claims against Johns Manville was more than 50,000; the total liability was estimated to be at least $2 billion. The lawyers received $1.71 for every dollar that went to the victims, and Johns Manville's long-term legal costs could have been as much as $90 billion. Its insurers refused to pay, arguing that the damage had been inflicted on the victims years ago. Long latencies with respect to the onset of the disease meant that different insurers had been around when the victims first suffered exposure.

The company's filing for Chapter 11 reorganization was a surprise. It was the first time a company had used bankruptcy laws to stay the claims of a group of creditors who were the victims of the company's past actions. Under the bankruptcy filing, Johns Manville created a separate fund under which all present and future asbestos claims would be reimbursed. In the meantime, the company could continue normal business operations. The fund for the reimbursement of victims was to receive $2.5 billion over 25 years, and it had the right to at least 50 percent of the common voting shares of the corporation. The company had to pay up to 20 percent of its operating profits into the fund over 20 years. Johns Manville would divest itself of its asbestos divisions, which were its most profitable; but victims could no longer sue the company.

Some believed that this use of bankruptcy laws to evade punitive damage awards was unjustified and that Johns Manville deserved to be punished. The company defended itself by claiming that asbestos brought many advantages to society (for example, fireproofing and insulation and better brake linings, which added to automotive safety). The company did not intend to cause harm; and it took the position that it only knew of the asbestos problem with certainty in 1964, after a major study showed illness among asbestos workers (a claim that much of the evidence against the company contradicted). Johns Manville relied on a state-of-the-art defense, which is typical in tort cases of this kind: at the time of production, the company was conforming to what it believed to be the best practice in the industry.

The plaintiffs presented evidence that the company had to have known that asbestos caused health-related problems. The reason? One of Johns Manville's founders from many decades past, Henry W. Johns, died of chronic lung disease, later labeled asbestosis. Medical studies going back 50 years showed that people who had been exposed to asbestos were likely to have severe pulmonary problems, with damage to the lungs and increased difficulty breathing. As early as 1918, insurers refused to sell health insurance to asbestos workers because the insurers understood the health problems. In 1933, top officials of asbestos manufacturers, including Johns Manville, met to discuss the health risks to asbestos workers. (The Metropolitan Life Insurance Company had revealed the health risks in a report commissioned by companies in the industry.) Copious notes were taken during the meeting. Those notes were locked away in a safe in one of the companies. A former doctor for Johns Manville said that he had informed top company officials in the 1940s that only 4 of the 708 asbestos workers he had X-rayed had healthy lungs; but company officials refused to do anything about it.

That evidence was used to show that the asbestos companies acted in reckless disregard of the health of their workers. The companies deserved to suffer punitive damages, and they would serve as a deterrent for others contemplating such activities. With the filing of Chapter 11, the imposition of punitive damages would be out of the question.

Aside from the damage claims and judgments against the company, in all other ways, it was solvent. Representatives for Johns Manville justified the use of Chapter 11 by saying that the procedure was not set up for companies that were currently insolvent but might become so. Still, Johns Manville was a very healthy company in all other respects when it declared bankruptcy. It declared bankruptcy to escape liabilities under the tort system and, in that way, was permitted to avoid both legal and moral consequences for its actions.[26]

The mere threat of bankruptcy is often enough to compel a class action settlement—not just in products liability cases, but in all areas of litigation against corporations, including securities fraud, insider trading, and other financial corruption cases. A similar ploy has been used by corporations in recent times to avoid payment of retiree pensions and other earned benefits. The safe harbor of bankruptcy reorganization for corporations engaged in wrongdoing is ethically questionable on grounds of foreseeability and obligation; that is, should the company have foreseen the problem?

## Beyond Compliance

Responsible manufacturers of consumer goods understand that their primary obligation is to create and sell a product that will function as intended and not cause harm. Injuring or killing customers isn't good business practice, regardless of the bottom line.

While bankruptcy may provide a financial safe harbor from responsibility, it is not necessarily an ethical one. Instead, the ethical path to protection in products liability exists in the basic deontological premises of dignity and respect for the individual, free will, and the right not to be treated as a means without the individual's informed consent. Society admits a reasonable

---

26. Dow Corning, a subsidiary owned 50 percent by Dow Chemical and 50 percent by Corning Glass, tried a similar bankruptcy move to avoid paying damages to successful plaintiffs in suits involving its defective silicone breast implants. Both parent companies were solvent at the time. In that case, the court found that due to the control wielded over Dow Corning by its two corporate shareholders, the corporate veil should be pierced to determine solvency and the parent companies might bear some indirect liability for payment.

level of acceptable risk in its consumer products. A potential victim's informed consent to the risk is a defense to *all* three of the potential causes of action for a defective or unreasonably dangerous product. The safest course for most companies is to put all of the information on the table, disclose and warn, and *then* let the buyer beware. Armed with that knowledge and information, the consumer is free to choose whether or not to use the product.

From an ethical perspective, the quid pro quo for the safe harbor of assumption of risk requires an affirmative obligation on the part of a company to test, monitor, and research to discover what the potential risks are—to make the consent of the user truly "informed." Producers must take a proactive approach to the safety of the products they offer to the public, even when independent science has yet to discover a problem.[27]

---

27. Traditional smoke screens of "lack of conclusive scientific evidence"—used effectively for so many years by the tobacco companies, chemical industry, breast implant makers, etc.—can no longer be the standard corporate response.

# Chapter 9

## Obligations to Community and Society— Technological Progress and Environmental Safety

*"Time and time again warnings are ignored, unnecessary risks taken, sloppy work done, deception and downright lying practiced... Better organization will always help any endeavor. But the best is not good enough for some that we have decided to pursue... There is no technological imperative that says we must have power or weapons from nuclear fission or fusion, or that we must create and loose upon the earth organisms that will devour our oil spills."*
— Charles Perrow[1]

*"A human being is a part of the whole called by us universe, a part limited in time and space. He experiences himself, his thoughts and feelings as something separated from the rest, a kind of optical delusion of his consciousness. This delusion is a kind of prison for us, restricting us to our personal desires and to affection for a few persons nearest to us. Our task must be to free ourselves from this prison by widening our circle of compassion to embrace all living creatures and the whole of nature in its beauty."*
—Albert Einstein

### Technological Progress and Costs

Economic growth—the capacity of a nation to produce the goods and services its people want and can afford—is dependent on an array of factors: the quantity and quality of labor and natural resources; capital, machinery, and equipment; and values that encourage hard work, diligence, and thrift. Technology leads to increasing mechanization and gives rise to an efficient division of labor that improves productivity and permits the accumulation of capital. It, too, is among the most critical of factors that affect economic growth. The economic prosperity of the post-Second World War period was built on waves of technological innovations, as shown below.[2] Technology improves standards of living, provides knowledge, and stimulates hope that the next generation will be better off than the current one.

The promise of technology seems limitless. Yet on a practical level, technology poses risks to the environment. Unintended side effects are a cost of progress. Growth may have its limits. A 1972 book titled *The Limits to Growth* ignited controversy by arguing that growth had reached

---

1. Perrow, C. (1984). *Normal accidents.* New York: Basic Books, Inc., pp. 10–11.
2. Rothwell, R., & Zegveld, W. (1985). *Reindustrialization and technology.* Armonk, NY: M.E. Sharpe, Inc.

---

**Waves of Innovation**

1782–1845
  steam power, textiles

1845–1892
  railroads, iron, coal, construction

1892–1948
  electrical power, automobiles, chemicals, steel

1948–present
  semiconductors, consumer electronics, aerospace, pharmaceuticals, petro-chemicals, synthetic and composite materials

---

its limit.[3] Population and consumption were threats to the vitality of the global economy. The book predicted that if the world's consumption patterns and population growth continued at the same rate, the resources of the earth would be nearly depleted by the end of the century. The book called for reduction in the level of resource consumption and a reevaluation of humans' attitudes toward the environment.[4] Opponents of the views expressed in the book contended that technological innovations and policies could push back the limits and continue indefinitely to raise global living standards.[5] The book's forecast did not come to pass. Its message, though, was not totally unheeded. The 1970s saw an increase globally in environmental consciousness. The UN had it first Conference on the Human Environment in Stockholm in 1972, which launched that organization's program on the environment. That program has been the source of many international environmental agreements. Many countries, including the United States, passed laws and created environmental protection agencies. U.S. regulation is based on the legislation passed in the early 1970s, including the Clean Air Act, the Clean Water Act, and the Safe Drinking Water Act. This chapter discusses technology's impact, environmental statutes and regulations, and the ethical obligations managers have to the environment.

## Technology's Impact

*They hang the man and flog the woman
that steal the goose from off the common,
But let the greater villain loose
that steals the common from the goose.*

*The law demands that we atone
when we take things we do not own,
But leaves the lords and ladies fine
who take things that are yours and mine.*

—English Nursery Rhyme ca 1764

Corporate managers have an obligation to consider the *commons*—land and resources belonging to and affecting the whole community.[6] The commons are public goods and resources shared by all. Harm to the commons hurts everyone. The obligation of corporate managers is not to cause avoidable harm to the public goods. This obligation is no different than the injunction against causing harm in other contexts. As with worker safety and product safety, a necessary determination is the level of acceptable risk. Are the advantages gained from a technology worth the costs to the air, water, and other resources in the public domain. (See the following feature.)

---

3. The book was put out by the Club of Rome, an organization comprised of scientists, economists, businesspeople, high-level civil servants, heads of state, and former heads of state from all five continents who, according to its charter, are convinced that "the future of humankind is not determined once and for all and that each human being can contribute to the improvement of our societies." The 1972 book sold 12 million copies in 37 languages.

4. The disproportionate consumption of the world's resources by the richest nations was a significant part of the analysis in the 1972 book. The disproportionate consumption ratio continues today—with the world's richest 20 percent consuming 86 percent of the goods and services, over half of the energy, and nearly half of the meat and fish. Meadows, D. H., Randers, J., & Meadows, D. (May 2004). *Limits to growth: the 30-year update.* White River Junction, VT: Chelsea Green Publishing.

5. Those in this more optimistic camp included the late Herman Kahn, who, with a group consisting of H. Brown, O. Helmer, W. Harman, B. Fuller, and others, was among the first to develop modern forecasting.

6. *Oxford American Dictionary.* (2001).

## The Tragedy of the Commons

In 1968, Garrett Hardin published a classic article in *Science* called "The Tragedy of the Commons." The article explored the conflict between individual interests and the common good. Hardin's thesis was that problems, like overpopulation and pollution, were beyond technical solution and required a change in consciousness and institutions for their long-term resolution.[a]

The *tragedy* of the commons occurs when the use of a public good is guided by principles that maximize individual utility, without regard to the costs borne by others. Hardin illustrated his point with an historical example of the grazing of cattle on the English Commons.

> Picture a pasture open to all. It is to be expected that each herdsman will try to keep as many cattle as possible on the commons.... As a rational being, each herdsman seeks to maximize his gain. Explicitly or implicitly, more or less consciously, he asks, "What is the utility to me of adding one more animal to my herd?" This utility has one negative and one positive component.
>
> The positive component is a function of the increment of one animal. Since the herdsman receives all of the proceeds from the sale of an additional animal, the positive utility is nearly +1.
>
> The negative component is a function of the additional overgrazing created by one more animal. Since, however, the effects of overgrazing are shared by all herdsmen, the negative utility for any particular decision-making herdsman is only a fraction of -1.
>
> ...The rational herdsman concludes that the only sensible course for him to pursue is to add another animal to his herd... But this is the conclusion reached by each and every rational herdsman sharing a commons. Therein is the tragedy. Each man is locked into a system that compels him to increase his herd without limit—in a world that is limited. Ruin is the destination toward which all men rush, each pursuing his own best interest in a society that believes in freedom of the commons. Freedom in a commons brings ruin to all.
>
> But what does 'freedom' mean? When men mutually agreed to pass laws against robbing, mankind became more free, not less so. Individuals locked into the logic of the commons are free only to bring on universal ruin; once they see the necessity of mutual coercion, they become free to pursue other goals. I believe it was Hegel who said, 'Freedom is the recognition of necessity.'" [b]

In Adam Smith, private vice leads to public virtue. According to Hardin, the opposite occurs. Pollution means disposing of one's waste into the commons, without appropriate accountability.

"The rational man finds that his share of the cost of the wastes he discharges into the commons is less that the cost of purifying his own wastes before releasing them. Since this is true for everyone, we are locked into a system of 'fouling our own nest,' so long as we behave only as independent, rational, free-enterprisers."

How is this tragedy avoided? Where once the commons seemed limitless, modern population growth and relatively unrestrained fouling of the environment revealed the limits of the commons and required a change in attitude and approach.[c] That change requires sacrifice of some previously enjoyed "rights" or "freedoms" valued by Americans and others. Unfettered use of cars, boats, and supersonic transport; methods of farming and manufacturing; and the creation of energy and other technologies that affect the commons need to

---

### The Tragedy of the Commons (continued)

be tempered. According to Hardin, social coercion resulting in the mutually agreed sacrifice of some freedom is necessary and justified for human survival.

"But what does 'freedom' mean?... Individuals locked into the logic of the commons are free only to bring on universal ruin."[d]

> a. "A technical solution is one that requires a change only in the techniques of natural sciences, demanding little or nothing in the way of change in human values or ideas of morality." Hardin, G. (1968, December 13). The tragedy of the commons. *Science,* 162, 1243.
> b. Id, p. 1244.
> c. "A hundred and fifty years ago a plainsman could kill an American bison, cut out only the tongue for his dinner, and discard the rest of the animal. He was not in any important sense being wasteful. Today, with only a few thousand bison left, we would be appalled at such behavior." Id, p. 1245.
> d. Id, p. 1248.

---

### *Acceptable Risk*

Introducing new technologies may be risky. What happens when the risk is catastrophic in nature? It has the capacity to take many lives at once and do irreparable harm.[7] Should such technologies be banned? Some maintain that those technologies are not acceptable; while others hold that to prevent risk taking would decrease safety, health, and well-being.[8] Risk taking depends on courting technological dangers; without the willingness to take those risks, society would be impoverished. Technologies such as bridges, natural gas lines, and commercial air travel would not have become widespread. When first introduced, they appeared to be very dangerous; but today the risks associated with them are tolerated and manageable. To enhance the wealth of society, risk taking is needed; only wealthy societies can adequately protect the environment. Poor people have to meet subsistence needs. They do not have the luxury or foresight to consider long-term environmental impact. The problem is courting technological

dangers without the consent not only of people today, but also of future generations.

Therefore, the law limits the use of technology. It provides warnings, bans, and penalties for possible harm. Yet determining where to draw the line with regard to the benefits of a technology and the damage it inflicts is difficult. The benefits of the technology must be balanced against the risks. This is a utilitarian calculation where the point at which the benefit exceeds the costs is not the only important factor. The rights of particularly sensitive minorities and individual also must be taken into account.

"Consider the harm that results from the production of automobiles. We know statistically that about 50,000 persons per year will die and that nearly 250,000 others will be seriously injured in automobile accidents in the United States alone. Such death and injury, which is harmful, is avoidable... Because of the advantages of automobiles, society accepts the possible risks that go in using them. Society also accepts many other types of avoidable harm.

---

7. Some people maintain that no matter how effective management practices are, certain technologies such as nuclear power plants, chemical plants, aircraft and air traffic control, ships, dams, nuclear weapons, space missions, and genetic engineering will always fail under some conditions. Better operator training, safer designs, more quality control, and more effective regulation cannot eliminate the risk. One of the foremost advocates of that position is sociologist Charles Perrow. See, for example, Perrow, C. (1984). *Normal accidents.* New York: Basic Books, Inc.

8. They maintain that the welfare of a society is a function of its wealth and that its wealth increases in proportion to its willingness to take risks. One of the foremost advocates of this position is Aaron Wildavsky. See, for example, Wildavsky, A. (1988). *Searching for safety.* New Brunswick: Transaction Press, pp. 125–147.

We take certain risks—ride in planes, build bridges, and mine coal—to pursue advantageous goals. It seems that the high benefits of some activities justify the resulting harms."[9]

## Environmental Statutes and Regulations

*Only within the moment of time represented by the present century has one species—man—acquired significant power to alter the nature of his world.*
—Rachel Carson

### Common Law Obligations

Before the enactment of environmental protection laws in the early 1970s, legal recourse for preventing harm to the environment was limited to common law actions for negligence or nuisance. Common law remedies against nuisance remain available today. A *nuisance* exists when an activity interferes with community health and welfare. The remedy may be cessation of the activity. Where an activity causes personal injury or direct economic loss to an individual, the harmed party also may sue for compensatory damages. If, for instance, a company negligently discharges harmful toxins into a water supply and unusually high instances of illnesses such as childhood leukemia ensue, those harmed can bring suit. They must prove that there is a link between the toxic disposal and the wrongful death.[10] An *actionable nuisance* unreasonably interferes with or threatens health, safety, peace, comfort, or convenience of the public. Traditionally, it was the only impetus for abating problems of noise, odors, and other side effects of production. Governments often sued on behalf of affected citizens. Private individuals who were victims also could sue—for example, adjacent landowners who wanted to protect themselves from unreasonable interference with the use and enjoyment of their property. Whether the defendant was ordered to cease or modify the activity often was determined by weighing the activity's utility against the harm it caused.

Sophisticated environmental protection laws in the United States diminished the importance of nuisance suits. Common law actions have procedural requirements and formalities that make them a cumbersome and inefficient means of dealing with most environmental issues. Environmental protection statutes, in contrast, provide the government with a more direct regulatory means in combating activities that pose a risk. Nonetheless, common law retains its vitality for activities that are not yet regulated, such as global warming, as the following feature shows.

## U.S. Regulations for Environmental Protection

The U.S. legal and regulatory regime for environmental protection is among the most complex and comprehensive in the world. The following table provides in chronological order some of the major environmental statutes that the EPA administers and enforces.

Other federal environmental laws have been enacted in response to impacts of particular industries. The Noise Control Act of 1972 regulates aircraft noise so as not to unreasonably disturb people living in flight paths. The Surface Mining Reclamation Act of 1977 requires the mining industry to restore land surfaces ravaged by indiscriminate extraction practices. The Asbestos Hazard Emergency Response Act of 1986 requires schools to monitor and contain the threat of asbestos in building materials. The Oil Pollution Act of 1990 imposes cleanup costs and penalties on oil spills. Its enactment was in direct response to the catastrophe in Alaska when the oil tanker Exxon Valdez ran aground, spilling more than 11 million gallons of crude oil.

Congress enacts environmental protection laws, but the EPA is the agency charged with developing and enforcing regulations. The EPA has administrative rule-making power to promulgate regulations that set air and water quality standards and to identify hazardous substances, among others. It must give public notice of the proposed rules, invite public comment and tes-

---

9. Bowie, N. (1990). Money, morality, and motor cars. *Business, Ethics and the Environment: The Public Policy Debate.* Hoffman M., & Petry, E., Jr. (Eds.). New York: Quorum Books.
10. This was the scenario in the true case of Woburn, Massachusetts, depicted in the book and film *A Civil Action*, by Jonathan Harr.

## Global Warming: A Modern Nuisance

In late summer of 2004, the attorneys general of eight states—New York, Connecticut, California, New Jersey, Iowa, Rhode Island, Vermont, and Wisconsin—filed suit against five U.S. energy companies on grounds of "public nuisance."[a] The suit alleged that the activities of the companies—Cinergy Corp., Southern Company, Xcel Energy, American Electric Power Company, and the Tennessee Valley Authority—contributed unreasonably to global warming, thereby creating harm in the form of a public nuisance. The suit seeks no monetary damages; instead it is requiring the energy companies to begin reducing their $CO_2$ emissions immediately by 3 percent per year for the next ten years.

The suit is a fairly novel legal use of the centuries-old common law protecting "the commons" absent statutory authority. In previous cases, state attorneys general have sued the EPA for failure to promulgate and enforce regulations restricting $CO_2$ emissions. The failure of federal protection prompted the states' direct suit against corporate polluters. Proponents of the case believe the legal foundation is solid. According to one of the plaintiffs, Connecticut Attorney General Richard Blumenthal, the public nuisance claim is "not arcane or anachronistic; 'nuisance' law is still routinely used in modern court decisions… It says everyone shares a duty to avoid harming people when there are achievable ways to avoid that harm."

Ultimately, the goal of the suit is to encourage a settlement whereby the energy companies voluntarily agree to reduce $CO_2$ emissions and to refrain from lobbying efforts that thwart regulation in the area. The plaintiffs have indicated that they would happily drop from the suit any company that comes to them with an offer to voluntarily reduce emissions within a viable time frame.

The case is reminiscent of the tobacco lawsuits filed by a small group of states' attorneys general in the 1990s for reimbursement of state healthcare expenses associated with the use of tobacco. Proponents hope the energy industry will learn from the tobacco saga and willingly take the high road of managing beyond mere compliance with regard to the current laws on $CO_2$ emissions.

a. Griscom, A. (2004, August 3). Public nuisance no. 1. *Grist Magazine.* Additional information taken from the press releases issued by each of the involved states attorney general (July 2004). The suit was filed in the U.S. District Court for the Southern District of New York.

timony, and issue the rules in final. The EPA sets standards; but in many cases, the states have to implement them and achieve statutory objectives within a given time frame.[11]

A brief summary of some of the key provisions of the major environmental statutes and their operation is provided below.

The *Clean Air Act* sets national ambient air quality standards for various pollutants by determining their maximum concentrations. It prohibits further deterioration of air quality in areas already meeting the standard. It requires preservation of natural visibility in parks and wilderness areas. It also establishes emission standards for hazardous pollutants through the use of individual source emissions limitations. The EPA administers the act, but states make their own implementation plans. Amendments

---

11. In addition, all of the states have their own environmental protection laws. To the extent the state laws are more protective of the environment than the federal standards, the state laws are not *preempted* under the Supremacy Clause of the Constitution. Instead, they are allowed to exist alongside the federal law. For example, the California Clean Air Act has more stringent limitations for vehicular emissions than the Federal Clean Air Act; accordingly, for automobiles licensed in California, the tougher state standard applies.

| Federal Statute | Year Enacted | Scope |
| --- | --- | --- |
| National Environmental Policy Act (NEPA ) | 1969 | Requires federal agencies to account for impact of proposed actions with environmental impact statements (EIS) |
| Clean Air Act | 1970 amendments gave enforcement authority to the original 1963 law | Established to preserve and improve ambient air quality throughout the nation |
| Federal Insecticide, Fungicide, and Rodenticide Act (FIFRA) | 1972 amendment turned it into a comprehensive regulatory statute | Regulates the distribution, packaging, labeling, and sale of all forms of pesticides |
| Clean Water Act | 1972 Federal Water Pollution Control Act was renamed in 1977 to the Clean Water Act | Established to preserve and improve the quality of navigable and recreational waters |
| Endangered Species Act | 1973 | Identifies and protects endangered terrestrial and marine species through protection of habitat |
| Toxic Substances Control Act (TSCA) | 1976 | Regulates toxic substances that are used in everyday products, as well as by-products of hazardous activities |
| Resource Conservation and Recovery Act (RCRA) | 1976 | Systematically monitors and controls hazardous waste through a manifest program that tracks waste classified as hazardous throughout its life |
| Comprehensive Environmental Response, Compensation, and Liability Act (CERCLA) | 1980 | Imposes strict liability for cleanup costs on owners and operators of environmentally degraded property; established the Superfund |
| Safe Drinking Water Act (SDWA) | 1986 | Establishes bacterial and chemical contaminant limits for public drinking water; regulates underground injection of contaminants into groundwater |
| Pollution Prevention Act (voluntary) | 1990 | Provides matching funds to states to encourage business technology cleaner and more efficient production |

to the Clean Air Act in 1990 substantially strengthened penalties for noncompliant regions, allowing the withholding of project permits and federal funds for those regions behind schedule. The 1990 amendments addressed the problems of acid rain, urban smog, airborne toxins, and ozone-depleting chemicals. The amendments also introduced a market incentive for reducing sulfur dioxide emissions. Each year the EPA auctions a limited number of allowances for $SO_2$ emissions; firms holding the allowances use them to emit $SO_2$. Firms also may bank them for later use or sell them. The market for trading in $SO_2$ allowances encourages companies to reduce emissions and trade them on the market. By doing so, they earn a reward for operating beyond compliance.

The *Clean Water Act* aims to restore and maintain the chemical, physical, and biological integrity of the nation's waters. The EPA restricts effluent discharges into navigable waters by means of a permitting system known as the National Pollutant Discharge Elimination System (NPDES). The agency may require a discharger to pretreat its discharge depending on the toxicity of the pollutant. Restrictions are more lenient for discharges into sewer systems because the discharge undergoes further treatment. A separate statute, the *Safe Drinking Water Act* (SDWA), regulates drinking water. The EPA sets the standards for public water supplies by establishing limits on bacterial and chemical contaminants and by regulating the underground injection of contaminants into groundwater that contributes to public drinking water sources.

The *Resource Conservation and Recovery Act (RCRA)* is a comprehensive national program for systematic control of hazardous waste. Before it was passed, disposal of hazardous waste was a matter of state regulation, as is the case with solid waste, including garbage. The generation and disposal of hazardous waste is subject to strict liability. It cannot be safely undertaken; so the burden of risk of harm is placed on those who generate the waste. Accordingly, RCRA imposes *cradle-to-grave* liability on the generator; the generator is responsible for storage, transportation, and final treatment or disposal. Under RCRA, the EPA identifies what waste is hazardous and establishes standards governing generators, transporters, and owners/operators who store or treat the waste. The agency maintains a manifest system that tracks waste classified as hazardous throughout its life.[12]

The *Comprehensive Environmental Response, Compensation, and Liability Act, (CERCLA)* set up Superfund—a multibillion-dollar appropriation funded by many sources. Superfund permits the government to undertake abatement and cleanup of a dirty site prior to establishing who is responsible. The EPA may remediate the hazard, issue cease and desist orders, and bring actions for reimbursement of the costs from potential defendants. The pool of people responsible for the cleanup costs include (1) everyone in the chain of activity that created the hazard—generator, transporter, disposal authority; (2) those who owned or operated the property at the time of the offensive activity; *and* (3) those who currently own or operate the property. Few defenses are available; and the liability is *joint and several liability*, meaning that any of the defendants may be held liable for the full cost of cleanup.[13]

---

12. RCRA imposes heavy paperwork and costs on those generators seeking to transport and dispose of hazardous waste. That regulatory framework is layered with state and local paperwork and licensing requirements. The burdensome and costly requirements of RCRA compliance is a disincentive to generating the toxic stuff. However, some U.S. companies (and the U.S. government itself) avoid the problem by exporting their hazardous waste abroad.

13. The inclusion of current owners and operators of the property creates a dangerous trap for the uninformed. By taking title to property without first examining the history of its ownership and use, a person can be held liable for cleanup of the problem even though he or she had nothing to do with its creation. Accordingly, the acquisition of commercial real estate by a business requires due diligence to ensure the absence of potential environmental problems with the property. Buyers also may require contractual representations and assurances from sellers regarding the environmental integrity of the property. While those contractual arrangements may provide for reimbursement from seller to buyer for cleanup costs incurred, they do not protect the buyer from liability as a responsible person under CERCLA. The inclusion of current owners in the chain of responsible persons resulted in many banks and mortgage companies becoming defendants in CERCLA suits. In the acquisition of most real estate, a lender provides a loan to the borrower to acquire the property and takes back a mortgage as security for repayment. If the borrower defaults, the lender then forecloses on the mortgage and takes back title to the property. In the case of dirty property, a lender's foreclosure puts it in the chain of title as the current owner of the property. To mitigate the harsh effects of that application, amendments to CERCLA in 1996 provided a safe harbor whereby lenders could take back title to foreclosed property without liability as responsible persons, provided the lenders' activities with respect to the property were limited.

## Laboratory Earth

*"Better Living through Chemistry"*... One great leap in modern technological advancement has been the chemical revolution. For the past 60 years, the social progress wrought by chemistry seems almost magical. The role of chemicals in modern life is ubiquitous. Now, decades into the business of chemicals, the full cost of this technology is just becoming apparent. As science advances, so does knowledge of the causal links between exposure to certain chemicals and harm to humans and their environment. The universal moral obligation to not cause preventable harm counsels that when these risks become known, reasonable efforts must be made to contain their harmful effects. This obligation binds individuals, groups, organizations, and governments. Yet, the evidence shows that this moral minimum has not always been honored by the chemical industry.

### The Chemical Revolution

The resurgence of the American economy in the post-World War II era may be attributed in large part to the birth of the chemical industry. The defoliants and chemical weaponry developed for the war proved the perfect tonic to revive agricultural lands devastated by the Great Dust Bowl of the 1930s, which ravaged topsoil and made dust of much of the nation's "breadbasket." Chemical fertilizers and pesticides revitalized arable lands and produced ever greater yields. With the advent of plastics, the very fabric of American life was transformed as plastic and its derivatives became the material of choice. Solvents and sprays, cosmetics and clothing, implements and toys, indeed, the very taste of processed food is all chemicals.

The fallout from chemical technology did not begin to appear until a few decades into the revolution. It began with a few dead fish and fowl, and toxins that moved up the food chain to human consumption; moved on to contaminated soil and carcinogens; and has moved now into genetics and the reproductive systems of animals and humans. Where the fallout will end depends in large part upon how the chemical industry itself approaches the issue. Historically, the industry has not been forthcoming.

### Industry Knowledge of Risks—Industry Response to the Knowledge

More than a million pages of documents chronicling the inner-workings of the chemical industry, dating from its very beginnings, were made public by discovery in a civil action for the wrongful death of a chemical worker. The documents detail a long history of industry knowledge about the risks of its product—risks that the industry took great pains to keep secret from governmental regulators and the public. The documentary, Trade Secrets: A Moyers Report, provides a detailed examination of the decades of deception practiced by the industry.[a]

Among the known risks documented by the industry's own scientists:

### *Vinyl chloride*

Confidential inter-company correspondence between Union Carbide, B.F. Goodrich, Dow Chemical, Monsanto, and other chemical manufacturers beginning in 1959, revealed industry suspicions about the level of worker exposure to Polyvinylchloride (PVC) monomer, acknowledging the chemical to be much more toxic than originally believed. By 1966, the industry knew that exposure to the substance would cause the bones in hands and feet to dissolve and by 1969 it had evidence that it may cause systemic disease. The industry, fearing a public expose, kept the information to itself. Not only did it not warn workers of the risks, but it also rejected recommendations by its own researchers to reduce the level of PVC

### Laboratory Earth (continued)

monomer exposure on the factory floor by 90%.

In the early 1970s, European scientists discovered that exposure to PVC monomer caused a rare cancer of the liver and likely was absorbed into body fats and carried to the brain. The US chemical industry responded by entering into an agreement for secrecy and confidentiality for the European findings. "Conoco, BF Goodrich, Dow, Shell, Ethyl, Union Carbide—some of the founding fathers of the chemical revolution—were among those who signed the secrecy agreement, even as they were admitting to themselves the bad news: Working with vinyl chloride—even at low levels of exposure—could cause cancer." The industry withheld this information from government regulators and still did nothing to warn the workers—many of whom were already suffering with dissolving bones and cancer of the liver.

At about the same time, the industry discovered that the use of PVCs in aerosol cans sold to the public exposed users to the same health risks as its workforce. Recognizing that the aerosol segment constituted but a small part of the PVC market, and that its liability for marketing a defective or dangerous product would be potentially unlimited, the industry quietly pulled out of the aerosol business, without giving any public warning. The workers, to whom company liability would be limited by Workers Compensation, still were not warned of the risks.

In 1974, four workers at BF Goodrich died of the rare liver cancer discovered by the European researchers three years earlier. In 1975, over the objections of the industry, the government finally ordered workplace exposure to PVC reduced to a negligible risk of one part per million—fifteen years after the industry first knew of the harm.

### Benzene

A widely used additive in gasoline, by 1958 all the science indicated a clear link between benzene exposure and leukemia. The petrochemical industry's own research supported that finding. Nonetheless, in the late 1970s, when OSHA moved to reduce the permissible levels of benzene in the workplace, industry fought it, arguing that the cost of reducing exposure outweighed the benefits of doing so. Through the use of court challenges, the industry delayed implementation of the regulation for a full decade. Hundreds of preventable cases of leukemia are documented from the delay.

### DBCP

DBCP was a pesticide produced by Dow, Occidental, and Shell. Internal documents show that the producers knew as early as 1958 that the chemical had the effects of testicular atrophy. Evidence that the chemical was a reproductive toxicant began to surface in the following years. Those working with the chemical—a large percentage of whom would find out that they were sterile—were not warned of the risk. In 1975, it was discovered that the manufacture of DBCP had contaminated all of the wells in the surrounding area of a plant to the point of toxicity to humans and animals. Still, the companies utilized all of their resources to challenge federal regulation of DBCP and delayed its ban from the market for nearly another decade.[b]

### The Use of Political Influence

In addition to secreting the known risks of these chemicals from affected workers, the public and the government, chemical companies also sought to thwart government oversight of the industry itself. When proposed in 1971, the Toxic Substances Control Act (TSCA)—which

## Laboratory Earth (continued)

would burden industry with the obligation of registering marketed chemicals and proving them safe, or at least testing toxicity, before sending them to market—threatened the pocketbook of chemical manufacturers like nothing before. Industry waged a five-year battle to block the legislation before TSCA was finally passed by the Congress in 1976.

The internal documents of the chemical companies and their trade association, the Chemical Manufacturers Association, reveal a change in strategy after the passage of TSCA. A 1979 memo lays bare the approach: "Gentlemen, this is a campaign that has the dimension and detail of a war. This is war – not a battle. The dollars expended on offense are token compared to future costs... The rewards are the court decisions we have won, the regulations that have been modified, made more cost effective or just dropped. The future holds more of the same."[c]

New strategies for collecting and distributing the "token" dollars for offense were developed. Through the use of political action committees, the industry collected and distributed more than $6 million to chemical-friendly candidates in the 1980 elections. The biggest return on this investment was the election of Ronald Reagan to the Presidency. In his first month in office, Reagan issued an executive order that precluded the promulgation of EPA regulations unless and until each proposed change could be shown to be "cost-effective." The order effectively turned the role of TSCA upside down—instead of the manufacturer of the chemical having to show its safety, the EPA had to establish that it posed a risk and that the risk outweighed its economic benefits.

Environmentalists, consumer activists, health advocates, and others argue that the obstacles to banning, regulating use, or even just limiting exposure to chemicals under TSCA has been made so burdensome as to render the statute useless. In the first 25 years of the existence of TSCA, only 5 types of chemicals, out of thousands, have been banned. The low number is due to lack of information. The risk posed by the vast majority of these chemicals remains unknown.

> "Of the 100,000 existing registered chemical worldwide, only about 400 have complete toxicological profiles. In the more limited chemical universe of what are called High Production Volume (HPV) chemicals, there are at lease 2500 chemicals used heavily in global commerce. At least half of these were identified in the mid-1990s as being insufficiently profiled from a hazards standpoint. . ."[d]

The chemical industry used its political clout on the state level as well. In 1986, California voters put onto the ballot and passed Proposition 65—a law that required companies to provide a conspicuous warning of any health hazard or toxic risks posed by its chemicals to virtually anyone affected by them. Proposition 65 is a right-to-know law—giving individuals the information they need to knowingly and voluntarily decide the risks to which they will expose themselves. Despite millions of dollars spent by industry to fight the initiative, it passed. Since that time, industry has stepped up its political contributions to chemical-friendly state legislators and groups and has defeated every subsequent state ballot initiative modeled on California's right-to-know law.[e]

### The Chemical Industry in the 21st Century

Preferring "self-regulation" to governmental regulation, the chemical manufacturers agreed in 1998 to voluntarily undertake the testing of some chemicals.[f] Although US companies vol-

## Laboratory Earth (continued)

unteered in 1998 to screen some 3,000 HPV chemicals for environmental and health hazards by 2005, US policy still allows the use of some 30,000 chemicals that predate testing requirements under TSCA.[g] Moreover, even for those on the schedule for testing, the industry has yet to make public any of its results.

Nonetheless, many in the industry have put forth a convincing case that they have seen the light of sustainable chemical development and mended their ways. DuPont is a good example. DuPont made a commitment to sustainable development nearly a decade ago by pledging to reduce waste, emissions, and energy usage. Since that time, it has deepened its commitment by seeking businesses that can be conducted in a sustainable manner, without irrevocably depleting natural resources. The company spun off its Conoco petroleum business in the largest IPO of 1998, and invested the proceeds in a seed technology that not only produces food but also renewable materials for commercial use. DuPont took an active role in the World Summit on Sustainable Development in Johannesburg, S.A. in 2001, and used the principles set forth at this meeting to benchmark its progress. To date, it has been very successful in this effort. It has reduced greenhouse gas emissions from global operations by 65 percent since 1990. Over the same period, it has reduced global energy use by 6% per year, saving an estimated $1.5 billion. Further, DuPont now satisfies 3% of its total energy needs from renewable sources, with a target of 10% for 2010. Finally, toxic releases and total waste are down 79% and 40%, respectively, from 10 years ago.[h]

Yet, DuPont continues to face repercussions from past sins: in August 2000, DuPont settled a $1.5 million lawsuit with the EPA and the Department of Justice over a release of sulfuric acid at a Kentucky plant; in August 2001, DuPont lost an $88.5 million lawsuit brought by two Costa Rican-based plant nurseries for birth defects and crop destruction caused by its fungicide; in August 2002, DuPont settled a $47.2 million class-action lawsuit for damage caused by leaking polybutylene pipes manufactured by the company. Looming on the horizon is a potential bombshell involving DuPont's signature substance "Teflon." In June 2004, internal DuPont documents were made public which disclosed that, as early as 1981, the company had indications from its research of the risk of birth defects posed by the synthetic chemical perfluorooctanoic acid (PFOA), an essential ingredient in Teflon. The EPA has indicated that it will seek millions of dollars in fines from the company for not disclosing the findings.[i] It is not yet clear whether private suits will also be brought against the company. Until 2000, when it left the business, the American company 3M was the biggest supplier of PFOA. Samples taken by 3M from the public blood supply in the 1990s revealed that PFOA was present in the bloodstream of more than 90% of Americans.[j]

### The Precautionary Principle

How are social values to be weighed when it comes to technology? Who shall determine what constitutes acceptable risk? One response to these questions, which is gaining popularity with European policy-makers and many in the American public, calls for application of a precautionary principle when it comes to toxic risk. The precautionary principle holds

> "When an activity raises threats of harm to human health or the environment, precautionary measures should be taken even if some cause and effect relationships are not fully established scientifically."[k]

## Laboratory Earth (continued)

The dramatic increase in human disease patterns since the chemical revolution provides some support for a better-safe-than-sorry approach:

Rates of breast cancer have risen steadily over the last four decades; in total, by more than 50% in the past half-century. More than forty thousand women die of the disease each year.

Rates of brain cancer among children is up by 26% per cent.

Rates of testicular cancer among older teenage boys has almost doubled.

Infertility among young adults is up.

Chronic diseases now affect more than 1/3 of the US population (100 million men, women, and children).

Nearly 12 million US children suffer from one or more developmental disabilities.

Between 5% and 10% of US schoolchildren suffer from learning disabilities and the number is increasing.

The incidence of asthma has doubled in the last two decades.

The incidence of cancer generally, and certain kinds of cancers specifically, has risen. In addition to breast cancer, cancers of the liver, prostate, kidney, thyroid, testis, esophagus, bladder, and skin cancers have all increased in the past 25 years.

Disorders in human reproduction and the human endocrine system are on the rise—including the discovery of "endocrine disruptors." Endocrine disruptors include a wide range of chemicals regularly used in modern society, which pose a dramatic risk of harm to developing animal embryos and fetuses, as well as risks to human fetuses, children, and even adults.[l]

The future of Laboratory Earth and its inhabitants rests in large part of the ethics of corporate stewards of technology like the chemical industry. Whether the industry's purported new commitment to transparency and sustainable development is sincere or a mere public relations attempt at greenwash remains to be seen in the 21st century.[m] Only future generations will know for sure.

---

By Sheryl Kaiser, @2006, NorthCoast Publishers, Inc.

a. *TRADE SECRETS: A Moyers Report* by Bill Moyers and Sherry Jones, Center for Investigative Reporting (2001). This documentary is highly recommended as an accompaniment to this text. It covers issues of workers' rights to know, consumers' rights to know, obligations of business to the environment, the use of political influence to thwart regulation, the precautionary principle, and the challenge of keeping science nonpolitical. The video is available from PBS.

b. The archival evidence of industry knowledge about the risks posed by these three chemicals—vinyl chloride, benzene, and DBCP— as well as other manufactured chemicals, is detailed in *Trade Secrets*.

c. Id.

d. *Trespass Against Us: Dow Chemical and the Toxic Century*, by Jack Doyle, Common Courage Press, Environmental Health Fund (2004)

e. Trade Secrets

f. A 1992 memo from the industry trade association, the CMA, recommended that "A general CMA policy on voluntary development of health, safety and environmental information will...potentially avert restrictive regulatory actions and legislative initiatives." Id.

g. *Trespass*, Doyle, at pp. 247-248. Doyle notes that the EU version of TSCA, called REACH-Registration, Evaluation and Authorization of Chemicals, requires manufacturers to re-register and establish the safety of the 30,000 chemicals already on the market, in addition to any new substances that are developed. The American chemical industry has said that the costs of compliance with REACH would create an undue economic burden.

h. http://www1.dupont.com/dupontglobal

---

**Laboratory Earth (continued)**

i. "EPA to Fine DuPont Millions over Teflon," The Associated Press July 8, 2004

j. "DuPont, Now in the Frying Pan," by Amy Cortese, *The New York Times*, August 8, 2004, Section 3.

k. Wingspread Statement on the Precautionary Principle (1998); "The Rise of the Precautionary Principle: A Social Movement Gathers Strength" by Nancy Myers, *Multinational Monitor*, September 2004. The Maastricht Treaty of 1994, which established the European Union, uses the Precautionary Principle to guide EU health and environmental policy. Australia uses it for hazardous waste permitting.

l. Statistics from: Myers, id.; "System Failure" by Jon R. Luoma, *MotherJones Magazine* July/August 1999; and *Trade Secrets*

m. "Greenwash" was a term coined in the early 1990s for corporations that talked the talk of environmental responsibility, but failed to walk the walk. See, e.g. Greenwash: *The Reality behind Corporate Environmentalism*, by Jed Greer and Kenny Bruno (1993)

---

The *Toxic Substances Control Act (TSCA)* gave the EPA the power to require that chemicals be registered and screened for toxicity before being used. The statute covers toxic substances used in everyday products and their by-products. TSCA put the burden of proof of a chemical's safety on those proposing to use it. Before TSCA, chemicals were presumed innocent until harm had been caused.[14]

### Ethical Obligations

The ethical obligations of business to the environment have minimalist and maximalist versions. A minimalist approach is compliance with the law and ethical norms. A company should meet the negative injunction against causing harm. It should not interfere in the political arena to defeat and weaken environmental legislations.[15] But beyond mere compliance with the law, business possesses special knowledge, expertise, and resources, which are invaluable in dealing with environmental issues.[16] According to the maximalist approach, then, business should work with government to identify risks and find solutions. It should share its knowledge and expertise in moving toward the goal of environmental sustainability.[17]

### The Limits of Teleological Ethics in Managing Technology

Teleological ethics, or utilitarianism, focuses on *ends*—if the end result maximizes the good for the most and minimizes harm, then the end result justifies the means. Deontology, a rights-based approach, focuses on the means—people are entitled to be treated as an end in themselves, not merely a means, regardless of the circumstances. Thus, the means used to pursue any goal or result (including the most happiness for the most people) cannot transgress basic human rights. For deontologists, the ends are less important than the means of achieving them. A company must respect basic human rights and dignity.[18]

---

14. As one commentator put it, "The whole theory of TSCA was that we're not going to keep waiting until we can count the bodies in the street. We're going to do some preliminary steps early on, catch the problems in the laboratory, get rid of them, identify the really bad actors, take some steps to reduce exposures, to find substitutes for these. That was the theory." Jacqueline Warren, Former Attorney for the Natural Resources Defense Council, in *TRADE SECRETS: A Moyers Report*, by Bill Moyers and Sherry Jones, Center for Investigative Reporting.That was the theory. It just in practice has never worked.

15. As with all such limited approaches to responsibility, however, the position assumes a meaningful role for government to protect the public interest. "Environmentalists frequently argue that business has special obligations to protect the environment. Although I agree with the environmentalists on this point, I do not agree with them as to where the obligations lie. Business does not have an obligation to protect the environment over and above what is required by law; however, it does have a moral obligation to avoid intervening in the political arena in order to defeat or weaken environmental legislation. Bowie, N. (1990). Money, morality, and motor cars. In Hoffman, M., & Petry, E., Jr. (Eds.). *Business, ethics and the environment: the public policy debate.* New York: Quorum Books. Bowie calls this the corporate "cake-and-eat-it-too argument"—no business social responsibility and no business regulation.

16. Hoffman, M. (1998). Business and environmental ethics. In Shaw, W., & Barry, V. (Eds.). *Moral issues in business* (7th ed.). Belmont, CA: Wadsworth.

17. Id.

18. The Means-Ends dilemma is the subject of Chapter Two.

### Everyone Has His or Her Price?

How much is a life worth? That question may appear abhorrent and absurd since human worth cannot be truly captured in monetary terms. Nonetheless, human lives are valued in monetary terms every day for many purposes. Compensation for wrongful death requires a calculation of the monetary value of one's lost life. As well, monetary value is placed on human life in many aspects of public policy making as well as private business decisions. The government considers the value of a human life when making decisions ranging from highway construction to space exploration.

Callous calculations in the pursuit of maximizing profits aside, ascribing some economic value to life is essential for society to make rational assessments of how to expend its resources. Decisions on how much money to spend on new medical technology, whether to ban a chemical with economic value, which Superfund sites should have cleanup priority, what emissions standards to institute for air quality, etc., require a measurable estimation of the human benefit or human suffering produced by the activity. For that reason, human life is given a monetary value. The difficulty is in determining the factors that should be included in the calculation.

Until the late 1960s, society had a simple answer to the problem of how much a human life was worth.[a] A person was valued according to the net present value of his or her expected lifetime earnings. Calculations in 1986 dollars showed that an American man in his late twenties was worth about $500,000; a woman, about $350,000. Today that number is considerably higher, although it still varies widely depending on the distinguishing characteristics of the victim.

"The median award to a plaintiff who wins a wrongful death case is about $900,000, according to Jury Verdicts Research, a Horsham, Pa. firm that has analyzed 200,000 personal-injury jury verdicts. But a life's value has a wide range, as shown by the Victims Compensation Fund, the U.S.-funded commission to compensate Sept. 11 victims and stave off lawsuits. The fund's compensation grid starts at $250,000 and maxes out at about $7 million; the average payout has been about $1.8 million.... Currently, the Department of Transportation values lives at about $3 million when making road improvements"[b]

Different approaches to valuation yield different results. For example, the government may make the calculation based on wage-risk surveys, which attempt to measure the value of life by determining the additional compensation that a worker would demand for a more dangerous job. Another approach is known as the Human Life Value method, often used in wrongful death suits, which attempts to measure the economic value of a person's lifetime contributions to his or her family. The value of annual income until retirement; fringe benefits; and contributions to family life, including cooking, cleaning, and taking care of dependants are tabulated. Against this are deducted the costs of personal consumption by the deceased, taxes, and the time value of money. That was basically the method used by the September 11 Victims Fund to determine compensation to survivors of those killed in the terrorist attacks. An alternative to the approach is a "willingness to pay" criteria, where economists attempt to establish value by determining people's willingness to pay to extend life or to reduce risks posed to their health and safety.[c]

Both the discounted future earnings approach and the willingness-to-pay approach cast human value in purely materialistic terms. There are some obvious shortcomings with an approach that values life based only on earning power or direct economic contribution. It may be argued that the quality of life is not meaningfully measured when the only factor taken into account is one's paycheck. Some jurisdictions have moved away from this strict

---

**Everyone Has His or Her Price? (continued)**

earnings consideration to include the value of the deceased to the family in terms of emotional caregiving and other noneconomic activities, as well as the value of the deceased to the larger society—for example, in charitable and community works.

Further, given the nature and structure of the American workforce, a purely economic approach statistically ends up valuing women less than men and minorities less than majorities—since, statistically, they have considerably less earning power. Even greater discrepancies arise in the valuation of non-American deaths.

For the determination of compensation to the thousands of victims of the toxic gas leak at Bhopal, India, Union Carbide fought mightily to keep the proceedings in India, where the typical award for wrongful death would be no more than a few hundred dollars. In the United States, juries can award damages in the millions for these kinds of cases. Union Carbide succeeded in keeping the case out of the U.S. courts, eventually paying each Bhopal victim an average of $3,200.[d]

People in other countries that are wrongfully killed by the U.S. government are also valued differently.[e]

a. Geyelin, M., & Marcus, A. D. (1991, March 27). Dollar valuation of life pleasures set back, *Wall Street Journal*, B6; Dyer, L. (1986). Environmental policy and the economic value of human life. *Journal of Environmental Management*, 229–243; Leape, J. (1980). Quantitative risk assessment in the regulation of environmental carcinogens. *Harvard Environmental Law Review*, 86–117; Selegman, D. (1986, March 3). How much money is your life worth? *Fortune*, 25–27.

b. Torpy, B. (2004, March 15). Life—hard to know what price is right. *Atlanta Journal-Constitution*.

c. A 1986 study examined people's willingness to pay extra for homes in areas with little pollution and came up with a $600,000 to $900,000 price tag for a human life in 1986 dollars. A study of risk-time trade-offs among seat belt bucklers and nonbucklers calculated that the worth of a human life was about $625,000 in 1986 dollars.

d. *The Times of India* sarcastically noted that approximately $40,000 was spent on the rehabilitation of every sea otter affected by the Exxon Valdez oil spill, making the value of an Alaskan sea otter worth more than ten times the value of an Indian citizen of Bhopal.

e. Herold, M. W. (2002, September 11). The bombing of Afghanistan as reflection of 9/11 and different valuations of life. University of New Hampshire.

---

The teleological tradition of ethics—utilitarianism and/or cost-benefit analysis—employs a balancing technique to determine what will maximize the good of the most, weighing the relative values on each side of the good/harm ledger. While extremely useful in setting policy goals and evaluating initiatives to achieve them, the approach is problematic for issues involving goods that cannot be quantified and compared in monetary or other commonly shared terms. A healthy environment is the kind of value where traditional utilitarian analysis falls short. Steven Kelman provides a critique of cost-benefit analysis in a celebrated and well-known essay.[19] Kelman's position is that accurate and effective cost-benefit analysis requires that all components and factors be weighed on a common scale or denominator. However, some "goods"—such as human life and clean air—have no precise market valuation that can be balanced against other inputs. Unlike the costs of labor and materials, human life, breathable air, drinkable water, and edible food cannot be assigned an exact dollar value in benefit or cost.

---

19. Cost benefit analysis: an ethical critique. (1981). Included in numerous anthologies of business ethics studies and reproduced in full in Birsch, D., & Fielder, J. (1994). *The Ford Pinto case: a study in applied ethics, business, and technology*. Albany, NY: State University of New York Press.

Environmental regulation in the United States was hamstrung for many years by the controversy over whether the regulation required cost/benefit justification. In 2001 in *EPA v. American Trucking*, the U.S. Supreme Court ruled that the failure of the EPA to consider the cost of implementing national ambient air quality standards (NAAQS) in setting standards was not a sufficient ground upon which to challenge the regulation.[20] The Court found that the Clean Air Act directs the EPA to set NAAQS at whatever level is necessary "to protect the public health... with an adequate margin of safety." Yet some utilitarian ethical analysis is essential for decision making about the environment. And some notion of relative values is required to facilitate that analysis. What is the value of a human life? What is the value of common goods such as breathable air, drinkable water, and edible food? Given the risks of technological progress and the good that it brings, how are those competing values to be accounted for? Deontological ethics address the risks of technological progress with the notion of "acceptable risk." Human beings may not be treated as a means to an end *without their consent*. For the sake of providing for themselves and their families and improving their lives and the lives of others, people, individually and collectively, may agree or implicitly assent to levels of "acceptable risk."[21] For further discussion of the issue of teleological versus deontological ethics in environmental decision, see the following feature.

## Homocentric versus Biocentric Approaches to Environmental Ethics

The rights-based approach to environmental ethics is divided between two approaches: homocentric and biocentric. A *homocentric* approach determines the value of the natural world and the "rights" to be accorded it in terms of its value to human beings. That is, under the homocentric view, the natural world possesses no intrinsic value save for how it may benefit humankind. Accordingly, its ethical use is determined in accordance with maximizing its value to humans. A *biocentric* view holds that the natural world—flora and fauna—possesses an intrinsic value, apart from its value for use by humans. The biocentric approach views humankind as but one stakeholder in the planet, albeit one very key stakeholder. The place of humans in the universe, then, is as a responsible, integral participant and partner—neither master, nor exploiter.

The homocentric approach supports environmental ethics on the basis of human rights. The human *right to life* is a universally accepted moral norm. The natural right of humans not to be unfairly deprived of life has been embodied as a primary, preeminent political principle since the Enlightenment and the birth of government by the people. More recently, it was unanimously accepted as a basic moral tenet in the UDHR, adopted by the UN in 1948.[22] Presumably, the right to life includes the right to the necessities to sustain life—drinkable water, breathable air, and healthy food. Without those prerequisite needs met, the rights to liberty, security, property, and happiness are rendered meaningless. Threats to the common goods that facilitate life—whether by contamination, depletion, or denial of access by privatization—thus, pose a threat to the human right to life.[23]

The *biocentric* approach confers a moral value on the natural world, seeing animals and plant life as worthy of respect beyond their use to humans. The level of respect or "rights" to be accorded to the natural world does not approach that accorded to humans—animals are not viewed as intrinsically entitled to due process; the forests have no rights of free speech. Nonetheless, biocentrism recognizes some basic

---

20. *EPA v. American Trucking* 531 US 457 (2001). The Court noted that "Nowhere are the costs of achieving such a margin made a part of the initial calculation." It concluded that the EPA may not consider implementation costs in setting air quality standards under the Clean Air Act.

21. The approach to environmental ethics under the deontological theory depends, in part, on how one perceives *rights*: who possesses them, how they arise, and what degree of respect they are to be accorded.

22. The Universal Declaration of Human Rights (UDHR) is discussed in detail in Chapter Ten.

23. Express recognition of a human *right to a livable environment* has come about only in the past few decades. Although the UDHR does not specifically include such a right, it is included in the Stockholm Declaration of 1972 and many later-enacted environmental compacts. What constitutes a *livable* environment remains a point of contention, however.

innate rights for all living things; for example, in the case of sentient life, the right to be free from unnecessary pain and suffering. The key principle of biocentrism is conservation and restraint. The approach does not counsel against all use of the natural world by human beings; instead, it demands a nonexploitative attitude that recognizes the value of nature's perpetuity.

The homocentric/biocentric schism is not merely a philosophical one, but, instead, holds significant implications for the ability to protect the environment by law. The U.S. legal system protects legal rights and interests. American property law takes a homocentric approach and recognizes rights to protect property as inhering in the humans who own it or are affected by the use of it. It is their rights in the property or use of it that deserve protection, not the property itself. In a legal sense, the *rightlessness* of the natural world means that property can be given no protection beyond its highest and best use for humans and can be protected only at human behest.

The homocentric limits of environmental protection were raised in the 1970s by Christopher Stone, an eminent law professor, in his work "Should Trees Have Standing?" Stone pointed out that protection under the American legal system requires the right to sue for relief. In order to bring suit, a complainant must have *standing*—that is, a legally protectible interest. To establish a legally protectible interest, one must generally establish that his or her rights have been interfered with unreasonably. Standing to sue requires legally recognized rights. As a result, the only complainants with standing to protect the environment are those with a recognized property right in it.[24] No rights beyond those of its human owners and users are recognized for the natural world.

While the idea of conferring some form of legal rights on trees and animals and the like may seem far-fetched, there is precedent in the U.S. legal system for the issue of conferring rights on nonhu-

mans. In 1992, the Supreme Court decided the case of *Lujan v. Defenders of Wildlife*.[25] In that case, Defenders of Wildlife (DOW) attempted to bring suit against the Department of Interior for failing to properly promulgate regulations under the Endangered Species Act. The high court had to decide whether DOW had *standing* to bring the suit. That is, did the environmental group have a legally protectible interest in the protection of endangered species sufficient to permit its request for relief? The Court acknowledged that standing would be more difficult to establish for DOW because the law did not directly regulate the activities of DOW. Instead, DOW had to establish a legally recognizable interest in its membership in the regulation of endangered species. DOW provided affidavits from its members, stating that the members had visited foreign regions and observed the habitat of endangered species and planned to return to do so again. It made a showing of a "vocational nexus" with the object of the regulation and DOW's members who studied endangered animals and habitats for a living—scientists, researchers, scholars, documentarians, etc. It made an argument for an "ecosystem nexus"—a position stating that it had a protectible interest in what happens anywhere in the world to endangered species because all parts of the ecosystem are inextricably interconnected; acts in one part of the globe invariably have an impact on others. The Supreme Court rejected all of those arguments and ruled that DOW did not have standing to challenge the EPA's regulation.[26] Accordingly, suits to protect endangered species could be brought only by those directly impacted by the protection of endangered species (or the lack of it).

However, in 2000, the high court addressed a similar issue in *Friends of the Earth v. Laidlaw Environmental Services*.[27] In a citizen suit under the Clean Water Act, Friends of the Earth (FOE) attempted to sue Laidlaw for its illegal discharges of mercury into the North Tyger River in South

---

24. So far as the common law is concerned, there is no general way to challenge the polluter's actions save at the behest of the lower riparian—another human being—able to show an invasion of "his" rights." Stone, C. D. (1974). *Should trees have standing? toward legal rights for natural objects*. Palo Alto, CA: TIOGA Publishing Co. Original essay in *Southern California Law Review 45* (1972).

25. *Lujan, US Secretary of the Interior vs. Defenders of Wildlife*, 504 US 555 (1992).

26. "It goes beyond the limit and into pure speculation and fantasy to say that anyone who observes or works with endangered species anywhere in the world is appreciably harmed by a single project affecting some portion of that species with which he has no more specific connection." Id.

27. *Friends of the Earth v. Laidlaw Environmental Services*, 528 US 167 (2000).

Carolina. Like the DOW case, FOE did not have a direct property interest in the river. In the FOE case, the Supreme Court again applied the homocentric approach to environmental protection, stating that "the relevant showing for purposes of standing is not injury to the environment, but injury to the plaintiff." Nonetheless, the Court found that FOE established a protectible interest in the river and, thus, had standing to sue. One FOE member, who lived a half mile from the river, provided an affidavit that he could not make recreational use of the river as he would otherwise, due to its contamination. Other members living close to the Laidlaw facility and the river testified about their concerns for the health hazards that it posed to the community. Other members testified that their choice of residence was affected by the river's pollution and that the contamination had affected property values in the region. The Court held that those sworn statements were sufficient to show injury to protectible rights. The Court held that the discharges into the river "directly affected those members' recreational, aesthetic, and economic interests."[28] Although the Court did not disaffirm its holding in the DOW case—distinguishing those claims as "general averments" and "speculative some-day intentions"—the effect of the decision somewhat liberalized the interpretation of "standing" for purposes of private enforcement of the environmental laws.

## Beyond Compliance

Whether perceived through a homocentric or a biocentric view of the world, environmental ethics play a key role. Socially responsible management is essential both domestically and globally, even though globally there is little international law governing the effects of business on the environment. Each country makes its own rules, though national borders are imaginary with regard to pollution. The carbon emissions that fuel global warming, for instance, affect the whole of the planet. The Kyoto Protocol on Global Warming seeks to limit the release of greenhouse gases worldwide. Despite the fact that most of the developed world and many underdeveloped nations have ratified the treaty, the U.S. government has rejected its terms. And although U.S. companies are not legally required to comply with its terms, several major U.S.-based companies have voluntarily agreed to meet the standards of the Protocol.

The bottom-line returns on voluntary action toward sustainable development are mostly long-term. The measurable effects may take years. In an immediate sense, they return to shareholders an improved image of the company and an improved environment in which to live. In the longer term, many companies find that reducing their consumption of energy, eliminating or mitigating their production of waste, and operating with greater safeguards and controls result in cost savings that translate directly to the bottom line.

Examples of ways that companies have modified their views to environmental concerns include the following:

- The UPS fleet includes 1,800 alternative-fuel vehicles; FedEx plans to convert all of its trucks to hybrid electric-diesel engines.
- Nike has removed vinyl, which has been linked to cancer, from almost all of its footwear.
- Starbucks is buying more organic and shade-grown coffee, which minimizes disruption of rain forests; it is also buying more "fair-trade" coffee, which gives the owners of family farms an agreed-upon price for their harvest.
- Since the late 1980s, McDonald's has reduced waste by 300 million pounds a year and has been using recycled materials. The company offers incentives to its fish, beef, and potato suppliers to support sustainable practices. In 2003, the company became the first fast-food restaurant to commit to using refrigerants that do not contain freon or hydrofluorocarbons, which contribute to global warming.[29]

See the following feature for another example.

---

28. Id.
29. Gunther, M. (2003, June 9). Tree huggers, soy lovers, and profits. *FORTUNE* (all examples).

## The Precautionary Principle in Action – SC Johnson's Greenlist

SC Johnson is one of the world's largest manufacturers of household cleaning, home storage, air care, personal care, and insect control products. In an effort to "make measurable improvements in the company's ecological footprint," the company developed a process for classifying and screening the ingredients used in all of its products.[a]

The system the company developed, called the "Greenlist," screens and rates the environmental and human health impacts of all of the company's manufacturing ingredients and packaging. The rating system evaluates materials according to several criteria, including aquatic toxicity, biodegradability, and human toxicity. The classification of the ingredient under the EU Dangerous Substances Directive, which regulates the use of dangerous chemicals, is also considered. Substances are given a score based on the combined criteria. Ingredients that score highest are the safest. Those that score poorly are eliminated from or restricted in use while the company seeks safer alternatives. SC Johnson's Greenlist currently rates surfactants, solvents, propellants, insecticides, resins, and packaging. The company soon hopes to implement the program for fragrances and personal healthcare products.

When the Greenlist was established in 2001, the company set a goal to reduce its use of ingredients, aiming for an environmental impact of 8 percent over the following year. The company exceeded that goal by more than half. The company's senior management is strongly committed to the program, and employee compensation is directly influenced by the achievement of corporate environmental objectives. Further, the effects of the program extend beyond SC Johnson to its suppliers and business partners, who are also encouraged to produce more environmentally sustainable ingredients.

a. World Business Council for Sustainable Development (WBCSD). (2004, September 15). SC Johnson: easing our ecological footprint. Geneva. A full case study on the SC Johnson "Greenlist" is available at the WBCSD web site at http://www.wbscd.org.

Environmental law in the United States provides incentives for voluntary environmental responsibility. The establishment of a trading market for SO₂ allowances under the Clean Air Act is just one example of the government using incentives to promote cleaner technology. Similarly, the Pollution Prevention Act of 1990 provides matching funds to states (and the companies that do business with and in them) that use source reduction techniques for clean and efficient production. Other economic incentives for environmental responsibility are provided by the U.S. tax code through credits and expense deductions for research and development of cleaner or more environmentally sound technologies.[30]

Of course, the greatest economic incentives for environmentally responsible business come from informed consumers. If you build it clean and green, will they come? Will average consumers buy green products and services? There can be little doubt that guiding consumer choices toward greener products and socially responsible investing can steer huge chunks of the national economy in a sustainable direction."[31] Consumers as well as businesses and governments have a responsibility to show the way.

---

30. The fueling of the modern transportation society in which we live is one of the key sources of modern pollution. Two of the case studies in Part 3 examine efforts by companies to create a cleaner, greener product: ADM is involved in the development of alternative fuels and GM is involved in the development of alternative vehicles. Both of these business activities are encouraged with tax incentives that translate directly into bottom-line savings.

31. *State of the World 2002*, The Worldwatch Institute, Norton, New York 2003.

# Chapter 10

## Ethical Considerations in Multinational Operations

*"The second half of the 20th century has seen the growth of the importance of finance, the consolidation of wealth, and the emergence of the multinational corporation, which owes its allegiance to no government whatsoever and is completely immune to the needs of the society in which it flourishes."*
—Joseph Heller[1]

The means and ends of globalization and the global economy are primarily political questions: What are the obligations of rich nations to poor? How should "fair" trade be defined when the playing field slopes so unevenly? Is universal human freedom and democracy a precondition for an integrated global free market? The primary obligation for addressing those issues lies with international institutions and national governments operating multilaterally. Nonetheless, no one could deny the pivotal role multinational corporations (MNCs) play in the process—both directly, as the purveyor of development, and indirectly, as an influence on global economic policy and law. As but one institution, "international law" is an amorphous and uneven concept—varying widely among countries—as will be seen in this chapter.

The narrow focus of this chapter is the moral obligation of corporations operating in countries with little developed social regulation. The shareholder-centric model of corporate social responsibility, as espoused by Friedman, counsels that management should maximize profits within the limits of the law and ethical custom. The applicable "law" in multinational operations is the law of the host country in which the corporation is operating. Where the host country has yet to evolve a meaningful regulatory system—where legal protections do not yet address the health and safety of workers or consumers, discriminatory or compulsory labor conditions, environmental hazards, and similar issues of social welfare—the model leaves unanswered the question, What is the limit for profit maximizing? How low can you go? What are the moral limits, if any, to exploiting the lack of law in a developing country in the service of private profit making? Almost by definition, for the ethical operation of a corporation, managing "beyond compliance" is essential in developing countries.

Reasonable minds may disagree about whether business has an affirmative duty to proactively serve the public good in the host

---

1. Author of *Catch-22*. From an interview on the book that he gave to The Learning Channel (TLC) shortly before his death in December 1999.

country or a duty to operate in such a way as to contribute to the improvement of the lives of the citizens. The controversy is not much different in a global context than it is in a domestic context. Undisputed, however, is the business obligation to mind the negative injunction: to avoid doing harm to and in the host country, regardless of the limits or lack of them in law. It is from that premise that notions of *moral minimums,* an ethical floor for commercial operations, find their origin.

## The Relationship between the Corporation and the Stakeholders

"First World multinational corporations (MNCs) are both the hope of the Third World and the scourge of the Third World."[2]

There is little disagreement that MNCs represent the best chance and the most effective vehicle for development in underdeveloped nations. The resources available to investing MNCs far exceed those available within a country or from foreign aid, and they are available with no political purse strings attached. MNC investment in third world countries appears to be a win-win proposition—for the developing country and for the shareholders of the company undertaking development activities. Yet MNCs also pose some of the greatest threats to people and the environment in developing countries. Moreover, MNCs often encounter a double-edged sword of criticism for their activities. With respect to employment practices, providing jobs to needy third world citizens is criticized for dislocating American workers. Pay at less than a minimum or living wage, which may be a part of the draw to the host country, is criticized as "sweatshop" labor by those in the United States, while pay above the average host country wage is viewed as unfair by local competition. With respect to the choice of where to do business, MNCs seek to uphold their obligations to shareholders for prudent management and security of shareholders' investments by locating in countries with "stable" regimes; yet

they are often criticized for doing business in repressive countries with right-wing leadership that present less risk of political upheaval or government appropriation.[3]

### The Nature of MNCs

In simplest terms, MNCs are corporations with production facilities in more than one country. When a company decides to engage in transactions in the global marketplace, there are basically three ways to go about it:

- The company can manufacture at home and export goods abroad, an approach that is constrained by trade and tariff barriers and locational limitations.
- The company can license its technology or other intellectual property for production by foreign entities overseas, an approach that is risky at best given the spotty and poorly policed international protection of patents, copyrights, trademarks, and similar intellectual assets.
- The company can make a direct investment in the host country by buying or building a subsidiary.

Only the last option constitutes an MNC. The advantages of direct investment include not only the ability to protect proprietary technology and intellectual assets, but also favorable conditions for access to markets, transportation, lower costs of labor and materials, accommodation of protectionism in local markets, preferential tax environments, appeal to consumer preferences for home market goods, the ability to take advantage of economies of scale and more rationalized production, and favorable currency exchange rates.

MNCs account for more than one-quarter of all global production and more than one-half of all U.S. imports. Some MNCs enjoy annual sales that exceed the GNP of many countries (and not just underdeveloped countries). For example, Wal-Mart's annual revenues of $220 billion in 2002 exceeded the entire annual GDP

---

2. DeGeorge, R. (1986). *Ethics and the multinational enterprise.* Lanham, MD: University Press of America.
3. Id.

of Israel and Ireland combined. Thus, MNCs may be wealthier and more powerful that the host country.

The nationality of MNCs can be a murky and inconsistently resolved issue. Companies may be headquartered in one country, may be managed from another country, may count its majority shareholders from a different country, may maintain its production facilities and the bulk of its workforce in another country, and may house its research and development activities in yet another country. The question of nationality may arise for purposes of determining law applicable to the corporation as well as for the protections to be afforded to it. For example, U.S. law provides protection for "U.S. producers" under its antidumping laws. (*Dumping* involves a foreign company selling product either below the current price in the exporter's home market or selling below production cost. The United States may impose a duty on dumped goods equal to the difference between the price charged in the United States and the price charged in the exporter's market if harm is shown to have occurred to U.S. producers).

Two typewriter manufacturers, Smith Corona and Brother, each alleged unfair competition by the other and sought a remedy against the other under the U.S. antidumping laws. At the time of the complaint, Smith Corona was headquartered in the United States, its major stockholder was British, and its manufacturing operations were conducted primarily in Singapore. Brother maintained its corporate headquarters in Tokyo, where its major stockholders were also domiciled, but conducted the vast majority of its manufacturing operations in Tennessee. Both companies claimed to be entitled to protection under U.S. law. In that particular dispute, the tribunal held Brother to be entitled to relief on account of its production facilities in Tennessee. Soon thereafter, however, in a different case involving Smith Corona and another "foreign" company, the same tribunal ruled Smith Corona to be a U.S. producer entitled to relief.

There is some question about whether national trade protection is warranted in such a case. Where MNC ownership, operations, and activities are so widely diffused and globally connected, with the companies owing no national allegiance to any country except that which is most efficacious for its business at that point in time, national boundaries and national law seem artificial concepts to apply. From a practical perspective, the issue is often resolved on the basis of where the corporate operations are taxed (an issue unto itself, especially in the context of international transfer pricing and the ability of MNCs to manipulate profit reporting to take advantage of differential tax rates in various countries). There is some logic to that approach, insofar as tax payments are, at least in part, paid in exchange for the protection and security of governmental policies.

## Considerations in Investing Abroad as an MNC

A plethora of strategic considerations must be taken into account in determining whether, where, and how to invest and operate abroad. A partial list of some of those factors, as compiled by Harvard Business School Professor Constance Bagley, follows.

Added to those strategic business considerations are some overarching ethical considerations involving the host country's political and legal profile vis-à-vis its citizenry. Of prime concern is whether the host country abides by fundamentally accepted principles of human rights and whether the country abides by fair and conscientious labor and environmental standards. Where a host country regime operates under martial law, engages in religious prosecution, punishes political dissent, permits forced labor, or otherwise oppresses its population, the calculus for investment becomes morally muddied.

These ethical considerations generally mirror those of national trade policy. The political questions of whether to engage in trade with a country—whether to grant it preferred or even completely free trade status—hinge on a variety of factors. Among them are whether the foreign country is engaged in fair trading and whether it accepts and abides by fundamentally accepted principles of human rights and fair and conscientious labor and environmental standards. The human rights issue arose repeatedly in the decades of the 1980s and 1990s as Congress annually debated whether to grant an increasingly repressive regime in China the most favored nation trading status that would entitle it to preferential tariffs and duties. In the negotiations for the North American Free Trade Agreement (NAFTA), which sought to add Mexico to the existing free trade pact between the

United States and Canada, one of the main sticking points was Mexico's failure to enact and enforce labor and environmental standards in line with those otherwise prevailing in the North American region. Strange bedfellows consisting of U.S. and Canadian manufacturers, labor unions, and human rights and environmental advocates argued against Mexico's admission to the free trade zone. This alliance was brought about because of the unfair advantage gained by a company producing in a country with lax regulations, competing directly with those operating under regulatory limits; because of the likely migration of jobs to a country that lacks worker protections and sustainable wages; and because of the potential harm to the North American environment and beyond engendered by the lure of a business climate devoid of environmental protections.[4]

Even where no controversy exists over whether a country suffers oppressive or irresponsible policies, reasonable minds still differ on the proper response. Engage or ostracize? Is it more effective to enter a country and conduct business in and with an oppressive regime in the hope of producing change or progress by working within the system? Or is it more effective to boycott the regime, imposing economic punishment in the hope of leveraging a change in policy? A policy of engagement often enriches and perpetuates oppressive governments. However, a policy of boycott punishes both the local citizenry, which is deprived of goods and commercial opportunity, and U.S. companies hoping for a share of the market. The multilateral boycott of apartheid South Africa proved a successful inducement to political change in that country. A similar boycott of Cuba by the United States, now more than three decades old, has produced no such results.

The decision regarding whether to engage or divest presents corollary ethical issues of universality and consistency as well. Should the same standards for the decision apply—regardless of the size or power or resources of the country

---

## Thinking Internationally

### Market Conditions and Competition
- Product/service market fundamentals
- Distribution/operational realities
- Personnel and management
- Location
- Currency
- Competitors
- Achieving "local touch"

### Legal Mores of Foreign Country
- Rule of law
- Corruption
- Judicial integrity

### Substantive Foreign Law
- Exchange controls
- Import/export costs and controls
- Employment law
- Taxes, both foreign and domestic
- Securities
- Antitrust
- Formation, governance, and dissolution of foreign entity

### Sociopolitical and Economic Climate of Host Country
- Long-term economic stability
- Stable pro-market consensus
- Attitude toward foreign investors

Source: Bagley, C. (2002). *Managers and the legal environment: strategies for the 21st century* (4th ed). Mason, OH: South-Western, p. 439.

---

4. Ultimately, a side agreement to the trade pact was signed, providing for monitoring of labor and environmental standards in Mexico with a procedure for complaints. Enforcement authority of the tribunal was left essentially toothless, however. See the *North American Agreement on Labor Cooperation: Supplemental Agreement to the NAFTA.* (1993, September 14) and the *North American Agreement on Environmental Cooperation* (1993, September 10).

involved? China, which represents a potential multibillion-dollar market, is governed by a historically repressive regime that became even more iron-fisted after the 1989 uprising in Tiananmen Square. Although the issue was hotly debated in the halls of Congress throughout the 1980s and 1990s, China was, nevertheless, routinely granted preferential trade status year after year. Not so for Burma, a tiny country with a tiny market ruled by a military dictatorship under martial law. The United States imposed economic sanctions on Burma in 1996, prohibiting new investment in the country and most trading relations.[5]

Similar human rights issues were at stake in both countries, so why the difference in response?

There is also the question of the efficacy of unilateral action in U.S. trade policy. Where the United States stands alone in its decision to boycott or divest, the impact on the sanctioned economy is more limited; in addition, U.S. companies are placed at a particular competitive disadvantage. That was the case with Vietnam. As years passed after the Vietnam War, most industrialized nations gradually lifted their investment sanctions, permitting MNCs from their countries to get a foothold in the new Vietnamese economy in its nascent stages. By the time the United States lifted its ban (and it was among the last to do so), foreign competition had fairly secured its position in the Vietnamese market and U.S.-based competitors entered from a disadvantaged position.

Like those who craft foreign policy, MNCs undertake similar deliberations in deciding whether to engage or ostracize repressive or corrupt regimes. In most cases, major investment activities in an underdeveloped nation involve partnering in some capacity with the ruling government or an instrumentality of it. Many countries require local majority ownership; and especially for industries involved with natural resources, the government generally takes a large equity piece of the operations. The government's interest in the venture, at times, is the

main source of financial support for the regime. However, when the government is involved in repressive activities to further the business venture, the issue of corporate complicity in the repression arises. Even when the government is not a direct partner, the problem of doing business in the country without violating accepted international norms can be a challenge.

Like governmental foreign policymakers, MNCs face the ethical dimensions of universality and consistency. Can they craft a coherent transnational investment policy applicable to their investments everywhere? Should there be a difference in approach depending on the size or potential lucre represented by a given market? And what if MNCs stand alone among their competitors in choosing not to engage? What effect might that have on their ability to compete—indeed, even to remain in existence? That was the question Levi Strauss faced in deciding whether to engage with China. (The topic is explored in more detail in "Race to the Bell-Bottom," appearing later in this chapter.)

### Legal Obligations Owed by MNCs to Stakeholders

In general, there is very little international law. Traditional notions of sovereignty pose nearly insurmountable obstacles to forging universal governing rules and the authority to enforce them. There is virtually no international law governing the conduct or legal obligations of MNCs to stakeholders affected by the corporations' operations. MNCs operating abroad are subject to the laws and regulations of the host country only with respect to the way business is conducted there—home-country law does not travel outside the home country, and there are few uniform international standards that require compliance. The drawbacks to such a system for global operations are obvious: a regulatory cuckoo's nest for companies operating in many countries, all with different laws. Nonetheless, this piecemeal approach to stakeholder protection, entirely dependent on the laws and policies of the incumbent host govern-

---

5. See further discussion of this situation in the case study "Lying Down with Dogs...Getting Up with Lawsuits: Unocal and the Alien Tort Claims Act" in Part Three of this text.

## When In Beijing...

In 2001, AOL Time Warner planned to negotiate a joint venture in China to provide Internet services to the country. The provision of Internet services to the Chinese market presented the Chinese people with an exceptional opportunity for communication, education, and global socialization. The legal and logistical difficulties of doing business in China and the lack of existing infrastructure to support a "wired" country required the immense power and resources of an entity such as AOL Time Warner. The endeavor would be a mutually beneficial. China coveted the resources and know-how of AOL Time Warner as much as AOL Time Warner coveted the profits associated with such a vast market.

Nonetheless, engagement in China presents a classic case of the tensions and conflict that multinational companies face. The Chinese government does not abide by fundamentally accepted principles of human rights. It does not recognize the rights of freedom of speech and freedom of association, nor does it recognize any fundamental rights of privacy for its citizens.

*The Washington Post* reported that the company had drafted a memorandum for its executives in order to assist them with potential media questions about the venture.* One of the questions was "What would AOL do if the Chinese government demanded names, e-mails or other records relating to political dissidents?" The suggested corporate response was as follows: "It is our policy to abide by the laws of the countries in which we offer services . . . We will work closely with government officials and our partner in China to understand and comply with the regulations that govern online services in China."

In the article, Michael Lynton, president of AOL International, explained the response by pointing out that the company did place a value on privacy, but that "issues about privacy have to be looked at in a local context." He cited as examples AOL policies to respect local Australian sensibilities on pornography and German law on hate crime.

Critics point out that there is a big difference between, on the one hand, protecting populations and, on the other hand, turning over information about dissidents to an authoritarian government. The policy seems particularly troubling given that those "dissidents" would presumably be AOL's own customers. AOL Time Warner's decision to approach the issue of international engagement with a policy to "abide by the laws of the countries in which we offer services" could mean compliance with laws and regulations requiring AOL to share with the government the speech and expression of AOL users for purposes of punishment. The arrangement could effectively place the company in the position of serving as a conduit for governmental monitoring of its customers. The chilling effect on political expression and communication in such circumstances is total. There is also at least a hint of irony in that the twin media empires of AOL and Time Warner rest their very foundations on principles of free speech.

That scenario neatly illustrates the conflicting positions of engagement versus ostracism. Those who favor engagement with China argue that U.S. business operations in China, particularly those that serve to open communications with the rest of the world, will eventually have a democratizing effect, destabilizing the totalitarian regime. Others warn that such engagement, particularly in the context of the deprivation of human rights, amounts to complicity with the repressive practices of the regime and may serve to perpetuate it. An article in *The Washington Post* cited a recent study of China and Cuba conducted by two fellows at the Carnegie Endowment for International Peace that concluded, "far from hastening its own demise by allowing the Internet to penetrate its borders, an authoritarian state

---

**When In Beijing... (continued)**

can turn the technology to its advantage, using it to spy on its own people, uncover political opponents and spread propaganda."

*Mufson, S., & Pomfret, J. (2001, August 29). You've got dissidents? *Washington Post*.

---

ment, also provides ample opportunity to exploit for profit the lack of regulation and the lack of meaningful social and political institutions in developing countries.

*Sovereignty* means "supreme or preeminent power and authority." *National sovereignty* refers to the authority of each country to conduct its own affairs—political, legal, social, and economic—without interference by the government or laws of any other country. Countries and their governments submit to no higher authority than their own laws unless they explicitly consent to do so by signing a treaty or pact with other countries. Only by the voluntary consent of sovereign nations is international law made. Only countries that sign such agreements can be bound to their terms. And the conceded authority over those signatory countries is limited to the terms of the four corners of the agreement; only what the country specifically agrees to and cedes authority for is given preeminence over national law.

The situation is comparable to the legal structure underlying the system of Federalism in the United States. At the time the United States was founded, it consisted of a collection of sovereign states, each with its own laws and policies and self-determination. In forming the Union, each of the states agreed to voluntarily relinquish supreme authority for certain issues to the centralized federal government. The matters given over to national authority consisted primarily of entrusting to it the protection and preservation of the most fundamental rights of the citizens—life, liberty, security, due process, free speech and expression, equality, and protection of the common good—and the authority to develop and maintain a federal government. The Tenth Amendment makes

clear that this delegation of sovereignty is a limited one and that the consent of the states to submit to federal authority extends only as far as explicitly stated in the Constitution. "The powers not delegated to the United States by the Constitution, nor prohibited by it to the States, shall be reserved to the States respectively, or to the people." Authority over matters not ceded to the federal government remains the province of the sovereign state, to address as it sees fit without interference. For two centuries, American jurisprudence has sought to delineate the boundaries between federal authority and states' rights.

A modern example of the process of codifying international law may be seen in the development of the European Union (EU). The sovereign nations of Europe agreed to cede authority over certain matters to a higher central authority, the EU. They are still sovereign nations with the right to enact and enforce national law and conduct their affairs as they see fit. However, the authority of their national law on matters covered by EU law is preempted and submits to the higher authority of the multilateral organization.

Traditional notions of national sovereignty as the foundation for international law date back to at least the Treaty of Westphalia of 1648, signed at the end of the Thirty Years War. In the ensuing centuries, two doctrines in international law have evolved to reinforce the concept: the Doctrine of Sovereign Immunity and the Act of State Doctrine.

The Doctrine of Sovereign Immunity protects foreign governments from the imposition of another's laws upon it. The doctrine recognizes that each country is entitled to exclusive jurisdiction over its internal laws, operations, and people and provides that no country or government shall be subject to the jurisdiction of another country's laws or legal system unless it first consents to such jurisdiction.

While there may be some political logic to that doctrine, it can present a problem for MNCs conducting operations in underdeveloped countries. Invariably, most instances of major commercial development in third world countries—especially in the context of natural resource use, exploration, or extraction—involve private corporations partnering with the host government or government-owned companies to undertake such projects. The government partner's share of revenues generated from the joint enterprise is then used to fund governmental prerogatives—in the best case, to raise the standard of living for its citizens; in the worst case, to line the pockets of corrupt officials. Either way, private corporations contract with the government in order to do business there. However, because of the Doctrine of Sovereign Immunity, private corporations have little legal recourse against governmental partners in the case of a dispute in the arrangement or in the case of a deal going sour. One generally cannot haul a foreign government into court and sue it—the Doctrine of Sovereign Immunity prohibits that. Unless the contracting parties have secured the consent of the foreign government to suit, there are few avenues for redress. In 1976, the United States enacted the Foreign Sovereign Immunities Act (FSIA), which provides for some limited exceptions to protection under the doctrine. Noteworthy among them is the "commercial activity" exception, which denies immunity to a sovereign nation with respect to its commercial transactions. Unlike acts of state, *acts of commerce by the state*—such as sales of goods, loans, employment contracts, service contracts, and similar commercial activities—are not given sovereign protection. Interpretations of this exception have been very narrowly construed, and it remains very difficult to bring suit and enforce judgments against foreign nations.[6]

The Act of State Doctrine provides that the actions of foreign governments are to be respected by other nations, regardless of their illegality under home country law. The Act of State defense is often invoked in cases of expropriation, where the foreign government has confiscated privately owned property without compensation. Most often, such expropriation is viewed as beyond the jurisdiction of home country courts. There is, however, a commercial activities exception to the Act of State Doctrine that functions in the same fashion as the commercial exception in the FSIA.[7]

These long-standing principles of sovereignty are what make it so difficult to establish international law. There is no consistent or uniform standard for legal behavior save that which nations have agreed to bind themselves to. Often those take the form of conventions, pacts, treaties, and other forms of agreement. Among the few that exist, those that purport to govern corporate behavior are scant. In the absence of signing a formal international agreement among nations, a very difficult endeavor for even the best-intentioned negotiators, governments may resort to synchronized home country legislative enactments to effectuate the intent of international accord on a legal principle. This collaborative national approach was the means ultimately resorted to by the Organization for Economic Cooperation and Development (OECD) to implement an agreement among the most industrialized nations in the world to prohibit foreign bribery once and for all.

The free market model operates properly only when grounded upon certain fundamental moral assumptions about fairness and honesty and consistency of custom and trade practices. Global commerce requires the same basic assumptions and rules of play. In the absence of universal transnational law, voluntary membership organizations such as the OECD propound uniform rules and guidelines. The directives are voluntary; nonetheless, they are viewed as the standard-bearer and often are adopted by mem-

---

6. See, for example, *Argentine Republic v. Amerada Hess Shipping Co.*, 488 U.S. 428 (1989). (Sovereign nations are immune from suit in the United States, even in cases of clear violations of international law.)

7. See, for example, *Riedel v. Bancam*, 792 F.2d 587 (6th Cir. 1986). For certain types of international investments, corporations may seek to insure against expropriation through the Overseas Private Investment Corporation (OPIC).

ber nations as a part of home country law.[8]

The OECD has been called a think tank, a rich man's club, and a nonacademic university. The OECD is a club of like-minded countries. And it is rich in that the nearly 40 countries now counted as members produce more than two-thirds of the world's goods and services. The club is not exclusive, however; membership is open to any country that can prove commitment to a market economy and pluralistic democracy. The OECD works toward identifying and defining issues in global commerce and developing approaches to them. It has developed model legislation that includes establishing codes for free flow of capital and services, prohibiting foreign bribery, and ending subsidies for shipbuilding. It is one of the few international organizations to put forth guidelines for the conduct of MNCs (actually two sets of guidelines in the past three decades, both of which are discussed in more detail below). The OECD budget is financed by the member countries. The annual contribution of each member country is calculated according to the weight of its economy.

As discussed in the Lockheed Bribery Case in Chapter Two, in 1977, the United States enacted the Foreign Corrupt Practices Act, which prohibited corporate payments to foreign governments or officials for the purpose of influencing decisions affecting their business. In 1977, the United States stood almost alone among nations in imposing such a ban. Many industrialized nations not only still condoned such payments, but also permitted a tax write-off for them.[9] U.S. corporations complained that the law put them at an unfair competitive disadvantage. Acknowledging the validity of those complaints, for the next 20 years, U.S. representatives in the OECD lobbied their member nations relentlessly for a binding agreement to ban such practices. Finally, in 1997, representatives of all of the member nations (then numbering about 30) agreed unanimously to the ban. However, if the accord was to be codified as

an international agreement, ratification in each of the members' respective home countries could take decades. Each of the respective legislatures had the ability to alter and amend, and every alteration and amendment required a return to the OECD for agreement by the other member nations. Of course, each member nation approached the matter of ratification with an overarching reluctance to cede sovereignty on any issue to a higher authority. Mindful of those problems, the OECD took a two-pronged approach to implementation: First, a (voluntary and unenforceable) pact was signed by all of the member nations, agreeing in principle to the ban on foreign bribery and the elimination of any tax deduction for bribes paid. Each country signing the pact also agreed to use its best efforts to pass national (home country) legislation to effectuate such a ban as quickly as possible. The second prong of the approach required the passage of national legislation in each of the member nations to implement such a ban. (This is the approach taken by the FCPA in the United States as well: U.S. MNCs are prohibited from foreign bribery through the U.S. securities laws.) As of 2000, all member nations were in compliance with the pact, each having enacted a national law prohibiting foreign bribery by MNCs based in their country. In that way, an international ban on foreign bribery was effectuated, albeit, not as international law.

Whether national sovereignty deserves the reverence and sanctity it has traditionally been accorded is a matter of some controversy. Should governments led by tyrants and self-enriching dictators be afforded the same legal rights and international respect as those ruled by democratic processes? Should a government in power by military junta or bloody *coup d'etat* be granted the same legitimacy and legal protection as those who take office by democratic processes? Does the mere fact of being in charge give to a government sovereign power to abuse and oppress its citizens or to pollute the coun-

---

8. In similar fashion, voluntary membership organizations made up of the corporate members of a particular industry or others groups of businesses may develop transnational codes of conduct and rules of engagement, which member companies then adopt as their own through the corporate governance process.

9. For several European nations, the tax deductibility of foreign bribes lasted well into the 1990s.

try's environment for the generations to come? Moreover, the doctrine seems particularly inapposite for borderless issues such as environmental threats, which pay no respect to arbitrary lines drawn on geopolitical maps.

A critical eye toward national sovereignty in the context of international law may be appropriate; nonetheless, this firmly entrenched and long-standing principle is not likely to be altered in the foreseeable future. Because of that fact, it is quite unlikely that any form of Federalist-style world government that makes and enforces universal rules of global behavior will emerge. The current composition of world powers and concentrations of wealth and resources make it unlikely that those with mighty armies and full treasuries would willingly cede power to a higher authority except where it is clearly in their self-interest.

As such, the whole of socially responsible corporate activity in a global context lies in the ethics of the organization and its willingness to abide by moral minimums of business behavior, regardless of the requirements of law. National industries, individual businesses, and assorted coalitions of industry and business groups motivated for one reason or another to operate in a socially responsible way are left with voluntary guidelines, model transnational codes of conduct, and basic deontological principles to direct their activities in underdeveloped countries—with no legal accountability for compliance or disregard.

The next section of this chapter explores these theories of moral minimums for multinational enterprises (MNEs) and the practical implications of abiding by them.

## Ethical Obligations of MNCs to Their Stakeholders

### A Preliminary Note on Relativism

Like differences in language, differences in cultural norms create barriers to understanding and obstacles to successful commercial engagement. When doing business abroad, business management must recognize and respect cultural differences and conduct operations in context. The simplistic formulation is "When in Rome, do as the Romans . . ." In practice, however, reconciling cultural differences proves a bit more complicated than jumping on a Vespa and waving "Ciao."

A *culture* may be defined as "a set of beliefs that develops from shared history, custom, environment, religion, education, language, available resources, and other common experience." It is not necessarily bounded geographically, nor is it determined or defined by any incumbent ruling government. Cultural relativism posits that no one set of beliefs or culture should take precedence over another; that there is no right and wrong with regard to cultural issues; and that everyone has an obligation to respect local traditions and customs, even if a person doesn't embrace them. To impose one's own belief system on another amounts to *cultural imperialism.* Respect for local traditions may mean that McDonald's does not serve beef at its restaurants in India, where cows are considered sacred; that Muslim women be permitted to wear traditional head scarves in lieu of uniform caps; and that businesses close during certain holy days/holidays. The list goes on. Awareness, accommodation, and assimilation of cultural norms form a cornerstone for successful and socially responsible multinational operations.

Some take cultural relativism a step further and assert that because of cultural relativism, there can be no universal ethical principles—there can be no universal anything; it's all relative. Whatever the culture says is moral is moral for that culture, and there can be no true moral right and wrong. The problem with that argument is the leap from cultural relativism to ethical relativism without adequate support. Accepting that different cultural beliefs and norms are justified and that different cultural beliefs lead to different moral practices does not necessarily lead to the conclusion that all moral practices are justified. The fundamental premise of ethics is that there are some universal, unanimously agreeable principles by which all humans should abide as rational beings. For some people, to deny that there are basic right and wrongs—universally praised or condemned and, in fact, necessary for the perpetuation of civilization—would be to deny their very

## Lost in Translation

The name *Coca-Cola* was first rendered in China as *Ke-kou-ke-la*. Unfortunately, the Coke company did not discover until after thousands of signs had been printed that the phrase means "bite the wax tadpole" or "female horse stuffed with wax," depending on the dialect. Coke then researched 40,000 Chinese characters and found a close phonetic equivalent in *ko-kou-ko-le,* which loosely translated means "happiness in the mouth."

In Taiwan, the translation of the Pepsi slogan "come alive with the Pepsi generation" came out as "Pepsi will bring your ancestors back from the dead."

Also in Chinese, the Kentucky Fried Chicken slogan "finger-lickin' good" came out as "eat your fingers off."

The American slogan for Salem cigarettes "Salem—Feeling Free" translated in the Japanese market as "When you smoke Salem, you feel so refreshed that your mind seems empty."

When GM introduced the Chevy Nova in South America, it was apparently unaware that *no va* means "it won't go" in Spanish. It later changed the name in South America to the *Caribe.*

Ford had a similar problem in Brazil where the Brazilian term *pinto* was slang for "tiny male genitals." Ford substituted all Pinto nameplates with *Corcel,* which means "horse."

When Parker Pen marketed the ballpoint in Mexico, its ads were supposed to say "it won't leak in your pocket and embarrass you." Unaware that the Spanish word *embarazar* did not mean "embarrass," the company instead got "it won't leak in your pocket and make you pregnant."

A Miami T-shirt maker printed shirts for the Pope's visit to Mexico. Instead of "I saw the Pope," the translation read "I saw the Potato."

Chicken man Frank Perdue's slogan "It takes a tough man to make a tender chicken" was likewise mangled in its Spanish translation. A picture of Frank with one of his birds appeared on billboards all over Mexico with the caption "It takes a hard man to make a chicken aroused."

Colgate introduced a toothpaste in France called *Cue,* the name of a notorious porno magazine.

In Italy, a campaign for Schweppes Tonic Water translated into Schweppes Toilet Water.

Hunt-Wesson introduced its Big John products in French Canada as *Gros Jos,* which in slang translated to "big breasts." Interestingly, the translation problem did not seem to have a detrimental effect on sales.

Source: Anonymously circulated on the Internet.

humanity and that which distinguishes them from mere instinctual animals.

Genocide is a good example of a universal moral imperative. A country engaged in genocide is universally condemned. There are no "cultural" traditions of genocide; if there were, the culture wouldn't exist for long. Further, even those engaged in genocide deny their activities. Tyrannical dictators do not justify mass murder on grounds of custom and belief, nor do they defend such actions on the ground of utility. Instead, they hide the mass graves of dissidents and deny all knowledge when the graves are discovered. There is no moral relativity about genocide. The same can be said of slavery and torture—universally condemned, yet still practiced in many parts of the world. Those activities cannot be justified on cultural grounds; no group would willingly embrace such treatment. Thus, they are unambiguously considered immoral. The legal term for such acts is the Latin *mala in se,* "bad in and of itself."

There are, in fact, some fundamental moral values that cut across all cultures. Returning to the earlier definition of ethics from John Rawls—"...a conception of the person, the relations among persons, and the general ends and goals of social cooperation"—ethics and morality play a large role in making social cooperation possible, a necessity for a functioning society. In his book *The Elements of Moral Philosophy*, James Rachels posits that certain moral values must be universal; otherwise, society would cease to exist. The forms that they take and the exceptions that are made to them may differ in some respects, but the basic precepts are accepted by all. The point is illustrated with examples of three universal moral values embraced in some form by all groups: care for their young, the presumption of truth telling, and the prohibition of murder. Without those moral values, Rachels argues, a society could not long exist. Human infants cannot care for themselves and without care will perish, ultimately decimating the group. Without a presumption of honesty, communication is meaningless; without trust, mutual exchange is impossible. The ability to kill one another at will eliminates all notion of security and undermines the very reason that humans band together in societies and form governments to begin with. Different cultures may recognize different exceptions to the rule—human infanticide may be an accepted practice of last resort in a group without enough resources to feed and shelter all of its members; murder may be justified in cases of self-defense or when conducted by the state as capital punishment. Nonetheless, the basic moral value is universally embraced. As Rachel puts it:

> There are some moral rules that all societies will have in common, because those rules are necessary for society to exist. The rules against lying and murder are two examples. And in fact we do find these rules in force in all viable cultures. Cultures may differ in what they regard as legitimate exceptions to the rules, but

this disagreement exists against a background of agreement on the larger issues. Therefore, it is a mistake to overestimate the amount of difference between cultures. Not every moral rule can vary from society to society.[10]

The quest for ethics is to determine what those universal moral norms look like, what activities can be considered *mala in se*, what moral minimums of behavior are necessary for the progress of humanity. For companies operating in the global economy, the task is to discern and abide by that moral floor beyond which profits may not ethically be pursued.

Various approaches to defining the moral minimums are discussed in the following section. Without a doubt, however, the precept that all humans are born free and equal, regardless of race, creed, color, national origin, or sex, is universally accepted as a human right.

### Establishing Moral Minimums for Behavior

Virtually all theories and conceptions of moral minimums and the codes developed to implement them proceed from the deontological tradition of ethics. The fundamental premises of deontology set the framework for evaluating how low one can morally go. The Kantian categorical imperative sets forth these premises:

> Human beings are to be treated as an end in themselves, not as a means.
> All human beings are born equal in their freedom and rationality.

From this, the Kantian "Golden Rule" was derived: Ethical action is that which you would want to be a universal action in response to the situation in a world in which you'd want to live. Deontology embraces first the primacy of the person. Human security and freedom are the highest obligations owed in the society. Everything else proceeds from those values. This approach recognizes the ultimate sovereignty of human beings—above national rights and interests. And since the state derives its very legiti-

---

10. Rachels, J. (1998). *The elements of moral philosophy.* New York: McGraw-Hill.

### Missing Links at Mitsubishi Motors

Mitsubishi Motors, a large multinational automobile manufacturer, operated a plant outside of Chicago, with a notorious reputation for the mistreatment of female workers. Even after the filing of two major sexual harassment cases against Mitsubishi in 1996 (one by 29 female employees on its assembly line and the other by the EEOC), management maintained an openly belligerent and hostile approach to the charges. The company not only blatantly denied that anything illegal had occurred, but also mounted a public relations campaign against the plaintiff women and the EEOC that would ultimately blow up in its face. Many suspect that this reaction to the charges was due to the cultural values of the company's Japanese leadership. Cases actually filed by the EEOC are a rare occurrence and are usually a step the agency takes when the allegations are supported with strong corroborative evidence. Few American companies would respond to its charges with such public defiance.

Two weeks after the EEOC filed its lawsuit, Mitsubishi organized and funded a demonstration by nearly 3,000 of its employees in front of the EEOC's regional office in Chicago (at a cost to Mitsubishi of $35,000 for bus transportation and $15,000 for lunch for the demonstrators). The demonstration was orchestrated by Mitsubishi's *American* chief counsel. Employees who participated were paid for a day's work; those who did not take part were required to report for work or lose a day's pay. (Those who reported spent the day cleaning the plant.) Employees were encouraged to fill company billboards and newsletters with hostile reproaches to the charges and the employees making them, and the company refused even to reproach those found to be the most egregious offenders of the law.

Mitsubishi had been aware of complaints of sexual harassment on the assembly line for at least four years before the EEOC suit was filed. (Four separate grievances had been filed with the EEOC by female employees in 1992). And before that time, complaints had been lodged with Mitsubishi management in-house. After a four-year investigation, the EEOC turned up evidence of sexual harassment of 300 female employees (of the 800 employed by the company) by 400 different male employees (out of 3,200)—clearly a "pattern or practice" of discrimination under Title VII, exhibiting endemic, widespread discrimination and entitling the victims to a class action suit and potentially punitive damages.

The nature of the discrimination?

- As a part of Mitsubishi's training program, managers were sent to training in Japan and visited "audience participation" sex bars at which the Japanese hosts and American trainees participated in sex acts with prostitutes on stage.
- Women being instructed by Mitsubishi management on Japanese culture were told that they would not be welcome in the plant, that any direct eye contact they made with their Japanese managers or counterparts would be regarded as flirtation, and that the women could expect conditions of work that were considerably less favorable than those of their male counterparts.
- There was a "sexualized environment" on the assembly line—sexual graffiti was affixed to cars as they moved down the line; women were openly referred to as "bitch," "whore," and "cunt"; and male employees regularly exposed themselves to the female workers (one incident taking place in front of the plant's employee relations officer, who was inquiring into an alleged incident!).
- Male employees and managers came to the plant with pornographic pictures depicting Japanese executives and American managers and employees engaged in sex acts with prostitutes at sex parties organized by company management on company time

---

**Missing Links at Mitsubishi Motors (continued)**

(defended by one manager as being no different than guys coming back from a hunting trip and showing pictures of slain deer).

- Women at the plant were subjected to both physical and verbal attacks, unwanted touching and rubbing, threatening phone calls, assaults in cars, and other lewd behavior.

Women who complained were threatened with the loss of their jobs, and many were put into physical danger at the plant through intentional and malicious meddling with safety devices designed to protect them while working. The plant had no meaningful complaint system, and the women were forced to first take a complaint to their immediate supervisor (many of whom had taken part in the offensive activities). The employee relations department did nothing with the grievances it received, and not one of the dozens and dozens of complaints of harassment that were made ever resulted in any disciplinary action except against the employee who made the complaint. Occasionally, employee relations would require a harasser to view a half-hour video on the issue. The video was a joke, and the fact of having been ordered to see it was worn like a badge of courage among the male plant workers.

After two years of litigation—and a public relations disaster when the facts of the situation began to be revealed—Mitsubishi finally settled with the EEOC in 1998 for $34 million (nearly four times the previous record settlement by the EEOC). Further, Mitsubishi agreed to allow a panel of three independent monitors to observe its workplace for three years to ensure no retaliation and no further harassment problems. Moreover, the EEOC will determine how the damage award will be divided among the women; Mitsubishi will have no say in the decision.

Perhaps the most astounding feature of this case is the Neanderthalian-like position taken by Mitsubishi management in fighting it in the face of overwhelming evidence, in the post-Anita Hill/Clarence Thomas, and in the post-Tailhook era. Did they just not understand? Is it possible to view this as a reasoned strategy for the company? Can there be a cultural explanation or justification for the maintenance and defense of such a workplace by a modern MNC?

For a detailed study of Mitsubishi's legal battle and its attempts to correct the problem in its workplace, see Sharp Paine, L., & Coxe, D. O. *Mitsubishi Motor Manufacturing of America: the quest for a model workplace.* Harvard Business School Publications, No. 9-398-028 (1998).

---

macy from the consent of the sovereign citizenry, from its members' willingness to cede their inherent authority over to that national government, this seems appropriate.

The teleological tradition of ethics—utilitarianism and/or cost-benefit analysis—has a place in the reasoning and decision making of MNCs trying to discern the ethical path, but only after moral minimums have been satisfied. With that moral floor laid, one may proceed to other eth-

ical and strategic considerations. Consequentialist ethics are always open to criticism for injustice to the few. But for the two issues at the heart of moral minimums in international law—human rights and environmental responsibility—cost-benefit analysis falls especially short. While everyone may have his or her price, not everyone has a fair market value.

Steven Kelman made the argument convincingly in his still widely read and cited essay

---

### U.S. Companies Promote Gender Apartheid in Saudi Arabia

McDonald's, Kentucky Fried Chicken, and Burger King all promote sex discrimination in Saudi Arabia as the restaurants "all have two designated areas: one for families and the other for singles, all males," said Ann Rozenich, an employee of McDonald's in the communications office. "The restaurants also have two separate entrances."

In a letter written to *Washington Post* columnist Colbert I. King, an American official just having returned from Riyadh, Saudi Arabia, also cited Pizza Hut and Starbucks as two other U.S. companies that have segregated dining areas. The official said, "The men's sections are typically lavish, comfortable and up to Western standards, whereas the women's or families' sections are often run-down, neglected, and, in the case of Starbucks, have no seats. Worse, these firms will bar entrance to Western women who show up without their husbands." The official also suggested that this segregation and discrimination may not be an enforced law, as Dunkin' Donuts did not have sex-segregated eating areas.

King compared U.S. companies' policies in Saudi Arabia to apartheid in South Africa. But he cited that many U.S. companies, following the lead of Leon Sullivan of General Motors, resisted implementing apartheid in the workplace and eventually used their influence to help eradicate apartheid altogether. So far, most U.S. companies in Saudi Arabia have shown no inclination to challenge sex discrimination there. According to Rozenich, McDonald's has to respect Saudi customs. King forces people to ask the question, Would McDonald's respect Saudi customs if the discrimination were against blacks or any other group? Would Americans tolerate McDonald's (or any other U.S. company) if it did?

Source: http://www.feminist.org/news/newsbyte/uswirestory, January 15, 2002.

---

"Cost-Benefit Analysis: An Ethical Critique."[11] Kelman's position is that accurate and effective cost-benefit analysis requires that all components and factors be weighed on a common scale or denominator and that for some "goods," such as human life and clean air, there really isn't a market valuation comparable to that of the other inputs of the equation (for example, the cost of labor, materials, environmental precautions, profits, and similar cost-measurable items). Some goods cannot be assigned a dollar value in benefit or cost. Some goods are priceless. And in those cases where true cost-benefit comparison cannot take place, it shouldn't.

### The Universal Declaration of Human Rights (UDHR)

The Universal Declaration of Human Rights (UDHR), reproduced at the end of this chapter, is probably *the* primary source for discerning the moral minimums accepted by modern civilization. The Declaration was approved unanimously by all members of the UN in 1948, amid much controversy and after much negotiation to arrive at universally agreed terms. The Declaration does not have the force of international law; nonetheless, given the unanimous and universal accord with its provisions, it serves as the standard bearer for global morality—delineat-

---

11. Kelman, S. Cost benefit analysis: an ethical critique. (1981). Included in numerous anthologies of business ethics studies and reproduced in full in Birsch, J., & Fielder, J. (1994). *The Ford Pinto case: a study in applied ethics, business, and technology.* Albany, NY: State University of New York Press.

ing the basic rights of people everywhere in the world and the obligations of individuals, institutions, and governments not to impinge on those rights. International conventions to codify the principles of the UDHR into international law have been signed by many member nations since the 1960s. The International Covenant on Civil and Political Rights and the International Covenant on Economic, Social and Cultural Rights are two such covenants, which, when ratified by signatory countries, give legal force to those provisions of the UDHR recognizing civil, political, economic, social, and cultural human rights. Promulgated for adoption in 1966, by 1976, the conventions had sufficient member-nation support through ratification to take legal effect. The glaring exception was the United States. Unlike the rest of the developed world (and much of the underdeveloped world) the United States did not ratify the Covenant on Civil and Political Rights until 1992 and has yet to ratify the Covenant on Economic, Social and Cultural Rights.[12]

Motivated by the horrors of the Second World War, the Declaration enumerates the basic, fundamental dignities that may be expected by every living human being regardless of where they were born; to whom they were born; or what their color, sex, culture, or religion is.[13]

The UDHR is structured as an international bill of rights in much the same fashion as national counterparts such as the 1689 British Bill of Rights, the 1776 American Declaration of Independence and Constitution, and the 1789 French Declaration of the Rights of Man and Citizen. It proceeds from the same deontological Enlightenment perspective that spawned those political documents, but it provides for significantly more in terms of social and economic human values. Like the U.S. Bill of Rights, the UDHR provides for equal protection under law, freedom from slavery, freedom from discrimination, rights of due process, rights of free speech and expression, rights to vote, and rights to own property. Yet the UDHR further recognizes a fundamental right to work, a right to equal pay, a right to unionize, a right to social security, a right to subsistence health and living standards, a right to free public education, and several other guarantees for a dignified quality of human life that are absent from the bills of rights of most sovereign nations.

Nations' noncompliance with the UDHR is not punishable—the Declaration alone has no enforcement mechanism, and principles of sovereign immunity would preclude such actions anyway. Yet the document serves as a benchmark reflecting the consensus, indeed unanimous, view of human rights in the late twentieth and early twenty-first century. In its half-century existence it has gained enough authority to be considered reflective of "international norms," a stature sufficient for some legal actions against individual actors or institutions (but not governments) that violate its terms.[14]

### The Moral Minimum for MNCs

Various theories about the morally minimum behavior required of MNCs have evolved from those basic theories and precepts of human rights. Virtually all such theories require a respect for human rights, regardless of the position of the host country government on the issue; and all recognize the fundamental moral negative injunction against causing harm and requiring compensation for harm caused.[15] Beyond those two moral imperatives, ethical theorists examine and posit various other maxims and measures for

---

12. The United States ratified the Covenant on Civil and Political Rights with several reservations attached to ensure that it could have no effect domestically. Glendon, M. A. (2001). *A world made new: Eleanor Roosevelt and the Universal Declaration of Human Rights.* New York: Random House, p. 213. See note below.

13. An excellent book on the history of the UDHR is Glendon, M. A. (2001). *A world made new: Eleanor Roosevelt and the Universal Declaration of Human Rights.* New York: Random House.

14. The legal status of the UDHR and legal claims citing it are discussed in more detail in the case study "Lying Down with Dogs... Getting Up with Lawsuits: Unocal and the Alien Tort Claims Act" in Part Three of this text.

15. Norman Bowie points out that this obligation is no different for MNCs than for domestic companies, given that the value of the health and safety of stakeholders does not differ by nationality. "The common fundamental principle is that we cannot impose avoidable harm on an innocent third party." Bowie, N. The moral obligations of multinational corporations. In Dienhart, J. (2000). *Business, institutions, and ethics.* Oxford University Press.

morally minimum behavior. The ideas of two such scholars are presented here.

*DeGeorge.* Richard DeGeorge places great faith in MNCs in the global marketplace, but recognizes that such a large role produces equally weighty responsibilities.[16]

> Multinationals are presently the most effective vehicle available for the development of the Third World. At the same time, critics complain that the MNCs are destroying the local cultures and substituting for them the tinsel of American life and the worst aspects of its culture.

According to DeGeorge, acceptance of cultural relativism and a heightened sensitivity to local custom will be required of MNCs if they are to accomplish this global task successfully. As well, this pivotal economic role comes with an obligation to abide by moral minimums. The charge for management of an MNC is to separate what is morally mandatory behavior from what is merely not "our way." It is a falsity to equate U.S. standards with moral minimums, according to DeGeorge. Unlike developing nations, the United States has highly developed sociopolitical, legal, and economic background institutions and a meaningful regulatory edifice—but not every OSHA regulation or FDA standard is "morally mandatory." Further, to impose such an obligation of identical treatment between domestic and third world production would eliminate the cost-saving motivation for locating there, an inducement that developing countries desperately need to barter with.

DeGeorge's moral minimums for MNC behavior are as follows:

> *Do no intentional harm*—The obligation not to cause avoidable harm is not peculiar to MNCs, but applies universally to anyone on the planet.
>
> *Produce more good than bad for the host*

*country*—This is a sort of utilitarian moral minimum; and as will all utilitarian ethics, the question remains, What is "good"? DeGeorge says, in general, that "more good will be done by helping those in need, rather than by helping those in less need at the expense of those in greater need." This moral minimum generally requires the host country to be more helped than harmed and that it not be exploited for the benefit of the home country.

> *MNC activity should contribute to development of host country*—Contributing to the progress and development of the country will help to counter any charge of exploitation.
>
> *Respect human rights of employees*—This moral minimum applies regardless of whether host law requires it and whether local companies do or do not; and it includes matters of discrimination, worker safety, and personal security.
>
> *Pay fair share of taxes*—This moral minimum refers to the ability of MNCs, due to the lack of transparency and national inconsistencies of the financial reporting laws, to manipulate tax payments among the various countries in which it conducts business. Developing countries, with limited resources for forensic accounting, often end up receiving far less than their fair share of an MNC's taxes.
>
> *Respect the local culture to extent it does not violate moral norms*—MNCs have an obligation to accommodate and assimilate local customs and traditions, but only to the extent that those practices do not violate moral minimums. For MNCs from socially developed countries, the onus is even weightier. DeGeorge has said, "An American multinational must respect the ethical norms and values of the home company wherever the company is located. It

---

16. DeGeorge, R. (1986). Ethical dilemmas for multinational enterprise: a philosophical overview. In *Ethics and multinational enterprise*. Lanham, MD: University Press of America.

must, of course, take into account local laws, traditions, and so on. But it cannot hire child labor, even if that is the local custom; nor can it discriminate against women, or follow apartheid laws, or buy goods made with slave labor, or fail to provide safe working conditions. The list goes on."[17] This distinction for DeGeorge puts a higher onus on MNCs from highly developed countries. Unlike local businesses, MNCs have a choice about whether to do business in a foreign country. If they opt to engage, "because of their powerful position, they have the obligation to help bring ethical practices into the marketplace and to help make the market fair."[18]

*Cooperate with the host government to develop and enforce just institutions*—DeGeorge argues that the underdeveloped world presents special moral problems because of the lack of just legal and social institutions in the host society—meaningful laws and judiciary and civil police, dependable banking and commercial systems, health and welfare initiatives, labor unions, and a tax structure that redistributes wealth to the neediest. He says that in the long term, MNCs have more to gain than lose by helping to implement such institutions, resulting in a more secure, stable, and predictable environment in which to conduct its business. The benefits of exploiting the lack of such institutions are both short-term and shortsighted. DeGeorge further suggests that MNCs likewise have more to gain than lose by propounding and supporting voluntary codes of conduct in the absence of regulation by just institutions.

While recognizing that the primary responsibility for ensuring the welfare of its citizenry lies with the host government, DeGeorge and others, nonetheless, impose an obligation on MNCs not to exploit a lack of such governmental concern for the sake of profit. With the decision to engage with or in such a regime, the MNC assumes the obligation to do so in observance of commonly accepted moral norms.

*Donaldson.* Like DeGeorge, Thomas Donaldson asserts that MNCs need to respect local traditions and to consider context in their operations abroad. He also recognizes the need for MNC management to identify morally mandatory behavior and distinguish it from mere differences in cultural practice.[19] Donaldson's guiding principles emphasize respect for core human values to set the moral minimum. Donaldson's conception of core human values reflect the Kantian/Rawlsian/deontological view of people as an end in themselves, born equal in their rationality and freedom and entitled to the basic dignities to ensure that equality. His view also encompasses an understanding of what it means to work toward a common good and not just the good of one's self, aiming toward the ethical goal of social cooperation. Donaldson identifies those values as "respect for human dignity, respect for basic rights, and good citizenship."[20]

Those core human values form the moral floor for MNC operations. Above it, the company is bound to respect local traditions and take into account the fact that context matters in determining one's ethical stance. Practices and policies that are perfectly reasonable in some countries or cultures may be abhorred or have unintended detrimental consequences in others. All aspects of the country and its mores must be taken into account when an MNC establishes rules of conduct or engagement in that country.

---

17. DeGeorge, R. *International business ethics and incipient capitalism: a double standard?* Presented to the Society for Business Ethics, May 1994.

18. Id.

19. Donaldson, T. (1996). Values in tension: ethics away from home. *Harvard Business Review.* In Donaldson, T., Werhane, P., & Cording, M. (2002). *Ethical issues in business: a philosophical approach* (7th ed.). Upper Saddle River, NJ: Prentice Hall.

20. Id.

Donaldson and Dunfee have referred to this area above the moral floor as "moral free space."[21] The moral free space allows for the generation of social and economic norms by local communities in conformity with their cultural beliefs and practices. The norms must be fairly grounded in public consent, but they need not conform to the norms of any other group or culture or locality in order to be legitimate. These are referred to as *micronorms*. An MNC has the obligation to accommodate and defer to such micronorms, local customs and rules and practices, to the extent that they do not conflict with moral minimums of respect for human dignity and respect for basic rights—called *hypernorms*. In the case of a conflict between the two, the hypernorm prevails and the micronorm of the local host yields to the hypernorm. It is within that area of moral free space that MNCs engage in cultural relativism. Like DeGeorge, however, Donaldson subordinates respect for cultural values to respect for core human values.

Navigating moral free space can be a treacherous endeavor for the managers of MNCs. How does one distinguish the morally mandatory from the merely multicultural? Donaldson puts forth an ethical algorithm to guide managers through the muddy waters of moral free space.[22] The algorithm provides one means of reconciling conflicts between the practices and policies of home and host.

Use of the ethical algorithm first requires that the source of the conflicting practice or policy be identified. Is the difference attributable to the fact that home and host are at different stages of economic development (a Type-I conflict), or is it attributable to a difference in cultural tradition (a Type-II conflict)? Conflicts of relative economic development include differences such as minimum wage and hour policies and the age at which employment is considered "child" labor. Conflicts of cultural tradition involve practices such as gender discrimination and denial of free speech rights, which are rooted in religious or cultural traditions or authoritarian politics rather than economic factors.

For a Type-I conflict involving relative economic development, the algorithm directs the manager to resolve the conflict by considering whether the practice would be acceptable in his or her home country if the home country were in a similar stage of development. If so, then accepting the practice in the host country is within the ethical free space available to MNCs. For a U.S. MNC operating in a developing country without any protective wage and hour laws, the manager could look to U.S. history to see that labor laws on wages evolved with economic development in the United States. Under the algorithm, then, paying low wages does not cross the ethical line for a Type-I problem, although the limits of "how low" may bring the wage into conflict with moral minimums. Slave labor, forced labor, or pay so egregiously low as to deny a subsistence standard of living would not be morally justified regardless of home country history.[23]

For a Type-II conflict arising from local tradition or custom, managers are directed to two questions. The first question is, Is it possible to conduct business in the country without undertaking the practice? If not, then the question becomes, Is the practice a violation of a core human value? Only if the practice does not violate a core human value—those moral minimums for human respect, security, liberty, health, safety, etc.—may the company ethically engage in business with the country.[24] Donaldson's example of a Type-II conflict is the practice of business gift giving in Japan, which is viewed in some nations and cultures as bribery, but is a commonly accepted and expected practice in Japanese business. For all intents and purposes, it is not possible to successfully con-

21. Donaldson T., & Dunfee, T. (1999). *Ties that bind: a social contracts approach to business ethics.* Harvard University Business School Press.

22. Donaldson, Values in tension: ethics away from home.

23. One criticism of this approach is that it seems to permit wide latitude for MNCs to exploit poor economic treatment based on the nascent stage of capitalism in whatever country an MNC is operating. Others believe that MNCs should be held to a higher standard and denied the benefit of moving throughout the world to take advantage of the low end of economic development over and over again.

duct business in Japan without engaging in gift giving. So the question becomes, Does gift giving violate a core human value? Donaldson concludes that it does not. Gift giving may not be entirely moral or ethical, but it does not rise to the level of a morally mandatory minimum for behavior.

The situation of racial apartheid in South Africa presents another example of a Type-II conflict. In that case, engaging in the practice of discrimination against the black majority would clearly violate a core human value. Accordingly, under the algorithm, it would not be ethically permissible to conduct business in that regime. Gender apartheid in the workplace in Saudi Arabia, as well as in other aspects of public life, presents a current problem for MNCs operating there. (See "U.S. Companies Promote Gender Apartheid in Saudi Arabia" presented earlier in the chapter). Using Donaldson's ethical algorithm, how does the proposed investment by AOL in China (presented earlier in this chapter) measure up?

The foregoing theories of moral minimums and others like them seek to provide guidance to international organizations and consortiums and to MNCs, individually and in groups, that attempt to develop a socially responsible approach to global business operations. The implementation of theories of moral minimums is facilitated through codes of conduct.

## Implementation of Moral Minimums for MNCs—Voluntary Codes of Conduct

Given the lack of international law governing the conduct of MNCs, society is left to depend on the moral fiber of companies and peer and public pressure to encourage responsible behavior in the pursuit of profit. Some multilateral international groups have developed codes for certain aspects of transnational corporate behavior, particularly in the area of human rights, with the earnest goal of persuading governmental adoption of the model as home country law. Most often, national adoption

does not occur. Nonetheless, the model codes for behavior serve two important purposes: First, they act as guidelines for companies and industries seeking to establish their own transnational code of conduct. Second, they are increasingly viewed as the normative standard by which MNC behavior is evaluated. "Corporate actions that transgress these principles are understood to be *de facto*, and in some cases *de jure*, unethical and immoral."[25] Whether legally enforceable or not, these codes reflect the social and political consciousness of society. Eventually, the law will evolve to reflect that fact. While waiting, socially responsible management looking to move beyond mere compliance with the technical letter of the law should be seeking direction from these principles.

William Frederick has identified six international compacts, which he believes collectively "proclaim the basic outlines of a transcultural corporate ethic. This ethic effectively lays down the specific guidelines for the formulation of multinational corporate policies and practices."[26]

The six compacts so identified by Frederick are as follows: the United Nations Universal Declaration of Human Rights (1948), the European Convention on Human Rights (1950), the Helsinki Final Act (1975), the OECD Guidelines for Multinational Enterprises (original version 1976, revised substantially in 2000), the International Labor Office Tripartite Declaration of Principles Concerning Multinational Enterprises and Social Policy (1977), and the United Nations Code of Conduct on Transnational Corporations (a work in progress since 1972 and still not yet promulgated, as discussed below). Those six compacts represent the perspectives of a broad international constituency, yet reflect common themes that may be viewed as a consensus on moral minimums.

The most consistent common theme among the codes is inclusion of basic respect for fundamental human rights. The only one of the codes missing an explicit nod to the principle was the original OECD Guidelines for Multinational

---

24. If the answer to the first question is yes, then the company should engage in the country without undertaking the practice; and presumably there would be no ethical conflict.
25. Frederick, W. (1991). The moral authority of transnational corporate codes. *Journal of Business Ethics, 10*.
26. Id.

Enterprises of 1976. The OECD Guidelines were subsequently revised in 2000[27] to explicitly include respect for human rights "consistent" with not only the host's law, but also international obligations. Given the purpose and mission of the OECD, its less-than-complete embrace of fundamental human rights as an explicit feature of the Guidelines is not surprising. The OECD is not founded on humanitarian impulses but, instead, consists of representatives of the most developed nations seeking to make global commerce in a global market economy as efficient, predictable, and stable as possible so as to enhance the nations' economies. Nonetheless, the change in the OECD approach between the 1976 Guidelines and the 2000 Guidelines reflects evolution of political consensus about human rights as a necessary plank for the construction of global capitalism. A brief comparison of some of the key provisions in each version is provided in the following table.

The codes also share common principles regarding worker rights to equality and equity, along with general observation of the principles of national sovereignty and the authority of each nation for self-determination and self-governance. In the majority of such codes, however, those precepts are subordinate to respect for human rights. Frederick attributes this universal acceptance of fundamental human rights as a moral minimum to the fact that such a concept is transcultural. It is a norm universally embraced as a cornerstone of modern civilization. Unlike norms of sovereignty, social equity, and market models, principles of fundamental human rights remain unchanged by cultural norms. The ever-widening global acceptance of the deontological norms that underlie democracy (in the very Kantian sense—that people are born equal in freedom and rationality; that humanity is an end

---

**The OECD Guidelines for Multinational Enterprises**
**Comparison of 1976 Version and 2000 Version**

| **OECD Guidelines, 1976** | **OECD Guidelines, 2000** |
|---|---|
| • Respect host country policy objectives | • Contribute toward progress and sustainable development |
| • Provide transparency of books and records of related entities | • Respect human rights "consistent" with host's law and international obligations |
| • Cooperate closely with local community and business interests | • Encourage human capital formation |
| • Do not discriminate in filling foreign assignments | • Refrain from avoiding or working against regulatory laws aimed at social ills |
| • Do not give bribes | • Ensure good corporate governance (financial disclosure and transparency) |
| • Do not make political contributions unless legally permitted | • Provide meaningful self-regulation |
| • Abstain from improper political activities | • Encourage business partners and contractors to embrace these principles |

---

27. The guidelines and annual reports on compliance and progress can be downloaded from http://www.oecd.org.

in itself, not a means) provides one explanation for common coalescence around the principle. Perhaps even more persuasive is Frederick's argument that the universal embrace of human rights principles derives from the fact that the world is shared. That shared experience of past and present history has shown unambiguously that respect for human rights reaps rewards beyond what is reaped by the repression of human rights—a safer, healthier, happier, more sustainable workforce and a more sustainable environment in which to operate in perpetuity.

The failure of the UN to lead the way with guidelines for transnational operations is noteworthy. The UN has had a mandate since 1972 to develop guidelines for MNEs and a means to implement them. Its efforts to date have been fairly ineffective—the initiatives it has produced have been the subject of criticism on the grounds of being too soft on global business due to the lack of any enforcement mechanisms and too hard on global business by the breadth and vagaries of its directives. The Global Compact, negotiated in Davos, Switzerland, in 1999, sets forth some noble principles for MNEs, but provides virtually no monitoring or enforcement apparatus to verify compliance. Many companies have signed on to the Compact, but very little actual behavior change is required of them in exchange for the imprimatur of the UN on their operations—only a description in their annual report of the way they are making "changes to business operations so that the Global Compact and its principles become a part of strategy, culture, and day-to-day operations." With respect to human rights obligations, the Global Compact counsels only that MNEs need to support human rights within their sphere of influence and not be complicit in abuses. The key legal and ethical issues regarding what constitutes "complicity" and what is within one's sphere of "influence" are considerable.[28]

The most recent initiative of the UN is its Human Rights Norms for Business, adopted in August 2003 by the UN's Sub-Commission on the Promotion and Protection of Human Rights. The Human Rights Norms for Business (the "Norms") set forth a more expansive view of the obligations of MNEs with regard to human rights. While acknowledging that the primary obligation for securing human rights lies with national governments, the Norms reflect more clearly the principles of the UDHR and the theories of DeGeorge and Donaldson. The Norms prohibit MNE benefit from direct or indirect human rights abuses and prescribe that their operations should contribute to host country development, including the realization of, among other things, "freedom of thought, conscience, and religion, and freedom of opinion and expression." The Norms have been criticized for being too lofty and too vague, given the complications of operations in countries ruled by regimes of all stripes. Businesses are reluctant to sign on to provisions that have no discernible boundaries for compliance, and their hesitance is understandable. Consider the implications of AOL Time Warner's investment in China under such a norm.

These global pacts and initiatives by international organizations are supplemented by voluntary agreements among businesses to abide by certain principles in their operations. Groups of businesses, intra- and inter-industry, may agree to abide by common principles in their operations. One example, the Caux Business Roundtable Principles, reflects a stakeholder-interest approach to corporate purpose and responsibility. As well, companies may voluntarily adopt common principles for engagement with certain regimes—for example, the Sullivan Principles governing the moral rules of engagement in apartheid South Africa. Or they may adopt principles for operations in certain industries—for example, the Kimberly Process for those engaged in diamond mining, the Harkin-Engle Protocol for the chocolate industry, the Valdez Principles for those engaged in transporting petroleum products globally, and the Fair Labor Alliance for global garment manufacturing.

International guidelines and codes are also supplemented and/or supplanted by individual

---

28. The topic is discussed in greater detail in the case study "Lying Down with Dogs... Getting Up with Lawsuits: Unocal and the Alien Tort Claims Act" found in Part Three of this text. In any event, that construction of human rights obligations does not rise to the level of the moral minimum. Indeed, it may not even rise to the legal minimum, depending on the outcome of some of the ATCA cases.

## Race to the Bell-Bottom

The difficulties of going it alone—with only an internal corporate code of international conduct and rules of engagement not universally followed by the industry—are exemplified by the experience of Levi Strauss & Company. Founded in the mid-1800s as a dry goods firm in San Francisco, Levi Strauss grew dramatically over the next century. It successfully went public in 1971. In 1985, the founders' descendants and company management took the company private again, paying a hefty premium over market price to do so. Private ownership by the family, management, and employees would permit the company to pursue long-term corporate strategies free of the fickle restraints of short-term expectations in the stock market.

Throughout its long history, the company had acquired a reputation for good corporate citizenship—as a community benefactor and a fair and conscientious employer. Levi Strauss's management believed that there didn't necessarily have to be a conflict between doing good and doing well, particularly over the long haul, and that fair treatment of all of its stakeholders would be rewarded in the marketplace. As the company evolved under private ownership, management's core values increasingly stressed utilizing ethical business practices and putting moral minimums above economic considerations where they conflicted.

In the early 1990s, several sweatshop scandals were publicized involving compulsory, involuntary Chinese labor and several name-brand U.S. apparel manufacturers. Levi Strauss was among them. The company broke ties with the offending contractors and undertook to reevaluate, from a moral perspective, its engagement in China and elsewhere abroad. Though the company's presence in China was limited at the time, the Chinese market was opening up, presenting tremendous growth opportunities for all apparel manufacturers. A task force of executives within Levi Strauss developed global sourcing rules covering the selection of countries in which it would do business and terms and conditions for engaging with business partners in the host country. The company's global sourcing code established minimum standards for worker health and safety, human rights, and the environment.

A second executive task force was convened to examine investment in China under the terms of the company's new global sourcing rules. The committee found that worker rights in China were virtually nonexistent—labor unions were illegal, and a "maximum wage" law prohibited pay above government-set levels. The use of uncompensated, compulsory prison labor by government personnel was rampant and included major textile operations. The human rights record of the country was notoriously repressive. Free speech, assembly, and association were severely restricted, with any political dissent grounds for imprisonment; and Chinese legal institutions did not provide any due process in arrest, charging, trial, or sentencing. Human rights organizations throughout the world, as well as the U.S. State Department and other governments, documented the existence of a totalitarian regime that ruled with an iron fist, particularly in the years following the tragic prodemocracy demonstrations in Tiananmen Square in 1989.[a]

In 1993, Levi Strauss finally reached a considered opinion on whether to "engage or withdraw." The company announced that it would defer any direct investment in China and begin an orderly withdrawal of its existing manufacturing contracts there for finishing and manufacturing the company line. The company explained that, given the human rights climate in China, it did not believe it could ensure that its employees or those working on its behalf would not be subjected to human rights violations. Further, the company calculated that doing business in China would pose reputational risks to its brands. Man-

## Race to the Bell-Bottom (continued)

agement acknowledged that its decision was not intended to change China's human rights policies or to impose the company's view on others. The move simply felt right to the company, its employees, and its business partners. In the ensuing five years, Levi Strauss decreased its direct production in China by approximately 70 percent. During that same time, the company suffered a substantial loss of market share, lagging sales, plunging profits, and domestic layoffs and plant closings. By 1997, more than 11 of its U.S. plants were closed and thousands of its workers were out of jobs.

Struggling financially and needing new markets with low-cost labor to remain competitive—indeed, to remain in existence—in 1988, Levi Strauss reversed its self-imposed restrictions on manufacturing in mainland China. In a press release, Levi Strauss's management explained that, given the repatriation of Hong Kong to China, the company once again had a direct investment in the country. Moreover, it was no longer practical to conduct business in Asia without being in mainland China. The company could no longer support the policy of staying out of China "while others are solidifying footholds in one of the world's fastest-growing economies." The company promised to "only pursue business activities in China that will allow the company to operate in a socially responsible manner and consistent with how it does business elsewhere in the world." Officials reiterated the company's dedication to its global guidelines and expressed confidence in its ability to "identify responsible business allies who will honor its Global Sourcing and Operating Guidelines" in mainland China.

In 2002, Levi Strauss announced that virtually all of its domestic production would cease. Since 1997, it had closed more than 24 U.S. plants and lain off 13,000 workers. The announcement in 2002 affected several thousand more workers—nearly 20 percent of the company's global workforce. Company management had attempted to retain domestic manufacturing facilities for as long as possible; and for a time, Levi Strauss was one of the few domestic apparel manufacturers still located in the United States. But paying U.S. wages of $9–$15 per hour, compared with what their competitors were paying abroad ($1 per hour or less), was crushing the company competitively.

The company attempted to mitigate some of the hardship to employees by providing a severance package that included two weeks pay per year of service, a $2,200 transitional allowance to be used any way they choose, extended medical coverage, and an enhanced pension plan. Activists who monitor trade and labor practices lamented the move by the company as striking a death knell for apparel manufacturing in the United States. One of the last manufacturers left standing, Levi Strauss had, at last, succumbed to join the race to the bottom.

Millions of U.S. manufacturing jobs have been lost to overseas relocation in the past decade. Since 1995, close to half a million jobs have been lost in textiles alone. It is predicted that the overseas relocation that has been taking place for decades will likely surge in the textile industry in 2005, when the Multi Fiber Agreement, which places restrictions on textile exports by third world countries, is fully phased out. China's current 20 percent of the global apparel market could grow to as much as 50 percent.[b]

While the availability of cheaper goods may benefit consumers, workers throughout the world will pay the price. Ever lower wages and deteriorating working conditions are the hallmark of the race to the bottom. For example, the Economic Policy Institute has documented that since the inception of NAFTA in 1994 (and the relocation of U.S. companies to

**Race to the Bell-Bottom (continued)**

Mexico), manufacturing wages in Mexico have dropped more than 20 percent. Relocating out of the reach of U.S. law makes monitoring working conditions and wages and bringing any pressure to bear for change more difficult. Consumer activism, such as the college anti-sweatshop movement, and reliance on voluntary compliance in the form of membership in the Fair Labor Association (FLA) and similar standards, are the only tools available. And they are not all that effective even when adopted.

In June 2003, the *Los Angeles Times* reported that factories making products in China and elsewhere for Nike, Inc.; Levi Strauss & Co.; and five other companies violated labor laws, ranging from inadequate pay to failure to provide proper hearing protection. The group of seven companies had agreed under the FLA to inspection of overseas operations. Between August 2001 and July 2002, the FLA published detailed results of its inspections in 48 factories in several countries. China accounted for more audits than any other country. Violations included a contractor for Nike in China that paid its workers less than the minimum wage of 31 cents an hour and a contractor for Liz Claiborne Inc. in China that failed to register workers ages 16 to 18.[c] The article indicated that Levi Strauss dropped out of the FLA program in October 2002.

Engage or withdraw? in China? elsewhere? As one global watchdog put it, "If Levis can't make a living making clothing in a socially responsible way, the responsible thing to do would be to get out of the clothing business."[d]

In May 2004, the Gap took an uncharacteristic step for the transnational garment industry and publicly released a report on the working conditions in its 3,000 worldwide factories, a report detailing a wide array of workplace violations concentrated in plants in underdeveloped countries. Such a level of transparency in operations has not been previously seen among industry leaders.

> The Gap report represents a dramatic change in strategy for a retailer that has long been on the defensive about working conditions at the factories that make its clothing. It may also represent a deft strategic move. At the same time that the report exonerates the majority of factories making Gap clothes, its frank discussion of violations at a minority of plants is already winning praise from some of its most vociferous critics.[e]

Bolstering the credibility of the report and in keeping with the notion of "best practices" for the twenty-first-century multinational, the Gap invited input on the report from some of the groups that have been critical of its labor practices. Gap CEO Paul Pressler noted that the company has been working with NGOs and local authorities to develop meaningful standards and verification mechanisms.[f] The report is available on the Gap web site at http://www.gap.com.

a. Among the more troubling findings of the Levi Strauss task force was that the company would be responsible for enforcing China's one-child-per-family law—effectively forcing the company to monitor and report officially on the reproductive lives of its workforce.
b. Colwell, D. (2002, May 9). Levis: made in China? *AlterNet*.
c. Labor laws violated, group says. (2003, June 5). *Los Angeles Times*.
d. Colwell, loc. cit.
e. Merrick, A. (2004, May 12). Gap offers unusual look at factory conditions. *Wall Street Journal*.
f. Id.

codes of conduct for transnational operations adopted internally by individual MNEs. Many, if not most, major companies operating in the global economy have adopted some code of conduct for multinational operations. Such codes are voluntary and only internally enforceable (for example, by shareholder suit) and vary greatly in scope and coverage and the extent of corporate obligation recognized. As well, in the United States, many exist only on paper (for the appearance of propriety) and have no meaningful effect on actual corporate activities.

The downside of adopting and adhering to such codes is, again, the fact that operations above the legal floor come with costs and some built-in, at least short-term, competitive disadvantages.

## Beyond Compliance

Given the lack of international law to regulate the conduct of MNCs, socially responsible multinational operations of necessity exist in the realm beyond compliance. Moral behavior depends entirely on the fiber and leadership of companies and peer and public pressure to encourage responsible behavior in the pursuit of profit.

Shareholder consciousness and activism on human rights and global environmental issues have increased dramatically in the past decade, with scores of shareholder resolutions (albeit, nonbinding) on annual proxy statements directing corporate management to cease and desist objectionable operations. The effectiveness of such activism generally hinges on the level of enlightenment of corporate leadership and/or the volatility of the company's position in the market.

Accusation and trial in the court of public opinion is also an increasingly important tool for MNC accountability. Particularly for companies with much of their value in a recognized brand or trademark, public outcry over human rights abuses and environmental degradation coupled with consumer boycotts, campus activism, and letter-writing campaigns can have a significant bottom-line effect on targeted companies. Nike, the Gap, Wal-Mart, and many other household name brands and companies have suffered criticism and controversy over their use of overseas sweatshop labor, often at below living wage stan-

dards. Wal-Mart, the largest employer in the world, has been awarded the sardonic "Sweatie" award for several years running by the Canadian Maquiladora Solidarity Network (MSN) and Oxfam, which each year recognizes those MNCs engaged in the most egregious use of sweatshop labor in manufacturing.

The other key impetus for MNCs to operate beyond compliance is the steady evolution of law in the area of international human rights. Progress is inevitable, if not imminent; and unless a company has its finger on the pulse of where the law is going, it can get stung. The experience of Unocal in Burma is a good example of this. Victims of forced labor on Unocal's pipeline project in Burma brought suit against Unocal in a U.S. court, using an arcane eighteenth-century U.S. piracy and antislavery law, the Alien Tort Claims Act (ATCA). The case went all the way to the 9th Circuit and, ultimately, was settled by Unocal when the company was ordered to stand trial for complicity in slave trading. The case provides a good illustration of the evolution of law and its reflection of social and political consciousness. What is "legal" one day may not be "legal" the next day.

It is clear that well-settled international norms exist for morally minimum behavior. A more profound issue for MNCs is determining their core values and the fundamental corporate approach to social responsibility. If MNCs abide by the negative injunction only—respecting human life, health, and security as an end in itself and not causing avoidable harm in the pursuit of profits—that would be a step in the right direction. Companies willing to take a more affirmative view of CSR will also be asking what it can do, in the process of making money, to make itself better, cleaner, and safer and to help others.

## The Universal Declaration of Human Rights

### PREAMBLE

*Whereas recognition of the inherent dignity and of the equal and inalienable rights of all members of the human family is the foundation of freedom, justice and peace in the world,*

*Whereas disregard and contempt for human rights have resulted in barbarous acts which have outraged the conscience of mankind, and the advent of a world in which human beings shall enjoy freedom of speech and belief and freedom from fear and want has been proclaimed as the highest aspiration of the common people,*

*Whereas it is essential, if man is not to be compelled to have recourse, as a last resort, to rebellion against tyranny and oppression, that human rights should be protected by the rule of law,*

*Whereas it is essential to promote the development of friendly relations between nations,*

*Whereas the peoples of the United Nations have in the Charter reaffirmed their faith in fundamental human rights, in the dignity and worth of the human person and in the equal rights of men and women and have determined to promote social progress and better standards of life in larger freedom,*

*Whereas Member States have pledged themselves to achieve, in cooperation with the United Nations, the promotion of universal respect for and observance of human rights and fundamental freedoms,*

*Whereas a common understanding of these rights and freedoms is of the greatest importance for the full realization of this pledge,*

## Article 1
All human beings are born free and equal in dignity and rights. They are endowed with reason and conscience and should act towards one another in a spirit of brotherhood.

## Article 2
Everyone is entitled to all the rights and freedoms set forth in this Declaration, without distinction of any kind, such as race, colour, sex, language, religion, political or other opinion, national or social origin, property, birth or other status.

Furthermore, no distinction shall be made on the basis of the political, jurisdictional or international status of the country or territory to which a person belongs, whether it be independent, trust, non-self-governing or under any other limitation of sovereignty.

## Article 3
Everyone has the right to life, liberty and security of person.

## Article 4
No one shall be held in slavery or servitude; slavery and the slave trade shall be prohibited in all their forms.

## Article 5
No one shall be subjected to torture or to cruel, inhuman or degrading treatment or punishment.

## Article 6
Everyone has the right to recognition everywhere as a person before the law.

## Article 7
All are equal before the law and are entitled without any discrimination to equal protection of the law. All are entitled to equal protection against any discrimination in violation of this Declaration and against any incitement to such discrimination.

## Article 8
Everyone has the right to an effective remedy by the competent national tribunals for acts violating the fundamental rights granted him by the constitution or by law.

## Article 9
No one shall be subjected to arbitrary arrest, detention or exile.

## Article 10
Everyone is entitled in full equality to a fair and public hearing by an independent and impartial tribunal, in the determination of his rights and obligations and of any criminal charge against him.

## Article 11
1. Everyone charged with a penal offence has the right to be presumed innocent until proved guilty according to law in a public trial at which he has had all the guarantees necessary for his defence.
2. No one shall be held guilty of any penal offence on account of any act or omission which did not constitute a penal offence, under national or international law, at the time when it was committed. Nor shall a heavier penalty be imposed than the one that

was applicable at the time the penal offence was committed.

## Article 12
No one shall be subjected to arbitrary interference with his privacy, family, home or correspondence, nor to attacks upon his honour and reputation. Everyone has the right to the protection of the law against such interference or attacks.

## Article 13
1. Everyone has the right to freedom of movement and residence within the borders of each State.
2. Everyone has the right to leave any country, including his own, and to return to his country.

## Article 14
1. Everyone has the right to seek and to enjoy in other countries asylum from persecution.
2. This right may not be invoked in the case of prosecutions genuinely arising from non-political crimes or from acts contrary to the purposes and principles of the United Nations.

## Article 15
1. Everyone has the right to a nationality.
2. No one shall be arbitrarily deprived of his nationality nor denied the right to change his nationality.

## Article 16
1. Men and women of full age, without any limitation due to race, nationality or religion, have the right to marry and to found a family. They are entitled to equal rights as to marriage, during marriage and at its dissolution.
2. Marriage shall be entered into only with the free and full consent of the intending spouses.
3. The family is the natural and fundamental group unit of society and is entitled to protection by society and the State.

## Article 17
1. Everyone has the right to own property alone as well as in association with others.
2. No one shall be arbitrarily deprived of his property.

## Article 18
Everyone has the right to freedom of thought, conscience and religion; this right includes freedom to change his religion or belief, and freedom, either alone or in community with others and in public or private, to manifest his religion or belief in teaching, practice, worship and observance.

## Article 19
Everyone has the right to freedom of opinion and expression; this right includes freedom to hold opinions without interference and to seek, receive and impart information and ideas through any media and regardless of frontiers.

## Article 20
1. Everyone has the right to freedom of peaceful assembly and association.
2. No one may be compelled to belong to an association.

## Article 21
1. Everyone has the right to take part in the government of his country, directly or through freely chosen representatives.
2. Everyone has the right to equal access to public service in his country.
3. The will of the people shall be the basis of the authority of government; this will shall be expressed in periodic and genuine elections which shall be by universal and equal suffrage and shall be held by secret vote or by equivalent free voting procedures.

## Article 22
Everyone, as a member of society, has the right to social security and is entitled to realization, through national effort and international cooperation and in accordance with the organization and resources of each State, of the economic, social and cultural rights indispensable for his dignity and the free development of his personality.

## Article 23
1. Everyone has the right to work, to free choice of employment, to just and favourable conditions of work and to protection against unemployment.

2. Everyone, without any discrimination, has the right to equal pay for equal work.
3. Everyone who works has the right to just and favourable remuneration ensuring for himself and his family an existence worthy of human dignity, and supplemented, if necessary, by other means of social protection.
4. Everyone has the right to form and to join trade unions for the protection of his interests.

## Article 24

Everyone has the right to rest and leisure, including reasonable limitation of working hours and periodic holidays with pay.

## Article 25

1. Everyone has the right to a standard of living adequate for the health and well-being of himself and of his family, including food, clothing, housing and medical care and necessary social services, and the right to security in the event of unemployment, sickness, disability, widowhood, old age or other lack of livelihood in circumstances beyond his control.
2. Motherhood and childhood are entitled to special care and assistance. All children, whether born in or out of wedlock, shall enjoy the same social protection.

## Article 26

1. Everyone has the right to education. Education shall be free, at least in the elementary and fundamental stages. Elementary education shall be compulsory. Technical and professional education shall be made generally available and higher education shall be equally accessible to all on the basis of merit.
2. Education shall be directed to the full development of the human personality and to the strengthening of respect for human rights and fundamental freedoms. It shall promote understanding, tolerance and friendship among all nations, racial or religious groups, and shall further the activities of the United Nations for the maintenance of peace.
3. Parents have a prior right to choose the kind of education that shall be given to their children.

## Article 27

1. Everyone has the right freely to participate in the cultural life of the community, to enjoy the arts and to share in scientific advancement and its benefits.
2. Everyone has the right to the protection of the moral and material interests resulting from any scientific, literary or artistic production of which he is the author.

## Article 28

Everyone is entitled to a social and international order in which the rights and freedoms set forth in this Declaration can be fully realized.

## Article 29

1. Everyone has duties to the community in which alone the free and full development of his personality is possible.
2. In the exercise of his rights and freedoms, everyone shall be subject only to such limitations as are determined by law solely for the purpose of securing due recognition and respect for the rights and freedoms of others and of meeting the just requirements of morality, public order and the general welfare in a democratic society.
3. These rights and freedoms may in no case be exercised contrary to the purposes and principles of the United Nations.

## Article 30

Nothing in this Declaration may be interpreted as implying for any State, group or person any right to engage in any activity or to perform any act aimed at the destruction of any of the rights and freedoms set forth herein.

*Adopted on December 10, 1948, by the General Assembly of the United Nations (without dissent)*

# PART 3

## Case Studies and Exercises in Corporate Responsibility

Most of the case studies in Part Three are relevant to more than one chapter of the text, encompassing many issues of corporate responsibility. They also vary in scope and depth—ranging from case vignettes and exercises of a few pages to fully researched and cited analyses. Accordingly, they are grouped by chapter where they are relevant and by scope, starting with simpler cases and proceeding to more complex ones.

### High Value Discount Appliances
The case presents a short exercise on conflicts between individual ethics and loyalty to the organization and its long-term goals in the context of financial reporting.
*Relevant chapters: 1, 2, 5, 6*

### KPMG and David Duncan
The case makes a brief examination of one of the key figures in the Enron/Arthur Andersen meltdown of 2002. The short portrait considers the culture of Andersen, the close ties between Andersen's and Enron's senior management, and the role of the individual in organizational wrongdoing. The demise of the two companies involved is explored in greater detail in two additional case studies in Part Three: The Collapse of Enron: A Business Ethics Perspective and

No Accounting for It: The Demise of Professionalism in Public Accounting.
*Relevant chapters: 1, 2, 5, 6*

### Transforming the Soul of Business
The case presents a short exercise on conflicts in corporate views of social responsibility—the shareholder-profit-centric view versus corporate commitment to principles of sustainable development— and explores the role of individual ethics in the organization.
*Relevant chapters: 1, 3, 5, 6, 9*

### The Bhopal Disaster: Implications for Investments in Less Developed Countries
The case analyzes the Union Carbide gas leak in Bhopal, India, in 1984. The case looks at the risk posed by chemicals as technology advances, the role of multinationals in the global economy, and the role of governments in business regulation.
*Relevant chapters: 2, 3, 4, 9, 10*

### St. Valentine's Day Massacre Redux: The Human Cost of Chocolates and Diamonds
The case is a two-part study of the human rights abuses associated with the chocolate industry and the diamond industry. Child slavery in the Ivory Coast and rebel regimes in Sierra Leone and

Angola create the problem. The case study explores the response of businesses engaged in the production and sale of these commodities and assesses the efficacy of current voluntary pacts aimed to restrict the involvement of legitimate businesses with crimes against humanity: the Harkin-Engel Protocol for Cocoa Production and the Kimberly Process for Conflict Diamonds.

*Relevant chapters: 2, 3, 10*

## Lying Down with Dogs... Getting Up with Lawsuits: Unocal and the Alien Tort Claims Act

The case of Doe v. Unocal is examined in the context of corporate responsibility for human rights abuses in overseas operations. The legal requirements of the ATCA, current international law on human rights, and the activities of Unocal in Burma are explored in some depth. Other pending cases against U.S. companies under the ATCA are included.

*Relevant chapters: 2, 3, 10*

## The Collapse of Enron: A Business Ethics Perspective

The case examines the demise of Enron, then the seventh-largest company in the world, from the perspective of all of the affected stakeholders. It explores the rise and fall of the company, its corporate culture, its corporate governance, and its use of political influence to thwart regulation. A brief discussion of the provisions of the Corporate Fraud Accountability Act specifically targeted to Enron-type fraud is included.

*Relevant chapters: 3, 4, 5, 6*

## No Accounting for It: The Demise of Professionalism in Public Accounting

The case looks at the changing role and nature of accounting firms in modern business: conflicts in auditing and consulting, revolving doors with clients, and change in the very business model of the accounting firm itself. The alignment of the audit firms with industry clients on issues such as the expensing of stock options and consulting conflicts of interest reflect this transformation from the traditional independence and public-interest mission of the accounting profession.

*Relevant chapters: 3, 4, 5, 6*

## The Cigarette Controversy

The case looks at the post-multistate tobacco settlement transformation of Philip Morris Company into Altria. The case looks at the company's attempt to remake itself, as well as its continuing product liability litigation battle. Corporate culture, the perception of the company by consumers, the role of government relations, and the impact of its behavior on shareholders and employees in the tobacco industry are explored.

*Relevant chapters: 3, 4, 5, 6, 8*

## The Chilling Truth: Must Corporate Speech Be Honest?

The case examines the legal and ethical issues surrounding the California and United States Supreme Court cases of Kasky v. Nike, Inc. Issues examined include the first amendment rights of corporations, the different legal statuses of political versus commercial speech, and the ethics of corporate marketing and public relations.

*Relevant chapters: 3, 4, 8*

## A Big Fat Problem

The case analyzes some of the facets of corporate responsibility for the current health crisis involving obesity. The case examines some of the causes and considers the legal and ethical implications of the current spate of product liability litigation against purveyors of fast food and snack food. The second half of the case considers the response of Kraft Foods to the problem, with the initiation of health and wellness programs and products and self-restraint in its marketing to children.

*Relevant chapters: 3, 4, 8*

## ADM and Biodiesel

The case analyzes the environmental advantages and drawbacks to biodiesel and other alternative fuels, with a specific focus on one leader in the industry: Archer Daniels Midland. The case explores the corporate strategy of ADM and the key role of the government in the success or failure of competitors in this emerging market.

*Relevant chapters: 3, 4, 9*

## General Motors and Alternative Vehicles

The case analyzes the alternative transport market from the perspective of car manufacturers; specifically, General Motors, the largest. In its exposition of the company's alternative vehicles projects, the case considers the value of corporate technology for sustainable development, the role of government incentives, competitive industry pressures, and the level of consumer demand for green products.

*Relevant chapters: 3, 4, 9*

## Target and the Perception of Good Corporate Citizenship through Charitable Works

Although corporate charity is not the same thing as corporate social responsibility, the benevolent activities of business nonetheless enhance its reputation and the goodwill value of its brand name. This case analyzes the experience of Target and its struggle to assess the value of its nonbusiness contributions. In the industry of big-box retail, Target maintains a better record of charitable giving than its main competitor, Wal-Mart, yet lags behind in sales and reputation.

*Relevant chapters: 3, 5, 8*

## Auto Safety at Ford

The case analyzes the Ford Explorer/Firestone Tire litigation involving allegations of an unreasonably dangerous and defective product. The cause of the deaths of and injuries suffered by SUV passengers on rollover was alternately blamed on defective tires and a defective chassis design. The case compares Ford then and now—through a reexamination of Ford's Pinto product safety cases of the 1970s. The case also examines the relationship of Ford-Firestone, contrasting the American and Japanese management responses to the crisis.

*Relevant chapters: 3, 5, 8*

## Safety Audit at LAMC—USMNC's Newly Acquired Subsidiary in Latin America

The case is a short study of the obligations of a new parent company for workplace safety in its far-flung subsidiaries. Prior incidents and accidents prompt management to self-audit its safety practices.

*Relevant chapters: 5, 7, 10*

# Case 1

## High Value Discount Appliances

*This case presents a short exercise on conflicts between individual ethics and loyalty to the organization and its long-term goals in the context of financial reporting.*

*Relevant chapters: 1,2,5,6*

The High Value (HV) chain of discount appliance stores, started in 1988 with the merger of three smaller chains, had achieved sales in excess of $5 billion in a mere 15 years under the respected leadership of its CEO, George Sutherland. Investors included major banks, insurance companies, real estate developers, Fortune 400 companies and investment banking houses. High Value was touted by the business press as one of the most outstanding new companies in the United States during the last 20 years. It was especially praised for its internal culture. *BizEd Magazine* chose it as one of the 10 best companies for which to work. The culture of the organization was described as "fresh, dynamic, and exciting." High Value had managed to create a "protected, family feeling, without the stifling atmosphere that sometimes prevails inside families."

### Business and Sports

Sutherland came from old New England stock, was a pillar of the community, was active in his church, and had an impeccable reputation for business integrity. He was a major patron of the arts, an important contributor to the Republican party, and a part-owner of two major league sport franchises, one in Cleveland and the other in Oakland. A soccer player during college at Dartmouth, Sutherland had devoted much of his life to making soccer a national sport comparable to baseball or football. In 1989, he founded the USA Soccer League, which now has teams operating in eight cities. High Value and the USA Soccer League were indistinguishable to many people; as the league's main corporate sponsor, High Value attached its name to nearly all of the league's activities.

You are a former college soccer star from the University of Illinois and a continuing soccer enthusiast who was introduced to Sutherland after a 1996 match in New York City. Although nearly 20 years his junior, you immediately developed a rapport. It so happened that your wife's first cousin was a close associate of Sutherland's and an investor in a number of the same businesses. Sutherland invited you to a weekend aboard his yacht. You also played ten-

Case study exercise developed by Alfred A. Marcus, Univ. of Minnesota. ©2006, NorthCoast Publishers, Inc.

nis and golf with him. You were amazed at Sutherland's skill in both these games.

Not only did you like Sutherland, but also the group of young, athletic and talented men and women whom Sutherland gathered around him – up-and-coming lawyers, accountants, marketing and advertising people, and journalists. You fit right in with this hard-working, hard-playing crowd. You were surprised that, contrary to expectations, none of this crowd was callous or self-centered. They were a warm, caring group, extremely supportive of one another, devoted to Sutherland, and accepting of you.

You grew up in the Midwest and had no extended family or friends in New York City, where you now work. For six years, a major accounting firm employed you, but you did not become a partner and you were let go. Then, you had an unchallenging job in a large bank, but saw no future for yourself in banking,

### Promoting Sport to Benefit Business

On August 3, 1999, after a fairly brutal tennis game, Sutherland asked whether you would like to become Sutherland's personal assistant. The work sounded a little nebulous, but the salary didn't. You had to support two young children and a wife, and though you lacked experience in retailing, you could leave the bank with no regrets. The bank never felt like home. It was a place to punch a clock. Everything was bound by dry and impenetrable rules. The people barely said hello. You were bored stiff and had only started there. You accepted Sutherland's offer.

Your new job was a whirlwind of excitement. What you did had scarcely any connection with High Value. You were the company's liaison to the world of professional soccer. You were in contact with major celebrities and became a central figure in promoting the success of the new soccer league. You even came up with the idea of changing High Value's logo to a soccer ball, to make the connection between the company and the soccer league even clearer in people's minds.

On July 4, 2003, after a tennis game at his estate, Sutherland asked you to go into Sutherland's private office and bring him some files to look at by the pool. You tripped on a chair in Sutherland's office and the contents of the files

scattered across the floor. Upon picking them up, you inadvertently saw a memo from Sutherland to the CFO. The memo reads as follows:

There are no irregularities in the statements of inventory or accounts receivable, as alleged by Garcia. These are judgments calls, as we all know. There is no reason to be conservative in making these calls and to make it appear as if our profits are any less than they are. You realize as well as I do that every year we are subject to an independent audit by the respected firm of DuPers and LienBold. How can we fool such experienced auditors into believing that our inventory and accounts receivable are less than reported? Explain the situation to Garcia, thank him for his diligence, transfer him to a part of the company where he no longer can be concerned with these matters, and provide him with appropriate remuneration for his efforts. The so-called issue of irregularities is not an issue, as we both know.

### Pessimism and Decline in the Sport League

Despite the U.S. recession, High Value's reported profits the prior year had suffered little. Sutherland earned a substantial bonus and was able to cash in on stock options worth more than $8 million. The soccer league, on the other hand, was having difficulties. It had always been hard for professional soccer to take off in the United States. Sutherland again dipped into his personal fortune to provide it with an infusion of cash.

The next year was not an especially good one for High Value. Maybe the company overextended itself by opening too many new stores. Sales continued to climb, but the competition intensified, and margins and profits were way down. Still, most investors continued to have faith in the company and there was no dearth of funds for additional expansion. However, investors had started to ask more questions. Why had High Value been so successful? Analysts were beginning to carefully scrutinize the company's records. It didn't seem to add up.

The situation at the USA Soccer League also

was deteriorating. American fans were losing interest. Attendance was down and a number of franchises were near bankruptcy. Without a major infusion of new money, the league was in jeopardy of folding. Sutherland had been on the telephone for days trying to persuade his wealthy friends to commit more dollars, but they saw the league as a losing proposition and refused to cooperate.

After your tennis match with Sutherland on July 4, 2003, you found Sutherland in an uncharacteristically pessimistic mood. Sutherland said: "There is not much more I can do. My bonus and stock options this year will be nowhere near what they were last year. From now on, we are going to have to start playing things a lot closer to the vest at High Value. The league could fold. I have sunk as much cash as I can into this endeavor. We both know that High Value has plenty of cash. We could borrow $10 to $15 million *temporarily* to keep the league going. What do you think? No one would have to know."

What should you do?

## Discussion Questions

1. How should you respond to Sutherland? What would you do?

2. If a friend presented this dilemma to you, what would you tell him to do? What are the issues? What is at stake? What is the appropriate way to behave?

# Case 2

## KPMG and David Duncan

*The case makes a brief examination of one of the key figures in the Enron/Arthur Andersen meltdown of 2002. The short portrait considers the culture of Andersen, the close ties between Andersen and Enron senior management, and the role of the individual in organizational wrongdoing. The demise of the two companies involved are explored in greater detail in two additional case studies in this Part Three:* The Collapse of Enron: A Business Ethics Perspective *and* No Accounting For It: The Demise of Professionalism in Public Accounting.

*Relevant chapters: 1, 2, 5, 6*

KPMG faced a dilemma. It had been hired by Levi Strauss to replace Arthur Andersen in 2002 as its outside auditor. In a suit for wrongful termination, two former employees from Levi Strauss' global tax department charged that KPMG staff working on the account had questioned the appropriateness of some of Levi Strauss' tax treatments and the way it had set up balance sheet reserves under Ander-

sen. A Levi Strauss executive asked that the KPMG accountants be taken off the account, a request to which KPMG acceded. Other charges of this nature were being made against KPMG. At the start of 2003, the SEC accused the company or removing staff when Xerox asked. One of the KPMG staff that had been removed questioned elements of a fraudulent scheme, for which the SEC was suing Xerox in a civil suit. So far, KPMG had denied all these charges.[1] KPMG did not know how to respond to these incidents. As it considered what to do, it reviewed the story of Arthur Andersen and David Duncan. What could it learn from this story?

David Duncan had been a typical Andersen employee. His values were consistent with where Anderson wanted to go. The accounting firm wanted to please its clients. The more the company pleased its clients, the larger would be its consulting and accounting fees.

David Duncan had lost his father, a manager at a chemical plant in Beaumont, Texas, at the age of 18. Graduating with honors from Forest High School in Beaumont, Texas, he was consid-

Case study developed by Alfred Marcus, based on "Accountable: How a Bright Star At Andersen Fell Along With Enron --- Like His Firm, David Duncan Basked in Glow of Client On a Decade-Long Roll – `All the Ammo I Can Get'" *Wall Street Journal;* May 15, 2002; By Anita Raghavan ©2006 NorthCoast Publishers.

1. Ex-Executives' Suit Against Levi Raises Questions About KPMG, *Wall Street Journal;* April 18, 2003; By Sally Beatty and Cassel Bryan-Low.

ered to be an ambitious young man. Duncan completed a degree in accounting at Texas A&M University, the school his father attended. Graduates of the school had the reputation for loyalty and an unparalleled work ethic. Andersen recruited heavily there and Duncan went to work for Andersen in 1981. His personality was to blend in. He was a courteous and respectful man who did not challenge people. Duncan wanted to be liked. He played by the rules, did not question the practices in the firm. At Andersen he met his wife, also an accountant. At Andersen, he became a partner. By 2001, he was earning more than $1 million a year. He was acclaimed at the firm's annual partners' meeting that year, but by January 2002, he was fired for shredding Enron-related documents. In April 2002, he pleaded guilty to obstruction of justice. To protect Enron from federal investigators he admitted that he had destroyed critical audit documents that might have incriminated his client.

Duncan had worked with Enron for more than 10 years. For the last five he had been lead partner on the Enron account, for which he had been amply rewarded. His ties with Enron were extremely close. He had an office in Enron's building, often had lunch with its chief accountant, and regularly attended major golfing tournaments with the chief accountant.

The chief accountant was one of a number of top ranking officials at Enron with whom Duncan closely associated. The whole group had gone to Texas A&M. They were very close. These relationships were the keys to Duncan's success at Enron. His loyalty was intense. His loyalty may have led Duncan to dismiss warnings he had heard from accounting-standards specialists at Andersen that Enron's approaches to its off-book partnerships were problematic. Other instructions from Andersen Duncan took quite literally. An e-mail from an Andersen lawyer reminded him about the firm's document "retention policy" and led him to order his staff to shred documents immediately after Enron received a request from the Securities and Exchange Commission for information. Between Oct. 23 and Nov. 9, 2001, Duncan led a frenzied effort to do away with as many sensitive Enron documents as possible.

Andrew Fastow, Enron Chief Financial Offi-

cer (CFO), had first approached Duncan in 1999 about setting up the off-book partnerships. Fastow called them "special-purpose vehicles." The first one, LJM1, was a partnership that gave Fastow millions of dollars in compensation and allowed Enron to conceal millions of dollars of debt off of its balance sheet. LJM1 was followed by LJM2 and other partnerships of this nature. To approve the partnerships, Duncan had to get around Andersen's Professional Standards Group. When Duncan first consulted this group, the firm's source of advice on such issues, one of the members raised a number of serious objections. He said that it was not right for Enron to be recording "gains" from the sale of its assets to LJM. He said that the venture should not be managed by the company's CFO because of conflicts of interest. He also said it was unclear if Enron's Board of Directors should approve the partnerships. Duncan replied that he was not completely comfortable with the arrangements, either. However, there was nothing he could do about them.

Duncan then told Fastow that Andersen would only work with Enron on the partnerships if the company's CEO and its Board went along. Fastow got their permission and the matter seemed settled. After this, Andersen's total fees from Enron rose from $46.8 million in 1999 to $58 million in 2000.

Personally, Duncan continued to have some reservations about the complexity of the transactions in which Enron was engaged. Nevertheless, when Carl Bass, an accountant based in Houston, who was part of Andersen's Professional Standards Group, objected, Duncan had him removed from the account. Bass went to his boss, a senior partner at Andersen, complaining that the removal was unfair. Duncan's response was that Enron had given Bass a negative review and that it was Enron and not Duncan who was responsible for Bass' removal.

In 2002, Duncan again was forced to defend Enron to the Professional Standards Group. He assured them that the LJM partnerships were not an issue, but some members of the group refused to relent. One wanted to know if the partnerships met a "non-consolidation" test. What would happen if Enron had to merge the partnerships' results with its own (the partnerships were running huge losses)? Duncan tried to reassure the members of the standard group that special-purpose vehicles would not have to be amalgamated into Enron's financial statements so long as they had independent external ownership of at least 3% and that the Enron's partnerships met this test. However, a member of Duncan's team, Debra Cash, called a member of the standards group the night of the meeting and said testily that she did not agree, that Duncan was wrong about this point and that ultimately Enron would not be able to hide its losses in the special purpose entities. Enron and the standards group remained "miles apart" on the issue of the "outside equity needed for Enron's joint ventures," but never resolved the matter. Duncan stood up for the Enron position and intimated that Andersen could lose the account if the professional standards group decided against the company.

At "Andersen U.," the campus where Arthur Andersen trained new employees, there was a shrine to ethical accounting. In 1914, months after Arthur Andersen founded the company, a client demanded that Andersen approve a transaction to lower expenses and boost earnings, but Andersen said there was "not enough money in the city of Chicago" to make him do it. The client promptly fired the accountant. Later, Leonard Spacek, head of Andersen from 1947 to 1963, led a campaign to clean up the accounting industry.[2] His main focus was on eliminating conflicts of interest. Now, it was this very same issue that had started an ethical crisis that was affecting every firm in the industry, including KPMG.

Enron was not the first scandal in which Andersen had been involved. In the 1990s, there had been other scandals — from Sunbeam Corp. to Waste Management Inc. Facing obstruction-of-justice charges in the Enron case, Andersen was nearing its end as a company, a sad conclusion to a firm that had been considered one of the world's most successful accounting firms and one that personified integrity. Its 85,000 employees, who had generated $9.3 billion in revenue in 2002 would have to live with the consequences. Andersen had gone from the accounting industry's conscience to an accused felon.

What had gone wrong at Andersen? Could the same thing happen at KPMG? Now that it faced its own challenges, KPMG was trying to understand what it could learn from the Enron experience?

### Discussion Questions

1. What best explains David Duncan's actions?

2. To what extent is KPMG similarly at risk, as was Arthur Andersen? What can be done to prevent a similar fate?

3. How would you reform the way KPMG does business?

---

2. "Sad Account: Andersen's Fall From Grace Is a Tale of Greed and Miscues — Pushed to Boost Revenue, Auditors Acted as Sellers, Warred With Consultants — `Three Pebbles and a Boulder'" *Wall Street Journal*; Jun 7, 2002; By Ken Brown and Ianthe Jeanne Dugan.

# Case 3

## Transforming the Soul of Business

*The case presents a short exercise on conflicts in corporate views of social responsibility—the shareholder-profit-centric view versus corporate commitment to principles of sustainable development – and explores the role of individual ethics in the organization.*

*Relevant chapters: 1, 3, 5, 6, 9*

Darlington Foods is an integrated wholesaler and retailer of high-quality food products. It provides gourmet foods to supermarket chains and specialty stores in the United States and Europe under the well-known brand names of "Fuller Flavor," "Good-For-You," and "Healthy Delite." Partly through acquisition, its sales have more than doubled in the past 10 years, but profits have been disappointing.

The top management team consists of: company president and CEO Robert Dennis, 39, an undergraduate engineering graduate with a Ph.D. in educational administration from the University of Kansas; executive vice president Carl Martin, 49, who attended the University of Utah and worked for the Albertson and Super Value grocery chains; retail sales vice president Kevin J. O'Brien, 31, a graduate of the Harvard Business School; marketing vice president Jane Wyman, 40, who attended the University of Houston and worked for Dayton Hudson; and chief financial officer (CFO) Benson Siegel, 59, a CPA from the University of California, Berkeley, who used to run his own business.

The founder of the company, Maxine Chu, and the former CFO, Brian Kensington-Fuller, were forced to resign because of the company's poor performance.

Before the monthly executive team meeting in November 2003, O'Brien proposed to send five senior employees to a conference on "Transforming the Soul of Business: Profit, Competition, and Conscience on the New Fron-

|      | Sales (000s) | Operating Income (000s) | Net Loss (000s) |
| ---- | ------------ | ----------------------- | --------------- |
| 2001 | $28,380      | $1,554                  | $ (1,043)       |
| 2002 | $35,595      | (6,351)                 | (10,353)        |
| 2003 | $49,020      | (4,155)                 | (6,975)         |

Case study exercise developed by Alfred A. Marcus ©2006, NorthCoast Publishers, Inc.

tier," which would be held in Hilton Head Island, South Carolina, February 8-12, 2004. This proposal was part of O'Brien's ongoing effort to make the company a more socially responsible entity, along the lines of Ben and Jerry's and the Body Shop.

O'Brien believed that the key to restoring Darlington's profitability was to align it with upscale consumers that would appreciate a socially conscious profile. Doing so was not only a way to restore profitability, but the right thing to do. "This company should be governed by conscience," O'Brien was fond of saying. "It should not be a slave to short-term profits. If we do the right thing, everything will work out for the better."

The cost of sending the five employees to Hilton Head would be about $16,000. However, Darlington had not provided conference trips to employees in the past, so this marked a break with precedent.

Benson Siegel, the newest member of the executive team, had about a week until the next meeting to look over the conference brochure. On the title page, it advertised "Innovative Techniques for Making a Profit While Making a Difference," "How to Make Your Business a Positive Agent for Social Change," and "Step-by-Step Strategies to Build Your Company and Make it Thrive."

The mission of the conference sponsor, the National Institute for a New Corporate vision, was "to foster an evolution that encourages balance: a thriving corporate life, self-fulfillment, and meaningful personal relationships." Other companies that would be represented at the conference were Stonyfield Farm, Seventh Generation, Crip Publications, Reebok, Deja Foods (a maker of footwear from recycled soda bottles, tires, and latex), After the Fall Products, Odwalla (all-natural fruit juices), Motherwear, and Republic of Tea. The conference promised sessions that would address topics such as extraordinary customer service, incentives that work, employee empowerment, thinking globally, fostering creativity, employee ownership, collaborative communication styles, entrepreneurial spirit, reengineering, systems thinking, teamwork, and giving back to the community.

Siegel did not know what to think. A liberal Democrat, a successful entrepreneur, and philanthropist, he also had been known as a hard-driving person when he owned his own business. He felt that he had kept his priorities straight: "When in the office, use your head – keep your heart at home" was his motto.

Siegel was not inclined to support O'Brien's initiative and considered it his duty to bring some common sense to the executive team. He had been brought in to tame the youthful, disorganized exuberance of Maxine Chu, the company's talented but flawed founder, and Kensington Fuller, the prior CFO. O'Brien had been Chu's favorite and Siegel felt that the initiative was a left over that should no longer be part of Darlington's way of doing business.

Siegel was unsure how other members of the executive team stood on the conference. Though all of them had been hired by Chu, none completely shared her point of view. They were competent professionals who had done what Chu asked, but had not displayed much leadership. Darlington never had gone far in implementing the "creative capitalism" ideas O'Brien promoted. Chu believed these ideas were a matter of personal conviction and had been careful not to let them intrude deeply into the business. One reason she did not push hard was her fear of antagonizing customers, especially the large supermarket chains.

Siegel thought the culture at Darlington was a bit flaky and rather disorganized. He joked that it gave him a mild sensation of being captured by a cult. Chu was not dogmatic; O'Brien was another matter. No doubt about it, Siegel thought, O'Brien was extremely bright, but he was also arrogant and self-righteous, qualities that Siegel detested. Siegel feared O'Brien. He considered him single-minded, intolerant, excruciatingly pure, a fanatic; there was no telling how far he might go.

Siegel then read an article about how several socially conscious businesses had been unable to live up to their ideals. Ben and Jerry's deserted its much vaunted pay scale, which had meant that the CEO could earn only seven times the salary of a person who scooped ice cream. Stride Rite took its factories out of inner city locations and shipped jobs to low-wage countries in Asia, like Nike, its rival. The most interesting part of the article concerned a glaring expose about the Body Shop that had appeared in *Business Ethics: The Magazine of Socially Responsible Business.*

Titled "Shattered Image," it told the tale of a disgruntled former Body Shop franchisee, who ended up losing over $10,000 a month because of alleged discrepancies between what the Body Shop owners promised and what they delivered. The Body Shop was being investigated by the Federal Trade Commission for its treatment of franchisees. The article also claimed that the Body Shop used outmoded product formulas that relied on nonrenewable petrochemicals, and that it had a history of quality control problems, which had led to the selling of contaminated products.

Though a multimillionaire with an estimated net worth of over $200 million and a yearly income of $1.30 million, Anita Roddick (CEO of Body Shop) had proclaimed that she saw herself not only as a creator of profits for her shareholders but as "a force of good, working for the future of the planet." She had sought "enlightened capitalism" as "the best way of changing society for the better:"

> I think you can trade ethically, be committed to social responsibility and global responsibility and empower your employees without being afraid of them. I think you can rewrite the book on business.

But the article claimed that Roddick was a master of hype and image building and not much substance. Siegel sent copies of this article to all the members of the executive committee. He could not wait for the executive meeting.

O'Brien was not going to be done in by Siegel. He decided to invite a guest to the meeting, Laura Scher, a former MBA classmate of his, a person he believed was above reproach and represented the best of the new capitalism. Scher had graduated from Harvard in 1985 near the top of her class, but like O'Brien had not chosen the path to easy and quick riches. She refused a lucrative Wall Street offer and created her own company, Working Assets Funding Service, whose purpose was to do well by doing good.

The company started by offering a donation-linked credit card. Then it came up with a charity-connected long-distance phone service. Both businesses allowed people to donate to various left wing, feminist, and environmental causes while carrying out their everyday transactions. *Inc.* magazine named Working Assets one of the 500 fastest growing privately held companies in the United States.

O'Brien wanted Scher to convince the members of the executive committee that Darlington Foods could succeed by doing good. The soul of the company, however, first had to be transformed. The company needed an entirely new business ethic. The way to start was to allow the five employees to go to Hilton Head.

Foreseeing the coming battle, the other members of the executive committee were not sure how to react. What should Darlington Foods do? How should it steer between the powerful points of views of its talented executive committee members? Who was right about this issue—Benson Siegel or Kevin O'Brien?

### Discussion Questions

1. If you were Benson Siegel, how would you prepare yourself for the next meeting of the top management team? What would be your goals? What would you hope to accomplish?

2. If you were Kevin O'Brien, how would you prepare yourself for this meeting? What would be your goals? What would you hope to accomplish?

3. As a member of the management team, what are your views about the future of Darlington Foods and the differences between key members of the management team? Should employees be sent to the conference in Hilton Head?

# Case 4

## The Bhopal Disaster: Implications for Investments in Less Developed Countries

*The case analyzes the Union Carbide gas leak in Bhopal, India in 1984. It looks at the risk posed by chemicals as technology advances, the role of multinationals in the global economy, and the role of governments in business regulation.*

*Relevant chapters: 2, 3, 4, 9, 10*

In order to compete in the increasingly global economy, corporations had to be prepared to take advantage of expansion opportunities in foreign countries. The risks of such expansion, however, had been highlighted for all business people by the industrial accident that occurred in Bhopal, India in 1984. The accident killed more than 2,000 people and injured hundreds of thousands.

No industry was more concerned with the implications of the accident for foreign operations than the chemical manufacturers. The worst industrial accident in history had drawn critical attention to the industry. Congress and administrative agencies had proposed tougher laws and regulations governing how the indus-try conducted its business. Numerous stories in the media had documented the events leading up to the accident and the horrible consequences it had for the impoverished Indians who had made their homes near the Union Carbide plant where the accident occurred.

What changes would American chemical companies have to make in their safety policies and procedures in order to prevent a repeat of the disaster?

### The Role of Chemicals in Feeding the World's People

American chemical companies had a lot to offer a developing country like India. The agricultural chemicals like fertilizers and pesticides that they produced were a vital part of the Green Revolution that had increased food production dramatically in the poorer nations where additional food was so vital.

In 1983, experts estimated the number of chronically malnourished people in the world at between 0.45 and 1.3 billion, and that the number was growing every year.[1] It was necessary to increase the yields of the food crops if

Written by Mark Jankus with the editorial guidance of Alfred Marcus. This case study originally appeared in *Business & Society: Ethics, Government, and the World Economy,* by Alfred A. Marcus, Richard D. Irwin, Inc. 1993 ©2006, NorthCoast Publishers,Inc.

1.  From David E. Whiteside, "Note on the Export of Pesticides from the United States to Developing Countries," Harvard Business School case 384-097, 1983, p. 127.

everyone was going to be fed, since there was little unused land left to be cultivated in the developing countries. According to Nobel laureate Norman Borlaug, increases in world food supply required the use of pesticides.[2] Pesticide use had increased the average yield of corn crops grown in the tropics on research plots from 30 bushels per acre to 440 bushels per acre. Rice plots grown with the aid of insecticides in the Philippines showed yield increases of 100 percent.[3] Pesticide use also helped protect the crops after they had been harvested, when they were in storage and vulnerable to rodents and insects. Around 25 percent of the harvest worldwide would be lost without pesticide use, according to experts.[4]

Increased food production was not all that agricultural chemicals had to offer the developing nations. Economic growth necessary to raise standards of living was facilitated by the increased agricultural efficiencies chemicals made possible. Less land was needed to produce the same amount of food, and labor was freed up for other productive purposes. The sale of crops like cotton provided a valuable source of foreign exchange funds necessary to purchase advanced, modern technologies. Some experts estimated that without the use of pesticides in the United States, the price of farm products would increase by 50 percent.[5] Pesticides had proven effective in making food more affordable in developing countries as well. Finally, pesticide use had been tremendously effective in reducing the incidence of a variety of pest-borne diseases like malaria, elephantiasis, and yellow fever.[6]

### The Risks of Chemical Use

Clearly, there were undisputable benefits for developing countries who adopted modern technologies like agricultural chemicals. Unfortunately, as the Bhopal disaster had shown, there were also risks involved. India was a very different place from the United States, where much of the industrial technology for producing pesticides had been developed. The Indian infrastructure was more primitive and the culture had different norms regarding the purpose and value of human life. That meant a complex technology like pesticide production was an awkward fit.

The dangers of pesticide manufacture and use were not understood in many developing countries. Many people in developing countries perished from pesticide use. Estimates of annual pesticide poisonings ranged from a quarter to three quarters of a million people, with more than 10,000 dying annually. While developing countries used only 15 percent of the world's pesticides, they reported more than half of the accidental poisonings and more than three-fourths the deaths. Over half the fatalities were children.[7]

These fatalities occurred because people did not use the pesticides appropriately. For example, fishermen living on the shore of Lake Volta in Ghana used them to kill fish. Local people ate the fish, drank the water, and used it for other purposes. Many developed the blurred vision, dizziness, and vomiting that were symptoms of pesticide poisoning. The boomerang effect meant that people in developed countries also were affected. They ingested excess amounts of pesticides on the fruits and vegetables that they imported from LDCs where pesticides had not been properly used. Pesticides, which were banned from use in the U.S. like DBCP, were sold by U.S. firms abroad and came back in the produce that foreign producers sent to the U.S. This impact on people in developed nations was very hard to control.

Moreover, over time the efficacy of the pesticides used declined. The insects that pesticides were designed to control developed tolerances and eventually become immune to the pesticides that were supposed to prevent their development. Insect resistance to pesticides meant

---

2. Cited in ibid., p. 128.
3. Ibid.
4. Ibid.
5. Ibid, p. 129.
6. Ibid.
7. Whiteside, 1983, p. 129.

that repeated spraying of more powerful pesticides with greater toxicity to humans, animals, and the environment was necessary. This pesticide phenomenon was called the treadmill. It greatly disturbed scientists who pointed to the increasing concentrations of very deadly pesticides throughout the biosphere.

The regulatory apparatus in third world countries was completely inadequate to deal with these problems. Besides permitting pesticides to be imported to their countries which were not allowed to be used in developed nations, these countries had no labeling or handling requirements. To the extent that they had regulations, these regulations were poorly enforced. Moreover they had no sense for the alternatives to pesticides that were available. As a legacy of their colonial pasts, they tended to put restrictions on foreign firms operating in their countries. The Indian government, for instance, had passed laws limiting the degree of control that a foreign corporation could exercise over an Indian subsidiary. However, after the Bhopal accident, the government had laid the blame solely on Union Carbide, filing a $3 billion lawsuit after ruling itself the sole representative of the victims of the accident.[8]

### The Bhopal Accident

While a multinational corporation had much to gain in the way of expanded markets for its products by setting up business in the developing countries, Bhopal made it clear that there were costs to consider as well. Bhopal, the most centrally-located city in India, is the capital of one of the least-industrialized states in the country. Although the area had a fairly good base of natural resources like water and timber, the feudal history of the region had contributed to its status as a mainly agricultural region. Beginning in the 1950s, the Indian government had actively encouraged industrial development in the region, though it had not engaged in a comprehensive planning effort and as a consequence the infrastructure of services like roads, utilities, and communications services was poor.

By the 1980s, stagnation in agricultural production in the country's rural areas had driven thousands of people to the cities to look for work. Bhopal's population grew six-fold between 1961 and 1981, almost three times the average for the country as a whole. The resulting severe housing shortage forced the migrants to build shantytowns wherever there was open space,.Areas near industrial plants where work might be found were favorite choices.

The walls of Union Carbide's Bhopal plant were crowded with such squatter's dwellings. The plant was originally built in the 1960s in open fields within two miles of the local commercial and transportation center. At the time of start-up, the plant was used to mix chemical components that had been manufactured overseas and shipped to Bhopal into the final pesticide formulations that would be marketed. As a "finisher" in the manufacturing chain, the plant did not pose much threat to neighboring residential areas.

However, by 1978 the company, under pressure from the Indian government to manufacture the precursors to the pesticide in India and competitive pressures to backward-integrate its pesticide production, had built and begun operating the facilities necessary to manufacture those precursors. The plant was now much more of a health hazard than before, and although some local authorities objected to the continued siting of the plant at its present location, state and national government officials overruled them.[9] The plant was too important a part of the local economy to risk losing.

Among the pesticide components manufactured at the plant was a highly toxic compound called methyl isocynate (MIC). Used to make the active ingredient in the pesticide Sevin, MIC is highly unstable. It was manufactured in batches and stored in three refrigerated tanks set in concrete. Each tank was equipped with pressure and temperature gauges, a high-temperature alarm, a level indicator, and high- and low-level alarms.[10]

---

8.  Paul Shrivastava, *Bhopal: Anatomy of a Crisis,* (Cambridge, Ma.:Ballinger Publishing Co., 1987) p. 59.
9.  Ibid., p. 41.
10.  Ibid.

There were several safety systems designed to handle accidental leaks: a vent-gas scrubber which neutralized toxic gases with a caustic soda solution, a flare tower which could burn off the gases, the refrigeration system to keep the chemical at low, stable temperatures, and a set of water-spray pipes which could control escaping gases or extinguish fires.[11]

### The Evening of December 2, 1984

When Suman Dey, a control-room operator at the Bhopal plant, came on duty at 11:00 pm on the evening of December 2, 1984 everything seemed normal. He performed a routine check of the gauges in the control room and noticed that the pressure in the MIC storage tanks was within the normal range of 2-25 pounds per square inch (psi). At about 11:30, however, a worker noticed an MIC leak near the vent gas scrubber and notified Dey. A tea break was due at 12:15 am and the workers planned to fix the leak afterwards. By the time the break was over at 12:40 am it was too late. The pressure in one of the tanks, labeled E610, shot up to 30 psi shortly after the break began and minutes later exceeded the gauge's upper limit, 55 psi.

Dey ran outside to the storage area to investigate. He heard a tremendous rumbling sound beneath the concrete, and as he watched sixty feet of concrete six inches thick cracked open, unleashing heat so intense that Dey couldn't get close.[12] A white cloud of MIC began to shoot out of the vent gas tower attached to the tank and settle over the plant. Within a few minutes the fire brigade arrived and began to spray a curtain of water in the air to knock down the cloud of gas. The tower from which the gas was escaping was 120 feet high, however, and the water only reached about 100 feet in the air. The system of water spray pipes was also too low to help. Dey ran inside the control room and turned on the vent gas scrubber. It did not work. The scrubber had been under maintenance and had not been charged with a caustic soda solution. Experts later noted that even if the scrubber had been operational it would have been ineffective since the temperature of the escaping gas was at least 100 degrees fahrenheit hotter than the system was designed to handle.

By this time the plant superintendent had raced to the plant on his bicycle and he and Dey conferred on what to do next. They were afraid to turn on the flare tower for fear of igniting the large cloud of gas that had enveloped the plant. The superintendent then remembered that the flare tower was also being repaired and was missing a four-foot section. Likewise, the coolant in the refrigeration system had been drained weeks before to be used in another part of the plant. They considered routing the escaping gas into an empty MIC storage tank, but there were no empty tanks available, contrary to established safety procedures. There seemed to be nothing to do.

As the gas began to escape, a warning alarm was sounded but was shut off shortly afterwards. Four buses parked near the entrance which were intended to be used for emergency evacuations of plant workers and nearby residents were left sitting as workers fled the plant in panic. By 1:30 am the gas had permeated the control room and Dey dashed for his gas mask and oxygen tank. The few remaining control room workers fled, one of them breaking his leg as he scrambled up and over the barbed-wire-topped fence surrounding the plant. Dey left the control room and waited upwind for the cloud of gas to disperse, periodically putting on his mask to enter the control room and check the pressure gauge. By 2:30 am the gas had stopped shooting out of the vent stack. By 3:30 am the gas had dispersed from the plant.

Meanwhile, in the shantytowns and neighborhoods outside the plant, chaos reigned. The gas seeped into the rooms of the sleeping population, suffocating hundreds in their sleep and driving others out into a panicked run through the narrow streets where they inhaled even more of the gas. Blinded by the cornea-clouding effect of the gas, lungs on fire, thousands of people fled the city. Forty-five tons of MIC spread over 25 square miles of the city, killing

---

11. Ibid, p. 45.
12. Diamond, Stuart. "Workers Recall Horror," *New York Times*, January 30, 1985, p. I-1.

over 2,000 residents and seriously injuring 40,000 more.[13]

### The Costs of the Accident
Long after the accident victims continued to suffer from breathlessness, coughing, lung diseases, eye disorders, abdominal pain and vomiting, and menstrual disorders, as well as psychological trauma. The psychological problems were most severe for women of childbearing age, many of whom suffered from reproductive illnesses as a result of the accident. These women were afraid to tell their families or spouses about the problems because of the cultural prejudices against infertile women.[14]

The economic consequences of the accident were as devastating as the physical. Many victims were physically unable to work and their families suffered as a consequence. Estimates of business losses ranged up to $65 million. The Union Carbide plant was closed and 650 high-paying jobs were lost, as well as 1,500 government jobs that were peripherally related to the presence of the plant. In addition, the business reputation of the city and the whole developing world suffered as a consequence of the accident.[15]

Union Carbide was hard hit by the accident. Besides the $3 billion lawsuit filed against the company by the Indian government on behalf of the victims, the company's reputation came under attack from the worldwide news media. Activist groups undertook a variety of campaigns against the company, and communities where UC had proposed building plants canceled the plans.[16] The company's stock dropped from $48 per share to a low of $32-3/4 within a few weeks (though it rallied to $52 by the end of August 1985).[17] The company's debt rating was reduced to the lowest investment grade by

Standard and Poors. The company was sued by its own stockholders for not informing them of the risks of doing business abroad. Further damaging the company's and the industry's reputation was the revelation in early 1985 that there had been 28 major MIC leaks at the Union Carbide plant in Institute, West Virginia during the five years preceding the Bhopal accident.[18]

### The Investigation
In the weeks and months after the accident a horde of reporters, Indian government officials, and Union Carbide technical experts descended on the plant to find out what had gone wrong. Gradually it became apparent that the accident was the result of not just technical malfunctions in the plant's equipment, but also stemmed from human errors and organizational shortcomings.[19] The unprepared ness of the emergency infrastructure of the local government exacerbated the problem further.

The Union Carbide scientists that analyzed the residue that remained in tank E610 after the accident determined that the chemical reaction that led to the leak was caused when approximately 1100 pounds of water was somehow introduced into the tank. Water reacts exothermically with MIC to produce a hot, highly pressurized mixture of liquid, foam and gas. The pressure in the tank had reached 180 pounds per square inch, more than enough to blow open the safety valve and allow the deadly gas to escape. The question that remained was how the water had gotten into the tank.

There were two main theories. Most experts believe the water leaked into the tank on the evening of December 2nd when an employee washed out some of the pipes leading to the tank. Investigations revealed that the employee had failed to use a device called a slip blind to

---

13. "The Union Carbide Corporation and Bhopal: A Case Study of Management Responsibility," *Business Ideologies and Social Responsibilities*, p. 303.
14. Shrivastava, p. 74.
15. Ibid., p. 72.
16. Ibid., p. 76.
17. Ibid., p. 78; see Alfred A. Marcus and Robert Goodman, "Corporate Adjustments to Catastrophe: A Study of Investor Reaction to Bhopal," *Industrial Crisis Quarterly*, 3 (1989): 213-34.
18. Ibid., p.77.
19. Ibid., p. 48.
20. Ibid., p. 51.

ensure that water could not leak past a series of valves leading to the tank. Union Carbide argued that the accident was the result of sabotage by an unhappy employee who deliberately unscrewed a gauge and stuck a water hose into the tank. As support for this theory, Carbide cited the statements of some employees who remembered seeing a running water hose near the tank after the accident. The company also argued that it wouldn't have been possible for the large quantity of water introduced into the tank to have leaked past the series of valves between the pipes being washed and the tank.

Whatever the proximate cause of the accident, it was clear that the magnitude of deaths and injuries was the result of more than a few leaking valves or an act of sabotage. The safety policies and procedures which were intended to prevent such an accident were not followed, and the reasons they were not were rooted partly in the deteriorating financial condition of the Bhopal plant.

Simply put, the Bhopal plant was an unprofitable unit in an unimportant division of the company.[20] Competitors in the country's pesticide market had introduced new, inexpensive products and the Indian economy had been in a downturn for a few years. The Bhopal plant had been losing money for three years in a row. As profits fell and the plant's budgets were cut, maintenance was deferred, employees were laid off, and training programs were scaled back. Half the operators in the MIC unit were laid off between 1980 and 1984, leaving only six. Because of the layoffs and because of rumors that the plant was a candidate for divestment, morale was low and many of the best employees quit. Labor-management conflicts were common. A 1982 company safety inspection determined that many basic safety rules were being ignored; for example, maintenance workers were signing permits they were unable to read and others were working in prohibited areas without permission.[21] Safety training was inadequate—there had been many small accidents and one death in the past—and workers had no training in dealing with emergencies. There were in fact no emergency plans for the plant at all, so when the MIC leak occurred employees reacted in a disorganized manner, shutting off the warning siren, for example. The plant management and workers knew little about the toxic effects of MIC and couldn't supply the local authorities with any information to deal with the accident.[22]

The plant relied on manual operating systems to a much greater degree than its counterparts in the United States. The construction and final technical engineering of the plant had been done by Indian workers and engineers, and the Indian engineers had designed the plant to use more manual labor than comparable plants overseas, partly to generate more jobs. The communications system of the plant relied heavily on runners to bring messages between parts of the plant or outside the plant. The local police were not notified of the accident until 3 am, more than two hours after the release of gas began, partly because the phones weren't working, and partly because the plant management had an informal policy of not involving the local authorities with gas leaks.[23]

### The Indian Government's Role

While the Indian Government laid responsibility for the accident completely at the door of Union Carbide, it played a significant role in contributing to the conditions that created the disaster. Like many developing countries, India had strict rules regarding the degree to which foreign companies were allowed to own and operate businesses within its borders. Intent on developing the self-sufficiency of Indian industry, the government placed restrictions on the equipment that could be imported, the source of the raw materials used in manufacturing processes, and the makeup of the labor force.

Because of these regulations, control of the Bhopal plant was turned completely over to its Indian subsidiary, Union Carbide India Limited

21. Ibid., p. 49.
22. Ibid., p. 50.
23. Diamond, "Workers Recall Horror."
24. Ibid.

(UCIL) in 1982, and the plant was operated solely by Indians. UC's top management in Connecticut received monthly reports concerning the plant and continued to make major decisions concerning financial, maintenance, and personnel decisions, but the Indian personnel were responsible for making safety inspections and operating the plant, including the MIC unit, according to the processing manuals supplied by headquarters. Many aspects of the relatively primitive local and national infrastructure also contributed to the severity of the accident. The Department of Labor of the state where the accident occurred was responsible for safety inspections of the industrial facilities located there. Grossly understaffed, the Department had only 15 inspectors to cover the more than 8,000 industrial plants in the state, and some of the inspectors lacked even typewriters and telephones to assist them in their duties.[24] The two inspectors responsible for the area where the Bhopal plant was located were trained as mechanical engineers and had little understanding of the hazards of a chemical plant. The government, fearful of discouraging job-producing industries, was reluctant to place a heavy burden of safety and environmental regulations on business.

When a journalist from the Bhopal area wrote a series of articles in 1982 detailing the death of an employee that was caused by a chemical leak at the plant and warned of the possibility of a catastrophe, neither the plant management nor the government took action, even after the journalist wrote a letter to the Chief Minister of the state to warn him of the danger. A top government bureaucrat who requested that the plant be moved to another location because of the threat it posed to neighboring slum residents was transferred to another post.[25] When migrants began building dwellings adjacent to the plant, government officials allowed them to do so and in 1984 issued deeds allowing the squatters the right to stay for 30 years.

Besides an indifferent bureaucracy, the primitive state of the local social services infrastructure contributed to the severity of the accident. There was only one telephone per 1,000 residents, and dead lines were common. Running water was only available a few hours per day and was of poor quality. There was only one, government operated, radio station. The streets in the older parts of the city were only twelve feet wide and were crammed with animals, carriages, scooters, cars, buses, bicycles, and people, making evacuation difficult. The hospitals and dispensaries were not equipped to handle the flood of victims.

### Inappropriate Technology?

Some critics argue that a highly complex technology like pesticide production is inappropriate for a country like India, whose people are largely unfamiliar with the hazards of such technologies. The squatters who lived around the plant thought that it produced some kind of beneficial plant medicine and had no idea that there was any threat to their safety.[26] The employees of the plant were unfamiliar with the nature of the health threat posed by MIC and were unable to advise the doctors treating the injured. Further, preventative maintenance is a somewhat foreign concept in a subsistence economy, where the idea of spending money now in order to save money later is unfamiliar.

Others argue that modern technologies like pesticides are the developing world's best hope of achieving a better standard of living and that without such technologies to increase the food supply, millions would die. A Bhopal-like accident, they contend, is part of the price developing societies pay for modernization.

The Bhopal disaster demonstrated that the actions of one small plant in a distant subsidiary could threaten the survival of a whole multinational corporation. There was a definite need for a list of guidelines for corporate involvement in the developing world that would help ensure that the mistakes contribut-

---

25. Hazarika, Sanjoy, "Indian Journalist Offered Warning," *New York Times*, Dec. 11, 1984, p. I-9.
26. "Slumdwellers Unaware of Dangers," *New York Times*, January 31, 1985, p. I-8.

ing to the Bhopal disaster would not be repeated. A plan was needed and it was urgent – as the legitimacy of the industry was in question.

### Discussion Questions

1. If accidents consequences are severe when might it be worth the risk to engage in foreign production?

2. What were the causes of the Bhopal accident? How could it have been prevented?

3. What should the chemical industry do to avoid the repeat of such a disaster in the future?

# Case 5

## St. Valentine's Day Massacre Redux: The Human Cost of Chocolates and Diamonds

*The case is an analysis of human rights abuses associated with the chocolate industry and the diamond industry. Child slavery in the Ivory Coast and rebel regimes in Sierra Leone and Angola create the problem. The case study explores the response of businesses engaged in the production and sale of these commodities and assesses the efficacy of current voluntary pacts aimed to restrict the involvement of legitimate businesses with crimes against humanity: the Harkin-Engel Protocol for Cocoa Production and the Kimberly Process for Conflict Diamonds.*

*Relevant chapters: 2, 3, 10*

*"If I had to say something to them it would not be nice words.*
*They buy something that I suffer to make.*
*They are eating my flesh."*

— Victor, a child slave in the Ivory Coast cocoa fields, to the chocolate-consuming public—from the documentary *Slavery*, by True Vision (2000)

Nothin' says lovin' like somethin' sweet or sparkly. Attempts to materially express love and affection often take the form of indulgence in luxuries like chocolates and diamonds; especially on those special days that commemorate "love" like St. Valentine's Day and wedding anniversaries. As a culture we unquestioningly embrace as tradition that betrothal in marriage will be accompanied by the gift of a diamond ring to the bride-to-be; without realizing that the custom is the result of a decades-old (and very successful) marketing campaign by a diamond cartel. We reward our children and ourselves with chocolate in all forms; an affordable fix of sweet stimulation is available to just about everyone. We do this weighing the costs associated with the indulgence—the steep price of a diamond balanced against its value, both in what it represents and on resale; the calories and fat and carbohydrate count of a sweet gooey bar of chocolate balanced against... well, you know... What is not weighed by the average purchaser is the human cost of producing that product. In both of these industries—cocoa production and diamond production—the human cost of production is the ultimate price: payment in body and soul.

This case study was authored collaboratively by Prof. Sheryl Kaiser, Laura Daly (Loyola College'04), and Carolee Dobbins (Loyola College'04). @2006, NorthCoast Publishers, Inc.

Nearly one-half of the world's chocolate comes from cocoa beans grown in the West African country of Ivory Coast, where the use of child slaves to work the cocoa plantations is commonplace. In many of the diamond-producing countries of Africa, notably Angola and Sierra Leone, diamond production rests in the hands of rebel forces. These rebel regimes use the profits from sales to legitimate diamond distributors to fund their nefarious practices of forced labor, forced relocation, rape, recruitment of child soldiers, and the amputation of limbs from tens of thousands of children, men, and women.

### Like taking candy from a baby. . .

More than 43% of the world's chocolate comes from cocoa beans grown in the West African country of Cote d'Ivoire, the Ivory Coast. The cocoa trade in the Ivory Coast is a huge market with 600,000 cocoa farms—the cocoa industry constitutes fully one-third of the Ivory Coast economy.[1] Much of the field work on these Ivory Coast cocoa plantations is uncompensated and performed by children who have been either sold or tricked into slavery. The US State Department's *2000 Human Rights Report* estimated that more than 15,000 children have been sold into slavery to work on cocoa, coffee, and cotton plantations in the Ivory Coast from the surrounding countries of Mali, Togo, and Benin. The estimate is considered conservative by many child-rights advocates.

In July 2001, Knight-Ridder Newspapers ran a series of investigative articles in the United States that revealed the on-going slave-trading and slave-holding practices in the country. In its September/October 2001 issue, *Mothering Magazine* reported on children ages 7-18, who are purchased for $1.50 each and sold for up to $350 dollars each into West Africa's agricultural, domestic, and sexual industries, where they remain slaves all their lives. The children sold into such slavery are often the sons and daughters of poor street sellers whose parents sell them for just a few dollars; or they are aban-doned children of the slums, tricked into slavery by a promise of honest paid work— essentially kidnapped by slave-traders. The slave-children are brutally beaten, locked up at night, insufficiently fed, receive no medical care, and are made to work 12-hour days without any compensation. They are routinely and incessantly dehumanized. They are mere means to the end of cocoa production; considered to have no intrinsic human value beyond what they can produce for their owners' profit. Needless to say, most of these children have never even tasted chocolate.

There is a great demand for cocoa plantation workers. When plantation owners are faced with the choice of paying adult workers or using child slave laborers at no cost, the profit-maximizing owners will opt for the latter. The lack of development in the Ivory Coast—the lack of public education in particular—has only aided the plantation owners in slave-trading. Ivory Coast law stipulates that children must attend school until age 16; however, it is a rarely enforced law, given that more than 70% of Ivorian children leave school by the age of 12 or 13 years. According to the *CIA World Fact Book*, 37% of the people living in the Ivory Coast live below the poverty line (which is set at bare subsistence) and the impoverished families cannot afford the cost of schooling, books, uniforms, and school supplies. So these children, mostly boys, are sold by their parents to the plantation owners for cash needed for the survival of the rest of the family. The Ivory Coast government, well aware of the practice and the problem, has taken no meaningful action to stem child slavery on the plantations.

The nature of this slavery has changed a bit from that practiced in the antebellum South; though seemingly inconceivable, it has actually gotten *less* humane.

As John Robbins has explained:

> The ownership of one human being by another is illegal in Ivory Coast, as it is in every other country in the world

---

1. http://www.stopchildlabor.org/internationalchildlabor/facts

today. But that doesn't mean slavery has ceased to exist. Rather, it has simply changed its form. In times past, we had slaveowners. Now we have slaveholders. In both cases, the slave is forced to work by violence or the threat of violence, paid nothing, given only that which keeps him or her able to continue to work, is not free to leave, and can be killed without significant legal consequence. In many cases, non-ownership turns out to be in the financial interest of slaveholders, who now reap all the benefits of ownership without the obligations and legal responsibilities.

Kevin Bales is author of *Disposable People: New Slavery in the Global Economy* and director of *Free the Slaves*, an American branch of Anti-Slavery International. . . . He points out that one of the economic drawbacks of the old slavery was the cost of maintaining slaves who were too young or too old to work. Children rarely brought in more than they cost until the age of ten or twelve, though they were put to work as early as possible. Slavery was profitable, but the profitability was diminished by the cost of keeping infants, small children, and unproductive old people. The new slavery avoids this extra cost and so increases its profits.

In the United States, the old slavery consisted primarily of bringing people against their will from Africa. This represented a significant financial investment. Bales says that before the Civil War, the cost to purchase the average slave amounted to the equivalent of $50,000 (in today's dollars). Currently,

though, enslaved people are bought and sold in the world's most destitute nations for only $50 or $100. The result is that they tend to be treated as disposable. Slaves today are so cheap that they're not even seen as a capital investment anymore. Unlike slaveowners, slaveholders don't have to take care of their slaves. They can just use them up, in the cocoa fields for example, and then throw them away.[2]

Industry response to the initial revelations of the investigative reports ranged from sincere shock to disingenuous disbelief. Some of the smaller players in the industry were already aware of the problem and had responsibly addressed it by committing to purchase only Fair Trade Certified cocoa beans, which guarantees that slave labor was not used in production; or by using only organic beans, which are not grown in the Ivory Coast.[3] The larger industry players, however, were not so in touch with the issue until it touched them directly, and negatively. The $13 billion US chocolate industry consists primarily of a few big players with the lion's share of the market. Hershey's and M&M/Mars control 2/3 of the US market; Nestle and Cadbury Schweppes (the market leader in the UK) each have a substantial stake as well. When the story became publicly known, none of these companies had a handle on the issue or a policy approach toward it, despite the fact that the use of child slaves in the Ivory Coast was well-known in the trade and despite the fact that Cadbury Schweppes had a corporate human rights policy that supposedly would have addressed the issue.

For some time, several NGOs, including the Geneva-based International Labor Organization

---

2. "Is There Slavery in Your Chocolate?" by John Robbins, www.earthsave.org. Robbins is among the world's leading experts on the dietary link to the environment and health. He has authored many books on health and ecology, was awarded the 1994 Rachel Carson Award, and is the founder of EarthSave International. Robbins, incidentally, is the son of the founder of Baskin-Robbins. *See* also *foodrevolution.org*

3. See the mini-case on Fair Trade Certified coffee in Chapter 3. Companies already using only slavery-free cocoa included Cliff Bar, Cloud Nine, Dagoba Organic Chocolate, Denman Island Chocolate, Gardners Candies, Green and Black's, Kailua Candy Company, Koppers Chocolate, L.A. Burdick Chocolates, Montezuma's Chocolates, Newman's Own Organics, Omanhene Cocoa Bean Company, Rapunzel Pure Organics, and The Endangered Species Chocolate Company. The last two, Rapunzel and Endangered Species Chocolate buy only Fair Trade Certified cocoa, which guarantees fair pricing, long term trade relationships, living wages, and no child labor. See Robbins, *Ibid.*

(ILO) and the Fair Trade movement, have pushed for those in the chocolate industry to take some responsibility for their role in the problem by agreeing to purchase cocoa certified as child-slave-labor-free. The ILO forbids child slavery and is in coalition with the Fair Trade movement in asking chocolate manufacturers to buy only certified cocoa. The certified cocoa is a bit more costly at 80 cents a pound, but would go a long way toward putting the plantation slave-owners and the slave-traders out of business.

One of the ILO's biggest steps toward eradicating child labor was its Convention 182, introduced in 1999. The goal of this convention was to respond to the urgent need of the children who were being abused all over the world for labor, prostitution, and pornography. Convention 182 calls nations to recognize and eliminate practices involving child labor and to enact and enforce laws designed to protect children against mistreatment. The Convention also recognizes that ". . . child labor is to a great extent caused by poverty and that the long-term solution lies in sustained economic growth leading to social progress, in particular poverty alleviation and universal education."[4]

The Ivory Coast has not ratified the Convention, but the US and many other nations have. The enforcement mechanism for such a Convention is wanting, however, as is the case with so many international compacts. Without voluntary industry cooperation, the principles of Convention 182 have little chance of meaningful implementation.

The initial response of Big Chocolate and its lobbyists to the public revelations was predictably anachronistic—lots of resources focused on defeating any legislative regulation of the business of producing chocolate. In 2001, the US House of Representatives introduced a labeling requirement for slavery-free cocoa and an amendment to the 2002 agriculture appropriations bill to allocate funds for the special labeling. The FDA would set aside $250,000 to provide the slavery-free certification labels for compliant products. A similar effort undertaken to certify "dolphin-safe" tuna had previously met with considerable success. Despite the best efforts of the industry lobby, the measure passed. As the legislation moved toward Senate approval, the industry saw the writing on the wall and capitulated—agreeing to voluntarily abide by the principles of the measure. The resulting agreement is known as the Harkin-Engle Protocol, named for its Senate and House sponsors, respectively.

The Harkin-Engle Protocol sets forth a series of requirements for setting labor standards in the production of cocoa and monitoring for compliance, with targeted dates for implementation. First on the agenda after the signing of the Protocol in the fall of 2001 was the establishment of the International Cocoa Initiative Foundation, made up of representatives of the chocolate industry, international labor, child rights and anti-slavery organizations. The purpose of the ICI is to ensure the elimination of the worst forms of child labor and forced labor in cocoa growing. The ICI is charged with developing a long-term strategy for universal compliance with the anti-slavery conventions in the production of cocoa worldwide. By July of 2005, the Protocol requires full and final implementation of standards of public certification that cocoa has been grown without the worst forms of child labor, and should include independent monitoring and verification components.

Albeit belatedly, a few of the larger players in the industry have stepped up to the challenge of addressing the issue. For example, Cadbury Schweppes, which had a long-standing human rights policy prohibiting forced labor of any kind, including child labor, has joined forces with the Fair Trade movement, claiming on their website "We share with the Fair Trade movement a commitment to improve the livelihoods of cocoa farmers and their families. We want all farmers to receive a fair return for their cocoa crops and Fair Trade is one way of achieving this goal." The company also has avowed its commitment to the Universal Declaration of Human Rights. The Sara Lee Corporation stopped buying coffee beans from Ivory Coast several years ago in order to distance the com-

---

4. www.hrw.org/reports/2000/framework

pany from the child-slavery practices on those plantations, and likely takes the same stance with Ivory Coast cocoa.[5] Hershey's has a substantial portion of its corporate website dedicated to its "commitment to responsible cocoa growing" as well. While not expressly endorsing the Fair Trade certification movement, Hershey's nonetheless claims to recognize the importance of sustainable development to the business of chocolate. The company points to its participation in a series of pilot projects under the Sustainable Tree Crops Program in West Africa, launched in 2000:

> The pilots are designed to last three years and test the best ways to drive economic, environmental and social improvement in the cocoa-growing regions of these countries. While final results won't be available until next year, clear successes have been achieved. Radio messaging already is communicating the importance of appropriate labor standards to often-remote farming communities in Ghana, with plans for expansion in the Ivory Coast. Progress is being seen in providing vocational education opportunities, a clear need for young people ages 9 to 15. And Farmer Field Schools are proving a tremendous tool for teaching farmers across the region about labor standards and improved farming methods.[6]

The Protocol's voluntary standards on the use of "the worst forms" of forced child labor (a very limited mandate at the outset) were not due until July 2005. Until that time, and until meaningful standards are implemented and monitored for compliance, the only course for chocolate manufacturers who wished to be socially responsible was to move beyond mere compliance. Companies seeking best practices in the area would be well-served to follow the example set by companies like Equal Exchange. Equal Exchange is the leading company in the United States for Fair

Trade beverages and in 2003 added Fair Trade cocoa powder and hot cocoa mix to their line. These cocoa products carry the Fair Trade label as certified by TransFair USA, an independent, non-profit NGO that does all Fair Trade certification for goods sold in the US.

Nonetheless, Big Chocolate is moving in the right direction. Larry Graham, president of the industry's largest trade group, the Chocolate Manufacturer's Association, said of the Protocol "the industry has changed, permanently and forever." Let's hope he is true to his word. It is the only hope these children have.

### Goodness has nothing to do with it . . .

Woman: *Goodness, what beautiful diamonds!*
Mae West: *Goodness had nothing to do with it, dearie.*
— From the film *Night After Night* (1932)

Rough stones—mined, sorted, cut, polished, and marketed for a precious sum. The value of a diamond lies not in its intrinsic value—it is a stone—but in what it has come to represent in the social consciousness. Many natural commodities have enjoyed their era as most-valued—gold, silver, frankincense and myrrh, precious gems, oil, coffee, tea, even cocoa beans in earliest cultures—this era just happens to bestow extraordinary worth on the diamond.

The diamond is not naturally a rare gem. "Despite its elite status, the diamond, which can be found in abundance from southern Africa to Australia to northern Canada, is not the rarest of gems. With no intrinsic value, all a gem-quality diamond has to offer is the perception of its preciousness."[7] The creation and maintenance of that perception, coupled with the near-monopoly control of the diamond market by one company, DeBeers, has managed to elevate the status of diamonds to the pinnacle of dearness. That value translates into big dollars for those involved in the diamond trade.

DeBeers created value in diamonds with a dual strategy. First, beginning with the diamond

5. "How Can Something So Sweet Taste So Wrong?" by Athena Sydney, May 10, 2004, http://www.ritro.com/sections/worldaffairs
6. Hershey's website- Hershey's Commitment to Responsible Cocoa Growing
7. Emerling, Susan. "Not Forever." 27. Sept. 2000  http://www.salon.com/business

rush of the 1870s, company-founder Cecil Rhodes worked to expand and consolidate DeBeers Mining production.[8] Under the leadership of CEO Earnest Oppenheimer, DeBeers gained ownership of most of the Kimberley diamond fields in South Africa as well as mines in Angola, Botswana, and Zaire. "At the height of its powers, DeBeers controlled about 80 percent of the world's diamond supplies, striking joint venture deals with most producing countries that enabled the company to control the release of diamonds onto the world market."[9] As the demand for diamonds ebbed and flowed from the Roaring 20s through the Great Depression of the 1930s, Oppenheimer contracted to buy nearly all of the diamonds available in the world and then to limit their availability on the market. Thus, the diamond cartel was born with the control of supply.[10]

On the demand side, the company has been able to establish themselves as *the* source for diamonds and the DeBeers name has come to represent quality and prestige. DeBeers initiated its "A Diamond is Forever" advertising campaign in the 1930s in response to the decline in the demand for diamonds during the Great Depression. DeBeers as well established a brand in "The Diamond Engagement Ring," which has become its leading product. The campaign succeeded beyond anyone's wildest expectations, making DeBeers the preeminent source for engagement rings. The Diamond is Forever slogan has "become so entrenched in American culture that many people never realized it was an advertising vehicle... Almost eighty percent of all American marriages begin

with the gift of a diamond ring."[11]

DeBeers' strategy of holding a substantial stock of diamonds, controlling supply, and promoting final demand proved effective, but costly, because it enabled free-riders in the market, which then became competition. As a result, DeBeers has changed its modern strategy away from horizontal integration (aimed at controlling world production and marketing of unpolished diamonds) and toward more vertical integration (controlling the product from the mine all the way to the jewelry store)—so as to stem competition from all sectors of the diamond market.

A bit more than 40% of the world's diamond production value originates from Botswana, South Africa, and Namibia; countries in which DeBeers controls a major share of the mining, sorting and cutting stages of production. Ten countries in South Africa, including Sierra Leone, comprise 25% of world diamond production. The diamonds in these countries, known as alluvial diamonds, are found primarily along the river beds where the mining sites cannot be fenced or secured and controls are loose and frequently ineffective. This is where the problem of conflict diamonds arises.[12]

Alluvial diamond mining is poverty-driven work, usually done by uneducated people who have no other employment options. "Today, an estimated 13 million people in about 30 countries across the world are small-scale/artisan miners, with about 80 million to 100 million people depending on mining of gold and precious stones for their livelihood."[13] This type of

---

8. DeBeers. 10 April 2000  http://www.adiamondisforever.com

9. The International Consortium of Investigative Journalists, *Conflict Diamonds are Forever,* 2002

10. At one point, Nicky Oppenheimer, only partly in jest, declared, "I am chairman of DeBeers, a company that likes to think of itself as the world's best known and longest running monopoly." Indeed, due to antitrust violations in the US, DeBeers has no stores or concrete representation in the country, with the exception of NWAyer, its marketing firm. The company has battled antitrust charges in the US for decades. Until quite recently, if any DeBeers executive were to set foot on US soil, he would be subject to immediate arrest (Emerling, Susan, "Not Forever," Sept. 27, 2000, http://www.salon.com/business). In July of 2004, DeBeers pleaded guilty in the US to charges of price-fixing in the industrial diamond market, agreed to pay a $10 million fine, and ended the 60-year legal impasse. The $10 million payment means that DeBeers executives are now free to live and work in the United States, the largest diamond market in the world.

11. Griggs, Robyn, "For DeBeers, A Great Slogan is Forever," *Advertising Age,* 29 Mar. 1999, C21

* One stand-up comedian has noted that married men live longer than unmarried men, and unmarried women live longer than married ones; leading him to conclude that the diamond engagement ring is given by the man to the woman as a sort of payment "for the life I'm about to suck out of you."

12. Goreux, Louis, "Conflict Diamonds," Mar. 2001, *Africa Region Working Paper Series* No. 13.

13. Ibid.

work is generally dangerous, unhealthy, precarious, and poorly paid, but miners expose themselves and their families to these dangerous, harsh working conditions because they have no other choice. This is a highly unstructured and unregulated industry which diminishes the economic potential. It creates human rights concerns because, "labor laws, if they exist, are not enforced, including the use of child labor. Because of low pay, civil servants, if present, are often prone to corruption. Finally, 'law' enforcement in conflict diamond zones is in the hands of the rebel forces."[14]

In many African countries, including Sierra Leone, "diamonds have been, and are continuing to fund terrible human rights abuses either by insurgent groups or by unscrupulous governments who are equally brutal, to fuel conflict and carry out atrocities against innocent civilians."[15] According to the United Nations, conflict diamonds are "diamonds that originate from areas controlled by forces or factions opposed to legitimate and internationally recognized governments, and are used to fund military action in opposition to those governments, or in contravention of the decisions of the Security Council."[16]

The issue of conflict diamonds was brought to the attention of the world in 1992 during the war in Angola, when UNITA leader Jonas Savimbi, seeking new ways to finance his army, looked to the country's vast diamond fields to extend the smuggling business his rebel movement had pioneered in the 1970's and 1980's.[17] Over the course of the year, Savimbi was able to create one of the largest diamond-smuggling networks ever—selling directly to "legitimate" diamond exporters. One such company was De Decker Diamonds, which admitted to selling the diamonds directly to DeBeers.[18] Although the evidence points clearly to DeBeers' complic-

ity, the company adamantly denies any involvement with conflict diamonds.

That model for diamond smuggling to fund rebel operations has been replicated in many other African countries. One of particular note is the situation in Sierra Leone. Sierra Leone is at the forefront of the conflict diamond issue due to the extraordinary abusiveness of the rebel forces that control most of the country's diamond production. Since 1991, the civil war between the Sierra Leone government and the Liberia-backed rebel Revolutionary United Front (RUF) has crippled the country. The RUF has forced millions of Sierra Leoneans from their homes and committed tens of thousands of abuses, including rape, recruitment of child soldiers, and the amputation of hands of thousands of children, men, and women.

Diamonds are just about the only thing supporting the economy of Sierra Leone. Yet, much of the income from diamonds is taken by the rebel forces. "Export earnings from diamonds were estimated in 1999 at $138 million, of which $70 million went to the RUF and at least $10 million to the Civil Defense Force (CDF), a militia organization presently supporting government forces."[19]

It was not until 1998 that the United Nations first addressed the issue of conflict diamonds. The UN ultimately created a monitoring mechanism to investigate conflict diamond peddling in Angola, and the Security Council imposed sanctions on diamond dealing with UNITA in 1998, which were later extended to Sierra Leone.[20] In July 1999 the warring parties signed the Lomé Peace Agreement to stop the bloody fighting in the area. The UN Security Council established the Mission in Sierra Leone (UNAMSIL) in October 1999 to help implement the Lomé Agreement, but, despite UNAMSIL's presence, fighting continued. In May 2000 the

14. Ibid.

15. "Scheme to End the Trade in Conflict Diamonds-Regular Monitoring Not Agreed." 31 Oct. 2003. NGO Press Release. http://www.worldvision.org

16. http://www.un.org/peace

17. The International Consortium of Investigative Journalists, *Conflict Diamonds are Forever*, 2002.

18. Ibid.

19. Goreux, Louis, "Conflict Diamonds," *Africa Region Working Paper*, Series No. 13 (Mar. 2001).

20. The International Consortium of Investigative Journalists, *Conflict Diamonds are Forever*, 2002.

crisis peaked as the RUF took 500 UN peace-keepers hostage.[21]

The conflict diamond problem became of greater concern after the September 11, 2001 terrorist attacks on the US, when evidence was presented that diamonds were used by terrorist organizations, including al Qaeda, as a means of transferring their wealth globally.[22] Such concentrated attention on conflict diamonds, and the revelation of atrocities by those who trade in them, finally prompted the African countries to take steps to remedy the problem.

The Kimberley Process was established by southern African diamond-producing countries in 2000 to stem the flow of rough diamonds by rebels. Among its objectives was the protection of the legitimate diamond industry, upon which many of the affected countries depended. The Process aims to register the origin of all rough diamonds before they are sold, polished and cut. The premise of the Kimberley Process is that, if people are made aware of the atrocious human rights violations being committed in the diamond mining process, they will not want to purchase conflict diamonds and support the rebel forces.

Verification for the process is accomplished through the Kimberley Process Certification Scheme, which is an international certification scheme for rough diamonds based primarily on national certification schemes and on internationally agreed minimum standards. The aim of this program is to certify which diamonds have come from legitimate mines and to identify which diamonds are conflict diamonds. It also extends further to require that diamond retailers educate company employees about the self-regulation so that consumers can be given appropriate assurances that diamonds are conflict-free. All of this is to be regulated and overseen by the World Diamond Council.

However, even the Kimberley Process has been criticized for being inherently flawed:

The period after rough diamonds enter the first foreign port until the final point of sale is covered by a system of voluntary industry participation and self-regulated monitoring and enforcement. These and other shortcomings provide significant challenges in creating an effective scheme to deter trade in conflict diamonds.[23]

Research by Global Witness revealed that these flaws were indeed hindering the process and that diamond retailers were not carrying out the basic steps of self-regulation.[24] In addition to not complying with self-regulation, companies were also failing to educate employees about these practices, which means that consumers were not being informed about the origin of their diamonds. The Global Witness report showed that:

Salespeople were well-informed about their company's policy and the system of warranties in only 4 out of 33 stores.

Out of 30 companies, 25 have failed to respond to Global Witness in writing about their policies on conflict diamonds and the self-regulation. One of these [non-responsive] companies is Harry Winston, which buys directly from DeBeers.

The World Diamond Council, which is responsible for coordinating industry's efforts to combat conflict diamonds, has not adequately monitored compliance with the self-regulation, nor have other trade associations.

At a minimum corporations owe their consumers the basic right to know whether their money is being used to support a regime that commits such horrifying human rights violations This is true with respect to the obligations of those in the business of diamonds; and with respect to the issue of complicity by these companies in doing business with the rebels and

21. http://www.un.org/peace
22. Ibid.
23. The International Consortium of Investigative Journalists, *Conflict Diamonds are Forever*, 2002
24. *Global Witness* "Broken Vows: Diamond Jewelry Retailers Fall Short on Conflict Diamond Pledge" 30 Mar. 2004

thereby financially enabling them;. The issue of conflict diamonds is one of not only human rights, but corporate transparency, and basic moral minimums.

DeBeers sits in a peculiarly powerful position, dominating the market as a supplier and purchaser. In addition, they are a part of the World Diamond Council, effectively giving them regulatory authority over themselves. DeBeers' stance on conflict diamonds is set forth on its website as follows:

> The Kimberley Process officially comes into force on January 1st 2003. However, De Beers LV will be fully compliant with the new scheme from the day our first store opens in London, in November 2002.
>
> All our diamonds are sourced from guaranteed supplies governed by both the international certification regime and the system of warranties.
>
> Our Store Manager and trained staff will be happy to answer questions you may have about the efforts of the diamond industry to tackle the problem of 'conflict diamonds'.

Although DeBeers represents itself as fully compliant and cooperative with the Kimberley Process, its "opaque operating procedures make it impossible to trace the origin of its diamonds."[25] Diamond tracing is the backbone of the Kimberley Process; without it, the problem of conflict diamonds is virtually unsolvable; the tainted goods invisible. Contamination with conflict diamonds can be prevented only if all those with access to the pipeline respect strict compliance with the tracking system of the Kimberly Process—from mine to jeweler.

Given the power of DeBeers over the diamond industry, its failure to step up to the moral plate in its operations and openly and transparently assure that its diamonds are conflict-free suggests that independent monitoring of the Process is essential. The designated oversight authority, the World Diamond Council, is dominated by industry players themselves—the fox is guarding the henhouse. The stakes in human life and security are simply too great for such blind trust in a business trust.

Next anniversary? Say it with flowers....

### Discussion Questions

1, Compare the responses of Cadbury Schweppes, Sara Lee, and Hershey. Are they adequate? What more should they be doing?

2. Are these companies moving in the right direction.

3. What are the purposes of the Kimberly Process Certification scheme? Will it adequately achieve the goals it proposes to achieve?

4. Evaluate De Beer's response to conflict diamonds?

5. To what extent would independent monitoring of DeBeer' activities make a difference? Is independent monitoring the best long-term solution? What else can be done?

---

25. The International Consortium of Investigative Journalists, *Conflict Diamonds are Forever,* 2002
* Additional sources include the case studies prepared by the co-authors: "Child Slave Labor Conditions in the Ivory Coast and the Recent Efforts to Thwart its Progress" by Laura Daly, and "The DeBeers and Conflict Diamonds: Diamond Mining in Sierra Leone" @2006, NorthCoast Publishers, Inc.

# Case 6

## Lying Down with Dogs ... Getting Up with Lawsuits: Unocal and the Alien Tort Claims Act

*The case of Doe v. Unocal is examined in the context of corporate responsibility for human rights abuses in overseas operations. The legal requirements of the ATCA, current international law on human rights, and the activities of Unocal in Burma are explored in some depth. Other pending cases against US companies under the ATCA are considered*

*Relevant chapters: 2, 3, 10*

Thoughts from the turn-of-the-1st century:

*He who helps the guilty shares the crime.*
— Publilius Syrus, *Sententiae*

*He who profits by crime commits it.*
— Seneca, *Medea*

*He who does not prevent a crime when he can encourages it.*
—Seneca, *Troades*

Two thousand years later, the law is still evolving to reflect the moral concept of responsibility by complicity. In the international arena, where governing law is limited and mechanisms for enforcement are lacking, a new legal approach is emerging: the use of home-country national law and home-country courts to hold multinational corporations accountable for violating human rights on foreign soil, in a host country. In the United States, more than two dozen such suits have been brought by foreign nationals against multinational companies under the *Alien Tort Claims Act* (ATCA)—a law enacted in the US in 1789 to allow cases involving violations of the law of nations, or international law, to be heard in Federal court. None of the cases have yet gone through the full trial process, and a few have been dismissed on grounds of improper forum (deeming the host country instead to be the proper place for trial); but several of the cases remain pending and at least one of the cases has survived several rounds of motions to dismiss and seven years of litigation to make its way to the Ninth Circuit Court of Appeals. The case promises a sea change for the way American multinationals conduct business if it is decided in the plaintiff's favor. That case, *Doe v. Unocal*, is discussed in detail below.

The theory of the case in most of these lawsuits against the multinational companies is *complicity*—that the multinational companies were complicit in human rights abuses perpe-

Case study by Sheryl Kaiser, J.D. (2003); @2006, NorthCoast Publishers, Inc.

trated by the government. This complicity derives from the nature of their business relationship with the government—that they are active collaborators doing business with the regime, not merely companies conducting business in a repressive country. In most instances of major commercial development in Third World countries, such as pipelines or resource extraction, private corporations partner with the government or government-owned companies to undertake such projects. The nature of this business relationship as a common enterprise leads to a legal characterization akin to "aiding-and-abetting" illegal activity where the private company knows of the misdeeds undertaken by its confederates in furtherance of the goals of the business arrangement.

A partial list of the cases brought against multinational corporations thus far under the ATCA provides a picture of the nature of justice sought under the statute:

*ChevronTexaco for activities in Nigeria*—the suit alleges that the oil company encouraged and assisted the brutal Nigerian military in gross human rights violations associated with protecting ChevronTexaco's oil production in the Niger delta; including the shooting of peaceful protesters at a Chevron-Texaco offshore platform by soldiers flown in by ChevronTexaco and the destruction of two villages by soldiers in ChevronTexaco helicopters and boats.

*Shell Oil for activities in Nigeria*— the suit alleges that the oil company requested the intervention of and condoned the brutal tactics of the Nigerian military for protection of Shell's oil operations in the Niger delta and the lands of the Ogoni tribe; culminating in the summary execution of Ogoni leader, writer and businessman Ken Saro-Wiwa, and eight other Ogoni activists (the "Ogoni Nine") by the Nigerian military government in 1995, a case that elicited international outrage. Shell declined to use its influence with the Nigerian military regime to save the lives of the polit-

ical dissidents, stating "a commercial organization like Shell cannot and must never interfere with the legal proceedings of any sovereign state"

*ExxonMobil for activities in Indonesia*—the suit alleges the company's complicity in human rights abuses—murder, torture, kidnapping and rape— at the hands of the Indonesian military unit guarding ExxonMobil's natural gas field in Aceh, an impoverished region of four million people in western Indonesia. It is alleged that ExxonMobil knowingly provided barracks where the military tortured detainees and lent heavy equipment like excavators that were used to dig mass graves for its victims.

*Talisman Energy Company for activities in the Sudan*—the suit alleges that the Canadian oil company undertook a "joint strategy" with the Islamic government in Khartoum whereby "government troops and allied militia engaged in an ethnic cleansing operation to execute, enslave, or displace the non-Muslim African Sudanese civilian population from areas that are near the pipeline or where Talisman wanted to drill." Evidence includes a May 1999 memo from Talisman asking the Sudanese government to "conduct clean up operations" in villages near the oil drilling area. Two days later, the Khartoum regime launched one of the largest military offenses of the civil war, destroying villages and driving out or killing half of the population in the area.

*Drummond and others for activities in Columbia*—the suit alleges that Drummond, an American mining firm, along with two Coca-Cola bottlers, and two other multinational companies, employed paramilitary forces as their agents in the assassination of three Columbian labor leaders engaged in union organizing efforts of the companies' respective workforces.

*Texaco for activities in Ecuador*—the suit alleges reckless environmental degradation by Texaco in its efforts to exploit rich deposits of crude oil under the Amazon; including the clear-cutting of whole forests, uncompensated takings and relocations, and millions of barrels of crude carelessly spilled into the Amazon. Texaco is alleged to have ignored all state-of-the-art advances for more environmentally responsible extraction, resulting in the complete destruction of arable lands, disease and deformity among the population, and the near-extinction of several indigenous tribes; clean-up costs alone exceed $600 million. This case was one of the first of the ATCA suits filed and it languished in court for nine years. The case was finally dismissed from US courts on the grounds that Ecuador was instead the proper forum for the case, despite the fact that all operational decisions were made at the company's New York headquarters, and despite the limitations of the comparatively rudimentary judicial system in Ecuador.

## Claims under the ATCA

*The Alien Tort Claims Act* was enacted into US law in 1789. It permits "aliens"—non-US citizens—to bring suit in US federal courts against those who caused harm to them on foreign soil. The harm caused—personal injury or property loss—must be the result of a violation of international law. The statute provides, "The district courts shall have original jurisdiction of any civil action by an alien for a tort only, committed in violation of the law of nations or a treaty of the United States." Early cases under the ATCA involved claims for piracy and slave trading. Then, for many years, the statute lay dormant. But in 1980, the law was used to hold a Paraguayan police inspector living in the US liable to the families of dissidents he tortured and killed in Paraguay. A $10 million judgment was entered against him. Since then, other cases have been successfully waged against agents of foreign governments for torture and murder, including claims by victims from the Philip-

pines, Argentina, Chile, Guatemala, and Bosnia. The case against Ferdinand Marcos of the Philippines by a group of Filipinos tortured by the regime resulted in a $150 million judgment against the former dictator's estate. Actions by private individuals (non-government agents) found to be acting in cooperation with the government are also covered by ATCA. Corporations are covered under the law in the same fashion as individuals—they are treated as persons, albeit artificial persons.

Several procedural conditions must be met to bring suit under ATCA. The plaintiff must be a non-US citizen. The court must have personal jurisdiction over the defendant; either by the presence of the defendant in the country or, in the case of a corporation, that the defendant conducts business in the US or has sufficient commercial contacts with the country to be subject to the jurisdiction of its courts. In the case of obtaining jurisdiction over foreign governments themselves, the defenses of the Act of State Doctrine and Foreign Sovereign Immunity must be overcome. Both doctrines exempt a foreign government from the judicial reach of U.S. courts for governmental actions taken within its own territory. But both doctrines also have exceptions for commercial activity by the government—where the foreign government is engaged in commercial, as opposed to governmental, enterprise. For the most part, however, governments enjoy broad immunity. It is their agents who are not so well-protected; as evidenced in the case of Ferdinand Marcos and also Radovan Karadzic of Bosnia-Herzegovina, both individuals being found liable under the ATCA for acts of torture, rape, and genocide undertaken in their official capacity in the regime.

Apart from procedural prerequisites, the substantive elements to bring suit under the statute are formidable. One of the essential conditions for a claim under the ATCA is that the nature of the violation that caused harm be one that is prohibited by the *law of nations* –that it be specifically in contravention of the terms of a specific treaty or pact or convention or other accepted norm of international law. "The norms of the law of nations are found by consulting juridical writings on public law, considering the general practice of nations, and referring to judicial decisions recognizing and enforcing international law.... A court applying the ATCA must determine whether there is an applicable norm of international law, whether it is recognized by the United States, what its status is, and whether it has been violated." (*Doe v. Unocal,* discussed below.) In fact though, very little accepted international law or law of nations exists. Slavery and genocide are prohibited by international law, as is torture. There have also been several international conventions on the environment, which may serve as a basis for an ATCA claim. Thus, it is primarily only in the area of egregious human rights abuse and profound environmental degradation that grounds for violation of international law exist.

*The United Nations Universal Declaration of Human Rights,* though not legally enforceable, was adopted by the UN General Assembly in 1948 without a dissenting vote as an expression of universal international agreement among all nations with its principles.[1] The UDHR sets forth the basic rights to freedom and equality and security and fair treatment to which all peoples are entitled, regardless of any distinguishing natural characteristics like race, color, sex, religion or nationality. In 1966, the UN General Assembly adopted the International Covenant on Civil and Political Rights, which transferred the original principles of the UDHR into treaty provisions, thus providing for their legal enforcement. By the beginning of 1991, this covenant had been ratified by 92 of the UN's 164 members. Regardless of the state of ratification by a given country, the principles contained in the Declaration reflect "norms" of the law of nations for purposes of the statute. Similarly, in the environmental context, the ATCA case brought by Ecuadorians against Texaco alleged violation of the series of multilateral Declarations on the Environment, beginning with the Stockholm Declaration and including Rio and Agenda 21, which specifically recognize a livable, sustainable environment as a human right. Treaty language propounding that human beings are entitled to a "healthy and productive life in harmony with nature" was ratified by 178 nations at the United Nations Conference on Environment and Development in Rio de Janeiro. The Ecuadorian plaintiffs argued that, like the body of international laws and treaties establishing human rights, the Rio treaty was "one in a series of agreements showing that nations recognize environmental rights as being universal."

In bringing suit against the multinational corporations, perhaps the most difficult element of the case to establish is complicity by the company of a sufficient level to impose legal liability. The ATCA requires a knowing and voluntary complicity; merely doing business in a country with a repressive regime is not sufficient. There must be a partnership, collaboration, or cooperation with the regime or other evidence of informed support. Like all common law tort standards, the essential question of duty and the culpability of the defendant depend largely on what the defendant knew about the possibility of harm, when it knew it, and its action or inaction in response to the risk.

The new legal strategy with the ATCA has ruffled political feathers as well. The George W. Bush administration has come to the defense of some of the defendant companies, particularly in the energy sector, arguing that the lawsuits interfere with foreign policy. In the *Unocal* case, discussed below, a strongly worded brief in defense of the US-based company argued inexplicably that the case had "no connection whatsoever with the United States." The US State Department also filed a brief in the ExxonMobil case involving Indonesia, asserting that the suit, and any interpretation of the ATCA that would permit such suits, could interfere with the administration's War on Terrorism.

### The Case of Unocal in Burma

In 1996 a class action lawsuit under the ATCA was filed with 15 Burmese villagers as named plaintiffs (all identified as John or Jane Doe to protect them from retaliation) in the Federal District Court in Los Angeles, California. The named defendants included Unocal and its President, John Imle, and CEO and Chairman, Roger Beach; the French oil company, Total; the Burmese gov-

---

1. The UDHR appears in the appendix to Chapter Ten.

ernment, known as the State Law and Order Restoration Council (SLORC); and the government's wholly-owned oil company, MOGE (Myanmar Oil and Gas Enterprise). The complaint alleged violations of international law, as well as violations of US federal and state law, by the named defendants in the course of construction of a natural gas pipeline in Burma. Allegations included forced relocation of numerous towns and villages for the benefit of the pipeline; conscription and enslavement of thousands among the dislocated populations in order that they might work, uncompensated, as servants, porters, and human pack horses in support of workers on the pipeline; torture; rape; and wrongful death. Among many legal claims is one for the tort of "negligent hiring"—more than a bit of an understatement, if the allegations are true.

## Burma Politically

Burma (called "Myanmar" by the current government in power) has been under the rule of notoriously repressive military regimes for decades. After a popular uprising in 1988 against the existing military dictatorship, democratic elections were held in 1990 and won by Burmese democratic opposition leader and Nobel Peace Prize laureate Daw Aung San Suu Kyi. The military dictatorship (SLORC) nullified the election results, placed Suu Kyi under arrest, and has since conducted the affairs of the country with an even bloodier and more repressive hand. Suu Kyi, an outspoken activist for democracy in Burma who was popularly elected by an overwhelming majority, has remained confined and held incommunicado with the public since that time. Periodically, human rights watch groups reported sightings of her throughout the decade, confirming that she was alive. For a brief period in 2003, the dictatorship lifted Suu Kyi's confinement; however, when she ventured out publicly, her vehicle was ambushed, her bodyguards assassinated, and she disappeared for some time. She was later discovered being held in a government facility, and has been held

in detention and not permitted public contact since that time.

Unlike previous regimes, SLORC encouraged foreign investment in Burma, including exploration by multinational energy concerns. Opposition groups in Burma made public pleas for economic sanctions and isolation, arguing that doing business with the regime would only strengthen its stranglehold on the populace. Throughout the early 1990s, the US State Department and US Department of Labor each conducted independent investigations of the situation in Burma and found extensive corroborated evidence of forced relocation, forced labor and slavery. Human rights watch groups documented countless similar abuses as well as evidence of rape and murder and included infant and child victims. For more than a decade, Burma has been at or near the top of all official and unofficial lists of most-oppressive regimes in the world.

International awareness of the severity of the situation in Burma gained strength in the early 1990s. Shareholder activists and to a lesser extent, informed consumers, put pressure on corporate boards to retreat from investments in Burma. Such investments were invariably undertaken with the Burmese government in the venture as a partner. Most of the multinational corporations withdrew from Burma; including Compaq, Apple, Disney, Heineken, Levi Strauss, Motorola, and Pepsi. After much deliberation and debate over the appropriate trade policy—engagement versus divestment—the Clinton Administration in 1997 struck a compromise and imposed a ban on new investment in the country, though the sanctions applied only for new ventures and did not require divestment of existing projects and activities in Burma by US companies. Sanctions and bans on procurement of products from companies doing business in Burma had already been implemented by many developed countries, as well as by several US cities and states, universities, and similar institutions.[2]

---

2. See, for example, *Crosby v. Natl. Foreign Trade Council*, 530 US 363 (2000), wherein a Massachusetts ban on state contracts with companies doing business with the SLORC was challenged by the NFTC on behalf of its 550-member businesses. The USSC struck down the Massachusetts law as being in conflict with the Commerce Clause, which reserves authority for international policy-making decisions to the federal government.

### Unocal's Investment in Burma

By the 1990s, Unocal had been operating in Burma for several decades. In 1992, the SLORC formed Myanmar Oil and Gas Enterprises (MOGE) to serve as the state-owned energy company. In 1993, MOGE entered into a consortium with Unocal and the French oil company, Total, for the purpose of exploring and extracting oil and other resources of the country. Although oil exploration in the region proved unproductive, the group embarked on a $1.2 billion project, called the "Yadana Project," for the construction of a huge natural gas pipeline across the southern portion of the country and stretching into Thailand. Unocal holds a 28% stake in the joint venture. The SLORC is entitled to receive at least one-half of the project's revenue, estimated at approximately $400 million per year for the next several decades.

Far from divesting in the face of increasing human rights abuse and pressure from shareholders and the international human rights community, Unocal upped its investment in the project in 1997, mere weeks before the US federal ban on new investment in Burma formally went into effect. The move was widely condemned by the international human rights community as technically legal (just under the wire), but clearly not ethical. Bishop Desmond Tutu denounced the investment and likened the situation in Burma to apartheid South Africa.

Unocal defended its decision on the basis of the economics of the transaction and that the company's presence

could teach local workers new job skills and improve the local infrastructure. An electricity-generating plant and fertilizer-manufacturing plant planned for a later phase of the project would also "help meet the power demands of local residents, homeowners, small businesses and local industry, and provide domestic farmers with much-needed agricultural chemicals and fertilizers."[3]

Unocal had adopted an internal corporate code of conduct for transnational business.

**UNOCAL
STATEMENT OF PRINCIPLES
CODE OF CONDUCT FOR DOING
BUSINESS INTERNATIONALLY**

*Meet the highest ethical standards in all of our business activities.*

*Treat everyone fairly and with respect. Offer equal employment opportunity for all host country nationals, regardless of race, ethnic group or sex. Make sure that a very high percentage of the work force is made up of nationals. Train and develop national employees so they have full access to opportunities for professional advancement and positions at higher levels in the organization.*

*Maintain a safe and healthful workplace. As employees, value and protect each other's health and safety as highly as we do our own. Use local goods and services as much as practical, whenever they're competitive and fit our needs.*

*Improve the quality of life in the communities where we do business. Contribute — and not just economically — to local communities so that our presence enhances people's lives in long-lasting, meaningful ways.*

*Protect the environment. Take our environmental responsibilities seriously and abide by all environmental laws of our host country, as we do in the United States.*

*Communicate openly and honestly. Maintain our policy of encouraging meaningful dialogue with concerned shareholders, employees, the media and members of the public.*

*Be a good corporate citizen and a good friend of the people of our host country.*

---

3. See the Unocal website at http://www.unocal.com.

# UNOCAL
## STATEMENT ON INTERNATIONAL POLITICAL NEUTRALITY

*Unocal's participation in any international energy development project is based on resource potential, business economics and technical expertise — not political motivations.*

*Our commitment is to the people of a host country, not to a particular party or political group. Our goal is to help improve the quality of life in the communities — and countries — where we do business.*

*Neither Unocal nor any Unocal employee may make a foreign political contribution on behalf of the company. It is also inappropriate for Unocal or any Unocal employee to participate in or to support, financially or otherwise, public or private alliances with foreign political parties, opposition movements or other political organizations engaged in the domestic political affairs of a foreign country.*

## The Lawsuit against Unocal

In 1996, attorneys representing Burmese citizens filed a lawsuit under the ATCA in US federal court, which alleged Unocal's complicity in forced relocation, enslavement, killing, torture, and other human rights abuses of the population living near the pipeline.[4] The lead plaintiffs in the suit, villagers and farmers known only by the generic name "Doe" and a number to protect their safety, each had suffered grievous harm at the hands of the SLORC troops working on the pipeline—including rape, murder, and forced labor. The suit named as defendants Unocal and its chief executives, Total, SLORC, and MOGE, Burma's state-owned gas company. The claims against Unocal in the suit were based on its knowing support of the human rights abuses by its confederates—in the form of employing, funding, and benefiting from the illegal activities.

Unocal's initial public response to the lawsuit was not denial of the charges, but instead an explanation that the responsibilities for labor on the Project had been delegated to Total, its French partner, and that if there were problems, it was Total's responsibility. However, the common law views actors in a joint enterprise as jointly responsible for the activities of the endeavor, regardless of which particular member undertakes them. One member of a joint enterprise may not delegate liability for tortious actions to another. All members are responsible for all of the activities undertaken in furtherance of the business endeavor. Accordingly, Unocal changed its public approach to the charges and defended its activities on the grounds that constructive engagement in developing the Yadana project was the best course of action and the best hope for the Burmese people. It characterized the accusations as a political strategy to pressure Unocal to leave Burma.

In its legal response to the lawsuit, Unocal raised objections to the suit on procedural and substantive grounds.[5] In the initial round of motions to dismiss, heard by District Court Judge Paez, Unocal argued first that MOGE and SLORC were not subject to the jurisdiction of the US district court because of sovereign immunity, and the judge agreed, dismissing the suit as to those defendants. The judge did not agree that these parties were "indispensable" to the case against Unocal, however. The relief sought by the plaintiffs—cessation of work on the pipeline and compensation for harm caused—was unaffected by whether or not the government and its oil company were a part of the suit.[6]

Unocal also argued for dismissal of the suit on the grounds of Act of State, and that permitting the suit to go forward could interfere with the foreign policy initiatives of the US government. The judge denied this ground as well, citing a 1997 affidavit filed by the US State Department in the case that verified that the action would not interfere with US policy

---

4. Two suits were actually filed—one on behalf of a group of Burmese villagers representing a class of injured plaintiffs, and another by the Burmese government-in-exile and the National Trade Union in Burma, alleging the same types of abuse and atrocities against citizens and members. The courts eventually joined the two suits as one.

5. One legal defense not raised by Unocal but common in ATCA actions was proper forum. In the Texaco case, for example, the defendant successfully argued that the proper forum for the case was Ecuador. Given that there is virtually no judicial system in Burma, the tactic was not available to Unocal in this case.

6. Total was also dismissed from the suit on the grounds of lack of personal jurisdiction.

regarding the SLORC regime.

Unocal further argued that the violations of international law alleged in the suit—forced labor, murder, rape, and torture—were not actionable under the ATCA against private defendants, but instead were only covered where the activities occurred in conjunction with state action or in an official governmental capacity. The court rejected these arguments as well. There is precedent in ATCA cases for holding private individuals liable for a violation of the law of nations. Courts have recognized that there are categories of acts which could constitute violation of international law, even where committed by private parties—slave trading, genocide, war crimes.[7] The allegations of forced labor in the case rose to the level of slave trading, providing sufficient grounds for an ATCA case against private individuals (or organizations).

Further, with respect to Unocal's complicity with the government as grounds for liability, the judge found the allegations sufficient to hold Unocal over for trial. The judge noted that, had the plaintiffs done no more that merely allege the existence of a business relationship between Unocal and the Burmese Government, the case would be dismissed.. However, the suit alleged that the corporate defendants knew of, and benefited from, the human rights abuses of the government, including forced labor to build the pipeline. As a result, Unocal and its Project partners, including the Burmese government, had acted as joint participants to deprive plaintiffs of their internationally recognized human rights in order to further their financial interest in the pipeline. If these allegations could be proven, they clearly stated a claim under the ATCA.

In refusing to dismiss the claims against Unocal, Judge Paez found that

> The allegations of forced labor in this case are sufficient to constitute an allegation of participation in slave trading. Although there is no allegation that SLORC is physically selling Burmese citizens to the private defendants, plaintiffs allege that, despite their knowledge of SLORC's practice of forced labor, both in general and with respect to the pipeline project, the private defendants have paid and continue to pay SLORC to provide labor and security for the pipeline, essentially treating SLORC as an overseer, accepting and approving the use of forced labor. These allegations are sufficient to establish . . . jurisdiction under the ATCA.[8]

Motions for summary judgment at the district court level in 2000 were heard by a different judge, who granted summary judgment to Unocal and dismissed the plaintiffs' claims on the basis that Unocal's participation in the atrocities was not adequately shown to rise to the level required under ATCA.[9] The case was then appealed to the Ninth Circuit federal court, which affirmed parts of the lower court decisions and reversed others.

The Ninth Circuit affirmed the lower court's dismissal of SLORC and MOGE on grounds of sovereign immunity and Total on grounds of lack of personal jurisdiction. However, it reversed much of the summary judgment granted in favor of Unocal, reinstating the claims of Unocal's complicity in slave trading by forced labor, and rape and murder, and dismissing only the claim of torture, and only then because the particular plaintiffs before the court had not alleged that they personally suffered torture in the context of pipeline operations.[10]

The Ninth Circuit found that the evidence of Unocal's knowledge of the labor practices employed by SLORC and MOGE in building the pipeline was compelling enough to subject the

---

7. US law recognizes a somewhat analogous distinction—each of the amendments that comprise the US Bill of Rights prohibits deprivation of rights by state action and do not apply for individual action, with the exception of one: the Thirteenth Amendment, which prohibits slavery and involuntary servitude. The 13th Amendment is the only one that circumscribes individual action standing alone.

8. *Doe I v. Unocal,* 963 F. Supp. 880 (CD Cal 1997)

9. *Doe I v. Unocal,* 110 F. Supp. 2d 1294 (CD Cal 2000)

10. *Doe I v. Unocal Corp.,* Nos. 00-56603, 00-57197, 2002 U.S. App. LEXIS 19263, 2002 WL 31063976 (9th Cir. Sept. 18, 2002), *aff'd* in part, *rev'd* in part, and *remanded* for further proceedings

company to trial on the issues. The court found it undisputed that Unocal knew that the SLORC military regime was providing security for the pipeline, and that many facts supported the allegation that the Project specifically paid the military for such protection, creating an agency relationship. There was also factual evidence that the Project had directed the actions of the military with respect to its pipeline activities—in the form of regular meetings and briefings of the military by Project representatives and the provision of maps, aerial photographs, plans and other materials directing where helipads were to be built and facilities secured—as well as substantial documentary evidence of Total's close and regular monitoring of the activities of the military in accomplishing these tasks. The court also cited documentary evidence that Unocal's own attorneys and consultants had warned it about possible repercussions for the forced labor and other human rights abuses of its partners in the project, lending credence to allegations that Unocal had knowledge of the activities.

On the issue of the third-party liability of Unocal—its responsibility despite the fact that the company did not physically "pull the trigger"—the Ninth Circuit found that in addition to responsibility on the basis of partnering or joint venturing with the perpetrators and general principles of agency, the company might also be subject to liability for "aiding and abetting" the perpetrators. The Court defined this to include "knowing practical assistance or encouragement that has a substantial effect on the perpetuation of the crime." The standard for aiding and abetting in the case of crimes against humanity, such as those alleged to have occurred in the Yadana Project, can include "all acts of assistance in the form of either physical or moral support... that substantially contribute to the commission of the crime." Intent to aid or abet may be established where the defendant knew or reasonably should have known that its actions would assist the perpetrator in the commission of a crime. The accused itself need not have a "positive intention" to commit the crime, nor does the aider even need to know the *precise* crime that is being committed. Instead, it is enough if the accused is aware that one of such crimes may be committed, that such a

crime is in fact committed, and that the accused intended to facilitate the commission of crime. If the accused knows or has reason to know of the likely commission of the crime, it is not necessary that he himself possess the intent to commit it to be liable as an accomplice. A comparable standard is found in domestic tort law.

### Ethical Implications—Regardless of Legal Outcomes

Almost irrespective of the legal outcomes of the ATCA cases, they compel a shift in the political calculus required of companies doing business in and with underdeveloped nations. The global political and social consciousness has evolved to a consensus on the acceptable limits of human rights abuse, and the law will invariably follow, if not imminently, certainly eventually. At issue for business managers is the extent to which corporate capital will be put at risk in facilitating such regimes. Where law is absent or patently unjust—how low can a corporation go? What is the moral floor for economic benefit? Increasingly, the question is becoming a practical one for managers. Aside from potential legal liability, stakeholders with otherwise divergent interests have begun to coalesce around the issue. Shareholder resolutions seeking corporate withdrawal from repressive regimes proliferate. Organized labor has brought the issue into contract negotiations. International human rights activists pressure companies publicly and consumer response is measurable. Since 2000, more than 40 US companies, including dozens of major retailers, have voluntarily agreed to boycott products made in Burma. Even Wall Street has received the message—fund managers outside the realm of traditional "social responsibility" funds are beginning to factor a company's overseas business practices into their stock recommendations.

Business managers have two choices in responding to the issue. They can continue to pin their hopes on stemming the evolution of the law—putting corporate resources into hiring lawyers and lobbyists to thwart efforts at legal accountability for their actions abroad. Or they can awaken to their pivotal role in the development of these countries and attempt to operate responsibly, beyond mere compliance with the law.

Professor Elliot Schrage, of Columbia Law School, has argued that US courts are not in the best position to set either global standards of conduct or American economic policy toward underdeveloped countries. Nonetheless, the foreign victims so severely harmed by American companies are entitled to meaningful redress. He concludes that, over the long term, multinational corporations have much to gain by supporting and encouraging the development of just legal institutions and social reforms in the underdeveloped countries in which they do business:

> Over the long term, the most important step multinational corporations can take to protect themselves is to strengthen justice systems in foreign countries. Companies should fund programs to train foreign court officials and judges, and consider supporting legal aid clinics for workers and their families. This may seem like an odd mission for the private sector, but distant villagers and laborers are turning to U.S. judges because of the failure of local courts. The legal costs to U.S. companies in the Unocal or Saipan cases probably represent a sizable fraction of the national court budgets of many developing countries.... When foreign victims can find meaningful redress in their home countries, U.S. judicial activism will smack of judicial imperialism. In theory and in practice, local courts should be able to identify problems earlier, resolve them faster, and tailor solutions more appropriately to local conditions. And yes, those solutions will cost less, since they will not require payments to U.S. plaintiffs' attorneys.

### And the Law Continues to Evolve...

At the end of 2002, yet another lawsuit was filed under the ATCA, with implications for multinational business potentially much more expansive than those that have gone before.

The suit names as defendants more than 100 firms that did business with the apartheid regime in South Africa; including IBM, General Motors, Citicorp and ExxonMobil.[11] The named plaintiffs include a wide array of individuals who suffered at the hands of the apartheid regime. Among the plaintiffs is the family of a 13-year-old black student, the first shot by police in the 1976 uprising in Soweto that ultimately left more than a thousand black youths dead. Another plaintiff is the widow of a black schoolteacher and anti-apartheid activist whose burned and mutilated body was found with the charred remains of three other men. Ultimately, six police officers confessed to the unprovoked killing. Other plaintiffs include scores of those arrested, jailed, tortured, and consigned to years of hard labor by the apartheid regime merely for their political belief in freedom.

The legal theory of the case is complicity by the companies in an ongoing enterprise in violation of international law. The suit asserts that apartheid is included among the crimes against humanity recognized among the established norms that form the law of nations—along with slavery, genocide, torture, extra-judicial killing, lengthy arbitrary detention, unlawful medical experimentation, and other abominations. In 1973, the United Nations General Assembly adopted the International Convention on the Suppression and Punishment of the Crime of Apartheid, which declared apartheid a crime against humanity and called for the prosecution of persons and institutions engaged in the practice. The complaint alleges that: "The system of Apartheid as practiced in South Africa explicitly promoted extra-judicial killing, torture, cruel, inhuman and degrading treatment and consisted of elements of genocide and forced labour, all of which were and still are against the norms of Customary International Law."

Complicity with the regime is based on the "aiding and abetting" standard established in Unocal and other international cases. Examples of corporate complicity in the complaint include: IBM and ICL, which provided the computers that enabled South Africa to create the hated pass book system and to control the black

---

11. *Khulumani et al. v. Barclays Bank, et al.,* Docket No. 1:03-cv-04524-JES (E.D.N.Y, 2002).

South African population; car manufacturers, which provided the armored vehicles that were used to patrol the townships; arms manufacturers, who violated the embargoes on sales to South Africa, as did the oil companies; and banks, which provided the funding that enabled South Africa to expand its police and security apparatus. The suit alleges evidence that companies in the key industries of mining, transportation, armaments, technology, oil, and financing were not only instrumental to the implementation of the furtherance of the abuses, but were so integrally connected to the abuses themselves that apartheid would probably not have occurred in the same way without their participation—one of the requirements for aiding and abetting under the ATCA.

The findings of the Truth and Reconciliation Commission in South Africa stated:

> Business was central to the economy that sustained the South African state during the apartheid years. Certain businesses, especially the mining industry, were involved in helping to design and implement apartheid policies. Other businesses benefited from cooperating with the security structures of the former state. Most businesses benefited from operating in a racially structured context.

Plaintiff groups explained publicly that the suit was filed as a last resort, when all negotiations to cancel apartheid era debt had failed. In 1998, a wide-ranging campaign to cancel the massive debts incurred by the apartheid era regime was initiated. The "apartheid debt"—debt incurred by the apartheid government and inherited by the post-apartheid government in South Africa—was having a crushing impact on the economy of the country. Advocates for debt cancellation argued that it was morally unjust to hold the current government responsible for payment of the debts of their former oppressors; debts that were in fact incurred to facilitate the oppression. But the banks and other corporations and organizations holding the apartheid debt refused to negotiate any reprieve, leaving victims with little options for relief. The reparations sought as damages under the lawsuit

would serve to mitigate some of the harsh economic effects of the apartheid debt.

Advocates in the case justified the suit based on the complete lack of regret or atonement expressed by these multinational entities for their participation in apartheid. The Truth and Reconciliation Commission was established in South Africa in 1995 to investigate the nature, causes and extent of the gross human rights violations committed during the apartheid period. It was empowered to grant amnesty to those coming forward truthfully about their complicity with the apartheid regime. Thousands came forward with testimony, enabling the Commission to develop a clear picture of what went on during those years. The amnesty led to truthful answers about the activities of the apartheid regime to those who suffered under it, and began the process of forgiveness and reconciliation needed to re-unify the country. Yet, not one single foreign business person or entity appeared before the commission nor approached the TRC to ask for amnesty for their involvement in apartheid. At a minimum, then, the suit is designed to force these entities—their managers, employees, investors, and customers—to consider their moral role in the decades-long oppression of a people.

## UPDATE
### December 2004

*In August of 2004, the U.S. Supreme Court announced an opinion in an unrelated case involving claims under the ATCA that cleared the way for the Doe v. Unocal plaintiffs to proceed in the lower court. In September of 2004, a California judge ordered Unocal to prepare for a jury trial on the human rights charges. In December of 2004, Unocal and EarthRights International, the non-profit legal group representing the Burmese plaintiffs, announced in a joint statement that they had reached a settlement in principle in the case. The parties agreed to keep the terms of the settlement confidential, but said in the statement:*

> *Although the terms are confidential, the settlement in principle will compensate plaintiffs and provide funds enabling plaintiffs and their representatives to develop programmes to improve living condi-*

*tions, health care and education and protect the rights of people from the pipeline region... These initiatives will provide substantial assistance to people who may have suffered hardships in the region.*

*EarthRights International expressed that the plaintiffs were "thrilled" with the terms of the settlement. Although dollar amounts were not disclosed, Unocal's legal fees alone in the suit are estimated to be at least $25 million.*

## Sources

"New Peril for Companies Doing Business Overseas: Alien Tort Claims Act Interpreted Broadly" by Joseph D. Pizzurro and Nancy E. Delaney, *The New York Law Journal*, November 24, 1997.

"US Petroleum Giant to Stand Trial for Burma Atrocities" by Jed Greer, *The Ecologist*, January/February, 1998.

*The Price of Oil: Corporate Responsibility and Human Rights Violations in Nigeria's Oil Producing Communities*, Human Rights Watch (New York 1999).

"Texaco's Crude Legacy" by Alex Markels, *Mother Jones Magazine*, May/June 1999.

"A Long Way to Find Justice: What Are Burmese Villagers Doing in a California Court?" By Elliot Schrage, the *Washington Post*, July 14, 2002.

"Sudan: Mixing Blood and Oil" by Benjamin Bock, *Amnesty Now,* Summer 2002.

"The Price of Apartheid" by Lynne Duke, the *Washington Post*, December 3, 2002

Briefing on the Reparations Lawsuit Facilitated by the Apartheid Debt and Reparations Campaign of Jubilee South Africa, November 12, 2002, http://www.africaaction.org.

"Showdown for a Tool in Rights Lawsuits" by Alex Markels, the *New York Times*, June 5, 2003.

"De-Globalizing Justice: The Corporate Campaign to Strip Foreign Victims of Corporate-Induced Human Rights Violations of the Right to Sue in US Courts," by Kenny Bruno, *Multinational Monitor,* March 2003.

"Judge OKs Human Rights Suit against Unocal," *Associated Press*, September 14, 2004.

"Unocal Must Face Abuse Suit" *Los Angeles Times*, September 15, 2004.

"Energy Giant Agrees to Settlement with Burmese Villagers" by Duncan Campbell, *The Guardian,* December 15, 2004.

# Case 7

## The Collapse of Enron:
## A Business Ethics Perspective

*The case examines the demise of Enron, then the 7th largest company in the world, from the perspective of all of the affected stakeholders. It explores the rise and fall of the company; its corporate culture; its corporate governance; and its use of political influence to thwart regulation. A brief discussion of the provisions of the Corporate Fraud Accountability Act specifically targeted to Enron-type fraud is included.*

*Relevant chapters: 3, 4, 5, 6*

**Corporation** *n.* An ingenious device for obtaining individual profit without individual responsibility

— Ambrose Bierce,
*The Devil's Dictionary* (1909)

The essential questions posed by business ethics ask: Who in the society is the corporation responsible to for its actions and activities? What are the purposes and goals of the entity? And, by what means, within what limits, may these goals be pursued?

Two main schools of thought on these questions have developed in the study of business ethics. The first approach, developed in the 19th century and in modern times championed most ardently by economist Milton Friedman, is known as the maximizing profits model. The maximizing profits model posits that the sole purpose of the corporation is to benefit its shareholders by maximizing their profits, and that the means to achieving that end may include any activities not prohibited by law. In his famous 1970 article, "The Social Responsibility of Business Is to Increase Its Profits" (*New York Times Magazine*, September 13, 1970), Friedman argued that corporate executives are employees of the owners of the business and have direct responsibility only to them. "That responsibility is to conduct the business in accordance with their desires, which generally means to make as much money as possible while conforming to the basic rules of society, both those embodied in law and those embodied in ethical custom." Friedman goes so far as to assert that it is irresponsible for a corporation to act on social issues such as controlling pollution or training the unemployed, because these are political functions that should be left to the political processes of government. Corporations are simply not designed or equipped for such considerations. Hence, under the maximizing

By Sheryl Kaiser, J.D. Parts of this case study were previously published in *Contemporary Business Law in a Global Economy*, by Kubasek, Herron, et al. Lakeshore Publications. @2006, NorthCoast Publishers, Inc.

profits model, all areas of social concern and social responsibility should be left to governmental regulation. The sole corporate focus should be on making profits within the confines of these rules.

The second approach to corporate social responsibility is called the stakeholder interest model, and was developed in the mid- to late-20th century, partly in response to the harsh effects of the maximizing profit model. The stakeholder interest model recognizes that there are many constituencies with as great a stake in the effects of corporate activity as the shareholders, and that the shareholders are but one constituency to be considered in corporate decision-making. Other stakeholder groups include the corporation's employees, management, customers, business partners, and the communities in which the corporation operates. The stakeholder interest model posits that the interests of and impact on these other groups should also be considered when determining how a corporation will go about achieving its goals and making its profits. This approach does not trust the political process and the enforcement of law exclusively to ensure socially responsible behavior in commerce. Instead, it looks to internal accountability and values within the corporation to protect the legitimate interests of those affected by corporate actions.

The swift and messy collapse of the Enron Corporation, at the time one of the largest corporations in the United States, represents a failure of corporate business ethics and corporate responsibility under either model. Enron not only failed to serve the interests of its shareholders, but it did so in a manner that exploited and harmed all of its stakeholders.

### From Bricks and Mortar to a House of Cards

Enron was created in 1985, with the combination of two natural gas pipeline companies. With the deregulation of the industry, Enron executives developed a business in trading gas as well as being a gas supply company. As the profits from the trading business overtook that of the business of building pipelines and drilling wells, the company emphasis moved away from the nuts and bolts of providing the resource and into the realm of developing inno-

vative financial devices and arrangements to buy and sell the product. Enron management adopted an "asset-light" strategy for the business, emphasizing intellectual capital over hard assets. Profits and revenues climbed steadily from the company's natural gas and electricity trading in financial instruments and derivatives (financial instruments that derive their value from another financial instrument or commodity such as interest rates, stock prices, precious metals or other resources). These revenues were bolstered significantly by utilities deregulation generally, and also by special regulatory exemptions for the types of derivatives Enron traded in. Enron had lobbied hard for these accommodations, giving substantial political contributions to the decision-makers on those issues.

In the mid- to late-1990s, the company decided to expand its financial expertise to other diverse areas—water, coal, broadband, fiber-optic capacity, and several others. Enron's stock price rose steadily and it became a favorite with Wall Street as well as with its own employees, many of whom invested their entire retirement savings in company stock through the company-maintained 401(k) plan. For the most part, however, these new ventures were not profitable for the company, saddling it with vast quantities of debt; debt that would hurt the company's stock price if revealed to the public. Accordingly, the company took aggressive advantage of complicated loopholes in the accounting laws to keep these losses from public view. It engaged in questionable reporting practices including the utilization of a slush fund to shelter bad deals, the swapping of financial instruments to shift profits from one deal to another, and the use of unrealistic profit projections to mislead the markets as to the financial results of its trade deals.

Enron also embarked on a scheme to structure its riskier ventures in entities that would not have to be reported on its balance sheet (called "special purpose entities" or SPEs). These off-balance-sheet partnerships and subsidiaries permitted Enron to keep its mounting corporate debt off of its balance sheet, thus protecting its credit rating and its stock price from the effects of the debt. The problems with these off-balance-sheet entities were several. First, in simplified terms, any losses suffered by these entities were effectively guaranteed by Enron stock; meaning that Enron shareholders would be left holding the bag if the investment turned sour. As well, these guarantees were built on the assumption of Enron's stock price remaining high. Any drop in the stock price could trigger calls for repayment of the debt by these off-balance-sheet entities. The quest to keep the stock price high thus became essential not only to keep Wall Street impressed but, in fact, to prevent the entire financial edifice of Enron from collapsing. Indeed, it was just this mechanism that would ultimately bring down the entire house of cards and lead to the largest bankruptcy in US corporate history.

The other major issue with the off-balance-sheet entities was who invested in them and what they got. Many of the banks and investment houses that did business with Enron participated as venturers in the SPEs. Enron executives, as individuals, were partners in several of the entities, as well. Enron's Chief Financial Officer, Andrew Fastow, collected more than $30 million as a partner in SPEs that he himself had engineered. Michael Kopper, another Enron executive, garnered a return of more than $10 million. The fiduciary duty of a corporate executive is to act in the best interest of the corporation. The conflict of interest is clear where corporate executives partner with the very corporations they are bound to represent and negotiate with such corporations in their own interest. In the case of Enron's SPEs, Enron executives with a personal stake in the entities negotiated terms and conditions of the investment across the table from their corporate subordinates, obviating any chance of an arm's length transaction. When presented with these transactions, Enron's Board of Directors twice suspended the corporation's code of ethics in order to approve the self-dealing. The extent of the Board's understanding of the dubious accounting and financial practices of Enron management remains suspect. One thing is certain: no information regarding the existence of these entities, holding hundreds of millions of dollars of Enron debt, was made public to Enron's investors.

At the beginning of 2001, Enron's stock was

trading in excess of $80 per share. Early in the year, an energy crisis in California and a serious downturn in the technology sector caused Enron's stock price to dip. By early summer, the stock price had fallen to the $50-$60-range, a point that would trigger the repayment provisions for several of the off-balance-sheet partnerships that were keeping hundreds of millions of dollars of debt off Enron's public books. In mid-August, Jeffrey Skilling, Enron's CEO of six months, abruptly resigned citing personal reasons. Enron's Chairman of the Board, Kenneth Lay, who served as CEO prior to Skilling's appointment, resumed the CEO position. The day after Skilling's departure, Vice President Sherron Watkins sent a confidential memo to Lay outlining the problems with the off-balance-sheet financial structures and their imminent breakdown. The memo warned that the company would "implode in a wave of accounting scandals." Upon cursory review of Watkins allegations, Enron's lawyers opined that there was no cause for concern.

Enron's stock continued to decline in the aftermath of the September 11 terrorist attacks, though Lay and other executives actively sought to reassure outside investors and the employees invested in the company stock that the company was in great shape and that "the third quarter is looking great." In October, Enron reported a third quarter loss of more than $600 million and the following day restated its balance sheet, reducing its reported assets by more than $1 billion. That same day, the company froze all assets in the employees' 401(k) plan, preventing employees from selling the company stock in their retirement portfolios. The employees would not regain the right to sell Enron stock until its value had fallen to pennies per share. Within days, the SEC initiated an investigation into Enron's accounting and financial practices, the CFO was fired, and Enron reported overstated profits of nearly $600 million in the previous financial statements. Further damaging financial revelations ensued. The stock plummeted to near zero and at the beginning of December, Enron filed for Federal bankruptcy protection from its creditors and investors.

The breadth and depth of the investigation into Enron's "implosion in a wave of accounting scandals" is considerable. Soon after opening its investigation of Enron, the SEC expanded its investigation to Enron's accountant and auditor, Arthur Andersen. Evidence of secret destruction of Enron financial records and documents by Andersen personnel has led to a criminal indictment of the accounting firm by the Justice Department. Enron executives and members of the Board of Directors are under investigation by a variety of Federal agencies and are named defendants in dozens of lawsuits by shareholders, employees, and creditors. Many of the executives refused to testify when called before Congress, invoking their Fifth Amendment right against self-incrimination. Banks and investment partners involved in Enron financing schemes not only face suits from Enron plaintiffs for their role in the arrangements but also fallout from their own accounting improprieties and balance sheet problems arising from Enron's collapse. On the political front, the public call for legislative and regulatory reform to prevent another Enron has been met with unease and some trepidation by the many politicians who counted Enron and its executives among their largest financial contributors.

The ethical issues that emerged from the Enron debacle are copious and relate not only to Enron itself, but also to the many businesses engaged with it. The demise of Enron not only reflects a failure of regulatory oversight, but also a failure of internal corporate governance and checks and balances. A few of these key business ethics issues are examined below.

### Obligations to the Shareholders

Whether one embraces the maximizing profits model or the stakeholder interest model, the primary, if not exclusive, obligation of a corporation is to its owners, the shareholders. Corporate management, which consists of the company's directors and officers, are elected and appointed to represent the interests of the shareholders in running the company. These directors and officers, and the agents they hire, have a legal fiduciary duty to act prudently and in the best interests of the corporation and its owners and not in their own self-interest or for their own benefit.

In the case of Enron, officers of the corpora-

tion worked with the accountants and law firms hired to represent the company (and who were paid handsomely for such advice with corporate funds) to hide from the owners of the company the true status of the corporation's financial affairs. Grand and complex machinations between Enron executives, Arthur Andersen accountants, and Vinson & Elkins attorneys served to conceal from investors an accurate picture of the company's financial situation and how its business was being conducted. Further, many of these executives personally profited from the deception. The CFO and others involved in the off-balance-sheet partnerships profited by tens of millions of dollars. Similarly, top Enron executives cashed out of their Enron stock while continuing to publicly reassure investors of the soundness of the company. Between May 2000 and August 2001 when the company imploded, top Enron executives profited from the sale of more than $100 million of the company's stock. These insider trades were not reported to the public investors until long after the fact. Enron executives profited at the expense of those they were charged with representing and serving. Clearly, they breached their fiduciary duty.

There is plenty of blame to be spread. Gaping loopholes in the accounting rules permitted an opening for the chicanery; loopholes that business and industry and the accounting profession had fought hard to keep open. Internal controls that should have caught the problems did not. Enron's auditor, Andersen, and attorneys, Vinson & Elkins, helped to structure and then signed off on the questionable deals. Enron's Board of Directors failed to use the prudent care required of directors to inform itself about the transactions. The Board's audit committee failed to diligently examine the transactions and the full Board, when presented with transactions which clearly violated the company's policy on self-dealing by corporate officers, merely waived Enron's corporate code of ethics (not once, but twice).

In the absence of fraud, corporate directors and officers are generally indemnified and insured against personal liability for such negligence—a practice that raises ethical issues of its own, but is nonetheless necessary to attract people of means to serve on corporate boards. However, several of Enron's insurance carriers are exploring ways to rescind their policies on Enron directors and avoid their responsibility for paying legal judgments entered against the Enron directors. The enormous restatement of earnings by the company on account of the undisclosed partnerships (nearly $600 million and dating back several years), could serve to void the policies on the grounds of apparent fraud. If so, the Enron directors could be looked to individually for liability to creditors and shareholders.

The loss to Enron's shareholders from the beginning of 2001 to the bankruptcy filing in December of that year is estimated to be in excess of $60 billion.

### Obligations to the Other Stakeholders

Perhaps the most negatively affected stakeholder group in the Enron scandal was its employees. Not only did some 5000 of them lose their jobs at the outset of the bankruptcy, but more than 20,000 employees, loyally trusting the assurances of upper management, lost their retirement savings in Enron stock. Employees participated in a company-managed 401(k) plan. Inspired by management optimism, many Enron employees invested their retirement savings heavily in their employer's stock. On the date that the company went public with the first of its financial revelations and restated its assets downward by more than $1 billion, the company froze the employees' plans, ostensibly for a change in fund managers, which prevented the employees from conducting any trades. By the time the ban was lifted, the value of a share of Enron stock had fallen to mere pennies, rendering the retirement accounts worthless.

The fallout from Enron affected many other constituencies as well. Enron's trading partners suffered several billions of dollars in losses on uncollateralized derivative contracts. Enron's bondholders also lost several billions of dollars. Suppliers large and small were not paid. A negative ripple effect was experienced by the energy sector generally. The City of Houston, already reeling from the economic downturn, lost not only one of the largest businesses in the United States and a major employer, but a city

icon and the sponsor of its premier professional sports venue, Enron Field.

### Enron's Corporate Culture from an Ethical Perspective

Enron's collapse was not the result of missteps by one rogue actor. Within Enron's executive ranks, managers and directors, and many of Enron's advisors were privy to the trick accounting arrangements being used to cook the corporate books. Improbity to the degree exhibited in the Enron case requires a corporate environment that rewards results by any means necessary. Due to the fragile and complex nature of the company's off-balance-sheet financial structure, it was driven by the need to keep its stock price artificially high. Accordingly, as CEO, Jeffrey Skilling nurtured a corporate environment where risk-taking and creative, if shaky, deal-making that enhanced the immediate bottom line were rewarded with large bonuses and positive reviews, whereas concern for long-term growth and shareholder value were marginalized.

Skilling was reportedly a manager who surrounded himself with "yes men." In such an environment, the critical thinking required to sustain a multinational company such as Enron is absent. Lost is the key dialogic component that permits a company to realistically and effectively assess and react to the market and to its demands. Alternative views and perspectives are essential for real growth in any organization. Moreover, bad news travels up the corporate ladder badly in the best of organizations. In an organization led by those who refuse to hear bad news, it doesn't travel at all. And in such circumstances, no one wants to be the messenger. It was said that raising a red flag at Enron was a "ticket to exile."

Nonetheless, there were a few heroic souls in Enron's corporate environment willing to point out the lack of Emperor's clothes. Enron's treasurer, Jeffrey McMahon (who took over as COO of the company in Enron's bankruptcy), was reported to have raised issues regarding the propriety of the partnerships when they were initially established. He was promptly transferred to London. In early spring 2001, Jordan Mintz, an in-house Enron lawyer, raised issues with the chief accounting officer and chief risk officer for the company regarding the propriety of the off-balance-sheet arrangements. He was told to stay out of it. Later that spring Mintz would arrange for an independent review of some of the transactions by outside counsel. Sherron Watkins, Enron's vice-president of corporate development, submitted a powerful confidential memo to Kenneth Lay the day after CEO Skilling's resignation, outlining the nature of the off-the-books entities and the potentially devastating financial problems they presented. Presciently, she warned of the imminent "implosion" of Enron due to the accounting artifice. Watkins' memo was passed on to Enron's lawyers and promptly deemed to be of no real concern by them.

Business ethicist Joanne Ciulla has asserted that there is something wrong with an environment "where doing what is sensible or right takes an heroic gesture . . . morality in the workplace should not be that drastically different from the morality in the culture outside of it."[1] A corporate culture that suppresses, frowns upon, or punishes sensible questions and concerns by loyal employees regarding transparency and accountability is doomed to fail by its own sensory deprivation.

### The Use of Political Influence to Thwart Regulation

Political contributions on Enron's behalf to Federal candidates and parties totaled nearly $6 million in the decade from 1990 to 2000; $1.7 million was contributed in the 2000 election cycle alone. Hundreds of thousands of dollars were also contributed to state politicians, particularly in California and Texas. A substantial percentage of these contributions went to members of Congress holding powerful positions in the committees charged with oversight of Enron's business activities. Contributions to the parties generally and additional lobbying expenditures of $1-$2 million each year provided Enron access to all levels of the political process.

Throughout the 1990s, Enron lobbied hard for deregulation in the areas of its businesses, particularly that of the wholesale electricity market. The Federal government began deregulation of these markets in 1992, California in 1996, and Texas in 1999. Beginning in 1992, Enron also worked with the Commodities Futures Trading Commission (CFTC), then chaired by Wendy Gramm, wife of Texas Senator Phil Gramm, to exempt from regulation futures trading in energy derivatives. The CFTC exempted such transactions and they soon became one of Enron's most profitable activities. In 1993, Wendy Gramm stepped down from the CFTC and became a member of Enron's Board of Directors, where she remained through the 2001 collapse. Efforts in 2001 by the CFTC to reassert control over the trading in these derivatives were defeated by Congress, hindered largely by the Senate Banking Committee, then-chaired by Senator Phil Gramm.

With respect to the accounting sleights performed so artfully by Enron's advisors, attempts to close such loopholes were thwarted by the financial industry throughout the 1990s. A forceful effort by the SEC in 2000 to separate audit and consulting practices by accounting firms was swiftly derailed. This was a major ethical issue in the Enron debacle, as Andersen served as both consultant and auditor to Enron—two roles often in conflict—and its consulting revenues were many times greater than its audit fees.

So, what is wrong with a corporation using money to exercise its First Amendment freedom of speech, and, in the process, gain access to the political decision-makers that govern its activities? Well, it depends on what you do with the access.

In a stakeholder-interest approach to corporate responsibility, a corporation will take into account the effects of its actions on its various constituencies and self-regulate to ensure fairness to those interests. In making corporate decisions, it will take into consideration the social costs and social impact, as well as the effect on the bottom line.

In a maximizing-profits approach, a corporation need not take into account the effects of its actions on anyone save the shareholders, pro-

---

1. Joanne Ciulla, "Messages from the Environment: The Influence of Policies and Practices on Employee Responsibility", in Chimezie A.B. Osigweh, Yg., ed., *Communicating Employee Responsibilities and Rights: A Modern Management Mandate.* New York: Quorum Books, 1987.

vided it is acting within the confines of the laws in effect at the time. As Friedman observed, the social costs and social impact on the rest of society are left to the protections of the government that enacts those laws. Accordingly, with this narrow focus of obligation to the shareholders only, there is a corresponding obligation on the part of corporations to stay out of, and certainly not to thwart, efforts at social protection by other institutions, such as the government.

There is also a more profound ethical issue involved in efforts to deregulate a commodity that is a necessity, an "essential good" for the society, like natural gas and electricity. These commodities are in the nature of public goods—in limited supply, but necessary for the maintenance and progress of the society as a whole. Although the capitalist system permits private ownership of and profit from the sale of these kinds of goods, there is a paramount public interest in how and to whom these goods are distributed. Given the far-reaching social implications, the use of political influence to completely privatize the availability and cost of such an essential good is dubious under any construct of corporate social responsibility.

* * * * * * * * * * * * *

### The Aftermath and Aftershocks of Enron

The swift and messy collapse of Enron proved to be just the first wave in a tsunami of financial scandals that would deluge Wall Street in 2002 and beyond. Company after company revealed use of the same kinds of accounting artifice and financial reporting chicanery as that employed by Enron and its accountants and lawyers. The public learned that self-dealing and undisclosed self-enrichment was rife among corporate executives. Several of the largest, oldest, and most respected companies and firms revealed massive fraud—many of these resulting in the bankruptcy of the companies involved. Like Enron, most of these corporate disasters left employees, shareholders, and creditors holding the bag once again.

Among the reforms engendered by Enron et al. were several changes to the reporting requirements of public companies and, of course, the enactment of the Corporate Fraud Accountability Act of 2002—many provisions of which are directly aimed at Enron-type problems. Some of these reforms include:

- Corporate executives must now disclose their transactions in the corporation's stock within 48 hours of the trade
- The audit committee of the corporation's Board of Directors must consist entirely of outside, independent members to ensure diligence and autonomy.
- At least one member of the audit committee must have financial expertise
- Corporate CEOs and CFOs are now required to personally sign off on the company's financial reports and can be held personally liable for their veracity
- Accounting firms are more severely restricted in selling other services, like consulting, to their audit clients to prevent conflicts of interest. Enron's fees to Andersen for consulting services dwarfed its revenues from auditing Enron.
- Oversight has been imposed on the accounting profession generally with the establishment of the Public Company Accounting Oversight Board. Previously, for the history of the accounting industry, it had always been self-regulated, with only a peer-review process to provide checks on accounting excesses or irregularities.
- Companies are now forbidden to impose black-out periods on company-sponsored 401(k) retirement plans, as Enron did, unless a similar restriction on trading is placed on all insiders.

The pace of prosecution by the government in the Enron case has been predictably slow. By the end of 2004, more than 20 of Enron's top executives had been indicted criminally on various charges of securities fraud, insider trading, and obstruction of justice. The first big name indicted was CFO Andrew Fastow, along with his wife, Lea. The Fastows were permitted to plea to lesser charges in exchange for their cooperation with the authorities. CEO Jeffrey Skilling was indicted on 35 counts of fraud, insider trading, and conspiracy. Kenneth Lay,

Enron's Chairman of the Board and CEO, has been indicted on criminal counts of bank fraud, conspiracy, securities fraud, insider trading and lying to auditors.

Some of the cases against companies that aided and abetted Enron's fraud have been settled. Citigroup and JP Morgan Chase, two of America's biggest banks, paid $308 million in fines to settle charges for their role in disguising Enron's financial picture. The fines were actually "disgorgement of profits" and represented a small fraction of the profits realized by the companies. Evidence showed that the two banks provided at least $8.3 billion in credit to Enron "solely to obscure its true financial condition."[2] Since only the banks, and not any individuals within them, were prosecuted, it will be Morgan's and Citi's shareholders who bear the cost of the punishment, also a likely result for the owners of many of the companies implicated.

## Discussion Questions

1. What are SPEs? How did they work? How did Enron benefit from them?
2. What was the nature of Enron's offenses?
3. What led to the company's collapse?
4. Who are the responsible parties?
5. Describe Enron's culture. To what extent did it contribute to its collapse?
6. Please explain some of the different models of corporate responsibility and the relevance they have to this case. Why is Enron's collapse a failure under the various models?
7. What are the main lessons to be learned from Enron's collapse? Condense these lessons into an implementable plan of action that any company could pursue.

---

2. *The Economist*, August 2, 2003

# Case 8

## No Accounting for It: The Demise of Professionalism in Public Accounting

*The case looks at the changing role and nature of accounting firms in modern business: conflicts in audit and consulting; revolving doors with clients; and a change in the very business model of the accounting firm itself. The alignment of the audit firms with industry clients on issues such as the expensing of stock options and consulting conflicts-of-interest reflect this transformation from the traditional independence and public-interest mission of the accounting profession.*

*Relevant chapters: 3, 4, 5, 6*

O n June 15, a Houston jury convicted Arthur Andersen—the 89-year-old accounting firm once known as the gold standard of integrity in auditing—for obstruction of justice in the government's investigation of Enron, Andersen's biggest client. With the demise of Andersen, the American business landscape was forever altered. But something else was altered as well: the scandal surrounding Enron and Andersen, together with the wave of other major accounting scandals that have come to light in recent months, has dealt America's markets

*an unsettling psychological blow.*

*If we can't trust the auditors, investors wonder, whom can we trust?*[1]

### The Relationship between the Firm and Its Stakeholders

The profession of public accountancy is one that serves a variety of constituencies.

> The responsibility of a public accountant is not only to the client who pays his fee, but also to investors, creditors, and others who may rely on the financial statements he certifies . . . the auditor's function has expanded from that of a watchdog for management to an independent evaluator of the adequacy and fairness of financial statement issues by management to stockholders, creditors, and others.[2]

The role of auditors is to examine a company's financial books and records and, if appropriate, to certify that they are complete and "fairly stated." Auditing gained professional

By Sheryl Kaiser, @2006, NorthCoast Publishers, Inc.

1. Introduction to the documentary *Bigger than Enron*, produced by FRONTLINE and narrated by Henrik Smith in 2002. This video is highly recommended as accompanying material for this case study. It runs approximately 60 minutes and is available from www.pbs.org or Films for the Humanities. The documentary is cited throughout this case study.

2. *Rosenbloom, Inc. v. Adler*, 461 A.2d 138 (N.J. 1983)

standing along with the reforms of the 1930s securities acts, which were premised on the notion of accurate and transparent disclosure to the market. The standards by which financial books and records are evaluated are set by the Financial Accounting Standards Board (FASB), a private-sector organization, funded largely by the accounting industry and its clients.

Historically, the practice of accountancy has been viewed as a "professional" trade—subject to internal codes of conduct and professional responsibility much like law and medicine— and has been entirely self-regulated. Like law and medicine, however, the potential for conflicts of interest in practice abound. Most of these conflicts arise from the nature of the relationship between the firm, as independent auditor, and its client, the auditee.

The client chooses, hires, and pays the auditor for the audit. There is thus a desire on the part of the auditor to be sure to please the client, else it won't be a client for long. There is some inherent conflict in even identifying who the "client" is in this context. The client is the company and its owners. It is from corporate funds, belonging to the shareholders, that audit fees are paid. It is to the owners of the company that the books are certified. Nonetheless, it is incumbent management who hires the auditor and cuts the check for services rendered. In the event that the interests of incumbent management in financial reporting should conflict with the interests of the shareholders, the auditor has a problem if he wants to keep the client.

There is also often a familiarity between auditors and clients that transcends usual business relationships. Because of the revolving door between the firms, it is increasingly common to see former auditors and accountants hired in-house by companies. Enron, for example, hired a number of former "Anderoids" (as the Andersen people referred to themselves); among them Sherron Watkins, the whistle-blower. In the event of a dicey audit issue, one

is less likely to challenge former colleagues or a potential future employer.

Perhaps the greatest challenge for accounting conflicts of interest arose when the firms began to offer consulting services in addition to their auditing practice. In doing so, they transformed themselves from rendering a professional independent service to running the firm as an entrepreneurial business. No longer content to merely service big business, the accounting firms themselves became big business.[3]

Lynn Turner, chief accountant of the Securities and Exchange Commission from 1998 to 2001, says,

> Having been in one of these Big Five international accounting firms, I can tell you that over the last 10, 15 years, the mindset has evolved from one of looking out for the investor and placing their interest first—because [auditing] is truly a public function, a public franchise—to one of, "We're a great big international business, and business comes first."[4]

Throughout the 1990s, the Big Five—PricewaterhouseCoopers, Deloitte & Touche, Ernst & Young, KPMG, and Andersen—doubled their collective revenues, to $425 billion. A large part of the increase was attributable to consulting fees. "At some firms, like Andersen, auditor's compensation depended upon their ability to sell other services to clients: equity partners began to be paid like investment bankers. Inevitably, there were conflicts between the independent role required of an auditor and the supplicant role of a salesman trying to expand services."[5]

Well before Enron's problems became public, at least 14 of Andersen's top partners had raised serious questions about the financial schemes that eventually contributed to Enron's fall. Nonetheless "the partners concerns were outweighed by possible future rewards" because, it

---

3. The same can certainly be said of the profession of law and the way it is practiced by those representing business. Vinson & Elkins' role in strategizing and structuring Enron's off-the-books transactions is but one example of this.

4. "Bigger than Enron" FRONTLINE.

5. "The Accountants' War" by Jane Mayer, *The New Yorker*, April 22 & 29, 2002.

was noted, fees from Enron to the firm "could reach $100 million per year."[6]

The battle over whether accounting firms should be able to do consulting work for their audit clients remains controversial. In 2000, an effort by then SEC Chairman Arthur Levitt to ban the practice met with a war-like stance from the industry, which fought mightily against any attempt to limit consulting activities, and won. The post-Enron Corporate Fraud Accountability Act of 2002 placed strict limits on the practice of consulting for audit clients; however, proposed SEC regulations to implement the ban have been watered down considerably.

The manifestation of the accounting industry's transformation from business facilitator/overseer to major player in its own right became most apparent with the position taken by the industry over the accounting treatment of stock options in the early 1990s. Like the consulting issue, the accounting treatment of options remains contentious to this day.

### *The Options Craze*

Stock options gained popularity throughout the 1990s as the preferred form of executive compensation. The tax code drove much of this phenomenon. The Revenue Act of 1950 for the first time permitted companies to pay employees with stock options instead of or in addition to cash compensation. In 1993 the allowable deduction for cash executive compensation was capped at $1 million (a corporation could still pay its executives more than that, but would not get the write-off on its tax return). As total executive compensation packages increased dramatically, stock options made up a larger and larger portion of the remuneration. By 2001, options accounted for 60 percent of the pay package for the typical corporate CEO, helping to drive the average compensation package above $10 million.[7]

### **Theory versus Practice**

The benefits of paying management in stock, at least in theory, are several. Most cynical among

them is the fact that if managers are shareholders too, then even if they breach their fiduciary duty and act in their own self-interest, they will have the same interest as the other shareholders. Stock ownership was thought to *align* the interests of management and owners. Granting options and stock ownership to employees also was viewed as likely to increase their loyalty to the company and their commitment to its success. Stock options are characterized as pay for performance; a healthy motivator for everyone.

In practice, however, equity compensation has not proven the nifty package once thought. The ability of inside management to manipulate stock price and the CEO pay packages that increase steadily despite their company's dismal stock performance have proven problematic for this compensation scheme. Tying executive compensation to stock performance, especially where there are no limitations on when the executive can exercise the option, creates a powerful incentive for the executive to ensure that the stock price climbs: at whatever cost. The massive wealth to be reaped in executive stock options accounts for much of the financial chicanery and accounting impropriety witnessed in the last decade. The problem is putting such a laser-like focus on "the number" instead of actual company performance and the true value of the corporation.

> The stock price is now the overwhelming factor in determining the pay of top company officials, with tens of millions of dollars at stake every year. It is the yardstick by which Wall Street's analysts and money managers declare which companies are most worthy, and it is the cue for much of the financial press in deciding which managers are to be lionized and which are to be ignored, or even vilified. A rising stock price is the CEO's best defense against an unwanted takeover or an unceremonious sacking by the board of directors. And in an era when an increasing share

---

6. Id.

7. "Executive Privilege? Here's the New Take on Stock Options: They Reward Corporate Leaders for All the Wrong Things" by Steven Pearlstein, *Washington Post*, March 24, 2002.

of employees' retirement funds are tied up in their companies' stock, the direction of the share price has become a key factor in the motivation and loyalty of many employees.[8]

Management has become so focused on the short-term, so focused on the quarterly earning numbers, that they no longer see the larger picture of corporate health and viability. Whenever a leader fails to look beyond his own tenure, he ceases to lead.[9] Most options do not require an extended holding period by the executive, thus creating the temptation to boost stock price in the short-term only, and leave the issues of long-term competitiveness and viability to the next administration. Lawrence Mitchell, director of the Sloan Program for the Study of Business and Society at George Washington University, explains the effect of options-heavy compensation; "A CEO would do better using his tenure buying and selling divisions, laying off workers, ignoring environmental cleanups, and delaying investments in training, research and development."[10]

Recent analyses show that increases in executive pay, on average, do not translate into later gains for the shareholders.[11] Proposals to address the downsides of equity compensation include: imposing lengthy holding periods on executive options before exercise; disgorging option profits earned by executives in the year preceding a bankruptcy filing; and even removing the $1 million cash compensation cap.[12]

### The Accounting Treatment of Options

Irrespective of the merits and shortcomings of using stock options to compensate executives, the main controversy surrounding options is the way they are reported to shareholders (or,

more precisely, *not* reported).

The awarding of massive numbers of stock options to executives greatly dilutes the value of the shares already owned and outstanding by current shareholders. Shareholders have no say in the awarding of these options; that is left to the discretion of the Board of Directors. So, at a minimum, shareholders and potential investors in the company should be kept apprised of the size and value of the options packages being granted to company management, diluting the value of their interest. At present, such options are disclosed in the form of a footnote to the company's audited financial statement—the information that appears in very tiny print.

How options are financially accounted for makes their true value all the more opaque: they are not reported as an expense by the corporation when they are granted, as are other forms of employee compensation and benefits. Option costs are reported in very tiny footnotes and are not deducted as an expense against earnings—thus, artificially propping up "the Number."

In 1994, FASB—the group authorized to consider such things as the proper conventions for treatment of options—opined that the estimated value of options granted should be expensed against earnings. Industry roared "NO" and the Congress backed them up.

Few argue against the expensing of options on the merits of the accounting principles. Clearly, when granted, the company is parting with something of value in exchange for the employee's labor. Under the most basic principles of accounting, that cost should be reflected in the accounts. Instead, opponents argue 1) that it is too difficult to accurately gauge the value of options when granted, and 2) that the effect of expensing options would be devastating to company's earnings reports.

---

8. Id.

9. An excellent book on this phenomenon is *THE NUMBER: How the Drive for Quarterly Earnings Corrupted Wall Street and Corporate America* by Alex Berenson, New York: Random House, 2003. In tracing the history of how this short-term obsession came to be, Berenson, a *NYTimes* business reporter, says, "Earnings per share is the number for which all other numbers are sacrificed." He observes that earnings per share have come to represent "the distilled truth of a company's health... Too bad it's a lie."

10. "Executive Privilege? Here's the New Take on Stock Options: They Reward Corporate Leaders for All the Wrong Things" by Steven Pearlstein, *Washington Post*, March 24, 2002.

11. "Option Pie: Overeating is a Health Hazard" by Gretchen Morgenson, *NYTimes,* April 04, 2004.

12. "Mo' Money, Fewer Problems: Is it a good idea to get rid of the $1 million CEO pay ceiling?" by Janice Revell, *FORTUNE*, March 31, 2003.

With respect to the difficulty in estimating value, proponents point out that is the case with a great many items of revenue and expense that make up a company's financials: that doesn't mean you don't count them at all. A good faith estimate, determined in a consistent fashion, would more than do the trick. After all, the options are currently counted at $0.00 and they're certainly not free: a good estimate is better than nothing, literally.

With respect to the second argument, yes, no doubt about it, it will affect the earnings number—that's just math.

> [In 2001], according to those annual report footnotes, expensing would have reduced the earnings of the S&P 500 by 21%. That's partly because earnings were such a horror show last year. Merrill Lynch guesses that this year [2002] the S&P options bite would be more like 10%. At a lot of tech companies, of course, the bite would be much worse: Dell's 2001 earnings would have been reduced 59% if options were counted; Intel's 79%; Cisco's 171%. [13]

A more recent study by Prudential Financial focusing on the high tech industry revealed that expensing option costs would have reduced earnings at semiconductor makers in 2003 by an average of 40%. Options at these companies constitute 16% of the total shares outstanding.[14]

But proponents of expensing point to the fact that legitimate expenses should be factored into the earnings number. If the rule changed, *everyone* would be subject to it. There would not be a competitive disadvantage due to the lower earnings numbers because *everyone* would be subject to the same reporting requirement—the playing field would be level. For the high tech industry, which relies heavily on stock options to procure and keep talent and has taken especial affront to the options-expensing proposals,

just about every company in the industry would be affected in the same way. Moreover, analysts and investors are keenly aware of the issue and would likely be able to factor in the options effect without having some kind of panic-attack. They do so now from the information in the very tiny footnotes.

## The Accountants Join the Fight against FASB

In 1993, FASB proposed closing what has been referred to as the most gaping accounting loophole in the business by requiring options to be recorded as an expense on corporate balance sheets. Industry immediately mobilized to fight the new accounting standard.

> You had groups, mainstream business lobbies; you had the Silicon Valley lobbies; you had the accountants, who in theory shouldn't care what the rules are, they should just want to apply them. All calling on every senator and congressman, leaning on the SEC, visiting members of FASB, threatening the budget of FASB, threatening the budget of the SEC, working with any kind of trade association they could swing in, kicking in large campaign contributions.
>
> It was one of the most impressive lobbying efforts on earth. It was protecting CEOs' pay packages. . . I mean, there's nothing in CEOs' salaries that compares to the number of CEO stock options. It was protecting CEOs' pay packages. They were out in force.[15]

Corporate executives pulled out all of the stops to prevent implementation of FASB's recommendation; including turning to Congress for help, despite the fact that Congress has no jurisdiction over the technical rules for accounting standards. And their lawyers, investment bankers, and accountants stood with them shoulder-to-shoul-

---

13. "REFORM: The Only Option (For Stock Options, That Is)" by Justin Fox, *FORTUNE*, August 12, 2002.

14. "Litmus Test for Ethics: Options" by Gretchen Morgenson, *NYTimes*, March 21, 2004.
A separate study by Merrill, Lynch in 1992 showed that expensing stock options would have slashed profits among leading high-tech companies by 60 percent on average.

15. Sarah Teslik, Executive Director of the Council of Institutional Investors, in *Bigger than Enron*.

der, dollar-for-dollar in the battle.

Jim Hooten, then the chief of Andersen's worldwide auditing practice, observed: "It was the first time that accounting principles had become very, very much influenced by commercial interest and political interest . . . If you move accounting and accounting standards into the political environment, then you've lost control over whether those standards are the best standards."[16]

Arthur Levitt, then Chairman of the SEC, who personally favored the change and bore the brunt of the wrath of business and industry on the issue, has remarked that the role of the accountants in the fight was a "defining moment" for him: "The accountants were going beyond good accounting. They were advocating a business position. They wanted to keep their customers happy. It was quite unseemly."[17]

Ultimately, led by Senator Joseph Lieberman of Connecticut, the Senate passed a non-binding resolution condemning FASB's proposal by a vote of 88-to-9, and the political pressure caused FASB and its supporters in the government and investment community to back down. Former Chairman Levitt has said that he views losing this showdown as one of his greatest mistakes in office. "It used to be that if industries had a problem they would try to work it out with the regulatory authority. . . Now they bypass the regulators completely, and go right to Congress. . . . It's almost impossible to compete with the effect that money has on these congressmen."[18]

Casting their lot in the column of business management instead of public shareholders and investors in the stock options battle was the first major public unveiling of the newly-transformed accounting industry. Throughout the 1990s, the accounting industry would similarly wage battles against the other major regulatory efforts to increase transparency and protect the owners of corporations. In 1994 and 1995, the industry joined forces with industry to push through reforms in the tort laws to make it more difficult for defrauded shareholders to sue the companies responsible for the fraud. Led by Newt Gingrinch, the Congress passed a law denying rights of access to the courts for these kinds of securities fraud suits. President Clinton vetoed the legislation, but in an unusual move, Democrats in Congress crossed party lines to override the veto. The amount of campaign dollars contributed by business and the accounting industry to those leading the Congressional charge were unprecedented (especially given that many of these politicians were not even up for re-election). Again, in 1999-2000, when the SEC, chaired by Levitt, sought to require accounting firms to separate its audit and consulting functions, the accountants and their industry clients waged a war against the reforms. CEOs of the largest corporations in the country, including Ken Lay of Enron, used whatever political influence available to thwart the separation, claiming that consulting was a crucial aspect of their relationship with their audit firms. The fight ultimately got so nasty as to result in threats by Congress to de-fund the SEC in appropriations if it did not back down. Levitt had no choice but to blink. Auditor consulting as a policy matter remains unresolved today.

At the time of the battle over consulting, the rules governing auditors' independence hadn't been updated in two decades. Levitt made sincere efforts to obtain input from the accounting industry in formulating the SECs's approach: to no avail. "They were constantly deadlocked by differences of opinion. When I asked for support, I never got it. I never heard in any speech they gave the words 'public interest'—I realized it was an industry that completely lacked leadership."[19]

Despite the failure of the accounting profession and the government to vindicate the interests of public investors, there have been a few

---

16. *Bigger than Enron.*

17. "The Accountants' War" by Jane Mayer, *The New Yorker*, April 22 & 29, 2002.

18. Ibid., Mayer notes further that "Enron's campaign contributions and its political power have received much attention, but two of the top five accounting firms—Andersen and Deloitte—and the accountants trade association actually spent more during the 2000 elections."

19. Id.

leading companies that have voluntarily decided to expense the options granted to employees and make full disclosure of the transaction to shareholders, analysts, and the rest of the business world: among them, Coca-Cola, Wachovia, Bank One, and the Washington Post. Most European companies likewise report equity compensation when granted. And in some companies, shareholders are making it clear that they will not tolerate it any other way. In March of 2004, 55% of Hewlett Packard shares voted in favor of a proposal to require the company to expense options. Management had recommended a vote against the proposal.[20] And in May of 2004, 54% of Intel's shareholders voted the same way, despite management's opposition. Although shareholder resolutions are not technically binding on management, they nonetheless send a clear message on shareholder sentiment and satisfaction with management policies: one apparently much louder than the regulators.

### The Myth of the Few Bad Apples

As various financial schemes and scandals broke throughout the 1990s and then exploded beginning with Enron's demise, the mantra of industry was that there was no real cause for alarm by investors, that there will always be "a few bad apples" in the barrel. Nonetheless, it is now known what widespread deception and manipulation pervaded business at the turn of this century. Most of the deception and conniving were accomplished for the sake of pleasing Wall Street by meeting "the number" (often in furtherance of self-enrichment through stock options). Companies themselves bear the primary blame for such grifting, but their accountants facilitated the fraud. Andersen took the hardest fall for its misdeeds—a suicide plunge perhaps—but all of the Big Five engaged in the same types of activities and between them they represented the vast majority of large companies in the country. All four of the remaining Big Five are currently under scrutiny for at least one high-profile audit failure.

A study conducted by two Cornell law pro-

fessors in 2003—"Was Arthur Andersen Different? An Empirical Examination of Major Accounting Firms' Audits of Large Clients" by Theodore Eisenberg and Jonathan Macey—looked at financial restatements, or corrections to accounts, by the largest audit clients of the top accounting firms over the five-year period beginning in 1997.[21] Statistically, the study found that there was no significant difference among the firms; and in fact, that Andersen had the second-lowest number of restatements for revenue recognition—the kind of restatement that has the greatest impact on share prices. The frequency of restatements for all five firms rose significantly between the first year of the study and the last (and we know that after 2002 the numbers jumped dramatically again).

Enron may have been the ruin of Andersen, but it certainly wasn't the firm's first major modern accounting scandal. In the late 1990s, Andersen was squarely in the middle of two other major accounting frauds with clients. At Sunbeam, CEO Al Dunlap ("Chainsaw Al") used accounting tricks to cook the corporate books for his own self-enrichment. With a hefty grant of stock options in his pay package, Dunlap stood to make more than $200 million personally if he could keep Sunbeam's stock price high. To accomplish this, Dunlap overstated company losses when he took the helm and then used the numbers as a slush fund to shore up earnings when they failed to meet projections. Dunlap also played games with revenue recognition and timing to artificially bolster Sunbeam's stock price. Andersen was aware of much of the trickery. When Sunbeam finally corrected its books, the restatement was so severe as to cause the company's bankruptcy, and the stock price plunged from $53 at its peak to just pennies. As with its representation of Enron, Andersen's loyalty to Sunbeam was beyond zealous: upon investigation the SEC discovered that Andersen accounting documents in the Sunbeam case had been destroyed.

Waste Management was another of Andersen's misdeeds in the late 1990s. The SEC inves-

---

20. "Litmus Test for Ethics: Options" by Gretchen Morgenson, *NYTimes,* March 21, 2004.
21. "How Bad Was Andersen?" *The Economist,* December 6, 2003.

tigation of the company revealed an overstatement of earnings by $1.7 billion (the biggest, pre-Enron) and a long-running cover-up scheme by the company and Andersen to avoid detection and prosecution. The SEC fined Andersen $7 million for its part in the fraud, just months before the Enron scam made headlines.

In May of 2002, a month before the firm would be found criminally liable in the Enron case, Andersen settled a lawsuit with investors in its client, the Baptist Foundation of Arizona. The foundation, which managed retirement accounts for many elderly investors, was allegedly running a Ponzi scheme— using money from new investors to pay earlier investors—ultimately costing investors and an estimated $570 million when the Baptist Foundation of Arizona (BFA) collapsed in 1999.[22] Andersen agreed under the settlement to pay $217 million, though the firm's demise the following month made collection by the plaintiffs on the settlement highly improbable.

PricewaterhouseCoopers managed to avoid enforcement action against it for its role in the MicroStrategy accounting fraud. It paid $50 million to settle a suit by MicroStrategy investors, but was not prosecuted by the SEC. Its senior partner on the MicroStrategy account was not so lucky. More than three years after the massive restatement of earnings by the company and the plea deals made by the company principals with the SEC, PwC audit partner Warren Martin, without admitting or denying liability for failing "to act with due professional care" or "to maintain an attitude of professional skepticism," was fined and agreed to be barred from auditing publicly-traded companies.[23]

A wide-ranging investigation into the sales of tax shelters by KPMG has put that firm on the defensive. In May of 2004, the firm was ordered to produce documents relating to such sales, which the firm had claimed were confidential.

The judge ruled that corroborated evidence of the firm's attempts to hide and secrete all information regarding the shelter schemes undermined its claim of confidentiality for the documents.[24] In a related ruling involving the biggest bankruptcy in US history—WorldCom—the bankruptcy judge directed the reorganizing WorldCom (now known as "MCI") to stop paying its external auditor KPMG, following a request by 14 state governments to disqualify the accounting firm. Specifically pointing to the aggressive tax-avoidance strategy that KPMG sold to WorldCom in the years leading up to its 2002 bankruptcy, the states contended the KPMG is not sufficiently disinterested to act as an independent auditor or tax advisor. "KPMG, as an auditor, would have to evaluate the soundness of its own prior tax advice, posing a conflict of interest for the firm."[25]

Ernst & Young was the auditor of record for the scandal-ridden company, HealthSouth, which is still in the process of being sorted out. In addition, the SEC is trying to have Ernst barred from accepting new public clients for 6 months because of its inappropriate relationship and activities with the software company PeopleSoft in the 1990s.[26]

With all the scandal and investigation, it's hard to find good accounting help these days— no one wants to be represented by a firm embroiled in controversy and at odds with the regulators—it doesn't bode well for their clients.

The accounting industry claims to have reawakened to its responsibilities and revamped its practices in line with them; improving training for auditors, veering clear from riskier businesses, and disbanding some services that fall into the grey area of accounting propriety. But it may be too little too late. Indeed, the accounting profession is no longer trusted as a "profession" and no longer enjoys the privilege of self-regulation.

---

22. "Andersen Settles Foundation Lawsuit" by David Hilzenrath, *Washington Post*, May 7, 2002.

23. "SEC Settles with Audit Firm: PricewaterhouseCoopers Exits MicroStrategy Scandal" by David Hilzenrath, *Washington Post*, August 18, 2003.

24. "KPMG Is Ordered To Release Data Under IRS Probe" by Jonathan Weil, *Wall Street Journal*, May 5, 2004.

25. "WorldCom is Told it Must Withhold Pay to KPMG" by Jonathan Weil, *Wall Street Journal*, March 22, 2004.

26. "Surviving the Accounting Upheaval: Ernst & Young Changing in Response to Pressures" by Carrie Johnson, *Washington Post*, July 30, 2003.

Passage of the Corporate Fraud Accountability Act in 2002 brought with it the creation of independent governmental oversight of the accounting profession in the form of the Public Company Accounting Oversight Board. The PCAOB, which operates under the authority and supervision of the SEC, is charged with investigation and sanction in cases of intentional misconduct or repeated instances of negligent conduct in the accounting profession—a role previously reserved for the member-managed AICPA.

The PCAOB got off to a rocky start. Set up after the passage of the Act in the summer of 2002, the Board was left without a chairman after the first choice for the job, former FBI and CIA director William H. Webster, was forced to quit amid ethics charges. Webster served as the chair of the audit committee on the board of directors of a company under investigation for accounting improprieties and securities violations. SEC Chairman Harvey L. Pitt (a controversial choice from the start given his traditional position defending corporate criminals), had tapped Webster for the job without disclosing the legal and ethical issues engulfing him. Pitt, too, was then forced to step down.[27] Ultimately, William Donaldson took the position as SEC Chairman and ultimately he named William J. McDonough, retiring president of the Federal Reserve Bank of New York, to head up the PCAOB.

## Conclusion

The role of auditors in protecting the interest of the investing public is necessary but not sufficient. Others with responsibilities to the investing public include boards of directors, investment banks, credit rating agencies, and lawyers. Paul Volker, Chairman of the Federal Reserve Board from 1979 to 1987, who played a leading role in trying to salvage Andersen from total destruction during the Enron debacle, says,

You know, it's not just in the auditing profession. They're at the end of the line. That's very important; they have a public responsibility. But these breakdowns reflect pressures that are very strong and affect other professional groups, financial groups, as well. Andersen didn't make up all these things that Enron was doing. Other people sold those techniques to Enron, or they developed them themselves. Andersen's function was to rule on them in the end, but they didn't make them up.[28]

Arthur Levitt, former chairman of the SEC adds,

The Enron story was a story not just of the failure of the accounting firm, but also the traditional gatekeepers: the board, the audit committee, the lawyers, the investment bankers, the rating agencies. All of them had a part in this...[29]

In losing sight of their public obligations, accountants have lost sight of their purpose in the financial process. They were brought in with the securities laws; with the intent to bring transparency and disclosure to investors in business; and their mission for the 21st century needs to return to those precepts of the 1930s.

We need a lot more sunlight on the system, so that the public can see what's going on.... Because if the accounting profession is scared to operate in the public domain, out in the sunlight so people can see everything that's going on, then, quite frankly, that should tell you something—that there's something wrong. The accounting firms should recognize it; the public should understand it. And Congress, probably along with the SEC, needs to make reforms.[30]

27. "Birth of a Watchdog" *NYTimes* Editorial  April 28, 2003
28. *Bigger than Enron*
29. Id.
30. Lynn Turner, former chief accountant of the SEC, in *Bigger than Enron*.

## Discussion Questions

1. What is the historical role of accounting firms and public auditors?
2. Discuss ways in which accounting firm independence may be compromised. How serious is this problem? How can the issue best be addressed?
3. Why are so many executives paid in stock options?
4. How are options reported to shareholders? Why is this a problem?
5. What are the arguments for expensing options?
6. What are the arguments for and against eliminating options?
7. Explain the changes in the accounting industry after Enron. Assess the degree to which these will make a difference in accounting practice.

# Case 9

## The Cigarette Controversy

*The case looks at the post-Multi-State Tobacco Settlement transformation of Philip Morris Company into Altria. It looks at the company's attempt to remake itself as well as its continuing product liability litigation battle. Corporate culture, the company's perception by consumers, the role of government relations, and the impact on its behavior on shareholders and employees in the tobacco industry, are all explored.*

*Relevant chapters: 3, 4, 5, 6, 8*

### Introduction

The tobacco controversy has hit Altria (formerly Philip Morris) harder than any other tobacco company in the world. With more than 50% market share, Altria remains the largest target of ongoing public anger; resulting in numerous law suits, particularly in the state of California. Andre Calantzopoulos, president and CEO for Altria's tobacco businesses (Philip Morris), asserts that integrity and responsibility are just as important as economic success.[1] However, skeptics of the tobacco company want to know how he plans to live up to these promises.

The public outcry against all tobacco companies, and against cigarettes in general, has escalated in recent years. The amount of lawsuits continues to increase and stricter regulations on public smoking and tobacco sales are being enforced. New York City banned smoking in restaurants, bars, and public buildings—including Altria's Park Avenue headquarters. Philip Morris has born the brunt of these attacks. In the light of recent events what options are available to Altria and what are the implications of these options? What are the next steps that Altria should take? What are the "honorable" and "right" thing to do? What is "practical?"

### Evolution of the Cigarette Controversy

In the U.S. more than 400,000 people die annually from smoking-related diseases.[2] With 50% market share, Philip Morris is seen as being responsible for 200,000 of those deaths each year.[3] Each year more information comes to light regarding the tobacco companies' knowledge concerning the dangerous effects of smoking. Today, studies are widespread explaining the causal links of smoking cigarettes to cancer

This case study was originally written by L. Bavaro, S. Choi, A. Flaherty, T. Hase, G. Hernandez, N. Lee, V. Osipov, L. Palmisano, A. Schneider, and Z. Swanson, and was revised by Alfred A. Marcus. ©2006, Northcoast Publishers, Inc.

1. http://www.philipmorrisinternational.com Calantzopoulos Speech.
2. Byrne, John A., "Philip Morris: Inside America's Most Reviled Company", *BusinessWeek.com*.
3. Id.

and other health issues. In the 1990s, a number of reports were published showing that tobacco companies manipulated nicotine levels in cigarettes to addict smokers. The FDA also is increasing its efforts to try and regulate the tobacco industry.

Lawsuits have been the means by which Philip Morris and other tobacco companies have been "punished," culminating in the large 1997 Big Tobacco settlement. When the five major tobacco companies settled with 46 states, they not only had to pay the states $254 billion over 25 years, but in the interest of public disclosure, they also had to post millions of pages of previously secret internal documents on the Internet. Access to these documents has been crucial to the recent, negative advertising campaigns and increased litigation against Big Tobacco.

### Today's Challenge – More Lawsuits

With the big tobacco trial behind it, Phillip Morris was planning a new corporate identity—one that would stress the company's food businesses more, while reducing its association with tobacco. The new name, Altria, was intended to convey altitude and altruism. With its decision in 1998 to settle the Medicaid-reimbursement lawsuits brought by state attorneys general, Philip Morris agreed to pay half of the tobacco industry's $254 billion bill over 25 years. It hoped to put the worst litigation behind it. However, since 1999 seven plaintiffs claiming cigarettes caused cancer or other illness have won court cases against the company. The damages include a $28 billion punitive damage judgment, the largest award ever to any individual in United States history. It was later lowered to $28 million. Over the last few years, Philip Morris has lost a string of multimillion-dollar personal-injury cases on the West Coast.

A case in Illinois, tried by Judge Nicholas Byron in Madison County, was a new kind of class action.[4] The plaintiffs were 1.1 million Marlboro Lights and Cambridge Lights smokers.

They held that Philip Morris had deceived them by not stating outright that light cigarettes are just as dangerous to health as regular ones. Judge Byron's ruling in Illinois that Philip Morris had deceived smokers into believing its light cigarettes were less dangerous than regular ones was announced on March 21, 2003. Before appealing the $10.1 billion verdict, Philip Morris would have to pay $12 billion bond. The company was given until April 21 to pay the $12 billion bond, but rating agencies almost immediately downgraded Altria's debt. [5] Rating agency, Moody's Investor Service, downgraded Altria's rating two positions, just above "junk" bond status.

Altria could pay the plaintiffs a nonrefundable fee in exchange for a bond reduction, as it did in a Florida personal-injury class action, but the ruling left Altria threatening Chapter 11 bankruptcy. In that event Philip Morris possibly could cut off its annual multibillion-dollar payments to the states. The possibility that the states would not get these payments caused the rating agencies to also lower the ratings of state bonds, which were backed by future tobacco revenues. It prompted a massive sell off of these bonds.

Some analysts argued that the tobacco manufacturer was playing "hard ball" and that there were other means to solve the situation, but state governments started to support Altria, arguing that the size of the bond the company had to post in the Illinois case was too large.[6] If Altria was compelled to pay this bond, the company might have to file for bankruptcy and if the company filed for bankruptcy state governments could not be assured of their regular tobacco settlement payments: $2.5 billion was due to the states by April 15, 2003. In response to the Illinois ruling, Altria's lawyers sent a letter to the Washington State Attorney General warning that if the Illinois verdict went through Philip Morris would not be able to provide its next scheduled payment.

The budget crisis that states faced forced them to look for ways to cover their deficits, and

---

4. Sellers, Patricia "Altria's Perfect Storm: Hit by cut-rate competitors, taxes, and most of all, litigation, the company that owns Philip Morris faces its worst crisis in years," *Fortune*, April 14, 2003.
5. O'Connell, Vanessa, "Altria's Tobacco Paymnets in Doubt", *The Wall Street Journal*, Monday March 31, 2003.
6. Carr, Korein, Tillery Legal Firm, Press Release: "Financial 'Scare Tactics' Designed to Win Special Treatment; Confidential Court Documents, Expert Analysis Show Company Can Afford $12 Billion Appeal Bond, Payments to States." April 2, 2003.

tobacco money was a source they could not ignore. The collective deficit of the 50 states was $27 billion as February 2003. Some states including Virginia, Kansas, New York, Vermont and California, Philip Morris' worst enemy, had plans to sell bonds backed by tobacco payments to cover their deficits. As Scott Harshbarger from the Massachusetts state government commented, "Certainly many of us never anticipated that states would become addicted to tobacco money as a way to finance our operations."[7]

Chapter 11 would have another effect that was highly beneficial to Philip Morris. It would stop further litigation, unless the bankruptcy court allowed it. The threat of bankruptcy might have been posturing by Altria to lower the court's tobacco bond, but it worked, as Judge Byron gave in. He ruled that he would consider alternatives. However, two additional consumer fraud class actions of this nature were be tried in Massachusetts and Florida and two more personal injury cases were scheduled in California. The company, meanwhile, was appealing 10 separate verdicts that had gone against it. The Engle case awarded $145 billion to Florida smokers three years ago, of which Philip Morris must pay $74 billion.

The lesson that Philip Morris was learning from these cases is that it had to be less cautious in the courtroom. It would start to interview jurors more carefully, present more evidence, and call more witnesses. It would attempt to move cases out of cities like Los Angeles and San Francisco, where anti-smoking sentiment runs high.

From 1954 to 1998, only 3 of the more than 800 individual smokers who sued cigarette makers won their cases, and two of those were reversed on appeal.[8] But since 1999, smokers have won 10 of the 30 cases brought against tobacco firms in several states.[9] There had been four straight victories against Philip Morris in California in the past three years.

Numerous attorneys around the country were lining up to attack Big Tobacco. Fifty-five law firms in 26 states belonged to the newly created Tobacco Trial Lawyers' Association, up from perhaps a dozen willing to represent a smoker five years ago.[10] The cost of carrying out these lawsuits was decreasing dramatically due to the existence of extensive and easily accessed information and the sharing of strategy among lawyers.

Big Tobacco's decline in the courtroom could be traced to a few simple factors. One was the incriminating evidence in the documents. "Plaintiffs could marshal documents showing that tobacco companies knew for decades that cigarettes caused cancer and that nicotine was addictive even as they publicly denied the links." The outright lies of earlier decades made jurors mad and changed the dynamic in the courtroom. Documents alone did not necessarily influence juries. Plaintiffs' attorneys were drawing on tobacco insiders willing to testify. For instance, William Farone, who was a top tobacco scientist at Philip Morris from 1976 to 1984, testified in the Bullock case in California in November of 2002 against the company.[11]

### Is Bankruptcy Next?

But these were not Altria's only problems and the only reasons it had lost market value.[12] As state governments increased excise taxes on cigarettes by as much as 48% in one year, new discount competitors offered cheap cigarettes. The primary reason Philip Morris USA, that had sales of $18.9 billion in 2002, saw profits fall 13%, to $5 billion was that cigarettes were considered by many consumers to be too expensive. In New York City, a pack of Marlboros cost $7.68. Those prices were especially high for the average U.S. smoker, whose household income was just $35,000 a year.

High prices created an opportunity for competitors, cheap cigarettes selling under names like

---

7. O'Connell, Vanessa, & Fairchild, Gordon, "Once Tobacco Foes, States Are Hooked on Settlement Cash" ", *The Wall Street Journal*, Wednesday April 2, 2003. Page A1, A11.

8. Sherrid, Pamela, "Smokers' Revenge", Money & Business Vol. 133 , No. 17; Pg. 44.

9. Id.

10. Id.

11. Id.

12. Sellers, Patricia "Altria's Perfect Storm: Hit by cut-rate competitors, taxes, and most of all, litigation, the company that owns Philip Morris faces its worst crisis in years," *Fortune*, April 14, 2003.

USA Gold and Roger. They accounted for about 10% of the U.S. market in 2003, an increase from 2% in 1997. Even better bargains were available on Internet sites such as esmokes.com. and dirtcheapcigs.com. Counterfeit cigarettes—mainly fake Marlboros from China—grabbed another 1% of the market. In July 2002, Philip Morris had to raise promotional spending by $850 million for 2002. It funded buy-two-get-one-free offers and other incentives to buy its brands.

Philip Morris, officially became Altria on Jan. 27, 2003, when it engineered a $8.4 billion IPO of 16% of Kraft in the second-largest initial public offering ever. Kraft Foods, of which Altria now owned 84% consisted of well-known brands like Oreo, Jell-O, Maxwell House, Oscar Mayer. Miracle Whip, Entenman, Toblerone, Post Cereals, and Kool-Aid. The international tobacco division made $5.7 billion on $28.7 billion in revenue in 2002, the largest revenue of any division in the $80-billion-a-year company, Altria's planned acquisitions of additional assets in the food industry and overseas tobacco business, however, were put on hold because of the debt downgrades, which made these acquisitions much more difficult.

### Past Strategies: Defend and Attack

Philip Morris' former CEO, Geoffrey Bible, initially retreated from the public eye and created a defensive culture to protect the company from attack. Bible became CEO in 1994. He had spent his entire professional life in the tobacco industry and was determined to defend the tobacco industry at any cost. In his early press conferences, he demonstrably and incessantly chain smoked Marlboro menthols. He emphasized smokers' rights, the importance of liberty and choice, and the right of a person to choose whether he or she would enjoy the pleasures of smoking. He contested the scientific findings that linked smoking and the passive absorption of smoke to disease. The combative Bible was a proud smoker who had built international tobacco into an $8.5 billion business.

The 144,000 employees of Philip Morris consistently faced the dilemma of using their business expertise to sell products that could greatly harm its customers and those around them. Few corporations were so subjected to public outrage and attack as Philip Morris and few employees escaped the scrutiny that was heaped on their company. It was important for management to reinforce, in employee's minds, the value of working at Philip Morris. Bible's approach was to loudly and directly confront the issues and attacks regarding cigarette smoking. He earned a reputation for strongly defending the production and sale of tobacco products and the tobacco industry. He waged war with critics through Philip Morris' lawyers: by filing lawsuits against detractors, including the television network ABC and the Food and Drug Administration.[13] Philip Morris believed then that smoking was a lifestyle choice. Those who smoked were aware of the risks involved and made an informed choice. Philip Morris also believed that people could quit smoking if they resolved to do so, although it did recognize that it could be difficult to quit.

Under Bible, Philip Morris did not reach out to its critics to create a dialogue as to how to deal with the issue. Many executives felt cut off and ill-equipped to defend the company. In 1994, Stephen Parrish, senior vice president for external affairs, was quoted as saying:

> "...my daughter came home from school and said "...tomorrow we're going to talk about drugs...We're also going to talk about cigarettes and whether they are addictive..." I told her that a lot of people believe that cigarette smoking is addictive but I don't believe it...the Surgeon General says some 40 million people have quit smoking on their own...But if she asked me about the health consequences, I would tell here that I certainly don't think it's safe to smoke...But it's a choice. We're confronted with choices all the time..."

David Dangoor, executive vice president for corporate affairs, said:

---

13. Byrne, John A., "Philip Morris: Inside America's Most Reviled Company", *BusinessWeek.com.*

"Everybody knows that smoking must be a terrible idea...Yet they do it. Why?...People do all sorts of things to express their individuality and to protest against society. And smoking is one of them, and not the worst...In a lot of countries, its incredibly important to the whole welfare system that we sell our products to collect taxes."

Craig Fuller, senior vice preside for corporate affairs, said:

"We think smokers and nonsmokers alike have rights. And they ought to be accommodated...Among our strongest brands is Marlboro...It gives us cash flow, a financial base...."

William Campbell, president and chief executive officer of Philip Morris USA, said:

"My girls ask why I smoke. And I can only answer them that I enjoy it, and I think I'm informed about it. And I tell them, "You'll be facing decisions like this one when you're an adult....""

Victor Crawford, a lobbyist for the Tobacco Institute, said:

"I got the diagnosis of throat cancer...I have no animosity. I've got nobody to blame but myself...I'm not proud of having lobbied for them...Do I feel guilty about what I did? Yeah."

Through a large in-house survey, Philip Morris' employees clearly indicated the desire for senior management and executives to respond differently – to increase efforts to restore and improve Philip Morris' image as well as to communicate more openly with the public.[14] Employees wanted an end to what they believed to be the siege mentality that Philip Morris adopted.

In 1997, Bible changed his strategy. He joined the industry-wide talks and took part in an effort to gain a legislative settlement to the outcry against tobacco products. He agreed to eliminate Philip Morris' well-recognized Marlboro Man from its ads and to pay approximately $175 billion of a $368.5 billion settlement.[15] Some of Philip Morris' executives did not necessarily agree with the change, but at this point, the company had little choice. Bible's vociferous attempts to defend smoking had failed to quell the political and public opposition. The tobacco industry was forced into billion-dollar deal to settle lawsuits filed by 46 states to recover smoking-related medical costs.

### New Strategies – Overhauling the Company's Image

After settling the lawsuits with state governments, Philip Morris and the tobacco industry had to radically change their strategy. They moved from total non-compromise with anti-smoking forces to one of greater accommodation. Philip Morris publicly signaled the strategy shift from siege-mentality of defend and attack to one of change and accommodation. The company now believed that the way to end the controversy was to improve its relationship with the public and government by agreeing and cooperating. The first efforts were to carry out the terms of the June 20, 1997 settlement, which included reducing underage smoking and new health warnings. Philip Morris ended cigarette sampling and mail distribution of cigarettes, halted vending-machine sales, and banned mass-transit and outdoors ads. More than 30,000 retailers were trained by Philip Morris to recognize fake identifications.[16] During this period of time, Philip Morris increased its investment in youth smoking-prevention programs by tenfold to $100 million.

In an October 2, 1997 statement, (Attachment A), Philip Morris recognized that a substantial body of evidence existed supporting the judgment that cigarette smoking plays a causal role in the development of lung cancer and other diseases in smokers. In this same statement, Philip Morris also recognized that the

---

14. Id.
15. Id.
16. Id.

nicotine in cigarette smoke had mild pharmacological effects and that cigarette smoking could be considered addictive under some definitions. Philip Morris deferred to the judgment of public health authorities regarding the issue of environmental tobacco smoke, although it did not specifically agree with the evidence.

Philip Morris continued to donate heavily to community and charitable organizations in hopes of gaining positive headlines. Historically, the company always had supported such causes as the NAACP, the United Negro College Fund, the Boy Scouts, the Girl Scouts, the United Way, the national Multiple Sclerosis Society, and National Association on Drug Abuse. It gave to the Joffrey Ballet, the Morgan Library, the Guggenheim Museum, the Museum of Natural History, and the National Gallery of Art. The company claimed that its business activities had to "make social sense and that social activities must make business sense." Post-tobacco settlement, new initiatives ranged from Save Our Streams and Camp Heartland for children with AIDS/HIV to battered women's shelters, disaster relief, and scholarship programs.[17] In 1999, Philip Morris gave over $60 million to charitable organizations, such as hunger relief, domestic violence programs, museums, fine arts, etc.[18] In spending more than $250 million in an image rebuilding campaign, Philip Morris attempted to present itself as a valuable member of the business community and the community at large as well as to humanize it as a group of people who care. This message was evident in its advertising slogan, "Working to make a difference. The people of Philip Morris."

Critics attacked Philip Morris — not for giving to charities but for the fact that the source of the money given was unethical ("blood money...off the backs of millions of addicted smokers"[19]) and that the donations were a blatant effort to assuage the public's hostility toward Philip Morris. Critics believed that Philip Morris was just "postponing the day of reckoning", or rebuilding its domestic image just enough to allow it to build markets overseas in Russia, China and other developing countries. In recent years, Philip Morris was accused of promoting cigarettes to minors in other countries with less restrictive laws than those in the U.S.

Philip Morris was pulled in disparate and opposing directions by lawsuits and the FDA, by shareholders, and by the community. After Geoffrey Bible's famous taped oath "I believe that nicotine is not addictive," its management warmed to the idea that an open discussion on health and the company's past was the best strategy going forward. Corporate identity changes were intended to stop some of the bleeding, not just a change in name (Altria) but, to signal a change in values. The company proclaimed it was "a quality tobacco product for adults that choose to use them" (Altria Value Statement, Philip Morris homepage). Half the company's revenue was from Kraft Foods, but profit margins were not close to that of tobacco.[20] The new name and image were meant to help reinvigorate the non-tobacco parts of Philip Morris and sustain cumulative performance (See Attachment B for 5 year stock performance). While revenues continued to climb, earnings, severely compromised by legal settlements, were starting to plateau (See Attachment C).

Consultants found specific areas where the public wanted to see improvements: addressing youth prevention of smoking, helping the FDA with tobacco regulation, and two-way communication of the risks with the public (Philip Morris USA homepage). Beginning in January 2003, Altria openly addressed these concerns on its web page and in its corporate literature. It incorporated the new concerns in a revised mission which states that the company's "...goal is to be the most responsible, effective and respected developer, manufacturer and marketer of consumer products..."[21] Its prior mission had been to please shareholders and increase shareholder wealth.

---

17. Dreyfuss, Robert, "Philip Morris Money", The American Prospect Vol. 11 No. 10, March 27, 2000 - April 10, 2000.
18. Id.
19. Id.
20. DiPasquale, Cara B. "Behind the Philip Morris Name Change Plan". AdAge, 24 April 2002.
21. http://www.philipmorrisusa.com/home.asp  "Mission Statement".

With Bible departed, new CEO Louis Camilleri, considered a "diplomat," was at the forefront of these changes. Altria's top executives admitted that Philip Morris was now paying for its history of arrogance and denial. Camilleri went so far as to say the company had to get beyond "40 years of mistrust."[22] Altria created new board committees in response to Enron. Examples included: audit, public responsibility, social responsibility, compensation, and corporate governance.[23] Altria was trying to play a positive role in the debate about the government regulating tobacco use. A side benefit of FDA regulation was that complying with it would be costly for makers of cheap, generic-brand cigarettes that had been gaining on the major tobacco companies' market share.[24]

Representing the shift in approach in the tobacco industry, the current director of corporate affairs at Philip Morris noted:

> This isn't about press releases. It's about doing the right thing. It's about being a good citizen and a responsible marketer and manufacturer of a risky product. When we do these things, in a sincere and consistent manner, we build our reputation and protect our image in the eyes of society. When we do not, our reputation suffers.[25]

To foster better relations and to boost its public image, Philip Morris stated that it would stop publicly debating the effects on health of cigarette smoking or the issue of addiction to cigarette smoking. Even though differences continued to exist between Philip Morris' views and those of the public health community, the company wanted to ensure that a consistent public health message was delivered to the public. In February 2000, it signaled that it was willing to start a dialog with the Food and Drug Administration about regulating tobacco marketing. By fostering better relations and cooperation with the government, Philip Morris was trying to create a regulatory environment that was more favorable to its interests.[26]

Critics, such as the American Lung Association, saw this move as another cynical ploy by the tobacco industry to limit the terms of the debate on tobacco. The critics believed that Philip Morris' tactic was just to buy more time, to cooperate but in a limited way in order to slow down or stop the rate of change in the tobacco industry, and to ultimately sell more in the USA and overseas.[27] Again, the critics questioned Philip Morris' motives as being too self-interested (their purpose was to prop up Philip Morris' stock price and long-term business prospects) and not at all altruistic (protecting the public health). Critics noted that although Philip Morris seemed to be cooperating with FDA tobacco regulation development, it had challenged the FDA regulations through lawsuits.

In a March 4, 2003 press release Altria announced it was moving its headquarters from New York City to Richmond, Virginia. Corporate officials said it was a cost-cutting move that would save over $60M per year in operating costs, but employees were upset because they were not told about the move until the news was public. Many of the 682 affected employees said they would not relocate. Speculation was that the move was made because of aggressive, anti-smoking laws in New York City.[28]

After spending millions of dollars touting its philanthropic efforts, Philip Morris still ranked second to last, beating only exploding tire maker Bridgestone Firestone, in a survey of corporate reputations, conducted by The Reputation Institute and Harris Interactive.[29] What can Philip Morris do now? Federal legislation,

22. Sellers, Patricia "Altria's Perfect Storm: Hit by cut-rate competitors, taxes, and most of all, litigation, the company that owns Philip Morris faces its worst crisis in years," *Fortune*, April 14, 2003.

23. www.Altria.com  "Board Committees".

24. Gordon Fairclough and Vanessa O'Connell; Altria's CEO Faces a Pack Of Problems, *Wall Street Journal;* New York, N.Y.; Apr 14, 2003.

25. Renato Salud, Director, Corporate Affairs, Philip Morris Asia / IPRM/UiTM Public Relations Regional Conference 2001, Kuala Lumpur / 13 August 2001.  http://www.philipmorrisinternational.com/pages/eng/press/speeches/RSalud_200108.asp.

26. Garrison, John R., CEO, American Association, *lungusa.org* Public Statement February 29, 2000.

27. Id.

28. Berkowitz, Harry. "Philip Morris Confirms It's Quitting City". *Newsday* 4 March 2003.

which wouldl limit the liability of the tobacco companies for punitive damages was pending.

## Discussion Questions:

1. Why have tobacco makers like Altria lost so many trials recently? Why were they previously so successful in defending themselves? What could turn the tide again in their favor?
2. Explain the ties that exist between tobacco companies like Altria and state governments. To what extent do these ties preclude or impede fair resolution of tobacco cases.
3. What would Altria gain from a Chapter 11 bankruptcy filing? What prevents the firm from making this filing?
4. Why did Geoffrey Bible capitulate in 1997 and change his defend and attack strategy?
5. What do you think of the defense made by tobacco companies that people have right to smoke? Do not current laws take away people's liberty? How can these laws be defended?
6. What identity does Altria try to project about itself? Is the identity it promotes a believable one?
7. To what extent is Altria a socially responsible company? Can any tobacco firm be considered socially responsible?
8. What would you do if you were a member of Altria's top management team? What are your options? Which ones make the most sense to pursue? Which are financially prudent, legally sound, and/or ethically appropriate? Which are not?

## Attachment A

### PHILIP MORRIS COMPANIES INC. STATEMENT OF POSITION
October 2, 1997

### FROM THE CORPORATE WEBSITE
We are entering into an historic resolution of much of the controversy that has been focused on tobacco and its use in the United States. The resolution should be the beginning of a new era for the industry and its relationship with the public and government. Hopefully, it will be an era characterized by cooperation and agreement. We are fully committed to the objective of discouraging and reducing underage smoking, as embodied in the terms of the comprehensive agreement we entered into on June 20, 1997. We support and will work for passage of legislation incorporating all the provisions of that agreement, including the required new health warnings. In this regard, we have been asked by various Members of Congress, Attorneys General, representatives of the public health community, and others, to state our views on a number of issues related to tobacco, and we are pleased to do so.

### Causation
We recognize that there is a substantial body of evidence which supports the judgment that cigarette smoking plays a causal role in the development of lung cancer and other diseases in smokers. We previously have acknowledged that the strong statistical association between smoking and certain diseases, such as lung cancer and emphysema, establishes that smoking is a risk factor for and, in fact, may be a cause of those diseases. For example, of all the risk factors for lung cancer that have been identified, none is more strongly associated with the disease, or carries a greater risk, than cigarette smoking; a far greater number of smokers than nonsmokers develop lung cancer.

Despite the differences that may exist between our views and those of the public health community, in order to ensure that there will be a single, consistent public health message on this issue, we will refrain from debating the issue other than as necessary to defend ourselves and our opinions in the courts and other forums in which we are required to do so. For that reason, we are also prepared to defer to the judgment of public health authorities as to what health warning messages will best serve the public interest, as reflected in the proposed new health warnings.

### "Addiction"
We recognize that nicotine, as found in ciga-

29. Price, Tom, "Philip Morris Changes Its Name But Not Its Tactics", *Corpwatch.org* , March 14, 2002.

rette smoke, has mild pharmacological effects, and that, under some definitions, cigarette smoking is "addictive." The word "addiction" has been and is currently used differently by different people in different contexts, and the definition of the term has undergone significant changes over the past several decades. In 1964, for example, the Advisory Committee to the Surgeon General of the United States concluded that smoking, although "habit forming," did not fit within its definition of "addiction." However, in 1988, the Surgeon General redefined the term, and concluded that smoking is "addictive." We have not embraced those definitions of "addiction" which do not include historically accepted and objective criteria, such as intoxication and physical withdrawal, as important markers. We acknowledge that our views are at odds with those of the public health community, but in the last analysis there is little point to a continuing public debate about the definition of a word used both colloquially and technically to describe many different kinds of behavior. We continue to believe that people can quit smoking. if they resolve to do so, but we recognize that it can be difficult to quit. Accordingly, to ensure that there is a single, consistent public health message on the issue of addiction, we will refrain from debating the issue other than as necessary to defend ourselves and our opinions in the courts and other forums in which we are required to do so, and we will also defer to the judgment of the public health authorities as to what health warning messages concerning addiction will best serve the public interest, as reflected in the proposed new health warnings.

### Environmental Tobacco Smoke

The proposed warnings relating to environmental tobacco smoke (ETS) accurately reflect the views of the Environmental Protection Agency, the Surgeon General and certain health authorities. While we believe that the evidence with respect to ETS is not persuasive, nevertheless, we are again prepared to defer to the judgment of public health authorities as to what ETS health warning messages will best serve the public interest, as reflected in the proposed new health warnings.

## Attachment B
### Philip Morris (MO) 5 Year Stock Performance History

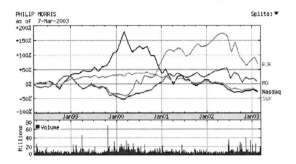

## Attachment C

### Philip Morris 5 Year Operating Revenue

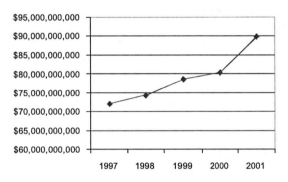

### Philip Morris 5 Year Net Earnings

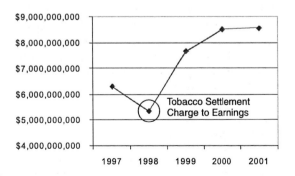

# Case 10

## The Chilling Truth: Must Corporate Speech Be Honest?

*The case examines the legal and ethical issues surrounding the California and United States Supreme Court cases of Kasky v. Nike, Inc. Issues examined include: the first amendment rights of corporations; the different legal status of political versus commercial speech; and the ethics of corporate marketing and public relations.*

*Relevant chapters: 3, 4, 8*

Freedom of Speech in the United States is sourced in the First Amendment of the Constitution, which states: *Congress shall make no law. . . abridging the freedom of speech, or of the press; or the right of the people peaceably to assemble, and to petition the Government for a redress of grievances.* This prohibition against governmental infringement on free speech by the federal legislature was extended to cover action by the states in the Fourteenth Amendment.

Although they are interpreted broadly, the free speech protections of the First Amendment are not absolute. Speech that constitutes a clear and present danger may be prohibited—certain types of hate speech, for example, and the fact that you can't yell "Fire" in a crowded theater. Speech that defames another may be actionable—false factual allegations about another that cause measurable economic harm may be the subject of a civil suit for damages. In many cases, malice or the intent to deceive must be proven against the speaker in order to recover.[1] Perjury—lying under oath—is another form of prohibited or punishable speech.

In addition, *commercial speech*—speech that has as its objective economic or financial gain—may be regulated as to time, place, manner, and to some extent, even content. Accordingly, most forms of advertising and marketing in furtherance of the business purpose may be subject to regulation. Thus, the government has imposed bans on certain forms of tobacco advertising and limitations on the marketing of certain products and services to children on television without violating the First Amendment

---

By Sheryl Kaiser, J.D., with valuable assistance from case briefs on *Kasky v. Nike, Inc.* prepared by Kristin D'Onofrio (Loyola '04), Crystal Baltimore (Loyola '05), John Dempsey (Loyola '05), and Matthew Glynn (Loyola '05). ©2006, Northcoast Publishers, Inc.

1. Malice must be shown in cases of defamation involving public figures and public officials. The argument has been made that the same standard should be applied for claims of defamation against publicly-traded corporations. An excellent example of the issue is presented in an award-winning documentary that looks at the suit for libel filed by McDonalds against two social activists—the longest-running trial in English history. The film is *McLibel: When Two Worlds Collide*, or you can read the story of the case on www.mcspotlight.com.

rights of the speakers. As well, laws and regulations that require truth in advertising impose on commercial speech a condition to which political speech is not so stringently subjected.

As distinguished from commercial speech, *political speech* may include speech critical of government officials or social policies or issues.[2] Some false or misleading speech is permitted in the political realm—a more liberal standard for political views is perceived as necessary for the free flow of ideas essential to the maintenance of a dynamic democracy. For political speech, the standard for First Amendment protection is that the speech, if false, was made without malice—that is, with out knowledge or reckless disregard of the truth or falsity of the statement. In commercial speech cases, there is no First Amendment protection if it can be proved that information was false or misleading. Citing the language of prior US Supreme Court cases, the Supreme Court of California quoted:

"[T]here is no constitutional value in false statements of fact. Neither the intentional lie nor the careless error materially advances society's interest in 'uninhibited, robust, and wide-open debate on public issues.'"... For this reason, "[u]ntruthful speech, commercial or otherwise, has never been protected for its own sake."

Commercial speech and political speech are treated differently in law for a couple of reasons:

The United States Supreme Court has given three reasons for the distinction between commercial and noncommercial speech in general and, more particularly, for withholding First Amendment protection from commercial speech that is false or actually or inherently misleading. First, "[t]he truth of commercial speech... may be *more easily verifiable by its disseminator* than... news reporting or

political commentary, in that ordinarily the advertiser seeks to disseminate information about a specific product or service that he himself provides and presumably knows more about than anyone else.... Second, commercial speech is *hardier* than noncommercial speech in the sense that commercial speakers, because they act from a profit motive, are less likely to experience a chilling effect from speech regulation.... Third, governmental authority to regulate commercial transactions to prevent commercial harms justifies a power to regulate speech that is "'linked inextricably' to those transactions." ...The high court has identified "preventing commercial harms" as "the typical reason why commercial speech can be subject to greater governmental regulation than noncommercial speech"... and it has explained that "[t]he interest in preventing commercial harms justifies more intensive regulation of commercial speech than noncommercial speech even when they are intermingled in the same publications".[3]

All of the states have some form of consumer protection laws and most of these include a law against misleading or deceptive advertising. The consumer laws are one attempt to prevent sellers from taking advantage of their superior knowledge of the wares offered to the detriment of the purchaser or consumer. The deceptive advertising laws generally seek to prohibit advertisers from engaging in material misrepresentations, omissions, or practices that are likely to mislead a reasonable consumer. The standard includes expressly deceptive information, as well as half-truths that do not provide the whole picture, or patterns of behavior that in and of themselves can be misleading. Whether commercial speech is materially deceptive often depends upon whether the

---

2. Pornography is a blurred area when it comes to First Amendment protection. Is it commercial speech or political speech? Is it Art? Does it matter if it is commercially sold versus hanging in a museum?

3. *Kasky v. Nike, Inc.,* 27 Cal. 4th 939; 45 P.3d 243; 119 Cal. Rptr.2d 296 (2002).

speech is factual in nature or just an opinion—and even that can sometimes be difficult to discern. For example, use of the term "100% Columbian coffee" would require that the coffee beans come from Columbia in order to be factual. However, a "Made in the USA" label requires only a government-mandated percentage of American participation in production to use that label. And what about "less filling, tastes great"—fact or opinion (or neither)?

That different standards of veracity apply for commercial speech versus political speech is well-settled; remaining murky is how to distinguish political from commercial speech. That thorny problem was presented in the case of *Kasky v. Nike, Inc.*

### Kasky v. Nike, Inc.

Nike, Inc. is an athletic shoe and apparel company based in Oregon, whose products are mainly produced in China, Vietnam, and Indonesia. In the fall of 1996, media reports of sweatshop practices by Nike in the Asian factories began to surface.

> Beginning at least in October 1996 with a report on the television news program *48 Hours*, and continuing at least through November and December of 1997 with the publication of articles in the Financial Times, the New York Times, the San Francisco Chronicle, the Buffalo News, the Oregonian, the Kansas City Star, and the Sporting News, various persons and organizations alleged that in the factories where Nike products are made workers were paid less than the applicable local minimum wage; required to work overtime; allowed and encouraged to work more overtime hours than applicable local law allowed; subjected to physical, verbal, and sexual abuse; and exposed to toxic chemicals, noise, heat, and dust without adequate safety equipment, in violation of applicable local occupa-

tional health and safety regulations.[4]

Nike attempted to publicly refute this claim about its labor practices in a pamphlet distributed to reporters, in press releases, on the Internet, in letters to organizations (including university presidents and their athletic directors who were parties to Nike shoe contracts), and in a letter to the editor. These communications all denied the allegations, stating that Nike's working conditions in the Asian factories met local laws and regulations.

California's unfair competition law (UCL), which covers deceptive and false advertising, defines unfair competition to include "any unlawful, unfair or fraudulent business act or practice and unfair, deceptive, untrue or misleading advertising."[5] The stated purpose of the UCL is to protect both consumers and competitors by promoting fair competition in commercial markets for goods and services. Nike operates in California and is subject to its jurisdiction.

The California law includes a "private attorney general" provision found in many such consumer protection statutes, which permits individuals to sue for violations in cases where the state has not brought charges. Given generally inadequate state funding or resource allocation to the agencies charged with enforcement of these statutes, many states allow private causes of action for prosecution.

> Not only public prosecutors, but also "any person acting for the interests of... the general public," may bring an action for relief under the UCL. Under this provision, a private plaintiff may bring a UCL action even when "the conduct alleged to constitute unfair competition violates a statute for the direct enforcement of which there is no private right of action." [Cite omitted]... In a suit under the UCL, a public prosecutor may collect civil penalties, but a private plaintiff's remedies are "generally limited to injunctive relief

---

4. Id.
5. Cal. State Statutes § 17200 et seq.

and restitution."[6]

San Francisco-based labor activist Marc Kasky claimed that Nike's refutation of the labor charges contained many false and inaccurate statements regarding its practices and the working conditions of its Asian employees. In 1998, Kasky filed suit against Nike for violation of the California UCL, as a citizen complainant. Kasky's complaint alleged that the statements made by Nike about its labor practices were in fact untrue and could be so proven. Further, he alleged that the communication of these statements—the purpose of this speech—was commercial; it was intended to effect economic or financial gain. "These documents were devoted almost entirely to praising and promoting Nike and its manufacturing practices and were replete with references to the athletic shoes it was trying to sell."[7]

Nike, Inc. defended its statements as political speech deserving of the full protection of the First Amendment, as well as protection under Article I, section 2(a) of the California Constitution. "California's free speech provision is at least as broad and in some ways is broader than the comparable provision of the federal Constitution's First Amendment."[8]

Before making a determination of the truth or falsity of Nike's statements, the California courts had first to decide whether the speech was even commercial. The California UCL would only be applicable if the speech is commercial. If Nike's communications were considered political speech, they would be protected by the federal and state constitutional free speech laws.

By the time the issue reached the California Supreme Court, the two lower state courts had ruled in favor of Nike. In a 4-3 decision, the California Supreme Court ruled in favor of Kasky, finding the nature of Nike's speech to be com-

mercial under prior US Supreme Court precedent. For more than two decades the US Supreme Court itself had struggled with the definition and description of commercial speech, and had sent conflicting signals in a series of cases. Nike appealed the California Supreme Court decision to the USSC and the case was granted a *writ of certiorari* for USSC review.[9]

The parties submitted written briefs to the USSC and presented oral arguments before the justices. Nike was ably represented by Harvard law professor and constitutional scholar, Lawrence Tribe, and enjoyed the benefit of a deluge of *amicus* briefs from business, the corporate media, and even the ACLU in support of its position. Kasky was also ably represented by Patrick Coughlin and his position was supported by consumer advocacy groups, the Sierra Club and other NGOs, and the attorney general of California (the state official charged with enforcing the California UCL). In an unusual move, after hearing oral arguments but before rendering an opinion in the case, the USSC abruptly changed its mind and dismissed the case—effectively revoking the grant of *certiorari*. The case was thus sent back to the California Supreme Court, with its original opinion intact, for a determination of the truth or falsity of the commercial statements made by Nike.

In September of 2003, before trial on the issue of the truth or falsity of the statements, Nike and Kasky settled the case; with Nike paying $1.5 million to the Fair Labor Association, a worker advocacy group based in Washington.[10] The FLA enforces the voluntary code of conduct for international labor standards discussed in greater detail in Chapter Ten. Its activities include surprise inspections at factories with high risk of worker abuse. The joint statement issued by the parties in the settlement explained: "Investments designed to strengthen workplace monitoring and factory worker programs are more

6. *Kasky v. Nike, Inc.* 27 Cal. 4th 939; 45 P.3d 243; 119 Cal. Rptr.2d 296 (2002)
7. Kasky brief to USSC on certiorari
8. *Nike v. Kasky, writ of certiorari granted,* 537 US 1099 (2002); *dismissed,* 539 US 654 (2003)
9. A rare occurrence—less than 1% of the cases that apply for USSC review are granted review—the grant is known as a *writ of certiorari*. The grant is generally made only to cases felt by the Supremes to have great national significance beyond the mere facts of the instant dispute.
10. "Nike Settles with Activist in False-Advertising Case" by Anitha Reddy, *Washington Post,* September 13, 2003

desirable than prolonged litigation."[11]

With the high court's demurrer on the issue and the parties' settlement, the distinction between political versus commercial speech remains somewhat unsettled. Although perhaps mooted by the parties' settlement, review of the reasoning of the California Supreme Court and its construction of USSC precedent on the issue is instructive. The controversy is bound to arise again and again until the law speaks definitively.

### Was Nike's Speech Commercial?

The California Supreme Court looked to USSC precedent to discern a method of testing whether Nike's statements should be considered commercial:

> The United States Supreme Court has not adopted an all-purpose test to distinguish commercial from noncommercial speech under the First Amendment, nor has this court adopted such a test under the state Constitution, nor do we propose to do so here. A close reading of the high court's commercial speech decisions suggests, however, that it is possible to formulate a limited-purpose test. We conclude, therefore, that *when a court must decide whether particular speech may be subjected to laws aimed at preventing false advertising or other forms of commercial deception*, categorizing a particular statement as commercial or noncommercial speech requires consideration of three elements: the speaker, the intended audience, and the content of the message.[12]

The court applied this tripartite analysis to the facts of Nike's speech and found that the speaker, the intended audience, and the content of the message all met the commercial speech characterization.

With respect to the commercial nature of the speaker, this element was satisfied because the company and its officers, directors, and management—those responsible for the statements—are all involved in the business of manufacturing, importing, distributing and selling consumer goods for profit—clearly a commercial endeavor.

The intended audience for the speech was also determined by the court to be a commercial audience: "Nike's letters to university presidents and directors of athletic departments were addressed directly to actual and potential purchasers of Nike's products, because college and university athletic departments are major purchasers of athletic shoes and apparel." Similarly, Nike's letters to the editor, written by its director of communications, included statements such as "[c]onsumers are savvy and want to know they support companies with good products and practices" and "[d]uring the shopping season, we encourage shoppers to remember that Nike is the industry's leader in improving factory conditions." These statements were viewed as clear evidence of the intent of Nike for the statements to reach its commercial audience.

With respect to the third prong, the content of the message, the court found that in Nike's factual representations about its own labor policies and working conditions, Nike was "addressing matters within its own knowledge. The wages paid to the factories' employees, the hours they work, the way they are treated, and whether the environmental conditions under which they work violate local health and safety laws, are all matters likely to be within the personal knowledge of Nike executives, employees, or subcontractors. Thus, Nike was in a position to readily verify the truth of any factual assertions it made on these topics."

> The third element—representations of fact of a commercial nature—is also present. In describing its own labor policies and the practices and working conditions in factories where its products are made, Nike was making factual representations about its own business operations. In speaking to consumers

---

11. *Nike v. Kasky, writ of certiorari granted,* 537 US 1099 (2002); *dismissed,* 539 US 654 (2003)
12. *Kasky v. Nike, Inc,.* 27 Cal. 4th 939; 45 P.3d 243; 119 Cal. Rptr.2d 296 (2002)

about working conditions and labor practices in the factories where its products are made, Nike addressed matters within its own knowledge.[13]

The public statements made by Nike, a commercial enterprise, to its commercial audience, about facts of a commercial nature—wages paid, hours worked, ages of employees, records of abuse—that Nike could readily verify, all amounted to a characterization of the statements as commercial speech.

The court was not swayed by Nike's argument that its statements were made as a part of the larger public debate over the treatment of workers internationally and the effects of globalization. The court explained, "This argument falsely assumes that speech cannot properly be categorized as commercial speech if it relates to a matter of significant public interest or controversy. As the United States Supreme Court has explained, commercial speech commonly concerns matters of intense public and private interest." Commercial speech may often be intertwined or intermingled with political speech, but that does not change its commercial nature or quality. False or misleading commercial speech cannot be immunized against regulation or protected by free speech laws "simply by including references to public issues"—particularly where the actionable portions of the statements by Nike concerned specific assertions of fact about the company and its practices, not its opinions on the global labor situation.

The court's decision was a narrow one, with three judges dissenting. The dissents focused primarily on two issues. First, the dissent argued that the decision unfairly restricted Nike's ability to participate in the public debate that their opposition has started. Nike, because of its commercial nature and audience, was held to a different standard of truth than its critics.[14] The dissent also argued that the fact that commercial and political speech may be "inextricably intertwined" was not adequately addressed by the majority opinion.

The majority's attempt to parse out Nike's noncommercial speech—"*to the extent* Nike's speech represents expression of opinion or points of view on general policy questions... it is noncommercial speech" –is both unavailing and unhelpful.... Nike realistically could not discuss its general policy on employee rights and working conditions and its views on economic globalization *without* reference to the labor practices of its overseas manufacturers, Nike products, and how they are made.[15]

The decision of the California Supreme Court and the ultimate rejection of the case by the USSC dismayed many in the business community, who felt that the ruling would have a "chilling effect" on the kinds of public communication the company could engage in. A spokesman for the trade association, the National Association of Manufacturers, predicted that companies will be forced to limit their remarks to narrow factual issues when discussing corporate activities because, "It doesn't make sense to put yourself at risk for statements that are not required by law."[16] The same article reported that Nike's general counsel announced a policy that the company will no longer allow employees to discuss labor practices in California or to speak on academic panels where the topic could arise. Nike also planned to withhold from public dissemination its corporate responsibility report, detailing labor conditions, until the case was resolved.

---

13. Id.

14. Of course, had its critics made false statements about Nike, Nike could have sued them for defamation. At present, the laws of defamation in the United States protect political speech critical of public official and public policy, provided they are not made with malice. This free-speech right has not yet been extended to publicly-held companies, which for the most part are treated the same as human citizens under US libel and slander laws—that is, if the statement is untrue and causes measurable economic harm, it is actionable.

15. Kasky v. Nike 27 Cal. 4th 939; 45 P.3d 243; 119 Cal. Rptr.2d 296 (2002), Chin, J. *dissent;* and Brown, J. *dissent,* stating, "Nike could not comment on this public issue without discussing its overseas labor practices, the commercial elements of Nike's representations about its labor practices were inextricably intertwined with their noncommercial elements."

16. "Nike Settles with Activist in False-Advertising Case" by Anitha Reddy, *Washington Post,* September 13, 2003

Irrespective of legal obligations in the US or elsewhere, Nike has an ethical responsibility to be truthful about that which it knows, or at least to not report falsely or deceptively. As Patrick Coughlin, Kasky's attorney said, "I think that I want people to speak truthfully about working conditions overseas. If that chills some people that want to sell something here in California, I think that's too bad. Tell the truth and it'll be fine."[17]

Taking the California decision to its farthest extreme, would holding all corporate speech relating to factual representations about the policies and practices of the company to a standard of truthfulness be such an oppressive charge for corporations? The court thought not:

Our holding, based on decisions of the United States Supreme Court, in no way prohibits any business enterprise from speaking out on issues of public importance or from vigorously defending its own labor practices. It means only that when a business enterprise, to promote and defend its sales and profits, makes factual representations about its own products or its own operations, it must speak truthfully. Unlike our dissenting colleagues, we do not consider this a remarkable or intolerable burden to impose on the business community.

## Discussion Questions:

1. What is the meaning of commercial speech? How does it differ from political speech?
2. How did the California Supreme Court decide the Nike case?
3. Please assess the California Supreme Court's decision. To what extent was it fair to all the parties? On what was it based?
4. What is your opinion – were Nike's statements political or commercial speech?
5. What are the lessons that firms should take away from the California Supreme Court's decision?

---

17. *Kasky v. Nike, Inc.*, 27 Cal. 4th©2006, Northcoast Publishers, Inc.

# Case 11

## A Big Fat Problem

*The case analyzes some of the facets of corporate responsibility for the current obesity health crisis. It examines some of the causes and considers the legal and ethical implications of the current spate of product liability litigation against purveyors of fast-food and snack-food. The second half of the case considers the response of Kraft Foods to the problem, with the initiation of health and wellness programs and products and self-restraint in its marketing to children*

*Relevant chapters: 3, 4, 8*

Americans are bigger than ever. More than 60 percent of Americans fall into the categories of overweight-to-obese by government standards. The problem has in fact spread to most of the developed world—obesity rates in most western European countries as well as the former Soviet nations and Eastern Bloc countries approach those of the US, and are generally higher among women than men. More than 15 percent of American children aged 6-19 are overweight, which is triple the percentage from 20 years ago. This alarming rate of growth has led the Centers for Disease Control (CDC) to declare the massive problem an epidemic.

In the context of human health, bigger most definitely is not better. Obesity raises the risk of diabetes, heart disease, high blood pressure, strokes, kidney failure, and many types of cancer. The costs in preventable human suffering and early death may be incalculable; but the dollars spent on healthcare associated directly and indirectly with obesity are measurable and the amount is hefty. In 2003, Secretary of Health and Human Services, Tommy Thompson estimated the figure at $117 billion per year for direct and indirect costs. A study released early in 2004 documented $75 billion spent on direct obesity-related health costs in 2003, with taxpayers funding about half of the amount in Medicare and Medicaid.[1]

Several modern forces have conspired to bring about this distended result. Modern man gets less exercise than his predecessors—car-to-train-to-bus-to-cab, whatever the commute, it's rarely accomplished under one's own power. Unless one makes specific time to exercise, the modern daily routine does not burn off the modern daily intake of calories. As well, there is

Original case study written by Sheryl Kaiser (2004). Kraft Foods case study written by Kristin Grill (Loyola MBA '05); excerpted in part from "The Effects of Food Marketing on Childhood Obesity" by Kristin Grill (May 2005). ©2006, Northcoast Publishers, Inc.

1. "Obesity Expenses Tax States" by Jennifer Warner, *WebMD Medical News*, January 21, 2004

the fact that 70 percent or more of mothers work outside the home. As a result, the hours available to carefully shop for and prepare healthy food are dramatically reduced and prepared foods become a staple of life. For most working people, not just working parents, the convenience of food-to-go is too sizeable to ignore. For working parents too, there is the draw of fast-food as a treat; it assuages some of the inevitable guilt of being a working parent. The trend toward America becoming a "fast-food nation," as described by Eric Schlosser in his book of the same title, looms large.

So, where's the beef? The connection between obesity and diet is axiomatic. The choices among prepared foods tend to be heavy on fat, sugar, salt, and cholesterol and light on vegetables, fruits, and grains. The prepared foods cause the problems. McDonalds, KFC, Pizza-Hut, Burger King, Wendy's, Taco Bell, and similar establishments offer choices of limited nutritional value that are high in calories and artery-clogging agents. A steady diet of these options almost invariably leads to the problems associated with poor nutrition—obesity, illness and disease.

Modern science has made immense strides in knowledge about nutrition and its effects on human health. Public consciousness of the risks posed by a diet high in saturated and animal fats has broadened in recent years. The direct connection that "you are what you eat" is made with increasing regularity. Despite this, most of the choices available as food-to-go have changed little and remain unhealthy. The marketing of these limited food choices approaches bombardment, and often specifically targets children, who then develop an early taste for the grease of French fries and the sugary buzz of breakfast cereals. These favorites are often consumed without the benefit of healthy meals to balance their effects. Early food preferences are shown to continue into adulthood; they make for lifelong customers. Indeed, the savviest purveyors of fast food and junk food count on that. It is no accident that Ronald McDonald is as recognizable to children as Santa Claus, or that McDonalds is one of the few restaurants to offer indoor playgrounds to its customers. It is also no accident that the value of "pester power" as a marketing tool has been exploited by the fast-food industry.

What one eats is, of course, a matter of some choice. No one is force-fed Quarter-Pounders or Oreos. But the exercise of free choice presupposes an *informed* and *voluntary* decision. One needs to know the risks before they may actually assume them and one needs meaningful options if the choice is to be voluntary. Like Big Tobacco, Big Food loathes disclosure of what it knows about its product. The industry was dragged into compliance with nutritional food labeling laws—and the fast-food/prepared-food industry remains largely exempt from such disclosure unless a customer specifically asks for the information. Moreover, the relative low cost of fast-food makes it an appealing option for working class families. When the product is offered with the choice to "supersize" for just a few cents more, it is almost irresistible. Of course, the supersizing applies not only to the product but often to its consumer as well.

The issue of voluntariness is always present with products marketed to children, which is why cigarette and alcohol advertising are prohibited from targeting children. Children enrolled in school lunch programs provide a particularly captive and arguably nonconsensual group of consumers for unhealthy food. The National School Lunch Program is one of the main culprits behind the dramatic rise in childhood obesity.

*"School lunches are loaded with fat—and the beef and dairy industries are making sure it stays that way. . . . At a time when weight-related illnesses in children are escalating, schools are serving kids the very foods that lead to obesity, diabetes and heart disease. That's because the National School Lunch Program, which gives schools more that $6 billion each year to offer low-cost meals to students, has conflicting missions. Enacted in 1946, the program is supposed to provide healthy meals to children, regardless of income. At the same time, however, it's designed to subsidize agri-business, shoring up demand for beef and milk even as the public's taste for these foods declines."*[2]

---

2. "Unhappy Meals" by Barry Yeoman *Mother Jones Magazine* (Jan/Feb 2003)

More than 27 million children eat a school lunch daily. Heavy on cheeseburgers, fries, pizza, hotdogs, and cheese on the broccoli, menus for most of the subsidized school lunch programs across the country routinely fail the government's own nutritional standards for fats and saturated fats. Nonetheless, the US government spends $800 million per year on farm products for school meals. In 2001 alone, it spent $350 million on surplus beef and cheese for schools—the very ingredients at the heart of the problem.

The government-funded food programs are influenced by powerful interests in agri-business to maintain demand for meat and dairy. Schools are under intense budgetary constraints, and nutrition simply cannot be a priority. Schools depend on the federal funds to subsidize their budgets and they must take whatever is offered. Most districts simply do not have the financial luxury of purchasing from the open market. Attempts to change the standards to require healthier purchases for government-subsidized school lunches have faced challenges from the powerful lobbies of agribusiness—the National Cattlemen's Beef Association, the Dairymen's Association, the National Frozen Pizza Institute, and similar interest groups. Government proposals to establish scientifically supportable standards for nutrition are subject to legal and political battles that invariably, sometimes indefinitely, delay implementation. Even when the standards are changed, compliance with them by the industry is often optional.[3]

Marion Nestle, chair of the Department of Nutrition and Food Studies at NYU and author of *Food Politics*,[4] says of the problem:

*"For at least the past 50 years public health authorities have wanted to deliver a simple urgent message to the American people: Eat less. They have been thwarted in doing so, however, by political pressure from the food industry. The meat industry alone spends millions a year on lobbying, apparently with*

*great success.... Food companies compound the confusion by advertising that their products can be "part of a balanced and nutritional diet" even though they know their products are not typically consumed that way. Any food can theoretically be part of a balanced diet if you keep the portions tiny enough and add lots of fruits, vegetables and grains."*[5]

A school lunch program designed around healthier choices, and less animal fats, could likely affect the lifelong eating habits of children: a bitter prospect for an industry that makes its living raising, slaughtering, and selling animals as human food. One insider explains the industry's concerns: "If they were taught, even subliminally, that beef wasn't a part of a healthy school meal, they would internalize that and eat less beef—or not eat beef as they grow up."[6]

Cash-strapped schools depend on outside funds to subsidize their budgets and are generally forced to take what is offered. From the National School Lunch Program, that means lots of animal fats in the form of beef, pork, and dairy.[7] Subsidizing meager school budgets often also means granting exclusive concessions and advertising rights for concessionaires within the confines of the school itself. On-site school advertising is a tempting revenue source for school districts in need of funds. Even districts that question the ethics of providing such a captive audience for marketing often succumb to the perceived lesser-evil of granting concessions, sometimes exclusive, for snacks and candy and sodas in school vending machines. As the connection between obesity and junk food has become clearer, schools that can are attempting to offer more balanced choices. State legislatures have awakened to the problem as well, and more than 30 bills around the country propose to ban certain snacks and beverages from school vending machines.[8]

Channel One, which provides educational programming used in many schools, derives its

3. Id., *Mother Jones* (Jan/Feb 2003).
4. *Food Politics: How the Food Industry Influences Nutrition and Health* (Univ. of Cal. Press 2002).
5. "Is Fat the Next Tobacco?" *FORTUNE* (February 3, 2003).
6. Yeoman, *Mother Jones* (Jan/Feb 2003).
7. Yeoman, *Mother Jones* (Jan/Feb 2003).
8. "If You Pitch It, They Will Eat" by David Barbosa, *New York Times*, August 3, 2003.

revenues from commercials for candy, soda and sweets, which it can virtually guarantee will reach the target audience repeatedly throughout the day. While the food industry contends that it is the responsibility of parents to guide their children's eating habits, few parents have the resources, time, or captive attention of their children needed to counterbalance these persuasive and pervasive tactics of kid-targeted marketing.

Some leaders in the industry, including Kraft and General Mills, have voluntarily agreed to give up in-school marketing.[9] However, self-regulation does not seem likely to resolve the problem when much of the industry is actively working against the imposition of any limitations.[10]

In 2004, the World Health Organization (WHO) proposed its Global Strategy on Diet, Physical Activity and Health. The proposal sought to encourage governments to adopt a number of common-sense steps to combat the worldwide spread of obesity, diabetes and other related diseases. The proposals included: clearer food labeling; limits on junk food advertising; the promotion of healthful diets with more fruits and vegetables, and less sugar; and assurances that schools promote healthy diets, and not just junk food and soda pop. Europe has embraced the proposal and in recent years has made it increasingly difficult for food companies to make nutritional claims about their products if they also have a high fat, sugar or salt content. The George W. Bush Administration blocked the proposal in the U.S., citing the need for personal responsibility in matters of choosing "a diet conducive to individual energy balance, weight control and health."

But what of the $100 million-plus health bill associated with these personal choices and the fact that taxpayers pick up at least half of that tab? Even assuming an informed and voluntary choice, the personal responsibility for diet becomes a collective responsibility for bad diet choices that is borne by all. Several approaches to the problem have been proposed—imposing

sin taxes on unhealthy foods in the same fashion as they are imposed on alcohol and cigarettes; higher insurance premiums for the obese (which may present its own issues of illegal discrimination); and similar proposals aimed at defraying the health costs of obesity. To date, such proposals have had little impact.

So what's a chocoholic to do?

### Enter the lawyers . . .

With the increased scientific knowledge of the risk to human health posed by obesity and the direct link between obesity and unhealthy foods, it was only a matter of time before lawyers began to ask: Is unhealthy food an "unreasonably dangerous" product? What is the duty of care owed to the consumer of one's food products? Is there a duty to warn of known health risks? What did the food companies know about the nutritional value of their foods (or lack thereof) and when did they know it? Can an unhealthy diet be proximately linked to the harm caused by obesity?

Where government regulation breaks down, there's usually a contingency fee law firm willing to take up the cause if it is one that's deemed winnable and if the pockets of the defendants are deep enough to make it worthwhile. Several such firms have looked at Big Fat and Big Food and taken up the challenge.

In July 2002 a class of obese and overweight children filed suit against McDonalds, claiming that the fast-food chain

*"negligently, recklessly, carelessly, and/or intentionally" markets to children food products that are "high in fat, sugar, salt, and cholesterol" while failing to warn of those ingredients' links to "obesity, diabetes, coronary heart disease, high blood pressure, strokes, elevated cholesterol intake, related cancers," and other conditions.*[11]

Similar suits have been filed in New York City against McDonalds, Burger King, KFC, and Wendy's. A lawsuit filed in May 2003 in San Francisco against Kraft, which sought to block

9. Id.

10. The political influence wielded by Big Food on both sides of the aisle is ponderous. The Sugar Association alone spread $406 million in political contributions among the Congress. "Tough Love for the Obesity Lobby" by Jonathan Rowe and Gary Ruskin, *www.alternet.org,* Independent Media Institute, January 23, 2004.

11. Id., *FORTUNE* (February 3, 2003).

the sale of Oreos to schoolchildren, was dropped and Kraft voluntarily agreed to stop promoting its products in schools.

The theory of the case against fat bears a striking resemblance to the case against tobacco.[12] Although junk food may not be as addictive as nicotine, childhood patterns set adult weight patterns and the longer weight is carried, the harder it is to lose. The health impacts are comparable; and childhood diabetes is irreversible. The health costs of the two are achieving parity, with obesity-related health costs estimated in the $120 billion-range and smoking-related health costs at about $140 billion. Although both involve an ostensible choice to consume or not, the informed and voluntary nature of the choice is suspect in both cases. The deep pockets of the potential defendants in both cases also appeals to contingency lawyers. And, like the tobacco industry, the fast-food and junk food-industries set up a large target for states' attorneys general seeking "reimbursement" for revenues spent to meet growing state health care costs. Perhaps the biggest difference between the two is the fact that tobacco companies cannot make their product safe and the fast-food industry can: it can either make a healthier product or at least limit its exposure to lawsuits by providing adequate warnings about nutritional value.

The fat suits against Big Food stretch the limits of the law and are viewed by many as excessive. Further, no one would argue that litigation is the best approach to resolving such a national, indeed global, problem. Inconsistency of results; potentially unfair windfalls to plaintiffs and their lawyers; potentially unfair unapportioned liability imposed on certain defendants and their shareholders; and the fact that we all end up paying for these suits in one way or another militate against this approach. Litigation is rarely the best approach to public policy making; but in the absence of government or industry self-restraint, there is often little alternative.

## Corporate Responsibility

The influence of schools on childhood nutrition and obesity has become apparent and several states and individual school districts have imposed restrictions on vendors—limiting the type and amount of junk food and soft drinks available in school vending machines, and requiring healthy substitutes. In response to this trend, in the summer of 2005, the American Beverage Association recommended a self-imposed limit on the availability of soft drinks in schools throughout the United States supplied by its members. President and CEO of the Association, Susan Neely, explained: "Childhood obesity is a real problem. The individual companies have been doing several things to be part of the solution and there was an agreement among all of our leadership that we needed to take another step and take it as an industry."[13] The ABA agreed to stock elementary school vending machines with only bottled water and 100% fruit juice; to add sports drinks and no-calorie soft drinks to middle schools; and to offer all types of drinks at the high school level, with a limit of 50% on soft drink products. The Association represents 85% of the bottlers involved in school vending.

Kraft Foods, Inc. is a company that has also moved beyond mere compliance with the law in recognizing and responding to its influence on childhood nutrition and obesity. The company's approach to developing healthier and more nutritious products and its restraint in some of the marketing techniques used on children are self-imposed obligations.

## The Health and Wellness Initiative of Kraft Foods, Inc.

The products of the largest food company in the United States, Kraft Foods Inc., can be found on virtually every aisle of the grocery store: from Kraft cheeses to DiGiorno pizzas to Oreo cookies to Post cereals to Maxwell House coffees. The company reported $32 billion in revenue for 2004.

In 2003, Kraft implemented a global Health and Wellness Initiative to promote a corporate strategy to "improve the nutrition of products,

---

12. Id., *FORTUNE* (February 3, 2003).
13. "Beverage Group Recommends Limiting Soda in Schools," by Rachel La Corte, *Associated Press* (August 17, 2005).

provide consumers with more information to help them make informed choices about food and exercise, adjust marketing practices and polices, and advocate for constructive public policy changes."[14] In implementing the Initiative, Michael Mudd, the Senior Vice-President of Corporate Affairs at Kraft stated: "We want to grow as a company, but unhealthy consumption is in no one's long-term interest."[15] At the time of development and implementation of Kraft's Health and Wellness Initiative, the company was facing intense pressure from lawyers, consumer groups and government agencies to address obesity through corporate policies and industry-wide leadership.[16]

The scope of the initiative includes product development, commercialization and marketing. In implementing guides for these areas, Kraft relies on a set of Healthy Living Principles, devised by its division of Health, Wellness and Nutrition Responsibility. These principles strive to encourage consumers of Kraft products to achieve and maintain a healthy lifestyle: *Eat Well, Be Sensible about Portions, Be Active,* and *Build Success.*[17]

Kraft has dedicated resources to develop new healthier products and to improve product nutrition by reformulating current products in an overall effort to reduce or eliminate trans-fats in its product line. Healthier new products such as *Veryfine* fruit juices, *Fruit2O* flavored waters, *Kool-Aid Jammers10* and the line of *Nabisco 100-Calorie Packs* of cookies also have a large appeal to the child market. In 2005, Kraft unveiled 70 new products that meet Health and Wellness objectives.[18]

Product labeling is another strategic focus in the Health and Wellness Initiative. Clearer labeling on smaller packages encourages consumers, both children and adults, to make informed decisions and be knowledgeable about what constitutes a single serving. Kraft developed the *Sensible Solution* label—a distinct green flag on the face of the package— to enable easy identification of better-for-you products. The Sensible Solutions flag indicates that the product will "provide beneficial nutrients while staying within specific limits on calories, fat, sodium and sugar; or meet specifications for *reduced, low* or *free* products."[19]

Responsible marketing is a key component for the success of the Health and Wellness Initiative. Kraft's global marketing practices recognize the "unique status of our children," aim to "avoid suggestion of over-consumption," and seek to "encourage an active lifestyle where appropriate."[20] Of its reported $32 billion revenue in 2004, Kraft spent over $6.5 million on research and development and $550 million on marketing.[21] Within the $550 million-marketing budget was an allocation of $90 million specifically dedicated to advertising and promotions targeted at children. That kind of spending qualifies Kraft as the third largest marketer to children.[22]

In 2003, in response to public and legal pressure, Kraft has ceased all marketing efforts in schools: including contests, posters, book cov-

14. Friedmann, Lance. "Marketing Strategies that Foster Healthy Food Choices in Children and Youth." Institute of Medicine Meeting #2 and Workshop on Food Marketing. Washington, D.C., 27 Jan 2005.

15. Thompson, Stephanie. "Kraft Tailors Marketing to Obesity Concern." Crain's Chicago Business. Chicago, Ill: 27 Jan 2005, Vol 26, Iss4; p15.

16. Thompson, Stephanie. "Food Fight Breaks Out." Advertising Age (Midwest region edition). Chicago, Ill: 17 Jan 2005: Vol 76, Iss3; p 1-2. In similar fashion, Altria Group, Kraft's parent company and owner of Phillip Morris, had assumed a similar role as a resource for the prevention of underage smoking and quitting smoking after acknowledging the role of it product in human disease and death.

17. www.kraft.com/responsibility/nhw_healthyprinciples.aspx

18. Friedmann, Lance. "Marketing Strategies that Foster Healthy Food Choices in Children and Youth," *Institute of Medicine Meeting #2 and Workshop on Food Marketing,* Washington, D.C., 27 Jan 2005. A list of these products is contained in the Appendix

19. www.kraft.com/responsibility/nhw_sensible solution.aspx. These products are also considered healthy enough to market to children and include: *Crystal Light, Kraft 2% Milk Mild Cheddar Reduced Fat* cheese, *Minute Rice* brown rice, and *Triscuit* whole grain crackers.

20. www.kraft.com/responsibility/nhw_marketingpractices.aspx

21. Arndt, Michael. "Why Kraft is on a Crash Diet." *Business Week.* New York, New York, 29 Nov 2004. Iss 3910, pg 46.

22. Ellison, Sarah. "Kraft Limits on Kids' Ads May Cheese Off Rivals; Company Plans to Stop Advertising Junk Food to Children Age 6 to 11." *The Wall Street Journal* (Eastern Edition) New York, New York. 13 Jan 2005: B3.

ers, product samples, and print and broadcast advertising; and has developed nutritional standards for the products it offers in vending machines on school grounds.[23]

In January 2005, Kraft announced a marketing initiative that emphasized nutritious products; specifically promising "a shift in the mix products advertised in television, radio, and print media viewed primarily by children ages 6-11." Kraft stated that "over the course of 2005, a number of well-known Kraft products— including regular *Kool-Aid* beverages, *Oreo* and *Chips Ahoy!* cookies, several *Post* children's cereals, and many varieties of *Lunchables* lunch combinations—will no longer be advertised in these media."[24] The announcement by Kraft came on the same day that the US Department of Health and Human Services and the US Department of Agriculture published the 2005 Dietary Guidelines for Americans.

The *2005 Dietary Guidelines for Americans* recommend that, in order to maintain a healthy lifestyle and avoid being overweight, children must:

- "Consume a variety of nutrient-dense foods and beverages within and among the basic food groups while choosing food that limit the intake of saturated and trans-fats, cholesterol, added sugars, salt and alcohol
- Engage in regular physical activity (at least 60 minutes on most, preferable all, days of the week) and reduce sedentary activities to promote health, psychological well-being, and a healthy body weight
- Consume whole-grain products often
- Drink 2 to 3 cups per day of fat free or low

fat milk or equivalent milk products
- Keep total fat intake between 25 and 35% of calories
- Choose fiber-rich fruits, vegetables, and whole grains often."[25]

Kraft's announcement of voluntary restraint in its marketing to children should improve its image among parents and public-health advocates and serve to shield the company from some public criticism and lawsuits. Under the new initiative, approximately ten percent of Kraft's total product portfolio, which equates to roughly $3 billion in sales, will no longer be promoted to children.[26] But Kraft executives are careful to point out that its self-imposed limit on marketing certain products in certain media will not reduce its overall marketing to children. According to Kraft Executive Vice President for Corporate Affairs, Mark Berlind, "the company does not plan to reduce its advertising spending to children, simply to shift the focus."[27]

By addressing only the television, radio, and print media vehicles and school as a distribution channel, however, Kraft's announced child-marketing limits fail to modify many of its child-marketing practices, including: the Internet, in-store display promotion vehicles, packaging, and cartoon endorsements.[28] For example, www.candystand.com, featuring *Life Savers*, *Planters* peanuts, *Crème Savers* hard candy, and similar products, is a promotional website created by Kraft to entice children to play their games and participate in their contests. Currently, nominal industry-wide regulation exists for internet websites and games directed at children; and this remains an area

23. Friedmann, Lance. "Marketing Strategies that Foster Healthy Food Choices in Children and Youth." Institute of Medicine Meeting #2 and Workshop on Food Marketing. Washington, D.C., 27 Jan 2005. The Guidelines for vending machine products are as follows: "35% or less total calories from fat (excluding nuts and seeds, given their nutritional benefits), 10% or less of total calories from a combination of saturated and trans fat, 35% or less of total calories from sugars (excluding those sugars naturally occurring in fruits, dairy or vegetables), inclusion where practical, of fiber, whole grains, fruits, dairy and vegetables." www.kraft.com/responsibility/nhw_marketingpractices.aspx

24. Kraft Press Release. 12 Jan 2005. www.kraft.com/newsroom/01122005

25. U.S. Department of Human and Health Services and U.S. Department of Agriculture. "Dietary Guidelines for Americans 2005." Rockville, Maryland: National Library of Medicine Cataloging, 2005. http://www.health.gov/dietaryguidelines/dga2005/document/html.

26. Thompson, Stephanie. "Kraft's Kid Ad Cuts Enrage its Rivals." *Crain's Chicago Business*. Chicago, Ill: 24 Jan 2005: Vol 28, Iss4; p 1c.

27. Ellison, Sarah. "Kraft Limits on Kids' Ads May Cheese Off Rivals; Company Plans to Stop Advertising Junk Food to Children Age 6 to 11." *The Wall Street Journal* (Eastern Edition) New York, New York. 13 Jan 2005: B3.

28. www.kraft.com/responsibility/nhw_marketingpractices.aspx

for future advocacy and corporate responsibility initiatives.

Kraft is the first major food company to replace unhealthy advertisements with more nutritious alternatives in media targeting children.[29] Some of Kraft's competitors view the move "as a tacit acknowledgement of guilt in fueling the country's obesity epidemic—and one that damns them by implication."[30] Though few companies openly acknowledge the nexus between advertising and childhood obesity, many are nonetheless addressing the problem.

PepsiCo joined the fray with a commitment that 50% of its new products will fulfill "healthy" requirements. The company also introduced *Smart Spot* labeling, which distinguishes healthier products and provides additional nutritional information.[31] The results of the strategy were impressive: in 2004, Pepsi reported a 56% growth in healthy products such as *Gatorade* sports drinks, *Aquafina* bottled water, and *Quaker Oats* cereal in the North American market.[32] As well, Pepsi has been a leader in the introduction of healthier beverage products in school vending machines.

Similarly, General Mills, the cereal giant, converted all of its Big G cereals to whole grain for the nutritional advantage. The switch to whole grains was at least in part an effort by the company to convince the health-aware consumer that old favorites like Cinnamon Toast Crunch, Trix, and Cocoa Puffs—cereals previously known to be high in sugar and empty carbohydrate calories—could be a part of a healthy diet. The company also maintains a website that provides weight-control information and materials for consumers who want to develop a healthy dietary lifestyle.[33]

Some have been critical of Kraft's plan to limit television, radio and print advertising to its youngest customers; claiming it does not go far enough. Nonetheless, the policy represents an awareness of Kraft's role and influence on child minds and preferences. Allen Kanner, a child psychologist and a member of the Campaign for a Commercial-Free Childhood, says of the initiative: "this shows that companies like Kraft are beginning to recognize the harmful impact of marketing unhealthy products to kids."[34] "It's a step, but it's a small step." According to psychologist Susan Linn, "What they really need to do is stop using cartoon characters to market food to children."[35]

Kraft is just beginning to position itself as a responsible food corporation. Kraft's Health and Wellness Initiative puts customer health and happiness at the heart of its corporate vision and strategy. Currently, Kraft's announcement regarding marketing limits for its youngest customers is just a promise; only future actions will reveal Kraft's true dedication to the health and wellness of its consumers. There are other marketing channels that socially responsible food sellers need to consider: Internet and in-store promotions, cartoon endorsements, community involvement projects, educational support, and collaborative industry reform. Kraft will need to operate beyond compliance in these areas if it is to achieve its new corporate vision and strategy. It has positioned itself, however, as a potential leader and benchmark for the industry. After the Kraft child-marketing announcement, industry analyst Dave Nelson predicted, "the industry is going to have to further restrict

29. Anonymous. "Kraft takes lead in Responsibility." *Advertising Age* (Midwest region edition). Chicago, Ill: 24 Jan 2005: Vol 76, Iss4; p 24.

30. Thompson, Stephanie. "Kraft's Kid Ad Cuts Enrage its Rivals." *Crain's Chicago Business*. Chicago, Ill: 24 Jan 2005: Vol 28, Iss4; p 1c.

31. Thompson, Stephanie. "Kraft's Kid Ad Cuts Enrage its Rivals." *Crain's Chicago Business*. Chicago, Ill: 24 Jan 2005: Vol 28, Iss4; p 1c.

32. Buss, Dale. "Is the Food Industry the Problem or the Solution?" *New York Times* New York, New York: 29 Aug 2004: p3.5.

33. Friedmann, Lance. "Marketing Strategies that Foster Healthy Food Choices in Children and Youth." Institute of Medicine Meeting #2 and Workshop on Food Marketing. Washington, D.C., 27 Jan 2005.

34. Thompson, Stephanie. "Kraft's Kid Ad Cuts Enrage its Rivals." *Crain's Chicago Business*. Chicago, Ill: 24 Jan 2005: Vol 28, Iss4; p 1c.

35. Ellison, Sarah. "Kraft Limits on Kids' Ads May Cheese Off Rivals; Company Plans to Stop Advertising Junk Food to Children Age 6 to 11." *The Wall Street Journal* New York, New York. 13 Jan 2005: B3.

itself in terms of marketing to avoid criticism and, potentially, regulation."[36] Kraft has market power and position that permit it to "increase pressure on the rest of the food industry to alter its marketing ways."[37]

With $15 billion spent on marketing food and beverages to children each year, corporations have a substantial influence over the eating habits of American children.[38] Competitors in the food industry work hard to appeal to consumers in their most-tender years. Establishing customer loyalty at an early age means long-term customers and dependable long-term revenue. It seems self-evident that keeping these customers alive and healthy for that long-term benefit is in the interests of all the stakeholders. Increasingly, food companies are starting to understand that connection. And the more far-sighted among them are engineering an entirely new and rapidly growing food and beverage market in healthy alternatives.

## Discussion Questions:

1. Why did Kraft and General Mills give up school their in-school marketing programs?
2. What do you think of these firms' health and wellness initiatives?
3. What is your opinion of the suit against McDonald's and other fast food companies?
4. How should McDonald's and the other fast food firms respond?

## APPENDIX

### KRAFT FOODS UNVEILS HEALTH & WELLNESS, CONVENIENCE SOLUTIONS AT FMIMore Than 70 New Kraft Products Featured At Annual Food Convention

***A.1.* Teriyaki Steak Sauce** - This sauce combines the authentic flavors of teriyaki with the bold flavor of *A.1.* for a new twist to an old favorite.

***Back to Nature* Cereal, Granola, Dinners, Crackers, and Cookies** - The *Back to Nature* line of wholesome food items has now expanded to include an Organic Shells & Cheese dinner free of hydrogenated oils; new Cinnamon and Honey Graham Sticks, a first in the natural/organic segment; new Organic Apple Cinnamon Harvest cereal made with orchard-ripened apples; as well as new crackers in Crispy Cheddars, Tomato Herb Rice Thins, Harvest Whole Wheats and Organic Stoneground Wheats.

***Balance* Trail Mix Energy Bar** - Looking for energy that lasts? This new convenient *Balance* Bar provides 14-15 grams of protein and 23 essential vitamins and minerals with three satisfying varieties, including Chocolate Chip, Cinnamon, Oats and Honey, and Fruit and Nut.

***Boca* Meatless Chili** - For the first time consumers now have a soy-based chili entrée that goes from the freezer to the microwave to the table in less than 5 minutes. With 90% less fat and 90 fewer calories than the leading meat chili, *Boca* Meatless Chili features *Boca* Ground Burger mixed with kidney and black beans, green peppers, onions, and a perfectly seasoned tomato-based sauce.

***Bull's-Eye* Sweet Homestyle Blend** - A perfect blend of brown sugar, molasses and spices makes this sweet and savory BBQ sauce the perfect topping for meats or vegetables.

***California Pizza Kitchen* Crispy Thin Crust** - No reservations are required for the great new taste of *California Pizza Kitchen's* restaurant-style thin crust pizza. It comes in three Neapolitan-influenced varieties, including the first nationally available "white" pizza featuring an olive oil base.

***Chewy Chips Ahoy!* Snack 'n Seal** - This innovative new "peel back and re-close" packaging is just what you need to keep your cookies fresh tasting.

***Christie Crunchers* Crackers** - Available in Canada in four light and crispy flavors (Ched-

36. Thompson, Stephanie. "Kraft's Kid Ad Cuts Enrage its Rivals." *Crain's Chicago Business*. Chicago, Ill: 24 Jan 2005: Vol 28, Iss4; p 1c.

37. Ellison, Sarah. "Kraft Limits on Kids' Ads May Cheese Off Rivals; Company Plans to Stop Advertising Junk Food to Children Age 6 to 11." *The Wall Street Journal* New York, New York. 13 Jan 2005: B3.

38. Mayer, Caroline E. "Minding Nemo: Pitches to Kids Feed Debate About a Watchdog." The Washington Post. 27 Feb 2005: F1,F6.

dar, Spicy Thai, Bold Barbecue and Sour Cream & Onion), these baked corn-rice crackers have zero grams trans fat and about 70 percent less fat per serving than the leading regular potato chip.

***Delissio* Balance Harvest Wheat Rising Crust Pizza** - Being introduced in Canada, this great-tasting pizza is made with whole wheat, part-skim mozzarella, reduced-fat grilled chicken, reduced-fat pepperoni and premium-roasted vegetables.

***Fruit$_2$O* Plus 10 and *Fruit$_2$O* Splashzone** - The refreshing, ready-to-drink flavored water with zero calories and no carbs per serving is now available in a special *Fruit$_2$O* Plus 10 variety that is fortified with 10 vitamins and minerals and features Natural Berry, Natural Apple and Watermelon Kiwi flavors. For the younger consumer, *Fruit$_2$O Splashzone* is a brand new line of naturally flavored waters specially formulated to be low in sugar and calories and packaged in a kid-friendly, portable pouch.

***Good Seasons* Premium Liquid Salad Dressings** - Made with quality ingredients including extra virgin olive oil, aged cheeses, poppyseed, ginger and roasted red bell peppers, this new line of bottled dressings are available in six delicious varieties.

***Jell-O* Sugar Free Reduced Calorie Pudding Snacks** - The first-ever sugar-free pudding snack in the refrigerated ready-to-eat category comes in three popular flavors of Chocolate, Chocolate/Vanilla Swirls and Vanilla and has just 60 calories per serving.

***Jell-O* Sundae Toppers Pudding Snacks** - Rich, creamy chocolate or vanilla *Jell-O* pudding with sundae toppings of chocolate or caramel. A sweet, satisfying reward with 110 calories and zero grams of trans fat.

***Kraft Mayo* Big Mouth Jar** - Featuring the same great Real Mayo and Light Mayo, this new shatterproof plastic packaging has an opening more than 100 % larger than the traditional jar and a convenient snap-top lid with flavor fresh seal.

***Kraft* 2% Natural Cheese Sticks** - When you need a nutritious snack on-the-go, reach for these great-tasting single-serve, one-ounce cheese sticks, in Cheddar and Extra Sharp Cheddar. They are an excellent source of calcium and *South Beach Diet* recommended.

***Lunchables* Lunch Combinations Chicken Shake Ups** - Made with white meat, these breaded pieces of chicken come with fun flavor packets to help "shake up" lunchtime boredom for kids — with less than 25% of calories from fat and zero grams of trans fat.

***Nabisco KidSense* Fun Packs** - These three new varieties of *Teddy Grahams* Cubs (Cinnamon), *Kraft Cheese Nips* Sport Crisps and Smilin' *Ritz Bits* are made with 3 grams of whole grain, zero grams of trans fat and no artificial flavors or sweeteners.

***Oscar Mayer* Deli Style Shaved Luncheon Meats** - Now you can create even more deli-quality sandwich combinations in your own kitchen with the introduction of new thinly shaved Slow Roasted Roast Beef in pre-packaged re-closeable Stay-Fresh plastic containers.

***Oscar Mayer* Ready-to-Serve Breakfast Meats** - Enjoy the taste of a weekend breakfast during the week with new Canadian Style Bacon and Pork Sausage Patties. These fully-cooked meats can be served straight from the box or heated in the microwave for less than a minute.

***Peek Freans* Lifestyle Selections** - This new line of biscuits is just what consumers in Canada are looking for when it comes to a snack choice that has zero grams of trans fat and is low in saturated fat.

***Philadelphia* Swirls** - Rich and creamy soft *Philly* cream cheese is swirled together with two delicious flavors for the perfect spread on bagels, crackers and vegetables; available in Brown Sugar Cinnamon & Spice, Peaches 'N Cream, Triple Berries 'N Cream, and Garlic 'N Herb.

***Planters NUT-rition*** - *Mr. Peanut* is putting the "nut" in nutrition with four new fresh-tasting snack nut mixes (Heart-Healthy Mix; Cashews, Almonds & Macadamias Mix; Lightly Salted Almonds; and Smoked Almonds) that complement a diet low in saturated fat and cholesterol.

***Post Alpha-Bits* Cereal** - The only letter-shaped cereal is now an excellent source of whole grain and re-formulated to contain zero grams of sugar, 2 grams of fat per serving, and 14 essential vitamins and minerals.

***Post Honey Bunches of Oats* Cereal Bars** - Consumers can now enjoy their favorite flavors of *Honey Bunches of Oats* cereal on-the-go with three new varieties of Cereal Bars – Banana Nut, Cranberry Almond and Oatmeal Raisin – featuring real fruit pieces, crunchy oats clusters and as much calcium as an 8-ounce glass of milk.

***Seattle's Best* Coffee** - Beginning this year, Kraft Foods has expanded its partnership with Starbucks to include distribution of *Seattle's Best* Coffee in grocery stores across the country. Available in both regular and decaffeinated, there are 25 varieties of traditional coffeehouse blends, organic blends and flavored coffees.

***South Beach Diet* Cereals, Cereal Bars, Frozen Pizzas, Meal Replacement Bars, Wrap Sandwich Kits, Frozen Entrees and Snacks** - With nearly 30 convenient and great-tasting food items, this expansive new line of healthful products is just what the doctor (Dr. Arthur Agatston, the creator of the diet) ordered for consumers following the *South Beach Diet* program or just looking for delicious, nutritional menu options.

***Tassimo* Hot Beverage System** - This revolutionary one-cup, on-demand brewing system brings the coffeehouse experience to consumers' kitchens at the touch of a button. Featuring proprietary "smart" technology and specially designed T-DISCS, the *Tassimo* Hot Beverage System creates a variety of hot beverages, including coffee, tea, cappuccino, espresso, latte and hot chocolate, in 60 seconds or less and with minimal clean-up.

***Wheat Thins* Chips Multi-Grain** - One of America's favorite crackers has now been oven baked into a delicious multi-grain chip that boasts 60 % less fat than leading potato chips and zero grams of trans fat per serving.

Excerpt from Kraft Food's Press Release: May 1, 2005
http://www.kraft.com/newsroom/05012005.html

# Case 12

## ADM and Biodiesel

*The case analyzes the environmental advantages and drawbacks to biodiesel and other alternative fuels, with a specific focus on one leader in the industry: Archer-Daniels-Midland. It explores the corporate strategy of ADM and the key role of the government in the success or failure of competitors in this emerging market.*

*Relevant chapters: 3, 4, 9*

ADM (Archer Daniels Midland) buys grain from farmers and resells it to exporters and processors. It makes agricultural commodities into valuable products for food, feed, and industrial uses. It transports, stores, and trades agricultural products such as corn, wheat, soybeans, peanuts, cottonseed, sunflowers, barley, flaxseed, rice, and canola around the world. It owns many U.S. grain elevators and has a complex of barges and rail cars that constitute one of the world's best grain collection and transport systems. Though it makes animal feeds, pasta, and malt, HFSC (corn syrup) is its most important product. An area of great promise for ADM has been bioproducts, which are food and feed additives such as vitamins, amino acids, and flavor enhancers derived from corn and soybeans rather than petrochemicals. As a major producer and processor of agricultural commodities, ADM has been involved in alternative-fuel markets, which use plants and byproducts as their source of raw materials. The company is a leading producer of ethanol, a corn-based petroleum substitute. It supplies 25 percent of the biodiesel used in Europe.[1] Biodiesel is a next generation fuel with potentially huge benefits for ADM and the environment. These benefits include: fuel from a renewable source that is biodegradable, lower American reliance on foreign oil, and growth in the American economy. ADM has been politically active via PAC and lobbyists to advance legislation that supports alternative-fuel incentives.[2] Because the use of such alternative fuels as biodiesel can reduce U.S. reliance on foreign oil and have a less damaging impact on the environment than fossil fuels do, the alternative-fuel industry has achieved support in the form of subsidies and tax incentives from the federal government. However, there are some significant obstacles that may prevent biodiesel from reaching its full potential, particularly in the United

This case study was originally written by D.Crain, N.Cho, T.Goodlow, B.Hillins, J.Kantor, Y.Takenaka, and J.Tobey – all of the University of Minnesota, and was revised by Professor Alfred Marcus.@2006, NorthCoast Publishers, Inc.

1. "Ethanol's Bright Future," *Agri Marketing*, October 2001, v. 39, i. 9,p. 52.
2. EV World, http://www.evworld.com/databases/shownews.cfm?pageid=news090502-12

States. Biodiesel is expensive to produce—it costs approximately three times the price of gasoline—which is a formidable obstacle to widespread adoption while cheaper alternatives exist.

This case reviews the history of biodiesel, examines the environmental advantages and disadvantages of its use, presents the legislative issues that ADM faces, discusses the industry's competitive dynamics, and considers ADM's options. With respect to biodiesel, ADM's top management has to decide what to do next. Whatever it decides, it must align the company's business strategy with its political strategy. The challenge the company faces consists of both elements: (i) the business challenge of what is the best business model for biodiesel development; and (ii) the public policy challenge of what package of incentives and encouragement does ADM need from political authorities.

### History of Biodiesel

Biodiesel is a renewable fuel made from vegetable oils and animal fats. It is created by separating the fat into two products — biodiesel and various byproducts that mainly are used for soap. The fuel can be used in unmodified diesel engines at 100 percent purity or in blends. Under the 1990 Clean Air Act Amendments, the EPA monitors biodiesel pollution.[3]

Rudolf Christian Karl Diesel (1858-1913), a German engineer, built the first successful diesel engine.[4] A diesel engine is a type of internal-combustion engine in which heat, caused by air compression, ignites the fuel. Diesel engines are more efficient and less expensive to operate than gasoline-powered engines, partly because diesel fuel costs less. Diesels consume less fuel and emit fewer waste products than do gasoline-burning engines. Most modern buses, trucks, trains, and ships are powered by diesels. These engines have become popular in some automobiles as well.[5] Although Rudolf Diesel discussed the use of biodiesel fuel for his engine, its use wasn't commercialized until the 1920s, and the term biodiesel wasn't coined until 1992,when the National Soy Diesel Development Board started work to broaden the commercial use of the product.

Biodiesel's major competitor in the alternative-fuels market is ethanol, which is derived from corn. Ethanol (which in effect is alcohol) has been considered as a potential fuel for cars since the early twentieth century.[6] Both it and biodiesel gained attention and increased use in the U. S. in the 1970s, during the energy crisis and the start of the environmental movement. Ethanol, however, has been the major focus of federal subsidies and tax incentives, enjoying breaks that have amounted to $10 billion since 1979.[7]

ADM's interest in the U. S. biodiesel industry stems from the attractiveness of a potentially large market, and a new, more profitable use for soybeans, which in recent years have been in excess supply. ADM's 2001 revenues from biodiesel were $300M, or about 1.5% of the company's total annual revenue of $20 billion, but almost all of its sales were in Europe.[8] The challenge ADM faces is what — if anything — should it do to encourage biodiesel development in the United States. If ADM proceeds with U.S. biodiesel development, it will need to justify any assistance it gets from the government. How can it do so given the fact that some see the subsidies to biodiesel as unwarranted? (see Appendix A)

A major decision for ADM is whether to enter the U.S. market, but there are many obstacles to its entering this market and reasons why it should not do so. First, while biodiesel is a cleaner-burning fuel than petroleum-based products, its primary input, soybeans, require more land to be used for farming. Production of soybeans involve the use of pesticides and herbicides, which can harm the environment in ways that can offset the benefits derived from

3. National Biodisel Board — http://www.biodiesel.org/resources/biodiesel_basics/
4. "Diesel, Rudolf Christian Karl," Microsoft® Encarta® Online Encyclopedia 2003
   http://encarta.msn.com © 1997-2003 Microsoft Corporation.
5. "Diesel Engine," Microsoft® Encarta® Online Encyclopedia 2003
   http://encarta.msn.com © 1997-2003 Microsoft Corporation. All Rights Reserved.
6. "Will Green Alternatives Do? The Use of More Plant-Based Fuel is on the Horizon," Motorhome, November 2002.
7. "Ethanol's Bright Future," *Agri Marketing*, October 2001, v. 39, i. 9,p. 52.
8. Archers Daniels Midland – http:// http://www.admworld.com/investor/pdf/adm_annual_report_2001.pdf

having a renewable resource as the basis for the fuel. Biodiesel also emits a higher level of the air pollutant NOx than fuels being used now. There are other alternative fuels that are cleaner burning. A watchdog for the environment, the Sierra Club, views natural gas as the optimal fuel.[9] There also is controversy over any proposed cut in the federal gasoline excise tax and other subsidies for alternative fuel production. ADM does not want to be seen as a corporation that gets its way mainly because of its reliance on PACs and lobbyists. Another issue is soybean prices. In 2001, more than a three-year inventory surplus of soybeans existed, which is why the price was so low. Increased demand would raise prices, which ADM wants low because soybeans are a raw material for many of its products.

### Environmental Impact

According to the EPA, biodiesel can be blended with petroleum diesel to create a more environmentally friendly fuel. In a 2002 report, the agency stated that biodiesel can reduce emissions of particulate matter by 47 percent compared to petroleum diesel in unmodified diesel engines. In addition, there is a 67-percent reduction in unburned hydrocarbons and a 48-percent reduction in carbon monoxide when pure biodiesel (B100) is used. The positive environmental impact of the use of 20-percent biodiesel, the most widely-used blend, is significantly less. For the mix (B20), unburned hydrocarbons are reduced 20 percent and carbon monoxide and particulate matter emissions are reduced 12 percent. However, the use of biodiesel in any blend increases the emission of NOx.[10]

In addition to the above-mentioned environmental benefits, biodiesel is renewable. Because it can be made from agricultural products and waste products, such as used cooking oil, its use conserves resources beyond non-renewable oil supplies. The U. S. has produced a surplus of soybean oil for years, and competition from the GATT and NAFTA agreements have affected the U. S. market for this commodity. Using the surplus for fuel could alleviate the soybean price pressure on farmers, thus strengthening the rural economy.[11]

Production of soy-based biodiesel has a positive energy balance (as much as 3:1). The high-energy value of ester-based feed, the low energy requirements of production, and the nitrogen-fixing characteristic of soybeans, which reduces the need for fertilizer, all contribute to the positive energy results.[12]

Biodiesel blends require no modification of engines, thus providing a competitive infrastructure cost. While not as efficient a fuel on a BTU basis as either ethanol or straight diesel, it does produce between 15,000 and 16,375 BTUS per pound (between 9 and 17 percent less than #2 diesel).[13]

Biodiesel is biodegradable and non-toxic—studies have shown it to degrade as quickly and with as little harm as sugar and to accelerate the degradation of diesel in the environment when present in a blend. Its fumes, which smell like french fries, do not produce harmful physical effects in humans, such as nausea.[14]

The negative impact of biodiesel use includes the increased emission, compared to fossil-fuel emissions, of NOx. Another disadvantage is its high production costs. According to one study, which was undertaken when agricultural commodity prices were much lower than they are now, oil would have to cost between $40 and $50 per barrel before biodiesel production could be viable without government subsidies.[15]

Biodiesel is even more expensive to produce when the costs of the energy consumed to manufacture fertilizers and pesticides used on the crops converted to fuel are considered. Additional costs include the price of energy used to cultivate, harvest, and transport the crop to the production facility. The impact of agriculture on the land is also significant. Run-off, soil ero-

---

9. Sierra Club - http://www.sierraclubri.org/globalwarm/

10. National Biodiesel Board Press Release, November 14, 2002.

11. Canadian Renewable Fuels Association web site, www.greenfuels.org/biopres.html.

12. Ibid.

13. "Will Green Alternatives Do? The Use of Plant-Based Fuel is on the Horizon," *Motorhome*, November 2002.

14. Canadian Renewable Fuels Association web site, www.greenfuels.org/biopres.html

15. Ibid.

sion, and pesticide and herbicide use all compromise the environment.[16]

Performance challenges also exist with biodiesel. According to a study by Cyto-Culture, a bioremediation company in Richmond, CA, plant-based biodiesel supports the growth of the algae and anaerobic bacteria that can grow in diesel fuel systems and produce a sludge that can clog filters.[17] Finally, biodiesel has a higher viscosity than conventional diesel and doesn't perform well at low temperatures. In northern parts of the U. S. and in Canada and large portions of Europe, biodiesel is most effective when kept below ten percent of the blend with conventional diesel fuel.[18]

### ADM and the Alternative-Fuels Market
In 1997, there were 32 ethanol plants in six Midwestern states with a production capacity of 1.4 billion gallons of fuel-grade ethanol. Five of these plants were owned by ADM and accounted for 44 percent of the national ethanol production capacity. ADM also has entered into a merger agreement with Minnesota Corn processors, which operates ethanol-production facilities in Minnesota and Nebraska and accounts for another 110 million gallons of production capacity.[19]

The entry into ethanol production has proved profitable for ADM. According to an SEC filing, ADM's corn-products division saw a 34.4 percent increases in gross sales during one quarter of 2002 as a result of "increased sales volumes and higher average selling prices of the company's fuel alcohol arising from increased demand from existing sales markets, expansion into new markets and to higher gasoline prices."[20] ADM also receives tax savings in the millions of dollars as a result of federal incentives.

Cargill and Ag-Processing led the entry into the U.S. biodiesel market. ADM ran a feasibility study for six months in 2002. The study examined the economic viability of processing fuel from soybean oil in Mankato, Minnesota, where the state had passed legislation encouraging the use of biodiesel.[21] Having completed the study, however, ADM had not decided to complete a production facility in Mankato.

But others have gone ahead. West Central Soy, a farmer-owned cooperative, has built a $6 million plant in Ralston, Iowa, which it claims to be the largest and most technologically advanced facility in the U. S. The plant has a capacity of 12 million gallons[22]. Agua Mansa Bioenergy LLC, in which Southern States Power Company is a major investor, is developing a biodiesel production facility in Riverside, CA. Southern States is coordinating the development of the 30 million gallons-per-year plant.[23]

Golden LEAF, a North Carolina foundation, announced plans in 2002 to invest in a biodiesel plant. Golden LEAF will invest $10 million in the plant, located in eastern North Carolina, which is supposed to produce 10 million to 12 million gallons of biodiesel per year.[24]

### Current Legislative Issues
In order to increase the use of renewable fuels, members of Congress have introduced legislation to increase the use of biodiesel as an eligible fuel to meet this goal. One of the most important bills includes a tax incentive. The biodiesel tax incentive (S. 355) would provide one-cent in the diesel fuel excise tax for each percentage of biodiesel blended with petroleum diesel up to 20 percent. This special tax break would make biodiesel more competitive with petroleum diesel and would help biodiesel producers to receive subsidies during the first years. Other members of Congress, however, think this tax break is not temporary and that biodiesel producers would unfairly benefit from prolonged subsidies.

16. Ibid.
17. "Will Green Alternatives Do? The Use of Plant-Based Fuel is on the Horizon," *Motorhome*, November 2002.
18. Canadian Renewable Fuels Association web site, www.greenfuels.org/biopres.html.
19. "Will Green Alternatives Do? The Use of More Plant-Based Fuel is on the Horizon," *Motorhome*, November 2002.
20. "Will Green Alternatives Do? The Use of More Plant-Based Fuel is on the Horizon," *Motorhome*, November 2002.
21. "ADM Takes a Closer Look at Biodiesel," Industrial Bioprocessing, April 12, 2002.
22. "U.S. Biodiesel Sees More Production in New Plants," *Chemical Market Reporter*, September 16, 2002.
23. "U.S. Biodiesel Sees More Production in New Plants," *Chemical Market Reporter*, September 16, 2002.
24. "U.S. Biodiesel Sees More Production in New Plants," *Chemical Market Reporter*, September 16, 2002.

Other pending legislation includes:
- EPACT Reform (S.356, H.R.316)—would removed the 50-percent limit on alternative fuel credits earned with biodiesel under the Energy Policy Act of 1992, which applies to federal, state, and public utility fleets.
- CMAQ (H.R. 318)—would allow biodiesel use under the congestion mitigation and air quality improvement program.
- Renewable Fuel Standard (S. 385)—would create a nationwide standard that would more than double the use of renewable fuels during the next 10 years, with biodiesel as an eligible fuel.[25]

The introduction of new legislative measures designed to increase the use of biodiesel has created opposing opinions about who would benefit from the legislation. One of the main benefits of the use of biodiesel is the reduction of harmful emissions, compared to petroleum diesel, to improve air quality, which has obvious benefits to the public. Leaders of the alternative-fuels industry, such as ADM, expect a partial tax exemption to make biodiesel more price-competitive with petroleum diesel, which would lower U.S. dependence on foreign oil. Soybean farmers would benefit from higher priced soybeans due to an increased demand for biodiesel. Taxpayers, on the other hand, could end up paying the price for a better environment and greater energy security because of the prolonged tax exemptions that might be given to private companies like ADM.

Parallels can be drawn with the ethanol industry. Here subsidies have driven production, which in turn has increased demand for corn (ethanol producers consume six percent of the U. S. corn crop[26]) and raised prices by 15 to 30 cents per bushel. Although soybeans, the popular commercial base for biodiesel production, are in surplus, growing demand for the fuel could eliminate the surplus and increase prices for this commodity. Biodiesel production has grown

from 500,000 gallons nationwide in 1999 to 5 million gallons in 2001.[27] Further growth was almost certain to drive up soybean prices.

## Future of Biodiesel

### Tax Breaks
The main factor that will determine the extent that biodiesel gains acceptance in the United States is the cost. The only alternative fuel that has gained significant acceptance is natural gas, and the reason is that natural gas is anywhere from 10 to 25 percent cheaper than heating oil. The first step to drive up the use of biodiesel is to provide tax incentives for its consumption.

### Political Unrest in the Middle East
The current landscape of the Middle East has an impact. To much of the world, the United States has interest in a country like Iraq only because of its massive oil reserves. A mantra of many anti-war protesters is, "No Blood for Oil!" There is political pressure, both inside and outside the U.S., to reduce the country's dependency on foreign oil. Biodiesel is one route for doing so. The United States imports 58 percent of the petroleum it uses. When OPEC decides to raise the prices of crude oil, it translates into higher gasoline prices at the pump for American consumers. Oil prices have a large impact on the U. S. economy.[28]

### The Need for Sustained Support to Make Biodiesel Competitive
In Germany, biodiesel is available for consumers at many gas stations. One major reason it has been more readily accepted by European nations is that gasoline is far more expensive than in the United States and biodiesel can compete more easily on price. In the United States, the energy-distribution infrastructure would have to be overhauled, and the price of gasoline would have to dramatically go up. But unless there is an emergency, a sustained effort to establish biodiesel might not be forthcom-

25. "Biodiesel Tax Incentive Makes a Comeback," National Biodiesel Board Press Release, February 14, 2003.
26. "Ethanol's Bright Future," *Agri Marketing*, October 2001.
27. Ibid.
28. *LIVING WITHOUT OIL* , By: Lavelle, Marianne, *U.S.News & World Report*, 00415537, 2/17/2003, Vol. 134, Issue 5.

ing. President Carter was a huge proponent of solar power and other alternatives, such as wind power. While some headway was made on these issues, government-led efforts ended with a new, Republican administration. The dependence on oil became greater than before.

Refineries will have to be built to convert soybeans to biodiesel. The costs associated with constructing these facilities raise the price of biodiesel to as much as three times that of oil. Without subsidies, biodiesel in the U.S. will not be competitive with conventional petroleum based diesel.

## ADM's Role

As the leading producer of alternative fuels in the U.S. and a major producer in Europe, ADM has a lot riding on the growth of the biodiesel market. Oilseed accounts for the majority of ADM's sales; revenues from biodiesel in 2001 already were $300 million. Most of these revenues came from Europe. To develop the U.S. market would require legislation that supported the infant industry until sales were sufficient for ADM to take advantage of scale economies and lower costs.

The environmental advantages of selling a biodiesel blend in the U.S., however, were not clear-cut. While biodiesel offers many advantages over conventional diesel, it has drawbacks, such as increased NOx emissions. Environmental groups have opposed ADM's lobbying efforts for subsidies for biodiesel.

ADM also continues to face questions about its integrity and ethics as a price fixing scandal in the lysine and citric acid markets involving people at the top of the company—including the son of long-time ex-CEO's Dwayne Andreas—that severely damaged the company's reputation. ADM has been a constant target for critics of "corporate welfare" because of how much it benefits from federal agricultural subsidies.

ADM has several options with respect to the U.S. biodiesel market. The first is to push biodiesel as a wide-scale, viable energy source through contracts with public and private fleets and legislation that provides incentives. ADM would therefore be investing its resources to grow the market, much as it did for ethanol, and therefore it could position itself to be a market leader, as it is for ethanol. However, dramatically increasing the use of soybeans for biodiesel production would drive up prices of this grain-based protein, which is an essential component of human diets in many parts of the world and is used by ADM for other processes as well. Higher priced soybeans would not be in ADM's interest.

On the other hand, a broad coalition could be formed in support of biodiesel subsidies. The coalition would include those who care about U.S. energy security, about the health effects of air pollution, and about the plight of the U.S. farmer. The disadvantages for ADM of pressing its case are ADM would be using up its scarce political resources for a benefit that it would have to share with current and future biodiesel competitors. ADM foots the bill for the lobbying and reaps a reward that it cannot keep for itself. Another disadvantage for ADM of pressing its case is the inevitable opposition of environmental groups.

Could ADM partner with the oil companies? Perhaps, they might offer a biodiesel-petroleum mix as an alternative to conventional fuels. The market for an "eco-friendly" fuel, if competitively priced vis-à-vis regular diesel, could be quite large. Government would have to provide a tax break or some other measure to equalize the price of biodiesel and conventional petroleum based products. ADM would have to build refining capacity to meet demand without any assurance that this demand would emerge.

ADM might not be able to realize a profit. Was there not better likelihood of high return from other investments? Perhaps, ADM should stick to the European market for now. There already was strong and steady demand and there was every indication that this demand would continue to grow. In the U.S. the market was much more uncertain. The lessons ADM learned from its European operations it could apply to the U.S. when the U.S. was ready to adopt the fuel.

ADM must decide whether the potential benefits of alternative fuel development in the U.S. outweighed the risks. Appendix A is a summary of an article that appeared in the *Wall Street Journal* about ADM's interest in biodiesel.

## Discussion Questions

1. What is the best business model for biodiesel development? Should ADM delay or move forward quickly in the U.S. market?
2. What public policy incentives does A DM need to achieve successful biodiesel development?
3. How should ADM go about obtaining these incentives?
4. What coalitions should it form?
5. What arguments should it be prepared to make? What forums should it use for making these arguments?

## Appendix A
## Comparison of Biodiesel to Petroleum

| | Biodiesel | | Petroleum | |
|---|---|---|---|---|
| **Advantage** | The fuel reduces known diesel carcinogens by 100%, smog-producing hydrocarbon by 95%, and particulates by 50% to 60%. | (1) | Petroleum is widely available and accessible. Unlike biodiesel, petroleum base fuel can be purchased easily by individuals and corporations. | (12) |
| | There are 3 billion gallons of excess vegetable oil on the market that can be used to make biodiesel. | (2) | The U.S. has existing infrastructure that allows the efficient delivery of petroleum to economy compared to biodiesel. | (13) |
| | 80-20 blended reduced unburned hydrocarbons by 30%, carbon monoxide by 20% and particulate matter by 22%. | (3) | It is far cheaper than biodiesel. ADM conducted the feasibility study that concluded that it is not feasible to produce, market and deliver the biodiesel at this moment. | (14) |
| | Lower vehicle emissions | (4) | | |
| | Better performance. E85 has an octane rating of 105. E85 is mixture that contains 85% methanol and 25% petroleum. | (5) | | |
| | Renewable, non-imported energy source. | (6) | | |
| **Disadvantage** | The researchers are not sure on long-term impact on diesel engine when biodeisel is used. They also found that the performance of biodeisel in a low temperature is poor. | (7) | The fumes from petroleum contribute more than half the carbon monoxide in the air, a third of the nitrous oxides, a quarter of the hydrocarbons, and nearly a third of the carbon dioxide. | (15) |
| | Any form of biodeisel is still cost prohibitive. It costs twice as much as gasoline. Without some subsidy from government, biodeisel is not profit making venture for ADM. | (8) | The price of the crude base oil depends on political landscape of Middle East. Thus, the crude oil price has been very volatile. This does not help the U.S. Economy to have sustainable growth. | (16) |
| | Overall cost is higher Ethanol has only 80% of the energy density of gasoline. One has to burn more ethanol to go the same distance as gasoline | (9) | If the government imposes high tax on the use of crude base oil, or provides the tax incentive for biodiesel, the cost advantage that petroleum has may be outweighed by the environmental benefit. | (17) |
| | Limited infrastructure. There are only about 40 ethanol pumps in the United States, mostly in the Midwest. | (10) | | |
| | Biodiesel increases the emission of Nox. | (11) | | |

## Appendix A Sources

1. Hawk, Jeff. "Soybean Powered Equipment May Help Clean Up Diesel Emissions." *ENR: Engineering News-Record*, 8/6/2001, Vol. 247 Issue 6, p31, 1p, 1c.
2. "Biodiesel blend helps county protect its air." *American City & County*, Apr2002, Vol. 117 Issue 4, p12, 2p, 1c.
3. Id.
4. Jewett, Dale "Ford opts for ethanol." *Automotive News,* 06/09/97, Vol. 71 Issue 5716, p34, 1/2p.
5. Id.

6. Id.

7. Hawk, Jeff. "Soybean Powered Equipment May help Clean Up Diesel Emissions." *ENR: Engineering News-Record,* 8/6/2001, Vol. 247 Issue 6, p31, 1p, 1c.

8. Lyman, F. "Clean cars." *Technology Review* (1997, May/Jun90, Vol. 93 Issue 4, p22, 2p, 1c, 1bw.

9. Jewett, Dale "Ford opts for ethanol." *Automotive News,* 06/09/97, Vol. 71 Issue 5716, p34, 1/2p.

10. Id.

11. Id.

12. Hertzmark, Donald; Flaim, Silvio; Ray, Daryll; Parvin, Greg "Economic Feasibility of Agricultural Alcohol Production within A Biomass System." *American Journal of Agricultural Economics,* Dec80, Vol. 62 Issue 5, p965, 7p.

13. N/A .

14. N/A.

15. Lyman, F. "Clean cars." *Technology Review* (1997) , May/Jun90, Vol. 93 Issue 4, p22, 2p, 1c, 1bw.

16. N/A.

17. Lyman, F. "Clean cars." *Technology Review* (1997), May/Jun90, Vol. 93 Issue 4, p22, 2p, 1c, 1bw.

## *How Green is Biodiesel?*

Strengthens rural economy =    ⇓
but more land under agricultural production

Renewable source = conserves    ⇑
resources/uses waste

Use surplus soybeans = reduces waste    ⇑

Production of soy-based fuel has a    ⇑
positive energy balance = reduced need
for fertilizer because of nitrogen-fixing qualities; low energy requirements for conversion

Bio-degradable and non-toxic =    ⇑
cleaner environment

Reduced tail pipe emissions =    ⇑
cleaner air

Increased NOx emissions =    ⇓
more harm

Better smelling emissions =    ⇑
better for human health

**Overall impact:**    ⇑

## *Impact of Biodiesel Market Development to ADM*

### Benefits to ADM

- Increased revenue—Currently has sales of $300 million in Europe alone

### Negative Impact on ADM

- Upward pressure on soybean prices
- Negative PR—from lobbying efforts

### Benefits to General Population

- Reduced noxious and toxic emissions
- Reduced reliance on foreign oil
- Some reduction in fertilizer use (compared to using land for corn-based fuels)
- Farmers: Increased return on soybeans

### Negative Impact on General Population

- Tax incentives divert funds from other public projects
- Increase in NOx emissions
- More land for agriculture/less land for conservation
- More herbicide and pesticide use

Overall **balance** for general population compared with ethanol; **positive** compared with petroleum production

Overall effect for ADM **positive**—Market size in Europe alone is $1.2 billion and could exceed that in U.S. Estimated demand for 2004 is expected to be between 30 and 50 million gallons, up from 12 million gallons in 2002.

Millennium Fuels Market Share Report, http://www.millenniumfuels.com/news/pdf/WhatistheBiodieselMarketToday.pdf

## *Biodiesel Production*

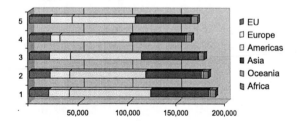

## *Biodiesel Product Growth Rate*

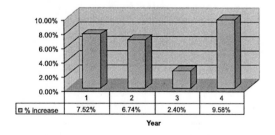

Data source: http://www.distill.com/world_ethanol_production.html

# Case 13

# General Motors and Alternative Vehicles

*The case analyzes the alternative transport market from the perspective of car manufacturers: specifically, General Motors, the largest. In its exposition of the company's alternative vehicles projects, the case considers the value of corporate technology for sustainable development; the role of government incentives; competitive industry pressures; and the level of consumer demand for green products.*

*Relevant chapters: 3, 4, 9*

The state of California recently scaled back its plan to require that 10% — or about 22,000 — of cars sold or leased each year in the state emit no pollution by 2003. In January of 2003, the state reduced that number to 10,000 and, later in the year, staff at the California agency recommended that the number be cut further to 250. General Motors was supportive of this reduction primarily because technology and the existing infrastructure did not exist to produce a zero-emission car and, as a result, consumer demand had been extremely weak. However, environmentalists were critical of GM and the auto industry because they felt that the

industry did not market the vehicles aggressively enough. They were critical despite the fact that GM had invested almost $1 billion in fuel cell technology research and was continuing to invest in this technology. Fuel cells promised to virtually eliminate the bulk of pollutants from auto exhaust.

Toyota, on the other hand, had successfully marketed an alternative vehicle, a hybrid, using batteries and a conventional engine. Unlike the electric car that GM offered in California as its zero emission vehicle, Toyota's hybrid, called the Prius, did not have limited range. Its batteries were recharged during driving by the conventional engine. The Prius was a mid-size passenger car, a low emission, not zero-emission vehicle, with fuel efficiency that could exceed 50 miles per gallon.

The question facing GM was where it should go next with alternative engine technologies? To what extent should it emphasize fuel cells, hybrids, or other options? In developing a strategy, the firm had at least two important factors to consider: its *business* plan — the approach it would take to researching and marketing alternative vehicles; and its *government* plan — how

This case study was originally written by Jesse Balok, Melissa Byrd, Corey Henry, Brigitte Klann, Helena Li, Dionne Meisterling, Selmer Moen, Rajesh Sekhar, Chad Tearle, and was revised by Professor Alfred Marcus with the assistance of Don Geffen. @2006, Northcoast Publishers, Inc.

it would approach the question of government support. Failure to align its business and political strategies could be detrimental to its efforts.

### Choices about Alternative Vehicles

Grounding in the basic facts about future automotive technologies is needed. There are four types of less polluting, more energy efficient vehicles:

1. Hydrogen-based fuel cell vehicles (FCVs).
   If the hydrogen comes from water, these vehicles would be virtually pollution free.
1. Hybrid vehicles (HVs) that have batteries, but also small, highly efficient internal combustion engines that currently use gasoline.
   Over time, other fuels including diesel or hydrogen can be substituted for the gasoline in hybrid vehicles.
3. An ultra efficient gasoline engine and auto body that relies on cutting edge technologies. This vehicle, though not free of emissions, might prove to be highly-energy efficient.
4. An advanced diesel engine that solves pollution problems that are specific to it, such as those from NOx.
   This approach also could yield lower pollution and more fuel efficiency, but progress would not be as dramatic as with the FCVs or HVs.

With FCVs, there are many uncertainties. Water is not currently a practical source for the hydrogen because of net energy loss when hydrogen is made. Methanol is a more practical source for hydrogen, but, if the methanol comes from natural gas, it is neither renewable nor pollution free. If the methanol is derived from plant material, the source of the hydrogen is renewable, but the extraction process is not pollution free and the costs are greater. Another issue is the trade-offs with regard to energy production and costs of the rare, precious metals that are fuel cells key components. Still other issues are the durability and longevity of fuel cells, the range of FCVs, and safe storage of the hydrogen, a volatile chemical that can explode.

Progress has been made on these issues but much remains to be done. Because of ties between HV and FCV technology, hybrid technology might provide a bridge to FCVs. A hybrid system has two parts – the internal combustion engine and the electrical motor system. Advances in the latter can carry over to FCVs or other systems relying on electrical motors. R&D funding for HVs might be more robust than funding for FCVs, because hybrids offer good current market opportunities, instead of opportunities in the future, as is the case with fuel cells. Widespread use of hybrids also might establish an infrastructure to service electrical systems and hence lay the foundation for FCVs.

With HVs, however, there are also uncertainties. One uncertainty is about battery longevity and cost. Another issue is space. Can an HV have as much room as a conventional auto? The first edition of the Prius had less trunk space than the gas-engine equivalent because of the need for space for the batteries, but the second edition was much roomier. How much more compression can there be in battery size? To develop an ultra-efficient conventional engine, additional advances would be needed in sophisticated electronic timing and sensing devices, advanced aerodynamic engineering, regenerative braking, and other areas. Many of these features could be incorporated into FCVs and HVs. They are not exclusive to conventional engines, but would their development trump the need for the FCVs and HVs? Advances in diesel might affect the outcome. If NOx emissions can be reduced and diesel engines made quieter and more efficient, they might be a more viable alternative in the U.S. In Europe and other parts of the world, they already are in widespread use. A world in which conventional engines and diesels continued to dominate could be as likely as a world in which HVs and FCVs play a growing role.

Unlike completely new technologies, where first users are very motivated and willing to pay high prices, HVs and FCVs replace existing technologies. This fact adds to the difficulty of coming up with a viable business model for bringing these vehicles to the market. How should GM approach this problem? Customers have to switch from a perfectly good technology (internal combustion) to one that is better. Hybrids might be a good transitional technology, if marketed properly. To really succeed in the market place, the auto companies might have to offer special performance or other features. They cannot just rely on the feel-good notion of owning a "green" vehicle. If these vehicles are relegated to a niche market of limited size (the "green" consumer), their significance is greatly diminished.

Eventually oil prices would have to send a clear signal of reduced supplies and much higher prices to make alternative vehicles compelling in the U.S. In Europe, Japan, and most of the rest of the world, on account of tax policies, the price of gasoline already is high. To consumers in the rest of the world, where gasoline prices average $3.50 per gallon or more, it is obvious that fuel economy pays. At $3.50 a gallon, a car getting an average of 40 miles per gallon (mpg), traveling 12,000 miles per year, saves $1,050 in fuel costs per year compared to a car only achieving 20 mpg. If a more fuel-efficient car cost an extra $3,000 over a conventional car, the pay back is less than 3 years.

European cars have had average mpg of about 30. A hybrid is capable of reaching averages of more than 50 mpg. Nonetheless, in the US with a payback of 6 years or so (in 2003), paying $3,000 more for a car to save on gas is not that attractive. Even in Europe and Japan, a high performance hybrid (better acceleration, traction and other road handling characteristics, etc.) would help with sales and overcome the widespread notion that "eco-vehicles" mean some type of sacrifice. In the US, high performance features might be essential given the then relatively low cost of gasoline.

Toyota has made a strikingly different decision than GM about its next generation vehicle system. GM has chosen to be a second or third mover on this issue, while Toyota has gone out on a limb and become a first mover. Why is GM apparently ceding the HV market to Toyota? Is it partly because of its beliefs about the size of the HV market and partly because it has been unable to catch up with Toyota's technology? What roles do the existence of the Asian — especially Chinese — and the European markets play in Toyota's calculations?

Also, what are some of the choices available to governments? What are the appropriate policies for governments to adopt – the appropriate tax policies, subsidies, consumer rebates, and energy efficiency mandates? Are there more coherent policies abroad – in China, the EU, or elsewhere? If GM wants to accelerate the development of alternative vehicles, which government incentives should it pursue? Which government policies should it promote?

### Electric Car Development

Early research into the feasibility and development of cars to reduce petroleum dependence started during the gasoline shortages of the 1970s. By 1990, electric cars were seen as an answer to growing pollution woes, particularly in cities like Los Angeles, which was plagued by smog. Electric cars were often hailed as an answer to existing vehicles that release hydrocarbons, carbon monoxide and nitrogen oxide. However, electric cars were not without their problems. They still required coal, oil, or natural gas to be burned to produce the electricity, and power stations, along with factories, continued to exceed motor vehicles with respect to the amount of pollutants that they emitted.

Electric vehicles were designed primarily as a response to new clean-air legislation enacted in select states. In September of 1990 California enacted new laws tightening emissions standards and targeting 2% of new vehicles sold to produce no exhaust at all (zero-emission vehicles). Zero emission vehicles (ZEVs) would necessarily be electric. No other alternatives met the California standard. Under the 1990 laws that California passed, the quantity of ZEVs being sold in the state had to increase to 10% by 2003 – about 180,000 electric vehicles per year were projected as being needed. At the time, the electric cars that were available had limited usefulness due to the small amount of energy that could be stored, restricting the distances that could be traveled. The new rules were designed to encourage research and technological advances to enhance development of electric vehicles. The laws were technology-forcing in a state that represented 14-18 percent of the U.S. new car market and 10 percent of the market for new cars sold worldwide.

Automakers lobbied the government heavily following passage of the legislation, claiming that battery technology was simply not advanced enough to allow commercial vehicle production. In 1995 the state government amended its laws. In exchange, the major automakers agreed to produce several thousand vehicles through 2000. The requirement for 10% of cars sold in California to be zero-emissions by 2003 for the time being was left in place, but whether it would be actually implemented was brought into question.

GM was a pioneer in developing electric automobiles, investing early research money in a wide variety of environmentally friendly, or "green", cars including electric and solar-powered automobiles. In the design of electric vehicles, GM employed the well known engineer Alan Cocconi, first to design the SunRaycer, GM's winning entry in the 1987 race across Australia of solar-powered electric cars. Cocconi then became involved in designing the Impact. The Impact was GM's prototype electric vehicle. It was revealed to the public in 1990. Cocconi's key contribution was the inverter, a piece of circuitry that converted DC from the car's battery to AC to run the engine and converted AC to DC to charge the battery. The prototype was then used to create the EV1, the electric vehicle GM released for sale in select markets in December of 1996.

When the California legislation was enacted, the most advanced prototype electric vehicle was GM's Impact prototype, which could accelerate from 0 to 60mph in less than 8 seconds, comparable to a petroleum-powered sports car. The Impact could achieve a top speed of 100mph, but was unable to maintain it. The prototype was designed to be aerodynamic with a light, very efficient motor, but suffered from a number of drawbacks. First, it contained only two seats, and secondly it used 32 conventional lead-acid batteries. An overnight charge would only allow the car to travel about 120 miles. The 32 batteries needed to be replaced every 20,000 miles, putting the cost of operation at about double that of a conventional vehicle of similar size.

At the same time, European automakers were developing their electric prototypes, including the Elettra, from Fiat, with a top speed of just 45 mph and a range of about 60 miles on lead-acid batteries at a price about twice that of the gasoline-powered version. Peugeot was still in the development phase with its electric vehicle, but was focused on "regenerative braking." This feature allowed the electric motor to function like a generator during braking. It eventually became a critical component of commercial electric vehicles.

**Launch of the EV1**

When GM launched the EV1, the commercial version of the Impact prototype, under the Saturn brand it was greeted with a significant amount of fanfare. The product was initially sold in select locations in California and Arizona and was supported by a massive $25 million marketing campaign, comparable to the advertising budget of traditional cars. In addition to GM's marketing plan, the vehicle received a lot of free publicity from its unique appearance, silent operation, and the fact that celebrities like Jay Leno and Alexandra Paul drove it.

The EV1 model that was commercialized had many of the features of gasoline-powered automobiles, including cruise control, anti-lock brakes, airbags, and keyless entry. Specific features of the EV1 were the twenty-six lead acid batteries required to power the vehicle, a braking system that recharged the batteries, and special tires to reduce rolling resistance. The car also had a backup beeper and a special, quieter horn for warning pedestrians, because the vehicle itself was so quiet.

The clean air mandates of states like Massachusetts, and New York, which followed in California's footsteps, spurred GM's development of the EV1. GM's early launch of the EV1 provided it with feedback from customers on the vehicle's positive attributes and limitations prior to 2003, the year the zero-emission law was to go into effect. At the same time that GM was introducing the EV1, Honda introduced its EV Plus and several of the other major manufacturers were getting their feet wet with sales to fleet buyers. GM subsequently added an electric version of the S10 pickup to its product line.

In 1997, amidst the media blitz on electric cars, a J.D. Power report indicated that only 23% of consumers would consider buying or leasing such a vehicle. Forty percent of those surveyed said that the technology was too new or untested and most felt that an electric vehicle had to meet the same purchase criteria as any other vehicle. In the same study, respondents indicated that electric vehicles did not get bonus points due to environmental friendliness, losing out to factors such as dependability, safety, price, and comfort. In order to overcome some of these issues GM offered the EV for lease. It thought more people would be willing to lease the vehicle rather than buy it given its high price and experimental features. The price tag was very high, but the lease agreement on the $35,000 vehicle included charger installation and roadside assistance to deal with the unique issues that cropped up with electric cars. An ongoing issue for all electric vehicles was the lack of infrastructure. Public recharging spots were just not available, so the vehicles were good only for short, predictable trips. Because of these limitations, electric vehicles tended to be an additional car, rather than purchased as an only car for an individual or family.

GM also took the unique tack of not just selling the cars to anyone with the money who wanted one. The process of leasing an electric vehicle included a screening comprised of test drives, a needs analysis, and a visit to the buye'rs home to determine if charger installation was even feasible. GM's initial sales targets were to lease about 300 EV1's for the first several years. The company found from market research that the right consumer for the EV1 was well-educated, with a household income of more than $125,00, who was environmentally conscious. These early tests were key, because if EV1's did not catch on with early adopters, they likely would not make it with the rest of the population.

One of the key challenges for GM and other electric auto producers at the time of market introduction was that gasoline prices were relatively cheap. The low cost of gasoline prevented drivers from being too concerned about fuel economy. And while several states followed California and adopted strict emissions standards, other states did not.

### Electric Cars Post-Launch

As indicated above, GM entered the market with the modest sales goals comprised of selling about 300 vehicles per year. In the first month the cars were available, December 1996, GM leased 76 of the vehicles. By February of 1997, the monthly sales number was down to only 31, leaving GM with a 240 day supply of the car. The precipitous drop in sales led industry experts to speculate that GM could halt production for the remainder of the year and still have adequate inventory to meet demand. GM stated at the time that the high inventory levels and slowing sales were not worrisome; stating that with new markets it was very difficult to predict sales and they could, in fact, be seasonal. Many speculated that the monthly lease price of $480 to $640 was just too high for a two-seater that was plagued with so many limitations. Despite the advertised 70-mile range, there were publicized complaints from some customers who maintained that they were only getting about 45 miles per charge.

GM had spent six years and $350 million to develop the EV1. In that time it already had once cancelled the program and reinstated it. The company contended that it could overcome the car's limited range with new battery technology. The car's range could be doubled, but the price tag for the technology was still $10,000 per battery pack. The target of the US Advanced Battery Consortium, a program sponsored by the U.S. government's Department of Energy and the automakers, was to get the technology down to $4,500 per battery pack. This 4-year $260 million project on advanced battery technology came out with a report in 1998 that indicated that the $4,500 price tag would be a stretch even by 2003. The best that could be expected would be a $7,000 price tag in the near future, but that would require 20,000 battery packs being made per year, which was unlikely by anyone's estimates. By the end of 1997 only 288 vehicles were in use and critics were angry. They contended that the US automakers lagged in environmentally friendly technology and were not sufficiently committed to it. The automakers responded that if there was any lag, it was due in part to US consumers' lack of concern with fuel economy, which rated 19th in product purchase criteria in a 1997 survey of car buyers.

Despite cumulative sales figures in 1998 of only 216 EV1s and about 200 electric S-10 pickups, GM indicated that the company would continue to work on electric vehicles due to the essential learning that could be gleaned for next-generation technology in the form of hybrid vehicles and/ or fuel-cell technology. Aside from the inherent limitations of electric vehicle technology, the image of the EV1 among potential customers was likely hurt by the numerous recalls it experienced, two in 1997 alone. First, in March of 1997 GM announced that it would recall all vehicles due to a charging receptacle that could short out due to water getting into the circuit board. In addition to the short, this situation could potentially cause a fire. Months later, the majority of the vehicles were again recalled, this time for a faulty O-ring that could allow fluid leakage, reducing braking capability.

GM continued to invest about 10% of its annual R&D budget in environmental car research, comparable to the other major US auto manufacturers. Prior to the introduction of the EV1, and continuing after its launch, GM sponsored races and competitions in order to advance green car technology and to recruit top engineering talent to work on low-emission vehicles. A technology Toyota championed was two-stroke engines working in conjunction with advanced fuel injection systems. GM took a license on this technology and incorporated the generator into a number of different engine technologies on which it was working. Because of the problems GM had experienced with electric vehicles in California, it became increasingly committed to other types of green, fuel-efficient alternatives. So, too, did policy makers. The successful implementation of the two-stroke engine, as well as the advent of cleaner burning fuels, were making the hurdle rate for electric cars very high. For many, hybrids came to the forefront as a much better option.

## Hybrids

In 1998, GM unveiled a prototype hybrid vehicle and started to do serious research on fuel cell powered cars. It announced that it would try to create a workable hybrid by 2001 and that its aim was to produce a fuel-cell prototype by 2004. A hybrid car is powered by both a traditional internal combustion engine and electric power. There are different types of hybrids, but GM's early focus was on designing an electric car with a small gasoline engine to top off the batteries. VW, in contrast, tried to combine a diesel and electrical unit, which together powered the vehicle.

During the 1990s, the federal government spent $240m per year for six years funding the Partnership for a New Generation of Vehicles (PNGV), a group comprised of US car manufacturers. The objective was to develop a new fuel-efficient vehicle. In 2000, GM showed the Precept, which was its hybrid prototype, at the Detroit auto show. Like Ford's Prodigy prototype, the Precept achieved 80 mpg, which had been the PNGV's aim. The Ford and GM prototypes were "American cars," not tiny vehicles, but roomy mid-size sedans. This feat was achieved through hybrid technology combined with energy conservation. In a standard fuel-powered vehicle over 70% of the fuel's energy is wasted. The Precept prototype was designed to be extremely aerodynamic and was comprised of lightweight materials such as aluminum and polymer composites. The internal pumps were more efficient and the tires more rigid to reduce frictional losses. The Precept was unique in that it was powered by two electric motors in addition to the diesel engine, which allowed the car to run about two-thirds of the time without the diesel. Of course all of this came at a cost and a commercial model was likely to be significantly more expensive than petroleum-powered vehicles. In the US, where fuel was relatively inexpensive, the fuel savings would amount to only about $500 annually. Americans appeared to like the idea of more fuel-efficient vehicles, but most were unwilling to pay extra for them.

Nonetheless, by the year 2000 hybrid vehicles had grown in popularity. The advantages of hybrids, such as longer driving ranges and automatically recharging batteries during driving, were often unknown to consumers — who still associated them with the electric car. Hybrids were being marketed with an emphasis on the environmental benefits of the technology. Some even called them "vehicles of peerless moral standing." Honda was the first to actually sell a hybrid to the public with its two-seater Insight hybrid. The Honda model, which achieved 70 miles per gallon, was priced at about $18,800, as compared to the $35,000 two-seater EV1. By 2002, Honda had a hybrid version of the Civic. Toyota's Prius compact hybrid, which got 52 miles per gallon in city driving, proved to be more popular than either the Insight or the Civic hybrid. The Prius was introduced in the U.S. in 2000 and in Japan in 1997. In 2002, Americans bought 36,000 Honda and Toyota hybrids. Viewed as a percentage of total U.S. vehicle sales, this amounted to just 0.2% of the 2002 market, but compared to the 3,300 electric cars of all types sold in the U.S. during the 1990s, the success of the hybrids was quite amazing. Toyota's second edition of the Prius was a huge success. Toyota could not make enough. Consumers experienced long waits before they got their cars.

As we look beyond 2003, . General Motors, Ford, and Daimler Chrysler announced that they probably would enter the market in the 2004 model year. General Motors first introductions would be hybridized versions of the Chevy Silverado and GMC Sierra pickup trucks, Ford's would be hybridized Escape SUVs, and Daimler Chrysler's would be a hybridized Dodge Ram pickup truck. Toyota announced that it would introduce a high-performance hybrid version of the luxury Lexus SUV in 2005.GM said it would introduce a small SUV under the Saturn name in that year. Moderate, hybrid-like features were planned on many vehicles for the year 2006-2007. GM, for instance, planned to have features in its Chevrolet Equinox and Malibu trucks in 2006 and 2007 that would gather energy and store it in a battery when slowing down, add power when accelerating, and start the engine when a driver gets in.

While Japan, like the U.S., had a hybrid market, Europe was moving towards diesel. Neither Mercedes nor Volkswagen had plans to introduce hybrids. Instead, they developed new-generation diesels that used electronic controls and fuel injection systems to increase fuel efficiency and reduce noise and pollution. These vehicles, however, did not comply with U.S. pollution rules.

Hybrids were fueled by gasoline. Their power trains had ordinary piston engines but incorporated additional electrical components — an electric motor filled with complex circuitry and a large battery. Hybrids could yield fuel-economy improvements of 10% to 50%, depending on their design and how they were driven. The gains came from: (i) the electric motor providing power at speeds when an ordinary engine was not efficient, (ii) capturing the wasted ener-

gy from braking, and (iii) shutting down the engine at stoplights. Hybrids were more expensive to make than other vehicles and the more the fuel efficiency built-in the greater the cost. Toyota's Prius and the planned Ford Escape and GM Saturn added more fuel efficiency at a higher cost. As opposed to other vehicles that might be sold under the hybrid name, they were considered "pure" in that they used parallel designs that permitted propulsion at low speeds by solely using the electric motor.

It was estimated that the Prius costs $2500-3,000 more to make than a conventional vehicle, but there was a $2,000 tax credit in place, which unfortunately would be phased out by 2006.Utah Senator Orrin Hatch had introduced a bill that would increase the tax break for hybrid buyers to $4,000, but it had not made much headway. Concerned about the tax credit lapsing, Toyota was pursuing the luxury-car segment, where it expected consumers would be willing to pay the full cost for having a hybrid.

Toyota and Honda were having a relatively easy time complying with corporate average fleet economy, or CAFE, standards, but GM, Ford, and Chrysler, which earned most of their profits from SUVs and light trucks, were having trouble meeting these standards. Hybrids would help them meet a proposed 1.5 mpg increase in truck CAFEs.

The most important factor affecting the further diffusion of hybrids would be driver concern about fuel economy. In turn, this concern would be influenced by geopolitical and other events that were hard to predict. If the earth really heated up because of global warming, with effects like the loss of low lying coastal areas in Florida, or the Arabs really did decide to hold the rest of the world hostage in exchange for oil, the price of gasoline could rise rapidly. If petroleum prices rose very rapidly, hybrids would probably gain wide acceptance. If fuel economy became a major issue, automakers would have other options than hybrids. They could further shrink the size and weight of conventional vehicles, overcome the pollution hurdles standing in the way of diesel, and move towards fuel cells.

No matter what happened, hybrids ultimately would serve a very useful purpose. Their components — electric-drive, power-control, and battery systems — would be *key* elements in fuel-cell technology. By 2013-15, there was some likelihood that fuel cell vehicles would replace conventional vehicles. The experience gained in using the above components would assist in the design of these vehicles. Hybrids came under fire for not being completely pollution-free.

On the other hand, fuel-cell technology, which combined hydrogen and oxygen, created only energy and water. In 2002 GM introduced an approach hailed as one of the most innovative in the industry utilizing only fuel cells, electronics, and a hydrogen tank. Of course, the potential safety hazards of hydrogen were a major drawback to the technology. The hydrogen could explode, unless great care was taken. Nonetheless, the popularity of fuel-cell technology had grown and all of the major US automakers had demonstrated prototypes. Though fuel-cell cars were promoted as the technology of the future due to their running entirely on renewable fuels and zero emissions, no company had plans to sell the technology to the public until 2010, at the earliest. While little existing legislation supports fuel cells, President Geore W.Bush had proposed tax incentives for their introduction.

### Next Steps at General Motors

Moving forward, GM faced two highly interconnected challenges. First, it had to make sure it had a sound business plan. Second, it had to make sure it had a sound strategy with respect to public policy. Government support or the lack of it could totally derail its ambitious plans for new vehicle development. What should it do next? How should it proceed?

### Discussion Questions

1. Explain hybrid technologies and other technological choices that auto companies have. What are the advantages and disadvantages of these options?
2. Why role does environmental policy play in inducing automakers to change the technologies they use?
3. How effective has environmental policy been in the past in bringing about such change?
4. Why hasn't the change taken place?
5. Why was the introduction of the electric car in California not successful? What should

General Motors do now about hybrids and other alternative vehicles?
6. What should General Motors learn from the failure of its past efforts to commercialize an electric car?
7. What kind of plan should General Motors have for the adoption of new automotive technologies?
8. What kind of public policies should it have in support of this plan?
9. How should it make the case that the government should support these policies? What arguments should it make to public officials? What arguments should it make in the media? With whom should it collaborate on its public policy agenda?

### References

ELECTRIC CARS AND PTEROSAURS ARE MY BUSINESS , By: Zorpette, Glenn, Scientific American, 00368733, May97, Vol. 276, Issue 5

GREEN RECRUIT , By: Sedgwick, David, Automotive News, 00051551, 02/23/98, Vol. 71, Issue 5754

ELECTRIC VEHICLE WORKSHOP, By: Vandenberg, Victoria, Tech Directions, 10629351, Mar96, Vol. 55, and Issue 8

HOW CLEAN IS THE PLUG-IN CAR? , Economist, 00130613, 10/13/90, Vol. 317, Issue 7676

ELECTRIC CARS GET JOLT OF MARKETING , By: Murphy, Ian P., Marketing News, 00253790, 08/18/97, Vol. 31, Issue 17

CAN YOU HAVE GREEN CARS WITHOUT THE RED INK? , By: Naughton, Keith, Business Week, 00077135, 12/29/97-01/05/98 Double Issue, Issue 3559

ROUGH ROAD AHEAD FOR GAS-ELECTRIC HYBRID SALES , By: Halliday, Jean, Automotive News, 00051551, 02/07/2000, Vol. 74, Issue 5860

LOOK, MOM, NO GAS , By: Cook, William J., U.S. News & World Report, 00415537, 9/30/96, Vol. 121, Issue 13

DEALERS LEASE 155 EV1S IN 3 MONTHS , By: Child, Charles, Automotive News, 00051551, 03/10/97, Vol. 71,

GM EVS ADD RANGE—AT A COST , By: Sedgwick, David, Automotive News, 00051551, 01/12/98, Vol. 71, Issue 5748

ROBERT STEMPEL , By: Flint, Jerry, Linden, Dana Wechsler, Forbes, 00156914, 8/1/94, Vol. 154, Issue 3

A PLUG FROM JAY? , Automotive News, 00051551, 01/06/97, Vol. 71, Issue 5694

124 GM ELECTRICS ON LEASE , Automotive News, 00051551, 02/10/97, Vol. 71, Issue 5699

THE INFORMER , By: Barrett, William P., Kellner, Tomas, Fisher, Daniel, Novack, Janet, Forbes, 00156914, 03/06/2000, Vol. 165, Issue 6

GM'S COMMITTED TO EVS , By: Smith, David C., Ward's Auto World, 00430315, Sep97, Vol. 33, Issue 9

ELECTRIC CARS MOVE CLOSER TO THE SHOWROOM , By: Estok, David, Maclean's, 00249262, 7/29/96, Vol. 109, Issue 31

DEALERS TO FIX EV1 SHORT, NUMMI CARS' AIRBAG SENSOR, By: Stoffer, Harry, Automotive News, 00051551, 06/02/97, Vol. 71, Issue 5715

GM RECALLS EV1 AGAIN, By: Stoffer, Harry, Automotive News, 00051551, 09/01/97, Vol. 71, Issue 5729

HYBRID VIGOUR?, Economist, 00130613, 01/29/2000, Vol. 354, Issue 8155

REPAIRS FOR RECALLED EV1S ARE DUE IN 2001, Automotive News, 00051551, 04/03/2000, Vol. 74, Issue 5868

A LIGHTER SHADE OF GREEN: HYBRID CARS , By: Newman, Richard J., U.S. News & World Report, 00415537, 4/29/2002, Vol. 132, Issue 14

MEAN CLEAN MACHINES , By: HAMILTON, ANITA, Szczesny, Joseph R., Time South Pacific, 08180628, 9/2/2002, Issue 34

ENVIRONMENT: AUTOMAKERS DROPPING ELECTRIC CARS AS SALES SAG, By: Stapp, Katherine, Inter Press Service, 9/30/2002

PULLING THE PLUG; CARMAKERS SCRAP ELECTRIC VEHI-CLES, By: Hall, Carl T., San Francisco Chronicle, 10/10/2002

GM AND TOYOTA TURN UP THE HEAT ON HYBRIDS, By: Truett, Richard, Automotive News, 1/6/2003

GM, TOYOTA BETTING ON GASOLINE-ELECTRIC HYBRIDS: THEY BOTH PLAN TO APPLY THE FUEL-SAVING TECHNOLOGY TO HIGH-VOLUME VEHICLES, By: Cato, Jeremy, Vancouver Sun, 2/7/2003

PULLING THE PLUG; GM'S DECISION TO END EV1 LEASES SHOCKS OWNERS, By: Sabatini, Jeff, Autoweek, 11/25/2002

HYBRID CARS DUDE, WHERE'S MY HYBRID? DETROIT IS JOINING TOYOTA AND HONDA IN THE HYBRID-VEHICLE MAR-KET. IT'S TRENDY, BUT IS IT A BUSINESS? By Stuart F. Brown, Fortune, 4/14/03

# Case 14

## Target and the Perception of Good Corporate Citizenship through Charitable Works

*Although corporate charity is not the same thing as corporate social responsibility, the benevolent activities of business nonetheless enhance its reputation and the good-will value of its brand name. This case analyzes the experience of Target and its struggle to assess the value of its non-business contributions. In the industry of big-box retail, Target maintains a much better record of charitable giving than its main competitor, Wal-Mart, yet lags behind in sales and reputation.*

*Relevant chapters: 3, 5, 8*

Target Corporation has a long and distinguished history of good corporate citizenship; however, according to Harris poll rankings, Target is perceived to be less generous than its closest competitor, Wal-Mart. A review of publicly available information on philanthropic gifts reveals that Target gives $2 million per week and Wal-Mart gives $3.5 million per week. However, a comparison of giving versus revenues indicates that Target gives 5% of pre-tax profits while Wal-Mart gives just 1.7%. Through strategic corporate giving, companies

attempt to thoughtfully align business interests with charitable donations. Still, the benefits of strategic giving programs are not well understood. Should the focus be on benefits to the recipients or public relations benefits for the company? Target was considering how best to approach the issue: was it obtaining enough corporate benefit from its contributions? Was that the purpose of its charitable giving? Was not the purpose of giving to "do good," plain and simple, not to help the company's bottom line?

### Target's Goals

It is Target's belief that philanthropy activity is motivated by a simple desire to be a good corporate citizen; that is, it is giving back to the community simply because it views it as the "right" thing to do. However, there are, admittedly, benefits flowing to its business operations as well. Benefits include; increasing customer preference, increasing employee satisfaction and decreasing turnover, improved relationships with suppliers, and support from the community at large. With current sentiments against big business, corporations are faced with many difficult decisions as they strike a balance

This case study was originally written by K. Choic, J. Fletcher, L. Harbinson, K. Kosuge, P. Peterson, M. Rainford, A. Scaglione, and S. Sundquist,, and was revised by Alfred A. Marcus. ©2006, Northcoast Publishers, Inc.

between corporate social responsibility and maximizing shareholder value.[1] Target Corporation has a long and distinguished history of good corporate citizenship; proudly giving back 5 percent of federally taxable income to communities it serves. However, in a recent Harris Interactive/Reputation Institute survey, Target was the 13th ranked U.S. company for social responsibility—behind its closest competitor, Wal-Mart (ranked number 3).[2] These survey results prompt several questions:

1. Why is Target perceived to be less generous than Wal-Mart?
2. Does Target obtain enough benefit—or return on investment—from its corporate giving?
3. Can Target increase recognition of its good works without crossing the line and being viewed as doing so only for public relations reasons?

These questions are reviewed by examining the benefits derived from social responsibility and by examining Target's position.

### *Corporate Social Responsibility*

Corporate social responsibility has been defined as an organization's ability to meet the demands and expectations of external constituencies—or stakeholders—beyond those linked directly to its products and services.[3] Many statements have been made about social responsibility. For instance, H.B. Atwater, former CEO of General Mills, referred to it as the "activities a company engages in outside the normal line of business: community and involvement and direct philanthropy." William Norris, former CEO of Control Data, called it "participation in public/private collaborations to address major social needs." Ralph Nader said that it was "first to obey the law...second to invest (corporate) funds and train their workers for future prosperity...(and) third to go beyond the law and exercise exem-

---

**A Corporation's Stakeholders**

- Employees and their families
- Consumers
- Customers
- Investors
- Business partners
- Competitors
- Governments
- Civil society
- Communities
- The environment

---

plary achievements in consumer, worker, environmental, and community progress." Doug Tompkins, a "deep ecologist," said that it was "an oxymoron." Roger Hale, ex-CEO of Tenant Corporation said that social responsibility was treating "employees, customers, vendors, shareholders, and the general community in the same way he or she would like to be treated." Jay Lorsch, of Harvard Business School, has written that "a socially responsible business is not only one that provides a return to investors...but also creates high quality products and/or services, provides rewarding jobs,...and does all this within the laws and mores of the countries in which it operates."

Key characteristics and underlying principles of social responsibility include:

- Compliance with laws and regulations
- Voluntary commitments
- Principle of inclusiveness and engagement of affected and/or interested parties
- Accountability
- Transparency
- Ethical behavior
- Flexibility to reflect diversity and needs.[4]

---

1. A recent article in the *Harvard Business Review* by Michael Porter and Mark Kramer summarizes the situation: "Executives increasingly see themselves in a no-win situation, caught between critics demanding ever higher levels of "corporate social responsibility." Michael E. Porter and Mark R. Kramer, "The Competitive Advantage of Corporate Philanthropy," *Harvard Business Review*, December 2002.

2. A summary of a recent article in the *Wall Street Journal*, attached as Appendix A, discusses these developments. Also see Ronald Alsop, "Perils of Corporate Philanthropy—Touting Good Works Offends The Public, but Reticence Is Misperceived as Inaction," *Wall Street Journal*, January 16, 2002.

3. M.A. Keeley, "Social Justice Approach to Organizational Evaluation," *Administrative Science Quarterly 23* (1978), pp. 272-92.

4. International Institute for Sustainable Development, www.iisd.org.

given the important role the Dayton family historically played in the Twin Cities.

The question facing Target was how it should focus and highlight its corporate giving programs. Going forward, what role should they play in the company? What was the right, honorable, and practical thing to do?

### Discussion Questions:

1. Why was Target lagging Wal-Mart on some indicators of corporate responsibility? Were not its program superior to those of Wal-Mart?
2. Why should Target care about corporate social responsibility?
3. What was the relationship between corporate social responsibility and charitable giving?
4. Should Target align its giving with other corporate goals? Or was giving a separate area that should not be strategic in nature?
5. What advice would you give to Target about the directions in which it should take in philanthropic efforts?

### APPENDIX A
**Target's Partners in Corporate Giving**

Each year, Target team members help improve the quality of life in their communities by supporting United Way. Its programs focus on the most critical needs in their communities. The generosity of our team members continually places Target Corporation among national leaders in dollars contributed to United Way.

The American Red Cross reaches out to help whenever a disaster strikes. So Target is proud to support the American Red Cross Annual Disaster Giving Program, helping the Red Cross respond to immediate needs of victims and their families. Target also provides disaster assistance through volunteer and in–kind support.

By making your pharmacy and health purchases at Target, you help support St. Jude Children's Research Hospital, the single largest center in the United States for the treatment and research of pediatric cancer and other life—threatening childhood diseases. And each holi-

day season you can purchase gifts for the kids at St. Jude from their wish lists on target.com.

Target has raised more than $27 million for St. Jude and for Target House, where families of St. Jude patients can make a comfortable home away from home during their children's life–saving treatment.

Target has teamed up with the Tiger Woods Foundation to create Start Something, a program focused on self–improvement for kids ages 8–17. Start Something encourages kids to follow their dreams, find the necessary tools to reach their goals and achieve success.

The Target Stores Ready. Sit. Read! program includes sponsorship of the *PBS KIDS Share A Story* literacy campaign. This initiative uses on–air and online programming to inspire adults to help children develop language and literacy skills through daily activities, including book reading, storytelling, rhyming and singing.

Target is pleased to sponsor the Kennedy Center's *Millennium Stage*, showcasing artists from across the country and featuring music, dance, theater, puppetry, standup comedy and more. Free performances take place daily at 6 p.m. in the Kennedy Center's Grand Foyer and online at www.kennedycenter.com/programs/millennium.

The Elizabeth Glaser Pediatric AIDS Foundation helps young victims of HIV and AIDS by making grants to scientists researching prevention and treatment of HIV infection in children. Target supports the foundation's annual fundraiser, which has raised almost $2 million in 2002.

Target is proud to support the United Negro College Fund, the nation's most successful education assistance organization for African–Americans. In 2002 Target is providing assistance through scholarships, raising operating funds for colleges and universities and giving students and faculty better access to technology.

The Hispanic Scholarship Fund, the largest Hispanic scholarship–awarding organization in the country, has awarded scholarships totaling nearly $60 million to more than 45,000 students. Target is providing financial assistance through scholarships to hundreds of deserving students in 2002.[15]

---

15. Target.com.

# Case 15

## Auto Safety at Ford

*The case analyzes the Ford Explorer/Firestone Tire litigation involving allegations of an unreasonably dangerous and defective product. The cause of the deaths and injuries suffered by SUV passengers on rollover was alternately blamed on defective tires and a defective chassis design. The case also compares Ford then and now through a reexamination of Ford's Pinto product safety cases of the 1970s. The case also examines the relationship of Ford-Firestone, contrasting the American and Japanese management responses to the crisis.*

*Relevant chapters: 3, 5, 8*

As William Clay Ford, Jr. sat in his Detroit, Michigan office, he contemplated the string of events that had occurred over the last few years. The following were the notes he wrote down on the legal pad in front of him.

### THE CURRENT CHALLENGE THAT FORD FACES
- Fatal rollovers have occurred.
- Many large lawsuits had been in process due to the fatal rollovers.

- Ford had a history of "cover-ups."
- The evidence made consumers think the cause of the rollovers was due to Ford.
- This is because other Firestone tire users, GM and Nissan, did not experience the problems, which Ford experienced with the Explorer.
- Ford depended on the Explorer's success.
- Since Explorer was the most successful SUV ever, Ford would find it very hard to admit a possible design failure with the Explorer.

The string of events and actions that occurred had cost Ford millions of dollars and ended a century long relationship between Ford and Firestone. It caused serious damage to the image of both companies, and led to William Clay Ford, Jr. taking over the company reins after the ousting of the prior CEO, Jacques Nasser.

As William Clay Ford. Jr. contemplated these events, he thought about previous auto safety episodes at Ford that had hurt the company. He wondered how these issues could have been handled differently. Had the company made mistakes on the legal front? Had it made public relations mistakes? What guidelines did it need

The original case study on auto safety at Ford was prepared by Prof. Alfred Marcus and Mark Jankus, University of Minnesota. Additional contributions were made by Michael Cox, Takafumi Hayashi, Hans Hinrichs, Melinda Pavek, Ana Ponguta, Sara Roslansky, Benjamin Seffrood, Taku Watanabe, Chris Whealy, and Janel Wittmayer; all of whom worked in the spring of 2003 at the U.of M.  to provide the background material on the current Ford crisis.@2006, Northcoast Publishers, Inc.

to put in place to prevent crises of this nature from taking place in the future? If they did take place, how could Ford manage them better?

## Ford's Current Crisis

When Jacques Nasser became CEO in January 1999, Ford was ready to overtake General Motors Corp. as the top carmaker in the world.[1] Nasser had tried to radically reshape the company. He made changes in the bureaucracy to assure that it would be faster moving. He partnered with the software company, Microsoft, and the Internet firm, Yahoo. He purchased Volvo and Land Rover, and other businesses including repair shops, a driving school, and the Hertz rental car company.[2] Nasser built Ford into a company that was widely regarded as the best managed U.S. auto manufacturer, but he made so many changes that nearly everything he did he encountered some resistance.[3] The performance review system he installed, for instance, was greeted by a class action lawsuit from 42 employees who claimed it was biased against older, white males. A large group of marketing executives left the company for Chrysler. Six Sigma, designed to fix Ford's quality problems, was not doing the job. The company's quality declined in comparison to that of its competitors, and in a June 2000 rating of the efficiency of Ford's factories, its labor productivity also was off 7%, while that of its major competitors was improving.

A major source of Ford's problems was reports of people dying in accidents when the treads of Firestone tires, installed in Ford Explorers, separated. In August 2000 Firestone, under pressure from Ford, announced a recall of 6.5 million tires, after the National Highway Traffic Safety Administration reported a rise in accidents involving the Firestone tires, mostly on Ford Explorers and light trucks.[4] The agency reported greater than 1,400 complaints, 88 deaths, and 250 injuries from accidents in 1900-2000. In Venezuela 46 deaths were reported from similar causes. The government of that country was conducting its own investigation. Ford and Firestone executives had to appear before congressional committees to answer questions about what had happened. Ford executives blamed the accidents on the tires, while Firestone executives held that the design of the Ford Explorer was the main culprit.

Tire pressure was a crucial issue in the controversy. Low tire pressure, while it might provide a vehicle with greater stability, could build up heat in a tire, leading to tire failure. Ford wanted the tires on its SUVs to run at low pressure because of concerns about potential rollovers. It told drivers they should keep tires inflated to 26 pounds per square inch, while Firestone recommended a tire pressure of 30 pounds per square inch. Ford disputed Firestone claims that Firestone tires were only likely to blow out when driven in Ford Explorers. It maintained that Firestone tires suffered 167 tread separations in vehicles other than Ford Explorers.[5] Firestone, however, held that there were only 5 separations involving vehicles other than Ford that had rollovers, while with the Ford Explorer there were 149 rollovers.

In 1989, when the Explorer was in the process of development, Ford had an independent research lab measure the performance of Firestone's tires. The report said that tread separations had occurred in 5 of 17 test runs.[6] Ford's main concern was vehicle stability. It lowered the recommended tire pressure to improve stability. It did so after engineering simulations had shown that the Explorer was likely to fail an emergency-avoidance maneuver. Lower tire pressure would improve handling; Ford was so convinced of this fact that it debated adding a

1. "Ford: Why It's Worse Than You Think," *Business Week*, New York, June 25, 2001.
2. Ibid.
3. Ibid.
4. Executives at Ford, Firestone Will Field Questions From House on Tire-Test Data , *Wall Street Journal*; New York, N.Y.; Sep 18, 2000; By Stephen Power and Timothy Aeppel
5. Ford, Firestone Spar Over Data Ahead of House Panel Meeting , *Wall Street Journal*; New York, N.Y.; Jun 14, 2001; By Joseph B. White and Timothy Aeppel
6. Ford, Firestone Deny There Was Coverup in Venezuela — In U.S., Estimate of Deaths Allegedly Tied to Flaws In Tires Increases to  88, *Wall Street Journal*; New York, N.Y.; Sep 1, 2000; By Jose de Cordoba and Joseph B. White.

warning sticker that said that tire inflation *had to be* 26 pounds per square inch to help prevent "loss of control, rollover and serious injury."[7] In the end, Ford did not add this warning. Instead, it made design and suspension modifications just prior to the Explorer's 1990 launch. It lowered the vehicle by a half inch and stiffened the front suspension springs, but decided not to widen the vehicle by 2 inches to lower the center of gravity even further. According to Ford, the changes it made achieved its goal of being "a safety leader."[8]

In January 2001, Ford launched a major effort to settle all 200 pending injury, death and class action suits in the U.S. caused by Explorer rollovers.[9] It offered victims and their families large settlements and went so far as to apologize for equipping the vehicles with Firestone tires. This effort to settle these cases came a month before a scheduled launch of a redesigned Explorer.

Ford's apologies laid the blame for the rollovers on Firestone's tires, which, Ford said, had been linked to 148 deaths in the U.S. Ford refused to make any concessions about the Explorer's design. Plaintiff attorneys attributed Ford's desire to settle to a concern that Firestone might file for bankruptcy. If it did, all suits against Firestone would be frozen, with Ford potentially at risk for damage awards against the tire maker as well as itself.

In light of the controversy with Firestone, Ford's market share shrunk. The company lost 1.7 percentage points in market share in the first five months of 2001.[10] Sales were down 11 percent in the first nine months of that year, from the same period the previous year. Ford lost $692 million, while the prior year it had earned $888 million.[11] To restore confidence, Jacques Nasser concluded that he had to recall another 20 million tires, at a cost of more than

$3 billion. In addition to the recall, he decided to cut all the company's ties with Firestone.

Nasser's style put him at odds with employees and dealers, whose support was needed as he tried to tackle the crisis.[12] The board named William Clay Ford, Jr. CEO in October of 2001, when it heard that the two men were bickering.[13] Ford, Jr. became CEO at a very difficult time in Ford's history, as the company's ability to come back from the auto safety problems it confronted was in question.

### Prior Auto Safety Episodes

The issue of auto safety was not a new one at Ford.

In April 5, 1990, the company had been hit with a very large settlement in a personal injury lawsuit. It had to pay $6 million in a case involving the safety of lap-only rear seat belts.[14] This problem had been emerging as a product liability issue for many years for the automakers, and a number of companies had reached multimillion-dollar settlements with litigants, but the Ford settlement was one of the largest in such a case. The lap-only rear seat belt case presented Ford with many of the same dilemmas it had confronted nearly 15 years earlier in the Ford Pinto case: the company believed that in *good faith* it was adhering to *state-of-the-art* technology with regard to safety – it was a safety leader. Nevertheless, attorneys for victims afterward maintained that the company knew that features of its automobiles could not adequately protect occupants, but Ford did not want to spend the extra money to do something about it. This claim had been made in the Pinto case and again was being made in the lap-only rear seat belt case where attorneys for the plaintiffs argued that shoulder belts, not just lap belts, should have been installed.

The Escort, ironically was Pinto's successor. Just as the reputation of the Pinto had been destroyed

7. Role of Ford Explorer Design Is Studied In Connection With Firestone Tire Suits , *Wall Street Journal*; New York, N.Y.; Sep 20, 2000; By Milo Geyelin.
8. Ibid.
9. Ford Will Try to Settle All Pending Rollover Suits, *Wall Street Journal*; New York, N.Y.; Jan 4, 2001; By Milo Geyelin
10. Ibid.
11. http://enquirer.com/editions/2001/10/30/fin_ford_dumps_ceo.html
12. "In the Lead: In Times of Trouble, The Best of Leaders Listen to Dissenters", Wall Street Journal, Nov. 13, 2001.
13. "Ford: Why It's Worse Than You Think", *Business Week*, New York, June 25, 2001.
14. Neal Templin, "Ford Settles Big Lap Belt Injury Suit," *Wall Street Journal*, April 5, 1990, B1.

by the controversy over its safety so, too, the reputation of the Escort was hurt. In both instances, Ford's subcompact challenge to Japan's dominance was challenged because of a safety issue. The similarity between the cases did not end there. In both instances, when the vehicles were first marketed there were no government regulations requiring that Ford do anything other than it was doing either in regard to the placement of the gas tank with the Pinto or the installation of lap-only belts with the Escort. Only after the Escort was on the market did the government mandate this safety feature in the rear seats of vehicles. In the meantime, more than 140 million vehicles had been sold in the United States with the lap-only rear belts. The fact that the government did not mandate rear seat three point belts, however, did not prevent attorneys for the plaintiffs from bringing successful suits.

Most American automobile executives had come around to the conclusion that safety helped sell automobiles. Since Ralph Nader's 1963 book, *Unsafe At Any Speed*, information about the relative safety of cars had increased. Foreign automakers had introduced many high-tech safety features, and consumers appeared to reject autos with poor safety records. For instance, Suzuki's Samurai sport's utility vehicle lost 70 percent of its sales after claims were made that it easily rolled over during sharp turns. However, in 2001-2002, U.S. automakers had become extremely cost conscious and were using rebates to sell cars. In Germany and Northern Europe, more than 50 percent of the vehicles were fitted with electronic stability control (ESC) systems, while only about 6 percent of cars in the U.S. were fitted with similar systems.[15] Nearly one quarter of U.S. deaths were due to rollover accidents, but only about 3 percent of these involved tire problems.[16] About 20% involved loss of control, which ESC could ameliorate, especially in SUVs like Ford's Explorer, whose center of gravity is very high. Road fatalities in Germany had

fallen from 21,000 in 1970 to 6,949 in 2001.[17] The U.S. decline was not nearly as steep, from 52,627 in 1970 to 42,116 in 2001. While European firms like Mercedes fitted ESC in its vehicles as a standard feature, Ford and other U.S. automakers offered it as an option on some higher-end SUVs and not on lower-end vehicles. Mercedes had seen a 15 percent decline in accidents after making ESC mandatory.[18] Toyota provided ESC as either an option or standard feature, but U.S. manufacturers, being more concerned about cost, did not follow.

The issue for the U.S. automakers remained how much safety and at what cost. At Ford, the issue of containing costs was especially acute, as the company's losses mounted in the post-Nasser era. A new plan for reducing vehicle development time was highly critical of "over-engineering," especially in safety. A Ford executive was quoted in the *Wall Street Journal* as saying: "That design (for pickup trucks) did give us a superior crash performance, but we could have gotten a top government 'five-star' rating in safety with much less expensive technology."[19] With these controversies in mind, William Clay Ford, Jr. reviewed the history of the Pinto case (See Attachment A).

*Ford's Relationship with Firestone.* After reading the Pinto case, Henry Clay Ford, Jr. turned to the current problem involving Firestone. He examined a very damaging opinion article had appeared in the *Wall Street Journal* on September 1, 2000. Firestone was a subsidiary of Bridgestone Americas Holding, Inc. It is a Nashville, Tennessee-based company that was formed in 1990 when Bridgestone merged with Firestone. Firestone has 38 manufacturing facilities in the United States, and 1,500 directly owned and operated retail outlets; it employs nearly 45,000 people.[20] Ford first chose Firestone to make tires for its autos in 1906. Shojiro Ishibashi created Bridgestone in Japan in 1931.[21] Bridgestone entered the U.S. market in 1967, consolidated the Firestone

15. Ibid. p. 96.
16. Ibid. p. 96.
17. Tierney, C., "American Drivers: Stiffed on Safety," *Business Week*, April 28, 2003, p. 96.
18. Ibid. p. 96.
19. Norihiko Shirouzu, "Ford's New Development Plan: Stop Reinventing Its Wheels," *Wall Street Journal*, April, 16, 2003, p. A.14.
20. http://www.bridgestone-firestone.com/corporate/profile_fr.html.

corporate headquarters with the Bridgestone headquarters in 1992, and moved the Firestone headquarters from Akron to Nashville. In Japan, Bridgestone was very closely integrated with the Japanese automakers to which it supplied tires. Its design teams worked closely with the automakers. Under Nasser, Ford pushed its suppliers hard, and the Explorer design team had only an arms length relationship with Firestone.

An associate handed William Clay Ford, Jr. a comparison she did on the different styles of crisis management in the U.S. and Japan (see Attachment B). She also did an issue time line of the Ford-Firestone case (see Attachment C). The question that lingered in William Clay Ford, Jr.'s mind was: What lessons should he learn from both current and past safety issues at Ford? What could Ford do to prevent such incidents from taking place in the future? If such incidents did take place how could they be better managed?

## Discussion Questions:

1. What were the root causes of Ford's persistent safety problems?
2. How could they be corrected?
3. Is cost-benefit analysis immoral or just imprudent given the way it would be perceived externally?
4. Design new safety policies and a new safety program that would try to eliminate the safety concerns that have plagued the company.

## Attachment A
### The Pinto Case

Shortly after Lee Iacocca took over as Ford's president in 1967, the company started an accelerated development program that was designed to bring the Pinto to market for the 1971 model year. Ford had a fairly strong position in the small car market with its Falcon and Mustang models. Iacocca knew something about small cars and their appeal, having masterminded the introduction of the highly popular Mustang in 1964, and he wanted a new, competitive small car brought

to market quickly. In 1967 it appeared that foreign imports like the Volkswagen were posing a threat to Ford's small-car niche. The company needed an inexpensive, fuel-efficient subcompact in order to be fully competitive. According to some Ford executives, who believed the company should compete in the small-car market, doing so was the socially responsible thing to do. It saved American jobs, conserved on energy, and reduced pollution. It provided people with the chance to obtain inexpensive transportation. Other Ford executives thought the company should stick to producing the large models where the profit margins were much higher.

To help clearly define what Iacocca wanted, he developed the "rule of 2,000." The car should not weigh more than 2,000 lbs or cost more than $2,000. Even at that price, the car would be more expensive than the subcompacts offered by foreign producers, who did not have high labor costs.[22] Pinto's product objectives were as follows.

- True Subcompact
  - size
  - weight
- Low Cost of Ownership
  - initial price
  - fuel consumption
  - reliability
  - serviceability
- Clear Product Superiority
  - appearance
  - comfort
  - features
  - ride and handling
  - performance

Critics later pointed out that passenger safety was not on the list.

Pinto made it into production in time for the 1971 model year as Iacocca had wanted. Rather than the usual 43-month development period, it was in dealer showrooms in 38 months. In the six years following its introduction in August 1970, Pinto fulfilled many of the compa-

---

21. *http://www.firestone.com/*
22. Davidson, Dekkers L., "Managing Product Safety: The Ford Pinto," Case #383-129 (Harvard Business School: Boston, 1984), p. 114.

ny's expectations and became one of Ford's all-time best-selling models. The 2 million Pintos sold between 1970 and 1977 helped retain Ford's market position during a period of rapidly escalating gas prices. The Arab oil embargo had caught the other major American auto manufacturers without an adequate line of small, fuel-efficient cars.[23]

The first public criticism of the Pinto came from Byron Bloch, an independent auto safety expert. He warned on national television in 1973 that the fuel system was very vulnerable to minor damage and called for a recall. The Nader-funded group, the Center for Auto Safety, demanded that the newly formed National Highway Traffic Safety Administration (NHTSA) investigate, but NHTSA maintained that statistical studies did not show a greater problem with Pintos than with other vehicles. The Insurance Institute for Highway Safety released a 1975 study showing a growth in the number of fire-related incidents. Ford had a disproportionate share: Ford manufactured 20 percent of vehicles on the road, while the company's cars had 35 percent of the fire-related incidents. In August 1977, the magazine *Mother Jones,* at a news conference in Washington, D.C., announced the publication of an article called "Pinto Madness."[24] Although not the first article to suggest that Ford executives had known about the Pinto's explosive defects before the car was produced (columnist Jack Anderson had written on the subject in late 1976), it generated additional attention to the issue.[25] The article contained a number of serious allegations:

1. Pinto's accelerated development schedule meant that crash tests were conducted after assembly tooling had already begun, making changes in design prohibitively expensive;
2. the safety of the car was not a serious consideration in its design because top executives like Iacocca believed "safety doesn't sell;"
3. Pinto's designers knew of the car's defects but chose not to remedy them (even though the

modifications might have cost as little as $1 per car for materials) based on a cost/benefit analysis that crassly assigned a dollar value to human life; and
4. Ford mounted a concerted campaign to delay implementation of the relevant safety standards, succeeding in postponing their final adoption until the 1977 model year.

Top Ford officials said the article was "unfair and distorted."[26] It made no pretense of objectivity, concluding with this question: "(o)ne wonders how long the Ford Motor Company would continue to market lethal cars were Henry Ford II and Lee Iacocca serving 20-year terms in Leavenworth for consumer homicide."[27] Still the article did raise some troubling questions about the company's behavior.

Ford executives continued to consider the allegations misrepresentations and the controversy a public relations disaster. The opponents held that many Ford customers had died fiery deaths, but how many people actually had died? Mark Dowie in the *Mother Jones* article claimed 500 deaths, but the National Highway Traffic Safety Administration (NHTSA) in its investigations of the Pinto counted only 38 cases of rear-end collisions of Pintos which resulted in fuel tank damage, leakage, and ensuing fires, and in these 38 cases, NHTSA reported 27 fatalities and 24 instances of non-fatal burns.

Ford's argument was that its placement of the car's gas tank between the rear bumper and the differential housing on the rear axle was *state-of-the art* for the period in which the car was introduced. Only well into the design process, did an engineering study suggest an alternative, that the "safest place" for the fuel tank might be directly above the rear axle. This option, which was diligently considered by Ford, was rejected for *safety* reasons. First, Ford rejected it because moving the tank closer to passengers actually increased the threat that they would be consumed by fire. Second, doing so required the use

23. Ibid. p. 14.
24. Dowie, Mark, "Pinto Madness," *Mother Jones*, Sept./Oct. 1977, pp. 18-32.
25. Anderson, Jack, and Whitten, Les,"Auto Maker Shuns Safer Gas Tank," *Washington Post*, 12/30/76, p. B7.
26. "Ford is Recalling Some 1.5 Million Pintos, Bobcats," *Wall Street Journal*, 6/12/78, p. 2, cited in Davidson, p. 111.
27. Dowie, "Pinto Madness," p. 32.

of a circuitous filler pipe that could be easily dislodged in an accident. Third, if the fuel tank was placed further to the front, it would change the car's center of gravity making it more difficult to control, precisely the problem with the Corvair that Nader so vigorously protested in *Unsafe At Any Speed*. Finally, if the fuel tank placement was different, then the car could not be serviced as easily, which presented another safety hazard. Additional reasons as to why the fuel tank was not moved was that it would reduce trunk size and make it harder to offer a station wagon or hatchback option in the future.

Ford was not violating any existing government regulations. In January 1969 under NHTSA's proposed rear-end fuel efficiency standard, the vehicle was tested with a 4,000 pound barriers striking it at 20 MPH. The vehicle was supposed to leak less than an ounce of fuel per minute. In the four tests Ford conducted, the vehicles slightly exceeded this limit in three cases and in the fourth there was massive leakage because of improper welding (the fuel tank split at the seams). However, before production began Ford made modifications so that its car would conform to the 4,000-pound *moving barrier* test. The government, though, did not go with this standard. Instead, it considered pushing the limit upward to a 4,000 pound *fixed barrier* test, which Ford considered to be the equivalent of a 4,000 pound moving barrier test at 40 MPH. Auto engineers believed that such a standard was highly unrealistic. More than 85 percent of rear end collisions took place at speeds of less than 20 MPH. The cars did not strike stationary objects, but hit other moving vehicles. In any case, only .45 percent of all auto injuries were a result of ensuing fires. At speeds of 40 MPH or more, the occupants would die or be hurt because of the impact, not because of the fire.

At that point in time (1971), Pinto already was on the market and many cars already were being driven. Ford did not want to unduly alarm people about a contentious issue that still was in the very early stages. Still it re-tested the Pinto using the 20 MPH and 30 MPH fixed barrier tests

that the government was proposing. When it found excessive leakage and concluded that it would have to completely tear-up the car and modify the design, it decided to stick to the 20 MPH moving barrier standard for current models and to do the engineering work that would enable it to meet a future 30 MPH moving barrier test, which it believed NHTSA would adopt.

In early 1971 a junior engineer named Pricor conducted a study that explored various ways to meet the 30 MPH moving barrier standard. Almost all the options (an over-the-axle gas tank, a repositioned spare tire, installation of body rails, and a redesigned filler pipe) involved extensive redesign of the vehicle. Only a rubber bladder (estimated to cost $5.80 per vehicle) could be installed without extensive redesign, but it would not work in cold weather, where it became stiff making it difficult to fill the gas tank, or hot weather, where it simply failed.

Nonetheless, though the incidents were few where Pintos were struck from behind at closing speeds between 30-35 MPH, when they did occur, they received wide media coverage. In these incidents, the gas tank was smashed between the bumper and differential housing, and fuel sprayed over the pavement and inside the vehicle. It ignited from a spark, perhaps from sheet metal scraping the pavement and caused enormous fires killing or maiming the vehicle's occupants in a hideous way. Two such incidents were reported very widely. In 1972, a Pinto was rear-ended on a California freeway at 30-50 mph. The woman driving the car, Lily Gray, died from the subsequent fire. Her 13-year-old passenger, Richard Grimshaw, suffered from burns over 80 percent of his body, losing his nose, an ear, and much of a hand as a result. The boy underwent scores of reconstructive skin grafting operations and was scarred for life. A California jury awarded the boy $2.8 million in February 1978 for wrongful injuries and set punitive damages at $125 million, the largest punitive damage award ever at the time. The court later reduced the punitive damages to $3.5 million.[28] The jury was strongly influenced by the films of

---

    28.  Mokhiber, Russell, *Corporate Crime and Violence:Big Business and the Abuse of the Public Trust*. (Sierra Club Books:San Francisco, 1988) p. 378.

the Pinto crash tests performed before the car went on the market in 1970. The tests showed a Pinto being backed into a wall at 20 mph and the nonflammable liquid in the car's gas tank spraying into the passenger compartment as a result. A juror told a reporter that "(i)t looked like a fireman had stuck a hose inside the car and turned it on. In my mind, that film beat the Ford Motor Company."[29]

In a 1978 accident in Indiana, three teenaged girls were burned to death in a Pinto when they were struck from behind by a van. A part-time prosecutor for the county where the accident occurred brought charges of reckless homicide against the company (the first time a corporation had been charged with murder), and the subsequent trial drew national attention. A jury found the company not guilty of the charges, but significant harm had been done to the company's reputation.[30] Under pressure from consumer advocate Ralph Nader and others expressing outrage over the Pinto's explosive potential, NHTSA finally opened an investigation into the Pinto in the fall of 1977. Dowie claimed that NHTSA would

> never force the company to test or recall the more than two million pre-1977 Pintos still on the highway. Seventy or more people will burn to death in those cars every year for many years to come. If the past is any indication, Ford will continue to accept the deaths.[31]

In late 1977 Ford issued a press release responding to the Dowie article and the issues it raised. In part, it said that

> (t)he truth is that in every model year the Pinto has been tested and met or surpassed the federal fuel system integrity standards applicable to it....it

is simply unreasonable and unfair to contend that a car is somehow unsafe if it does not meet standards proposed for future years or embody the technological improvements that are introduced in later model years.[32]

NHTSA informed Ford that a public hearing on what it had determined were safety defects in the fuel system would be held in June, 1978. Shortly before the hearing was to begin, Ford announced a recall of all 1971-1976 model Pintos in order to remedy the defect. The cost to Ford of the recall was estimated at $20 million. This cost was to be borne by a company that at the time earned $1.5 billion after taxes.[33]

Shortly after the recall announcement, the CBS news program <u>60 Minutes</u> aired a segment on the Pinto controversy. Correspondent Mike Wallace discussed the Grimshaw accident and interviewed a former Ford engineer who said Ford had known of the safety defect but hadn't remedied the problem because of the cost involved. Wallace's interview with Ford's executive in charge of environmental and safety engineering, Herbert Misch, made Misch appear unable to answer pointed questions about the controversy.[34] A public image of Ford as a company that willfully sacrificed the safety of its customers in return for larger profits had taken hold. Production of the Pinto ceased in 1980. Attachment A summarizes the charges and countercharges that were made in the Ford Pinto case.

### A Summary of the Charges and Countercharges Made in the Pinto Case

*Charge 1: The accelerated development program was partly responsible for the design flaws.* According to Mark Dowie, the author of the "Pinto Madness" article, the Pinto was rushed into production in 25 months instead of the usual 43. Ford records indicated that it actually took 38

29. Harris, Jr., Roy. J. "Why the Pinto Jury Felt Ford Deserved $125 Million Penalty," *The Wall Street Journal*, 2/14/78, p. A1.

30. See Cullen, Francis T., Maakestad, William J., and Cavender, Gray, *Corporate Crime Under Attack: The Ford Pinto Case and Beyond*, (Anderson Publishing Co.:Cincinnati, 1987) pp. 245-308.

31. Dowie, "Pinto Madness," p. 32.

32. Cited in Davidson, "Managing Product Safety," p. 117.

33. Ibid., p. 118-119.

34. Cullen, et.al., "Corporate Crime and Violence," p. 167.

months to bring the Pinto into production, and that the early introduction of the vehicle provided competitive advantage — five months of market dominance when the car's leadership was uncontested by any rival.[35] That the car was developed more quickly than normal to meet the competition meant that assembly tooling (where the machines that will make the parts of the car are themselves made), had to start before crash tests occurred.[36] Tooling usually took place after crash tests were completed. Still, Ford was able to make adjustments in the gas tank design before production that allowed the car to meet the federal safety standard for rear-end collisions that was designed to protect passengers from rear-end fires.[37] According to Dowie, secret company documents showed that the company had also crash-tested eleven Pinto prototypes before production at an average of 31 mph, and that only three had escaped with gas tanks intact. Dowie argued that Ford refused to adopt modifications because assembly tooling had already begun, and modifications to the machine tools would cut into profits. The pre-production test-crash films introduced as evidence in the Grimshaw trial, which showed Pinto gas tanks spraying fuel profusely when backed into a wall at 25 mph, suggested that engineers within the company were aware that the tanks were vulnerable. Still, at that time the applicable proposed federal standard was for a moving 20 mph test, not a fixed 25 mph test. According to Ford, the physics involved with crash tests meant that a car backing into a solid object (as in the fixed tests) was subjected to almost twice the stress of a car struck by a moving object.[38] According to Ford, Pinto was involved in fewer fire-related collisions than would be expected given the number of Pintos on the road.[39] Dowie, however, claimed that the studies commissioned by NHTSA showed that more than 3,000 people were burning to death in 400,000 auto fires per year and that the rate was increasing five times faster than building fires. He asserted that Ford made 24 percent of the cars on the road, yet these cars accounted for 42 percent of the collision-ruptured gas tanks.[40]

*Charge 2: Ford placed little importance on safety considerations in its design process.* According to Dowie, design engineers who learned of the Pinto's explosive faults were loathe to inform Lee Iacocca of their findings. He quoted several former company officials on the subject, one of whom told him: "Safety wasn't a popular subject around Ford in those days. With Lee it was taboo. Whenever a problem was raised that meant a delay on the Pinto, Lee would chomp on his cigar, look out the window and say 'Read the product objectives and get back to work.'"[41] The emphasis was on styling and price considerations, not safety, said another engineer. And another recounted how no one showed up when he gave a presentation on safer gas tank design.[42] The company's design departments seemed to take to heart a maxim attributed to Iacocca: "Safety doesn't sell." Undoubtedly, the Pinto controversy helped bring the importance of automobile safety design into the public consciousness, as did Ralph Nader's book on automobile safety, *Unsafe at Any Speed*. Still, there may have been some truth to Iacocca's adage that "safety doesn't sell" in 1967-70, when the Pinto was being developed.

*Charge 3: the Pinto's designers chose not to incorporate inexpensive design modifications that could have saved the lives of many of the burn victims, and made this decision on the basis of a cost/benefit analysis which assigned a value to human life.* Dowie's article claimed that four design changes the company tested in preproduction could have reduced the chances of fatal fires occurring. First, a $1 plastic baffle could be placed between the tank and the differential housing, shielding the tank from the sharp bolts on the housing that tended to pierce the

---

35. Davidson, "Managing Product Safety," p. 114.
36. Ibid.
37. Ibid., p.115.
38. Ibid.
39. Ibid., p. 115, 117.
40. Dowie, "Pinto Madness," p. 28.
41. Ibid., p. 21.
42. Ibid, p. 23.

tank in crashes. Second, a piece of metal could be placed between the tank and the rear bumper to absorb some of the impact of a crash. Third, a $5.08 rubber liner could be placed inside the gas tank to keep gas from spilling out if the tank was pierced. Fourth, the gas tank could be placed above the drive shaft, away from the rear axle and bumper altogether. Ford had a patent on this tank design and used it on its Experimental Safety Vehicle, which had withstood rear-end impacts of 60 mph. Ford denied that these were the options it considered in the pre-production stage. Still, a former engineer testified at the Grimshaw liability trial that 95 percent of the people who had died as a result of the Pinto fires would have survived if an alternative tank placement had been used. He estimated the additional cost at $9.95 per car.[43] Ford never explicitly used cost-benefit analysis in evaluating different methods for containing damage from rear-end collisions. Yet, Dowie attacked Ford in a deceptive way by using the 1973 NHTSA proposed standard for fuel leakage in roll-over accidents as an example of where Ford did use cost-benefit analysis. As part of its case against this standard, Ford presented a cost/benefit analysis purporting to show how the money spent to put an $11 valve on every car it made to prevent leakage in a roll-over would greatly exceed the social benefits that would occur as a result. The analysis assumed that 180 people would die in auto fires if the valve were not installed, and that another 180 would be seriously burned. Using a NHTSA-supplied figure of $200,000 in lost productivity per death (including $10,000 for the victim's pain and suffering), and $67,000 in lost productivity for a surviving burn victim, Ford calculated that requiring installation of the valves on the 12.5 million vehicles sold that year would mean a net loss to society of $87.5 million dollars.[44] The roll-over cost/benefit calculations were widely publicized in the press and made the company appear to be valuing profit over human suffering and death. The fact that NHTSA approved of this method of calculating the social costs of a proposed regulation did not receive much attention, nor did the fact that this cost-benefit analysis had nothing to do with the controversy about exploding rear fuel tanks with which it was associated.

*Charge 4: Ford mounted a campaign against the rear-end safety standards that delayed their adoption for 8 years.* When a federal agency like NHTSA proposes a new regulation, it requests public comment on the effects and feasibility of the regulation. During the evolution of Standard 301, Ford submitted evidence supporting its contentions that various aspects of the standard were unnecessary, unrealistic, or otherwise excessive. Dowie characterized Ford's actions with regard to the standards with cynicism:

> There are several main techniques in the art of combating a government safety standard: (a) make your arguments in succession, so the feds can be working on disproving only one at a time; (b) claim that the real problem is not X but Y...; (c) no matter how ridiculous each argument is accompany it with thousands of pages of highly technical assertions it will take the government months or, preferably years to test.[45]

There was no doubt that Ford's top management was hostile toward some aspects of federal safety regulation. NHTSA was a new, inexperienced agency. Its leadership during the Carter administration came from the ranks of ex-Naderites (Joan Claybrook), and it lacked not only the capacity to be objective but the technical competence to do a good job. Combined with the effects of inflation, foreign price competition, and the cost burden of complying with other regulations concerning fuel efficiency and pollution controls, the costs of safety regulations added significantly to the automakers' competitive worries.

43. Mokhiber, "Corporate Crime and Violence," p. 377.
44. Dowie, "Pinto Madness," p. 24,26.
45. Ibid., p. 27.

## Attachment B

## A Comparison of Crisis Management Styles in the U.S. and Japan

| | US Expectation | Japanese Expectation | Conflict that Resulted |
|---|---|---|---|
| **Public relations tradition** | Highly coordinated and used frequently by businesses as a way of building brand and reputation. | Collectivist nature of the culture means the PR field developed later than in other countries. Not widely used. | Ford understood the importance of quickly reacting to the issue and using PR to protect its image. The pledge to do the recall without Firestone's agreement would have come from this tradition. This was like a slap in the face to Firestone and put them on the defensive. |
| **Media relations tradition** | Decentralized and informal, adversarial relationships with am aim to expose the truth. | Press clubs serve as a means to restrict media coverage of events in Japan. Formal and cordial relations. | The information about the tire caused rollover deaths was not widely covered in Japan and the Bridgestone parent company was able to avoid confrontations with the media regarding the topic. Ford was facing questions each day from the media and was under pressure to respond. Ford may have felt that Firestone was not cooperating out of shame. |
| **Crisis management differences** | Open communication style is preferable. The CEO or other ranking official is required to apologize and explain to the stakeholders. | Consumers have few rights and management hunkers down and waits for the cloud to blow over. The less reaction the better. | The company did not feel any public pressure in Japan because of the recall. No Japanese lives were lost and the recall was very limited in Japan. In contrast, Ford faced questions daily and the alienation of its core consumer market. |
| **Public relations strategies** | Requires symbolic organizational responses to advance own interests. | "Laying low" is an appropriate, face-saving response to a crisis. | Bridgestone held only one news conference on the day of the recall. The silence was deafening and communication limited to terse written remarks. This limited communication did not build faith in the US government or consumer and signaled guilt to the stakeholder groups. |

## Attachment C
## Issue Timeline of the Ford-Firestone Case

| Date | Issue |
|------|-------|
| 1972 | A Firestone quality control manager warned of an 'adhesion problem' and reported a test tire in which "the rubber peeled cleanly from the wire."[46] |
| 1977 | Firestone recalled 400,000 tires after it determines that some 25,000 tires produced at its Decatur, Illinois plant were defective. The recall was voluntary but it followed some arm-twisting by the government.[47] |
| 03/78 | The National Highway Transportation Safety Administration (NHTSA) announced a formal investigation into Firestone 500 defects. Firestone balked at cooperating.[48] |
| 08/78 | Firestone argued before NHTSA that its steel-belted radial 500 was safe, despite what the public may have thought. Meanwhile, civil and class actions were pouring in, and NHTSA threatened to order a recall.[49] |
| 10/78 | Firestone took action and issued a recall.[50] |
| 10/78 | Firestone recalled 10 million of its steel-belted radial 500 tires. Richard Riley, chairman of what was then known as Firestone Tire and Rubber Co., said at the time that the company agreed to a recall not because the tires were proved defective but because of negative publicity.[51] |
| 1990 | Bridgestone purchased and integrated Firestone's US operations. |
| 01/99 | Mr. Jacques Nasser became CEO of Ford.[52] |
| 08/00 | 6.5 million 15-inch ATX, ATX II and wilderness AT tires are recalled and replaced.[53] |
| 10/00 | The Associated Press declared "The chief executive of Bridgestone/Firestone Inc. told attorneys during an eight-hour deposition Monday that the company recalled 6.5 million tires in August for safety purposes and that the decision did not mean the company was admitting to any product defect."[54] |
| 10/00 | According to James Fell, former head of research at the National Highway Traffic Safety Administration, the study provides "an indication that there may be a factor with the Ford Explorer beyond the tire issue. It's a first indicator that they may have a stability problem."[55] |
| 10/00 | John Lampe became Chairman, CEO, and President of Firestone. He pledged to speed up the process of recall, and overhauled the management team.[56] |
| 12/00 | A recall of 846,591 Explorers was announced to replace faulty parts on the suspension system.[57] |
| 12/00 | 10 days after the previous recall, Ford recalled 110,633 Explorers and Mercury Mountaineers for a problem with the speed limitation device.[58] |
| 01/01 | Nasser vowed to begin an ``early warning system'' to ensure such tragedies as deadly rollover accidents involving Firestone failures on Ford Explorers never recur again. Ford started to |

46. "The power of public opinion." *Risk Management*. May 2001
47. Ibid.
48. Ibid.
49. Ibid.
50. Ibid.
51. Ibid.
52. "Ford and Firestone's bitter legacy." Economist.com / Global Agenda, London - Jun 18, 2001
53. "The power of public opinion." *Risk Management*. May 2001
54. "Two sides to every story: In defense of Bridgestone/Firestone," Public Relations Quarterly – Rhinebeck. Spring 2001
55. Ibid.
56. "Is it the end of the road for Firestone?" *The Journal of Business Strategy*, Sep/Oct 2001
57. Ibid.
58. Ibid.

include tires under its vehicle warranties, and began to build its own database.[59]

04/01   With a national ad campaign entitled "Making it Right," Firestone tried to reassure the public that Firestone was committed to quality and safety.[46]

05/01   Ford's announced that it would replace an additional 13 million Firestone tires on its pickups and sport-utility vehicles with the cost of $3 billion.[60]

05/01   Bridgestone/Firestone ended its century-long supply relationship with Ford.[46]

06/01   A $1 billion claim for damages was launched for the family of a Florida couple who were killed the previous year when the tread separated from the rear tire of their 1997 Ford Explorer and the vehicle overturned.[61]

06/01   Regulatory Agents commented that "Ford is rushing to replace Firestone tires with other tires, some of which have been worse records for tread failure than the Firestones."[62]

06/01   Ford counterclaimed that it will continue the recall program while analyzing the data suggesting that some replacement tires have a higher rate of thread.[63]

09/01   In response to the recent poor rating of the Ford F-150 pickup, Ford's best-selling vehicle by the insurance institute, Ford asked the Insurance Institute to delay crash-testing the redesigned 2002 Explorer in hope of a better score by adding steel to the truck's body.[64]

09/01   Wall Street journal reported that "Ford has settled about 200 lawsuits with plaintiffs suing for serious injury and wrongful death in Explorer accidents involving failure of a Firestone tire".[65]

10/01   Firestone announced another recall of 3.5 million tires. The NHTSA, however, closed further investigations of Firestone's tires, thus reducing the uncertainty of Firestone's future.[66]

10/01   William Clay Jr. was assigned as CEO of Ford, replacing Jacques Nasser.[67]

11/01   A federal Judge granted class-action status to consumers who bought or leased a 1001-2001 Explorer equipped with Firestone tires.[68]

12/01   Ford announced a major restructuring including 35,000 job cuts after running its first annual loss in nearly a decade.[69]

02/02   Ford unveiled the TV commercial featuring William Clay Jr., CEO of Ford, in order to restore its battered public image.[58]

03/02   WSJ reported that "[Firestone] orchestrated what may be the most unlikely brand resurrection in marketing history by leveraging its powerful dealer network, rolling out splashy new tires and repositioning the brand slightly down-market."[70]

05/02   Ford and Firestone claimed victory, when a federal appeals court threw out nationwide class-action status for plaintiffs suing the both companies.

---

59. "Ford's Gamble: Will It Backfire? Blaming Firestone invites new scrutiny Ford can ill afford" *Business Week*

60. "Ford: Why It's Worse Than You Think- Quality, morale, and market share are down. Can Jacques Nasser get this company out of reverse?" *Business Week* Jun 25, 2002

61. "Ford and Firestone's bitter legacy." Economist.com / Global Agenda, London  - Jun 18, 2001

62. "Agency to Comment on Ford Tire Safety, While Inquiry Into Explorer Is Considered." *Wall Street Journal*, Jun 20, 2001

63. "Ford Analyzes Data Concerning Safety Of Tires Chosen to Replace Firestones," *Wall Street Journal*, Jun 22, 2001

64.  "Ford Asks Insurance Institute to Delay Crash-Testing 2002 Redesigned Explorer," *Wall Street Journal*, Sep 11, 2001

65. "Ford Settles Suit Filed by Family Of a Victim of Rollover Accident," Wall Street Journal, Sep 19, 2001

66. "Firestone Broadens Recall of Defective Tires," *Wall Street Journal*, Oct 5, 2001

67. "It's Curtains for `Jac the Knife'," Wall Street Journal, Oct 31, 2001

68. "Suits Against Ford, Firestone Are Given Class-Action Status," *Wall Street Journal*, Nov 29, 2001

69. "Ford to Unveil Ads For TV in Effort To Restore Image," *Wall Street Journal*, Feb 19, 2002

70. "Flats Fixed," Forbes, New York, May 27, 2002

71. "Court Ruling Favors Ford, Firestone -- Class-Action Status Denied Plaintiffs in Suit Alleging Breach of Warranty, Fraud," *Wall Street Journal*, May 3, 2002.

# Case 16

## Safety Audit at LAMC—USMNC's Newly Acquired Subsidiary in Latin America

*The case is a short study of the obligations of a new parent company for workplace safety in its far-flung subsidiaries. Prior incidents and accidents prompt management to self-audit its safety practices.*

*Relevant chapters: 5, 7, 10*

USMNC, Inc. of Sharpsburg, Pennsylvania has just purchased Latin America Metallurgy Company (LAMC) from a European (joint UK-Dutch ownership) firm Chemecon. There has been a sudden spike in worldwide demand for the sheet metal and coil that LAMC makes.[1] The acquisition substantially bolsters USMNC's capacity to meet this new demand. The financial press, therefore, greets the acquisition of LAMC with enthusiasm but shows concern about whether a company as large and diverse as USMNC with its history can effectively integrate LAMC into its operations. LAMC had not been well-managed under Chemecon, whose focus was elsewhere. Chemecon did not pay much attention to its Latin American subsidiary.

For the acquisition of LAMC by USMNC to succeed, USMNC has to be able to move LAMC's products out-the-door quickly. With worldwide demand soaring, it cannot afford delays in production. Yet, it seems to be an inopportune moment for USMNC to take on the complex integration of a foreign subsidiary that had been poorly managed by its prior owner given the fact that USMNC itself still was reeling from an accident at one of its Asian facilities. All the issues regarding this accident had yet to be resolved. How can USMNC bring product to the market quickly at its new Latin America facility, while at the same time it does so in as safe a manner as possible?

### Background on USMNC

The CEO of USMNC was now on record that all the company's facilities worldwide had to meet or exceed "to the extent possible" state-of-the-art U.S. standards in all areas including production, health and safety, labor, and the environment. Ethical and other requirements could not be compromised regardless of local practice. The CEO called this policy one of "zero tolerance."

The top management of USMNC learned this lesson the hard way. In the past, it had some problems with its foreign subsidiaries, but it never considered these problems unusual or out

---

Case study exercise developed by Alfred A. Marcus. ©2006, NorthCoast Publishers, Inc.

1. LAMC was located near Managua, Nicaragua.

of the ordinary until it had a major accident at an Asian facility in 1996.[2] It still was recovering from this accident. The accident caused 36 deaths, 100 or so people had to be taken to the hospital and treated for injuries, and there was substantial property damage at the site that was estimated to total more than $600 million in U.S. dollars. The accident also endangered the local population with a chemical cloud for a period of 36 hours and more than 25,000 people in the vicinity of the plant had to be evacuated because of the explosion and fire that ensued. A thin mist of the toxic pollutant, ethylene oxide, lingered in the air for a period of more than 30 days. Lawsuits still were going on as workers and people in the community claimed that they had respiratory and other serious ailments as a result of their exposure to the toxic mist.

This accident was not the only one USMNC had experienced at its facilities in the U.S. and abroad in the pre-1996 period but certainly it was the worst. Management viewed it as a wake-up call to do better. Following the accident, USMNC went through a period of soul searching. The CEO had a retreat in which he invited members of the top management teams of subsidiaries in all locations to attend. He followed up with an audit of all the companies' facilities worldwide. USMNC discovered that it had many small incidents and near misses, information about which it had not systematically collected and analyzed, sometimes out of a concern that if the information was readily available, it could hurt the firm's reputation or be used by attorneys who might sue it. Most troubling was the fact that the company had not carefully analyzed the incidents for the lessons that could be learned and applied the analysis to make worldwide improvements. It had not set up a database to track the occurrence of the incidents and to examine trends, nor had it introduced other programs for accident prevention and control.

Until the accident took place, there had been a sense at USMNC that it was on the leading edge technically. It had some of the best engineers in the world and though some of its processes were highly dangerous there were enough backups and redundancies that the chances of serious damage to people or the environment were very low. Talk of the risks of what USMNC was doing generally was suppressed. Most of the firm's efforts were devoted to rapid expansion. The company's ambition was to create a large global enterprise that had the size and scope to realize economies of scale in an industry that was extremely competitive and faced overcapacity. The conventional thinking at USMNC had been that only aggressive global expansion would permit the company to survive. Anything less would lead to extinction. Anything that stopped the rapid expansion was not an option. The audit, which was done after the accident in Asia, however, showed that USMNC had many warnings that an accident like the one that took place could have happened and that more attention should have been given to accident prevention.

USMNC had to acknowledge that its global safety, health, and environmental practices until recently were not as strong as they should have been. Before the accident, the corporate officers in Pennsylvania had granted USMNC's far flung global subsidiaries substantial discretion to run their safety, health, and environmental policies on their own in accord with local practice. After the accident, the company tried to centralize control of safety, health, and environmental policies and continued to have regular audits to bring local affiliates into compliance with corporate policies and practices.

### The Audit at LAMC
The main focus of the health and safety audit that USMNC initiated after it purchased LAMC was on respirator use. LAMC engaged in a variety of operations that required that workers wear respirators. These operations included welding, cutting, smelting, and casting molten materials; sanding, grinding, crushing, drilling, machining, and sandblasting; and cleaning, spraying, plating, boiling, mixing, and painting various pieces of metals and metal parts that

---

2. The accident happened in the Philippines in a small industrial town outside of Manila.

LAMC produced. These activities resulted in all kinds of fumes, dusts, and mists that could endanger human health and the environment. Gas and vapor contaminants that were present included: inert gases like helium, argon, and neon; acidic gases like sulfur dioxide, hydrogen, sulfide, and hydrogen chloride; and organometallic compounds like tetraethyl lead and organic phosphates. Unfortunately, the European Union's (EU) standards to which Latin American Metallurgy had aimed to conform (recall that LAMC's former owner was Chemecon) were not in harmony with U.S. standards. For example, particulate respirator standards, under EU regulation, fit into 5 very general categories, while U.S. standards (National Institute of Occupational Safety and Health) had 9 very specific categories of strictness and rigor. Gas and vapor respirator standards in the European Community had 3 levels, while the U.S. standards required approvals at many different levels. What was worse was that the nations of Latin America, especially Nicaragua, had a reputation for very weak enforcement, even when they aimed to meet standards such as those promulgated by the EU.

Though this had been the case in the past, government officials in Nicaragua assured USMNC management when they acquired LAMC that they would be trying to start to toughen their enforcement and that USMNC should not assume it could get away with anything by locating in their country. A very sensitive issue often brought out in the local media and discussed by intellectuals and academics worldwide was the abuses companies like USMNC perpetrated when they located in countries like Nicaragua. USMNC already had been pillaged in the press for its accident in Asia and it did not want bad publicity. Radical groups in Nicaragua riled up the local population and could incite violence. LAMC was a large company in the Nicaraguan context and a natural target. In absorbing LAMC, USMNC had few degrees of freedom. It could not afford to make mistakes that might jeopardize the corporation.

The audit team discovered that many different types of respirators were available for use by LAMC workers. LAMC had purchased many different kinds of respirators over a long period of time, some of them more functional than others. The main types of respirators were (i) maintenance-free and replaceable part half-mask and full-face respirators; and (ii) air-purifying negative and positive pressure units. The latter had air-supplied devices attached to them and they required considerable maintenance. The audit team was not convinced there was a sufficient number of either kind of respirator at the facility. It also was not convinced that the maintenance was being done on a regular basis on the latter type. It was quite apparent upon visual inspection that many of the respirators actually were not functional. Even more alarming was that many workers routinely took off their respirators. Others refused to wear them under any circumstances. Supervisors did little or nothing to stop them. Even when the workers wore the respirators it was not at all clear to members of the audit team that the right respirator was being worn for the right job. A very specific type of respirator had to be worn based on the risk of the job, and workers were not adjusting their wearing of the respirators to the jobs that they performed. What the audit team observed was a collection of respirators of various kinds and in diverse condition piled in a corner of the plant and workers deciding on their own if they would wear a respirator or not and when.

The audit team concluded that that LAMC management had not assessed the particular inhalation hazards and understood the specific use limitations of available equipment to assure proper selection of a respirator to fit the job. This principle that each job required a different respirator was not being applied. When queried on this point, LAMC management showed the audit team a copy of the EU standards and said it was in conformance with them.

Overall, the audit team was not at all satisfied with the hazard assessment and hazard control practices at LAMC. It found LAMC deficient in:

- supervision to assure that respiratory devices were properly used; and
- classroom and field training to recognize and cope with emergency situations.

The audit team reported that training in the use and maintenance of respirators was especially weak. It was very critical of the training

workers received in:
- recognizing respiratory hazards;
- understanding what can happen if the proper device is not used;
- understanding what should be done to avoid the need for the devices;
- understanding why particular devices are suitable for particular purposes;
- understanding devices' capabilities and limitations; and
- understanding how to use the devices.

Other findings in the report were that:
- respirator fit, inspection, maintenance, and repair was not up to par.
- medical surveillance was not in place to assure that workers were not having regular symptoms like wheezing, coughing, and chronic bronchitis.
- written procedures similar to those found in other USMNC locations did not exist.

The audit team had many negative findings in its report. It also found improper air sampling. Without appropriate sampling of the air in various locations in the plant, it was impossible to correctly assign inhalation protection devices. The audit team wrote that LAMC was not taking breathing zone samples. It was not sampling the air with sufficient frequency to assess average exposure.

The cause of these deficiencies did not seem to be just LAMC's reliance on European standards or its lack of spending on hardware. The audit team wrote that management had spent money to purchase respirators, but visual inspection showed that the respirators were almost uniformly not well maintained. Many of the respirators that team members saw were torn, had dents, had cracks, and had broken parts. Even if a worker was diligent and wore the respirator, it was not likely to matter. Workers, their supervisors, and managers did not seem to care. A number of workers in the facility persisted in behaving unsafely and the efforts their supervisors made to change their behavior were lackluster.

When questioned, the workers made many comments about the respirators, including.
- They were not comfortable.

- They could interfere with their getting the job done, and they were under a lot of pressure to do their jobs quickly.
- The respirators, which were made in North America and Europe, did not take into account the intense heat where they worked.
- Without removing the respirators they could not communicate.
- Without communication they could not do their jobs.
- Strenuous work for long periods of time could not be performed while wearing the respirators.
- The risk entailed in not wearing the respirators was not great.

A summary of what supervisors said to the audit team was the following
- Their reward came from meeting production goals.
- Safety was secondary.

The comments of plant management showed that it, too, did not have an understanding of safety or its importance. The audit team reported that
- Management's main concern was cutting costs, even if it might jeopardize safety.
- No matter how much management tried, neither the workers nor their supervisors believed that safety policies ever would be taken seriously.

In its recommendations, the audit team proposed focusing on monitoring, training, communicating, recognition, and awareness — all with the intent of tightening up discipline, establishing direction, and achieving focus in the area of safety. The audit team raised the question of how the safety function was organized.
- Should a separate safety group continue to exist?
- If it did exist, how could its efforts be better integrated with daily work activities.

Overall, the findings of the audit team were very troubling. The final sentence said that USMNC should consider shutting down the facility for a period to reassess worker safety issues and change policies and practices.

The main advantage of the purchase of LAMC had been to meet the growing spike in international demand for the products LAMC produced. The temporary closing of the facility would cost USMNC a substantial amount of money. What should USMNC do?

## Discussion Questions:

1. What were the main issues that USMNC faced at its new subsidiary?
2. How should it address these issues?
3. Was a shutdown of the facilitiy necessary? Why? For how long? For what purpose?
4. What other ameliorative measures should LAMC consider?
5. Draw up a plan of action for the company.

# Index